SPECIAL E   ~~~~~~~~~
IN EARLY CHILDHOOD
AN INCLUSIVE APPROACH

MARGRET WINZER
University of Lethbridge

Prentice Hall Allyn and Bacon Canada, Scarborough, Ontario

Canadian Cataloguing in Publication Data

Winzer, Margret, 1940– .
        Special education in early childhood

Includes bibliographical references and index.
ISBN 0-205-26564-2

1. Special education. 2. Early childhood education. 3. Mainstreaming in education. I. Title.
LC3965.W565 1996   371.9'0472   C96-931665-8

 © 1997 Prentice-Hall Canada Inc., Scarborough, Ontario
A Division of Simon & Schuster/A Viacom Company

Allyn and Bacon, Inc., Needham Heights, MA
Prentice-Hall, Inc., Upper Saddle River, New Jersey
Prentice-Hall International (UK) Limited, London
Prentice-Hall of Australia, Pty. Limited, Sydney
Prentice-Hall Hispanoamericana, S.A., Mexico City
Prentice-Hall of India Private Limited, New Delhi
Prentice-Hall of Japan, Inc., Tokyo
Simon & Schuster Asia Private Limited, Singapore
Editora Prentice-Hall do Brasil, Ltda., Rio de Janeiro

ISBN 0-205-26564-2

Vice President, Editorial Director: Laura Pearson
Acquisitions Editor: Cliff Newman
Developmental Editor: Imogen Brian
Production Editor: Kelly Dickson
Copy Editor: Matthew Kudelka
Production Coordinator: Jane Schell
Permissions/Photo Research: Marijke Leupen
Cover Design: Monica Kompter
Cover Illustration: Helen D'Souza
Page Layout: Niche Electronic Publishing

1 2 3 4 5   cc   01 00 99 98 97

Printed and bound in the United States

CONTENTS

CHAPTER 5
Intervention with Infants and Toddlers   109

SECTION 3
Preparing for instruction   150

CHAPTER 6
Models in early childhood special education   152

CHAPTER 7
Creating the environment   186

CHAPTER 8
Assessment Practices in Early Childhood Special Education 211

CHAPTER 9
Individualizing Programs for Children with Special Needs   247

SECTION 4
Presenting the program   266

CHAPTER 10
Generic teaching strategies   269

CHAPTER 11
Children's play   300

CHAPTER 12
Promoting social skills   325

CHAPTER 15
Promoting Skills Speech and Language   415

C H A P T E R 1 6
Transition to the school system   451

P R E F A C E

When young children with disabilities are in early childhood programs, the terms *early intervention* or *early childhood special education* are often used. The field of early childhood special education is relatively new, particularly that portion related to infants and toddlers.

This book is about young children with special needs. It is designed for those individuals intervening with young children in a variety of settings but most especially in daycare centres and preschools that cater to groups of young children. The focus of the text is on services for children with exceptionalities under the age of five. The material is directed toward those already teaching and those aspiring to work with children in this age group.

We see the education and care of young children with special needs as an integral part of, not separate from, regular early childhood education. Information is presented within the parameters of early childhood education; the typical curriculum and its themes and concepts is the framework within which special goals are addressed for children who are exceptional. The best practices in early childhood education and early childhood special education are stressed throughout and we present the findings of recent investigations and theoretical and practical perspectives. The reported research is current and reflective of today's trends and events in the field.

The text moves from theoretical constructs to practical considerations. Topics that include early childhood education, special programming for young children with disabilities, the development and future of early childhood special education, and the importance of educational integration are discussed in this text. The focus, however, is on a number of areas of particular importance to people working with young children with special needs. What teachers can do to facilitate the development of skills is the crux. The emphasis is on the manner in which very young children with exceptionalities—infants, toddlers, and preschoolers—can receive special education. For the preschool child, the stress is on normalized settings that integrate the child with an exceptionality with normally developing peers.

ORGANIZATION OF THE TEXT

The text is divided into five sections that move from theoretical perspectives to practical applications. The opening section of the text is designed to serve as an introduction and lay the groundwork for concepts and themes that will be discussed in greater detail in later chapters. In the opening section, we introduce some of the basic terminology and classifications employed in current special education and provide an overview of the concept and practice of early childhood special education. We examine the children to be served by early childhood special education; the philosophy, rationale, and underlying principles of the enterprise; and the special skills that educators may develop as they integrate children with special needs into regular early childhood settings.

We cannot discuss the child with an exceptionality in isolation. The primary environment for the very young child includes the family, educational program, and community and other resources such as medical services that are provided for the child and the family. As the family is so vital in the care and socialization of the young child, programs are most successful when parents are involved, and those intervening with disabled preschoolers will inevitably collaborate with parents, we devote the second section of the text to the families of children with disabilities.

Chapter 4 overviews the various models for looking at families and the way that a disabled member can alter family functioning. The second chapter in this section relates directly to intervention with infants and toddlers and how parents are central to the early intervention process. We discuss how family needs— defined as a family's expressed desire for services to be obtained or outcomes to be achieved—can best be met. We also discuss some of the types of early intervention that are available to help parents cope with and enhance the prospects for optimal development in their exceptional child. Parent involvement and parent training are focused upon: research shows that early childhood special education is not as effective if parents are not involved and supported.

Preparing for instruction is the theme of the third section. We begin by examining the theory and practices of early childhood special education, grounded in current best practices in regular early childhood education. Successful integration requires thoughtful planning and decision making prior to placement, and then careful monitoring once the child is enrolled in the mainstream program. Because all children do not flourish equally well in the same curriculum model, preplacement decisions should be influenced by the program's curricular approach and the extent to which staff are willing to individualize for children's special needs. We examine and discuss the major models employed in the field of early childhood education and show their relevance to programming for young children with disabilities.

We next examine modifications of the environment—the preparation of the environment in ways that will enhance the physical and social integration of children with disabilities. We then turn to individual program planning and its prerequisite, effective and comprehensive assessment.

Children with special needs require both educational and psychosocial development founded on a carefully task-analysed individual education plan. In designing a program for a child with a disability, or one who is potentially gifted, it is important to know the skills that the child must master and the sequence in which the skills should be taught. This depends upon proper measurement of a child's strengths, weaknesses, acquisition of skills, areas of deficit, interests, and likes and dislikes. We present an overview of the assessment process and a number of the tools available for different types of testing. The stress, however, is on those aspects of the identification process in which early childhood personnel may be involved.

Prior planning in the form of an individual program plan (IPP) is important to successful programming for young children with disabilities who may need more structured, systematic, and teacher-directed programs. Individual education plans contain long-term goals and short-term objectives, as well as an indication of the techniques that will be used in the intervention and the way that skill attainment will be evaluated. Within the individual plan, goals and objectives are founded on observation and assessment of the child and directed toward that child's unique individual needs.

The teacher is a key variable in determining the success of children with disabilities in regular preschool classrooms—a "facilitator" of child development who assists the children in their learning and stimulates their attempts to initiate new activities and learn new skills. Although teachers develop their own styles, there are common techniques and strategies; the mastery of these is an important aspect of preparation. We outline a number of generic techniques and methods that are appropriate for children with disabilities in regular early childhood settings.

Section 4 gives details on presenting a program to children with disabilities in integrated environments. We stress instruction in various domains of learning, beginning with play and moving into the motor, cognitive, language, and social domains. Keep in mind that this is an organizational structure. We divide curriculum into domains even though it is clear that most acts are rooted in multiple developmental domains.

We look first at play, as this is the fundamental mode for all early childhood instruction. We then move to behavioural considerations. One of the challenges to early childhood personnel is the refinement of interventions that improve the peer interactions of young children who are delayed in their social development, particularly in naturalistic settings, such as classrooms, playgrounds, and homes. An important chapter in this section discusses the promotion of social interactions among children with disabilities and their normally developing peers; teaching social skills; and managing inappropriate and deviant behaviour.

We also discuss the development of fine and gross motor skills and examine a number of related curriculum areas and how adaptations may be accomplished. We also discuss cognitive functioning and the stimulation and improvement of all aspects of communication. While much will seem familiar to those trained in early childhood techniques, it is the modifications that can be made to accommodate children with special needs that are the core of this section.

The final chapter in the book examines the transition process and the manner in which early childhood personnel can assist children with disabilities and their families in the transition to the public school system.

SPECIAL FEATURES OF THE TEXT

There are many texts that describe the characteristics of children with exceptional conditions and this book is not designed to present portraits of children. Nevertheless, before professionals can begin to work with families, develop programs, or collaborate with other professionals, two of the initial tasks are to understand the nature of a child's disabilities and recognize how a disability impacts on a child's day to day functioning. Each chapter therefore opens with a case study describing a child with a particular disability. Boxed items within the chapter provide a brief description of the disability and its developmental consequences. While it is important that intervenors understand a condition and how the impact of a particular disability on a child hampers behaviour and learning, it is equally important to be able to plan and program for the unique strengths and weaknesses of the child. For each child presented in the case studies, an individual program is presented with major goals and learning objectives and broad techniques for individualization. Each chapter includes a list of "Helpful hints" to help in the integration of the child in the case study. As you read these, do be aware that in many cases they can apply to any child who requires extra assistance in learning and behaviour. Also be aware that the case studies present only a few examples of the huge range of disabilities that may be seen in children.

To assist the reader in reviewing and comprehending the material presented, learning checks are found throughout. There are also additional activities for readers to pursue.

New terms are marked in bold face and their definitions are found in the margins where they appear and again in the glossary. And finally, as the work is based on best practice and recent research, an extensive bibliography accompanies the text.

ACKNOWLEDGEMENTS

A number of people contributed to the text. Helen Taylor's help and encouragement was invaluable. The three students who helped with the finishing touches, Tanya Collins, Dean Johnston, and Wade Johnson, provided valuable assistance. Marta Tomins at Allyn and Bacon was gracious and patient and made the task easier.

DEDICATION

This book is for Harry, a very special person to me.

SECTION 1

Foundations of Early Childhood Special Education

Section introduction

EARLY CHILDHOOD SPECIAL EDUCATION is a new term that emerged in the 1980s to refer to a melding of early childhood services, special education, and ameliorative programs. The enterprise of early childhood special education is directed specifically at meeting the needs of young children with disabilities and their families; it serves a wide range of children. The potential population includes children with established disabilities such as Down syndrome and deafness as well as those who are at increased risk for developing conditions that will impair learning or behaviour.

Young children with special needs are accommodated in a variety of settings, ranging from the home to a clinic to a segregated preschool program. However, we consider the optimal setting for early childhood special education to be one where children without disabilities are found— that is, the regular day care program or nursery school.

There are many advantages to the inclusion of children with disabilities in regular early childhood education. These include the growth of social interaction and the development of friendships among children, an improvement in self-concept among children with disabilities, a greater tolerance and respect for children with disabilities on the part of normally developing children, and an enhanced opportunity for children with disabilities to learn new skills by observing and imitating their peers' language, behaviour, skills, and social interaction.

Most teachers in community-based programs for young children are not specifically trained to handle children with disabilities. (Throughout this text, we use "teacher" as a generic term, implying that all intervenors are teaching, whatever their formal qualifications.) Nevertheless, teachers who have experience with young children will find that special education is neither a magic form of intervention, nor something completely new or different. Special education for most young children is simply an extension of what good teachers do every day.

The curriculum in early childhood special education conforms to that of regular early childhood education, and with few exceptions, most activities in early childhood programs can be made appropriate for children with disabilities. Children with disabilities should have the same toys and activities as other children, although teachers may need to adapt these to facilitate partial participation. The goal is to assist children to participate in activities to whatever degree possible (Baumgart et al., 1982).

Teachers will need to expand their skills and competencies if they are to accommodate young children with disabilities successfully. They will need knowledge of the disability and its developmental consequences, an awareness of methods that promote effective socialization and learning, and an understanding of procedures for collaborating with families and other professionals. An examination of these additional skills forms the core of this text. In almost all cases, however, the skills are built on a base that early childhood educators already possess. The one disclaimer concerns children with significant disabilities. In some cases, interventions with these children do require specialized techniques, and we explain these carefully as they arise.

In this opening section, we focus on the foundations of the philosophy and practice of early childhood special education. The first chapter presents an overview of the various ways to accommodate young children with special needs. The second chapter paints a broad picture of childhood exceptionalities and the responsible risk factors. We then examine the rationale, the efficacy, and the progress of the new field of early childhood special education. Especially important here is the focus on the skills and competencies that teachers will need to develop as they program for and accommodate young children with disabilities in natural settings.

CHAPTER 1
Early Childhood Special Education

CASE STUDY
Darrin

Four-year-old Darrin is affected by a severe motor disorder known as spastic cerebral palsy. The condition restricts especially his movement and his use of speech. Darrin has slow, laborious, and poorly co-ordinated voluntary movements. He is not ambulatory, and can move only by pulling himself along on a scooter board with his arms. Darrin has so far developed very little speech. To communicate his needs and wants, he uses head movements and consistent vocalizations.

This is Darrin's second year at the centre. Although he is an easy, friendly child, he was very shy and reticent at first, and his lack of speech and mobility made peer interactions even more difficult. Darrin has become comfortable at the centre only recently, but he is now beginning to get along well with the other children and the staff and participating in a wider variety of activities.

A short time ago, a new indoor activity was introduced in the preschool classroom involving a small climbing frame with an attached slide. Groups of children were soon busy going up and down the slide, often carrying with them balls, pillows, and other soft toys. They would push a toy down the slide, and then follow themselves.

For days, Darrin watched this activity. One day, he wanted to play, so he took a ball and rolled himself over to the ladder. The teachers were apprehensive, but did not stop him from participating. They realized that children learn socialization, sharing, and respect for the feelings of others through play. They understood that play and exploration of the world are closely intertwined, and that both activities have a central role in the adaptability, learning, cognitive development, socio-emotional development, and early education of young children. They were aware that climbing can be a confidence-building experience and that the skill can facilitate general mobility around the classroom and the community. Finally, they knew that children with physical disabilities must be given a chance to discover their own limitations.

Darrin waited his turn, and then started up the ladder. He soon found that pulling himself up while holding the ball was too difficult. Still, Darrin kept the other children waiting, albeit patiently, and refused any help. However, when another child asked if he could carry the ball up the ladder, Darrin finally agreed. The other child carried the ball up the ladder, and waited at the top while Darrin pulled himself up. Darrin then pushed the ball down the slide and quickly followed himself. As soon as he reached the bottom of the slide, Darrin got into line again. He was excited about his new skill and indicated that the other child should carry the ball to the top again.

Scooter board

DARRIN'S PLACEMENT IN THE PRESCHOOL did not "just happen." Much preparation went into the intervention. As both teachers and parents of preschoolers can be apprehensive when faced with the prospective enrolment of a child with a disability, a number of initial meetings were held. The parents visited the centre to become familiar with the staff and the routines, and were reassured that the teachers were willing to work with Darrin.

Staff members observed Darrin before he came to the centre, read about his condition, talked to the parents about management, and talked to other centres. Discussions with various therapists gave staff members a clearer understanding of Darrin's condition, the skills he needed to develop, and the limitations placed on his activities by cerebral palsy. The therapists also demonstrated special techniques for positioning, handling, toileting, and feeding Darrin. Darrin was prepared for the preschool experience as well. He had received early intervention in a clinic setting, knew how to move on his scooter board, and knew his own limits. Darrin visited the centre before formally starting, and brought home photographs of staff members.

After Darrin's first visit, the other children had some questions about him. The staff answered these honestly and gave simple explanations of Darrin's condition. To develop and enhance accepting attitudes further, the teachers led discussions and role plays.

It has been suggested that the accurate information provided by such a training package may reduce the fears and misconceptions that normally developing children often have of children with disabilities. This may help establish a foundation for social interaction between children with special needs and their peers (Guralnick, 1981). The New Friends Program was the training package used at Darrin's centre. It is a preschool/kindergarten-level curriculum of learning activities related to specific disabilities. The package contains a number of dolls that are used to encourage questioning and increase knowledge about disabilities, initiate simulation activities, and point out the strengths and similarities of children with disabilities (Raab et al., 1986).

Once the children were aware of the nature of Darrin's disability, they realized that even though he needed a little extra assistance at times, he still needed to develop independence. Teachers were also on guard against the possibility of Darrin developing a dependency upon a teacher or a non-disabled peer.

The environment was carefully prepared for Darrin's arrival. Preschool children with physical impairments have special furniture and equipment needs; adaptive equipment as well as mobility aids are crucial to their physical and educational development. A special chair was designed for Darrin, and rails were added in the bathroom. Shelves and dividers were spaced so that Darrin could easily manoeuvre his scooter board. There was a set path around the room that the other children knew to keep clear of obstructions.

All of those involved with Darrin worked together to plan an individualized program for him. A number of assessment techniques and interviews with Darrin's parents were used to identify some specific and general skills that Darrin needed to develop. These broad goals were broken down into short-term attainable objectives that the staff could follow when planning activities for Darrin.

PROGRESS CHECK 1

Before Darrin arrived at the centre, a number of interventions were used with the preschool teachers, the children, and Darrin himself. List these in three columns headed Darrin, Teachers, and Children.

Cerebral palsy a condition character- ized by damage to the brain before, during, or after birth. A neurological impairment, and one of the most common crippling conditions in children.

Contractures the shortening of the tendons to which children with cere- bral palsy are prone.

The activities of the regular classrooms did not change. Rather, Darrin's activities were struc- tured to facilitate his competent participation in the activities of the regular preschool, to en- courage him to learn from his non-disabled peers, and to promote positive social interaction among all of the children. Darrin participated in the on- going activities of the regular education class- rooms, learned in small, integrated instructional groups, and ate lunch and snacks with his non- disabled peers. In other words, Darrin was a reg- ular member of the group.

Even ten years ago, Darrin might have been excluded from a nursery school designed for normally developing children. Darrin has cerebral palsy, a motor disorder caused by damage to the brain that usually occurs prenatally or during the birth process (see Box 1–1). Depending on the type, degree, and location of the damage, a child's functioning will be affected in different ways. Darrin has spastic **cerebral palsy**, and both his mobility and his speech are hampered.

In the past, Darrin's lack of mobility, his unintelligible speech, and his spe- cial positioning, handling, feeding, and toileting needs would have been enough to send him to a specialized centre for children with physical disabilities. To be sure, in such a specialized setting, Darrin would have received individualized and intensive training from physical and occupational therapists to improve his mobility as much as possible, and to teach him to use his scooter board and pos- sibly a wheelchair. Special exercises would have helped prevent the develop- ment of **contractures**—a shortening of the tendons to which children with cerebral palsy are prone. Darrin might also have received consistent attention from a speech therapist to improve his articulation and start him on a commu- nication system, such as Bliss symbolics.

LEARNING ACTIVITY 1

Many of the interven- tions used with Darrin are described in greater detail in other parts of this book. You will find information about therapists and their roles in Chapter 3, on adaptive equipment and positioning and handling in Chapter 13,

and on augmentative communication in Chapter 15. Divide the class into four groups; each group is to read ahead for additional information on the topics mentioned. They are then to discuss the information in relation to Darrin. For example, what is positioning and how would they position Darrin? How would the speech therapist introduce a system of augmentative communication? How would the teacher use this at the centre?

In the regular preschool setting, Darrin still receives these services, although the therapists are not on site. In an integrated setting, however, he also has

BOX 1–1
Cerebral palsy

Neurological impairments occur when there is damage to the brain. There is a wide range of neurological disorders; some are associated with impairments of the nervous system; others result from diseases or accidents. Most birth injuries result from deprivation of oxygen to the immature brain. If supplies of oxygen to the nerve cells of the brain are too greatly reduced, brain damage or death can result. Brain damage results because destroyed brain cells cannot regenerate themselves. When a portion of the brain is damaged, the part of the individual that is controlled by that portion of the brain is also damaged.

Cerebral palsy, a condition characterized by damage to the brain before, during, or after birth, is a neurological impairment, and one of the most common crippling conditions in children. The most frequently cited incidence figures range from 3 to 6 cerebral palsied children per 1,000 live births (Apgar & Beck, 1974). There are more boys than girls within the cerebral palsied population. The condition occurs more often with mothers whose socioeconomic circumstances are poor (Hallahan & Kauffman, 1991).

Spasticity, athetosis, and ataxia are the most common types of cerebral palsy. Spastic cerebral palsy, which affects approximately 50 percent of the affected population, results in slow, laborious, and poorly co-ordinated voluntary movements. Athetosis is characterized by constant, involuntary writhing movements, especially in the hands and wrists; children with athetoid cerebral palsy are unable to stop moving when they want to. Ataxic cerebral palsy is characterized by poor co-ordination of the movements associated with balance, posture, and spatial orientation. Children with ataxia tend to show a generalized inco-ordination of both fine and gross motor movements, and walk with a wide gait, their legs spread well apart to compensate for poor equilibrium.

Cerebral palsy results in motor problems. Within twelve to fourteen weeks of birth, normally developing children achieve control of head movements. Within six months, they are able to pull themselves up into a sitting position. At about twelve months, they begin to walk unaided. As children pass through these developmental stages, they acquire more sensory experience, gain greater perceptual awareness, and learn to manipulate themselves and the objects around them. Children with cerebral palsy have abnormal movement patterns—their co-ordination movements are inefficient, and they retain primitive reflexes. These children will meet with difficulty in moving, grasping, and doing things with their hands.

The motor movements necessary for speech are often affected by brain damage. The motor dysfunctions that affect the speech organs may make intelligible speech impossible. With cerebral palsy, the muscles of the face, mouth, and diaphragm that are generally responsible for speech production tend to reflect the child's overall postural tone. In children with spastic forms of cerebral palsy, for example, the speech characteristics may include articulatory defects, laboured speech with distortions of sound, uncontrolled pitch changes, and husky voice quality. Other children may display listening, breathing, voice, articulation, or language disorders.

The presence of extensive motor disorders alone is sufficient to interfere with normal development. However, the brain damage that results in cerebral palsy is not always limited to motor areas. Because a high percentage of the cerebral palsied population exhibits one or more additional impairments, cerebral palsy can generally be seen as a multiple handicapping condition. Additional conditions include mental retardation, learning disabilities, sensory loss, epilepsy, and emotional and behavioural problems.

ongoing interaction with his normally developing peers and the opportunity to model their behaviours, both good and bad. Language input from the other children and the staff is constant.

Darrin's situation is not unique. The need to serve young children with disabilities early in their lives has been recognized in Canada. In the past twenty years, special services for young children with disabilities and their families have become relatively widespread. Before that time, there were some services and facilities available, but they tended to be sporadic and scattered. Some special-needs preschool and clinic programs were created to serve discrete populations of children such as those with hearing impairments or physical disabilities; other programs catered to a variety of handicapping conditions. All tended to be segregated, however, and grouped children with special needs together to be instructed by specialists trained in a specific area of exceptionality. Children played, socialized, and learned with other disabled children, not with their normally developing peers.

For both preschool-aged and school-aged children today, the trend is away from segregated programs. Increasing numbers of children with special needs are being integrated into programs with their normally developing peers in a process that is referred to as mainstreaming or integration but more often today as inclusive schooling or just inclusion.

While segregated classes and centres can be expected to continue, many educators believe that most regular preschool programs are ideal for children with disabilities since these programs are now designed to allow each child to learn at his or her own developmental level and pace. As far as possible, program policies, structures, and practices should be designed to support the inclusion of young children with disabilities in settings designed for their same-age peers without disabilities. Right across the country, regular daycare and nursery school programs are being adapted to serve the special needs of preschoolers with disabilities and their families.

Early childhood special education any program or service within the early childhood period. It can include home training, clinic-based programs, child care facilities, and nursery schools.

Ameliorative programs programs designed to assist children who are at risk for learning or behavioural difficuties, such as Head Start in the United States.

The practice of adapting programs for young children is popularly known as ***early childhood special education***. Early childhood special education is a relatively new field. Its beginnings can be traced to the 1960s, when ***ameliorative programs***—compensatory early childhood programs for culturally and economically disadvantaged preschoolers, such as Head Start in the United States—were implemented. Compensatory education merged rapidly with special education and early childhood education. By the mid-1980s, research, anecdotal reports, and experience had demonstrated the effectiveness of the amalgamation, and the new term, *early childhood special education*, or ECSE, was introduced. Today's ECSE is neither an extension of the fields of early childhood education and special education, nor an additive combination of the two (Peterson, 1987). Rather, ECSE integrates the fields of special education and early childhood education within a strong child developmental framework.

In this chapter we set out to do two things. First, we examine the three components of ECSE. We look separately at early childhood education, ameliorative programs, and special education, and then see how these fields were joined together to form a new discipline in the 1980s. Second, we present the rationale for ECSE, and illuminate ECSE with research in the area.

A New Field for Early Childhood Education

Early childhood education in North America can be traced back, if somewhat tenuously, to the 1820s. Programs invariably were designed for children who were developing normally. The young children who are the focus of this book—those who are at risk for learning and behavioural problems and those with disabling conditions—were often excluded. Special but separate programs for children who were exceptional were developed in the 1880s (Winzer, 1996), but it was not until the middle decades of this century that any real merging of early childhood education and early childhood education for children with special needs occurred.

> **Early childhood education** a program that is concerned with the development and special needs of young children and their families, with particular emphasis on the preschool years.

Although early childhood education for normally developing children traditionally was focused at the preschool level, it now encompasses children up to about grade three. The National Association for the Education of Young Children defines the period of early childhood as birth to eight years. Alberta Education (1982) defines *early childhood education* as a program that is concerned with the development and special needs of young children and their families, and that places particular emphasis on the preschool years. Isabel Doxey (1990) notes that early childhood education is "any program or service for children within the early childhood period: a child-care facility, a nursery school, a kindergarten or an early primary grade" (p. 10, preface). The birth to eight years perspective ensures a developmental framework for the design of services. However, the Early Childhood Division of the Council for Exceptional Children recommends a birth to five years age range for ECSE, and we stress this age range in this book.

The experiences of preschool-aged children are quite different now from what they were thirty years ago. In the past, parents were routinely advised against encouraging or allowing involvement in school learning too early, and children nearly always stayed at home until they were about six years of age. The programs for young children that did exist were viewed primarily as caregiving facilities. The overriding concern was socialization: the extent to which children were mastering concepts or developing skills was considered less important than whether they participated appropriately in daily routines and learned to get along with others. The adults in the programs had to be patient and caring, but technical and professional teaching skills were not usually expected or required.

In recent decades, the commitment to the needs of young children and their families has increased dramatically. Educators have been encouraged to accept new levels of responsibility for the education and care of young children by parents, politicians, and public leaders. They have also been prompted by research findings of the 1970s and 1980s and by the need for expanded daycare. Today, most children enter some form of school during the time still referred to as the preschool years.

The history of early childhood education for normally developing young children and their families has been marked by numerous and significant changes. These progressive changes have often been made in response to demands created by the ebb and flow of politics, social policies, economics, parent advocacy, and public demand. Of the many reasons for the new emphasis on intervention at the preschool level, three stand out. The first two revolve around the dramatic shifts our society has witnessed in both family patterns and work patterns; the third is related to research findings and experience.

First, large numbers of women, many of them mothers of young children, are now members of the work force, for reasons of personal satisfaction, or economic necessity, or both. Current reports indicate that more than half of the mothers of young children are actively involved in the work force. There is no doubt that the changing role of women has significantly altered traditional family child-rearing patterns and created the impetus for expanded child care facilities.

Second, major changes in families and family stability have led to a dramatic increase in the number of single parents. In the United States in 1940, there was one divorce for every six marriages; by 1980, the ratio had reached one for two (Zigler & Ennis, 1989). In Canada, the proportion of single-parent families has risen by 130 percent in the past twenty years. Most single parents are women, and most of them are in need of competent child care.

Third, research in child development has clearly demonstrated that the early years are a time of rapid learning.

The combined effect of changing social and demographic forces and new research findings in the field of child development began to make itself felt in the 1960s. David Elkind (1986) observed that in this period, early childhood education was "abruptly shoved into the economic, political and social spotlight." It became a target for educators and social scientists endeavouring to prepare children to cope with a rapidly changing technological society.

The events of the last thirty years in early childhood education have led to vast increases in our knowledge of how to provide effective and efficient services to young children and their families. However, the changes have also created a great deal of confusion about the philosophy, the process, and the appropriate practices of early childhood education. Isabel Doxey (1990) writes that "since the 1960s the early childhood span has been a battleground for theorists, educators, politicians, and researchers from a plethora of disciplines—psychology, sociology, neuropsychology, anthropology, economics, and political science." Research has produced somewhat contradictory findings so that today, people hold different ideas about daycare facilities and their influence on young children, about program models, about the vitality of training for normally developing children, and about the efficacy of early intervention for children with disabilities.

Nevertheless, the use of centre care for young children has increased substantially since the 1970s and is expected to become the predominant form of child care in the future (Hofferth & Phillips, 1987). Currently, various types of facilities for education and care, founded on a variety of models and having different program orientations, proliferate, and can be found right across the country. Training for the personnel staffing these facilities has expanded into systematic and professional programs at universities and colleges. Researchers and educators are engaging in intense research to generate new theories about how young children grow and develop, and are creating a body of professional and research literature that underlies and guides the practice of early childhood education. Books and magazines are readily available for parents, teachers, and others who wish to explore different aspects of young children and their care and education.

CARE AND EDUCATION

Distinctions between the care and the education of young children have plagued the early childhood field for years (Mitchell, 1989). Defined in the narrowest terms, education refers to academic skills instruction, while child care refers to custodial or protective services. Traditionally, programs and services for the *care* of young children have fallen under different sponsorship and responsibility from those concerned with the *education* of children. Child care was long seen as nurturance, and education as teaching. Personnel had different training, different qualifications, and different designations. Also, kindergarten programs were clearly differentiated from preschool programs.

Such a distinction is increasingly perceived to be inaccurate and inconsistent with the needs of young children and their families. Today, the formats, the rationales, the purposes, and the staffing of daycare and nursery school programs have become blurred, and many authorities no longer differentiate between the two programs but include both under the heading of early childhood education. Anne Mitchell (1989) points out: "Programs for young children cannot be one or the other; any early childhood program provides both education and care." In any situation where there are groups of children and a caretaker, learning of some type takes place. Daycare programs may be longer in duration, having lunch and rest time, and some daycare programs do focus on care rather than early education, but most are indistinguishable from preschool programs.

Child care is now regulated in all the provinces and territories, and the same regulations that apply to nursery schools apply to daycare centres. With respect to funding and regulations, kindergarten is considered part of the formal educational system.

Small children are curious about their environment.

Child care any arrangement for caregiving other than that provided by the parents.

Child care may be defined as any arrangement for caregiving other than that provided by the parents. Some children require child care because they have working mothers. Others are enrolled in child care programs because their families believe that preschool programs provide socialization and other valuable experiences, and that they prepare children for school.

Daycare is a type of child care that was developed to assist parents who were working or going to school. Working parents make many kinds of arrangements for their children's care and early education, and there are advantages and disadvantages to each arrangement. Parents' choices for different kinds of care are usually based on availability, cost, parental judgments about the quality of the care, the age of the child, and the number of children involved.

There are three basic types of daycare—family daycare, in-home daycare, and centre daycare. In-home daycare and family daycare involve an adult, usually the mother of young children herself, looking after a small group of children in her home. Sometimes the caregiver's own children are included in the group. In centre daycare, children receive care at a centre that may be private, but that frequently is affiliated with a church, university, or community agency. Programs are typically staffed by paraprofessional and early childhood specialists.

Nursery schools came into being because of educators' and physicians' concerns that the complexities of urban life could overwhelm young children and hinder their development. At the outset, nursery schools were usually privately run, and although they remained outside any formal educational or social service system, they served primarily educational purposes. Nursery schools focused on providing an environmental experience that was an extension of what children had at home.

Today's kindergartens, as part of the educational system, span the preschool and school years. When kindergartens were first established in the nineteenth century, however, they served a social rather than an educational function (Hill, 1987). It was only in the 1940s that the kindergarten began to extend downwards to include three- and four-year-olds. Until the 1950s, kindergartens tended to be privately operated, and were attended by middle- and upper-class children. Their primary function was to provide a comfortable, child-centred group experience outside the home (Connell, 1987). Gradually, many kindergartens and junior kindergartens became part of the public school system. Today they are staffed by professionals who often hold different qualifications from professionals in daycare centres and nursery schools.

ISSUES ABOUT CARE

The fact that child care centres provide the opportunity for many social experiences outside the home both pleases and concerns many parents, for the effects of child care are not uniform. Despite nearly twenty years of careful research, the psychological literature on child care is replete with contradictory results.

A good deal of empirical and anecdotal evidence points to the positive effects of child care. These findings come primarily from research done with economically disadvantaged children (Zigler, 1987). The daycare experience may have a positive influence on social development. Some studies show that children who participated in daycare are more socially skilled, more co-operative, and more task-oriented than children who spent their preschool years at home (Phillips, McCartney, & Scarr, 1987). Daycare children, for example, are more likely to share their toys. Infants who have been in programs are more peer-oriented and play at higher developmental levels. In fact, the longer children are in daycare, the more time they spend participating socially and playing constructively, as opposed to being unoccupied or watching others play (Schindler, Moeley, & Frank, 1987).

According to several thorough reviews, good preschool education advances cognitive development as well as social development. When preschool students are compared with other children from the same background who stay at home, the preschool children generally fare better (Haskins, 1989; Scarr, 1984). Quite consistently, researchers have found that when children are given intelligence tests any time between eighteen months and five years, those who have been in daycare as infants score higher than those who have not (Clarke-Stewart & Fein, 1983).

Socio-economic factors play a role as well, however. Children from middle-class families tend to do as well at a good daycare centre as they do with parental

Many children today attend daycare, preschool, or kindergarten.

care at home (Clarke-Stewart, 1982a,b; Kagan, Kearsley, & Zelazo, 1977). Children from homes with poorly educated parents who have low incomes tend to benefit intellectually from their daycare experience (Ramey, 1981).

There is some evidence, albeit tentative, that high-quality preschool programs affect other areas of children's future lives. For example, children from preschools were significantly less likely to be placed in special education by the end of their school careers than controls in one group of studies (Haskins, 1989). Henderson (1989) reported that low-income and minority graduates of preschool programs with high levels of parental involvement are still outperforming their peers when they reach senior high school. In a review of preschool intervention programs, Ronald Haskins (1989) mentioned several programs whose participants grew up to be less involved in crime and the welfare system and had lower rates of teenage pregnancy. These results are not found in all programs, however, and they should be seen as a reflection of what programs may do, not necessarily what they *do* do.

On the other hand, the research literature points to a number of negative effects of the daycare experience. In some studies, children from daycare are considered less compliant and more aggressive when they reach elementary school (Haskins, 1985). Other studies have found that daycare children are more impulsive; more aggressive toward adults and peers; more egocentric; less co-operative; and less able to cope with frustration. In one study (Baillargeon & Betsatel-Presser, 1988), teachers reported that child care children had difficulty respecting class rules, were aggressive, and had a tendency to form cliques. The teachers qualified their views by indicating that the type of child care and the child's family background contributed to such behaviour.

Infant daycare is an area of special concern since it is a relatively new practice. According to some studies, infant daycare places children at risk for long-term socio-emotional difficulties. Others dispute this claim, and assert that there is no risk associated with high-quality daycare. Daycare for preschool children has generated less controversy than daycare for infants. Different aspects of daycare are discussed in Box 1–2.

BOX 1–2

What the research says about daycare

Although daycare centres and nursery schools have existed nearly as long as elementary schools, they have generally not been universally available, and have been provided largely by the private sector. With recent increases in two-career families and single-parent households, more and more children are spending part of their daily lives in group settings outside the family. Some parents leave children with a sitter or a relative; others leave them in someone else's home; many children attend daycare centres.

As mounting numbers of women enter the labour force, the demand for expanded daycare facilities is becoming more insistent. In Canada, trends in maternal employment, family income, and reliance on child care have not gone unnoticed at the federal and provincial levels. Alan Pence (1989) observed: "It is an exciting and active time for child day care in Canada. After decades of neglect and a history of containment on the periphery of social concern, day care is now a central political and social issue" (p. 140). Politicians and other policymakers have begun to appreciate the magnitude of the child care problem facing society and the need for action (Morrison, 1989). However, despite the demonstrated need for more daycare in Canada and a growing body of research that supports the institution of high-quality daycare and suggests appropriate means of providing that care, the development of an expanded system of quality child-care services in Canada is proceeding along a tortuous path that appears likely to meet neither quantitative nor qualitative requirements (Pence, 1989).

Even when parents can obtain adequate care outside the home, they have concerns about the practice. A chief worry of parents is whether day-care will affect their children's attachment to them. The child is spending many hours away from home at a vulnerable age. The daycare environment is the child's environment for months or years, and inevitably will influence that child's development. Moreover, children in daycare form relationships with, and attachments to, their substitute caregivers (Lewis, 1987).

Babies must develop affective relationships with their mothers during infancy or they will be unable to develop normally. The critical factors are the amount of child/caregiver interaction and the timing of the interaction. Some researchers have claimed that full-time maternal employment disrupts bonding, an essential part of healthy infant development, and thus puts infants at risk for developing emotional insecurities and becoming socially maladjusted.

In 1986, Jay Belsky, a prominent developmental psychologist, published research on daycare and attachment. Belsky (1986) concluded that an extended daycare experience (more than twenty hours a week) during the infant's first year is a risk factor for the development of insecure attachments with parents. It may be, he argued, that daycare has long-term effects, such as an increase in aggression and noncompliance in preschoolers. This occurs because infants are not prepared psychologically to cope with extended separations from their mothers (see Belsky, 1986, 1987).

Because many people intuitively believe that daycare may be harmful, Belsky's paper caused a considerable controversy, which has not yet been resolved. Some researchers have concluded that there is insufficient evidence to support Belsky's claims (see Clark-Stewart, 1989). Others argue that infant daycare is still fairly new, and that we cannot yet determine the conditions that favour certain outcomes (Ritchers and Zahn-Waxler, 1988). Other studies have found that daycare does not disrupt the child's emotional bond with the mother even if the child is placed in daycare before his or her first birthday. This research finds that children who have attended high-quality,

Children who attend preschool programs tend to interact with their peers in both positive and negative ways.

dren, the most clear-cut influence of daycare seems to be on social development. Daycare can promote interest in peers and the development of social skills, but children frequently do not receive the individual attention and resources they would like.

Children who attend preschool programs tend to interact with their peers in both positive and negative ways (Belsky, 1984; Belsky & Steinberg, 1979). Some results indicate that these children may be more aggressive toward peers and adults. With their peers, they share more, but they also fight more; in fact, they may fight a great deal. They are also less polite, less compliant with adults, and more aggressive (Clarke-Stewart & Fein, 1983). The effect of this aggression in later years has not been conclusively determined. Some follow-up studies of children who participated in daycare programs showed increased levels of aggression when the children were ten years of age. Children tended to be less tolerant and more socially withdrawn (Belsky, 1987; Zinmeister, 1988). Nevertheless, compared to home-raised children, children in daycare have also been described as more assertive, self-confident, socially mature, self-sufficient, co-operative with peers, comfortable in new situations, and outgoing.

part-time daycare do not have substantially different measures of socio-emotional development from children reared at home (Chess, 1987; Phillips et al., 1987). Further studies of dozens of infants between three and twenty-nine months of age in various settings have led researchers to conclude that daycare does not necessarily weaken infant/parent ties or cause undesirable changes in the child's behaviour (e.g., Bradley, 1982; Kagan, Kearsley, & Zelazo, 1977; O'Connell, 1983). It seems that children of working mothers had just as much one-to-one contact as children of mothers who were at home. In addition, infants with previous daycare experience adjusted more quickly, explored more in unfamiliar settings, and performed better on verbal and nonverbal tasks than did children without such experience. However, if daycare begins before the child has developed a secure attachment to the mother, the quality of that attachment may be affected in some cases.

There seem to be some common themes in research on daycare for preschool children, and the effects of good daycare and preschool programs are generally positive. For preschool chil-

In the final analysis, daycare can be seen as an acceptable experience. Where the quality of the care is optimal, it becomes an enriching and stimulating experience. Most experts recommend home care for infants and group care for older children (Scarr, 1984). And whatever the conclusion, the debate highlights the need for affordable high-quality daycare for infants and toddlers.

AMELIORATIVE PROGRAMS

In the 1960s, widespread concern that social barriers were creating a dangerous situation in the United States led to pressures for an improvement in the status of ethnic and racial minorities. These pressures combined with a variety of scientific facts to create a great interest in the potential of preschool environments to increase the educational chances of the poor. This led to the development and implementation of ameliorative programs for disadvantaged preschoolers across North America. One of the best known of these early intervention programs was Head Start, a compensatory program for disadvantaged children that began in the mid-1960s.

When Head Start began in 1965, it set out to compensate for the poor living conditions of many American children. Its major goal was to reverse the poverty cycle by reducing school failure in low-income children, enabling them to be competitive in school and in the marketplace.

Three crucial assumptions formed the basis of Head Start. First, environmental conditions in poor homes were believed to be insufficient to prepare children to succeed in school. Second, schooling was seen as a social mechanism that would permit children to succeed in society. Third, extra assistance in the preschool years was viewed as a means of helping poor children succeed in school and thereby overcome poverty (Cole & Cole, 1989).

Head Start programs were funded under the Elementary and Secondary Education Act (ESEA), passed in 1965. The passage of the act was the first indication in the United States of legislative concern for the early education of children with special needs (those stemming from disadvantage), and the beginning of a national expansion and consolidation of early intervention efforts (Noonan & McCormick, 1993).

The original legislation for Head Start (ESEA) made no mention of children with disabilities. However, in 1972, Public Law 92-424 required Head Start programs to reserve at least 10 percent of their openings for preschoolers with disabilities.* Under PL 92-424, the target population of Head Start was expanded. It grew vertically to include toddlers and infants, and categorically to include impaired and high-risk children. By 1989, 13.3 percent of the children enrolled in Head Start programs were children with special needs (Hymes, 1991). Further details on Head Start programs are found in Box 1–3 and Box 1–4.

LEARNING ACTIVITY 2

Many pros and cons of daycare for infants and preschoolers are presented in the text and in Box 1–2. Use this information as a basis for a class debate on daycare.

---

* Public laws in the United States are laws that have been passed by Congress and are in force. The numbers refer to the law and the Congress. For example, PL 92-424 means that it was the 424th piece of legislation passed by the 92nd Congress of the United States.

BOX 1–3
Head Start programs

In the United States in the early 1960s, at the urging of Presidents Kennedy and Johnson, legislation was introduced that had far-reaching effects on social services for people in the lower socio-economic bracket. This legislative action was known as the War on Poverty, and represented an effort to eradicate social inequalities. The War on Poverty brought a substantial increase in the number of programs addressing the medical, financial, social, and educational needs of people living in poverty. It included job training programs, provisions for increased welfare benefits, and preschool education for disadvantaged children. Social scientists and social reformers in the United States argued that low-income children were often disadvantaged by their home environments or deprived by their community, and advocated that these children be provided with some form of compensatory education during the preschool years.

Head Start's planning committee had fourteen experts in the areas of preschool education, medicine, child development, and mental health. These policymakers based their decision to concentrate on preschool children as a strategy for social reform on the scientific evidence available at the time, particularly in the area of cognitive psychology. Studies dating back to the 1930s revealed that favourable changes in the environment brought about marked changes in children, and that the IQ levels of young children could be raised by environmental stimulation. By the 1960s, much evidence pointed to the influence of early experiences on cognitive growth. Policymakers concluded that if this were true, economically disadvantaged children,

as a result of the dearth of appropriate experiences in the home, were likely to suffer from deficits that would only worsen as they grew older. Hence, from its inception, Project Head Start had two prongs. The notion that early childhood was the prime learning period was joined to a social-political concern for populations of children who seemed to be in need of supplemental nutritional, health, and educational services.

Project Head Start began in 1965 as a summer program for four- and five-year-olds. Eventually, the program was extended to a full academic year. In the first year, more than 20,000 children from many racial and ethnic backgrounds attended a variety of programs. Some programs were full-time, some part-time; some concentrated on classroom activities, and some taught parents how to educate their own children in the home.

Despite the somewhat improvised nature of its beginnings, Project Head Start initially had encouraging results. Studies showed that participating children later scored higher on elementary school achievement tests, and had more positive report cards that non-Head Start children. By junior high school, children who had been in Head Start were significantly less likely to be placed in special classes or retained in grade. As adolescents, Head Start children had higher aspirations and a greater sense of achievement than did their non–Head Start peers.

Early research on the effects of Head Start programs also indicated that participating children gained about 5 points in IQ. However, these increases seemed to fade by grade three. This was one of the reasons that Head Start and other similar programs became political footballs. One of the most famous critics, the psychologist Arthur Jensen, wrote a controversial article in 1969 in which he began with the comment that "Compensatory education has been tried, and it apparently has failed." Jensen believed that programs such as Head Start might have generated some short-term IQ gains, but that these were not sustained over the years. Moreover, some minority children (for example, African Americans according to Jensen) inherited their IQ disadvantage; it followed that early education programs, since they were unlikely to affect the genes, were too time-consuming and financially burdensome. Jensen's paper gained national attention because of his contention that 80 percent of the variability of IQ scores was inherited. If this was true and IQ was genetically determined, then IQs were immutable and no amount of compensatory education would bring about lasting changes.

Many disputed Jensen's contentions on the grounds that they were racist. Moreover, later evaluations of the programs suggested more promising outcomes in the area of IQ. These studies attributed the earlier and more pessimistic results to faulty methodology, such as improperly matched control groups. Other researchers felt that it was shortsighted to place so much emphasis on IQ scores as an index of program effectiveness.

Since its inception, Head Start has provided comprehensive services including health, education, and social services to more than eleven million children, and has created many opportunities for parents and families to get involved (Lombardi, 1990). The strongest long-term impact has been on children's physical health and well-being. Nevertheless, by the late 1980s, only about 16 percent of eligible children were being served in programs such as Head Start (Children's Defense Fund, 1987).

Today, Head Start includes more than 2,000 programs that vary in the type and quality of services they render. These programs differ in their goals, methods of intervention, duration, and age of participants.

For young children, Head Start is a unique, integrated delivery model. Its major purpose is to provide enrichment to prepare children for success in elementary school. Head Start planners do not focus on the deficits of economically disadvantaged children; rather, they see the children as coming from a wide range of backgrounds, and stress an approach that respects these various backgrounds. Head Start programs do not focus on promoting intellectual performance alone; the emphasis is on developing the whole child, from nutrition and general health to verbal skills.

In Head Start programs, children are exposed to letters and words, to numbers and books, and to exercises involving drawing, pegs and pegboards, puzzles, toys, and materials that other children take for granted. For five-year-olds, Head Start programs are the same as regular preschool programs, although there is now more emphasis on academics, consistent with the public school curriculum.

Current Head Start programs differ from those of other preschools in the level of community involvement, family involvement, and availability of professionals from a variety of disciplines such as nursing, special education, and speech and language pathology. Parental involvement has become a standard aspect of most Head Start programs. In fact, parental membership on policy and advisory boards is mandatory as a condition of federal funding (Zigler & Valentine, 1979).

Learning to Learn programs are similar to Head Start; they too focus on small-group instruction, the child's use of language, and the fostering of parental involvement. These interventions educate parents about the goals of the program, provide them with information about their child's program, and repeatedly emphasize that a partnership between the home and the school is necessary to ensure the program's success.

BOX 1-4

Sammy and me in Head Start

Meeting Sammy

I remember Sammy—bursting through the door of the classroom at the beginning of the school year. The aides and myself, his Head Start teachers, smiled, his enthusiasm infecting us immediately. We were to remember that day when later we thought about and discussed how we could best help this young person gain a "head start," or at least catch up with the learning of his peers.

Sammy was of average size for a five year old and in good health. His use of language was appropriate and helped him communicate interesting questions and responses to others. Since he was smart and curious this was an important tool for him. In addition, he listened well when engaged in activities of a highly structured nature.

Sammy, however, found it difficult to stay engaged. The very energy and enthusiasm that fuelled his interactions with others and the learning environment were hard for him to direct and focus. He preferred to run in the classroom; during lunch time (which was served to all the children and adults) he was out of his chair an average of eight times; during family grouping time he could not remain seated for more than a few minutes; often he took his arm along the top of bookshelves and knocked down all books, materials and equipment; he hit other children and grabbed toys from them. Any one of these behaviours when demonstrated occasionally and as an isolated incident is not cause for alarm in a five year old child. However, when they are grouped and make up the majority of the child interactions they become problematic for the child and others in the learning environment.

Sammy's Family

Sammy's family included a mother, a few aunts and uncles and older siblings not living at home. His mother and he lived in a third floor apartment where the aunts, uncles and older siblings occasionally stayed. The father had not been a presence in Sammy's life for many years. In order to qualify for Head Start the family had to have an income below poverty level, be willing to participate in parent education activities and send Sammy to the Head Start classroom four days a week.

Mostly, the adults in Sammy's family had minimal education, thus their skill level for employment was low and work was inconsistent. They often bounced between employment and governmental financial aid. They were in their own desperate struggle to survive and gain a foothold in society.

They loved Sammy. This was demonstrated in their stated desire for him to have a better education, in their daily commitment to ensuring he attended Head Start and in the care they took with his personal appearance and clothing. The mother attended parent education meetings and helped in the learning environment. And yet the weight of poor education, sometime employment and very little income—in other words, poverty—left Sammy's family, particularly his mother, with poor coping and parenting strategies.

When days were unmanageable for the family, it was not uncommon for Sammy to spend the entire day outdoors devising his own play activities and living by his own rules. Inside the apartment, when the adults were unable to concentrate on their own behaviour, much less Sammy's, he was provided few guidelines on what was appropriate or not appropriate interaction. Behavioural expectations were inconsistent and it became very hard for Sammy to watch for clues and respond positively: When did he make decisions or when did the adults? Thus, his frustration level was reached quickly and he "acted out" with energy and enthusiasm—at home and at Head Start.

Important questions

As Sammy's inconsistent and often inappropriate behaviour emerged in the learning environment our first response was to do a series of focused and open observations. We needed to have a "picture" of his behaviour so we could answer questions like: When was he most in control of his own behaviour? What were his primary interactions with the environment, children and adults? What strategies did he have for changing his behaviour? In addition, we needed to have him tested for seeing, hearing, use of language and social skills. As the data indicated, Sammy was one of those children who would not be classified with any intellectual or physical problem, but rather social and emotional. He had learned a set of behaviours that helped him cope in one environment and not in another and in trying to adapt to both he was frustrated and aggressive.

The Head Start staff needed to consider what to do next. How could we change behaviour in the learning environment, particularly when it would not be reinforced at home? This was a real concern since part of Sammy's frustration was adjusting, on a daily basis, to two sets of environment with very different behavioural expectations. And yet, we believed that if Sammy was to continue in a school system he needed better coping and learning skills.

But the questions became even thornier. How could we gain the support of Sammy's family to change some of their behaviours with him? More important we had to answer this ethical question: What right do we have, as representatives of an institution—i.e. school—to imply and then request a family to change based on our value system? We discussed and discussed this question and it was not easy to answer. Our conclusion was this: it was our responsibility as educators to provide the family with feedback (not judgements) about Sammy's

learning potential in Head Start and future classrooms; then it was our role to ask the family if they would like us to help future classrooms; then it was our role to ask the family if they would like us to help them and Sammy improve his chances for learning in the school system. We knew the answer would be yes, and yet it had to be their decision and they had to be part of preparing a plan. We knew that no matter how constructively we worked in the Head Start learning environment, without the family cooperation our success was limited.

Family strategies

The first step was to gain the family's trust. Part of the Head Start program required the lead teacher, myself, to make regular home visits to each family. In the beginning this was very difficult with Sammy's family. I represented an "authority figure" from an institution in which they had experienced negative and possibly debilitating interactions. Also, I was of a different race and culture. It took us many visits to find common ground. Sammy was our link and we both were deeply interested in his future.

In the beginning home visits were often cancelled or changed by the family but I persisted and the early visits we did have were about general Head Start information, *nothing* evaluative or judgmental, and were kept short. In other words, we just chatted over coffee or tea. Then, as we became more comfortable with each other, and as I learned to listen better, Sammy's family members, particularly his mother, would ask questions related to Sammy's progress. This was the opening I had hoped for.

At that point in the relationship it became very important to follow up on all the questions and concerns noted by the family. I would try to provide answers during the home visit but often the information they needed wasn't with me to share. In this case I would call them between home visits, send written notes or possibly make an extra stop at their house to drop off materials. We were beginning to appreciate each other and establish a communication system.

The next step was delicate. I needed to describe suggestions we, the Head Start educators, had for improving Sammy's learning and coping strategies and how it would impact their family life. We agreed to a number of activities. They were interested in having me bring to their home children's books, games and materials that they could learn to use with Sammy. From then on, during each home visit, I introduced a different piece of equipment and made suggestions about how it could be used. At the next home visit I would ask general questions about how the interactions went and try not to be too evaluative of their efforts.

The mother agreed to participate in the classroom monthly. At first she was nervous and stayed in the background. I had, initially, made the mistake of not planning anything structured for her to do. I quickly learned that saying, "Would you take this game and introduce it to this group of five children, then let them play with it and you help where appropriate" was better than asking "What would you like to do?" She became more actively involved and then relaxed in the classroom.

During the first few times of her participation I remember her saying "All of you really talk with the children differently." We chatted about that observation and I believe she thought carefully about this because it did seem she slowly changed her own verbal interaction with Sammy. This was a great help to us.

In addition, she, and occasionally other family members, agreed to participate in parent education evenings with other parents. During these evenings there needed to be a delicate balance between presenting educational information and socializing. We planned evenings around activities that would produce something for the classroom such as games, books, toys, etc. As we all sat around a table making something, the Head Start educator's role was to infuse information about how this "something" could be used and how it fostered developmental learning. However, we also chatted about the weather, the latest basketball scores and where to find cheap children's clothes!

Team work

We had to work as a team. All the adults involved with Sammy—the Head Start educators, family members, special education person, social worker, nutritionist and psychologist—were considered part of the team. Each person collected and/or communicated information about Sammy to all the other team members. Sometimes this was done personally and sometimes in written communication. After receiving input from all these persons, the team needed to have at least one general meeting to develop a plan for Sammy.

In designing a program for shaping much of Sammy's behaviour in the classroom we discussed two points of view. The constructivist point of view suggested that children "construct" their own knowledge base and set of learning and coping skills when provided with an enriched learning environment that includes adults to facilitate this development. Our classroom arrangement and organization was based on the constructivist approach. And, for most of our children, this approach facilitated their learning—or constructing!

It requires, however, that the children have a repertoire of cooperative social skills they use most of the time (no one is perfect!). Because of his high frustration and aggression level, Sammy could not demonstrate these skills most of the time. Then we turned to the behaviourist point of view that suggests behaviour can be shaped and ultimately changed given the appropriate reinforcing environment. As a team we identified which of his behaviours was the most destructive to him and others; set some realistic expectations for his behaviour and devised a plan for reaching these expectations. If Sammy had been older we would have included him in these discussions.

Head Start classroom strategies

Because children require nutritional food daily to help learning occur, and because we were concerned that this was not occurring for Sammy, we agreed that he needed to stay seated to eat lunch. We devised a step by step plan that included expectations and consequences to shape Sammy's behaviour. I then explained to Sammy what our new expectations were and what would happen if he continued to leave his chair during lunch time. I don't believe he understood me, and why should he? The adults in his life had so often reinforced his leaving his chair. But it is an important step to verbally communicate the changes in order that children have a "sense of fair play."

Over the next months Sammy learned to stay at his chair during lunch time. Please don't assume that he became a leisurely eater who carried on conversations with his peers and teachers. He still was "Speedy Sammy." However, the goal was achieved; he did stay long enough to eat a nutritional meal. In addition to this targeted behaviour, Sammy learned to not dump books, games, etc. from their shelves; to stay seated increasingly longer during family group time and to refrain from running in the classroom. We believed he was successful when he behaved *most* of the time in this manner.

We made special efforts to keep Sammy's family informed about the progress, not necessarily the failures, and to ask their cooperation. We would send home notes commenting on his positive behaviour and ask them to talk with him about how pleased they were. During home visits I would ask Sammy to demonstrate to his family this behaviour and tell him, in front of them, how important this was to me and the other educators and children in the classroom. Also, I would ask the family if they could help me by continuing to expect this behaviour at home.

Also, the team met a few times to review progress and reevaluate the goals and objectives of the plan. In order to make a decision about the next appropriate action it was often necessary for the team members to collect more information about Sammy's behaviour. Classroom educators and family members collected observational and anecdotal data, the special education person engaged him in assessment activities, the social worker kept records of family, school and community interactions, the nutritionist kept a diary of his eating habits and the psychologist observed his behaviour at key times during the day. We needed everyone's input to get a clear picture of a very complex and interesting young person.

As hard as Sammy was trying and as hard as his little body was incorporating the changes, there were days when we all "lost it." Maybe he had a bad day, maybe I did, maybe the other educators did, or maybe we all did. However it happened, there were days, fewer and fewer in number, when Sammy could not stay in the classroom. We had made an agreement with the family that if this occurred he would be brought home. As Sammy valued his classroom experiences more and more he did not want to leave and worked hard to adapt. And so did we. As Sammy adapted more and more to the classroom social expectations he began to behave more in the constructivist mode. He had longer engaged play times; became more focused on activities; interacted with his peers more appropriately. The changes in scheduling bothered him less and less. We became better at identifying his interests and supporting his play time with materials and suggestions. We sincerely hoped he was beginning to construct a knowledge base and positive coping strategies that would support him throughout his schooling.

The future for Sammy

But the awful thing about teaching is we were never quite sure of his future. In one year we saw Sammy change his behaviour. But was it enough? Would it stick? Or, would he enter the school system and fall further and further behind? He still haunts my memory.

Until recently there had been very little to indicate the long term effects of Head Start enrichment programs on children's elementary, junior and senior high school experiences. However, a recent report lends credence to our notion that Sammy was going to make it.

In the 1960's David Weikert, who developed the first Head Start programs, identified a group of children who had Head Start experiences and matched them with a group of children who were the same age and family background and who had not had Head Start experience. He researched these two groups for 18 years and found that children who had Head Start experience were more likely than children who did not have Head Start experience to:

- *not* be classified as special education students
- complete more grades in school, and
- graduate from high school.

I believe Sammy was one of those students.

Submitted by Linda Jones.

SPECIAL EDUCATION

Children who are exceptional require special assistance. This assistance may be necessary periodically or continuously throughout their educational careers, and it should begin as early as possible—even in infancy.

> Special education programming and instruction designed especially to suit the needs of an individual child who is exceptional.

The process of designing programming and instruction for an individual child who is exceptional is known as *special education*. Of the many assumptions underlying special education, the most fundamental is the belief that every individual is unique. The essence of special education is to provide for that uniqueness through what is often referred to as individualization. We saw this in the case of Darrin. When he entered the program, few modifications to the overall curriculum of the regular preschool class were needed. However, Darrin's own program was individualized within the general curriculum to provide a focus on his special needs and unique strengths. These adaptations were written down in an Individual Program Plan (IPP), shown in Box 1–5.(Ideas for adaptations for a child with cerebral palsy are shown in Box 1–6.) As well, staff responsibilities were changed in order to promote the idea that integration was the responsibility of all staff members.

> Ancillary services areas and disciplines that support and complement special education.

Because the needs of children with exceptionalities are so varied, special education cannot exist in isolation. Other forms of intervention may be necessary as well—medical, technical, or therapeutic intervention, for example. The areas and disciplines that support and complement special education are known as related services, or *ancillary services*. (A number of related services are more fully discussed in Chapter 3.)

Until quite recently, special education was chiefly identified with the school system and with school-age children and their teachers. This is no longer true. In the past two decades, special education has expanded dramatically. It now includes infants and preschoolers as well as adolescents and young adults. Today, special education could be a mother using sign language with her deaf infant in the home, a caregiver in a nursery school modifying an activity for a preschooler, a classroom teacher using remedial techniques in the schoolroom, or a counsellor setting up a work experience program for a young disabled adult (Winzer, 1996).

BOX 1–5
Darrin's IPP

NAME: *Darrin*

CENTRE: *Sunshine*

DATE OF BIRTH: *January 12, 1988*

CHRONOLOGICAL AGE: *4 years, 2 months*

Present levels of functioning

Darrin is diagnosed as having spastic cerebral palsy. The major problems are in the motor area that affects ambulation and speech. There does not appear to be any impairment of intellectual functioning or any secondary condition such as a behaviour disorder. Darrin is, however, very shy. Throughout the early years, a child's interpersonal relationships are vital to his or her emotional and social development and to the emergence of his or her personality, so initiating and sustaining interaction between Darrin and his peers should be an important component of Darrin's program.

Persons responsible

The speech/language therapist will introduce Darrin to an alternative system of communication, although staff will monitor his use of the system in daily situations. At the same time, teachers will work on the goal of stimulating peer interactions within the setting.

The physical therapist will demonstrate ways to handle, lift, and position Darrin.

Teachers will focus on the goals outlined in the plan below within the context of daily routines and events in the setting.

Adapted schedule for Darrin:

1. *Daily classroom activities to promote gross and fine motor development and other long-term goals.*

2. *More individualized motor programming activities and exercises in small groups.*

3. *Physical or occupational therapy activities blended into classroom group activities (calendar, music, and so on).*

4. *Individual therapy with a therapist on a pull-out (removed from the regular class) basis (see Radonovich & Houck, 1990).*

Long-term goals

1. *Develop Darrin's basic skills in the use of an alternative communication system such as Bliss symbolics.*

2. *Teach Darrin to participate in centre activities daily, first with teacher direction and then more independently.*

3. *Help Darrin learn to play associatively and co-operatively with peers.*

4. *Enhance Darrin's motor skills and develop his manipulative skills, fine motor skills, manual dexterity, and eye/hand co-ordination through activities such as art and modelling with clay and Play-doh.*

5. *Build on Darrin's already established gross motor skills.*

6. *Develop Darrin's small motor skills through therapy and small group work.*

Short-term goals (one month)

1. *Speech therapist will work with Darrin to determine a form of augmentative communication.*

2. *Encourage Darrin to go to the play centre and select a toy. Play with the toy with him. Encourage him to select another toy. Reinforce his choices.*

3. *Encourage Darrin to join in centre activities that require two persons, such as building a tower with large Styrofoam blocks. Reinforce appropriate play behaviour and social interaction.*

4. *Allow Darrin to select a story or song during circle time by having him point to his*

choice from a selection shown in pictures on a chart.

5. *Further encourage Darrin to climb large equipment, specifically the ladder and slide. Generalize to other equipment. Assign another child as a buddy if necessary.*

6. *Provide Darrin with tools that require free-flowing movement of the fingers, hand, and arm such as large crayons and large paint brushes.*

7. *Develop Darrin's tearing skills to strengthen and encourage the use of both hands.*

BOX 1–6
Helpful hints

- Children with orthopedic, neurological, or musculoskeletal difficulties may require special equipment such as prosthetic devices, or special positioning or handling techniques and special feeding techniques. Learn the skills of positioning and handling a child with cerebral palsy.

- Investigate the use of bolsters and special seating.

- Be aware of any medication and any schedules for medication.

- Use adapted equipment such as adapted spoons and forks.

- Be aware of individual needs related to limited mobility and privacy.

- Learn procedures for positioning and moving wheelchair users.

- Leave enough room to store crutches or manipulate wheelchairs.

- Be alert to the possibility of a child building up a dependence on staff or other children.

- Keep expectations high but commensurate with the child's capabilities.

- Expect the child to adhere to the ground rules set for all children. In situations where this is not possible, explain the exceptions to the special child and to other class members.

- Avoid urging the child to engage in an activity that requires more complex behaviours than those you have already observed in that child's repertoire.

- Avoid urging or encouraging the child to engage in any activity that is already well-integrated in his or her repertoire. A child does not need to practise a skill he or she has already mastered unless it is part of a more complex behaviour.

- Encourage a child to participate in new activities or use new materials that require skills quite similar to those you have already observed him or her displaying.

- Provide opportunities for the child to observe others using slightly more advanced skills than he or she has mastered to date.

- If the child has an aide in the classroom, schedule that person's time carefully. Always ensure that the child is a member of the class and not working with the aide individually too much of the time.

- Provide large soft toys, or at least toys without sharp edges.

- Ensure that toys are very sturdy.

- Use lighter equipment for children with physical disabilities, as these children may not have the strength of their peers.

- Adapt mechanical toys with special switches.

- To strengthen hand use, encourage play in activities that require two hands, such as finger painting or Play-doh.

Mainstreaming

Most people have come across the term mainstreaming in relation to children with special needs. Mainstreaming is actually quite new in special education; it has evolved since the 1960s.

In the 1960s, the great majority of students with special needs were educated in separate, segregated classes, schools, or institutions. In the same decade, however, parents, researchers, and legislators began to attack the traditional models of special education on a number of different fronts. Their arguments can be grouped in three categories: ethical and humanitarian, legal and legislative, and psychological and educational.

A series of efficacy studies of the educational system in the 1960s demonstrated that children in special education classes were achieving no better than special needs students in regular classes. Legal arguments were linked to the civil rights movement of the 1960s. Critics of special education held that persons with disabilities had a civil right to live, attend school, and work in the same environment as others. They pointed to the discrimination inherent in providing separate schooling for children based on presumed mental, physical, or behavioural incapacities. Others castigated special education programs for the disproportionate number of ethnic and minority group children who were placed in special segregated classrooms. Critics deplored on ethical grounds the practices of labelling children and separating them from their normally developing peers.

Prompted by these changes in public and educational perceptions, attitudes toward people with disabilities began to change dramatically. There was an ideological shift from segregation during the 1960s and the 1970s toward the belief that community settings were superior in their effects on social, vocational, and academic learning. By the mid-1970s, the treatment of persons with disabilities in nonrestrictive, normalized settings had gained priority.

Legislative documents in the United States and Britain had an enormous impact on the course of special education. Britain's Warnock Report suggested new ways of talking about, treating, and educating persons with disabilities. In 1975, U.S president Gerald Ford signed Public Law 94-142, the Education for All Handicapped Children Act, probably the most important piece of federal educational legislation ever passed in the United States. PL 94-142 gave school-aged exceptional children the right to a free, appropriate education in the least restrictive environment supported by a cascade of educational services and an individual education plan (IEP).

PL 94-142 meant that many children moved from segregated settings into regular classrooms. The legislation also influenced many countries, including Canada, to reassess their special education practices and to pass their own legislation regarding students with disabilities. Canadian educators were already developing a deep regard for the principles of normalization and mainstreaming at this time. However, there is little question that the American legislation provided another strong incentive for legislators and policymakers in some provinces to pass mandatory special-education legislation.

Special education has travelled an enormous distance since 1975, although the road has been bumpy and full of hazards. Currently, special education is in a state of flux, both in the school system and in our area of concern, early childhood special education. Both disciplines are replete with competing ideologies and lack a clear research base to support any one process, setting, or intervention.

Inclusion

The hottest debate in special education today is about **inclusion**. There are many definitions and versions of inclusion, but essentially, it means that all children will be placed in the classrooms they would attend if they did not have a disability.

There are subtle but real differences between inclusion and the older terms that it has displaced: **mainstreaming**, least restrictive environment, and integration. Mainstreaming, as we saw, means providing all exceptional students, regardless of type and severity of disability, with an appropriate education alongside their normally developing peers as far as possible. The term *least restrictive environment* (LRE) is frequently used interchangeably with *mainstreaming* (although this is not entirely correct), and generally refers to the practice of placing students in settings that are as normal as possible and that permit students to have optimal interaction with their normally developing peers. Educational integration is simply another term that is used almost synonymously with mainstreaming and LRE.

Today, many advocates prefer the term *inclusion*, or *inclusive schooling*, and its underlying philosophy. In inclusive programs, the diverse needs of all children are accommodated to the maximum extent possible within the general education curriculum. Procedures such as collaborative teaming and teaching and shared planning are central to the success of inclusion.

Where school-age children and youth are concerned, the philosophical ideal of inclusion remains the subject of heated debate among special education and mental health professionals, teachers and teachers' federations, parents, and the public. However, many of the problems that surface with older students are not relevant in the case of students under the age of five. For example, inclusion on a full-time basis may not be appropriate for an older adolescent with a disability who needs to learn skills for the adult world. In this text, however, the emphasis is on the inclusion of young children in regular kindergartens and community-based preschool programs. One of the most important considerations with respect to intervention for young children with special needs is that it take place in programs that cater to normally developing children. Inclusion means that all children are part of the classroom. In large-circle time, for example, the child with a disability sits next to other children, sings the songs, and participates in other planned activities as far as possible.

This text holds that the more natural the learning environment, the greater the opportunity for using newly learned behaviours with different people and in different situations. The opportunity to interact with other children of the same age is necessary for a child's normal social development. Children with disabilities are more likely to develop limited horizons if they are segregated from normally developing children. Furthermore, the presence of advanced peers may cre-

To grow and learn, young children require many stimulating experiences.

ate a more developmentally complex environment, which, if the complexity is not too great, can give children with disabilities a developmental "push" toward acquiring and practising advanced skills (Jenkins, Odom, & Speltz, 1989).

EARLY CHILDHOOD SPECIAL EDUCATION

The history of early childhood special education is short—less than two decades. Few organized programs existed for young children with disabilities until the early 1960s. It was during this period that early childhood programs, ameliorative programs, and special education began to merge into the new field of ECSE. The merger was prompted and guided by impulses similar to those that directed early childhood education—a matrix of social, economic, demographic, educational, and humanitarian forces.

We pointed out that in the early 1960s, concerns about the impact of high-risk conditions on children's later cognitive, linguistic, and social functioning led to the development and implementation of ameliorative programs across North America such as Head Start. At the same time that Head Start was being initiated, early childhood education was undergoing fairly drastic changes. It not only was expanding rapidly, but also was seeing its whole orientation change. Historically, the care of young children was not generally viewed as a task that required a great deal of preparation. By the 1960s, however, what we might call the babysitting mode of child care was quickly yielding to models based on theory and research that sought to develop children's functioning across all domains.

Special education was also undergoing a rapid transformation. Until the 1960s, special education for school-aged children was offered almost exclusively in segregated settings—residential schools or special, separate classrooms within regular school buildings. Complaints and criticisms from parents and educators, action in the courts, efficacy studies on special education, and the new sensitivity to ethical and humanitarian issues that was an outgrowth of the civil rights movement impelled educators toward the concept and practice of mainstreaming.

Legislative change in the area of special education was directed at school-age children with exceptionalities. In early childhood services, interest in typical preschool children preceded interest in preschoolers with disabilities. However, with the growth of programs such as Head Start, the rapid expansion of early childhood education, and the dramatic movement toward mainstreaming in special education, a new discipline emerged.

Early efforts to combine young children who were disabled and their normally developing peers in a single program began in the 1970s (Bricker, 1978) with a process known as developmental integration. By the mid-1980s, ECSE had become a primary method of intervening with young children with disabilities and their families.

ECSE is embedded in regular early childhood education. It is not a separate entity, an add-on, or a parallel enterprise, as special education often is in the school system. ECSE practices share a general concordance with those of early childhood education. Indeed, there are numerous similarities between the two.

When children with special needs are placed in community-based centres, they become the responsibility of the regular staff and their education is in the context of the regular early childhood model and curriculum of the particular centre. This can be seen in Table 1–1 which shows the correlates of high-quality programs for children who are normally developing and programs for children with disabilities.

Table 1–1: Comparisons of quality indicators

Early childhood education	Early childhood special education
Curriculum	
Concrete, real, and relevant materials and activities	Functional
	Age appropriate
Integrated content	Integrated content and setting
Values/respects diversity	Values uniqueness of individual
Developmentally appropriate	
Adult/Child Interactions	
Facilitates child success	Intentional, concurrent instruction
Accepting and responsive environment	Prevention and remediation of learning difficulties
Facilitated engagement	Responsive to learner needs
Child initiated and directed	Optimize engaged time
Meets diverse needs	Child and family centered
	Individualized, integrated teaching and therapy
Age-based groupings	
Assess for program planning	Heterogeneous grouping; role of peers
Evaluate for curriculum effectiveness	Assess for program planning
Multiple sources of information	Programming changes based on formative evaluation
	Variety of outcome measures
Home and school relationships	
Family involvement	Family focus
Regular communication	Systematic communication
Role in decisions and planning	Full partners in planning and decision making
Support to family	Support to family
Co-ordinated sharing of information	Transition planning
Structure, staffing, and organization	
Properly trained staff	Integrated preparation and experiences
Adequate staff/child ratios	Individualized instruction
Continuing professional development	Professional development required and promoted
Co-ordinated sharing of information	Comprehensive, collaborative teaming and decision making
Staff beliefs about children, families, and learning	Parent and professional team membership
Respect, accept, and value children's actions	Outcome focused; integrated setting
	Administrative support
	Beliefs about children, families, teaching, and learning
	Educative approaches; naturalistic teaching

Source: From *Mainstreaming During the Early Childhood Years* by C.L. Salisbury, Exceptional Children, Vol. 58, 1991, 146-155.
Copyright 1991 by The Council for Exceptional Children. Reprinted with permission.

Early intervention the establishment of educational and support services for young children with or at risk for disabilities, and their families.

The underlying theme of ECSE is early intervention. ***Intervention*** may be defined as "care and education aimed at influencing the direction and scope of children's developmental processes" (Doxey, 1990, p. 143). ***Early intervention*** refers to the establishment of educational and support services for young children with disabilities or at risk for disabilities and their families. (The term "early intervention," although strongly associated with active educational programming, can also include medical intervention and welfare provisions for the family and the child.) Both early intervention and its natural corollary, early identification, rest on the belief that children with disabilities can make positive gains if their problems are identified and diagnosed as early as possible, and if they receive educational and therapeutic services tailored to their special needs.

PROGRESS CHECK 2

How have ECSE and special education changed since the 1960s? What led to the emergence of the new discipline of ECSE? What influence did Head Start and other ameliorative programs have on the development of ECSE?

The term early intervention has had a number of different meanings over the past twenty years. At the present time, a number of people believe that early intervention should be used to refer only to infant and toddler programs, and that early childhood special education or preschool special education are the terms that should be used for three-, four-, and five-year-old children (Bricker, 1993). In this text, we use the terms early intervention and early childhood special education interchangeably. We see ECSE as a subset of early intervention, and believe that both terms are applicable to all children in the early years, from infancy to kindergarten. We define ***early childhood special education*** as any program or service within the early childhood period. It can include home training, clinic-based programs, child care facilities, and nursery schools.

PROGRESS CHECK 3

Make sure that you can define intervention and early intervention. Then describe the early intervention initiatives used with Darrin. What should be the results?

The Rationale for Early Childhood Special Education

Early childhood education a program that is concerned with the development and special needs of young children and their families, with particular emphasis on the preschool years.

There is compelling evidence for beginning intervention early. For young children with exceptional conditions, early and sustained educational intervention is vital to help them achieve some measure of independence and develop skills in the social, cognitive, and communication domains. Moreover, both developmental and educational intervention are likely to be more effective if they occur before the child's deficiencies worsen and are compounded by the numbing effects of extended school failure (Satz & Fletcher, 1979). Children who have not had the benefit of early intervention face greater difficulties once they reach the regular school system, and their families often do not develop the confidence and skills necessary to assist them optimally. Early intervention also has benefits for society in the form of potentially significant reductions in the numbers of children who might otherwise require, in later life, extensive special services involving large public expenditures. The provision of early supportive services for children with disabilities and their families can lessen the debilitating effects of handicapping conditions, as well as the subsequent costs of care for individuals who are disabled (Marfo et al., 1988).

ECSE is now accepted in the educational community as an effective intervention strategy for lessening or ameliorating the negative effects of disabling conditions (Edmister & Ekstrand, 1987) and for supporting families. The current interest in ECSE rests on a matrix of factors, some of which are listed below:

- People have become more aware of the importance of the childhood years and of children in general, and realize that the early childhood years are the optimal time for development. This perspective is supported by a body of educational, psychological, and medical research that documents the critical importance of the first five years of life.

  For example, Benjamin Bloom (1964) summarized a large group of studies on intellectual growth. He suggested that a stimulating environment in the early years is critical to children's optimal cognitive growth and that a lack of proper stimulation can inhibit development. Bloom proposed that intellectual development has a negative growth curve; as a child grows older, the richness and diversity of his or her environment has a decreasingly positive effect. Psychologists use the term *plasticity* or *trait plasticity* to refer to the extent to which an individual can be modified by environmental influences.

  By the time children are six years old, almost two-thirds of their ultimate cognitive ability is formed. That is, "by the time children arrive in grade one, their educational futures are already shaped to a significant degree by their early learning experiences." After the age of six, the child's potential for further intellectual growth is slowed. Thus, children at the age of three will benefit more from enrichment activities than children aged eight to ten. Unless we take advantage of this most important time for child development, a unique and important opportunity will be lost. It is a particularly tragic loss, because later efforts cannot compensate for early deficiencies (Bloom, 1964).

  The same growth pattern is seen in the area of language development. About twice as much language growth occurs between the first and third years as between the third and fifth years (Cratty, 1986). Children learn to comprehend more than 14,000 new words, or about 9 words a day, from 18 months through the preschool years (Rice, 1989). In this early learning stage, both research and experience show that young children can learn at least as well outside the home as in it.

- Quality early childhood programs give children a solid base for later learning, a strong self-concept, an interest in learning, and an enthusiasm for later schooling.

- For children with disabilities, education is directed toward developing all of the child's senses and skills, not only those affected by the disability. Early integrated intervention aims to take a synthetic approach in which all developmental areas are addressed in conjunction with each other. All of a child's needs must be taken into account, not just those that are exceptional.

In general, early childhood programs aim to promote the healthy growth of each child, and each child is considered a unique individual with distinctive experiences, needs, and potential.

All children, regardless of their abilities or disabilities, are encouraged to acquire the skills they need to discover their own individuality and reach their full potential. Early childhood settings are one of the prime places to provide inclusive schooling and early intervention, and properly prepared settings can help young children grow and learn together.

One of the major reasons that placement in normalized settings is promoted for all young children is inclusion with normally developing peers.

- It has been clearly established that early intervention with children who are disabled or at risk in some way can have significant long-term benefits in terms of maximizing a child's ability to function at the highest possible levels. Research indicates that initial educational placements for children with disabilities are highly predictive of later placements (see, e.g., Edgar, Heggelund, & Fisher, 1989). Early intervention fosters more positive attitudes about school achievement, improves children's chances of succeeding in the regular school system, and may reduce the extent to which special placement is required in later years.

  Children with mild disabilities who were provided with early stimulation have been found to be significantly less likely to require special education in their later schooling than children who were not (Weber, Foster, and Weikert, 1978). The same is true of children from poorer socio-economic backgrounds. Studies of these children (Lazar & Darlington, 1982) found that those who received early intervention were less likely to be held back in school, and less likely to be in special education. These children also tended to be more achievement-oriented, and their mothers frequently had higher aspirations for them.

- Social skill development and peer interaction, two major areas of difficulty for young children with disabilities, can be improved through early intervention. As a learning process, socialization starts well before an infant is a year old, and in many ways, it is a process that continues throughout the course of a lifetime. Children with disabilities do not engage in as much social interaction as do children who are not handicapped. In an integrated setting, this imbalance can be redressed. Teachers can stimulate social interaction by structuring play situations and giving positive reinforcement to disabled and non-disabled children when they interact with one another (Denonay & Guralrich, 1974).

- Children do not seem to be rejected at the preschool level. Young children are very tolerant of individual differences, and integrated settings reinforce this acceptance of disabilities.

Self-concept the perceptions of self that underlie, illuminate, and direct personality.

- ECSE enhances a child's self-concept. Every child has a ***self-concept***—the perceptions of self that underlie, illuminate, and direct personality. Self-concept begins to form in infancy, and is shaped by experience with parents, peers, and others in the environment. A child's self-esteem can be enhanced by an environment in which positive attitudes toward self are promoted and individuality is respected.

- For children with behaviour disorders, early intervention works to lessen deviant behaviours. Children are more malleable and more open to positive influences in the early years.

- Young children with disabilities integrate more easily because the gap between their skills and those of regular children is smaller. Placing children with developmentally comparable peers is feasible only in preschool, however. A four-year-old child in a three-year-old class is not unduly noticeable, and even a four-year-old in a two-year-old class attracts little attention from peers. The situation would be very different if a ten-year-old were placed in a second grade classroom (Rule et. al., 1987).

- Labelling does not occur in an integrated setting. Rather, each child is viewed as an individual. The philosophy of integrated early intervention evolved from the concept that all children, regardless of ability or disability, are children first and foremost. The disability is seen as only one aspect of the child's overall strengths and weaknesses.

- Placing children with disabilities and normally developing children in the same classroom is believed to enrich the environment, setting into motion complex modelling, reinforcement, and expectation effects. Modelling is an important medium for learning. Non-disabled peers provide good models and are readily available in integrated settings. Children with disabilities can acquire social and communication skills through observing and imitating their developmentally advanced peers—interactions that occur naturally in a classroom setting.

- Integrated settings can provide more challenging experiences for children with disabilities. Children with disabilities may spontaneously attempt tasks that have been set for other children. We saw this with Darrin and his attempts to imitate the other children using the ladder and slide.

- Teachers and parents may have higher expectations for the child in an integrated setting. An integrated setting provides a developmental framework for monitoring the progress of all of the children involved in the educational program. This may help teachers and parents to develop more appropriate expectations for children with disabilities based on the performance of their non-disabled peers.

- Normalized experiences increase the likelihood that children will learn and generalize new skills (Bailey & McWilliam, 1990).

- An integrated educational setting prepares the children with disabilities for the "real world of adulthood, by teaching them in and about the real world of childhood" (Galloway & Chandler, 1978, p. 286).

- Early intervention programs may identify at-risk children through teachers' observations of their behaviour and development.

- Early intervention supports parents. In one study of parents of preschool children with disabilities (Winton & Turnbull, 1981), approximately two-thirds of the parents surveyed felt that a major benefit of early intervention was the assistance they received with the continuous responsibility of caring for their child.

- Legislation in the United States has had, and will continue to have, a profound impact on Canadian policies and practices. The passage of Public Law 99-457 in 1986 as an amendment to Public Law 94-142, the Education for All Handicapped Children Act (1975), extended services to children with disabilities down to the age of three. Part H of PL 99-457 stressed the importance of the family, and in so doing gave added legitimacy to parental perspectives regarding necessary services and support. In response to the recent legislation in the United States, early interventionists in both the United States and Canada are re-examining educational philosophies and practices.

- Integrated education also has benefits for normally developing children. The complete absence of disabled or non-disabled peers is not a culturally normal situation. The presence of children with disabilities causes other children to develop more realistic perceptions of what is normal in society and of the abilities of their disabled peers. Research has shown that contact with severely disabled students results in improved attitudes among their peers (Voeltz, 1980).

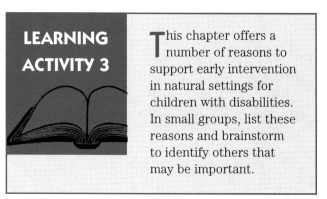

LEARNING ACTIVITY 3

This chapter offers a number of reasons to support early intervention in natural settings for children with disabilities. In small groups, list these reasons and brainstorm to identify others that may be important.

- In most areas, there are no specialized programs available to serve children with identified disabilities. As well, increasing numbers of children with special needs are members of single-parent families or families in which both parents are employed. These families need child care during parents' working hours, which rarely correspond with the operating hours of specialized services for children with disabilities (see Rule et al., 1985).

CONTEMPORARY EARLY CHILDHOOD SPECIAL EDUCATION

In the 1990s, intervention for infants, toddlers, and preschoolers with disabilities is a vibrant and rapidly expanding field, characterized by innovation and creativity, and by a range of program models and options. Vastly increased interest is manifest in the rapid expansion of programs, new and innovative initiatives in personnel training, and the wider population of children served. Today's early intervention programs serve a broad range of children from birth to school age. They serve children with all manner of handicapping conditions, children whose handicaps vary in severity and degree, and children considered to be biologically or environmentally at risk for developing conditions that hinder learning and behaviour.

The body of research and literature on ECSE is growing as well. For example, there was only one textbook on ECSE in 1977. By 1988, more than a dozen had been published (Odom, 1988). Three major journals in the area also appeared in the 1980s—the *Journal of Early Intervention*, the *Journal of Early Childhood Special Education*, and *Infants and Young Children*.

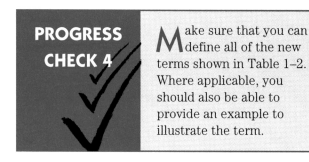

PROGRESS CHECK 4

Make sure that you can define all of the new terms shown in Table 1–2. Where applicable, you should also be able to provide an example to illustrate the term.

This increasing respect for the area of early intervention is reflected in changes made by professional organizations that represent the field. The Council for Exceptional Children (CEC), the encompassing body of special education personnel, opened a special division for early childhood in 1973. The Division of Early Childhood is the only national professional organization whose primary aim is to advance and improve the quality of services to the wide array of young children with special needs and their families. By 1990, the Division for Early Childhood had nearly 7,000 members, making it the fourth-largest of the CEC divisions.

TABLE 1–2: New terms and ideas

ameliorative programs	early intervention
ancillary services	inclusion
cerebral palsy	intervention
child care	mainstreaming
contractures	self-concept
early childhood education	special education
early childhood special education	

SUMMARY

1. This text is about children with exceptional conditions who require special consideration and assistance to stimulate and enhance their learning.

2. Early childhood education for normally developing children has rather a long history, albeit one punctuated by many halts and changes of direction. For years, middle-class children have attended preschools designed to provide them with social and intellectual stimulation for a few hours a week.

3. Early childhood programs for normally developing children remained relatively scarce until the 1950s, when a series of new social, economic, and demographic trends led to a rapid expansion of services and the emergence of new educational philosophies. In particular, the entry of women into the work force significantly altered traditional family child-rearing patterns, and increased the need for care and educational facilities for young children.

4. Studies of the effects of daycare are generally encouraging, although there are contradictory findings on the short- and long-term effects of daycare for infants and preschoolers. Generally, research findings seem to favour daycare for preschool children, but are not quite as clear about the long-term effects of placing children in daycare facilities before the age of one.

5. Today, daycare centres do more than simply care for children, and it is becoming increasingly difficult to distinguish between child care centres and preschools (nursery schools). There is no clear distinction between a daycare centre and an early childhood education program or nursery school. Generally, children tend to have similar experiences in both kinds of programs. Good-quality daycare programs promote the social and intellectual development of children as much as early childhood programs do.

6. In the 1960s, empirical and theoretical research convinced scientists, policymakers, and educators that early childhood is a critical time of development. The importance of early experiences for the development of personality and the intellect has been stressed by many researchers.

7. The practice of assisting disabled children and their families is a recent innovation. The term for it, *early childhood special education*, did not emerge until the 1980s. We use this term synonymously with early intervention, although some researchers prefer to reserve early intervention for the birth to three age range, and ECSE for preschoolers.

8. Today's ECSE can be seen as a melding of regular early childhood education, ameliorative programs such as Head Start, and special education.

9. Current ECSE is not simply an extension of early childhood education or special education but a combination of the two that integrates them within a strong child development framework. The development of programs for young children with exceptional conditions did not parallel the growth in care and education for normally developing children. Rather, it followed it.

10. Head Start began with the goal of eliminating poverty and promoting social equality. Although Head Start programs initially focused on young children from economically and culturally disadvantaged backgrounds, their clientele soon expanded. In 1972, when Head Start programs were mandated to reserve 10 percent of their places for preschoolers with disabilities, the target population for early intervention expanded. Head Start is a multifaceted intervention that includes both child and family. As a social program, Head Start was a success; as an experiment, the results are more difficult to assess.

11. It was once thought beneficial to segregate children with special needs in programs designed to accommodate their particular problems. More recently, normal participation with peers in everyday school and neighbourhood environments has been found to improve the functioning levels of children with disabilities far more than placement in special settings. Providing service to children with disabilities in mainstream daycare centres is desirable for many reasons. One such reason is that exposure to the language and social skills of more highly developed children can enhance the skills of children with disabilities in these areas.

12. There is an essential conceptual difference between inclusion and integration that has important implications for pedagogical practice and program delivery. *Integration* is the process by which physical, social, and academic opportunities are created for a child with a disability to participate with others in typical school or community environments. *Inclusion* accepts children as part of the regular population; program policies, structures, and practices are designed to support the inclusion of young children with disabilities in settings with their non-disabled peers.

13. Special services for infants and young children with disabilities are predicated on the dual prongs of early identification and early intervention.

14. In several countries, legislation pertaining to children with special needs has supported the development of programs for preschool children. In 1986 in the United States, PL 99-457 amended the law (PL 94-142) to extend rights up and down. It is not unreasonable to expect that the interest in ECSE generated by PL 99-457 will rapidly add to the vitality of the field in Canada.

15. Contemporary ECSE is a vibrant area. There is a growing body of evidence indicating that well-designed programs can promote development, prevent future problems, and improve family functioning.

16. Sometimes, teachers need new or adapted measures to meet the needs of special children. However, there is no magic in special education; what is good early childhood practice for typical children appears to be equally good practice for those with special needs. The presence of children with disabilities in the classroom does not necessitate a different style of teaching from that which is appropriate for non-disabled children. Teachers can learn to adapt and modify techniques and strategies without unduly interrupting regular programming. Many of the modifications made for exceptional children are also valuable for normally developing children.

17. Contemporary early intervention practices with young children with disabilities are clearly family-oriented. Teachers may work even more closely with the family of a child who is exceptional than they would with that of a non-disabled child.

CHAPTER 2

The Population of Children Who Are Exceptional

CASE STUDY

Nancy

Nicole, Ada, and Nancy are four years of age. They attend a daycare centre in a large suburb just west of Toronto. Each of the little girls enjoys the daycare experience, and each is progressing across a number of crucial domains.

Nicole comes from a stable, middle-class, Canadian family. She is a tall child, very adept physically. Her parents provide her with many experiences and much stimulation, and this is reflected in Nicole's language, physical and motor skills, social interactions, and increasing maturity. Nicole is beginning to teach herself to read. She constantly prods the staff with questions like, "What does this word say?" and "What letter is this?" She often proudly reads small books to the daycare staff and to other children.

Ada is a small, delicate child. Her parents have been in Canada only a short time, and this is Ada's first experience in a setting with some fixed expectations and rules and a large number of children. At home, Ada's parents speak their native Vietnamese. Although Ada is picking up English quite rapidly and seems to understand much of what is said to her, her expressive language seems to be developing more slowly. So far, Ada has experimented with only a few common words, and she continues to be very reticent about speaking in a group.

Nancy does not communicate with words at all. She has been diagnosed as having a *profound sensori-neural hearing loss* due to meningitis (see Box 2–1). She can express her wants and needs with gestures and vocalizations, and she uses some sign language. One of the daycare teachers is learning sign language, and Nancy is delighted to have someone with whom she can communicate. The daycare teacher is also teaching the other children a few signs.

The three girls are great friends. They play together at their favourite activity, dressing up, and the lack of a common communication mode does not stop them from giggling and laughing together. In other areas, the girls are demonstrating steady progress, although each is advancing at a different rate. For example, their fine and gross motor skills are developing rapidly, but Nicole tends to be ahead in fine motor activities such as cutting and tying.

One major difference the teachers have noticed is in the way the girls do small and large group work. The difference is especially noticeable during circle time, when the whole group meets together with an adult for ten to fifteen minutes to play games, sing songs, do finger plays, perform basic movement exercises, play musical instruments, listen to stories, and so on. Nicole is always attentive and involved. Ada tends to participate little, perhaps because of her limited English proficiency. Nancy does not appreciate being with the group, and wriggles and squirms throughout. Because she obtains all her information visually, sustained attention during linguistic activities such as story time is too difficult for Nancy right now.

Profound sensori-neural hearing loss **loss that affects the inner ear and the auditory nerve.**

NICOLE, ADA, AND NANCY ALL FUNCTION at similar developmental levels, save in the language domain. The three young girls are much more alike than they are different. Each enjoys the learning experience, and each has her favourite activity. Like all young children, Nicole, Ada, and Nancy are active, questioning, curious about their world, and anxious to explore. They are gaining independence and self-confidence, but are still forming ideas about themselves. Each is developing language, although Nancy's is in a visual, not a spoken, mode. Like most children at this age, the three girls are responsive to the sights, sounds, tastes, and feel of things around them. They show genuine wonder and delight in simple things;

snow falling, a snail crawling, or a new pet in the classroom will capture their attention and elicit comments.

But while we see many similarities among Nancy, Ada, and Nicole, there are also differences. Nicole comes from a stimulating environment and demonstrates precocious development. Given encouragement and continual stimulation and challenge, Nicole should proceed through the educational system with ease.

For Ada, the only obstacle to learning at this time is her limited English proficiency. This is not a serious concern, because research has shown that cultural differences per se do not inhibit learning. During the late 1960s and early 1970s, a number of studies examined academic achievement among different ethnic groups. The results indicated that given equal opportunity, students from different ethnic and cultural backgrounds performed as well academically as their classmates.

Ada's quietness is a normal stage in second-language development. Priscilla Clark (1988) observes that many children learning English go through a silent period when they do not speak, either in English or in their first language. Clarke's research shows that much language learning is still going on during this time, and that pressuring the child to speak will only interfere with language development. The quality of the child's interactions with adults is critical during this stage. Ideally, the child should be allowed to remain silent, but should also be encouraged to maintain an involvement in the program. Studies indicate that Ada will acquire adequate face-to-face communication skills within two years. It may take her longer to acquire the language skills she needs for academic pursuits—about five years—but as long as teachers are aware that Ada is still learning English, she too should proceed through the school system with little difficulty.

It is Nancy who faces the greatest obstacles to learning and socialization. Nancy's profound hearing loss will hinder her normal development, especially in the areas of speech and language, and could prevent her from attaining her full potential. If Nancy is to achieve her optimum levels of development, she will require special education. Special services should begin as early as possible. They should extend through the preschool years and will probably be necessary throughout Nancy's school life.

Nancy's hearing loss, the resulting difficulties she experiences with speech and language, and her attendant need for special services and special education make her a child with an exceptional condition or with special needs. Nicole, who appears to be functioning above the norm, may now or later also be considered as exceptional, in the category of giftedness. She too may require special education if she is to reach her potential, although the educational services provided for her would be quite different from those provided for Nancy. Ada, who is not yet proficient in English, is not seen as falling within the broad category of exceptional children. Many of the ideas that we present in this text for enhancing communication and developing language are appropriate for Ada, but she is not a child with special needs who requires special education.

Children Who Are Exceptional

All children differ from one another to varying degrees. The colour of their eyes, hair, and skin differs; the way they dress and speak differs; and their cognitive and social

BOX 2–1
Childhood hearing loss

Hearing loss or hearing impairment is a generic term that encompasses two major groups of individuals—those who are deaf, and those who are hard of hearing. The difference lies in the intensity of the hearing loss and the amount of auditory input that the individual can hear. People who are deaf cannot, even with the use of a hearing aid, hear speech. People who are hard of hearing can hear speech with or without amplification (hearing aids).

The physical aspects of deafness and hardness of hearing affect the child's development of speech and language, the most important components of interpersonal communication. The effects of hearing loss on speech and language development correlate with the degree of hearing loss, although other factors come into play. These include the early and consistent use of amplification, training in and use of alternative communication systems if necessary, the child's cognitive skills, the extent of parental communication with the child, and the amount and type of early intervention and stimulation the child receives. The time of onset is particularly important, because the later in life a hearing impairment occurs, the greater the child's linguistic capabilities are likely to be. Children who are deaf from birth are highest at risk for

serious lags in language and speech development. Children whose hearing impairments occur after they have developed speech and language will probably find it much easier to develop communication skills.

For deaf children, most loud speech is inaudible even with the most sophisticated hearing aids. Congenital hearing impairment inevitably affects every aspect of communication development from birth onwards. Children with congenital hearing losses cannot practise the listening skills essential to developing speech and language, and because they cannot hear the words of people around them, they have no language models.

Deaf children have significant problems in learning language; even with optimal intervention, the language levels of most deaf children are seriously retarded. Speech is another area of great difficulty; deaf children have significant articulation, voice quality, and tone discrimination problems. The majority of children who are deaf fail to acquire understandable speech (Winzer, 1996).

Because they are cut off from auditory means of acquiring and using speech and language, deaf children rely on visual modes, including speech reading and sign language. Lip reading or speech reading involves understanding speech by watching the lips and face of the speaker. It is not true that deaf children can naturally speech read. As with any other skill, speech reading must be learned, and it is a particularly difficult skill to acquire as only

skills and emotional development differ. Every child possesses a unique combination of abilities and problems, and interests and fears. Every child experiences a unique set of successes and failures. Some of the differences among children are apparent as we observe children; others we hear in their communication with peers and adults; still others become evident only after extensive interactions with children.

Many of the differences that we can observe among children do not dramatically affect learning and behaviour. This does not mean that all children learn, behave, and respond to their environments and the people in them in the same way. What it does mean is that most children who are provided with a stimulating early environment and appropriate later education learn and respond quite well.

For some children, however, the differences that distinguish them from other children are more pronounced. Some of these differences are the product of

about 30 percent of the sounds of English are actually visible on the lips.

Some deaf children communicate through speech reading and their own speech (called oral communication). The practice of teaching very young children sign language as a means of communication (manual communication) is becoming increasingly common. In some provinces, young deaf children are taught American Sign Language (ASL); in others, they are presented with what are generically referred to as school-based systems such as Signing Essential English (SEE). Whatever sign system is selected, the goal is to provide the young child with a means of communication (see Chapter 15).

For children with mild and moderate hearing losses, the effects on speech and language are not nearly as drastic as for deaf children. Hard of hearing children can use spoken language to receive and transmit information, and will develop speech and language skills, although they may use speech reading to supplement auditory input.

Deafness is not common in childhood; it is a low-incidence disability. Early childhood teachers are much more likely to encounter children who are hard of hearing, and more likely still to encounter children who have mild but recurrent hearing losses. The most common form of ear infection in children is called **otitis media**. In this condition, the lining of the middle ear becomes inflamed and the cavity fills with fluid. This hinders the conduction of sound from the outer ear to the inner ear. The peak time for children to develop otitis media is the period from 6 to 36 months of age, although many four- and five-year-olds have the condition as well. After the age of six, the prevalence of otitis media decreases.

Recurrent or persistent otitis media with effusion (OME) during early childhood has been implicated as a factor in later speech disorders. The mild to moderate fluctuating hearing losses associated with OME during the language-formative years are presumed to be responsible for these subsequent speech difficulties (Roberts et al., 1988).

Mild and moderate hearing losses are often difficult to identify. Teachers should be alert for some of the behaviours that suggest a hearing loss. These include:

- Talking too much, and seeming to want to control the conversation.
- Singing and talking too loudly or too softly.
- Giving incorrect answers to simple questions.
- Needing questions or directions repeated.
- Appearing to be inattentive when spoken to or in group situations; often responding with "Ay?" or "What?"
- Having physical problems such as earaches, discharge from the ears (effusion), or frequent colds and sore throats.
- Making physical movements, such as cocking the head or turning the body, in an effort to hear more accurately.

Otitis media the most common form of ear infection in children. The lining of the middle ear becomes inflamed and the cavity filled with fluid; thus, the conduction of sound from the outer to the inner ear is hindered.

mental and physical disabilities; children with developmental delays and disabilities may be limited in their ability to interact with the environment and the people in it. Other differences stem from various social and cultural patterns that may be useful in some environments but are not necessarily useful or acceptable in early childhood care and educational programs.

The study of children with exceptionalities is necessarily the study of differences, because the child with an exceptionality is different from the norm in one or more areas of functioning. However, it would be a mistake to focus the study of children with exceptionalities solely on differences. It is equally important to recognize the similarities among children.

Children with exceptionalities do not differ in every way from their normally developing peers. They are children first, and exceptional second. Children with

Like this nondisabled child, children with exceptionalities have the same needs for approval and affection.

disabilities have the same feelings, interests, attitudes, and perceptions that other children have. Their need for care, stimulation, education, and appropriate activities is similar to that of other children, and they desire acceptance, approval, and affection as much as do their nonexceptional peers (Winzer, 1996). These similarities are important as we must always be aware of the danger of seeing only a disability and losing sight of how much children with exceptional conditions resemble other children.

DEFINITIONS OF EXCEPTIONALITY

Children who have differences that substantially affect the way they learn, respond, or behave have been described in many ways. If you have been reading carefully, you will remember that we have thus far referred to these children as children with exceptionalities, children with exceptional conditions, children who are handicapped, children with special needs, and children with disabilities or disabling conditions. Another popular term for children with disabilities is "challenged." All of these terms are used more or less interchangeably, although the term "children with exceptionalities" tends to be the most encompassing.

> Exeptionality when the physical, cognitive, emotional, sensory, or behavioural development of an individual child is not within the norms that are established for all children of a particular age.

An ***exceptionality*** is a deviation in the physical, cognitive, emotional, sensory, or behavioural development of an individual child from the norms that have been established for children of that age. ***Children with exceptionalities*** may be defined as "those whose physical, cognitive, or emotional development falls above or below the norm. They require special education and related services in order to attain their full potential" (Winzer, 1996).

> Children with exceptionalities those whose physical, cognitive, or emotional development falls above or below the norm. They require special education and related services in order to attain their full potential.

These are very broad definitions, in that they include children who have disabilities, such as those who are deaf or visually impaired, as well as children who are functioning above the norm and who may be described as gifted or talented.

However, they are also restrictive definitions in the sense that they refer solely to the educational outcomes of exceptionality. For example, while the medical profession might see a child with Type 1 insulin-dependent diabetes as having a serious medical problem that distinguishes him or her from the norm, educators would not see such a child as exceptional because there is no reason why the diabetes should affect the child's learning and behaviour. Children are considered exceptional in educational terms only when their educational program must be altered to meet their needs. They must demonstrate a clear need for support services to reach their full human potential.

Many other definitions of children with exceptionalities exist, and the terminology is varied and sometimes contradictory. A number of generic terms and descriptions are listed in Table 2–1.

TABLE 2–1: Describing children who are exceptional

Atypical	Children who do not reach the norm in some functional area or areas are described as atypical.
Disabilities	Disabilities are the consequences of impairments in an individual's functional performance and activity.
Disabled individual	A disabled individual is one who suffers from a disability or impairment of function in one or more areas such as vision, hearing, and mobility.
Dysfunctional	A person who is below the norm in some domain of functioning is described as dysfunctional in that respect.
Handicap	A handicap relates to environmental or functional demands placed on a disabled person in a particular situation that are not met.
High risk	A child who is more prone to developing a disabling condition because of biological or environmental factors is described as high risk.
Impaired	A person who has abnormalities of body structure and system function resulting from any cause is described as impaired.
Special needs	Special needs is an educational term used to designate pupils who require special education—that is, students who require additional help and adaptations to ensure the best developmental outcome.

Source: Winzer (1996).

Over the years, the way that both professionals and society in general describe people with exceptionalities has changed in a positive way. In the past, the terms that were used to describe people who were exceptional were value-laden and emphasized the handicap, disorder, or disability. Today, a more humanistic perception holds sway, and the handicap, disorder, or disability is seen as only one aspect of the total person. It is now customary to use terms that refer to the child first and the disability second. Hence, we speak of children with Down syndrome or children with intellectual disabilities rather than Down syndrome children or mentally disabled children. The flexibility of the terminology reflects the ongoing efforts of educators to develop new systems that better describe or profile children's behaviour patterns. It also means that descriptions of children's needs, not etiological labels, drive intervention efforts.

CLASSIFICATION SYSTEMS

In the past, students were placed in categories according to their disabilities for a host of political and social reasons. Currently, classifying and categorizing children is becoming less popular in special education, especially in the evolving area of early childhood special education (ECSE). It is now considered unhelpful to label children early in their educational careers, and thereby slot them into immutable categories. There is also a growing recognition that many of the skills needed for self-help, independence, socialization, and so on are required by all young children regardless of their exceptionalities. Consequently, planning and instruction tend increasingly to cut across categories.

Most integrated early childhood programs adopt a generic or noncategorical approach. Children are accepted and instructed according to their functioning and needs rather than on the basis of some preassigned label. You will notice that in this text we sometimes use specific descriptions such as deafness or cerebral palsy. Just as often, we refer to children who have mild or significant (or severe or profound) disabilities. In the broadest terms, children with mild disabilities include those children traditionally categorized as mildly mentally retarded, mildly behaviourally disordered, learning disabled, hard of hearing, and so on. These categories are in many ways related to the environment and to observer distinctions, and are therefore somewhat problematic. Children with significant disabilities include those whose conditions are undeniable and readily subject to classification, such as those with moderate and severe intellectual handicaps, infantile autism, and multiple disabilities. Sometimes, children with these disabilities are described as developmentally delayed. These terms should be used with care, however. As is clear from the definition of developmental delay provided in Table 2–2, deafness and blindness are significant disabilities, but are not developmental delays.

Although the use of a rigid classification system for preschool-aged children can be very destructive, there are instances when labelling can help ensure that children receive appropriate services. Certain conditions are associated with specific and discrete learning needs. If personnel are to accommodate children with these special needs, they must acquire some knowledge of the functioning and developmental consequences of broad categories of exceptionality.

Labels may be of value if they assist a child in obtaining appropriate services. We can illustrate this point with Nancy, Ada, and Nicole. The three girls will require different educational strategies and instructional emphases. In the area of language, for example, each girl has different needs. Nicole requires further stimulation of her already precocious language; Ada needs assistance in using her second language with confidence while retaining her first language; Nancy needs structured and systematic intervention in order to develop basic competency in speech and language.

Classification systems remain fairly well entrenched in special education. A simple classification system that groups the major types of exceptionalities that early childhood educators may encounter is shown in Table 2–2.

Adaptive behaviour the ability to respond to and function in the environment according to age and social standards. Behaviour that allows the child to interact with the environment and those in it in ways that are appropriate to age, context, and culture.

Primary disability the major condition affecting a child.

This is only one way to describe and classify children who are exceptional. Additional qualifiers may be used to add specificity to these general classifications. Degrees of severity are the most commonly used qualifiers. Conditions are described as mild, moderate, severe, or profound. The term "mild mental retardation" is used to describe children whose IQs are between 55 and 70, and who demonstrate deficits in **adaptive behaviour**—the ability to respond to and function in the environment according to age and social standards. The term "profound mental retardation" applies to children whose IQs are below 25 and who display extreme deficits in adaptive behaviour. Nancy has a profound sensorineural hearing loss. This means that the hearing loss is greater than 90dB—so great that Nancy cannot obtain information through auditory means. In other words, Nancy cannot hear the speech of those around her with or without a hearing aid.

For some children who are exceptional, the differences will be in only one domain of functioning; for others, the differences will cross-cut a number of domains. The major condition that causes a child to differ in learning or behaviour is referred to as the **primary disability**. Other conditions that are present or

TABLE 2-2: Summary of categories and definitions

Children with intellectual differences include those who are intellectually superior (gifted, creative, and talented) and those who are intellectually disabled.

Gifted	Individuals function above the norm. Good IQ level, creativity, and task commitment.
Mental retardation	Individuals have a tested IQ of 70 or below and deficits in adaptive behaviour, manifested during the developmental period.

Children with sensory disabilities include those with auditory impairments (deaf and hard of hearing) and those with visual problems (blind, low vision, and visually impaired).

Deaf	Individuals cannot hear speech, even with the use of a hearing aid.
Hard of hearing	Individuals can hear speech with or without amplification (hearing aids).
Blind	A visual loss of 20/200 with a field of vision restricted to 20 degrees. For educational purposes, blind children need special reading assistance, such as Braille.
Low vision	A visual loss of more than 70/200 and a restricted visual field. Can use large print and other aids for reading and writing.

Children with communication disorders include those with speech difficulties, language problems, and learning disabilities.

Speech disorders	Problems in the oral production of language that interfere with communication. Speech is impaired when it is ungrammatical, culturally or personally unsatisfying, or injurious to the speech-producing mechanisms.
Language problems	Encompass a range of difficulties with the linguistic code, or with the rules for linking the symbols and the symbol sequences.
Learning disabilities	Children show a marked discrepancy between potential as measured on standardized tests and actual performance. They may display deficits in academic performance, especially in language and reading.

Behaviour disorders include conduct disorders, anxiety and withdrawal, personality disorders, social maladjustment, juvenile delinquency, and Attention Deficit Hyperactivity Disorder (ADHD).

Behavioural disorder	Children who chronically and markedly respond to their environments in socially unacceptable and/or personally unsatisfying ways but who can be taught more socially acceptable and personally gratifying bhaviour (Kauffman, 1977, p. 23).

Children physical disabilities and impaired health include those with neurological defects, or-thopedic conditions, birth defects, and conditions that are a result of infection and disease.

Physical disabilities	Disorders of physical development or musculo-skeletal development.
Neurological disorders	Disorders resulting from damage to the brain.

Children with developmental disabilities include those with pervasive disorders. Different types of conditions, including childhood psychoses, childhood schizophrenia, and infantile autism, are found under the umbrella of developmental disorder. This category also includes children with multiple handicaps, such as cerebral palsy and mental retardation, or deafness and blindness.

Pervasive developmental disorder	A general term used to describe children suffering from chronic and severe conditions that affect every aspect of their development.
Developmental disorder	A chronic disorder than can be manifest in mental or physical impairment.
Developmentally delayed	Individuals with conditions that represent a significant delay in the process of development and that present indications that the process of development is significantly affected.
Developmentally disabled	Those who suffer from chronic disabilities attributable to mental and/or physical impairments, or a combination of these that are manifested before age 22 and that result in functional limitations in major life activities requiring special services and treatment that are of extended duration or are lifelong.
Multiply disabled	Children suffering two or more handicaps that hinder their attainment of their full potential.
Medically fragile	Children who need much medical intervention. This category also includes children who demonstrate a wide range of chronic and progressive illnesses and severe disabilities, such as cystic fibrosis, congenital malformations, neuromuscular diseases, and many others.
Technology dependent	Those who rely on technology for functioning.
Infantile autism	A developmental disability significantly affecting verbal and nonverbal communication and social interaction, generally evident before age three that adversely affects educational performance.

Secondary conditions other conditions that are present or arise after the primary disability.

arise as a result of the primary disability are known as ***secondary conditions***. Nancy's deafness is her primary disability. If she were later to develop a behaviour disorder, it would be a secondary disability.

PROGRESS CHECK 1

There are differences between the terms *handicapped* and *disabled*. Define each term and give examples to show the differences.

LEARNING ACTIVITY 1

In recent decades, the causes of disabilities have altered somewhat so that researchers talk about "the new morbidity," that is, new causes. Pediatric AIDS, drug abuse, and alcohol abuse responsible for fetal alcohol syndrome (FAS) are part of the new morbidity. As well, tiny, premature infants can be disabled from technology, as in the case of retinopathy of prematurity.

Select one of the above — pediatric AIDS, maternal drug abuse, FAS, or retinopathy of prematurity. Research information on your topic and present an essay.

Nature the range of traits, capacities, and limitations that each person inherits genetically from his or her parents at the moment of conception.

Nurture all the environmental influences that come into play after conception, beginning with the mother's health during pregnancy and running through an individual's life span.

The Causes of Disabilities

To intervene successfully with young children with disabilities, personnel in early childhood settings need to increase their knowledge and skills in a number of ways. One of the most important things early childhood intervenors can do is acquire both practical and theoretical knowledge of the characteristics of young exceptional children in all domains of development. This will increase their understanding of, and their tolerance for, a child's condition. Early childhood intervenors will also find it helpful to learn some of the terminology used to describe exceptionalities and their respective causes. A working knowledge of relevant terms and etiologies will allow intervenors to collaborate with parents and other professionals, and will enhance their understanding of professional reports and literature. Finally, early childhood intervenors should familiarize themselves with risk factors. This will enable them to provide more effective early intervention.

A large and diverse range of agents are responsible for disabilities in children. Since the 1950s, advances in biochemical knowledge and technology have virtually eliminated potentially disabling diseases such as polio, measles, diphtheria, scarlet fever, and whooping cough. Today, however, a different group of disorders related to new etiologies and new technology has emerged. Children are at risk from such things as pediatric AIDS, maternal use of drugs and alcohol, and extreme prematurity (see Winzer, 1996). Indeed, there is substantial evidence that conditions fostering handicapping conditions and developmental disabilities are on the upswing in North America.

The discussion of childhood disabilities identifies both environmental and biological causes. However, the demarcation between the two is not always clear. In fact, it is almost impossible to determine the relative influence of heredity and environment for any form of human behaviour, since every human life is shaped by a complex interplay of hereditary and environmental factors.

The range of traits, capacities, and limitations that each person inherits genetically from his or her parents at the moment of conception is referred to as ***nature. Nurture*** refers to all of the environmental influences that come into play after conception, beginning with the mother's health during pregnancy and running across the whole of an individual's life span. Both hereditary and environmental factors are crucial to a child's development. Genes alone cannot produce a human being; an environment must also exist to provide nourishment, warmth, stimulation, and protection.

MAJOR RISK FACTORS

> **Etiology**   the causes of a disabling condition.

> **Risk factors**   the causes of potential disabilities. They are divided into three major categories: established risk, biological risk, and environmental risk.

There are a number of different ways of looking at the causes of potential disabilities in children. ***Etiology*** refers to the causes of a disabling condition. One way to examine handicaps is to look at specific etiologies and their effect on development. Another method involves studying these same etiologies throughout the developmental period, for a child's disability can occur prenatally, perinatally, or postnatally. A third approach considers disabilities in terms of risk factors. This is the approach that we take, as shown in Figure 2–1.

Risk factors are the causes of potential disabilities. A child exposed to any risk factor is referred to as high risk. Therefore a child may be at risk or high risk for a disability, for child abuse, or for dropping out of school (see Winzer, 1996). The thousands upon thousands of risk factors are divided into two major categories: established risk and high risk. The category of high risk is further subdivided into biological risk and environmental risk (Tjossem, 1976). These categories overlap considerably.

Risk is essentially a statistical concept. Specialists use the concept of risk status to classify young children in terms of the type and severity of potential disorders. Researchers who study risk identify the agent or situation and specify the effect, and then estimate the probability that the two are associated.

LEARNING ACTIVITY 2

In small groups, brainstorm to find as many reasons as you can why it is important for early childhood personnel to understand risk factors, the causes of disabilities, and the developmental consequences of disabilities.

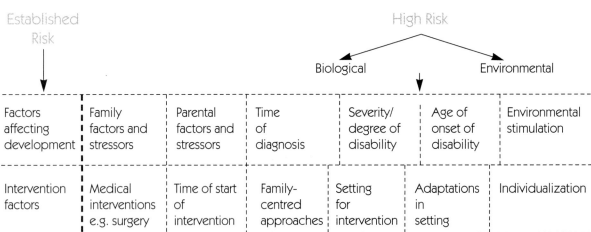

FIGURE 2–1

Risk factors and mediating influences

Established risk

Established risk   a diagnosed medical disorder with a known etiology (cause) that bears relatively well-known expectancies for developmental outcomes within varying ranges of developmental disabilities.

Continuum of reproductive casualty refers to reproductive factors; problems may range from relatively minor thought to major difficulties.

The first category of risk is ***established risk.*** Established risk refers to medical conditions and anomalies that invariably result in a disability or developmental delay. It is defined as a diagnosed medical disorder with a known etiology (cause) that bears "relatively well known" expectancies for developmental outcomes within varying ranges of developmental disabilities (Tjossem, 1976). This means that certain causes are known to relate to certain conditions. Established risk status is measured along a ***continuum of reproductive casualty***. The problems may range from relatively minor through to major difficulties.

Established risk is the most easily identified of all risk statuses. It is most often related to genetic and chromosomal problems. The category includes conditions such as Down syndrome, genetic deafness, and infantile autism.

About 3 to 5 percent of babies are born with a chromosomal abnormality, a clearly defined genetic disease, or a genetically influenced defect such as malformation of the spine. Among these children, about 3 percent of all newborns have some genetic birth defect and about one newborn in 200 has a chromosomal abnormality (Plomin, DeFries, & McClearn, 1990). There are more than 150 known gene defects that may result in mental retardation and other disabilities (Scarr & Kidd, 1983; Vandenberg, Singer, & Pauls, 1986). These problems are generally present at birth. When this is the case, they are referred to as ***congenital abnormalities.***

High risk

Congenital abnormalities problems that are generally present at birth.

High risk   children who have increased vulnerability; they are more prone to developing some form of disabling condition.

Biological risk relates to infants and toddlers with a history of prenatal, perinatal, neonatal, or early developmental events that result in biological insults to the developing nervous system.

When children are considered to be ***high risk*** or at risk, they are said to have increased vulnerability; that is, they are more prone to developing some form of disabling condition.

It is important to remember that not all children who are deemed high risk become disabled. In fact, the majority of children in the two high-risk categories of biological and environmental risk develop normally (Shonkoff & Meisels, 1991). But when compared to the general population, a greater proportion of children who are exposed to biological and environmental risk factors develop significant developmental difficulties. Present estimates indicate that between 30 and 70 percent of infants classified as at risk at birth eventually develop problems that require some form of intervention.

The two main groupings of high-risk factors, biological and environmental, overlap. Environmental risk factors such as poverty can compound problems associated with biological risk, such as prematurity and prenatal drug exposure. For example, premature babies are considered as part of the high-risk category because of their gestational age and their low birth weight. These infants may experience central nervous system (CNS) difficulties that can inhibit development. These difficulties can be overcome in a stable family environment. For infants in unstable or low-income family environments, however, where food and shelter are insufficient, the difficulties present at birth may result in developmental delays and learning problems (see Sameroff et al., 1987).

Biological risk   Infants and toddlers with a history of prenatal, perinatal, neonatal, or early developmental events that result in biological insults to the developing nervous system are said to be at ***biological risk.*** These biological conditions do not inevitably lead to developmental delay or disorder. For high-risk children, however, the probability that these conditions will lead to delay or disability is

Teratogens
environmental agents that may harm the developing fetus. Teratogens that can cause damage include prescription drugs, hard drugs such as cocaine and crack, nicotine, and alcohol.

Critical period a part of the life cycle during which the organism is particularly sensitive or responsive to specific environmental forces. Outside this period, the same event or influences are thought to have few if any lasting effects.

greater than it is for the general population (Shonkoff & Meisels, 1991). As we just pointed out, research has clearly established that premature infants have a higher incidence of developmental problems in childhood than do full-term infants (Cohen et al., 1982).

Two important aspects of biological risk are the causes (etiology) and the concept of critical periods. Etiologically, environmental agents that may harm the developing fetus are known as **teratogens,** from the Greek *teros,* meaning monster. Teratogens include prescription drugs, hard drugs such as cocaine and crack, nicotine, and alcohol. Chemicals can cause a wide range of congenital abnormalities and are said to account for about 10 percent of birth defects (Schwartz & Yaffe, 1980).

A **critical period** is a part of the life cycle during which the developing organism is particularly sensitive or responsive to specific environmental forces. Outside this period, the same events or influences are thought to have little if any lasting effects.

During critical periods, exposure to a teratogen is especially harmful to the fetus. Maternal rubella (German measles), which is carried by extremely small organisms that pass through the placenta, is an excellent example of a teratogen with a critical period. The fetal organs likely to be affected when the rubella virus crosses the placenta are those whose development is underway when the mother contracts the virus. The eyes, ears, nervous system, and heart are especially vulnerable during the early stages of fetal development. It is estimated that 50 percent of fetuses are damaged by a first-month contraction of the disease, and 20 percent of embryos from a second-month contraction (Rosenblith & Sims-Knight, 1985). The risk of eye and heart defects is greatest in the first eight weeks, whereas deafness is more common if the mother contracts rubella between the sixth and thirteenth weeks of pregnancy.

Continuum of environmental (caretaking) casualty environmental factors that range from healthy families to particularly adverse situations.

Environmental risk
applies to infants and toddlers who are biologically sound but whose early life experiences are limited.

Environmental risk   Children at environmental risk are those whose pediatric histories, caregiving circumstances, and current family situations contain risk factors that do not lead invariably to developmental delay, but that carry a greater probability of delay or disability than what is found in the general population (Shonkoff & Meisels, 1991). These risk factors fall along a **continuum of environmental or caretaking casualty** ranging from healthy families to particularly adverse situations.

Environmental risk is a term applied to infants and toddlers who are biologically sound, but whose early life experiences are limited by environmental factors such as a restricted use of language, poor family attitudes, low motivation, inadequate facilities, and poor maternal and family care, health care, and nutrition.

Poverty is far and away the greatest environmental risk factor. In general, children from poor communities are more likely to suffer from developmental difficulties than are children from affluent communities (Rutter, 1987). In fact, children who live in poverty are estimated to be one-and-a-half to two times more likely than affluent children to suffer from one or more disabilities. Children from lower socio-economic strata are at greater risk of incurring brain damage as a result of malnutrition, poor prenatal and postnatal care, and environmental hazards during infancy (Baumeister, Kupstas, & Klindworth, 1990; Dunlap, 1989).

Audiologists assess the hearing status of young children.

Researchers are increasingly able to identify the environmental conditions that increase the likelihood that a child will have a learning or a behaviour problem (Werner, 1986). The two environmental problems that have been studied most are a lack of early psychological stimulation and severe malnutrition. These two factors are not always independent: in many cases, children suffer both from malnutrition and from a lack of early stimulation.

The mother's diet and nutrition play a significant role in the growth and development of the fetus. The importance of nutrition is underscored by the relationship that has been established between the mother's diet, the newborn's weight, and the child's eventual learning ability (Salt, Galler, & Ramsey, 1988). Nutrition in the mother seems to be particularly important in the third trimester, when the fetus should be making rapid gains in weight.

Nutritional deficiency is responsible for a wide range of gestational problems and developmental consequences. In general, malnourished women are much more likely to produce low-birthweight babies. Severe malnutrition also increases the risk of congenital defects, prolonged labour, stillbirth, and infant mortality during the first year.

The period of intra-uterine development and the first eighteen months after birth are crucial to the physiological development of every organ system, but especially the brain. Inadequate prenatal nutrition can affect the relationship between the infant's biochemistry and the functioning of the brain. Postnatal malnutrition, especially during the first six months of an infant's life, is also a critical factor in brain development. Research indicates that severe chronic deprivation of either general nutrition or certain special dietary substances can cause behaviour disorders as well as physical disorders and mental retardation (Lahey & Ciminero, 1980). When malnutrition occurs both prenatally and postnatally, problems are likely to be much more severe.

LEARNING ACTIVITY 3

Risk status is a difficult concept. Make a chart with the headings Established, Biological, and Environmental. Then take the conditions outlined in Table 2–2 and slot them into the appropriate columns. Explain your reasons.

Obesity a body weight that is more than 20 percent greater than the average for one's age, sex, and body size.

In Canada, undernutrition is far more prevalent than malnutrition, and can also lead to cognitive difficulties. Most experts define **obesity** as a body weight that is more than 20 percent greater than the average for one's age, sex, and body size (Epstein, 1985). While the problems associated with obesity are not as life-threatening as those caused by severe malnutrition, obesity in children can have serious medical and psychological implications. Orthopedic and respiratory problems are especially associated with obesity. As well, children begin to develop negative beliefs about fat people even as preschoolers (Fritz & Wetherbee, 1982), although it is not known if being fat themselves affects their self-concept.

Prevalence Estimates

Reported figures on children with special needs almost invariably refer to school-aged children. Recent Canadian estimates (Nessner, 1990) indicate that about 6 percent of Canadian children between the ages of 5 and 14 are disabled as compared to 3 percent of children under the age of 5. This discrepancy may be the result of disabilities that affect children postnatally. Accidents and cancer are still the major causes of childhood mortality and morbidity.

In Canada, about 15.5 percent of school-aged children will require special education assistance at some point in their school careers. Of these students, the great majority demonstrate mild disabilities—more specifically, mild mental retardation, learning disabilities, and mild behaviour disorders. Less than 3 percent of special education pupils have significant disabilities such as deafness, severe visual impairment, infantile autism, and cerebral palsy.

The 15.5 percent figure is only an estimate, because it is extremely difficult to determine the number of children with exceptional conditions accurately. This is especially true for children under the age of five. One major reason for the difficulty in obtaining prevalence figures is that only a relatively small proportion of young children with special needs receive a clear diagnosis of disability.

Severe and profound disabilities in children are almost always identified during infancy or toddlerhood, but mild disabilities are rarely diagnosed in the early childhood years. Many mild learning problems show up only as children face the complexities of reading and mathematics in formal school situations. The category of learning disabilities is the largest special education category within the school system. However, since a learning disability is, by definition, a disability that causes difficulties in academic-related areas such as reading and math, it is not really possible to diagnose such a disability accurately before a child begins formal schooling. Nevertheless, children who are hyperactive, who show attention deficits, who demonstrate developmental lags and difficulties in speech and language, and who are inattentive or distractible above what is normal for their age may be at risk for learning disabilities.

Implications for Care and Education

It is not enough for educators to know about the etiologies of disabling conditions. If they are to contribute to a child's functioning and positive progress, they must also be aware of the developmental consequences of these conditions and the implications for learning and educational integration. Educators need to understand the interrelationships between the characteristics of the developing young child, the child's disabilities or special needs, and the elements of the

BOX 2-2

Helpful hints

Teaching children with mild hearing loss.

- Learn as much as you can about hearing loss and its developmental consequences.
- If the child uses sign language, learn some basic signs and use them consistently.
- Use frequent eye contact, and communicate nonverbally with many gestures.
- Keep group time short, lively, and interesting.
- Use a half-circle arrangement in groups so that the child can see everyone.
- Point out the child who is talking to keep the deaf child cued in.
- Be careful with directions—phrase directions carefully, give them one at a time, and repeat them.
- Squat to the child's level when speaking to him or her.
- Do not wear jewellery or earrings that will distract the child.
- If the child wears hearing aids, check every morning that the batteries are working.
- Keep a spare supply of hearing aid batteries on hand.
- Learn how to insert the ear mould of the hearing aid.

- Because understanding the speech of others is difficult for a child who is deaf, make sure that the light is on your face when you speak to the child.
- Speak only when the child is looking at you.
- Hold objects near your face so that the child will focus on the objects and on your lips, but make sure you don't cover your mouth.
- Don't exaggerate mouth positions. Speak in a normal tone and at a normal pace.
- When using sentences, place the important word at the end of the sentence. For example, "Do you want a *cookie*?"
- Accept and reinforce all of the child's consistent vocalizations.
- Be patient when the child is trying to tell you something. Use drawing or dramatization if you do not understand the message at first.
- Label things in the classroom. However, do not go overboard; half a dozen labels is enough at any one time.
- Remember that the deaf child will like the same toys that hearing children like. Toys that make noise (preferably with different levels of pitch and loudness) can provide a form of auditory training.
- Signal changes of activity or calls for attention by flicking the lights on and off.
- Expect the child to follow the same rules as everyone else.

child's environment that may support or impede his or her development and learning (Peterson, 1987).

As Figure 2–1 showed, a child may be disabled or high risk as a result of a variety of factors. These factors include the extent to which parents accept the child's condition and its implications, as well as the whole host of stressors that affect the family. The time of diagnosis is also important, because the earlier the diagnosis is made, the earlier intervention can begin. Age of onset is a factor as well; children who have congenital conditions—those present at birth—will generally experience more difficulties than those with later-onset conditions. This seems to be particularly true of sensory disabilities—hearing impairment and visual im-

BOX 2–3
Extract from Nancy's IPP

NAME: *Nancy*
CENTRE: *Maple Day Care*
DATE OF BIRTH: *2 April 1989*
CHRONOLOGICAL AGE: *4 years, 4 months*

Background information

Nancy's hearing loss was suspected by her mother when Nancy was about five months of age. Nancy's mother noticed that her daughter never reacted to the sound of the vacuum cleaner. When she was 14 months old, Nancy was medically tested and referred for audiological assessment. The results confirmed her mother's suspicions. Further audiometry performed when Nancy was 16 months old gave consistent results. Pure tone testing indicated a severe to profound hearing loss in the right ear and a profound loss in the left ear. The most recent report from the audiologist (January 1994) shows that Nancy has a bilateral sensori-neural hearing loss in the severe to profound range. She retains some residual hearing in both ears at the lower frequencies, but no usable hearing from 1000dB in either ear.

Nancy has not suffered any physical lags. She walked early (10 months), and currently does not appear to have any motor problems. A psychological assessment shows Nancy to be within the normal ranges in the development of cognitive skills.

It is Nancy's language that is seriously lagging. Language and speech assessment showed that Nancy is at the single word stage in terms of her receptive language. Her expressive language has not developed beyond the use of a few consistent vocalizations, although she has begun using some single signs to express her needs. Nancy uses about 20 consistent vocal approximations to name people, things, and needs in her environment. Now that she is developing a sign language vocabulary, she is attempting even more vocalization. Nancy has also learned to compensate for her disability by developing a unique set of gestures and actions to convey meaning.

In understanding the speech of others, Nancy appears to try to speech read, but she understands far more when the speech is accompanied by a natural gesture, a sign, or a concrete object. It is not possible to tell at this time how much she actually understands through speech reading alone.

Nancy brings many strengths to the preschool experience. She has good physical and cognitive skills, is friendly and socially aware, shows a sense of humour, and is willing to co-operate and learn. Her greatest need is the development of language.

Present levels of functioning

- *language: Nancy uses single words, and has a vocabulary of about 20 consistently used (signed) and understood words.*
- *speech: Nancy uses consistent vocalizations for specific wants such as milk*

pairment. And obviously, the severity of the condition is correlated with functioning. A child with a mild hearing loss, for example, will encounter far fewer problems in the acquisition of speech and language than will a deaf child (see Box 2–1). Finally, functioning is affected by the type of early intervention the child receives. Early intervention includes medical interventions such as surgery and drug therapy as well as therapeutic and educational interventions. Other important parameters of early intervention include the amount of family focus, the time that intervention starts, the intensity of the process, the setting, the cur-

or cookies, for people in the environment, and for favourite toys and activities.

Annual goals

Nancy's program will target speech and language development within the regular early childhood curriculum and with specialized assistance from a speech/language therapist and a trained teacher of deaf children. Her speech skills will improve through individual lessons with the specialized teachers.

In the classroom, teachers will stimulate language and communication skills through environmental arrangements, interaction with other children, modelling, and specific language intervention.

Long-range goals

1. To increase Nancy's awareness of sounds through play activities and listening exercises.
2. To expand vocabulary related to the classroom environment.
3. To train Nancy to follow simple, spoken directions within classroom routines.
4. To increase Nancy's use of speech through structured and unstructured play times.
5. To further enhance communication by learning signs; staff and children will use simple signs consistently in the classroom.

Short-term objectives (one month)

1. Stimulate residual hearing through auditory training and amplification.

- Nancy will wear her individual hearing aid at all times.
- To develop responsiveness to the on and off of sound, present sounds in small-group settings. For example, let Nancy place her hand on the piano and tell whether there is sound or not. Use a loud alarm clock and have Nancy tell when it is ringing.
- To increase responsiveness to tempo and rhythm, use finger plays in a small group. Once the finger play is well known, omit words for the children to fill in.

2. To increase environmental awareness, teach the names of body parts.

- Use flannel board stories and games such as "I put my fingers on my face," "I put my hand on my head."
- Use dolls; have Nancy respond to "Show me the head," "Where's her leg?"

3. To increase responsiveness to simple classroom instructions within general routines.

- Pair a gesture or sign with speech, gradually eliminating the gesture. For example, "Sit down for circle" can be first paired with a gesture that is slowly faded.

4. Structure play activities so that Nancy must use speech. If she is painting, for example, ensure that she must collect or ask

riculum model, the child/adult ratio, the amount of individualization, and the targeted skills.

There are far more children with mild disabilities in preschool settings than there are children with more significant problems. Personnel find children with mild disabilities far easier to accommodate in regular settings. It is children with more severe difficulties who require responsibilities, environmental and instructional planning, and teaching techniques. The greater the intensity of the disability, the greater the adaptations that will be necessary. (See the extract from

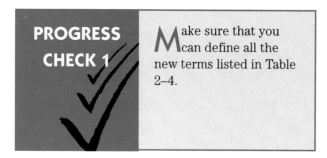

Nancy's individual program plan in Box 2–2.) The degree of disability is also related to progress in integrated classes; lower-functioning children make the smallest gains, students with mild disabilities the biggest (Galloway & Chandler, 1978).

PROGRESS CHECK 1

Make sure that you can define all the new terms listed in Table 2–4.

TABLE 2–3: New terms and ideas

adaptive behaviour	high risk
biological risk	nature
children with exceptionalities	nurture
congenital abnormalities	obesity
continuum of environmental casualty	otitis media
continuum of reproductive casualty	primary disability
critical period	profound sensori-neural hearing
environmental risk	loss
established risk	risk factors
etiology	secondary conditions
exceptionality	teratogens

SUMMARY

1. All children are at different developmental levels, and all have varying personal and social characteristics. There are many similarities between children with exceptionalities and normally developing children. There are also many differences among children with exceptionalities. However, all children with exceptionalities share a need for skilled intervention and special care from trained professionals.

2. In order for teachers to enable children who are disabled to function with their normally developing peers, they must know about the characteristics and abilities of each child and the developmental consequences of each condition.

3. Classification systems can enhance the quality of intervention and service delivery. The goal is not to do away with labels, but rather to develop the most useful and least harmful set of labels.

4. The causes of childhood disabling conditions are changing. With the rapid advances in medical science made over the last several decades, certain conditions have disappeared, but new ones have emerged to take their place. Survival rates for premature babies have risen dramatically, but so has the incidence of mental retardation and other disabilities associated with the wide range of insults to the nervous and organic systems that may occur when babies are born prematurely. As well, a frightening proportion of the next generation will be impaired by preventable problems such as pediatric AIDS and the various conditions that result from the use of drugs by pregnant women.

5. High-risk factors are categorized as established, biological, and environmental.

6. Mild cognitive difficulties and potential learning problems are difficult to uncover in the preschool years, because children at this stage have had little opportunity, if any, to engage in academics. Consequently, children with mild learning or behavioural difficulties may not be identified until they begin formal schooling.

CHAPTER 3
Issues in Early Childhood Special Education

CASE STUDY

Matthew

Before Matthew's parents decided to enrol their son in the half-day program of the local Montessori nursery school, they pondered long and hard. Their caution was understandable, for Matthew suffers from cystic fibrosis (CF), a serious health disorder that is the most common genetic condition found among Caucasians. To cope with its immediate effects, Matthew requires medication and a special diet, as well as therapy at least once a day. He is often ill as a result of the disorder.

The director recognized and respected Matthew's parents' concerns. When talking with them about their needs, she kept in mind that they were trying to do the best for their child. Every set of parents develops a different way of coping with a child's disability and a unique ideology to guide decision making, and attaches a unique meaning to the child's special needs. The director listened to the parents, answered their many questions, and reassured them that the staff would help Matthew socially and be alert for any symptoms of medical distress.

Because of his condition, Matthew had little experience with children his own age. The large-group situation, the many adults and children in the setting, the range of activities and materials, and the necessary rules and routines were all new to him. While Matthew had no cognitive defects, he lacked some of the social and co-operative skills for functioning effectively in the setting. Matthew needed help developing social skills. At the outset, the staff made sure Matthew had access to many materials for exploring and manipulating the environment. They also provided him with new materials to try out, with simple props for dramatic play, and with books and stories.

Matthew needed security, stimulation, and encouragement, along with the time and the space to explore freely and safely. Teachers encouraged him to participate, suggested to him ways to become involved, and physically assisted him as necessary. Matthew's individual plan is outlined in Box 3–4.

Cystic fibrosis a genetically determined inborn error of metabolism that primarily affects the respiratory and digestive systems.

Muscular dystrophy a condition characterized by wasting away of muscular tissue and consequent progressive muscle weakness.

Asthma a variable, reversible obstruction of the airways characterized by the narrowing of bronchial tubes, swelling of tissues, and clogging of mucus.

EARLIER IN THIS BOOK WE MET NANCY AND DARRIN, both of whom had fairly serious disabilities that will certainly hinder them as they try to reach their full potential. In this regard, Matthew's condition is quite different: while **cystic fibrosis** is a serious disorder (see Box 3–1), it does not negatively affect other areas of functioning such as cognition and language. This is also true of most other serious health disorders such as childhood cancer and **muscular dystrophy**, and of more common complaints such as **asthma** and allergies.

Children with health disorders are considered exceptional only when their condition requires a special individualized program. Such a need may arise when the child misses much school because of the condition or has limited vitality or a short attention span. Also, a health condition may sometimes interfere with the development of independence and socialization. We see this in Matthew: the intensive therapy he requires has hindered his ability to interact normally with peers. Thus, Matthew must also be helped to develop more mature and appropriate play skills and peer interactions.

BOX 3–1
Health disorders

Essentially, health disorders are medical conditions that require complex and sophisticated interventions; these may include surgical procedures, prosthetic devices, drug therapy, diet management, and ongoing medical treatment. Health disorders are not necessarily correlated with impairments in other domains of functioning. Generally, children with health problems demonstrate normal development in cognitive, communication, and socio-emotional skills. However, there may be disruptions attributable to the condition, such as long periods of illness, hospitalization, absence from school, and loss of peer interactions. As a result, special accommodations and programs are sometimes required. There are thousands of health disorders that can affect children. Some of the most common are listed below:

- **Cystic fibrosis** (CF) is a genetically based error of metabolism that mainly affects the respiratory and digestive systems. Children with CF require intense medical and therapeutic intervention—diet management, therapy for and management of respiratory disease, and various regimes of drug therapy.

- Musculoskeletal impairments are those that affect body movement and functioning but are not caused by neurological damage. Some of these conditions, such as **muscular dystrophy**, are caused by a wasting away of muscular tissue, which in turn leads to progressive muscle weakness.

- **Diabetes mellitus** is a metabolic problem caused by the inadequate secretion or utilization of insulin, a hormone needed to metabolize glucose. Diabetic children can participate in all school activities unless a physician advises otherwise.

- Allergies are the most common chronic disease in pediatrics. An **allergy** (hypersensitivity) can be defined as "an abnormal and varied reaction which occurs following a contact with substances or agents which normally do not cause symptoms in other individuals" (Kuzemko, 1978).

- **Asthma** is defined as a "variable, reversible obstruction of the airways characterized by the narrowing of bronchial tubes, swelling of tissues, and clogging of mucus" (Smith, 1978, p. 48). Asthma attacks are characterized by wheezing, paroxysmal coughing, and shortness of breath. Asthma can occur at any age, but it is found most frequently in children. Boys are twice as likely as girls to exhibit the condition (see Winzer, 1996).

For children with health disorders, few if any curriculum and environmental adaptations are necessary. Teachers will, however, need to be alert for particular medical correlates. Children with cystic fibrosis, such as Matthew, will have reduced vitality and will need many snacks; also, they may need to have their drugs monitored and may have a constant cough. Children with muscular dystrophy may be confined to a wheelchair; also, the physical environment will have to be adapted (e.g., barrier-free access to play centres). For children with asthma, teachers must be alert for the wheezing of asthma attacks and know the measures to take with inhalators. When children suffer allergies, especially food allergies, teachers need to be familiar with the problem-causing agents. Children with diabetes will probably be on a special regime that balances diet, exercise, and insulin.

LEARNING ACTIVITY 1

Allergies and asthma are very common and becoming more so. People are allergic to three general categories of agents—inhalants such as dust and pollen, contactants such as wool, and food and drugs such as peanuts and penicillin. Conduct a survey of your class (and perhaps other classes) to find out how many people suffer various allergies. Look at the results in terms of sex, age, place of birth, and place of domicile.

Allergy (hypersensitivity) an abnormal and varied reaction that occurs following a contact with substances or agents which normally do not cause symptoms in other individuals.

When a program is individualized for a child, we are looking at special education. In Chapter 1 we pointed out that early childhood education and early intervention are synonymous terms that are used broadly in reference to intervention practices for children from birth to five or six years of age. We also stressed that almost all young children with disabilities, such as Nancy, Darrin, and Matthew, should be integrated into programs designed for children who are developing normally.

There is a vast literature on special education and on early childhood education; there is much less on the subfield where these two disciplines overlap—that is, on early childhood special education (ECSE). The field of ECSE is so new, in relative terms, that there is much we do not yet know about it.

Most practitioners and researchers agree that early services should be characterized by the following: service delivery options that meet the individual needs of children and families; settings that demonstrate a commitment to integration; and program models that provide normalized experiences in natural environments (Canning & Lyon, 1990; Noonan & McCormick, 1993). Nevertheless, specifics on the best models, on the most appropriate curricula, and on the most effective strategies remain elusive. Further, while research clearly indicates that personnel who are well trained are more effective than those who are not (Tingey-Michaelis, 1985), it is not yet clear which specific skills and competencies count most for those intervening with young children with disabilities. There is also little consensus on how to best train people to help young children with disabilities, and their families.

Our lack of a really clear direction in ECSE opens the door to a host of issues and unresolved problems. Many facets of implementation remain murky and clouded in controversy.

Issues in Early Childhood Special Education

Diabetes mellitus a problem of sugar metabolism caused by a pancreatic disorder in the production of insulin, a hormone needed to metabolize glucose.

The major issues in ECSE are far-reaching and encompass almost every part of the enterprise. One crucial issue centres on the increasing recognition that the goals of ECSE must be broadened, that the entire family must be targeted, and that the parents must be deeply involved. Just as crucial is the issue of inclusion. So highly controversial is the inclusive approach, even at the preschool level, that Diane Bricker (1995) characterizes the inclusion of young children in community-based programs as "troubling because of its complexity and dramatic because of the emotional responses it engenders" (p. 180). A further critical issue is how to intervene most effectively with infants and toddlers, especially those with serious and multiple disabilities. Other controversies and debates revolve around whether early intervention is really effective; how much early intervention there should be; how early intervention should begin; what components characterize high-quality programs; the advantages of a child-directed curriculum compared to one that is teacher-directed; and how best to facilitate the transition from early intervention programs to early childhood and school programs. There are two final particular concerns: establishing which skills children need to succeed in daycare or preschool settings, and which additional skills and competencies early childhood personnel must have.

All these issues are outstanding, and the research and practice regarding most of them is relatively inconclusive. We will discuss some of these areas below; however, the major focus of this chapter is on the skills teachers require in various programs. This is because the effectiveness of efforts in ESCE depends greatly on the personnel involved. In the final analysis, the practitioners who are responsible for the children's day-to-day experiences and activities are the ones who make integration succeed or fail. As well, the competencies and the related services we will discuss in this chapter form the basis of many later discussions in this book, especially in the final section on classroom practice.

SEGREGATED OR INTEGRATED SETTINGS?

Writers in the area of ECSE have pointed out that "the issue of mainstreaming is very ambiguous and complex when considered relative to preschool handicapped children" (Edmister & Ekstrand, 1987, p. 133). A mainstreamed preschool may provide a challenging and developmentally appropriate social and communicative environment for a child with a disability—one that cannot be replicated in segregated programs because of the linguistic and social limitations of the children with disabilities themselves. Yet many questions remain concerning the effects of integrated educational settings and the strategies that facilitate social interaction. Research in the area is at best inconclusive, although it tends to favour integration.

While many early childhood educators avidly promote integrated or inclusive education for young children, regardless of the type or degree of exceptionality, segregated programs are still found throughout Canada. In fact, very young children with disabilities—especially those with significant disabilities—are more likely than children who have reached school age to attend separate schools. A range of possible programs is shown in Table 3–1.

TABLE 3–1: **Types of program settings**

Infant stimulation	Programs usually take place in the home, with the object of teaching the parents and those intervening with special needs infants.
Home visiting programs	Assist the child and the family in the home setting. Professionals visit the home on a regular basis.
Nursery programs	Traditionally refers to private or parent co-operative programs rather than to publicly supported programs. Today, however, nursery schools may be private or public. They generally provide half-day programs for children aged two or three to five or six.
Daycare centres	Programs of four or more hours' duration. They may accommodate varying ages, from infants through to preschoolers, but are more generally restricted to preschoolers.
Montessori programs	These programs for preschoolers are based, often loosely, on the philosophy of the Italian educator Maria Montessori.
Head Start	An American program, federally funded, that is designed to support economically and culturally disadvantaged children before they enter regular school programs. Includes nutritional and medical services.
Co-operative daycare	Programs organized and run by parents.
Demonstration schools (lab schools)	Usually situated in university or college settings.
Hospital programs	May be in- or out-patient programs. Organized to assist the progress of children with very special needs.
Clinic programs	Designed to intervene with children with very special behavioural and learning needs.
Special needs programs	Serve discrete populations of preschool children with disabilities.
Prekindergarten	Programs for children in the year before kindergarten entrance.
Junior kindergarten	An option for four-year-olds offered by school boards and available in some provinces.
Kindergarten	Programs for children in the year before first grade.
Primary programs	School programs for children of about six to eight years (grades one to three).

Special education preschool classes are staffed by certified special education personnel. Classes tend to follow the regular school schedule and may be full-day programs. The schedule is typically organized by developmental domains, with specific activities designed to address children's individual needs. As well, a number of private social-service organizations provide services for infants and young children with specific disabilities. Typically, they offer instruction to children and their parents at a centre or in the home. Physical, occupational, and speech/language therapy are stressed, and co-ordinated with early educational training.

Children in specialized settings obtain assistance for their specific disabilities but often miss out on the social and cognitive benefits that integration offers. Further, some authorities are concerned that segregated early-intervention programs are making young children with disabilities depend too much on adults, and that their transition to school or kindergarten is made more difficult as a result. Because most early intervention programs have a very low child/adult ratio, children become accustomed to teachers, aides, therapists, and other support personnel being readily available. This often changes when the child moves on to a more advanced class (Hamachek & Kauffman, 1994).

Recent studies have found that young children may benefit socially and educationally from inclusion in classes with normally developing peers (e.g., Harris et al., 1990). However, much of this research tends to be inconclusive—if not contradictory—and much of it is based on anecdotal rather than empirical data. Moreover, little research has been carried out on individual children in integrated and segregated settings; the bulk of research has concentrated on group differences. Further, different people hold different attitudes toward, and perceptions about, the philosophy and practice of inclusion. Parents, professionals, teachers, administrators, and researchers may view the process quite differently.

Most parents accept the philosophy and practice of integration; others do not. When asked about inclusion, parents of both disabled and nondisabled children are concerned about whether the special child will receive adequate attention and instruction (Stoneman, 1993). As well, the parents of normally developing children may believe that their children will be denied teacher time and intervention. The parents of children with disabilities may feel that their children's needs can be better met in a segregated setting with a structured curriculum and a low child/teacher ratio. But generally, the parents of young children with disabilities are enthusiastic about integration and hold positive attitudes. Parents believe that the two greatest benefits of inclusion are these: children with disabilities have more exposure to the real world, and they enjoy more acceptance in the community (Green & Stoneman, 1989).

Teachers may hold negative attitudes about disabilities and are often less sanguine about the prospect of integrating a child with special needs. In fact, in a recent survey of various officials from preschool programs, nearly 60 percent of the respondents cited teachers' attitudes as a barrier to preschool inclusion (Rose & Smith, 1993). Clearly, some teachers believe at least some of the myths about inclusion that are shown in Table 3–2.

TABLE 3–2: Myths and realities of integration

Myth	Reality
Normally developing children may imitate the behaviour of disabled children.	Research clearly indicates that this does not happen.
Teachers will have to spend too much time with the special child.	If time is organized efficiently, no great amount of extra time is necessary.
Children with disabilities are extremely hard to teach and handle.	Children may require extra attention and more structured programming, but early childhood personnel can learn to provide these.
Children with disabilities learn differently from normal children.	Generally, these children learn in the same way and in the same progression as other children. What is different is the pace of learning and the complexity of the material they can handle.
Teachers should have different expectations for the behaviour of the exceptional child.	It is important that behavioural expectations be the same for all children, regardless of disability.
Children who are disabled should always be treated in exactly the same way as other children.	There will be times when different treatment is necessary to take into account the consequences of the disability.

In general, teachers in early childhood settings are finding that they can successfully accommodate and teach children with special needs. They appear willing to accept their new roles, and there are only a few reports which suggest that early educators' attitudes are unfavourable. We outline some of the studies conducted in this area in Box 3–2.

IS EARLY INTERVENTION EFFECTIVE?

Despite the many advantages of early intervention in integrated settings, there is still debate within ECSE as to whether early intervention for children with disabilities, and for those considered at high risk, is truly effective. Advocates argue that early intervention can have a positive effect on the development of children in both categories. Critics of early intervention complain that too much has been claimed for early intervention, and too little proven.

The data supporting early intervention are not entirely persuasive. The crucial question is whether an early intervention program can produce better outcomes than no intervention. Studies that evaluate early intervention programs must demonstrate that advances in performance were the result of educational activities rather than maturation that would have occurred anyway over the period of intervention. This is a major hurdle, in that it is often unclear whether the progress

BOX 3–2

What the research says about teachers' attitudes

Intensive research has been conducted to determine the attitudes of regular classroom teachers toward children with exceptionalities and the concept of mainstreaming. Much less information is available regarding integration at the preschool level and how staff react and respond.

In general, studies at the preschool level indicate that experienced mainstream daycare staff often favour integration (Rule et al., 1985). However, a large number of staff are concerned about their lack of training for working with children with disabilities. Reporting about an effort to mainstream visually handicapped preschoolers, Simon and Gillman (1979) wrote: "Pupils and teachers, although well intentioned, become anxious, resort to stereotypic behaviours, and demonstrate avoidance of handicapped students" (p. 464). These tendencies were said to have increased over time (Rule et al., 1985).

Richarz and Peterson (1990) asked 211 teachers and 63 administrators in Washington state about mainstreaming at the preschool level and noted three general categories of concerns: about adequate preparation for integra-

tion; about adequate resources for program operation; and about conflicts between parents and staff relating to goals, philosophies of integration, and control of the child's time. An interview study was conducted in the same state with parents, teachers, and administrators (Peck et al., 1987). The ability of regular preschools to recognize and respond to children's individual needs was one of the most frequently expressed concerns about mainstreaming.

A study of the attitudes of preschool directors in New South Wales, Australia (Bochner & Pieterse, 1989), found concerns relating to the availability of support and resource facilities, the number of children with special needs enrolled at one time, and the severity of disabilities. The integration of children with mild or moderate visual or hearing disabilities presented no difficulties; the directors were less enthusiastic about integrating children with severe sensory impairments. They were most confident that they had the skills to integrate children with milder, less specific problems; they were least confident about their ability to assist children who were intellectually, physically, or sensorily disabled.

Children with severe or multiple disabilities are certainly more difficult to integrate. Bagnato, Kontos, and Neisworth (1987) found that these children were perceived by early childhood teachers as having more difficulties in social skills than in any other area.

LEARNING ACTIVITY 2

Many of the people reading this book are already expert in early childhood education and are aware of the many issues in the field. Use your background knowledge to discuss Day's (1988) observation that what is happening in early childhood programs can be summarized in two words—growth and uncertainty.

Now, on a chart, make two columns headed childhood education (ECE) and early childhood special education (ECSE). In the ECSE column, list all the issues mentioned in this section as stirring debate or controversy. Now list areas of debate in ECE. Do the columns match at all?

In British Columbia, the integration of handicapped children in early childhood settings has been taking place for some time. In 1990, Denholm examined the attitudes of directors in that province toward integration. Each of the 530 centres listed by the Ministry of Health as a licensed nursery school was mailed a questionnaire. The survey included questions relating to the director's educational background; the experience and characteristics of the early childhood centre; attitudes toward a given list of characteristics of disabled children; and stated roles and functions. Denholm found that directors were most positive toward children with impaired language skills, and least certain about children with moderate disabilities where the centre did not provide easy physical access. A wide range of specialist support staff were available for consultation; however, it was the perception of almost two-thirds of directors that most support staff were inaccessible. Although the directors expressed a belief in integration for some categories of children with disabilities, overall their support was rated as "medium." This was a result of several perceptions: that support staff were not accessible enough, and that their staff hadn't been adequately trained to work with handicapped children (Denholm, 1990).

There are suggestions in the literature that preschool teachers have more favourable attitudes toward special children than teachers of older students. Peck and Cooke (1983) report that the attitudes of mainstream preschool teachers are "largely positive." One study on mainstreaming at the preschool level (Rule et al., 1987) indicated that teachers found teaching children with disabilities to be more work than teaching nondisabled children; even so, all felt that mainstreaming benefited both exceptional and normally developing children. When asked if they would advise other daycare centres to include special needs children, one teacher was neutral and nineteen said they would strongly encourage other centres to join them. In another survey (Eiserman, Shisler, & Hesley, 1995) the investigators found moderate agreement among preschool teachers that children with special needs should be served in regular classrooms. Providers discriminated between different types of special needs and based their discussion on where children should be served accordingly.

Marchant (1995) interviewed teachers in integrated preschools and found that teachers viewed early childhood as the foundation on which to build integrated preschools. All of the teachers interviewed were committed to integration and made positive statements about the effects of integration on children and families. There were some concerns; these centred on ensuring interaction among children, and on whether teachers had enough time to assist the special child.

LEARNING ACTIVITY 3

Read Box 3–2 on teacher attitudes and Table 3–2 on myths about inclusion. How many of the myths (and truths) appear when teachers are talking about mainstreaming and inclusion? Do any myths stand out as being of particular concern to teachers? Do teachers hold different attitudes depending on the type and severity of the disability?

was the result of the intervention, or some particular aspect of the intervention, or other, outside factors not related to the intervention.

Although difficult, many studies have been conducted to evaluate the effectiveness of intervention for young children with disabilities. The results of well-controlled studies show that children do make developmental progress while enrolled in early intervention programs. For example, in a review of 27 studies, Simeonsson, Cooper, and Scheiner (1982) concluded that there was qualified support for the view that early intervention was effective. In a study of 18 autistic children, Fenske and colleagues (1985) found positive results for most children who received services before the age of five. Casto and Mastropieri (1986) conducted a meta-analysis of 74 studies and concluded that early intervention produces moderate gains in cognitive, linguistic, and academic development for a variety of disabled populations, although there is little evidence of gains in social and personal development.

Longitudinal studies have examined the extent to which early intervention fosters cognitive development. Initially, studies focused on children from economically deprived environments. It was found that early gains, measured in terms of intellectual ability, were not maintained over time unless intervention strategies were continued. Further, this continuing intervention had to involve the child's parents.

These results are contradictory; however, we must not foster the impression that programs which do not yield significant or measurable developmental gains in children are of no value. There may be more subtle, unmeasurable effects that relate as much to the parents and the family as to the child with a disability.

Parents of children with disabilities need the assistance provided by early intervention activities. With deaf children, for example, parental child-rearing attitudes appear to be the best predictors of positive self-concept in severely to profoundly impaired children (Warren & Hasenstab, 1986). Several researchers have suggested that the full impact of early deafness is felt by parents only in the preschool years, when the communication gap between children who are deaf and those who can hear becomes more evident (e.g., Lederberg & Mobley, 1990). In the early years, professionals can help parents of deaf children adjust to the impairment and overcome their initial reactions. They can help parents appreciate the role of the family in achievement, social and personal adjustment, and post-school adjustment.

Questions about program efficacy are not as important as they were even five years ago. Today questions about the overall effectiveness of early childhood programs for children with special needs have given way to questions that focus on specific curricula and teaching practices, and on which factors, alone and together, determine child and family well-being. Peck and Cooke (1983) noted that "the task of researchers vis-à-vis mainstreaming is not to prove, but to improve the quality of integrated programs" (p. 17).

HOW MUCH AND HOW SOON?

Some research has indicated that increased hours of programming are associated with greater gains. Moreover, earlier is better—that is, children seem to do better if intervention is begun before 36 months of age. Shonkoff and Hauser-Cram (1987) studied a group of newborn to three-year-old children and found that more mildly disabled children had better outcomes if they were enrolled in intervention programs before six months.

Some investigators found that the more intense the services, the more favourable the impact on cognitive development (Black, 1991; Reynolds, 1995). Other studies did not find this relationship—in other words, they did not find that intense and very early intervention was truly beneficial. Casto and Mastropieri (1986), for example, provided no support for the principle that "earlier is better"; they also found that children's progress did not vary with the time that intervention was initiated.

A recent study in Ontario (Musselman, Wilson, & Lindsay, 1988) failed to find evidence that lasting gains were associated with intervention during infancy, or with intensified programming, or with direct instruction by parents. The researchers used a sample of 118 three-, four-, and five-year-old children with severe to profound hearing loss and measured expressive and receptive language. Children were first tested at three, four, and five years and then again three or four years later. Another study of three- to five-year-old communicatively disordered and mentally handicapped children found some (i.e., not dramatic) improvement in expressive language scores because of the extra time provided in full-day rather than half-day programs. To contradict this, another study of mentally handicapped children found that those in half-day programs scored higher on cognition and expressive language than those in full-day programs (Taylor, White, & Pezzino, 1984).

WHAT TO TEACH?

For children who are developing normally we know the best practices, although there is no consensus about what form early childhood education should take or what children should be doing in early childhood education environments to enjoy maximum benefit (Doxey, 1990). Although there are many examples of good practice, ECSE does not yet have an identified body of "best practice," as is found in special education and early childhood education. For children with disabilities, there is debate about what to teach (i.e., the actual skills that children need), and about how to teach skills—most specifically about the amount of teacher-directed teaching.

Some educators of children with disabilities believe that one of the major differences in their field relates to the greater importance of teacher-directed learning. They see children with disabilities as requiring more adult direction to acquire skills. Now that the integration of children with disabilities into regular classes is increasing, the issue of how much teacher direction should be used is heating up. As with the other issues discussed in this section, there can be no easy resolution, for the research is contradictory.

For children with disabilities, early intervention is a complex process; furthermore, the complexity increases with the severity of the disability. For teachers of preschool children with mild disabilities, the normal develop-

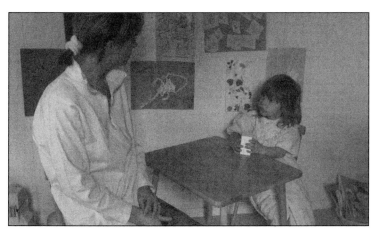

Children with learning or behavioural difficulties require more teacher direction than do normally developing children.

mental processes of children provide the most critical reference; the actual curriculum objectives will be the same as for normally developing children. Children with mild disabilities need the same skills as their peers, and they usually acquire those skills in the same sequence. Curriculum in ECSE for these children is a function of individual needs but generally includes cognitive, social, language, motor, and life skills development, and sub-areas such as fine and gross motor skills and eating, self-feeding, dressing, and undressing skills. What may be different is the way in which these children learn the various skills and the time required.

When the children involved are severely disabled, many problems occur. Little is known about how to train these children in integrated settings. For severely disabled children, or those with more than one disability, instruction is often hindered by the presence of interfering maladaptive behaviours, or the absence of suitable materials and techniques, or difficulties in identifying reinforcers to use in skill instruction programs. Training may have to emphasize early developmental skills of the type usually considered too routine or too basic to be part of a regular program—for example, feeding.

According to the developmentally appropriate guidelines devised for regular early childhood education (Bredekamp, 1987) teachers are to "guide," "support," and "encourage," and to structure the environment so that children can explore, interact, and learn on their own (see Chapter 7). Children who are developing normally will not experience difficulty with an unstructured instructional style; usually, they will profit from developmentally appropriate activities and from the typical experiences of childhood, and will learn a variety of functional and adaptive skills.

The skills that a child learns should generalize to other situations, such as the home and neighbourhood.

Some ECSE professionals are reluctant to endorse developmentally appropriate practice (DAP) for children with disabilities. They criticize the guidelines as merely promoting the development of "well-planned, safe and nurturing environments" (Carta et al., 1991, p. 8). At the same time, they see DAP as placing "undue restrictions on the options for teaching young children with disabilities" (Carta et al., 1991, p. 6). They therefore conclude that a program based on the DAP guidelines may not be sufficient for many children with disabilities (Wolery, Strain, & Bailey, 1992).

Young children who are exceptional do not benefit as easily from experience. Mere proximity interventions, in which children with disabilities are placed in settings with nondisabled peers, are not enough. Many times, these children do not learn by osmosis. And when they do learn, it is not enough that they acquire desired behaviours: teachers must ensure that the child's performance is maintained and generalized.

If children with special needs are to be successfully integrated into early childhood programs, individual, structured, and carefully planned learning experiences must be provided for them. How much teacher intervention to include in a program is, however, undecided. When considering this question, we must take into account the effects of too much teacher intervention. If teachers initiate most of the interactions, children may learn that they have a relatively passive role in their education—that is, that they do not need to seek information or assistance, because it will be offered to them. Huston-Stein, Friedrich-Cofer, and Susman (1977) compared highly structured (high percentage of adult-directed activities) programs for Head Start children with loosely structured classroom programs; they found that children in highly structured classrooms were more attentive during circle time and helped to clean up more after free play, but did not show more independent, task-oriented behaviour.

Other studies have found that preschool children in classrooms in which teachers are directive and intrusive are relatively low on task persistence. Apparently, helping young children to complete tasks can actually inhibit their willingness to persist in problem-solving situations where help is not offered. Also, frequent interactions with teachers may inhibit peer interactions (Stipek & Sanborn, 1985).

CHILDREN'S SKILLS

At present, literature that addresses the performance of children with disabilities in preschool environments for non-disabled children is relatively scarce. Observations of the behaviours and skills of normally developing children in daycare settings generally provide the information about what children with special needs should know in order to participate successfully with typical peers. However, there is little data available on what skills are needed for successful performance, or where, when, and how these skills should be taught (Murphy & Vincent, 1989).

A number of writers have tried to outline the skills that children with disabilities need for entry into preschool programs, and for success once they get there. Child care workers and directors have likewise pinpointed the skills they view as necessary for success. These are presented with a caveat: we hold that most regular preschool classrooms can be considered ideal for children with disabilities, since they are designed to allow each child to learn at his or her own developmental level and pace. Natural environments are the most appropriate for nearly all young children with disabilities, as long as adequate support—for the child and for the staff—is readily available.

Basic entry skills for preschools are seen as including the following:

- Mobility, or the ability to ambulate within the classroom (i.e., Darrin on his scooter board). If not mobile, is there an aide to assist mobility?
- Toilet trained or in training pants.
- Eating and drinking skills—the ability to sit and eat snacks and to drink from a regular cup.
- Readiness for associative and co-operative play.
- Attention span—the ability to sit at a table or on the floor for at least ten minutes.
- The ability to follow simple directions.
- The ability to communicate needs and to communicate with peers.
- Identification and discrimination skills (knows own cubby symbol).
- Fine motor skills.
- Basic dressing skills.

Murphy and Vincent (1989) were among the first to attempt to document the skills children needed in daycare. They designed and distributed a questionnaire to daycare centres in Madison, Wisconsin. The teachers were asked to rate for importance 57 behaviours or skills. Skills seen as important by the teachers for success in daycare related to behaviour that increased the child's ability to function in a large group—in other words, that made the child easier to manage. Also important were skills related to communication and independence—two difficult areas for children with disabilities.

In regard to the teachers' control over the children in a large-group setting, the Madison daycare teachers felt that children should be able to respond to their name, find the bathroom, ask for help from an adult, stay out of restricted areas, and respond to an adult's questions. In the communication area, communicating wants and needs and knowing when to ask for help were seen as important skills in settings where the care provider was not always available for immediate and direct attention. The skills with lower ratings were in the area of preacademics; these included the ability to follow routines such as sitting cross-legged in a circle. While these may be useful to a typical child, they may not be the skills chosen to teach to a child with a disability, who may develop a limited repertoire of skills.

Skills for Early Childhood Educators

A common assumption about early childhood education is that the younger the child, the easier the job. As every teacher knows, this is patently untrue. For one thing, it has been estimated that the typical early childhood professional in Canada will work personally and directly with a minimum of 12,000 children over the course of his or her career, spending approximately 2,000 hours with each child (Pence, 1990). For another, those who teach and care for young children in organized settings such as daycare, nursery schools, and kindergartens require a variety of special skills. So diverse are these skills that in the 1920s, when Ruth Stanton was asked, "What training does a nursery school teacher need?" she replied at some length. Nursery school teachers, said Stanton,

> should have about two years of study of astronomy because children are so very interested in the sun, stars and moon; then at least four of biology for nothing holds children's interest as much as the biological sciences; then four years studying the principles of democracy for the nursery school is a microcosm of a democratic society; then four years of English; two of finance; two of geography; four of history; and another four of mathematics.

On and on she went, from A to Z, listing all topics young children want to learn about. Stanton concluded by saying that "by the time the person is 98, she'll be ready to teach young children" (cited in Seefeldt, 1989).

Although we may detect a little exaggeration in the above extract, there is no question that those working with children at the preschool or kindergarten level require a range of skills, some of them learned in training programs but many learned "on the job." In general terms, these skills include organization and communication; also required are sensitivity and, of course, breadth of knowledge. More specifically, the abilities required of personnel in early childhood programs can be summarized as follows:

- To establish a safe and healthy environment.
- To advance the physical, social, emotional, linguistic, and intellectual competence of all children in the program.
- To ensure a well-run program that responds to participant needs.
- To maintain a commitment to professionalism.
- To accommodate a wide range of abilities, developmental levels, and socio-emotional needs in the preschool classroom.

SKILLS IN EARLY INTERVENTION

Accepting the integration of children who are exceptional into an early childhood education centre, and helping to integrate them, involves more than a verbal or written agreement. The process of integrating a child with a disability involves a range of issues possibly never experienced by the director, staff, or children of the centre (Denholm, 1990). Integration does not mean completely changing a program, denying normally developing children the teacher's attention, or giving special consideration to the behaviour of the child with a disability. Typically, early childhood personnel accommodate a range of children in their classrooms and direct programs geared to the developmental levels of participating children. In accepting children with disabilities into regular programs, we are simply working with a wider population.

When a child with a disability enters a program, the major changes are in two areas: staff responsibility, and the greater range of skills required by early childhood teachers. In a study of directors of preschools in New South Wales, Australia (1989), Bochner and Pieterse found that the following skills were essential for a director: the ability to assess children and plan individual education programs; the ability to co-ordinate resources; and the ability to work with parents and families. The general competencies found for teachers were these: a knowledge of techniques to use with children with learning and behavioural difficulties; and the ability to work with specialists, advisers, therapists, and so on. Others note that teamwork is critical. Peck and colleagues (1993) reported that intervention programs that survived over time were those in which there was collaborative planning and decision-making.

Personnel who intervene with young children with exceptionalities need to develop a range of new skills and competencies; these both overlap and extend the skills and competencies required of regular early childhood teachers. (Some very basic criteria are shown in Table 3–3.) The specific additional requirements can be summarized as follows:

- Ability to deal with both average and special-needs children.
- Awareness of normal child development.
- Awareness of the developmental consequences of specific disabling conditions.
- Awareness of the contributions of other professionals and paraprofessionals to the welfare of the child and the family.
- Skill in professional consultation and communications.
- Ability to interact with other professionals and paraprofessionals, and to work on a team.

- Ability to play a role in identifying children who are at risk or who have special needs.
- Involvement in writing individual program plans (IPPs).
- Knowledge of program models and curricula.
- Knowledge of techniques for small-group and individualized teaching.
- Extended skills in classroom management.
- Ability to interact with parents in parent conferences.
- Familiarity with **_adaptive equipment_**—that is, equipment customized to meet the physical needs of individual children.
- Knowledge of the technology that is used to enhance environmental stimuli for children with disabilities.
- Awareness of special arrangements that may be needed to accommodate seizure activity, medications, allergies, susceptibility to illness, poor muscle strength, and special feeding problems.
- Ability to liaise with other schools and agencies.
- Ability to assist in the transition process from preschool to the public school system.

Adaptive equipment equipment customized to meet the physical needs of individual children. It is any device designed or modified to lead individuals with disabilities to independence.

TABLE 3–3: Teaching tools and skills required for integrated programs

Teacher	Tool	Attitude/skill
Accept the child	Tolerance	Empathy; positive and humanistic attitudes
Learn about the condition	Reading, course work, discussions with parents and other professionals	Understanding
Learn about the child	Parent meetings	Understanding
Be part of a team	Work with other professionals	Collaborative skills
Assess the skills needed by the child in different environments	Checklists, developmental scales, tests—standardized and criterion-referenced, observation	Using assessment measures, understanding psychological reports
Target needed skills	Individual program planning, long-range goals, short-term objectives	Knowledge of child development
Integrate the child	Curricula presentation social skills	Modifications of environment, materials, and program; new instructional strategies
Focus on domains	Curriculum	Techniques to develop social, language, and motor skills
Evaluate progress	Your program, child's program	Informal and formal techniques

Early intervention also includes infants, who may participate in daycare, home-based, or clinic-based programs. Those working with infants and toddlers and their families require a different set of skills if they are to provide effective support. The specific requirements for working with families with infants include these:

- An understanding of family systems, and of both family and group dynamics.
- An understanding of the potential impact of disability on families.
- Knowledge of typical and atypical children and their development.
- The ability to build a trusting relationship.
- The ability to identify family concerns, priorities, and resources.
- The ability to provide information, and familiarity with medical, social, and educational services available locally.
- The ability to encourage family members to take an active role.
- The ability to develop parents' skills.
- The ability to model interactions with children and show how to modify activities.
- The ability to identify family outcomes.
- The ability to initiate, maintain, and terminate relationships with families effectively (see Beckman et al., 1993).

Although early-intervention professionals see working with families as important, many people in the field of early childhood education have little experience and training in intervention techniques. In many cases the shift toward family-centred approaches has been so rapid that the supply of trained personnel has not kept pace with demand (see Box 3–3).

SPECIFIC COMPETENCIES

Below we discuss in some detail the additional competencies needed by those intervening with children with special needs in early childhood settings. Keep in mind that this list of competencies is optimal; no one professional can be an expert in all possible areas. Moreover, the philosophy and orientation of the program, staffing arrangements, time and financial constraints, and so on will determine how many competencies can be developed.

Greater awareness of child development Developmental psychology studies the changes that take place in people as they age. People of different ages are qualitatively different from one another; growing up involves a sequence of stages that are characterized by specific and increasingly complex types of behaviour. Experts in child development talk about development *in* and *across* developmental domains. The major domains to which they refer are these: communicative, affective, cognitive, socio-emotional, and sensorimotor. Thus, abnormal development in any domain of functioning always has a referent in normal development. Children with disabilities can show delays or deficits in one domain or across domains.

BOX 3–3

The development of child care work

The emergence of a special "class" of childhood and youth was the first prerequisite for the development of child care in North America. The perception that children needed to be socialized and helped arose in tandem with the perception that childhood was a discrete stage of development and that children were separate beings (i.e., not miniature adults).

The term "child care worker" is more recent. Since it was first coined, its meaning has broadened so that it now applies to child care services in a variety of day, residential, institutional, and community settings. Today's child care workers are found in schools, in preschools, and in home visiting programs. In these situations child care workers may be teachers' aides with responsibility for helping teachers integrate and educate children with disabilities.

In preschool settings, child care workers may perform a number of roles, including that of teacher's aide. All too often, however, those involved with young children are regarded merely as babysitters. They earn low wages: in Canada, 66 percent earn less than $25,000 a year. They receive few benefits and often are not evaluated closely enough to ensure that they have the skills necessary to care for and interact with young children.

Within the child care field, there is a growing professionalism and a demand for greater knowledge and skills. However, appropriate training is still difficult to come by. In 1982, certification of early childhood personnel was in a state of confusion on such issues as minimum qualifications, and the types of personnel programs should require (Spodek et al., 1982).

Dickinson (1990) reports that professional requirements for child care workers vary across Canada. No training is required in Newfoundland and Alberta; in other provinces workers must complete some type of program. Only British Columbia requires child care staff to have early childhood training. In that province early childhood education in colleges consists of one year of study leading to a certificate. After graduation at certificate level, and after 500 hours of supervised practice, a supervisor's certificate is issued.

If children with disabilities are to be taught successfully, those who work with them must be equipped to deal with their unique characteristics and needs. The question is how to train personnel for work in integrated early-childhood settings; as yet, there is no clear answer, because the idea is still so novel. In Canada, many teachers who work with infants and their families have a two-year community college diploma and specialize in the developmentally disabled. As well, a number of community colleges are currently offering ECE diploma courses that include as a required component both theory and practical experience in working with special needs children.

In the United States, various agencies, professional organizations, and college and university preparation programs are seeking to develop reasonable standards and effective educational programs to train early-intervention personnel (Bailey et al., 1990). The issue is more pressing in the United States, where early identification and intervention is now required by federal law. There is presently a shortage of personnel. A national survey (Meisels et al., 1988) reported that that shortage is likely to continue into the next decade. A *severe* shortage of personnel with expertise related to infants and families is predicted.

To work efficiently with children who are exceptional, caregivers require a basic understanding of normal child development. Writers stress:

> Whatever the caregiver's or the teacher's context, and whatever the children's special needs, the most important preparation for working with special needs children is a thorough understanding of normal child development. In any situation, it is most important to know the normal stages and sequences of development, and the conditions, contexts, strategies, and relationships that promote it. (Canning & Lyon, 1990, p. 259)

Knowledge of exceptional conditions   Teachers need to understand the developmental consequences of various forms of exceptionality as well as what children can and cannot do at any given time. Such knowledge makes teachers aware of the extent to which children with disabilities vary from the patterns seen in normally developing children; of the special needs of these children; and of the types of instructional sequences to devise.

Identification and diagnosis   Early childhood programs would not be complete without a plan for evaluating children's growth and progress. For a child with a disability, early diagnosis is vital. Assessment procedures for very young children with special needs are based on the assumption that early identification will lead to an individual program plan that will either prevent or diminish the effects of an inappropriate education. If an early assessment is not conducted, a child may experience years of failure before a correct diagnosis is made. By then, secondary disabilities such as behaviour disorders may well have developed.

Children with special needs can be identified at any time through a variety of procedures. Assessment is a necessary and fundamental activity for teachers, therapists, and other professionals in early intervention (Bailey & Wolery, 1989). Assessment involves collecting data, and targeting skills that will further the child's participation in present and future environments. Early childhood teachers require at least basic diagnostic skills if they are to identify children with potential problems at an early age, make appropriate referrals for additional assessment, and develop programs for those children who can be served in the regular classroom setting. Assessment is discussed more fully in Chapter 8.

Intervention care and education aimed at influencing the direction and scope of children's developmental processes.

Curricula   The word "curriculum" has attached to it a number of underlying concepts. In a broad sense, the curriculum is the design and delivery of ***intervention***—that is, the care and education aimed at influencing children's development (Doxey, 1990). In this context, curriculum is the *content* of instruction (i.e., what we teach children). Pedagogy is the manner in which that curriculum is presented. For children with disabilities the term curriculum also includes the process of identifying curricular goals for teaching each child the skills needed for daily living, and for development in all domains.

Early childhood personnel must be able to set goals, and develop and modify curriculum materials for children with disabilities. While the curriculum is not greatly different for children with disabilities, it has a wider reach. The curriculum for children with disabilities must stress three very broad areas: performance and cognitive abilities, language and communication skills, and the skills needed for independent functioning.

Individual program planning   Some gains can be made simply by placing children with disabilities in mainstream settings; however, mere placement is not a substitute for well thought-out and systematic intervention. For children with disabilities, a curriculum must include long-term goals and short-term objectives; these are often formalized in an individual program plan (IPP). Essentially, an IPP is a management tool to ensure that the program is appropriate to the child's specific needs. It is also a chart of the child's progress. It outlines the child's long-term goals and short-term objectives, and may describe the methods and techniques that will be applied to those ends (Winzer, 1989). Ideally, the IPP is drawn up by a team, and various people assume responsibility for different goals. The planning process is examined in Chapter 9; an example is presented in each chapter of this book.

Classroom organization   The presence of a physically and socially responsive environment has been consistently related to cognitive growth. Such an environment promotes success and independence, and provides children with staff and materials that respond to individual needs. Early childhood personnel need to create a classroom environment in which the central features are respect for the learner and a willingness to arrange the environment to accommodate the needs of individual learners.

Environmental planning considers equipment and materials. *Equipment* includes furniture and other large items (easels, climbing structures, and so on). It also includes the space provided for play. *Materials* are the smaller items in a program, such as puzzles, games, books, and toys. Structural features of classroom organization include the daily schedule, staff assignments, transitions between activities, and the sequence of activities.

Because children with disabilities require more structured and systematic instruction, schedules and staff responsibilities should be adaptable. When the traditional preschool schedule is creatively modified so that direct instructional time is provided, children with disabilities are much more likely to succeed in the program (see Chapter 8).

Instructional techniques   In planning and implementing early educational experiences for children with disabilities, teachers must make many decisions. For example, they must select appropriate instructional strategies and plan time for using these procedures. **Teaching resourcefulness** is the ability to provide children with experiences and instructions that are specific to their interests, abilities, and developmental needs. Those intervening with young children with disabilities must expand their teaching resourcefulness and their repertoire of teaching techniques. They must know how to select a theoretical model; which procedures are most effective, and for whom; how to bring about broad and lasting changes; and how to incorporate various instructional strategies. By changing the rules, modifying materials, and using personal assistance strategies, teachers can adapt activities and routines so as to encourage participation.

Teaching resourcefulness the ability to provide children with experiences and instruction relevant to development that matches their needs, interests, and abilities.

There is no one "most suitable" way to teach all children with exceptionalities, any more than there is one way to teach only girls, or only children with red hair. Many if not most of the procedures employed with young children with disabilities are similar to those used with children who are developing normally. However, teachers must be able to plan and conduct group activities that encourage the participation and interaction of exceptional learners. The major difference between regular and special education relates to the extent to which the teacher directs learning activities (see Chapter 10). Teachers must often structure sessions and direct children—a role that some see as the antithesis of the facilitating, instructional model that is characteristic of most early childhood programs.

BOX 3–4

Helpful hints

- Learn as much as you can about the child's condition, including the etiology, developmental consequences, and the prognosis.
- Answer accurately questions other children ask about the differences in appearance and behaviour of the special child. Do this at the time questions are asked, whether or not the special child is present.
- Consult with parents, therapists, and medical personnel about handling the child.
- Be aware of the child's schedule for drug dosages and for special diet considerations.
- Keep an emergency list of telephone numbers close at hand.
- The physical layout of the classroom is important. Cubbies, bulletin boards, materials and chalkboards should be within the reach of all children.
- A familiar environment provides security for young children. Provide structure and predictability.

- Display the schedule prominently to reinforce a familiar pattern.
- Encourage the development of autonomy.
- Always let children succeed at some tasks daily.
- Give tasks that can be completed.
- Make children feel a part of the class even if illness keeps them absent for long periods.
- Be aware of drug dosages.
- Keep the parents' telephone numbers nearby.
- Ensure that all staff are aware of the child's medical needs.
- Accommodate special needs in vitality, attention, and mobility.
- Focus on the child, not the condition.
- Keep group time short, lively, and interesting.
- Allow children plenty of rest time.
- Help anxious, withdrawn, and immature children view themselves more positively. Children who lack a natural curiosity may require adult help and direction for play, as well as toys carefully selected to meet their needs.

Classroom management   Essentially, classroom management refers to the efficient management of schedules, instruction, materials, and child behaviours within the classroom. The goal of positive management is to keep children constructively involved in activities they enjoy and that will help them learn.

All early childhood educators must be skilled in classroom management and discipline, but when it comes to children with exceptionalities, they may have to expand their repertoire to include a variety of behaviour management techniques. Behaviour management is discussed thoroughly in Chapter 12.

Collaboration skills   In almost all preschool situations, the teaching is done by a team rather than by a single individual. The team usually includes an early childhood education supervisor, aides, one or more assistants, and sometimes volunteers, student teachers, and parents. Thus, early childhood personnel will have had some experience in teamwork. The integration of disabled children will involve expanding the team to include other professionals and paraprofessionals.

For their training and education, children with exceptionalities cannot rely on one person. More personnel will be involved, and teachers will interact with more professionals and paraprofessionals. As Diane Bricker (1993, p. 94) points out:

> Early childhood special education is composed of psychologists, physicians, nurses, special educators, early childhood educators, child development specialists, child development aides, communication and hearing specialists, vision and mobility specialists, dentists, counsellors, and parents. This array of people fill roles as teachers, practitioners, clinicians, evaluators, psychiatrists, administrators, and caregivers.

Early childhood personnel may consult with some or many of these professionals and paraprofessionals as part of a team. In a team approach, professionals from various disciplines assess and manage problems by sharing information and participating in decision-making. In this way, services are enriched, expanded, and made more comprehensive. When a team approach is followed, all members see the child as a total being. Roles and expectations are shared and experts train other members (see Landerholm, 1990).

It must be pointed out that in the human services area, the teaming approach is still in its infancy. A great deal must still be learned about the processes and procedures that make for effective teamwork. What is known is that teamwork demands collaboration that is "not mere cooperation or a matter of good will, but an agreed-upon distribution of power, status, and authority" (Weaver, 1979, p. 24).

The following attributes seem important to efficient team functioning:

- Each team has a leader, who may involve himself or herself in specific tasks related to team functioning.
- The size of the team varies according to the child's disability.
- While each team will differ from case to case, certain core people are usually involved. These include teachers, therapists, aides, and other paraprofessionals such as an audiologist. Family members should be encouraged to join the team; not only do they have the right to be included, but they are the people most familiar with the child.
- On a team, each team member has a role, and each role has a set of skills and certain expectations associated with it.

- Effective teams need to be nurtured over time. When membership changes frequently, the goals of both the child and the family are jeopardized.
- Team members have learned to communicate well on an ongoing basis.
- Personal characteristics that promote good communication and collaboration include empathy and openness, the ability to establish good rapport, respect for different points of view, and a positive and enthusiastic attitude (West & Cannon, 1987).

PROGRESS CHECK 1

Why are teams so important in early childhood education? In early childhood special education? Which people are generally on a team designed to assist a child with special needs? Discuss their roles. Apply this to Matthew's case.

Consultation The child with a disability may require the services of many specialists, including psychologists, physiotherapists, occupational therapists, speech pathologists, audiologists, and medical practitioners. In dealing with specialists, early childhood personnel need to develop two sets of skills: they need to learn enough of the specialist's terminology to talk about the particular child and interpret technical reports; and they need to know how to use these reports in their programming.

For many children with disabilities, physical, occupational, and speech/language therapists provide essential treatment. These therapists can help children develop hand skills, body co-ordination, and other physical skills; they can also improve gross motor development, muscle relaxation, and fine motor control. A communication therapist (speech/language therapist or speech/language pathologist) is skilled in assessing and training children in functional communication systems.

Ideally, therapists work together on a team, consulting with teachers and providing services to children in their classrooms in an integrated therapy model. Therapists can help teachers understand how a child's therapy will affect classroom behaviour. Children who seem to be at risk or whom teachers observe encountering difficulties can also benefit from a specialist's knowledge. A specialist is always a consultant and should be available for advice and assistance.

Occupational therapy   ***Occupational therapists*** come from a developmental rather than a medical base. Their training is in the biological and psychosocial sciences, which are the foundations of medicine, psychiatry, and prevocational skill development (Deiner, 1983). When occupational therapists work with children with physical disabilities, the main aims relate to motor development, sensory development, and the achievement of functional daily tasks. Occupational therapists work to enhance the child's potential for learning. They try to develop the child's vestibular balance, self-help skills, and tactile, kinesthetic, and perceptual co-ordination.

Occupational therapists **support personnel with training in the biological and psychosocial sciences, the foundations of medicine, psychiatry, and prevocational skills development.**

For a child with a visual handicap, the occupational therapist evaluates the effect of the impairment on daily living, play, and readiness for preschool and school programs. An important aspect of this branch of therapy involves teaching children with severe visual impairment the efficient use of residual vision and compensatory hand skills.

Physical therapy ***Physical therapists*** are trained in medically based programs. Usually they have studied the biological, physical, medical, and psychosocial sciences, and done in-depth work in neurology, orthopedics, therapeutic exercises, and treatment techniques (Deiner, 1983). Physical therapy is directed toward preventing disability—for example, developing, improving, or restoring more efficient muscular functioning, and maintaining maximum motor functioning. The physical therapist provides information about positioning and handling students and the use of adaptive equipment. Physical therapists work with children who need training in prosthesis management, wheelchair operation, and gross motor skills.

Speech/language therapy ***Speech pathologists*** or speech/language therapists are concerned with communication: with its normal development and its disorders. They focus on physical and behavioural characteristics that may contribute to disorders in a child's verbal expression, use of grammar, voice quality, social communication, dysfluency (e.g., stuttering), and so on.

In most provinces one must have a Master's degree and a year of closely supervised clinical work to become a speech pathologist. These clinicians work as consultants to centres, schools, and special education programs; they are also employed in hospitals and rehabilitation centres (Winzer, 1996).

The speech/language pathologist works with teachers to identify potential communication disorders; assesses and diagnoses communication disorders; and plans and recommends intervention activities for communication disorders. The pathologist works directly with children to teach them how to speak and listen effectively and how to overcome the effects of communication disorders.

In treating articulation disorders, therapists teach children to listen; to recognize and discriminate between consonant sounds; to produce articulated speech sounds; and to retain the memory of speech sounds (Winitz, 1975). Major emphases in voice therapy include listening skills, breath control skills, and articulatory adjustments. Breath control training includes learning to relax and reduce laryngeal tension.

Speech and language therapy may also be used with children who have difficulty controlling the fine motor muscles needed for eating. Therapists may also develop appropriate augmentative communication for children who cannot talk.

School psychologists Programs are accommodating more and more children with disabilities, and therapists and educators are becoming more familiar with the services that school psychologists can offer to intervention programs. This is creating a "market" for psychological services at the preschool level. A school psychologist reviews and assesses the cognitive, emotional, and socio-behavioural needs of children with disabilities, consults with centres and schools, counsels about behaviour management, and provides support for parents and teachers.

Not everyone agrees that psychological services are necessary or effective at the preschool level. For one thing, despite the growing number of programs that serve preschool children with disabilities and their families, few school psychologists have received formal training in working with this population.

Early childhood staff and school psychologists may have contrasting perceptions concerning the role school psychologists might play in infant and preschool programs. Two surveys (Widestrom, Mowder, & Willis, 1989) found that the two groups differed most in what they saw as the reasons for psychological consultation. Almost half the school psychologists believed that their primary responsibility on the preschool team would probably be conducting psychological assessments. However, that role was not a high priority for the early childhood educators, who stated that their greatest needs were assistance with behaviour and emotional problems, and with problems related to home and family.

Social workers   The social worker works with the child's caregivers. He or she helps the family deal with the child's impairment in the family situation and in financial matters, and in their efforts to encourage the child to develop as normally as possible. A social worker is often an advocate for both the child and the family.

Specialist teachers   Some specialized services are not provided within the context of a preschool program, yet are vital for the functioning of children with disabilities. We have already mentioned therapy for children with physical and speech/language difficulties. Children with a sensory impairment such as deafness or blindness also require additional intervention.

One of the major needs for children with a severe visual impairment is the ability to move at a reasonable rate between two places. Children need training in orientation (the knowledge of one's position in space) and in mobility (negotiating that space). Training in orientation and mobility allows children to move with confidence and independence within their environment. Orientation and mobility training, provided by a specialist in the field, can and should begin in the preschool years. Children as young as three years have been successfully taught to use a number of mobility aids, including the white cane.

Specialist teachers of deaf children are trained to teach language and develop speech. They can help children use and maintain hearing aids; they can also explain and demonstrate classroom amplification systems, such as the FM system, whereby the teacher wears a microphone that inputs into a child's amplification system.

Technical devices and adaptive equipment   More and more, professionals are recognizing the importance of assistive technology for young children with disabilities. In 1986, 26 percent of noninstitutionalized preschool and school children with disabilities used some form of assistive device. Most of these devices assisted mobility and/or agility (Nessner, 1990).

For disabled people of all ages, improved aids and devices are being developed to enrich education and improve the quality of life. With appropriate technologies, young children with disabilities can control their environment more directly; this reduces the likelihood and severity of socio-emotional and intellectual disabilities.

Handling medical conditions   Children with disabilities may have medical problems that affect their functioning. They may, for example, suffer heart defects that require the monitoring or curtailment of certain activities. Other children may need alterations in work, play, and rest schedules. Others may be on different regimes of drug therapy.

A number of students may be on occasional medication for any number of mild conditions, such as the common cold. Others will require the controlled and consistent use of medication. Pupils suffering from epilepsy, from allergies and asthma, and from other chronic childhood conditions will be on a medication regime. Teachers should be acutely aware of medication schedules, the reasons for the medication, and possible side effects.

Communicating with parents

In current early childhood education, the understanding of the family's role is undergoing a change. This is especially true when a child has a disability. In the past, parental input was not a major factor. Early programs concentrated almost entirely on the child and on the child's abilities and disabilities. Today, professionals are more likely to view the child as part of a system and to see that system as including the family, the community, and the culture. As well, professionals now realize that the assistance of parents in education, therapy, and advocacy is vital. Family members become partners, participants in educational and intervention endeavours, advocates for children, and decision-makers.

In a properly based preschool program, information will be shared and co-operative efforts between parents and centre staff will be integral. Parents may be involved through regular formal and informal conferences, parent education, and co-operative efforts between home and school in which objectives are clearly established. The establishment of positive relationships between parents and professionals depends on a number of factors. The professional must understand the parents' problems, be flexible, and demonstrate openness and empathy.

Transition planning

Transition the movement of children from one service program to another.

Transition is the movement of children from one service program to another. While it is only very recently that the issue of transition has surfaced in ECSE, transition planning is now an accepted part of early intervention. The goals of transition programming for young children are these: to select a placement that is appropriate for the needs of the child and supported by the child's parents; to ensure a smooth transfer of the child; to prepare the child to function in the next environment; and to ensure a smooth and rapid adjustment to that environment.

The child's transition from a preschool to a public school program is a time of change for both the child and the family. The transition involves two components: preparing children and family members for the move to a new program, and supporting children and family members as they adjust to the new program (Chandler, 1993). Transition is the subject of Chapter 16.

PROGRESS CHECK 2

Explain or define each of the terms in Table 3–4. Also, explain fully the responsibilities of the therapists—physical, occupational, and speech and language—discussed in the text.

TABLE 3–4: New terms and ideas

adaptive equipment	muscular dystrophy
allergies	occupational therapists
asthma	physical therapists
cystic fibrosis	speech/language pathologists
diabetes mellitus	teaching resourcefulness
intervention	transition

BOX 3–5
Matthew's IPP

Matthew has been at the centre for only a very brief time, but already his lack of social interactions with peers is evident. In the classroom, Matthew tends to wander, and to watch other children, but he does not play alone at a centre, nor does he join with other children. This is probably because the severity of his condition has kept him confined at home a great deal. However, Matthew is developing normally in the cognitive and language domains.

Long-range goals
The major goal for Matthew is to develop appropriate play behaviours. He should learn to play with toys appropriately, to co-operate in small groups, and to share.

Short-term objectives
Matthew will choose and use toys appropriately and play with sustained attention.

Matthew will choose a toy and play with it with the teacher.

Matthew will begin to play co-operatively with one other child, with teacher guidance.

The first objective involves helping Matthew select and use materials and sustain interaction with them. Bay-Dopyera and Dopyera (1990) suggest that play at the water table or sand area is a good way to allow children who lack confidence to experience satis-faction. The teacher should go with Matthew to the water or sand area and begin to play there herself. She smiles and praises Matthew if he begins to use the materials and continues making frequent visual contact, and smiling and offering periodic comment as long as the child remains occupied. Attention is contingent on continued activity. That is, Matthew receives individual teacher attention so long as he plays appropriately. With this initial positive experience built on adult support and attention, Matthew is likely to find that this type of involvement is within his repertoire; he will therefore be likely to independently initiate involvement on subsequent occasions.

To accomplish the second objective, a teacher will play with Matthew for specified periods daily. She will shape his individual play behaviour so that he will eventually select a centre, choose a toy, bring it to the mat, and initiate play himself. (The process of shaping is described in Chapter 10). The teacher will also verbally stress what other children are doing so that Matthew can learn to model his behaviour on theirs. For example, "What a great tower Chen has built. Can you build one the same?"

To help Matthew play and co-operate with a peer, the teacher will invite one other child to join the group using toys that require two players. Both children will be reinforced for co-operative play. For example, if they build a block tower together, the teacher may reinforce the behaviour by saying, "You helped Chen build a nice tower. Good for you, Matthew," and "I really like the way you and Matthew work together, Chen."

SUMMARY

1. Early childhood special education—more broadly, early intervention for children with disabilities—is a relatively recent phenomenon. ECSE has its roots in early childhood education, compensatory education, and special education for school-age children. It draws on the accumulated theory and methods in psychology, human development, nursing, and sociology.

2. Initially, early childhood intervention meant a select group of programs for young handicapped children. Almost always, these programs were specialized and segregated. Although specialized programs still exist, the current philosophy is that ECSE should generally not take place in settings separate from early childhood education. In both philosophical and pragmatic terms, the most appropriate settings for young children with special needs are comprehensive programs that promote regular contact between disabled and normally developing children.

3. Formal early intervention began in the late 1950s and blossomed in the 1970s. The 1970s and the 1980s produced significant findings concerning the outcomes of early intervention. However, even sophisticated analyses of early intervention programs cannot conclusively show positive effects for a range of problems and disability groups. Integrating children with exceptionalities with their normally developing peers is often very clearly the most appropriate option; even so, controversy still clouds the issue. In general, studies have indicated that children are not adversely affected by integrated programs, and that the outcomes are likely to be more positive when specific programmatic interventions are employed.

4. In accepting the responsibility of integrating children with disabilities, early childhood teachers are faced with the problem of programming for these children's cognitive, physical, and social needs, often with minimal advice and assistance.

5. Professionals require a range of skills if they are to work effectively with children with disabilities. These skills include the ability to work as part of a team and to manage classroom behaviour effectively. They must also know the characteristics and behaviours of children with disabilities, the concepts and skills those children need to learn, and the most appropriate techniques for teaching those skills. Finally, professionals must be able to serve as consultants to other significant individuals in the children's lives.

6. The skills required for working with infants and their families are different from those for working with three- to five-year-olds. Providing goals and services for individual families may be especially difficult for those early childhood workers whose training has focused on children. They are not trained in family assessment and intervention, which is a difficult area.

7. Different disciplines bring different skills and knowledge to early intervention; that being said, the nature of the individual child drives a need to blend roles, skills, and knowledge across disciplines. Early intervention services depend on a team of professionals working together.

8. Good communication skills are necessary for working with children, parents, and other professionals.

9. Physical and occupational therapists help to improve movement, fine and gross motor skills, positioning, and so on. Speech and language therapists improve the child's speech and language development.

SECTION 2
Parents and Families

ONE OF THE MAJOR CHANGES in early childhood education, for normally developing children and for those with special needs, is the new focus on the family and the role of family members. In the field of early intervention this change is echoed in a greater commitment to provide comprehensive, co-ordinated, and family-focused services to children with disabilities and their families.

In Canada the value of early intervention work with disabled or delayed children and their families is widely recognized (Marfo et al., 1988). Programs for infants and toddlers are becoming more prominent, and emphasize the role of the member with the disability in the family as well as the involvement of parents. Central to all this is the belief that an array of early intervention services can make an important difference in the lives of children with disabilities and their families (Guralnick, 1988).

Services may be based in the home, a clinic, a special setting, or a regular early-childhood setting. Multiple settings are possible. In various ways, parents are intimately involved in these programs. Their participation may include sitting on parent advisory boards, attending parent/teacher conferences, making use of family services, working as volunteers, and carrying out early intervention with their own children.

Infant programs offer parents intensive participation and usually continue until the child is about three years of age. These programs try to enhance a child's development by helping the parents become effective intervenors. While many infant programs are clinic based, programs in which workers visit the home are showing promise as a means to provide very young children with special services. Most of these home-visiting programs are based on consistent contact in the client's home between the child, the family, and a representative of a formal agency.

The awareness that early intervention is important to families with disabled children is quite recent. Traditionally, early intervention was viewed as a child-centred endeavour, the main purpose

of which was to enhance children's developmental outcomes. Only in the past five or ten years has the focus changed. It is now argued that a primary reason for early intervention is family support. This means that before professionals can work effectively with families in home settings, they must acquire a range of skills that differ in focus from those needed in centre-based settings (see Chapter 3). First, professionals must develop an appreciation of the impact the family member with a disability has on the family's functioning. Over the years, families and their functioning have been looked at in different ways. A systems approach is now seen as the most appropriate one for families with a disabled member. The systems approach is based on the premise that many factors in both the family and the community influence the child's development, and that the child in turn influences other areas of the system.

A second general skill professionals must acquire is the ability to interact with parents and to make parents an integral part of the intervention. There are a number of ways of looking at families, and a number of early intervention models, but all are based on the firm principle that parents and families ought to be the chief intervenors and advocates for their own children.

In this section we focus on families and very early intervention. In Chapter 4 we look at how a member with a disability can affect family functioning. In Chapter 5 we discuss the major practices in this exciting and expanding area. The focus in the latter chapter is on parent involvement and parent training. Research shows that early childhood special education is not as effective if parents are not involved and supported (Bricker, 1982).

CHAPTER 4
Parents and Families

CASE STUDY

Rollo

Roland James Michaels has always been called Rollo. His two-year-old sister found Roland too hard for her tongue to trip around, so Rollo it was. Within the family circle, Rollo is deeply loved. His two older sisters and his parents devote hours of their time to playing with him and talking to him. Sometimes Mr. Michaels is more reticent about Rollo and seems unsure of his role, but as time goes on, he is interacting more naturally with his son.

Rollo's birth was not a surprise: the parents had planned for one more child and hoped desperately for a boy. The pregnancy was uneventful, the labour fairly easy. It was a few hours later that life for the Michaels turned around. The doctor came to see the parents and announced, as gently as she could, that the child was a Down syndrome baby. Both mother and father were stunned and dismayed. Neither knew anything about Down syndrome except the ancient stereotypes: the words "mongoloid," "mentally retarded," and "idiot" immediately leaped into their minds.

The parents were now faced with handling an infant with strange and mysterious conditions about which they knew nothing. They were not only worried and frightened but also heartbroken. Their wonderful dreams and plans for their new child were shattered, and they realized that their lives and those of the rest of the family would change drastically. Rollo's two older sisters were disappointed. Both had been a little dubious about the impact of a new baby on their lives, but generally they had shared the parents' excitement about the new child. Now they did not have the cute and cuddly baby expected but instead, a brother with conditions that made him completely unlike any child they had encountered before.

The doctor tried to ease the parents' worst fears, as did a counsellor attached to the hospital. First, they confronted the most pressing issue. The child, the doctor explained, was born with a duodenal atresia—that is, the lack of an opening between the stomach and the intestine. Immediate surgery was necessary so that the infant could obtain nourishment. But, she pointed out, the surgery would not alleviate the physical and mental anomalies associated with Down syndrome.

In those early days, as Rollo recovered from the surgery in the neonatal unit, the parents demanded information about the condition, its consequences, and its prognosis. They found that Down syndrome is most likely to strike at the close of a woman's child-bearing years. Mrs. Michaels was only 28, and they asked, "Why us?" What had happened to make the chromosome split unevenly and give them a son with mental and physical anomalies?

The parents knew that Down syndrome was inevitably tied to mental retardation but could not accept the doctor's explanation that the degree of retardation was unknowable at that early date and that the physical anomalies characteristic of Down syndrome children bore no relationship to the degree of retardation. Mr. and Mrs. Michaels also found it difficult to believe that Rollo would learn anything, even though the counsellor explained that early and consistent intervention would improve and enhance the child's functioning.

An institution for the child was out of the question. Not only did the parents reject the idea, but Canadian institutions no longer accepted new referrals. Nevertheless, the Michaels worried deeply about how they would handle the child in the home, how the siblings would react, and how friends, neighbours, and the extended family would respond. Even at this early stage, the parents began to wonder what would happen to Rollo after they died.

In the first few months after Rollo came home, some of these fears grew stronger. For example, Rollo had some feeding problems that frustrated and worried Mrs. Michaels. While he was a good baby, he grew and developed slowly. He lay in his crib most of the time, reacting little to the environment or the people in it.

The two sisters soon accepted the child, but the grandparents on both sides asked many of the same questions the Michaels had asked. Mrs. Michaels tried to hide her grief under the mantle of everyday activities. The father had more difficulty accepting that his only son had a permanent condition that would affect all aspects of development and progress.

Two events brought about improvements in the family's functioning. First, the Michaels joined a support group of parents whose children had Down syndrome or other conditions that caused mental retardation. Before this, the Michaels had felt isolated and alone, as if they were the only people in the world facing such enormous problems. They soon learned that they were not alone, and this helped them greatly.

Second, a teacher came into the home once a week. A chief concern of this teacher was Rollo and his development, but she did not spend all of her time with him; she also intervened with the parents and siblings, providing information, support, and encouragement. The parents were especially eager for concrete information about the handicap and its impact on development, and about current and future educational options for Rollo.

With the parents, the teacher listed the skills that were important for Rollo to develop within the family context. Communication and social interaction were of particular importance to Mrs. Michaels. The teacher then demonstrated how to stimulate Rollo's social skills and communication, as well as his physical movement. She always demonstrated the procedures and invited the mother to participate. The teacher's aim was to help the mother develop a mutually satisfying relationship with the child. She used activities that Mrs. Michaels could continue, and ones that were reasonable within the context of the family.

For example, to initiate communication the teacher sat Rollo on her knee and babbled at him, and then responded to and reinforced any spontaneous vocalizations that Rollo made. At the same time, she reinforced eye-to-eye contact (gazing behaviour) and smiles. The teacher also demonstrated exercises to strengthen Rollo's abdominal muscles, to be done two or three times a day.

Although Rollo's initial progress was slow, the teacher could soon demonstrate improvements in his behaviour and overall functioning. Once Mrs. Michaels realized that Rollo could learn, her apprehension faded and she began to work with the child daily, following the model provided by the teacher. For example, she learned to reinforce Rollo's early vocalizations by smiling, talking back, and touching him; this encouraged him to continue vocalizing. The two sisters readily joined in this wonderful game.

By the time he was three, Rollo was walking. He had a vocabulary of about 50 words and understood some of what was said to him. He could feed himself—albeit somewhat messily— although he would only touch a restricted range of foods. He was not yet toilet trained. Nevertheless, the staff at the local daycare centre were willing to accommodate Rollo. They felt that integration with normally developing peers would benefit him intellectually and socially. The other children would provide appropriate models for many types of behaviour. As well, the other children would benefit from interacting with a child with a different learning style and abilities. The individual program that was designed for Rollo is presented later in this chapter.

THE GREAT MAJORITY OF CHILDREN are born healthy and well formed. However, some infants are born with serious disabilities that threaten their physical, intellectual, communicative, social, and emotional functioning. Rollo is one of these children. When the doctor diagnosed Rollo with Down syndrome, Mr. and Mrs. Michaels felt shock, dismay, and anger. Their hopes for a perfect child were shattered, and they were faced with raising an infant whose many problems would require intense medical and educational intervention. Yet the Michaels are not unique. A child with an exceptional condition can arrive to any family: no family, anywhere, is immune (Winzer, 1996). About 3 percent of newborn infants have a handicap that may result in developmental delay or disability; another 3 percent are born with significant conditions capable of causing medical or social handicaps (Berlin, 1983). Down syndrome itself occurs in about one in every 1000 live births (see Box 4–1).

The birth of any child has a significant impact on family dynamics as members adjust in a variety of ways to accommodate the new arrival. All families experience stress whether the new child is disabled or not; but when the new child *is* disabled, the stresses tend to be greater as they relate to acceptance, caregiving needs, and family variables.

It is only recently that professionals have begun to fully appreciate the confusion, uncertainty, guilt, and fear that are associated with the birth and parenting of a child with a disability. Changing social perceptions, new research, and parent and professional advocacy have brought about attitudinal changes. A major force promoting these changes was the passage in the United States of law PL 99-457. This legislation places the family at the centre of early intervention. Its main intent is to foster meaningful parent–professional partnerships to promote the optimal development of infants and toddlers (Summers et al., 1990). Technically, American laws have no validity in Canada; even so, their influence in education is pervasive. We explain PL 99-457 and its related laws in Box 4–2.

In the new climate fostered by changes in laws, perceptions, and programs, early intervention practices have improved dramatically. Today, professionals offer substantial support to families—support that is designed to provide parents with the energy, knowledge, confidence, and emotional resources they need to facilitate their child's development.

In this chapter we outline some of the reactions within families to the arrival of a child with a disability, and examine how a child with a disability affects the family. We also explore some of the approaches that are used to look at families and their functioning. These ways of viewing families are important because, at least to some extent, they determine how professionals intervene.

BOX 4–1

Down syndrome

Developmental disorders can result from an extra chromosome, or from pieces or fragments of chromosomes attaching themselves to other chromosomes. There are many different chromosomal disorders that affect children; the effects of the damage vary greatly in nature and severity.

Down syndrome was first described by John Langton Down in 1866. It is the most common and widely known chromosomal aberration, occurring in one in every 1000 live births. The condition has devastating effects on physical and intellectual development. The tiny fragment of extra chromosomal material somehow disturbs the orderly development of the body and brain and causes mental and physical anomalies.

There are three major types of Down syndrome: Trisomy 21, translocation, and mosaicism. Mental retardation is inevitable with Trisomy and translocation and possible but not inevitable with mosaicism. Trisomy 21 is by far the most common form of Down syndrome, accounting for more than 90 percent of all cases.

More than 50 physical signs have been listed as characteristic of Down syndrome. These include low-set ears, missing cartilage in the nose, and an epicanthic fold in the eyes. Some characteristics are apparent at birth, some appear much later, and some disappear with age. The number of physical features that a child displays bears no relationship to the degree of retardation. Few children have all the physical characteristics that are typical of the syndrome.

Among delayed preschoolers, Down syndrome is the most frequent specific diagnosis (Lojkasek et al., 1990). These children develop more slowly than others, both physically and intellectually. Children with Down syndrome often exhibit delayed motor development, hypotonia (low muscle tone) and a tendency toward obesity. Children with Down syndrome may be mildly, moderately, severely, or profoundly mentally handicapped.

Children with Down syndrome are often identified in the delivery room. For severely handicapped children, early intervention is crucial to later educational success; that is why the process of aiding these children's development should begin at the moment of birth. Children with Down syndrome seem to make the most progress when parents and other regular companions are persistent in their attempts to stimulate them while providing plenty of emotional support (Mundy et al., 1988).

With early support, Down syndrome children can make remarkable progress. At the University of Washington's Early Intervention Program for Down syndrome children, studies demonstrated this. Children who received no early intervention showed progressive declines in performance relative to their normally developing peers; those children who did receive early intervention showed positive developmental patterns. Those who participated in the program and were between three and four years of age typically performed about 95 percent of the tasks expected of their normal peers (Peterson, 1987).

BOX 4–2
Influence of American precedents and models

The United States has long relied on legislative and litigative remedies for social issues, including special education. When the U.S. government passes an education law, it is often a grant-in-aid law; this means that states must conform to the law in order to receive federal funding. For this reason, most states pass laws that mimic the federal mandates. In recent years a number of important pieces of legislation related to children with disabilities of both school age and preschool age have been passed and then amended in various ways.

The first federal education law aimed at young children with disabilities and their families was enacted in 1968. It established the Handicapped Children's Early Education Program (HCEEP). This program successfully provided services, assessment devices, curriculum materials, and parent training materials to young children and their families.

Public Law 94-142 was passed in the United States in 1975 to serve the needs of school-age students with disabilities. PL 94-142 provided all exceptional school-age children in the United States with a free and appropriate education, individual planning, related services, and nondiscriminatory assessment. Today more than 4 million children with disabilities are served under PL 94-142.

Since 1975 the original PL 94-142 has been amended several times; its mandate now includes infants and preschoolers and their families. In 1983, PL 98-199 established a state-level process designed to encourage planning and co-ordination of all early education programs, with particular emphasis on handicapped children and infants. States that had independently provided services for children between three and five, or for young adults between 18 and 21, had to also provide services for these age groups.

On August 5, 1986, Congress enacted PL 99-457, the Handicapped Children's Protection Act, as an amendment to PL 94-142. PL 99-457 deals specifically with children with disabilities under the age of five and their families. It has been described as "the most important legislation ever enacted for developmentally vulnerable young children" (Shonkoff & Meisels, 1990, p. 19) and has intensified concerns and interest about early intervention in the United States, Canada, and elsewhere.

Public policies for families with disabled children were once criticized for being unresponsive to family needs and unsupportive of familial care. PL 99-457 addresses the needs of both families and children; its mandates explicitly assume that American families with disabled children have a universal claim on public resources, and that

The Child and the Family

The family has been extolled as the cornerstone of our society. However, the word "family" means different things to different people, and in recent decades the modern family has changed dramatically. There is much we do not yet know about the impact of these changes on children's health, well-being, development, and learning.

In modern families, we no longer find the idealized version of mother, father, and several children living in their own home. Today the two-parent family is not the norm in our society. Many children today are born out of wedlock

the family's needs should be addressed in conjunction with the services provided to the child.

PL 101-476, passed in 1990, and otherwise known as the Individuals with Disabilities Education Act (IDEA), further amended the landmark special-education legislation passed in 1975. The title of the law was changed to embrace people-first terminology: thus, "a child with a disability" rather than "a handicapped child." The notion of empowering parents is central to IDEA, which reinforces rights for children regardless of their disability. Part H is the infant component of IDEA; section 619 of part B is the preschool component. Besides extending federal requirements for special education services to children between three and five, Part H of the law established a discretionary program to assist states in developing and implementing early intervention services for infants and toddlers with disabilities, and for their families.

In the United States, early intervention programs for young children with disabilities are rapidly expanding as states and local communities meet the service requirements established by PL 99-457. Preschool special education enrolment for 1989–90 rose 6.6 percent over the previous year. The total number of preschool children served was 382,434. The expansion is significant and should result in greater access to programs for previously unserved children and an increasingly broad array of service options.

This law is in force only in the United States. While early intervention has received much attention in Canada, we do not have a federal office of education, since education and social services are a provincial responsibility. Nor does Canada have legislation of a prescriptive nature for preschool children with disabilities and their families. Nevertheless, the American legislation is of crucial importance to Canada, which is so linked to the United States geographically, economically, and culturally that American practices have an enormous impact on Canadian policy.

Although prediction is a tricky business, past experience leads us to assume that Canadian jurisdictions will adopt at least some of the principles found in the American early childhood legislation and expand their commitment to young children with disabilities and their families. Further, early childhood special education programs are expanding and consolidating, and it seems likely that this trend will continue and accelerate.

As increasing numbers of children with exceptional conditions are placed in programs with normally developing peers, one official response may be some type of enabling legislation directed specifically toward infants and preschoolers with disabilities and their families. Early childhood education personnel are usually not trained in techniques for developing appropriate programs for young disabled children, so this facet of ECE may also be addressed. Such training may even become mandatory.

or to teenage mothers; others are in families where the parents have divorced or separated. The result of all this is an ever-increasing number of poor, single-parent families. Moreover, today's adult lifestyles are very different from those of earlier generations; this has also increased stresses on the modern family.

Nevertheless, whether families are traditional or not, they do tend to share certain characteristics, concerns, and needs. When a family has a disabled member, however, these shared characteristics are not as predominant—raising a child with a disability can make family life very different. Families with children who are disabled have important extra concerns, for there are no culturally available timetables for according independence and stimulating the development of physical and social skills (Baxter, 1980).

Most observers have concluded that raising a child who is disabled is often burdensome, tiresome, frustrating, and stressful. Abundant evidence indicates that parents of children with disabilities experience more than average amounts of stress. Parental stress is more evident when the diagnosis of a child's disability was delayed or is unclear (Goldberg et al., 1986). Stress is also more evident in families when the child has a severe or profound rather than a mild or moderate condition (Frey, Greenberg, & Fewell, 1989).

We can define **stress** as "the tension experienced when an event is perceived as harmful, threatening, or challenging to one's feelings of well-being" (Zeitlin & Williamson, 1988, p. 138). **Stressors** are the stress-inducing events or circumstances that give rise to stress—that is, the internal or external events that threaten, harm, or challenge personal feelings of well-being (Zeitlin & Williamson, 1988).

Stress factors and methods for coping with stress vary considerably among families. Many families adjust successfully to the stress; they find ways to meet personal needs and to respond to the demands of the environment. In other families, stress is pervasive and even debilitating. The families that are most stressed and have the most trouble meeting a child's developmental needs are also the families most likely to enrol their child in poor-quality care (Hayes, Palmer, and Zaslow, 1990).

The stress seen in families with disabled members is sometimes the result of one or more specific events: the initial diagnosis, the early impact of the news, the search for help, entry into the educational system, the arrival of puberty, the process of watching other children graduate from school or marry, and so on. More often, stress is cumulative, a result of the daily burden of caring for a child with a disability within the context of the family, the neighbourhood, and the culture.

The problems that create stress in families with a child with a disability can be placed in three broad areas: care and management, family factors, and social attitudes toward children with disabilities.

Stress the tension experienced when an event is perceived as harmful, threatening, or challenging to one's feelings of well-being.

Stressors the events or circumstances that give rise to stress; the internal or external events that threaten, harm, or challenge personal feelings of well-being.

CARE AND MANAGEMENT

When we examine the family problems associated with the care and management of a member with a disability, we see that some of the stresses arise directly from the child and relate to the child's temperament, rhythmicity (e.g., sleeping schedules, feeding times), caretaking demands, and behaviour, and to the severity of the child's handicap (Beckman, 1983). Other stresses arise from outside the child. Researchers have noted that many parents experience feelings of inadequacy when faced with the prospect of rearing a child who has been diagnosed as disabled (or even as gifted). These feelings of inadequacy may be reinforced by daily experiences.

Children with disabilities are often restricted in their ability to attend to, take in, and assimilate information from the environment; this makes them less responsive, less energetic, and less independent. When a child with a disability displays different and worrying social, behavioural, and physical responses, high levels of family stress may result. A particular child, for example, may show slower progress across all developmental domains. Or the child may have a more difficult temperament, or lack social responsiveness, or show stereotypic behaviour patterns, or present additional or unusual caregiving needs. We saw this in the case of Rollo, whose mother worried about his passivity and lack of development.

Some research has looked at child behaviours in the infant years—years that parents of disabled infants have identified as most difficult, stressful, and uncomfortable. The behaviours encountered include crying, resistance to being held, refusal to be soothed, passive nonresponsiveness, "tuning out," and production of atypical motor responses (Calhoun & Rose, 1989).

There are a number of outside agencies and support systems that help families and other caregivers manage and care for very young children with disabilities. These services are an important source of support and seem to mediate the effects of stress (Beckman et al., 1993; Stoneman & Crapps, 1988). In some cases, however, the support agencies may actually create rather than alleviate stress.

Most new parents of a child with a disability feel overwhelmed, and early intervention should include providing information about the child's condition and training in how to care for the child. Yet when parents are asked whether they found the services helpful, they often criticize the quality of the support and of the information received (e.g., Meyers & Blacher, 1987; Moses & Croll, 1987; Turnbull & Turnbull, 1986).

Christine Baxter (1987) examined the social-support function of professional services from the perspective of the parents. Her sample included 131 parents of children and adolescents classified as moderately or severely mentally handicapped. She found that parents of younger children were more likely to have received assistance than parents of teenagers, and that 90 percent of the parents believed that assistance was important or very important. Stress tended to result from worry about where to get help. Also, parents who did not receive support reported more stress than parents who did, even if the latter did not believe that the support was adequate.

Some families are unable to obtain adequate support, and this may create stress. There are many vivid anecdotal accounts in which affected parents describe their often extraordinary efforts to secure services for a child while also attending to the welfare of the family as a whole. For other families, the amount (as opposed to the availability) of support is inadequate and increases stress.

Even when parent services are available, some parents are more likely than others to gain access to help and assistance (Tomlinson, 1982). One differentiating factor is ethnicity, which is known to influence whether parents actually gain help from existing community services (Bennett, 1988; Smith & Ryan, 1987). Access to many services may be reduced by cultural and linguistic barriers. Families from different cultures often face many obstacles when trying to obtain assessment, respite, and other services from educational, mental health, and other agencies.

When parents discover their child has a handicap, they find themselves brought into the orbit of a number of professional disciplines. Gaining information about the exceptionality is only the first in a lifelong series of interactions; many families are plunged into the world of infant stimulation, early intervention, preschools, respite services, medical intervention, and so on. When a number of agencies are offering services to parents, stress may be created if the services are piecemeal and unco-ordinated.

Those providing early intervention services also note a lack of support. There is a large discrepancy between what service providers report as typical practice with families and what they perceive to be the ideal levels of family support

(Bailey et al., 1992). In part, this is because early intervention is such a new field that it is not yet clear what types of support are most likely to be of use to families.

FAMILY FACTORS   Stress also results from family factors. These include personal belief systems, the age of the parents, the level of psychological functioning, socio-economic status, spouse support, the need to care for siblings, and the amount of support from the extended family, friends, and neighbours (Dunst, 1985).

Stress may surface when parents have to provide support for other family members. The siblings' reactions invariably affect parental functioning, and vice versa. Remember that in the case of Rollo, the sisters' reactions—disappointment mixed with acceptance—mirrored to some extent those of the parents.

Until recently, professionals have either ignored or given secondary consideration to the impact of a special-needs child on his or her siblings (Seligman & Darling, 1989). We now realize that sibling relationships take on special significance when one sibling is handicapped (Powell & Ogle, 1985). The roles a

BOX 4–3
Rollo's IPP

NAME: *Roland*

CHRONOLOGICAL AGE: *3 years, 2 months*

BACKGROUND INFORMATION: *Rollo has Down syndrome, which was identified at birth. Since the age of four months, Rollo has been provided with sustained intervention through a home-based program. The intervention stressed stimulation to develop motor skills, achieve mobility, and engage in basic communication.*

Present levels of functioning:
Assessment indicates that Rollo is functioning in the range of moderately retarded. He is walking but has not achieved the motor skills of a child of three. Rollo is not toilet trained. He understands a small number of words and phrases such as "Yes," "No," "Get your coat," and "Snack time." He uses a few words, mostly related to food and other wants. Physical anomalies of the speech mechanism (tongue, teeth, and palate) will make speech difficult for Rollo to acquire.

In the playroom, Rollo tends to play with one or two boys. If he plays with others, it is with teacher direction. He prefers the younger group of children. Behaviour is not a problem; Rollo has learned most of the daily routines and joins in circle time and group activities, although his participation is limited.

Rollo needs many opportunities to expand his skills in fine and gross motor development and basic communication. Interaction with peers in free play situations should also be emphasized, so that he can develop play skills and also learn social and communicative behaviours.

Long-term goals:
* *To develop awareness of others and the ability to co-operate with others.*
* *To expand single-word expressive and receptive vocabulary related to food, clothing, and toys.*
* *To improve gross motor skills.*

  Personnel involved: Regular staff during free play and during small group sessions. Consultation with a speech therapist on language development.

sibling normally assumes are necessarily altered. A child who is disabled may not function as a playmate, a caretaker, or a socializing agent for his or her siblings. Parents may come to treat the child with a disability differently from the ones who are developing normally.

It is now fairly clear that siblings' major challenges relate to an increase in caregiving responsibilities, and to the requirement to make up for the limitations of the child with the disability (Dyson, Edgar, & Crnic, 1989). When 24 siblings of children with severe disabilities were interviewed, it was found that 84 percent had responsibilities for teaching, 79 percent for dressing, 71 percent for feeding, 71 percent for bathing, and 50 percent for discipline (Wilson, Blacher, & Baker, 1989).

Parents may come to treat the normally developing children differently from the disabled child. Because the parents feel uncertain about how to care for and manage a child with a disability, they may subject that child to patterns of socialization that are significantly different from those that operate for the other children. The child with a disability may not be given the same discipline

Short-term objectives:

1. *Rollo will need teacher direction to help him play for short periods with other children. The first step is to initiate parallel play with another child. To do this, sit Rollo and another child facing each other, and have them play with similar toys. The teacher can assist each child as necessary and comment frequently on each child's work.*

2. *At this time, work on gross motor skills should take in two areas: dressing and play. Rollo should learn the self-help skills of taking off his own boots and (later) his own coat, and be prompted to use clay and Play-doh to develop hand skills.*

   For undressing in the morning or after outside play, the teacher will first use a chaining method. That is, she will pull the boot almost all the way off and then praise Rollo for completing the task. Gradually, the teacher will do less and reinforce each step that Rollo completes.

   To encourage play with clay and Play-doh, the teacher will go with Rollo to the centre and make a model herself,

   commenting on her work and prompting Rollo to try. He should use both hands for this activity.

3. *To prompt Rollo to generalize the use of words for food and toys taught in small group activities, the teacher will again use a chaining technique. Thus, to prompt him to use a word, she will hold up a toy and say, "I have a _____." If Rollo completes the sentence, he will be reinforced with praise: "Good boy. Yes, I have a block." If he fails to respond, the teacher will model the sentence, "I have a block," and try chaining again.*

4. *To generalize names of foods, use a time delay procedure. (The methods for time delay are explained in Chapter 15.)*

5. *Rollo also needs to learn that language has a function and that one of its functions is to regulate others. To this end, allow him to lead a small group or even the whole group. For example, in circle time, have three pictures illustrating three known songs on cards. Let Rollo point to a card to choose a song for the group. Let him also choose other children, who will then choose a song in the same way.*

Sibling relationships are important in all families.

as the other children, or may always be treated as the "baby" of the family. As well, siblings share family resources, and relationships between siblings may be damaged when the child who is disabled draws on more of those resources (Dyson & Fewell, 1989).

Gifted and talented children may also cause disruption and stress within the family. Since giftedness is socially acceptable, most parents have few problems accepting their child's giftedness. Still, the gifted child may be both a blessing and a burden. It is generally accepted that parents and families must be highly involved in the development of their gifted children from a young age or the gifted child's potential will not be fully tapped. The downside, then, is the amount of time and energy that parents must expend on the gifted child.

Some parents of children who are gifted often feel inadequate in managing their children, uncertain about programming and placement decisions, and unsure about how to stimulate their children both in and out of school. Or they may be exhausted by constant questions and explorations. Others who try to stimulate and challenge the child may feel pressured to develop specific strategies for encouraging learning at home. They may feel that they have to make special accommodations, such as for special schools and extra equipment. These can be costly

PROGRESS CHECK 1

List the reasons why the siblings of a child who is disabled or gifted may feel resentment toward the special child and the parents.

and time-consuming. When special accommodations are made for the child, sibling competition and jealousy may result; siblings may resent the extra money and attention their parents are spending on the child who is gifted.

At the same time, if parents give the gifted preschooler too much attention, that child may later encounter difficulties in coping with sibling and peer competition (Rimm & Lowe, 1988).

Social factors   Because society's reactions to abnormality have a great impact on the development of the family unit and its members, social attitudes may be a source of stress. Too often, parents blame themselves for the problem behaviours of the child with a disability and are held at least partly responsible by friends and neighbours. Parents may also believe that negative societal reactions to their child's deviant behaviour amount to a criticism of their parenting skills, and of their status in general. As well, the discrepancy between the child's mental and physical age creates stress (and embarrassment) for the parents. For example, the child may be too big to fit into a shopping-cart seat yet still be at the mental age when he or she pulls things from supermarket shelves.

Dealing with stress   Although the sources of stress are extremely varied, most families do adapt, and in positive ways (Kazak & Marvin, 1984). The parents' history of dealing with problems will be reflected in their methods for coping with a child with a disability. If past crises have tended to produce major upheavals, then the discovery of a disability in a child will only add to the existing problems. If the parents have been able to make healthy adjustments to past difficulties, they will likely find it easier to accept a child with a disability (Winzer, 1996).

Ways of Looking at Families

Stage theory approach **suggests that the parents of children with disabilities pass through orderly stages from grieving to acceptance.**

There are a number of ways to conceptualize relationships between family members, the child with a disability, the extended family, and the wider culture. Each of these frameworks is a little different from the others, although the variables are the same; the real differences are in which components of family life are emphasized. This can be seen in Table 4–1. As we mentioned in the introduction, all these ways of looking at families are important because they undergird the manner in which professionals present early intervention programs and interact with parents.

STAGE APPROACH   **Stage theory** has long been a popular approach to examining families with children who are disabled. The basic principle here is that the parents of children with disabilities pass through orderly stages, from initial shock, fear, anger, and inadequacy, to acceptance of the child and the condition. Box 4–4 outlines the possible range of these parental reactions.

TABLE 4–1: Looking at families

Model	Principles	Major focus
Stage theory	Parents pass through discrete stages from grief to acceptance	Parent counselling Parent therapy Parent self-help groups Information about the condition
Life cycle theory	Families pass through cycles in which there may be crisis transition points	Transition support Liaison with other other agencies Family support Intervention with the child
Systems theory	The family is a system within the larger social context	Priorities set by the family Stress on all family members Functional skills for the child Improved functioning within family
Social support theory	Families are systems in themselves	Families helping themselves Families setting priorities Advocating for child

Not all parents pass through all of these stages, and each person works through them at a different rate (Eden-Piercy, Blacher, & Eyman, 1986). Parental reactions are mediated by various factors such as the severity of the disability, the parents' socio-economic status, and the quality of external and interfamily support systems (Ormerod & Huebner, 1988).

LIFE CYCLE APPROACH

Several authorities have questioned the validity of stage theory as it is applied to families of children with disabilities; in fact, they wonder whether parents go through stages at all. For parents, the stages are not always present (Allen & Affleck, 1985), and even when they are, they are not necessarily sequential (Darling, 1991).

Instead of adopting a stage approach, some researchers utilize a *life cycle* or lifespan approach. A life cycle perspective sees the family as a unit that is moving through time and experiencing a series of events, tasks, and transitions. When we look at a family's life cycle, we see that the impact of the child with a disability on the family changes over time.

Researchers have identified ten specific periods of the life cycle (i.e., "transition times") that result in increased stress in families (Wilker, 1981; Wilker, Wasow, & Hatfield, 1981). Five of these periods are shared by all families with children: the age at which the child should begin to walk; the age at which the child should begin to talk; entry into the public school system; onset of puberty; and the 21st birthday. For families with a child with a disability, there are extra dimensions of stress at certain periods. These are when diagnosis is made; when

Life cycle (lifespan) approach this perspective sees the family as a unit that is moving through time and experiencing a series of events, tasks, and transitions. By looking at the family life cycle, it can be seen that the impact of the disabled child on the family changes over time.

BOX 4–4
Parental reactions to the diagnosis of a disabling condition

Acute initial reactions	Chronic adaptive reactions	Mature adaptation
shock	withdrawal and isolation	refashioning expectations
denial and disbelief anger	depression ambivalence	coping with everyday practical problems
bitterness and shame	rejection	maximizing the child's potential
loss of self-esteem	overprotectiveness; self-sacrifice; defensiveness	
inappropriate guilt, projection of blame	doctor "shopping"	protecting the interests of the whole family
disappointment, sadness, grief bargaining		interaction with others

Source: See Winzer (1993)

Systems theory (perspective) recognizes that actions in any part of the system affect the other parts, and that solutions to problems can only be found when the problem is properly defined in its larger environmental context. Influences are seen as multidirectional: each adult and child influences every member of the household, and each family relationship affects all the other family members.

the development of a younger sibling surpasses that of the child with a disability; when placement outside the home is considered; when a child management crisis occurs; and when guardianship issues are discussed.

SYSTEMS APPROACH   The work of ecological theorists is exerting a great deal of influence on the early intervention movement. Today's interest in family-centred services has its basis in family systems theory, which emphasizes how the experiences of one family member affect the other family members.

It is now seen as crucial for professionals helping families with a disabled member to pay attention to the interactive functioning within the total family system and between the family and other systems (Elman, 1991). They must recognize that each family is unique. The same event will carry different meanings and arouse different responses for different families, so determining an individual family's responses and understandings is essential.

A *systems theory* or perspective recognizes that actions in any part of the system affect the other parts, and vice versa, and that solutions to problems can only be found when the problem is properly placed in its larger environmental

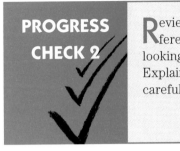

PROGRESS CHECK 2

Review each of the different models for looking at families. Explain each one carefully.

context. In a systems model, influences are seen as multidirectional: each adult influences every member of the household, and so does each child, and each family relationship affects all the other family members. Thus, the outcomes of any child-rearing patterns on any child depend on many factors, which interact with each other. These factors include the child's age, sex, and temperament; the parents' personality characteristics, personal history, and economic circumstances; the needs of family members; and the values of the culture. Infant and early childhood behaviours are interpreted in the context of cyclical interactions. The infant's behaviour affects the caregiver's behaviour, which in turn affects the infant's behaviour, and so on in a continuing cycle (Noonan & McCormick, 1993).

Within a systems framework, professionals consider the following:

- Basic family characteristics such as size, form, and culture. Also, the nature of the child's disability, the personal characteristics of the different family members, and specific conditions such as poverty or a single parent.

- Family interactions, which include modes of interaction (functional or dysfunctional) between parents and children, between siblings, with the extended family, with those outside the family, and so on. Also considered are family aspects such as how adaptable the family is to new and potentially stressful situations.

- Family functions, which include the many activities that families engage in to meet their diverse needs, such as economic needs and daily care.

- The family life cycle, which relates to the life cycle approach we referred to earlier. It addresses the fact that family needs change over time.

SOCIAL SUPPORT APPROACH

A systems approach considers events within the family as well as the broader social context. In many ways, the sys-

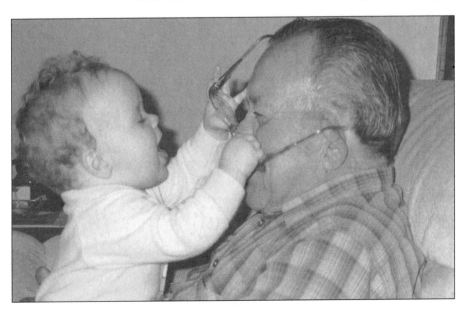

The extended family is important in the development of children.

Social support approach **focuses** on a family's functioning; stresses families helping themselves; sees informal support, such as the extended family and church, as more important than formal support.

tems approach overlaps with the social support approach; the difference is mainly one of emphasis. Whereas a systems approach focuses chiefly on the social context of the family, a ***social support*** approach focuses on a family's functioning. It stresses families helping themselves and sees informal support, such as the extended family and church, as more important than formal support.

The concepts of family support focus on the complex interactions of four family subsystems: marital, sibling, parental, and extrafamilial (Carter & McGoldrick, 1980). The two major concepts are embeddedness and social networks. *Embeddedness* refers to the fact that a developing child is enveloped within the family system and its members, and that the family unit is embedded in broader social units consisting of relatives, friends, neighbours, church members, and so on. These people—the family's *social network*—directly and indirectly influence both the family and the child (Dunst et al., 1990).

The families of children with disabilities often rely on an extensive network of social support (Marcenko & Meyers, 1991). In mothers, social support seems to decrease the incidence of maternal depression and increase a sense of personal competence (Gowen et al., 1989).

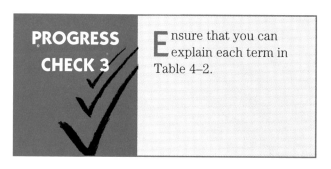

PROGRESS CHECK 3

Ensure that you can explain each term in Table 4–2.

TABLE 4–2: New terms and ideas

life cycle	stress
social support	stressors
stage theory	systems theory

SUMMARY

1. Modern families show great diversity.

2. It has been acknowledged for years that having a child with a disability in the family creates a difficult situation for all family members. However, the emphasis on the family as the crucial factor in the development of a child with a disability is fairly new in ECSE. Only in the past few decades have professionals begun to fully appreciate the pain and stress that parents feel when their child is diagnosed as disabled, and the amount of courage and outside help that parents need thereafter.

3. The effects of stress on the families of very young disabled or at-risk children are pervasive, multiple, and sometimes unsuspected.

4. Professional care providers tend to assume that services have a social support function and help to alleviate the problems parents face in caring for a child with a disability; however, this is not always the case.

5. Many researchers hold that most parents pass through similar stages before they accept the reality of their child's condition. Shock, denial, blame, guilt, depression, anger, and bargaining are all responses to the disabled family member. Other researchers look at families from a life-cycle perspective. The lifespan

approach sees families moving through time experiencing a series of events and tasks. These include transitions.

6. The most current way of viewing families is from a systems perspective, which takes into account how the family fits within the broader social context.

7. A family support-system approach stresses that the family is a system in itself, and that any change in a family that has a disabled child can cause stress in the system. Early intervention must take family dynamics into account.

CHAPTER 5
Intervention with Infants and Toddlers

CASE STUDY

Kasha

When Kasha was born she had a life-threatening heart defect and cataracts covering both eyes. Although heart surgery in the first few days of life was successful, the pediatrician explained to Kasha's mother that the cataracts would cause severe visual impairment and that the likelihood of deafness was great. The cause, explained the doctor, was maternal rubella, a virus that does most of its damage to the fetus during the first trimester (i.e., the first three months) of pregnancy. Kasha's mother could remember having a slight rash and sore throat for a few days in the early part of her pregnancy, but German measles (rubella), with its grave consequences for a child, had not even entered her head.

The mother brought Kasha home and focused immediately on caring for her new and disabled child. She was a good baby but required a great deal of extra attention, especially for feeding. Because of the thick cataracts, it was impossible to know how much Kasha actually saw. The mother did notice that even at four months, Kasha did not hold out her arms to be picked up as other babies do; nor did she begin to smile at faces or at the sound of her mother's voice.

Kasha's mother felt both inadequate and frustrated. She worried deeply about Kasha and her condition and grieved for her child. At the same time, she had two other children to care for. She was a single parent and did not have a great deal of family support to draw upon.

Personnel from the local branch of the Canadian Institute for the Blind tried to help Kasha and her mother. They did not intervene directly but suggested that the mother take Kasha once or twice a week to a centre designed to serve infants and toddlers with severe disabilities.

At seven months, the mother enrolled Kasha in the centre's program. At first, she was surprised that family goals took precedence over goals for the child. The centre's interest was not only in Kasha but in the functioning of the whole family and their hopes and priorities for Kasha. With the therapist, the mother discussed the major skills she wanted Kasha to learn so that the child could function more effectively within the home. The mother had two main priorities: she needed help with Kasha's feeding, and she wanted the child to become more mobile.

Kasha's visual, auditory, and motor functioning was assessed by specialists. In cases of visual impairment, two medical aspects of vision are taken into consideration: the physical and the functional. *Physical* aspects include visual acuity (how much a child can see), visual field (how widely the child's vision extends), and oculomotor control (how well the small muscles that control the eyes work). *Functional* aspects include the ways a child uses vision for purposeful behaviours.

An audiologist attempted to assess Kasha's hearing but could use only crude measures. Motor functioning was assessed by a physical therapist, who relied mainly on observation and developmental checklists. As well, the staff at the centre observed Kasha on the skills and abilities thought to be relevant to learning. Finally, a teacher visited the home and in that natural setting observed such things as how the mother interacted with and reinforced the child and how the siblings related to Kasha.

Immediately after the assessment, the mother received the results and interpretations of the findings. At a conference, those results were explained to her, any suspected problems or delays were identified, and Kasha's hearing and vision tests were discussed. The main point of the conference was to prepare a program for Kasha that would meet the family's needs, address the priorities the mother had set, and bring Kasha to her optimal functioning.

Service delivery, which refers to administrative arrangements for delivering assistance to exceptional children, was the first issue discussed—specifically, the site for intervention. The centre's staff felt, and the mother agreed, that two one-hour visits a week to the centre was too little intervention. Moreover, the travel was disrupting household routines. As a better alternative, a home visiting teacher was assigned to Kasha. Infants with a visual impairment have specific developmental needs that must be addressed by specialists, who work simultaneously with the infant and the parents (Friedman, 1989). In this case the home visitor was a specialist in visual impairments. From the outset, however, the focus was on the entire family and its needs, which were as important as attaining skills for Kasha.

The home visiting program proved very successful for both Kasha and the family. At sixteen months Kasha was reassessed, new goals and objectives were drawn up, and a new plan was put into action. Part of Kasha's plan is shown in Box 5–3 (pp. 141–142).

THIRTY YEARS AGO, PARENTS OF YOUNG CHILDREN with disabilities were virtually unaware that their children could benefit from intervention, that intervention should begin in the first months of life, and that services could be provided in local communities. Today there is a broad consensus that early identification and appropriate intervention are essential to both child and family.

For the child, the chances of ever catching up are directly related to how quickly intervention begins after deficits have been identified, and to the size of the discrepancy between the child's real and expected levels of performance (Peterson, 1987). Early services can maximize skill development and reduce or even remove the need for special services after a child enters school (Guralnick, 1989). For the family, early intervention serves as a support that enhances family functioning, provides crucial information for parents, and makes parents the primary players in their child's developmental progress.

Some of the most exciting advances in early childhood education practice are found in the new programs for infants and toddlers, which may precede, supplement, or substitute for preschool intervention. In Canada, a range of early intervention and parent education programs have been implemented. One 1985 survey (Kendall, Brynelson, & La Pierre, 1985) found as many as 50 infant development programs in Ontario alone. In the same year there were 27 programs in British Columbia, 20 in Quebec, 15 in Saskatchewan, and 12 in Alberta. New Brunswick had three programs, Nova Scotia and Manitoba four each, and Newfoundland and Prince Edward Island one each. Government funding in 1985 was available in all provinces except Nova Scotia. All provinces now offer some financial support to home-based programs, and many have developed or are developing guidelines for these programs (Brynelson & Cummings, 1987).

Service delivery
administrative arrangements for delivering assistance to exceptional children.

The program options for infants and toddlers vary widely. The variations are apparent in the types of services provided, the organizational structures through which these services are delivered, the sites of *service delivery*, the ages of the clients, and the amount of family participation. The agencies offering services differ in large part because traditionally a variety of disciplines have been involved in early intervention—albeit in quite different ways and often with quite different goals.

These programs exist under the aegis of both governmental and non-governmental agencies. They are administered by diverse organizations, and different types of programs are available in each community. Many of the current early-intervention programs are free-standing—that is, not combined with other programs. Philosophically, the different programs hold different ideas about family participation (i.e., how much is necessary, and what kind), although many are moving toward a family-centred orientation. Pedagogically, the programs use a range of models and techniques. Also, they can be in a variety of settings, though most are based in a clinic or in the home.

One characteristic of early intervention programs for infants with disabilities and their families is the involvement of professionals from diverse agencies and disciplines. These professionals bring multiple perspectives and are indispensable when it comes to providing the broad array of services needed by young children with special needs and their families. At one time or another, families may deal with professionals in education, psychology, medicine, physical and occupational therapy, speech and language therapy, counselling, public health, and social work.

Few exceptional children and their families will require all or even most of these professional services. However, the child with a disability will certainly encounter some of these services eventually. A child diagnosed in infancy as having a severe disability—Kasha, for example—will require careful educational, habilitative, and rehabilitative planning from birth through to adulthood. The child will encounter many of the medical personnel in hospital, while the parents meet with counsellors. Because of the complex situation, this child may require the services of many disciplines—education, psychology, physiotherapy, occupational therapy, speech pathology, audiology, medicine, and so on. After the child goes home, professionals may visit to provide infant stimulation, information for the parents, and the first steps for educational intervention. We saw this in the case of Rollo in Chapter 4.

A range of professionals and paraprofessionals with varied training are available to support the parents and to help the child through various stages of development. Intervenors go by different titles: home visiting teacher, rehabilitation counsellor, case manager, infant programmer, trainer, trained clinician, parent educator, parent therapist, resource teacher, and instructor. As well, programs designed to assist infants and preschool children with disabilities and their families are referred to in a variety of ways, including infant education, infant intervention, infant school, infant development, educational intervention, and, often, early intervention (Bricker, 1993).

The term *family centred* was first used in the health care field three decades ago as part of efforts to improve both obstetric and nursing practice (Trivette et al., 1996). Today, the same term is used broadly in reference to diverse types of social intervention. The term and the concept are increasingly used in early childhood programs. In a recent review of Canadian early education programs (Biemiller, Regan, & Lero, 1987), three trends relating to family-centred approaches were identified. First, early childhood education now considers family and parental needs as well as those of the child; second, parents are becoming genuine partners in early childhood programs and services; third, schools and the family are now being accepted as partners in the development of programs and

PROGRESS CHECK 1

Reread the case studies on Darrin, Rollo, and Kasha. Explain how professionals from the following fields may assist these children: education (including early childhood education), psychology, occupational and physical therapy, and audiology.

services for preschool children and their families.

In tandem with early childhood education, the clearest trends in infant and toddler intervention programs today are toward family-centred models and the involvement of parents. A review of the literature reveals three major principles of family-centred practice: establishing the family as the focus of services; supporting and respecting family decision-making; and providing intervention services designed to strengthen family functioning (McBride et al., 1993).

In Chapter 4 we discussed briefly how the inclusion of family variables in the intervention and treatment of young children with exceptionalities is a fairly recent innovation. Most professionals accept this innovation and much has been done to assist and include families. At the same time, there remains much to do and many questions are still unanswered. Paula Beckman and Donald Bailey point out:

> There is confusion about the ways to identify family strengths as well as needs, differences in the strengths and needs of different family members, changes in families and their needs over the life span, the best strategies for involving families from a wide range of cultural and socioeconomic circumstances, and the ways to provide support for families without becoming intrusive. (Beckman & Bailey, 1990, p. 195)

In this chapter we discuss intervention with infants and toddlers, with an emphasis on home-based programs. We examine some of the issues identified by Beckman and Bailey—identifying family needs, strategies for involving families, and providing support for the family and the child. We stress family-centred approaches and the ways in which parents may be involved in the development of a child with a disability.

Early intervention

Child a person undergoing the period of development from infancy to puberty.

Infant derives from the Latin for "not speaking."

Infancy the first two years of life or the period of life prior to the development of complex speech.

A ***child*** is a person undergoing the period of development from infancy to puberty. The word ***infant*** derives from the Latin for "not speaking"; thus, ***infancy*** is usually defined as the first two years of life or the period of life prior to the development of complex speech. Disabled infants and toddlers are defined as individuals from birth to two years who are in need of early intervention services because they are experiencing developmental delays (as measured by appropriate diagnostic instruments and procedures) in one or more of the following areas: cognitive development, physical development, language and speech development, psychosocial development, self-help skills. This category also includes children who have a physical or mental condition that is very likely to result in a developmental delay. Also included may be infants and toddlers who are at risk for substantial developmental delays if early intervention services are not provided (PL 99-457, section 672).

For infants and toddlers with disabilities, early intervention is crucial to later educational success. In this text, we use the terms early childhood special

BOX 5–1
Multiple disabilities

Children with multiple disabilities have two or more conditions that affect their learning and behaviour. The combinations of disabilities that are possible are almost endless; also, multiple disabilities are often the result of one major disability and additional handicapping conditions. Children with autism, or severe or profound mental retardation, or cerebral palsy, often have additional handicapping conditions; thus, we may meet a child who is blind and severely retarded, and another who is deaf and cerebral palsied. Within the broad category of multiple disabilities, Kasha is a deaf-blind child with dual impairments in vision and hearing.

When a child has multiple disabilities, one must remember that the conditions are not additive; rather, they combine to make a completely new type of disability, with each disability influencing the others in every area of a child's functioning. This means that Kasha will be taught using special procedures designed for a deaf-blind child, not instructional procedures designed for children who are blind *or* deaf.

Multiple handicaps result in large gaps in a child's functioning. Many children with multiple handicaps are very late in reaching developmental milestones. Walking, using first words, and toilet training may be severely delayed. As well, most children with multiple disabilities are deprived of orienting movements of the head and body, as well as a purposive gaze. This leaves them with no available modality through which to communicate; as a result, they tend to remain at early stages of communication development for a long time. These children also lag in social skills such as smiling and interacting with those in the environment.

Early intervention
The establishment of educational and support services for young children with or at risk for disabilities, and their families.

education (ECSE) and early intervention as synonyms. Specifically, *early intervention* refers to a variety of educational, psychological, or therapeutic interventions provided for handicapped, at-risk, or disadvantaged infants and preschoolers to prevent or ameliorate developmental delays of disabilities, or to provide support to children and families where disabilities exist (Michael & Paul, 1991, p. 202).

A number of salient points arise from this definition of early intervention:

- Early intervention can "help ensure that all young children reach their full developmental potential; that they can become valued and full participants in their families, schools and communities; and that their families benefit from consistent and supportive collaboration with service providers" (CEC Position, 1993).

- Early intervention encompasses a number of activities directed at a diverse population of young children with established disabilities and at those who are at risk because of medical or social disadvantage.

- Infants, toddlers, preschoolers, and very young schoolchildren all fit within the context of early intervention.

- Programs may be home based, clinic based, or centre based, and may be segregated or integrated. The rationale for early intervention with infants is the same

The learning and educational attainments of multiply disabled children depend on a matrix of factors. Not the least of these are the quality of education, the age at which education begins, the age of onset of the conditions, the nature of the combination of handicaps, and the severity of each condition. Also important are the family's response to the child, the educational setting, the amount of integration with nondisabled peers, the related services available for both the child and the family, and the amount of acceptance by the community (Winzer, 1996).

Many of the behaviour problems observed among children with multiple disabilities result from a lack of programs during developmental periods (Grunewald, 1974). The process of aiding the development of these children should begin at the moment of birth. Intervention during infancy and early childhood does much to prevent secondary problems, such as behavioural problems and developmental handicaps produced by experiential deprivation and understimulation.

At first, the focus is on obtaining responses to environmental stimulation. These responses include head and trunk balance, sucking, swallowing, chewing, grasping, movement of body parts, and vocalization. Later training focuses on imitation, language acquisition, self-feeding, ambulation, dressing skills, toilet training, social and recreational behaviour, and functional academic skills (Stainback & Stainback, 1977). For deaf-blind children, the stress is on visual stimulation and on visual perception skills as a basis for performing cognitive and academic tasks. The development of communication skills is a simultaneous activity. Psychosocial needs relate to adaptive behaviour, life skills, and a range of socialization activities.

as that for preschoolers; however, home-based and clinic-based programs differ from preschool programs on a number of dimensions, as shown in Table 5–1.

- The procedures used with young children with disabilities range from medical intervention to psychological assessment, therapy, and activities in schools and classrooms.

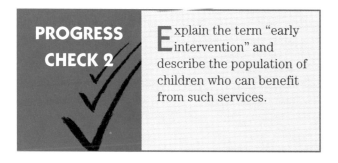

PROGRESS CHECK 2 Explain the term "early intervention" and describe the population of children who can benefit from such services.

- For children with established disabilities, activities are directed toward lessening problems. For children who are at risk, intervention serves to prevent or hinder the development of conditions that impair learning or behaviour.

- Activities are designed to support families to the greatest extent possible. Optimally, these family-centred activities include the siblings and the extended family as well as the parents.

For a number of reasons, concerns for young children and their families have achieved prominence in the past three to five years. Studies and anecdotal reports underscore the value of early intervention. Parents and teachers report its positive effects, and researchers are studying it carefully. Even physicians,

TABLE 5–1: Infant and preschool programs

Infant programs	Preschool programs
Individual services to children	Individual and group services to children
Organized by diverse agencies and differ in ages of clients, personnel, program orientation, and model	Organized by diverse groups, including parent co-operatives. Use different orientations and models
Rely heavily on inter-agency collaboration	Consultation and collaboration becoming increasingly important
Staffed by a variety of professionals and paraprofessionals	Professionals, paraprofessionals, and consultants
Recognize the importance of the family in early intervention	Recognize the importance of the family in early intervention
Develop written plans for each child with family input	Develop written plans for each child that include goals and objectives
Home based or clinic based	Centre based
Individual activities	Individual and small- and large-group activities
Strive for direct and intensive parent involvement and may use direct teaching by parents	May be parent volunteers
Child seen once or twice a week	Daily, semi-daily, half-week, or full-day programs

who are typically cautious in their judgments of early intervention, perceive that high-quality early intervention programs are of value to children and their families.

The expanded attention directed toward infants and toddlers with disabilities and their families is a result of these factors:

- Research has advanced in the field of infant behaviour. Recent information about infant development has resulted in improved understanding of the learning capacities of infants, the role of perinatal risks in compromising growth and development, and the enormous impact of life experiences on the psychological development of infants. One Ontario report on the outcomes of an infant stimulation program noted: "Infancy is the most malleable, rapidly changing, and least organized period of human development. Never again will there be the same potential for establishing the basic forms of understanding, style, and feeling in all domains of experience. Early experience is the primary matrix from which all later development is generated" (Fowler, 1975, p. 341).

- A child's development cannot take place independent of the caretaking experience. Early experiences influence every aspect of a child's functioning.

- Early intervention can reduce the effects of disabilities. It may halt or prevent declines in development and may do so more rapidly than later intervention. Down syndrome children, for example, have been shown to benefit from early and consistent stimulation; some children with Down syndrome approximate normal developmental patterns when intervention begins in infancy (Beers & Beers, 1980; Sharav & Schlomo, 1986). This seems to happen because early and sustained intervention halts the decline in cognitive development that typically occurs among these children during the first 12 to 18 months of life (see Guralnick & Bricker, 1987). It also appears to prevent further decreases throughout the remaining early childhood years.

  Similar outcomes have been observed regarding the motor development of children with cerebral palsy (Palmer et al., 1988). As well, some researchers and practitioners (e.g., Lovaas, 1982; Strain et al., 1982) contend that very early and sustained intervention can make some autistic children normal—that is, indistinguishable from their peers—by the time they reach elementary school.

  Decreases in declines have also been reported among children at biological risk, such as those born prematurely or at low birth weight. In 1990 the *Journal of the American Medical Association* reported on the results of the largest study ever done of an intervention for low birth weight infants. The researchers studied nearly 1,000 premature infants from birth to three years of age in eight American cities, and demonstrated that outcomes for premature low–birth weight infants known to be at risk for developmental, behavioural, and health problems can be significantly improved if there is comprehensive early intervention. Low birth weight infants in a control group who did not receive early education and developmental services were nearly three times more likely to have IQ scores in the range of mentally retarded.

- Early intervention can prevent secondary disabilities. Intervention during infancy and early childhood can do much to prevent secondary problems such as behavioural problems and developmental handicaps produced by experiential deprivation and understimulation.

- Early intervention provides a foundation for the early acquisition of cognitive skills, communication and language skills, motor skills, play behaviour, and functional and self-help skills. There may be critical periods for the development of certain skills, and most of these periods probably occur early in life. While some researchers have severely criticized the critical periods notion as a rationale for intervening early in life, most now agree that while all age periods are important, the early period of life is the most critical in terms of later development (see Wachs & Gruen, 1982).

- Early intervention may relieve at least some parental stress and improve overall family functioning. In retrospective reports, families who have had the opportunity to enrol their disabled babies in early intervention programs have expressed great appreciation for the positive changes in their children and for the sense that life has been made easier (Widerstrom & Goodwon, 1987).

- Early intervention provides critical information to parents. Sontag and Schacht (1993) interviewed 536 families about their needs in early intervention; the only item selected by the majority of parents was the need for information about the services available.

In a different type of study, teenage mothers (age 16 or younger) were given weekly classes on infant stimulation, nutrition, and family planning. They were also given supportive services. Significant improvements were found in both the mothers and the infants. The children showed higher scores on an IQ test than a control group, and the mothers were more responsive to their children (See Kaplan, 1995).

- In the United States, PL 99-457 and its amendments outline the rights afforded parents of preschoolers with disabilities (see Chapter 4). PL 94-142, reauthorized in 1986, included provisions for preschoolers with disabilities and their families. With the passage of PL 99-457, a new precedent in public policy for families with a handicapped child was created in law. U.S. legislation now mandates that families be fully included in any decisions relating to the preschool child or infant with a disability.

LEARNING ACTIVITY 1

Chart the major points in the two critical pieces of American legislation, PL 94-142 and PL 99-457. Explain how these have influenced Canadian programs.

PROGRAM SETTINGS

Services for infants and toddlers with disabilities can be placed in these categories: home-based therapy or education; clinic-based therapy or education; consultative services; and inclusion in regular early-childhood community programs. The younger the child and the more severe the disability, the more limited the availability of intervention services. Infants and toddlers with severe disabilities are more likely to receive home services.

Clinic-based programs

Clinic-based programs are typically specialized, serving only children with disabilities and their families. Although far less popular than in the past, clinic-based programs designed to serve discrete disabilities exist right across the country.

In these programs, families bring their infant or toddler to a setting where appropriate services are provided by professionals and paraprofessionals. Regular intervention sessions are scheduled either on an individual basis (for infants) or in small groups (for toddlers).

Most programs tend to follow developmental and therapeutic models in their curricula. A professional in a discipline in the child's area of most significant need is the primary interventionalist. As we saw in the case of Kasha, a specialist in visual disabilities worked with the child and mother.

Home-based programs

While clinic programs remain important, modern educators are more often supporting the idea that early intervention should take place in the home and/or use the home as a basis for curricular objectives. They argue that since the home is the natural environment for infants and toddlers, home-based programs are more normalized. As well, methods used in restrictive clinical settings are neither as effective nor as practical as those used in the home, since it is always difficult to transfer and generalize skills learned in a clinic setting to other situations. As an example, most training programs for young autistic children are based on the development of a therapeutic one-to-one relationship, and clearly parents are the most appropriate people to fill the position of primary therapist. Parental involvement in therapy ensures individual treatment for each child, and that therapy can take place throughout as much of the day as possible. Finally, when home-based therapy is used, the results don't have to be generalized from the clinic to the home; and when parents teach the skills, those newly learned skills are more likely to be generalized to other situations and settings.

Home-based programs are often referred to as ***home visiting***, which involves a professional or paraprofessional providing help over an extended time to a family in its own home (Wasik, Bryant, & Lyons, 1990). Home visiting programs have a long history in the health, educational, and social service traditions of Western Europe and North America. One of the first North American programs for school-aged children was initiated by Adela Smith in New York in the 1920s. For children deemed to be educationally disenfranchised, and for children with special needs, home-based programs began to play a major role in early intervention programs in the 1960s and 1970s (Powell, 1990). Some current programs begin early in pregnancy or infancy and have a health focus; others stress education.

In general, home-based early intervention involves consistent contact in the client's home between the child, the family, and a representative of a formal agency. The appeal of home visiting is that practitioners can work with individuals within the family context. In this way they can learn firsthand about the life conditions of the child and the parents (Powell, 1990). Also, instructional recommendations are more practical and realistic because the teacher can observe the family's lifestyle and available resources.

In home-based models, the person who visits the family regularly is the primary interventionalist. In some programs, specialists are matched to the child's particular area of disability; in other programs, children are assigned randomly or by geographic area; in still others, only paraprofessionals are assigned as primary interventionalists. Most programs use some combination of professional and paraprofessional home visitors.

Home-based programs are often found in rural areas, where transporting the children to a centre would take a lot of time and where the population of preschoolers with disabilities is small and scattered. Typically, services are directed toward infants and toddlers. Home visiting also serves individuals and families who are too distrustful or too disorganized to make their way to a centre-based program (Powell, 1990).

One of the best known of the home-based models is the Portage Project in Wisconsin, which began in 1969. The Portage program is a cross-categorical model for rural areas designed to serve children with special needs from birth to six years of age (see Shearer & Shearer, 1972). It places primary responsibility for intervention on the parents. A home teacher provides the parents with in-depth instruction on how to carry out home teaching (Cameron, 1989).

Many researchers have studied the outcomes of early intervention programs for infants and toddlers with special needs. So far, however, the value and rationale of home-based programs has not been intensely researched. Some studies do suggest that home visiting programs can improve outcomes for children and

Home visiting
a process whereby a professional or paraprofessional provides help over an extended period of time to a family in its home.

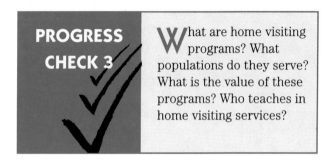

PROGRESS CHECK 3 ✓✓✓

What are home visiting programs? What populations do they serve? What is the value of these programs? Who teaches in home visiting services?

families. Studies of educational home visits have generally reported weak but positive effects when young children's cognitive gains are measured (Casto & Mastropieri, 1986). But as such programs are so diverse, it is difficult to evaluate the effectiveness of this one component of early intervention.

INTERVENORS   Many research studies confirm that specialized training in infant-related issues helps to ensure high-quality child development and child care services (Whitebrook et al., 1989). In infant programs, however, personnel standards and personnel preparation needs are not yet clear, and continue to be widely debated.

Many people in the field have not received any training in working with families on infant intervention. When they come from the field of early childhood, this is because most people who enter the field of early childhood education do so out of a desire to work with children; thus, training is focused almost exclusively on the child rather than the family. In Canada, many home teachers have a two-year community-college diploma and specialize in working with developmentally disabled individuals. In such programs there may be no family focus either. However, a number of Canadian college programs now offer a one-year post-diploma program that trains early childhood personnel specifically to work with children with special needs and their families.

As infant programs tend to focus sharply on the family, infant specialists require competencies and skills quite different from those typically taught in programs that train personnel to work with young children. These skills were discussed in Chapter 3. To reiterate and expand, we can say that those working with very young children and their families must have the following skills and qualities:

- They understand the uniqueness of infancy as a developmental phase.
- They hold a positive and proactive stance toward families. Intervenors should provide a safe context for parents to share concerns and feelings, to provide information, and to handle logistics. Effective intervenors understand family dynamics and systems and develop a relationship of rapport and trust with families. They increase a family's confidence in its own abilities, and contribute to the family's case management skills, providing encouragement, support, and feedback.
- They possess personal traits that encourage interaction with families. Intervenors should be warm, easy to approach, flexible, and nonjudgmental. They must communicate empathy, respect, and a willingness to listen. They must maintain confidentiality and establish and maintain appropriate interpersonal boundaries with families (Beckman et al., 1993).
- They are flexible. The role of the intervenor may change in different settings and at different times. The parents of a child newly diagnosed, for example, are often hungry for concrete information about the child's condition, the causes, and the prognosis. Parents who have had more time to come to grips with the diagnosis often worry more about long-term considerations—the correct ways of

teaching and caring for the child, preschool programs, later schooling, and even such future events as marriage and occupations.

- They are able to ascertain family priorities for service, and to assess family needs in a way that is acceptable to family members and that reflects important aspects of family functioning.
- They are able to discuss needs with family members, to provide direction in the specifying of family goals, to negotiate conflicts or competing priorities to develop acceptable goals, and to accept and support decisions made by families.
- They are able to foster family participation and to teach families the competencies they need to maximize their child's development.
- They are aware of the significant role families play in early childhood development and in early education and intervention. Early intervenors should possess specific skills for working with infants and toddlers. An early interventionalist works with the parents to identify child needs, strengths, and target objectives. Generally, he or she will work with the child, demonstrating techniques to the parent. After a demonstration, the parent is encouraged to try the same intervention.
- They are able to provide materials to assist parent interventions. Resources for parent training may include toy libraries; typically, these are associated with special needs programs, parent/child centres, and community organizations. The point of providing toys and games is to foster play and parent/child interaction (Mayfield, 1988, 1990).
- They are able to impart information about the child's condition, and about other agencies, schools, and so on. Parents need information about community programs, financial assistance, and their child's condition and physical health; and also about emotional adjustments, both the child's and their own (Gowen, Christy, & Sparling, 1993). Intervenors present information so that the parents can understand the child's disability and its effects on development and on families. They also provide useful and credible information about the educational process, preschool programs, other agencies, and self-help groups.
- They possess the knowledge and resources to make suggestions for linking families with needed support. Intervenors develop contacts with other agencies and assist the parents in accessing these agencies.
- They are able to provide assistance with transitions. As family involvement is imperative in the design and progress of transition programs, intervenors also provide information on transitions. We discuss transition planning and procedures later in this chapter and in Chapter 16.
- They understand the importance of culturally competent professional actions. Cultural beliefs are possibly the most static component of the family and can play an important role in shaping its ideological style, interactional patterns, and functional priorities (Turnbull, Summers, & Brotherston, 1986). Sensitivity to cultural and linguistic differences is the key to effective interactions with families and to successful co-ordination of services.

PROGRAM MODELS

The past decade has witnessed dramatic changes in early intervention, largely because of new ways of looking at families. However, no consensus exists about the best way to view families or the best program model or orientation. In fact, there will probably never be such a thing as a perfect or model parent program. Each family is simply too different from all others.

One common trend in early intervention models is toward family-centred approaches. A second, seen in programs for infants and toddlers, is toward the involvement of parents. The most successful programs involve parent participation and start before the child is two years old. Parents may be involved in a number of ways: in educational decision-making, advocacy, teaching, care managing, and program evaluation (Allen & Hudd, 1987).

Program approaches   The type of model selected for early intervention depends on which perspective on families is taken by the agency offering the services. If you remember our discussion in Chapter 4, there are a number of theories about how families develop and interact with the member with a disability. Researchers examine family functioning in terms of a stage theory approach, a life cycle approach, a systems approach, or a social support approach. Each of these ways of viewing families translates into a practical model for intervening and working with families. There is much overlap between the models, and many factors are considered before a particular type of program is matched to a family. These factors are shown in Figure 5–1.

As you can see, there are agency and program variables, of which the most important are the philosophy held by the service delivery agency and the training of the personnel. The next considerations are family and child variables. No two families are the same, and no two children have exactly the same needs, so programs must be flexible. There are, then, different program models; and embedded in these are different ways of delivering services, especially in relation to

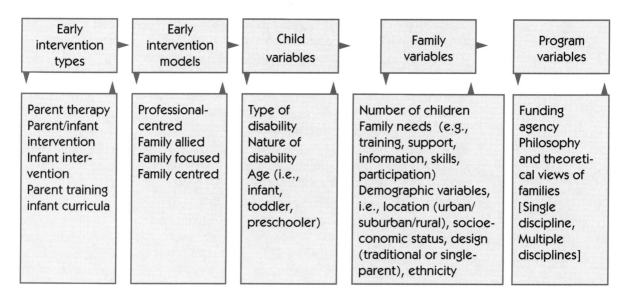

FIGURE 5–1

Variables in early intervention

the amount and type of parent involvement. In planning for parental involvement in early childhood programs, practitioners must consider the many variables that affect the lives of families with young children with disabilities. Parents should play a major role in determining the extent and degree of their participation; allowance must be made for differences in interest, skills, comfort, and the time available for case management.

The different models for early intervention include the following:

- In professional-centred models, professionals are the experts and determine the family's needs from their own as opposed to the family's perspective. Professionals determine the goals for the family based solely on their own assessment of the family's needs, even when (as often happens) the priorities of the family differ from those of the professionals. This is the traditional model, and falling out of use.

- In family-allied models, families are seen as agents of professionals. Families are enlisted to implement interventions that professionals see as necessary.

- In family-focused models, families and professionals collaboratively define what families need in order to function in a healthier manner.

- In family-centred models, professionals act as agents and instruments of the family, and intervene in ways that promote competency within the family (Dunst et al., 1991). Family-centred services are consumer-driven rather than professional-driven, and enhance the competency of the consumers, who are generally the parents.

    Family-centred models are the most popular in the present day. They are aligned with systems theory or a social support approach and are founded on a set of discrete principles. The most important of these is that the developmental needs of a young child with a disability can best be met by enhancing the family's effectiveness in caring for and managing that child (Mahoney, O'Sullivan, & Dennebaum, 1990). These models reflect the belief that parents must eventually learn to handle life events on their own, since professional assistance is not always going to be available or sufficient; in other words, parents must learn to do without the help of professionals and their systems (Dunst et al., 1991).

    In a family-centred model, families and professionals are partners in planning and implementing service delivery. Family members decide what is important to them and what outcomes they want for the child and for themselves, and what actions they will take to achieve the desired outcomes. The goal of training is to enable family members to achieve desired outcomes and to deal effectively with future concerns. The training activities build upon the skills and resources of the family members; the role of the professional is to create opportunities for family members to acquire any additional skills they will need to achieve desired outcomes (see Cordesco & Laus, 1993; Dunst et al., 1991).

    There are four broad classes of family-oriented early intervention programs. The

PROGRESS CHECK 4

Explain the systems approach and the social support approach as they are used to look at families with a disabled member. Then explain how agencies serving families translate these approaches into actual practice. In an ideal world, what are the end results of using these models?

class of intervention selected influences the roles of parents and therapists as well as the overall approach taken to address the objectives of early intervention. These classes are as follows:

- *Parent therapy* tends to be more parent than child oriented. It is the traditional approach and assumes that families need help, often through counselling. Thus, parent therapy seeks to promote competent parenting through counselling, and through guidance techniques that help parents to resolve their negative or ambivalent feelings and to cope with the initial stress that follows the birth of a child who is disabled. Parent therapy is often provided in conjunction with professional community and parent groups.

- *Parent/infant interaction models* focus on parent/child interactions and their enhancement by training parents to be sensitive and responsive to the child's weaknesses while developing responses.

- *Infant intervention models* stress the child's needs for training and stimulation. The infant is the direct beneficiary of intervention; intervention is between the infant and the professional intervenor. Sometimes toys or computers thought to stimulate development are provided.

- *Parent training infant curricula* are based on the assumption that parent training is as important for the success of early intervention programs as infant training. These programs set out to teach parents strategies for imparting specific skills and competencies in the belief that with instruction, modelling, and reinforcement, parents can become more effective teachers of their own children. Professionals assess the child to determine what skills he or she needs, help the parent plan the learning activity, and monitor progress of both parent and child. The goal is the optimal development of the child in these domains: motor, cognitive, language and communication, social, and self-help skills.

The parent training infant curriculum seems to be the most widely implemented model. In Canada, Marfo and Kysela (1985) found that 90 percent of early intervention programs involved training parents in program planning and/or teaching activities, either at home or in a centre.

Caregivers need assistance in understanding the nature and prognosis of the condition; in handling the child; in stimulating mobility, locomotion, and communication; and in responding appropriately to different or unexpected behaviours. Parent training sets out to teach parents how to develop flexibility and observational skills, how to challenge the child, and how to nurture present skills and teach new skills. Some specific areas of parent training include physical management; management of self-care and daily living activities; behaviour management; and communication.

PARENT INVOLVEMENT

One principle of infant service delivery that has long been generally accepted is the primacy of the family. There is no question that the nature of the home environment and involvement of parents are critically important factors in the social and educational development of a child. As one worker has said:

Infants learn from
parent/child interactions.

Effective parent involvement programs acknowledge the fact that parents are a child's earliest and most influential teachers. Trying to educate the young child without help and support from the home is akin to trying to rake leaves in a high wind (Gough, 1991, p. 339).

Parent involvement in early childhood education for normally developing children has a long and strong history that includes parents as program initiators, parents as volunteers, and parents as decision-makers about program models and curricula. Parallel to this, parent and family involvement in early intervention for young children with disabilities has evolved slowly since mid-century.

In the 1940s parent advocacy groups began to take root; many services at the early childhood level for children with special needs became available because of parent activism. However, in the actual delivery of services, parents tended to be ignored; they were not invited to participate to any degree. Until the early 1970s, parents were passive recipients of professional advice. Professionals held a monolithic view of families that assumed common structures, functions, and organization. Families were often treated as if they all had basically the same resources and needs. Service delivery tended to be professional-centred: professionals made the key decisions about a child's needs and educational placement, and then worked with the family and other agencies to attain set goals. Traditional notions of professional expertise, which denied that parents were competent to take the initiative, began to fade in the 1970s. Around this time, the early intervention movement began to co-opt parents as home teachers.

Parent/child interaction is the most important socializing agency for infants.

Today's thrust is far more family oriented than it was 20, 50, or 100 years ago. Perceptions about the role of parents in the educational process have shifted dramatically at all levels. Early intervention programs now stress the unique coping abilities of families; the newer approaches to education and treatment consider the family and social contexts as well as the child's.

Parents and families are seen as having needs and resources that directly affect the functioning of their children. Today's family-centred approach involves families in treatment and education. Parents of children with exceptionalities are major participants, as teachers and as educational decision-makers (Turnbull & Turnbull, 1990; Winzer, 1996). Also, approaches to family intervention now focus on informal rather than formal sources of support; the stress is on families helping themselves. This enhances the self-esteem of the family by setting up a situation in which the help seeker is less dependent than in earlier, more traditional times on the help giver.

The involvement of parents in intervention programs for infants and toddlers is promoted for a number of reasons:

- The effort to build professional/parent partnerships is consistent with the current thinking of child development theorists, who stress the importance of the social context within which child development occurs.
- Child development professionals have long recognized that the quality of care that young children receive from adult caretakers is the most important factor in their lives. Especially for children under three, interactions with parents and other caregivers are central to development. "To ignore the parent's position as the child's first and most natural nurturer," observes Shearer (1993), "is to lessen the chances for a successful intervention program" (p. 98).

- Efforts should be focused on the home because, for a very young child, the largest portion of time is often spent in that setting.

- During the first years of a child's life, the parents assume the primary responsibility for care and management. Parents are the primary instructors in most daily living activities. They are particularly good with naturalistic training strategies because they have substantial experience with adult/child interactions on which to draw.

- When parents are the principal therapists, children are trained by the people who care most about their welfare and progress.

- Early intervention is intensive in nature. In some studies, longer and more intensive programs have been associated with better outcomes (see Chapter 3). A child who is not developing normally needs more than 20 or 30 minutes one or two times a week. Parents can provide constant and sustained intervention.

- Children seem to develop more quickly when parents are involved. For example, parent training can benefit autistic children significantly. Howlin (1981) trained parents of autistic children in behavioural techniques to stimulate language at home and to deal with obsessions, rituals, phobias, temper tantrums, and hyperactivity. The parents also learned to teach constructive play and social skills. After six months, their children spoke more than before and used appropriate language.

- Involvement helps parents understand the condition and its implications. Parental attitudes have a great impact on a child's social and emotional development; early intervention can encourage healthy parent/child relationships and maximize the overall development of the child within the family circle. Programs may help parents deal with the grief and disruption associated with having a disabled child in the family, and can include the provision of information and training about care of the child. Programs may also foster advocacy skills so that parents can join with professionals in working toward ensuring the best programs possible.

- By taking part in their child's education, parents may more easily accept the disability. Parents' reactions to a disability may vary according to whether they think the condition can be improved and whether they feel they can participate successfully in the treatment program (Lavelle & Keogh, 1980). Involvement provides parents with an enhanced sense of control by allowing them to "do something." When parents are engaged throughout the process, and drawn more closely into the therapy of their own child, them feel less impotent. By the same token, parents who cannot accept their child's disability find it more difficult to consolidate efforts with schools and other support agencies, and this may interfere substantially with a child's growth.

LEARNING ACTIVITY 2

Imagine that you are the parent of an infant with a severe disability. Explain to the class the value to you and your family of early intervention services. Stress what you hope to gain from these services as a parent, for the family, and for the child.

- Involvement can prevent disruption of normal, mutually reinforcing parent/child interactions by encouraging the parents to be sensitive and responsive in ways that enhance reciprocal interactions (Marfo & Kysela, 1985). It is often difficult for significantly disabled infants and toddlers and their parents to establish mutually satisfying and rewarding interactional patterns. Parents need to feel competent in handling their child, to feel effective in meeting their child's needs, to feel love and affection, and to observe positive changes in return for their caregiving.

- Interaction with parents provides the child with models of behaviour, thereby smoothing the child's integration into the community.

The intervention process

Intervention for very young children with disabilities has many facets, including the setting for intervention, the intervenors themselves, the amount and type of parent participation, the goals set, the way goals are developed and ranked, and the manner in which the goals are attained.

ASSESSING FAMILY NEEDS Once a family has shown an interest in participating in an early intervention program, the first step for professionals is to assess needs. Here, *assessment* refers to ongoing procedures to identify the child's unique needs, the family's strengths and weaknesses relative to the child's development, and the nature and extent of the early intervention services that will be provided (Fewell, 1991).

Three closely related processes may be undertaken. Two involve the identification of family needs and priorities. Helping a family determine their needs and the extent to which they wish or are able to be involved in case management is a critical task of family-centred early intervention services. The third process focuses on the skills and deficits of the child with the disability. It considers the characteristics of the child that directly influence family functioning—such as temperament, behaviour, caretaking demands, and feeding—and how these affect the family routine.

There are three basic strategies for gathering data about children and their families: naturalistic observation, interviews, and testing. These may be used singly or in tandem. *Naturalistic observation* is useful in determining rates and patterns of behaviour, including parent/child interactions. *Interviews* help determine the parents' perceptions; *tests* determine a child's level of functioning.

Infant assessment The identification of atypical or high-risk infants and their needs is critical to the provision of appropriate early intervention. Observation is a primary assessment strategy. Intervenors may wish to observe an infant's interactions with caretakers. Other observations may indicate specific difficulties; for example, a highly trained observer may be able to distinguish signs of sensory or neurological problems. Observation can also provide an assessment of the child's strengths and needs relating to a particular activity—for example, feeding, or behaviour while shopping.

As a supplement to observation, intervenors may use checklists, which are completed with parental input. An example of a checklist is shown in Table 5–2. Readers will find further details about infant assessment in Chapter 8.

TABLE 5-2: Example of a parent checklist

		Yes	No	Additional
Training comments	• the child is toilet trained	☐	☐	
	• there are problems with constipation or diarrhea	☐	☐	
	• toilet training has been attempted	☐	☐	
	• the child gives signs of needing toileting	☐	☐	
	• training is a priority with the parent	☐	☐	
Feeding	• the child can cope with pureed/ chopped/mashed foods	☐	☐	
	• a special diet is required			
	• the child has strong likes and dislikes	☐	☐	
	• the child has a big appetite	☐	☐	
	• the child has a small appetite	☐	☐	
	• the parent is concerned with the child's feeding patterns	☐	☐	
	• the child's weight is a cause for concern	☐	☐	
	• the family eats together	☐	☐	
	• the child is fed separately	☐	☐	
	• there is a problem with behaviour at meal times	☐	☐	
	• particular meal times are more difficult	☐	☐	
	• anyone can feed the child	☐	☐	
	• spoon feeding is encouraged	☐	☐	
	• special equipment is needed, such as a special spoon	☐	☐	
	• the child attempts to finger feed	☐	☐	
	• there are difficulties with tongue thrust/ gagging/poor lip closure	☐	☐	
	• a trainer cup is used	☐	☐	
	• the child attempts to hold a bottle or cup	☐	☐	
	• the child drinks a lot	☐	☐	
	• warm drinks are preferred	☐	☐	
	• cold drinks are preferred	☐	☐	
Dressing	• dressing is an enjoyable activity for the child	☐	☐	
	• there is resistance	☐	☐	
	• there is passive co-operation	☐	☐	
	• there is active co-operation	☐	☐	
	• the child needs a special position for dressing	☐	☐	
Self-help	• teeth cleaning has been introduced	☐	☐	
	• it is a daily routine	☐	☐	
	• the child co-operates	☐	☐	

		Yes	No	Additional
Movement	• the child moves independently	☐	☐	_____
	• frustration is evident	☐	☐	_____
	• the child attempts to roll, pivot, crawl	☐	☐	_____
	• the child uses walkers or other devices to assist walking	☐	☐	_____
	• the child moves to reach parent or toy	☐	☐	_____
	• the child uses one or both hands together	☐	☐	_____
	• the child performs fine motor tasks	☐	☐	_____
	• there are positions that the child refuses to tolerate	☐	☐	_____
	• specialized seats or other equipment have been tried	☐	☐	_____
Language	• the child seems to understand general conversation, commands, names, routines, particular phrases	☐	☐	_____
	• the child responds to gestures, facial expressions	☐	☐	_____
	• the child vocalizes as a social response	☐	☐	_____
	• cooing is used	☐	☐	_____
	• babble or jargon is used	☐	☐	_____
	• other family members understand the child's needs	☐	☐	_____
	• the child provides consistent responses	☐	☐	_____
	• vision and hearing have been formally assessed	☐	☐	_____
	• glasses or hearing aids have been prescribed	☐	☐	_____
Play	• the child has favourite toys	☐	☐	_____
	• the child is happy to play alone	☐	☐	_____
	• the child enjoys television	☐	☐	_____
	• adult attention is always needed	☐	☐	_____
	• the child participates in simple games	☐	☐	_____
	• singing activities are enjoyed	☐	☐	_____
	• there are many opportunities for mixing with other children	☐	☐	_____
	• the child seems willing to join in	☐	☐	_____
	• the child attempts to imitate other people	☐	☐	_____
Routines	• the parent follows a basic timetable for naps, meals, etc.	☐	☐	_____
	• the child handles breaks in routine well	☐	☐	_____
	• the child naps regularly	☐	☐	_____
	• the child settles easily	☐	☐	_____

		Yes	No	Additional
	• there is a preferred sleeping position	☐	☐	
	• the child is generally easy to handle, placid	☐	☐	
	• the child is generally demanding, clingy	☐	☐	
Professionals	• the child has had contact with therapists and other professionals	☐	☐	
	• the child has regular visits to medical personnel	☐	☐	
	• there are special medical problems	☐	☐	
	• the child has allergies	☐	☐	
	• the child regularly requires medication	☐	☐	

Source: Adapted from anon.

Family needs

Family needs refer to the services the family wishes to obtain and the outcomes it wishes to achieve (Bailey & Blanco, 1990. Family needs are determined by a needs assessment process that helps to identify and examine both values and information. A **needs assessment** assesses current conditions and needs and provides information on the parents' goals for their child and on the potential for parent involvement in the program.

A parent interview is one tool for determining family needs. In interviews, intervenors can explore child-rearing methods, discipline, and opportunities for learning in the home, as well as parental attitudes and perceptions about the child's behaviour and skills. A parent interview can ask parents or caregivers and other family members to describe family routines, the child's participation in these routines, and what they would like the child to learn to better participate in family routines (Falvey, 1989; Kilgo, Richard, & Noonan, 1989). Such face-to-face discussions with the family focus on the skills that members would like the child to learn or to use more often. They also focus on the behaviours that the family would like to see *less* often, such as temper tantrums.

When families find it difficult to prioritize goals, professionals can ask questions such as, "If your child could pick one skill to learn, what would it be?" Professionals and family members can then explore questions such as these: Are there specific home and/or community activities that are concerns for family members? What skills would family members like the child to learn or to use more often? What behaviours would family members like the child to perform less often? Which of these concerns are priorities for family members? (Cordesco & Laus, 1993).

Testing can assess such variables as the parents' stress and their knowledge of infant development. However, few instruments are available

Family needs a family's expressed desire for services to be obtained or outcomes to be achieved.

Needs assessment assesses current conditions and needs and provides information on what the parents' goals are for their child and for potential parent involvement in the program.

LEARNING ACTIVITY 3

Role-play a situation between Kasha's parents and an early childhood intervenor using the case study that opens this chapter as a base. In the role play, use questions such as those above to help the parents prioritize their developmental needs for Kasha.

to use with families of disabled children. Murphy and colleagues (1995, pp. 28–29) have drawn a list of scales and tools used with families. One scale is the Parent Satisfaction Scale (Kovach & Kjerkland, 1989). It has 37 items for parents on growth in four categories: knowledge and skills for helping the child, growth in understanding normal behaviour and problems, utilization of community resources, and building a support system. Brass Tacks (McWilliam & Winton, 1990) has 147 items for parents and staff on various goals for intervention.

Over the past five years, much has been written about the inadequacy of existing models for family assessment (see Bernheimer, Galtimore, & Kaufman, 1993), and many challenges have been made to the idea of family assessment. Some current writers are concerned that educators might become overly involved in the assessment of family members. If this happens, "parents may legitimately question why providing such information is necessary when they thought the purpose of the early intervention program was to help their child. Many families perceive this process as an invasion of privacy" (Slentz & Bricker, 1992, p. 14).

Intervenors will be better equipped if they concentrate on collecting information that relates only to enhancing the child's development. It may be more appropriate for professionals to use only brief informal interviews to determine the needs of the family and child rather than administering a complex battery of tests.

Parent participation

Earlier in this chapter we spoke of the necessity of parent involvement in the intervention process, especially in the very early years. The degree to which parents wish to be involved is an important consideration for intervenors.

Parent involvement does not mean that parents should do the job of professionals. Nor is parent involvement a specific set of activities, such as teaching activities and attendance at parents' meetings. Rather, it is a point of view that consistently takes into account the needs and skills of the entire family.

> **Parent involvement** the process of actualizing the potential of parents; of helping parents discover their strengths, potentialities, and talents; and of using these for the benefit of themselves and the family.

In its broadest sense, parent involvement implies shared responsibility for a child's progress. **Parent involvement** may be defined as "a process of actualizing the potential of parents; of helping parents discover their strengths, potentialities, talents; and using these for the benefit of themselves and the family" (Morrison, 1978, p. 22).

Many parents *want* to be involved in teaching and therapy with their children; they *want* to help their children with skill development and *want* to know what specific steps they can take to ensure their child's progress. With proper training and support, parents can learn how to manage their child and how to stimulate social, motor, and communicative development. Parents can be highly effective therapists, developing and maintaining many skills in the child.

The family's active involvement is a sign that the early intervention program is contributing to the development of the child with special needs. But even though parent participation is highly valued, many difficulties can arise. For example, Bricker (1986a) found that only 20 to 40 percent of parents were involved in their child's early intervention program. The factors that influence parent involvement are diverse and often difficult to document. Some parents simply choose not to play an active role. Sometimes collaboration by parents is hindered by limited knowledge bases, skill deficits, lack of self-confidence, impaired objectivity, economic considerations, and the needs of other family members.

Even when the parents are eager to be involved, the process may be too expensive or too inconvenient (Turnbull & Turnbull, 1986). Parents enter programs with the expectation that they will get help for their child. When they find that in return they are expected to participate and/or make time-consuming commitments, they may feel guilty for not participating fully. They may see themselves as open to criticism for not having their child's interests at heart (Akerley, 1975).

The cultural background of the family can also have a profound effect on the intervention process. Culturally based beliefs affect how families adapt to the disabled child, as well as the family's willingness and ability to seek help. These beliefs also influence how families communicate with professionals, their level of trust in caregivers and caregiving agencies, the amount and type of participation, and the goals the family selects for the child. Finally, these beliefs often dictate which family members will participate in intervention activities (Hanson, Lynch, & Wayman, 1990; Schorr-Ribera, 1987).

Difficulties can also occur when there is poor communication between the families and the professionals who serve them. A lack of language-appropriate information about the nature of the child's condition and the intervention being undertaken can seriously affect parents and children at every point of service delivery (Smith & Ryan, 1987). Parents and intervenors can too easily misunderstand each other.

Very young minority children with disabilities require the same level of services as other infants and preschoolers with special needs. However, early intervention must meet the family's needs in a way that is culturally acceptable to that family. Attitudes toward professionals vary across cultures, so when entering into interactions with a family whose language, customs, and values are very different from those of the majority group, early interventionalists must demonstrate great sensitivity, patience, caring, and respect. After all, they may well be the first professionals the family has had to deal with in arranging appropriate services for the child.

Early intervention programs must also take into consideration different family types and changing roles within families. Even though the traditional family is not as common in modern society, infant and preschool programs are often directed toward the two-parent, middle-class family. Some programs have assumed that mothers are the primary caregivers, that children are raised by two biological parents, and that fathers show their concern for their children through participation in organized efforts such as fund-raising, advocacy, and so on. These assumptions are not based on data (Atkins, 1987). Intervention should not become the sole concern of the mother.

Most parents want a voice in *what* their child is taught, and *how*, and want to participate in the teaching (Dunst, Trivette, & Deal, 1988). When parents do not wish to be deeply involved, the interventionist cannot assume that they are "bad" parents. Parents' priorities can be different from those of professionals. The interaction between parents, children, and early intervention specialists is only one of many interaction situations encountered by families. While their child is in an early intervention program, parents continue to interact with relatives, friends, strangers, and other professionals. The parents must attend to the needs of the child, to other members of the family, and to themselves. In some cases, the demands of an early intervention program may even conflict with the family's pursuit of a normalized lifestyle in other areas. The professional may urge the parents to spend more time and effort on the child, but parents must weigh this against the needs of the family as a whole (Winzer, 1996).

Parents who feel accepted and understood may be more ready to get directly involved in subsequent efforts involving their child. When talking with parents about their concerns, intervenors should remember that parents are trying to do the best for their child. Each parent has a different way of coping with a child's disability, and has developed a unique personal ideology to guide decision-making, and has attached a unique meaning to the child's special needs (Winzer, 1996).

Parents and professionals

When an early intervenor (case manager) works with a family, she or he bears in mind a number of interrelated goals and objectives. The overriding concern is to provide services to the family that will meet the needs and priorities of that family. This can only happen when parents and professionals work together; when both sides respect and trust each other, a partnership is possible. The partnership between professionals and families is reflected in the way parents involve themselves in planning and in the way professionals recognize and respect the roles of parents.

Positive relationships between parents and professionals depend on a number of factors. Communication, flexibility, and time seem to be the key factors in solid parent/professional interactions. Good communication on the part of the teacher is central to the success of any intervention. Parent educators must work hard at being good listeners, and must be able to counsel the family. They should serve as a support system for the family; especially, they should reassure the parents that their feeling are valid.

Barriers to effective communication between parents and professionals are raised when advocates of parent intervention, perhaps because of too much exuberance, lose sight of all the other responsibilities of parents and fail to fully appreciate what it means to have a child with a disabling condition. Other barriers may be raised when parents and teachers disagree about approaches to learning. Some parents may prefer a more formal style and not see that young children learn through play and in the natural routines of the home. If professionals wish to facilitate parental involvement in case management activities, they must understand a family's competing needs. Whatever training is provided by parents and other family members at home must be compatible with the natural structure of the family's life—the family's routines, activities, and interactions. The professional must understand the parents' problems, must be flexible, and must appear open and empathetic.

More so than centre-based programs, home visits are fraught with ambiguity regarding the roles of the visitor, the child, the parent, and other family members (Powell, 1990). For one thing, the parent is in charge of the situation and the visitor is not autonomous in a home situation. As well, family roles often shift; whenever there are changes in family status, employment, finances, or similar, adjustments will be necessary in the services provided.

Teachers who serve children in the home have a unique opportunity to involve families in the educational process. Teachers who enter students' homes must be aware of differences in parent and family practices. They must consider the parents' point of view and be sensitive to the situations of individual families. Most importantly, they must understand that basic family needs must be met before education can become a focus of concern.

Heinicke and colleagues (1988) suggest that a trusting relationship between the family and the program worker is the essence of intervention and requires a certain number of sessions to develop. Their analysis of 20 studies indicated that interventions were more likely to succeed in the long term when they included eleven or more contacts over at least a three-month period.

Some hints for working with parents are presented in Box 5–2.

BOX 5–2

Helpful hints

- Respect the parents by not talking down to them. Respect the child as well.
- Listen carefully to parents.
- Parents are parents first, and parents of a child with a disability second.
- When offering suggestions, be tactful and task-oriented.
- Offer the parents help in locating additional sources. Don't be territorial.
- Hope that parents will help develop and maintain the child's potential, but don't expect them to fill the role of teacher.
- When you perform an activity with the child, explain why, how, and when.
- After you've explained or demonstrated an activity, let the parent take over.
- When possible, use items from around the house as toys. A coffee can and a wooden spoon make a wonderful drum.
- Include other members of the family, when possible.
- Stress the positive aspects of the child's development.
- Remember that the goal of the professional is to support, not supplant, the family.

- Involve parents in all aspects of decision making and planning.
- The parents, siblings, and extended family are as important to the child's progress as the child who is being helped.
- Be sensitive to and honest about the limits of your own knowledge and abilities.
- Be sensitive to the child's individuality, but remember that the parents are individuals too.
- If possible, fit visits into the family's schedule.
- Don't offend the parents by over- or under-dressing.
- A learning plan should be developed for a disabled child in the first two years of life.
- For children under two years, the family should be supported in its role as primary teacher and caregiver.
- Intervenors should be particularly sensitive to the needs of the entire family. They must step over territorial lines, as parents may have connections with four or five different groups and associations.
- Be positive. It is easy for parents to become defensive when teachers seem critical of a child's behaviour or abilities.

Source: Adapted from Winzer (1993a).

The IFSP   In the United States, early intervention (in tune with PL 99-457) is both more prescriptive and more binding than in Canada. Although the American federal mandates do not state exactly how parents should be involved in early intervention planning, they do specify that a specific plan must be written. Those working in Canadian settings do not legally have to complete individual family service plans (IFSPs); however, a closer look at these plans may be worthwhile here.

The purpose of an IFSP is to identify formal and informal resources and plan how they can be assembled to facilitate attainment of a family's goals. The law is explicit on the IFSP's content and development process. It must contain a statement of the child's present functioning in the following areas: physical development, cognitive development, language and speech development, psychosocial development, and self-help skills. It must also contain a statement of the family's strengths and needs related to enhancing the development of the family's handicapped infant or toddler.

Specific goals or outcomes for the family and the child must be written down, along with the criteria, methods, and timing for evaluating the plan's results. The services needed to achieve prescribed goals must be fully described, along with their frequency, intensity, and method of delivery; and the family's case manager, who will be responsible for implementing the plan, must be named. The multidisciplinary team that formulates the IFSP is required to review and revise the plan according to a preset schedule. The child's parent(s) must be part of the multidisciplinary team that constructs the plan. The team's decisions must be based on a multidisciplinary assessment of the child and family.

The IFSP must contain the following components:

- A statement of the infant's or toddler's present levels of development (physical, cognitive, speech/language, psychosocial, motor, and self-help)
- A statement of the family's strengths and needs as they relate to enhancing the child's development
- A statement of major outcomes expected to be achieved for the child and the family
- The criteria, procedures, and timelines for determining progress
- The specific early intervention services necessary to meet the unique needs of the child and the family, including the frequency, intensity, and method of delivering services
- The projected dates for initiating services, and the expected duration of those services
- The name of the case manager/service co-ordinator
- Procedures for transition from early intervention into the preschool program

FIGURE 5–2

Components of an individualized family service plan

Targeting skills

As we have stressed, every child and every family is different. However, parents of infants and preschoolers with disabilities seem to share some common perceptions of what they want their children to learn:

- They want the child to learn specific skills (how to walk, talk, feed himself or herself, play with other children, and so on). Parents see these life skills as vital. Hamre-Nietupski (1993) surveyed 192 parents of children with disabilities about the percentage of the typical school week that should be spent on the following: functional skills, academic skills, friendship-making skills, and other educational programs. The parents of severely disabled children wanted the greatest amount of time to be devoted to functional skills; friendship skills and social development came after. Parents of children with moderate disabilities favoured academic skills, then functional skills, and then friendship and social skills.

- They want the child to be helped in areas in which he or she is not progressing as expected.

- They want to keep the child from falling behind others of the same age.

- They want to help the child change certain behaviours that are at present difficult to manage (e.g., stubbornness, nonresponsiveness, temper tantrums).

- They want special therapy for the child in speech and language, motor development, and other specific areas (Peterson, 1987, p. 76).

The priorities the family sets for their child become the targeted skills for that child. For Kasha's mother, the priorities were feeding and mobility. Rollo's parents wanted their son to develop skills in mobility, language, and socialization.

For very young children, the emphasis should be on functional skills that are age-appropriate. A functional skill is one that will be useful to the child in many current and future environments. An example of an age-appropriate skill for very young children is the ability to form a satisfying relationship with caregivers.

Self-help skills (adaptive skills) are considered functional skills and should be an area of focus. To be self-sufficient, one must be able to care for oneself. In attaining self-help skills, children increase their ability to care for themselves; in turn, this allows more independent functioning. Self-help skills can be categorized as follows: eating, dressing, bathing, grooming, and toileting.

Many domains of learning require that the child be able to interact with the environment. Functional and adaptive skills are not enough: skills in mobility, and social and communication skills, must also be stressed.

Teachers may use a curriculum for assessing skills. Earlier, we mentioned the Portage Program. In this model the intervenor first assesses the child, often with the Alpern-Boll Developmental Profile. Then each week the teacher targets behaviours for learning (no more than three) and demonstrates the method for the parent. During the week, the parent continues the training.

The Portage Guide to Early Education (Bluma et al., 1976) is the curriculum guide of the Portage Program for children from birth to six years. This guide consists of a manual of instructions—a sequential checklist of behaviours including cognition, language, self-help skills, motor skills, and socialization. An infant stimulation section is also provided. A set of 50 curriculum cards matches each of the 580 behaviours stated on the checklist. The cards contain suggestions on materials and teaching procedures.

Similarly, a teacher might conduct an assessment using the criterion-referenced Carolina Record of Infant Behaviour. Skills can also be targeted and promoted through the Carolina Curriculum for Handicapped Infants and Infants at Risk (Johnson-Martin, Jens, & Altmeier, 1986).

Promoting skill development

Programs for infants and toddlers are individualized to address the child's unique needs, the family's priorities, and the amount of parent involvement. Most programs try to involve the parents in teaching and therapy for the child. Home-based programs use many resources found in the home; caregivers are trained in the context of play, and of caregiving routines such as feeding and diapering.

In intervening with infants and toddlers, the beginning steps for the professional are as follows:

- *Outline the major goals.* Generally, long-range goals will have broad parameters such as primary participation, co-operation, and expression. There are five domains of focus: motor development, self-help skills, sensorimotor and cognitive skills, communication, and social skills. The routines and activities selected as goals should reflect the child's capabilities, interests, and temperament. Intervention strategies should minimize the extent to which children will depend on others in the environment, and should promote active engagement (participation) and initiative (choice-making and self-directed behaviour). Goals are most effective when they are referenced to the unique needs and lifestyles of the child, family, peers, and community.

- *Select the skill.* For infants and toddlers with disabilities, skills and outcomes should be meaningful and functional. For an outcome to be meaningful, it must result in participation in daily routines according to the child's need areas and individual strengths. "Functional" means that instruction should result in the child having more meaningful control over personal routines and events in his or her life (Brown & Lehr, 1993). Intervenors may select ***keystone skills***—those which allow children to learn a multitude of important behaviours (Rincover, 1981). For example, by learning to imitate, children also learn to acquire other responses.

- *Select the strategy.* Repetition and simple conditioning are primary strategies in early intervention programs.

- *Select the setting.* It is best if instruction is carried out in the context of daily family routines. For example, with personal cleaning, the mother can tell Bobby that she's ready to wash his face, and then explain what she's doing.

- *Choose techniques and materials.* Intervention may consist of exposure to alternative strategies for achieving competence: for example, a special switch on a wind-up toy. Play or instructional activities should be carefully arranged so

> **Keystone skills**
> skills that allow children to learn a multitude of important behaviours.

that the situation attracts the infant's attention, is highly motivating, and is at a level of difficulty that is optimally challenging.

- *Demonstrate the skill.*
- *Involve the parent.* Exactly how to teach parents remains a matter of debate; this is among the most neglected areas of research in child development (Klein & Alony, 1993).

Parents can be shown general techniques for encouraging "responding" and interaction. They can also be shown how to stimulate skills in specific domains, such as language and mobility. Rebecca Fewell (1991) recommends that as much as possible, parenting be approached on the basis of the specific disability or impairment. Thus, parents would be provided with strategies for overcoming major deficits; for example, Kasha's mother would learn to stimulate residual vision.

Only an overview of strategies was provided in this section. In Chapters 10 to 15 we provide many examples of strategies that can be used with children in the sensorimotor stage of development. Many of these are incorporated into work with infants and toddlers.

GENERAL TECHNIQUES

General techniques include strategies to promote responding and interaction:

Focusing   This is defined as an act directed toward achieving a change in the child's perception or response (Klein & Alony, 1993). Many babies with developmental delays neither demand not reward parent attention. They do not consistently interact with the environment by attending to objects and events, and they fail to signal attention by visually tracking, by reaching toward objects, by vocalizing, or by manipulating objects. The child's signals may be inconsistent and difficult for the caregiver to read (as is often the case with infants with severe disabilities). Thus, the critical match between child and caregiver becomes difficult to establish and maintain. When tiny children are unresponsive, parents will have few opportunities for teaching that is contingent on the child's attention.

Parents are taught sensitivity and responsiveness to the infant's behaviour, as well as how to read the child's behaviour to see when the infant is ready to interact. Children with arched backs and furrowed brows are not ready to participate; calm, cooing children *are* ready. Parents are shown how to woo and interest the child, and how to provide the correct level of stimulation. These children take longer to interest and stimulate. Note that if there is too much stimulation, they may react poorly and then take longer to calm and settle down.

Affecting   This refers to behaviour that expresses approval or affection. The relationship that provides the ideal conditions for learning and for teaching includes a parent who knows the child's response repertoire, who is motivated to encourage the child's efforts, and who is likely to be attuned to changes in the child's behaviour; and a child who is motivated to respond because of the generally socially reinforcing nature of the relationship.

Adult interaction styles characterized by behaviours that are stimulating to an infant; that are nurturant, sensitive, and responsive to infant needs; and that show an awareness of individual temperament and styles, are associated with positive developmental outcomes. These include greater cognitive and linguistic abilities, increased motivation, secure attachments, and better social skills (Lussier, Crimmins, & Alberti, 1994). Infants and young children should live in "reinforcement-rich" environments where parents reinforce them with smiles, praise, frequent physical contact, and attention for every little thing they attempt or accomplish. When smiling, vocalizing, and attempts at social contact are reinforced, they become part of the child's repertoire. Over time the caretaker can shape primitive communication signals, such as smiling and touching, into more sophisticated communication behaviour.

Often, the teacher observes the infant and the caregiver and points out when the parent is showing approval and is effectively catching or maintaining the infant's attention. In this way, parents learn to become responsive to their infant, and the infant learns age-appropriate social skills (Noonan & McCormick, 1993).

Expanding This means broadening the child's cognitive awareness. The parent educator points out the baby's positive actions, no matter how small. This helps the family and the parent educator identify and align themselves with the baby's positive accomplishments (Ehlers & Ruffin, 1990).

> **Stimulus** an aspect of the environment that can be specified in such a way that two or more observers can agree on when it is present and when it is not.

Parents then learn how to stimulate cognitive development through activities that encourage exploration. A basic awareness of and sensitivity to a variety of stimuli is a prerequisite for learning more advanced skills. A ***stimulus*** is defined as an aspect of the environment that can be specified in such a way that two or more observers can agree on when it is present and when it is not (Becker, 1986). Any stimulus has the potential to exert some control over behaviour.

The more opportunities children are given to experience, touch, feel, manipulate, taste, listen, and smell, the more aware they become of their senses, and this awareness becomes the background for their development. Children must be allowed opportunities for exploratory and manipulative behaviours, such as handling, manipulating, and exploring objects. For example, the child can learn to reach for a hidden object under mommy's hand or behind mommy. This promotes bodily reassurance.

Rewarding This refers to the adult identifying specific pleasing components of the child's behaviour. Parents are taught to use natural consequences (objects and events that are highly salient and desired by the child). If a child requests a rattle, then the child is given a rattle. The objective is to teach the child that certain behaviours will result in the provision of desired objects, activities, and services.

Regulating This refers to the way parents model, demonstrate, or verbally suggest a behaviour or a change in behaviour. An infant's earliest efforts to control the environment involve simple, nonsymbolic behaviours such as eye contact, pointing, vocalizing, reaching, and touching. Parents are taught to teach new behaviours, and to modify inappropriate behaviours that interfere with learning.

SPECIFIC STRATEGIES

Normally developing infants acquire early language through social interaction. The way parents speak to their babies is believed to affect how children learn. Parents interact with their infants in regular and systematic ways. Parental speech around infants (often called "motherese") differs in pitch, pace, and intonation from the speech parents use with adults or older children.

Children with disabilities often do not react to linguistic input; as a result, parents may simply stop talking. But children must be talked to and played with, even if responses are not immediately forthcoming. Language development is important to parents, who often see it as an indicator of intelligence. For the child, some form of communication is critical to future development.

How soon and how quickly a child acquires language depends on the motor, perceptual, and cognitive skills that the child brings to this first social relationship between parent and child. For children with limited output and input modes, communication can be a viable goal.

The most important thing parents can do to initiate early communication is to consistently respond to the child's communication attempts. It is vital for the caregiver to develop an awareness of the child's interests and to tune in to the variety of things that will catch the child's attention. By responding to a glance from the child, by passing a wanted toy, by pointing to an object, by complying with the child's requests, by responding to comments, and so on, caregivers teach the child that communication is functional. The child discovers the fun of sharing experiences, as well as the power of his or her behaviour to control the listener's behaviour.

At first, caregivers respond to unintentional vocalizations "as if" they had specific social meanings. For example, when the child's arms are extended toward an object, the caregiver responds "as if" the child were indicating that he or she wanted the object: "Oh, you want the bottle" (Bruner, Roy, & Ratner, 1980). Later on, caregivers interpret inarticulate verbalizations, "fill out" simple utterances by modelling expanded forms, and prompt the child to provide more complete descriptions and requests.

Early language includes eye contact, touch, and attention-getting behaviour. Once the child begins to respond, the parent can attempt to establish an early communication signal system, such as one involving touch, to enhance the child's opportunities for interaction. For example, the mother holds the child in her lap and stops a

Toys help infants develop sensorimotor skills.

pleasurable activity such as rocking or listening to music; the child must then signal to have it back again (Goetz, Gee, & Sailor, 1985).

At this age, language needs to be transparent (simple) and repetitive. The adult needs to be perceptive and patient, to observe the child, and to encourage and stimulate all communication attempts.

Research findings suggest that play is vital for the cognitive development of young children. It is through acting on the world using developmentally appropriate skills during exploratory play that children build a meaningful understanding of their environment. Parents may need to teach children how to play, provide a variety of toys and stimulating activities, and demonstrate to the child how to use the toys. Caregivers should guide exploratory play toward playthings that allow infants to use all the play skills available to them (Caruso, 1988).

Children may not explore and discover for themselves, and their play may cease when the adult presence is gone. For this reason, toys should provide an immediate reward. Adults should ensure an appropriate match between the developmental level of the infant and the toys he or she uses. Toys should be chosen to match the stages of play rather than the child's age.

Particular disabilities may require more specific strategies. These are often provided by a specialist in the discipline. The parents of a child with a hearing impairment, for example, are taught to appreciate their crucial role in communication development. They are shown how to provide models of language, how to motivate language through conversational exchange, and how to elicit vocalizations. They are shown the use of hearing aids, and the various available modes of communication are discussed.

Like other infants, children with visual handicaps need to be stimulated and encouraged to develop curiosity and interest in the world outside their own body. Infants with severe visual impairments do not look at their parents, do not gaze at objects, do not reach out to be picked up, and do not visually follow activities around them. They are less able to orient themselves to the external environment through such skills as reaching, crawling, and walking. They have little or no motivation to lift their heads, or to roll or sit or stand.

Through gross kinesthetic stimulation, parents can heighten their infant's body awareness. A key to quality movement is the child's ability to use sensory information in conjunction with movement. To increase motivation and mobility, parents can place noise-making mobiles over the crib to encourage the child to move arms and legs in different ways; items at the side of the crib will encourage the infant to move sideways. They can place the child in different positions on a rug to foster a "feel" for movement. Whenever the child edges toward the end of the rug, the parent makes a comment and places the child back in the middle of the rug. Thus, the child begins to use his or her sense of touch for orientation and exploration. Later, parents may use auditory cues, such as the sound of a bell, to improve the child's location skills. Ringing a bell near the object is a useful way to attract auditory and later visual attention. Also useful to this end are "talking" toys. The feedback also enables the infant to determine how near or far from his or her grasp a toy may be; this leads to the cognitive question, "Do I reach with my hand or do I crawl to my truck?" (Fewell, 1993).

Children with visual impairments have poor head control. When they attain sitting balance, it is frequently with the head tilted down. They need help in attaining a head-up position. When parents carry the child, the child should face away from them. This removes the child's head prop (the parent's shoulder) and forces the child to hold up his or her head alone. This technique is also better for the child who has some vision, in that it enables that child to see more.

A number of these ideas for visually impaired children are applicable to children with multiple disabilities, such as Kasha; they can also be used in centre settings. An extract from an IPP for Kasha is shown in Box 5–3.

BOX 5–3:

IPP for Kasha and her family

Kasha is a child with dual disabilities in vision and hearing and may be categorized as developmentally delayed, multiply handicapped, or deaf-blind. However, she seems to retain much residual vision and hearing.

Kasha is now fifteen months of age. She began receiving early intervention at seven months, first at a centre on a one-to-one basis and then in a home visiting program. There are two older children in the family, a boy and a girl. The mother is a single parent. The family is not dysfunctional; however, financial constraints are severe. One of the main reasons the mother changed to a home program was the cost and disruption of bringing Kasha to the centre.

Present levels of functioning

Since birth, Kasha has been assessed a number of times. She is fairly unresponsive, and this, combined with her young age, makes accurate assessment difficult. She has quite restricted vision because of cataracts, especially on the left eye. She does seem to retain much usable acuity but needs to attain greater visual functioning.

Audiological assessment indicates some hearing loss. The best estimate is that Kasha retains much usable hearing and has a loss in the moderate to severe range.

There do not seem to be inherent motor problems. Kasha is lagging in motor development, but this is more likely the result of the sensory impairments than of a specific disability. The same can be said for cognitive functioning. The hearing and visual losses confound any estimates, but Kasha's learning in the past eight months indicates potential.

Language remains at a low level. She is a very quiet child and does not vocalize a great deal. However, she has given indications of babbling behaviour and consistently uses "mama" to refer to or call her mother.

Recent gains

For the past eight months, Kasha and her family have been part of an early intervention program. The mother originally set two goals for Kasha: better feeding (she wanted the time taken for feeding to decrease from one hour a session), and greater mobility.

To some extent, these goals have been or are being achieved. Kasha is still a messy, slow, and picky eater and largely needs to be fed; however, she is learning to scoop with a spoon and to hold a cup with assistance. Meal times are now shorter and more pleasant. Kasha has advanced well in mobility and is now learning to pull herself up on furniture and to stand unsupported.

The mother was at first reluctant to work on these goals with Kasha. However, with demonstration and feedback from the teacher, she is now intervening in Kasha's development. The mother quickly learned how to respond to Kasha's initiations, how to provide optimal reinforcement, and how to embed targeted skills within the context of daily activities and routines.

Current program

After discussion with the mother about family needs and priorities, the following long-term goals have been outlined for Kasha:

1. *Self-feeding.*
2. *Locomotion.*
3. *Skills in hand development (prehension).*
4. *Visual training and the functional use of residual vision. Fostering visual skills means encouraging Kasha to use her vision in the ways that are most advantageous to her. This includes encouraging her to wear her glasses.*

Short-term objectives

1. *Self-feeding and the reduction of feeding time to 30 minutes.*
   - *Will lift and return cup to the table after drinking.*
   - *Will continually use spoon to scoop food.*

   Mother will physically move Kasha's hand to the cup or spoon, help her to grasp it, and reinforce correct behaviour.

2. *Locomotion. Will gain in motor development by increasing skills in mobility—standing assisted and standing alone.*
   - *Will pull to a standing position.*
   - *Will stand supported.*

   Kasha has a favourite toy that she recognizes. This will be paired with touch and sound movements and placed on a small table within Kasha's vision. She must pull herself up to get the toy.

3. *Skills in hand development and the facilitation of appropriate searching and grasping behaviour.*
   - *During lunch, practise grasping cup and spoon, as in 1.*
   - *Teach the siblings to use three grasping toys with Kasha.*

4. *Visual training and active participation to aid attention and increase awareness.*
   - *Awareness of light (orient to the presence of stimuli).*
   - *Attention to light.*
   - *Localization of light source.*
   - *Light tracking.*
   - *Visual tracking of objects or persons.*

All children need to be as mobile as possible and to explore their surroundings to the best of their ability. Behaviours such as locomotion, reaching, grasping, and maintaining one's body position and orientation in relation to objects in the environment allow children to master, control, and interact with the environment (Bailey & Wolery, 1984). Loss of vision removes many of the cues that help children attain normal movement. The development of a normal walking gait is important.

Parents of children with physical disabilities and motor delays are given specific demonstrations and guidance for helping the child manage dressing, eating, bathing, and other self-care areas, and for enhancing mobility and play skills (e.g., Hanson & Harris, 1986). The parents of a child with cerebral palsy may learn how to hold or roll the infant. When there is a neuromotor disability such as cerebral palsy, special procedures such as tube feeding and suctioning may also be necessary.

For children who are autistic, there are three main categories of parent training. First, intervenors present the most accurate information to parents

Outline some of the training techniques than an intervenor may demonstrate for the parent of a child with a severe visual impairment; with a hearing disability; and with infantile autism.

about the disorder; second, they teach the parents strategies to cope with aggressiveness, tantrums, and noncompliance; third, social support from the family and the community is emphasized (Bristol & Schopler, 1983).

The transition process

One of the goals of early intervention with infants and toddlers is to prepare the child and the family for the next environment; very often the next program is a preschool program. Research on transition to preschool is limited. Transition has not been the topic of formal investigations, and until recently it has not been emphasized in the early intervention literature (Kilgo, 1990). Most of the work in this area has focused on transitions from preschool to kindergarten or primary special-education programs. The role of sending programs has been stressed over the role of receiving programs.

Placing young children with special needs in preschool programs can mean a difficult transition for parents. For one thing, transition means changing roles and expectations for families. Parents must cope with the realization that their child is no longer an infant and that developmental and learning expectations are different at the preschool level. Parents may also be apprehensive about being separated from their child during the preschool hours, and they may feel a loss of control over daily activities. Frances Hanline (1988) surveyed 38 parents about 19 areas related to transition from infant programs to preschool and found that the major concerns of parents centred on a lack of information about services, anxiety about working with an unfamiliar agency, and uncertainty as to whether the child would receive appropriate services.

Parents who have invested a great deal of time and energy in providing daily care for their child may not know what to do with their free hours during school time (Hanline, Suchman, & Demmerle, 1989). As well, the transition from the home or other services to a preschool program requires parents to spend a great deal of time and energy learning about the new educational system.

After their child begins to attend preschool, parents may worry about the child's adjustment to the new environment and be concerned about such matters as the competence of the teacher. They may fear that the new teacher does not know the child well enough to provide appropriate care and instruction. Parents must establish a trusting relationship with the child's new teacher and identify parent participation activities that best suit the family.

For the child, a move to preschool is a move to a larger program with more children and new expectations. Children must learn to get along with peers, and with adults in a position of authority; they must also get used to a variety of play materials. One-to-one attention is less possible than in the home, and the child is expected to initiate activities, to play with a variety of toys and peers, and to follow the rules and routines of the centre.

The transition process for young children with special needs and their families involves the following: selecting a placement appropriate for the needs of the child and supported by the child's parents; ensuring a smooth transfer of the child; preparing the child to function in the next environment; and ensuring a smooth and rapid adjustment to that environment. Family involvement is imperative in the transition process, and most parents want to be involved. An exploratory study of nineteen parents (Johnson et al., 1986) reported that most parents were involved in their child's transition.

In Edmonton, McDonald and her colleagues (1989) conducted a study to assess parents' perceptions of the transition from a home-based infant program to a preschool program. The program they studied was serving about 50 families of children under three who had identified special needs. After consideration of functioning levels, family preferences, available spaces, and program entrance requirements, children from the home program were, at the age of three, placed in various out-programs.

McDonald and her colleagues had teachers administer a questionnaire during their regular home visits. Analysis of the results led to four main recommendations:

- Begin transition planning at least six months to a year prior to the change in programs.
- Ask the families how they would like to be involved in the transition process, and respect their choices.
- Facilitate the transition by helping the families plan for future environments.
- Provide follow-up support to the families and staff of the new program.

Other studies have found that discussing how to plan and prepare for the transition before, during, and after the process may help reduce parental stress associated with the transition (Hanline & Knowlton, 1988). Parents have indicated a need for support services that provide information about available preschool services and how to evaluate them, particularly in decisions regarding their child's education.

Certain procedures help make the transition easier for parents and child:

- Parents always benefit from a pretransition visit. Since many things about the setting are new, and may be overwhelming, parents often have many questions. At this time, the teacher can describe the curriculum, philosophy, and daily schedule, and answer any questions the parents have.
- The early childhood staff should get to know the parents, allow them to become familiar with routines, and reassure them that they are willing to work with them.
- The staff should see the child before he or she comes to the centre; read about the particular condition; talk to the parents about management; talk to professionals dealing with the child; have case conferences on the child's program; seek out support; and talk to other centres.

LEARNING ACTIVITY 4

Reread the case study on Darrin on page 5. Now read the list of procedures suggested for making the transition to a preschool program easier for both child and parent. Note which procedures were followed with Darrin. Who was responsible for carrying out each procedure?

- The child can visit the centre before formally enrolling, and may take home photos of staff members for the sake of familiarity.

- When parents attend preschool with the child during the initial period of adjustment, rapport is developed among parents, child, and teacher. This practice also alleviates anxiety about whether the child will be adequately cared for, and reinforces continued parental involvement. Some parents may only need to visit on the first day; others may need a few days to get used to being separated from the child.

- At first, the child may attend for only part of the session. As well, in the first days more adults may have to be present in order to accommodate the child's attention needs.

- When parents are allowed to participate in preschool programs, they will feel more comfortable about sending their child to them. A study of 60 parents of children with exceptionalities in Greater Vancouver found that optimal parent involvement included the following: maintaining informal contacts with teachers; developing program goals with the teachers; holding parent/teacher conferences; and observing the classroom.

Participation helps smooth the transition by ensuring parents that they are making a vital contribution to their child's educational program. Also, it keeps parents informed of their child's daily progress and creates avenues for parent education and support. Because each parent feels comfortable with different amounts and types of participation, a variety of options should be offered to meet the needs of individual families. Sending a notebook between home and school that describes the child's day at school and activities at home on a daily basis is one form of effective communication.

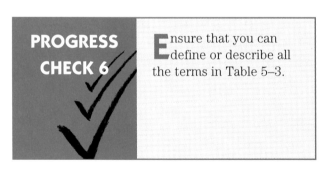

PROGRESS CHECK 6

Ensure that you can define or describe all the terms in Table 5–3.

TABLE 5–3: New terms and ideas

child	keystone skills
early intervention	needs assessment
family needs	parent involvement
home visiting	service delivery
infancy	stimulus
infant	

SUMMARY

1. Families raising a child with a disability in the 1950s faced many social circumstances that are different from today's. Until recently, parents looked to professionals and institutions to care for their disabled offspring. The field of early intervention is currently in transition; the focus of services is shifting from child-centred intervention directed by professionals to family-centred intervention directed by families. Families are now acknowledged as both unique and competent, and as able to identify their own concerns, priorities, and resources.

2. A family-centred philosophy changes how direct services are conceptualized and implemented. Today's early intervention is founded on the notion that the family can provide the most effective intervention for a very young child with a disability, but can only do so with appropriate support. Parents are seen as both constituents and consumers, and professionals give precedence to the wishes and needs of the family.

3. For children with disabilities, we find variations in when, how, and where early intervention services are provided. Early intervention programs focus on children younger than five or six, and have educational, psychological, and therapeutic components that are designed to assist children who are disabled or at risk. Intervention programs focus on strengthening and supplementing families as they adjust to the requirements of the member with special needs.

4. Because the infant years are so crucial to learning and development, programs for infants are expanding rapidly.

5. Programs for infants and toddlers and their parents hold different orientations vis-à-vis the involvement and collaboration of parents and professionals. All models assume that family involvement at some level is crucial. Professionals should focus on the child as a part of the family. The most popular methods for intervening with infants and their families include parent therapy, the parent/infant interaction model, the parent training infant curriculum model, and the infant intervention model.

6. Programs in which workers visit the home are becoming more common for children under three who require special services. Home intervention provides opportunities for full family participation. A teacher visits the home on a regular basis with the goal of helping parents enhance their child's physical, self-help, academic, and language development. Such programs must be flexible, and sensitive to the needs of children and their families; they must also develop innovative and creative approaches for encouraging and maintaining family involvement. Studies have found that home-based early intervention provides small but consistent benefits.

7. The skill priorities for both the child and the family can be established through a number of methods. The assessment should evaluate current conditions and establish the parents' goals for the child and the potential for parent involvement. The three basic assessment tools are direct observation, parent interviews, and behaviour/skills checklists.

8. A thorough understanding of the parents' role, as it is defined by the parents themselves, is essential to any intervention program. Parents play a major role that includes a variety of functions and activities.

9. Parents require accurate information and strong support to help them stimulate and interact with their disabled children. Parents should use interventions that capitalize on daily routines.

10. Family involvement is vital to the design and progress of transition programs. Teachers can ease the transition to preschool by recognizing and respecting the concerns of parents.

SECTION 3

Preparing for instruction

A PRESCHOOL ROOM IS OFTEN busy, noisy, and exciting. Materials are bright, colourful, and stimulating; many different activities are taking place simultaneously; and children are allowed great freedom of choice and movement. An untrained observer may perceive such classrooms as merely babysitting centres, with the main purpose being parent relief. Or the observer may see the setting as chaotic. Neither perception is true. The free and spontaneous preschool environment is a highly organized and meticulously prepared learning environment that is the result of much careful planning.

At any level, good planning is critical to effective instruction. Whether their students are preschoolers, elementary aged, or at the secondary levels, good classroom managers create environments that are warm and supportive, that produce optimal learning, and that show little evidence of behavioural misdemeanours or problems (Winzer, 1995). Environmental management is most important at the early childhood levels. Here, effective teachers are highly organized and consummate planners. They provide child-centred environments in which each child's interests and strengths are the starting point for learning. Teachers adjust to the child instead of forcing children to conform to preset standards.

When a child with a disability is integrated, environmental and planning factors expand somewhat. Researchers have identified specific program variables likely to strongly influence outcomes for young children with special needs. These include the physical and cognitive adaptation of the classroom to accommodate special children; the provision of multisensory learning stimuli and experiences; incorporation of the child's strengths and weaknesses in the development of curriculum; promotion of peer tolerance; a focus on independence and exploration of the environment; and the promotion of social interaction (see Guralnick, 1988).

Prior planning assumes even more importance and wider dimensions. Integration strategies will probably include early assessment, the development of an individualized program, the intervention of professionals and paraprofessionals, a range of teaching approaches and techniques, and adaptations of the environment.

In this section we examine some of these planning aspects—specifically, environmental arrangements, assessment, and individual program planning. Each is important to the integration of children with disabilities and should be carefully thought through in any attempts at integration.

In a properly functioning preschool class, the way a teacher plans is closely related to the theoretical orientation of the particular program. The many theoretical orientations in early childhood education and in early childhood special education (ECSE) are translated into program models, each of which has an identifiable configuration vis-à-vis time scheduling, space arrangements, facilities, teacher/child relationships, and objectives (Lay-Dopyera & Dopyera, 1990). The first chapter in this section examines some of the various models used in early childhood education and discusses how they can be adapted for children with disabilities.

It is vital that the environment be responsive to all children, regardless of their developmental level. If children with disabilities are to be successfully integrated, program teachers will need to guide, support, and encourage them, and structure the environment so that they can explore, interact, and learn on their own. While most children with disabilities play in ways that are similar to those of normally developing children, we need to plan materials and play activities carefully so that the young child with a disability can be led into experimenting with new skills in ways that capitalize on motivation and provide pleasure. Some

children may require special toys or other adaptive equipment. Chapter 7 discusses environmental planning and stresses the different types of specialized equipment that children may use for play, to improve mobility, and to get around sensory limitations.

A child with special needs requires an individual program plan (IPP). The first step in designing a program for a child with a disability (or one who is potentially gifted) is to determine which skills the child must master and the sequence in which the skills should be taught. To this end, the child's strengths, weaknesses, areas of deficit, interests, and likes and dislikes must all be determined. Assessment identifies target skills in terms of two criteria: appropriateness to the developmental sequence, and functionality in the child's environment.

Diagnosticians involved in early identification often use developmental checklists, rating scales, readiness measures, and basic concept inventories. The observations of parents and teachers are also considered closely, as they provide strong indications of the child's present skills and awareness. Chapter 8 discusses assessment in ECSE and the various tools, procedures, and adaptations that may be used.

Individualization is the essence of special education; individualized programs focus on the unique needs of the child with a disability. An IPP is the manifestation of the philosophy of individualization; it also provides a clear outline of what to teach, how to teach it, who will teach it, and how it will be evaluated. Chapter 9 discusses how to translate assessment results into long-term goals and short-term objectives for individual program plans.

CHAPTER 6

Models in early childhood special education

CASE STUDY

Juan

Juan is an only child, deeply loved, and the centre of his small family. Because she had only the one child, the mother could not easily compare Juan's language and behaviour to that of other developing children. Nevertheless, from the time Juan was about a year old, she harboured slight but nagging doubts about his development and progress.

By the time Juan reached his third birthday, the mother's fears and doubts had grown much larger—so much so that she finally consulted her pediatrician. Juan, she explained to the doctor, seemed a little slow in some things. Although he was three years old, he was only saying a few isolated words. He rarely used sentences, and when he did they were only simple two-word commands such as "me milk" or "mommy come." Juan was not fully toilet-trained and seemed to be lagging in the development of other motor skills. He did not run and jump and climb as mother saw other neighbourhood children do.

When the pediatrician examined Juan he found nothing amiss physically. However, he knew that Juan was a premature baby and that the labour had been long and arduous. Juan had always been in the high-risk category, and the pediatrician did not want to suggest to the mother that she was too protective or unduly concerned. He knew the child's history, and had watched his progress carefully, and now could elicit only a few responses and little language from Juan.

The pediatrician made a number of specific suggestions. First, he referred Juan for medical checks of vision and hearing and for a complete psychological assessment. He also suggested that the mother seek out a preschool setting for Juan, noting that being with other children in a stimulating environment would help him develop skills. This would be especially true if the facility could handle additional assessments and formulate an individual program. The pediatrician warned that some facilities would not accept children who were not toilet trained; however, he was confident that the mother would be able to locate an appropriate setting in her large urban area.

The results of the audiological and vision assessment showed that Juan had normal functioning in both areas. Examination of the structures needed for speech revealed no anomalies. The psychologist's report was less optimistic. The psychologist reported that Juan had come readily to the session and had shown interest and involvement in the materials and items administered. The psychologist warned that assessing young children is particularly difficult and that making predictions based on assessment results is hazardous. Having said that, he was fairly certain that Juan was functioning in an intellectual range that was equivalent to moderate mental retardation.

A speech/language therapist assessed Juan's speech and language skills. She reported that he was further ahead in receptive than in expressive language; that is, he understood more language than he used. However, his language levels were those of a child much younger and were not even commensurate with his mental age.

With the report in hand, the mother followed the pediatrician's advice about finding a preschool for Juan. She located three nursery schools in her immediate area and found that all were willing to accept Juan for a half-day program. The supervisors did not seem unduly concerned when they learned that Juan was a little slow in reaching some developmental milestones. All felt that he had the necessary skills to cope with their program without great modifications.

The three programs differed in style and philosophy. The first offered an academic curriculum, stressed discipline, and had a school-like atmosphere. The second emphasized social development and play and allowed children to exercise much initiative in their activities. The third adhered to a Montessori model. In each of the settings, Juan's mother was reassured by the respect the teachers showed for the individual needs of all children. The teachers displayed positive attitudes toward all the children in their care, and seemed confident of their ability to work with all children.

The mother now faced a number of dilemmas. She had to accept the diagnosis of Juan's functioning and alter her expectations of his progress. More immediately, she had to face being separated from her child as he participated in a program. Pragmatically, she had to select an appropriate program for the child. Each of the supervisors explained their program's orientation and curriculum to her, and she spent time observing in the classrooms; even so, she remained confused.

She could only hope that her needs conformed with the expectations of the preschool. She eventually chose the program that stressed social interaction, because she wanted Juan to fit in as much as possible among his peers.

As soon as Juan entered the preschool program, the supervisor arranged a team meeting. Present were the supervisor, the early childhood teachers, the psychologist, the speech/language therapist, and the mother. The main objective of the team meeting was to devise a program for Juan that would focus on the major domains in which he was demonstrating lags. Together, the team wrote out a program that stressed social interaction and the development of expressive and receptive language. Part of this program is shown in Box 6–2.

A RANGE OF PROGRAM MODELS AND curriculum orientations characterize current early childhood education, both for normally developing youngsters and for those with exceptional conditions. In one North American survey of preschools (Esterly & Griffin, 1987), six common models were identified. These were the developmental, the psycho-educational, the behavioural, the cognitive-developmental, the diagnostic-prescriptive, and the perceptual motor.

Programs have widely varying goals, methods, and philosophies. They also differ in type, emphasis, organization, structure, locale, and personnel. Programs may be called child development centres, children's centres, nursery schools, preschools, or child care centres. The most general designations are preschools (nursery schools) and daycare centres. However, this is rather professional terminology. As Hawes (1993) observes, "Families do not talk about going to child care. Instead, children and their families call child care various other names including school, preschool, nursery school, the babysitter, or Ms Jones."

The great variability in program organization is echoed in the curricula. A single early childhood curriculum simply does not exist, and many different curricula, based on diverse philosophies, have been developed and implemented. The differences exist because models in early childhood education are founded on various theories of development—theories which in turn differ in their relative emphasis. Some focus on innate, biologically determined differences, others on environmental differences. Also, the field of early childhood draws on a long history of educational thought and knowledge, and this in turn influences model development.

Some programs concentrate on play and the development of social skills. Others concentrate on cognitive development, and yet others on Montessori's methods. It is little wonder that Juan's mother became confused when she tried to locate a suitable preschool program for her son. She wanted the program that would best help Juan overcome his developmental lags, but she also wanted a program that would allow him much interaction with his peers in a natural setting. At this time, too, she needed assistance from the program staff in the form of personnel who would understand and accept her distress at facing Juan's disability and at being separated from him. She needed teachers who would appreciate how very difficult it was for her to place Juan in the preschool program, and who would also understand the dilemmas she faced in making educational decisions and confronting a variety of issues related to her child's disability and continuing education. Many things about the setting were new and overwhelming to her, and she had many questions. However, the classroom staff always made her feel welcome and attempted to answer her questions as fully as possible.

It is not possible to know whether the mother made the correct decision and whether Juan's social and language skills will improve if he is placed among his normally developing peers and given extra assistance in areas where he is demonstrating deficits. What works with a child developing normally is not necessarily best for a child with a disability. No consensus has been reached about the most effective program for children with disabilities; all that most educators agree on is that such programs should take place in integrated settings, with modifications and adaptations directed specifically toward the child's unique strengths and weaknesses.

In this chapter we provide an overview of the organizational and curricular models currently available in early childhood education and ECSE. Each of the major models currently seen in early childhood education is detailed; the ways these programs accommodate children with disabilities are outlined.

PROGRESS CHECK 1

So far in this text we have met three children with intellectual disabilities: Rollo, Kasha, and Juan. While children with intellectual disabilities share some common traits, they are no more homogeneous than are groups of normally developing children. Reread the three profiles and the boxes that discuss Down syndrome, multiple disabilities, and intellectual handicaps. Now compare and contrast those conditions in terms of etiology and developmental consequences in cognition, language, and social skills. Also discuss the type and intensity of early intervention offered to the three children and their families.

Early childhood education

Model **a pattern or design that can be replicated or repeated.**

Education and psychology are two disciplines that use many models to explain certain things and events. For example, we have models to explain how children learn, and how to manage classrooms, and how children develop in many domains. In a general sense, a ***model*** is a pattern or design that can be replicated or repeated. Models in educational psychology explain children's learn-

BOX 6–1
Intellectual disabilities

The American Association on Mental Retardation (AAMR) writes that

> ***Mental retardation*** refers to substantial limitations in personal functioning, characterized by significant subaverage intellectual functioning, existing concurrently with related limitations in two or more of the following adaptive skills: communication, self-care, home living, social skills, community use, self-direction, health and safety, functional academics, leisure, and work. Mental retardation is manifested before age eighteen. (AAMR, 1993)

In the context of the AAMR definition, subaverage intellectual functioning refers to an IQ of 70 or less on a standardized test of mental ability. The developmental period is the time between conception and the eighteenth birthday. *Adaptive behaviour* is behaviour that is appropriate for a person's age and social context and is defined as "the degree and efficiency with which an individual meets the standards of personal independence and social responsibility of his age and cultural group" (Grossman, 1977, p. 11). Adaptive behaviour encompasses social functioning and interpersonal relationships, functional academic competencies, and vocational-occupational competencies. The competencies dealing with functioning independently are perhaps the most widely accepted components of adaptive behaviour. Included in independent functioning are skills related to toileting, dressing, feeding, avoiding danger, and maintaining a minimum level of health and safety (Reschley, 1989).

Mental retardation implies deficiencies in cognitive development that are associated with or that result in a variety of physical, behavioural, and academic characteristics. However, mental retardation means slowing down, not stopping: the ability of people with intellectual disabilities to learn and to put their learning to use may be limited, but it certainly exists. More and more research indicates that retardation is quantitative, not qualitative. This means that children who are mentally disabled pass

---

Mental retardation substantial limitations in personal functioning, characterized by significant subaverage intellectual functioning, existing concurrently with related limitations in two or more of the following adaptive skills: communication, self-care, home living, social skills, community use, self-direction, health and safety, functional academics, leisure, and work. Mental retardation is manifested before age eighteen.

ing and development. In education, models are often used as templates for program and curriculum design. However, *all* educational models are designed to enhance the development and learning of children.

In early childhood education, models are founded on certain philosophies or beliefs about how children grow and develop and about the factors that best facilitate their development. An educational model in early childhood is "an ideal construction of a program in which both its theoretical and practical elements have been specified in a way so that the program can be copied or replicated" (SpodeK, 1973). Nancy Peterson writes: "An educational program model refers to a program for children in which its content and operational strategies are clearly conceptualized and defined in a manner that assures internal consistency and coherence" (1987, p. 371).

Two major points flow from the definitions of Spodek and Peterson. First, well-developed models include a clear definition of their theoretical orientation about development and learning in children, and consider carefully how knowledge, beliefs, and practices can be harnessed to produce desired outcomes. Second, an ideal model should be replicable in other programs, and should also provide a standard against which actual practices in a program can be com-

through the same developmental stages as other children, and in the same order, but they may do so later and more slowly.

There are a number of ways to classify intellectual disabilities. The most common is by level of severity: mild, moderate, severe, profound. Those who are mildly mentally handicapped (IQ 55 to 70) form the largest group of retarded learners; they also possess the widest range of skills and needs. In early childhood these children reach their developmental milestones, although a little late. They tend to be slower in developing language, motor, and social skills.

Individuals who are moderately mentally handicapped (IQ 40 to 55) have limited intellectual ability, difficulties in working with abstract ideas, and problems generalizing learning to new situations. These children demonstrate rather clear-cut deficits in adaptive behaviour and have problems with social relations and communication.

Children with severe disabilities (IQ 25 to 40) may demonstrate poor speech, inadequate social skills, poor motor development, and sensory impairments. In profoundly retarded individuals (IQ below 25), adaptive behaviour, social functioning, and speech and language skills are all extremely limited. These children show the highest incidence of additional disabilities such as deafness, blindness, and cerebral palsy.

The more pronounced cases of mental retardation are also accompanied by rather clear-cut organic and psychological signs. Maladaptive behaviours, which include both inappropriate behaviours and self-injurious behaviours, are found across the spectrum of the mentally disabled population but more commonly in severely and profoundly retarded persons. However, the frequency of maladaptive behaviours is extremely variable.

Inappropriate behaviours include aggression toward other people and objects, tantrums, and stereotypic behaviours such as meaningless repetitive movements, rocking, and hand waving. Finger and hand sucking is common. Self-injurious behaviour is defined as any self-inflicted, repetitive action that leads to laceration, bruising, or abrasions on the child's own body (Winzer, 1996).

pared. Many different components are included in early education models: objectives, teacher roles, scheduling, space arrangements, equipment, materials, and so on.

Effective programs are based on a theoretical model. Without a theoretical framework, there can be no consistency across the curriculum, and no rational means to choose among available materials and activities for young children (Grant, 1989). Many early childhood programs are indeed founded on a particular model; they have a well-defined philosophy and include firmly established procedures for working with children. However, too many early childhood programs suffer from weak planning and lack of direction; they have drifted into an amalgam of "typical" activities that as a whole lack theoretical underpinnings (Peterson, 1987).

Program models differ significantly in their basic assumptions and theoretical positions. And even when programs are founded on the same theoretical model, they will differ in how much that theory influences them and how it is applied in establishing various components, such as the curriculum, instructional methodology, and instructional materials to be used (Peterson, 1987). In this regard, see Figure 6–1.

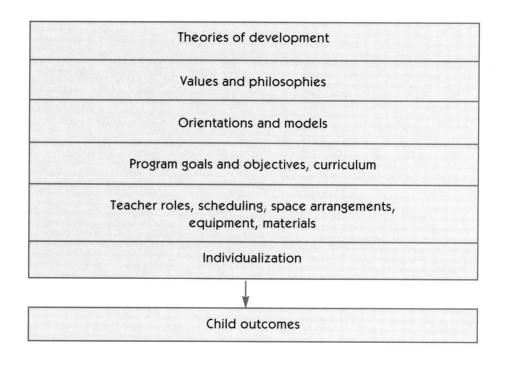

FIGURE 6–1

Components of Models

Curriculum an
organized and
sequenced set of
content to be
taught.

The model defines the ***curriculum***, a term that refers to an organized and sequenced content to be taught. It is the "what to teach," but it may also include the "how to teach." "Program" is often used interchangeably with curriculum. At other times, program refers to how the curriculum is made available to the child. Generally, early childhood education takes a developmental approach to delivering the curriculum—that is, an approach based on knowledge of child development and geared to the optimal development of the whole child (Doxey, 1990).

All educational endeavours begin with specifying the content of the curriculum. The content of the early childhood curriculum comes from two sources: knowledge of normal development, and the demands of the children's environment. The main elements of curriculum development are scheduling, allocating space, establishing a system of rules and routines, and selecting and sequencing learning opportunities (Doxey, 1990). For children with disabilities, there are certain additional elements. A good curriculum is comprehensive, individualized, developmentally and age appropriate, community-referenced, functional, generalized, and preparatory (Noonan & McCormick, 1993).

For children with disabilities, curriculum has generally been drawn from two sources: the content of the regular early childhood curriculum, and research findings on children with disabilities. Curriculum for children with special needs may be broader than for normally developing children. The main goal is always to increase the participation of infants and young children, and to increase their interaction with the social and physical environment.

MODELS IN EARLY CHILDHOOD SPECIAL EDUCATION

The theoretical position taken in an early childhood program becomes especially important when young children with disabilities are being integrated. These children may not reach developmental milestones as a matter of course. If left to their own devices, they will not necessarily explore and interact with the environment in those ways which promote learning in normally developing children. For this reason, the theoretical bases underlying programs that assist children with disabilities—particularly children with significant problems—may be different from those used for normally developing children.

In ECSE, the current trend is toward natural environments, and models that stress skills which are both functional and developmentally appropriate. But whether children are at risk, mildly disabled, or significantly impaired, a precise model for effective programming remains elusive. Phillip Strain (1990), a prominent researcher in the field of special education, wrote that "unplanned heterogeneity is the major characteristic of early intervention service delivery" (p. 295). Earlier (1981), he likened early intervention program development to "ten year olds building plastic model boats," in the sense that designing model programs with features expected to make them effective is not enough. After attaching "our idiosyncratic decals to the model," we must ask, "Does it float?" Unfortunately, says Strain, it is easier to answer this question for a boat.

One reason for the difficulty in establishing what works and what doesn't relates to the newness of the field. Preferences for a particular model in ECSE may not be driven by empirical evidence, because there is so little conclusive data (Cole et al., 1993). As well, children and families are all unique, and what suits one child may not suit another. Also, when people hold different perceptions and opinions, the result is heterogeneity and uncertainty. Concerned parties, including families served, intervention staff, and their professional colleagues, may not agree on what makes an effective model program.

There is apparent consensus in general early childhood education that high-quality programs for normally developing young children share these characteristics:

- Appreciation of the individuality found in emerging children.
- Many opportunities for young children to accelerate their rates of development, learn new behaviours, function more independently, and maintain positive advances. Children should be provided with a variety of activities designed to foster creative, motor, social, and language skills.
- Low teacher/child ratios. Very little research has been done on the effects of varying ratios on child behaviour. However, the type, number, and relative status of other people in the environment can affect children's behaviour. A caregiver who is responsible for too many children is forced to focus on basic custodial needs; the result is less time for affectionate and informational activities. Groups of between 15 and 18 children allow for more individual contact, more verbal interaction between children and adults, and more active involvement by children in group activities (McCartney et al., 1985).

- A clear curriculum. "The big dividing line between effective programs and ineffective programs is that the staff of the latter have not made a decision about the curriculum" (Weikart, 1986, p. 8).

- A curriculum geared toward cognitive development rather than behaviour control.

- An approach to curriculum delivery that is based on a knowledge of child development and geared toward the optimal development of the whole child.

- Staff with training and credentials in early childhood education. Caregivers with specialized training in working with young children often provide a richer experience than those without such training.

- An environment that fosters sustained interaction and a sense of community.

- Adults who often express positive emotions, who respond positively to children, and who provide opportunities for learning and conversation.

- Space and facilities that are organized to enhance creative and dramatic play. Greenman (1988) states that although the quality of interactions between staff and children is the most important determinant of quality in a program, it is the physical environment that most often distinguishes mediocre from very good child care centres.

PROGRESS CHECK 2

List the elements of effective early childhood programs. Which element do you feel is the most important? Explain. Is your choice based on a model of early childhood education?

- The providing of stable care. When staff turnover is low, the children have the opportunity to develop relationships.

These indicators of high-quality programs are generally accepted by early childhood teachers. However, there is little indication that professionals in the emerging field of ECSE have reached any agreement on the components that contribute to successful intervention programs.

A good environment for normally developing children is generally a good one for children with disabilities. In fact, a high-quality classroom environment may be even *more* important for children with disabilities. For example, the child/adult ratio assumes even greater importance when children with disabilities are integrated. There must be enough staff to conduct the necessary direct training sessions in such self-care tasks as toileting and feeding. If classroom staff are already fully occupied serving normally developing children, adding a child with a disability may necessitate hiring additional staff in order not to overburden existing staff.

Models in early childhood education

Every educator in every setting must possess certain knowledge. Teachers must know about the curriculum (*what* is to be taught), the pedagogy (*how* it is to be taught), and the environment (*where* and *when* it is to be taught). On this knowledge, the following process skills are based:

- Selecting a theoretical model.
- Specifying the content of the curriculum.
- Selecting and sequencing learning opportunities.
- Determining how to achieve broad and lasting effects.
- Determining the match between the needs and abilities of individual learners and the specified content.
- Manipulating the environment so that the important content is acquired.
- Identifying the tasks and activities the child needs to perform in order to function in the environment.
- Specifying the skills that will enable these tasks and activities to be performed.
- Determining the best arrangements for both teaching and supporting skill acquisition.
- Deciding which procedures are most effective, and with whom they are most effective.
- Ensuring that the learner generalizes the content (i.e., uses it when and where it is needed and desirable).
- Scheduling time efficiently for teachers and children.
- Allocating space.
- Establishing a system of rules and routines.

As this list of skills shows, the first step is to select a theoretical model. This is not an easy task: as we pointed out earlier, curriculum perspectives and models in early childhood education are presently evolving in many different directions. Different forms of early childhood education programs are now found; these are based on different orientations. These orientations arise from specific principles and procedures, which have arisen from different schools of psychology or educational thought. The major sites for the development of models are found in the fields of behavioural psychology and cognitive psychology.

Keep in mind two major points. First, the principles of behaviourism are quite different from those of cognitive psychology. Second, there is no such thing as a pure model in early childhood education, or in general education. While the influences of these essential orientations are retained in early childhood education today, as are many of the specific techniques, many programs are now thoroughly eclectic. Models are constantly evolving and changing, and teachers draw what is most efficient and appropriate from each of the psychological positions.

BEHAVIOURIST ORIENTATION

Behaviourism first emerged in North America in 1913 and dominated psychology until the 1960s. Behaviourism can be traced back to such famous philosophers, psychologists, and educators as John Locke, J.B. Watson, Edward Thorndike, and B.F. Skinner. All these people held to the notion that it was the environment that formed and shaped behaviour, not innate tendencies or features of temperament born with the child. John Broadhus Watson, for example, did not view children as actors within their environment. Instead, he saw children as passive—as reactors to environmental stimulation. According to Watson, the right environmental manipulation could condition children into doing, and choosing, almost anything.

Reinforcer an event or stimulus that increases the strength of a behaviour.

Behaviourists see all learning as resulting from environmental stimuli; they hold that learning can be better understood in terms of external and environmental causes as opposed to internal or intentional ones. That is, the ultimate causes of behaviour lie not within the organism but in environmental events, particularly those which reward or punish (Skinner, 1971). These events are referred to as reinforcers (or punishers). In Skinner's lexicon, a ***reinforcer*** is an event or stimulus that increases the strength of a behaviour.

Because they concentrate on external factors that shape, modify, and reinforce behaviour, behaviourists seldom consider such factors as a child's self-concept, internal thinking processes, or patterns of physical maturation. Rather, they consider only behaviours that are observable (i.e., visible) and measurable (i.e., that can be counted).

Behavioural models

Behavioural approaches are concerned with producing desirable behaviour. In behavioural models, teachers are interested in understanding how different conditions in the classroom determine the quality and quantity of learning. The idea that external influences can shape the developing child and should be carefully arranged to create desired outcomes is central to the tradition of behaviourism. Thus, teachers who adopt a behavioural approach to early childhood education recognize the importance of the environment. They arrange it to help children to learn and grow; and they do this not accidentally or through hoping, but intentionally and through professional actions. Thus, "the behavioural early childhood educator becomes a kind of engineer who manipulates environmental circumstances to build and elaborate child behavior" (Neisworth & Buggey, 1993, p. 116).

Early behavioural programs had an explicit goal: academic preparation. The stress was on acquiring predetermined skills and information along traditional subject lines. "Some early behavioral programs" observed Neisworth and Buggey (1993), "were characterized by teacher directed, fast-paced, task-oriented approaches that emphasized drill and 'repeated trial' sessions similar to animal training" (p. 133). While this type of strict behavioural model is no longer in vogue, today's behavioural models are a legacy of the habit-training models of earlier decades. The current behavioural curriculum model is primarily an instructional techniques model. Teachers use direct instruction procedures; the emphasis is on the teacher's active efforts to maximize the number of correctable or reinforceable responses.

The focus of behavioural approaches in early childhood education is repertoire expansion; the goal is to facilitate growth and development in a planned and sequential manner (Neisworth & Buggey, 1993). Educational programs based on behavioural principles are usually meticulously planned. The prominence accorded to environmental influences (stimuli) is reflected in the classroom's physical setting, the types of materials provided, the way those materials are presented and used, and the teachers' interactions with children.

For the program as a whole, and for each child, goals and objectives are defined in terms of observable behaviours. Behavioural programs rely heavily on continuous data collection. Instruction is highly individualized, and based on an initial assessment of the child's baseline behaviour or skills. The tasks to be learned are broken down into small steps (a procedure called task analysis); each child's specific objectives are stated in terms of observable behaviour. As children achieve each step, they are given systematic rewards such as teacher praise or a gold star. Progress is monitored through frequent data collection, and programs are modified based on that data.

In the behavioural model there is no organized system for selecting the skills to be learned, although basic skills (i.e., those thought necessary for success in elementary school) are often stressed. Generally, this means skills that are age appropriate and useful for immediate functioning. Instead of considering developmental sequences, behaviourists apply functional logic when selecting skills. In the programs most compatible with a behaviourist orientation:

- The focus is on very specific objectives.
- Teachers stress sequential skills.
- Teaching is in small "building" steps that flow out of task analysis.
- Activities are teacher directed, and there is heavy teacher involvement. Teachers direct, correct, and reinforce behaviours in desired directions.
- The child is shaped by the teacher through reinforcement.
- Children move rapidly from concrete to abstract manipulation of subject matter.
- Language is a vital component. Much instruction is verbal, either oral or written.
- Few materials are placed on open shelving for children to manipulate independently.
- There will probably be limited display space, and most of it will be devoted to children's best efforts (Lay-Dopyera & Dopyera, 1990; Noonan & McCormick, 1993).

LEARNING ACTIVITY 1

Task analysis is important in behavioural programs; it is also critical in preparing individual plans for children with special needs (see Chapter 9). Task analysis mean breaking an activity down into small "building" steps. The following task analysis was designed to teach a severely visually impaired child to wash his hands (Peterson, 1987, p. 461).

1. Step up on a foot stool to the sink.
2. Pull up the sink stopper.
3. Place hands on faucet handles.
4. Turn the water on.
5. Place hands in the water.
6. Find the soap.
7. Rub hands with the soap.
8. Place the soap back on the dish.
9. Rinse hands.
10. Push down stopper.
11. Turn off faucets.
12. Find or ask for a towel.
13. Dry hands.
14. Dispose of towel.
15. Step down.

Using the above as a guide, do a task analysis for each of the following activities. Make sure you have at least ten steps for each task.

- Styling your hair for the day.
- Getting to school.
- Helping a child to build a four-block tower.
- Teaching a child to help you hand out snacks at snack time.

Children with disabilities   Whether they are conscious of it or not, teachers use many behavioural principles in their settings. When they praise a child for appropriate behaviour, they are exercising a behavioural principle. Likewise, when they provide a reward or place a child in time out, they are applying behaviourism.

For children with disabilities, aspects of the behavioural model have long been important in instruction and management. Today's practices tend to be rooted in behavioural psychology and to be guided by research that supports the notion that direct instruction is effective. The behaviourist point of view suggests that developmental skills are best learned through direct intervention, systematic teaching, and contingent reinforcement. Even in texts that outline various philosophical underpinnings for early special education programs (including the Montessori model, the biological-developmental model, and the cognitive-developmental model), precise behavioural objectives pervade all discussions of screening, assessment, and general instruction (Heshusius, 1986).

Behavioural principles are particularly important in the instruction and training of children with severe and/or multiple disabilities. A great deal of research points out that for these youngsters, behavioural models succeed where other models fail. Behavioural programs have been successfully employed for teaching many skills, including self-help, eating, toileting, dressing, socialization, and language skills. Behavioural techniques have also been successful in eliminating maladaptive behaviours.

Functional approach   The functional approach—sometimes called life skills instruction—is an extension of the behavioural approach. As the term implies, ***functional skills*** are those which help children to get along in their environment. Functional skills include dressing, eating, and toileting. Also included are skills needed for participating in routine home and community activities, such as playing with siblings, helping with simple chores, and eating at a fast food restaurant.

Mark Wolery points out that functional tasks serve multiple purposes and are longitudinal. Functional skills will be useful to a child in many current and future environments. They are displayed throughout a lifetime and tend to be performed in progressively more complex and varied ways as children grow (Wolery, 1991). The functional approach becomes more important as children grow older.

Normally developing children learn many functional skills through observation and experience. Young children quickly learn to take the top off the cookie jar, to open the door to get outside, to pull off their socks, and to share a toy with a friend. Children with disabilities do not learn such skills as naturally, and may need specific instruction. The amount and type of intervention necessary will depend on the nature and the severity of the disability. For example, earlier in this book we met Darrin, Kasha, and Rollo. One of the objectives for Rollo was to teach him to take off his own boots—an important functional skill that he will generalize to other areas of dressing and undressing. Rollo will learn this skill rather easily; the teacher will first physically help him with the boots using a chaining technique, and then move to verbal prompts such as "Pull your boots off." Kasha will require substantially more interventions and much smaller building steps. It may take a number of interventions to teach Kasha to attend and then to grasp her boot or sock. Removing boots may simply be too complex a task for Darrin, given his severe motor disabilities.

Functional skills skills that help children to get along in their environments; behaviours that are critical for the completion of daily routines. These include dressing, eating, toileting, and participating in routine home and community activities.

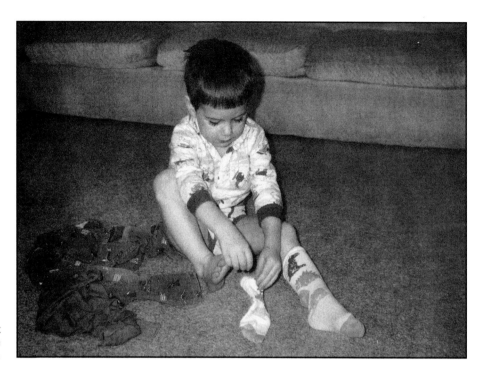

Functional skills assist children in independent living.

When goals are of a functional nature, attaining them will help the child control the environment. This is why teachers applying a functional approach select instructional items that are meaningful and important to the child. Functionality implies that a thing or action is useful for somebody (Clark, 1993). This suggests that the skills selected for the child to learn will be personal and individual.

When Juan first entered the centre, he consistently played with only one toy at a time and did not use toys in socially meaningful ways (e.g., he didn't roll cars on the floor or sweep with a broom). For Juan, playing with two toys at one time in socially meaningful ways became an instructional objective. Such toy play is functional because it allows for independent activities free of adult direction (Bailey & Wolery, 1984). Functional language is also a goal for Juan.

When a functional approach is taken, teachers identify specific skills that will immediately improve the child with a disability's ability to interact with the environment and increase the likelihood of future skills development. They then carry out a task analysis to break down important skills into small, building steps. Skills are chosen for generalization purposes as well as for functional usefulness. For example, teaching a child to grasp a toy may generalize to grasping a hair brush or a toothbrush. Both are necessary self-help skills.

MATURATIONAL-DEVELOPMENTAL ORIENTATION

The maturationalist or biological-developmental orientation is the traditional curriculum model in early childhood education. It arose from the child study movement that began in the opening decades of the twentieth century and from the work of child development researchers who were interested in finding patterns or laws to explain the development of both mind and body. For

BOX 6–2
Juan's IPP

Juan, whom we met at the beginning of this chapter, must learn certain skills to be able to function successfully in the early childhood setting. While naming and matching colours may be at his developmental level, a naturalistic approach would place greater priority on the skills he needs to participate in activities such as playing co-operatively with other children, eating a snack properly, and finding his own cubby.

Once these curricular goals have been identified, Juan's functioning relative to each is assessed in the natural environment—in this case, the preschool setting. After this assessment has been conducted, ways to meet the goals are specified. Note that the goals are not specific to the preschool: they should be set across all the settings in which Juan participates. Juan's participation and interaction must be encouraged across the full range of family routines and activities.

The ability to initiate and maintain social interactions is related to language skills. The development of functional language and the enhancement of social skills seem to be Juan's greatest needs at this time. Social interaction should start simply: with parallel play beside one other child. More socially involved activities should then be systematically introduced. Verbal cues and physical prompts accompany the initial stages of implementation and help Juan become familiar with each new activity. As soon as he is responding consistently without teacher intervention, he is ready to advance to the next step.

Present levels of functioning

Social: Is not yet engaging in play with peers. Tends to wander and to not choose toys or a centre. Will play, with teacher prompts and direction.

Language: Understands common words and phrases, but is using only a few words spontaneously.

Rules and routines: Has learned to follow the routines of the centre. Behaviour is not a concern.

Long-range goals

- *To increase self-esteem through success.*
- *To learn new vocabulary introduced in various activities.*
- *To use new vocabulary in social situations, with and without teacher or peer prompts.*
- *To develop more appropriate play behaviour.*
- *To use toys in meaningful ways without adult direction.*
- *To expand use of various centres.*
- *To learn to play with one peer. Will play with another child sharing manipulatives for up to 15 minutes.*

example, Arnold Gesell attempted to document the developmental milestones that children attained at certain ages. He carefully studied children's maturation and growth to arrive at a comprehensive list of milestones in the physical domain.

Many early childhood educators in North America still advocate a developmental approach to teaching. They perceive changes in children to be the result of both maturation and environment. One of the most important ideas underlying the biological-developmental stance (and also the cognitive-developmental stance) is the idea that there are stages in human development.

Short-term objectives

Activity	Strategy	Person responsible
Select a place to work.	Physically take and then verbally prompt centre choice.	Teacher
Clean up after an activity.	Verbal prompt; will replace toys on request.	Teacher peer
Model appropriate co-operative play.	Reinforce peers for social play; point out to Juan.	Teacher
Parallel play; Juan is aware of and will tolerate one other child playing next to or at the same activity.	Water play, sand play, puzzles, Play-doh. Seat children opposite each other; occasionally point out what one child is doing. Use telephone conversations. Two children face each other with their own telephones. Prompt in a typical conversation.	Teacher, peer
Physical contact; Juan will take part in activities involving physical contact with other children.	Hold hands and dance to music. Imitate teacher's steps—hopping, jumping, and so on.	Teacher, peers
Name and identify body parts.	Objects, picture cards.	Speech therapist, teacher
Spontaneously use new words.	Reinforce words introduced in all situations; create times to use words.	Teacher, all staff

These theorists contend that all people pass through a sequence of stages as they age. Parents often agree; for example, they talk about young children going through the "terrible twos'" or of adolescence as a particularly difficult stage.

Developmental theorists see stages as characterized by specific types of behaviour. A **developmental stage** is defined as age-related behaviour and changes that are predictable with increasing age. Researchers tend to disagree about exactly what characterizes each stage, about the ages at which particular stages occur, and about how learning affects stages; even so, they have demonstrated that

Developmental stage age-related behaviour changes that are predictable with increasing age.

Most children begin walking at about one year of age. This is a major developmental milestone.

all individuals complete stages characterized by simple behaviours before they advance to stages characterized by more complex ones (Winzer, 1995).

Using the framework of ages and stages, we can define **child development** as a series of predictable changes that foster a child's ability to cope with and master the environment. As they develop, children attain **developmental milestones** in various critical behaviours such as sitting, walking, and using first words. Most normal children accomplish the various developmental milestones at roughly the same age. Children who fail to develop within normal timelines are seen as having **maturational lags**. For example, most children say their first word at about twelve months. If twenty-month-old Brian has not yet uttered single words, he may be said to have a maturational lag in language development.

Maturational-developmental models

Normal physiological development produces steady, organized patterns of behaviour. This basic idea, together with the notion that normal development constitutes the most logical ordering of behaviours, underlies the developmental approach. Children follow a sequence of development, and develop many prerequisite behaviours, such as learning to vocalize before learning to talk. It is also held that children must be able to perform simple tasks before they can perform complex ones. To perform complex behaviours, children must learn to co-ordinate and modify components of simpler behaviours (Guess & Noonan, 1982; Haring & Bricker, 1976).

Educational programs based on this perspective stress readiness for learning, and self-expression in a warm and supportive environment. Programs that are designed to be developmental provide experiences that either compensate for deficits or enrich and extend the developmental process in all areas. The developmental perspective sets learning goals, not performance goals. Children are not pressured to perform beyond their current level.

Maturationalist programs are relatively nonspecific and unstructured. Instructional methods are designed to attract the child's interest rather than to compel involvement. Programs use a variety of materials, and offer activities that balance the active with the inactive, the group with the individual, the directed with the nondirected. In both work and play, there is minimum correction of children's efforts. The focus is sharply on the children's active involvement with materials and events in an appropriate setting.

Teachers in these programs believe that through interaction with and manipulation of the environment, children become progressively more skilled in basic developmental tasks and thereby increase their cognitive competence. It is assumed that

Child development a series of patterned and predictable changes that foster a child's ability to cope with and master the external environment.

Developmental milestones various critical behaviours, such as sitting, walking, and using first words.

Maturational lags occur when children fail to develop within normal timelines.

PROGRESS CHECK 3

Explain why a behavioural orientation is so important in ECSE. Also, discuss the value of a functional approach and explain how functional skills may be taught.

children will spontaneously select activities at their own developmental level; to help them do so, programs provide children with a setting in which they may follow their own interests and needs within acceptable (normative) frames of reference. Teachers encourage children to explore their environment freely and strive to keep direction to a minimum. They promote child-to-child interaction, and provide activities such as art and science projects, building with blocks, and playing house.

Children with disabilities A developmental model is the traditional model in early childhood education; it is also the original early intervention model for young children with disabilities. It was first employed with disadvantaged youngsters in the 1960s (e.g., in Head Start programs) as a means to give children an experiential foundation similar to that of their more privileged peers (Noonan & McCormick, 1993).

In a developmental curriculum, the objectives are grounded in stage theory, which holds that development progresses in a certain order. Intervention is designed to nurture and stimulate development and to help children become more competent and more autonomous. When extended to infants and young children with disabilities, the goal of the developmental model is to assist progress through the normal sequences of development. The basic strategy is to simulate activities engaged in by non-disabled infants, toddlers, and preschoolers. Assistance is given as needed, and the child is guided through activities.

Under a developmental model, the child's existing skills are considered in the context of the normal developmental sequence. Developmental milestones are emphasized; skills must be developed in a specific order regardless of the child's age. The developmental order of skills corresponds to what has been observed in younger children without disabilities (Bailey, Jens, & Johnson, 1983). Generally, the teacher follows these procedures:

- Observes the child.
- Compares the child's performance to described milestones.
- Records observations.
- Identifies emerging skills. These are skills that are either not mastered or not extremely advanced for the child's current developmental level.
- Identifies priority skills.
- Begins instruction where the child fails to demonstrate a skill in the normal sequence of development (Noonan & McCormick, 1993).

The content of the curriculum is based on developmental skills derived from standardized tests such as the Bayley Scales of Infant Development (Bayley, 1994); or from surveys of large numbers of children, such as found in the Gesell Scales (Knobloch, Stevens, & Malone, 1980). Content consists of sequences of physical development (gross motor and fine motor), adaptive development (self-help and daily living skills), social development, and communication development.

PROGRESS
CHECK 4

Explain the components and outcomes of the developmental model in early childhood education and ECSE. Why is this model criticized in relation to young children with significant disabilities? If you were one of the critics, which alternative model would you suggest? Explain.

Early interactions consist largely of sensory experiences, but as a child matures physically, more complex forms of interaction with the environment take place.

Although developmental models have long been employed with young children who are disabled, criticisms of this approach are legion. Most educators agree that developmental models are appropriate for children with milder disabilities, because they progress through the normal stages of development and can learn when their level of cognitive competence matches the kinds of experiences available to them. For children with severe and multiple disabilities, however, some educators see significant disadvantages to the developmental approach. Two major criticisms appear consistently.

The first centres on the contention that all children, regardless of disability, follow a logical progression of development. This may not be true for children with significant disabilities, who may not develop or acquire skills in a normal sequence. When there is a pathology of the central nervous system, the organization of behaviour is disturbed and the child's early development may well be uneven. Children with severe disabilities may learn in a different sequence, and the relationship between skills may be different (Snell, 1987). For example, a multiply disabled child may walk at a relatively early age but be severely delayed in language acquisition.

The second criticism has to do with the functional value of the skills taught. Critics of the developmental approach for children with severe disabilities argue that the goal of early intervention is not only to teach children with disabilities developmental skills but also to instruct them in the skills necessary to function in the home and community and in the next environment—that is, to teach them the functional skills we discussed in the previous section. Teaching skills directly from a developmental assessment rarely yields results that are useful to the child in the real world, or that reduce the child's reliance on others. If the child is much past infancy, a curriculum based on developmental sequences is not likely to help the child achieve the ultimate goal, which is self-sufficiency (Holveot et al., 1980). As well, time may be wasted on teaching prerequisite skills that are not really necessary for later steps.

COGNITIVE ORIENTATIONS

In the 1960s a school of cognitive psychology developed in direct opposition to behaviourism. The cognitive school of psychology is far more diverse and varied than the behavioural school in its ideas and theories. One common link among cognitive theorists relates to their general view of learning: they agree that learning does not take place merely through environmental stimuli and reinforcement; it is also a result of innate internal structures interacting with the environment. In other words, learning involves humans acting on the environment, rather than the environment acting on humans (which is the behaviourist's view).

The cognitive orientation most relevant to early childhood education is the cognitive-developmental (also referred to as the constructivist or interactionalist). The most general component of cognitive-developmental theory is the principle of constructivism. In the field of early childhood education, there are different interpretations of constructivism. Generally, we can say that constructivism is a theory of knowledge structures that captures both the *knowing* and the *doing*. Constructivists see progress as a series of stages that are the result of genetic patterns *and* of a child's own activities. Thus, constructivist theory has to do with "forming the mind, not just furnishing it" (De Vries & Kohlberg, 1987). Constructivists believe that real understanding occurs only when children participate fully in the development of their own knowledge; they describe the learning process as the self-regulated transformation of old knowledge into new knowledge.

Cognitive-developmental models   Cognitive-developmental models in early childhood education are concerned with how children derive the concepts through which they make sense of the world, and how their interactions with the environment help them move toward a higher state of development. The focus is on a better conceptualization of the physical and social world; emphasized are internal processes such as memory, language, thinking, and problem solving.

Educational practices that follow cognitive-developmental principles stress active involvement with the curriculum and the environment, rather than imitation or memorization of facts. Knowledge is not the object; rather, it is a means to an end. How the child uses skills and knowledge to solve problems is the key; in this light, experience is more important than the end-product. Teachers design and sequence activities to provide children with opportunities to try, to practise, and to master, not merely to memorize. In this way the *process* becomes more important than the *product* (Doxey, 1990). Isabel Doxey (1990) notes that when children are painting, it is the process of experiencing colours on paper, and how changes happen when colours are mixed, rather than the product (i.e., a painting), that is the essence of the experience.

In the cognitive-developmental framework, the teacher is essentially a guide. The teacher structures the environment, helps children to plan their activities, promotes exploration and thinking, provides maximum feedback, and clarifies a child's statements and problems. At the same time, the teacher attempts to keep in mind both the fields being taught and the characteristics of individual children.

Content in the cognitive-developmental model is similar to content in the developmental model, but places more emphasis on cognitive skills. A cognitive-developmental program is distinctive in the following ways:

- Instruction is motivating—that is, the objectives are slightly ahead of the child's present level of cognitive development.

- The child is an active participant in learning.

- The child's level of cognitive development both limits and determines his or her objectives for other developmental domains.
- The cognitive, language, and social domains are stressed over fine and gross motor development.
- All kinds of experiences are available, not merely "academic" ones.
- Long periods of unstructured activity are provided so that children can plan and execute projects independently.
- A variety of peers are available for social interaction.
- Adults provide input mainly on a one-to-one basis, or in small groups.
- Typically, classrooms have a central open area for group meetings and action games, with work areas around the perimeter. Learning centres have materials for art, block play, writing and drawing, dramatization, and exploration with raw materials such as sand and water (De Vries & Kohlberg, 1987).
- In cognitive-developmental and maturational programs, items considered particularly appropriate for display are children's artwork such as paintings, drawings, prints, and collages; charts, graphs, stories, and photographs developed with the children's participation; and informational materials such as "how to" charts (Lay Dopyera & Dopyera, 1990; Noonan & McCormick, 1993).

Children with disabilities For the child with a disability, in both the developmental model and the cognitive-developmental model content is established by assessing the child in the context of developmental skill sequences. Instruction begins where the child (or infant) fails to demonstrate a skill in the normal sequence of development.

Piagetian classrooms

Perhaps the most clearly articulated example of a theory-based developmental approach is the cognitive-developmental model founded on the theories of Jean Piaget, the Swiss researcher and writer. His work profoundly influenced education at all levels, but most especially in the early childhood years.

Piaget focused on how children adapt to and interpret objects, people, and events in their environment. He viewed cognitive development as composed of cognitive structures and intellectual functions and suggested that a child's acute observation and manipulation of objects form the basis for cognitive development. Children, held Piaget, construct their own knowledge by interacting with the environment. With this in mind, Piaget de-emphasized formal learning and stressed maturation and experience as the foremost factors in cognitive development.

Piaget discovered that children pass through specific stages of intellectual development and that they develop certain thinking skills in a predictable sequence. Children in a given age group will operate at different levels of thinking according to where they are in the sequence. We present a brief overview of Piaget's theories in Box 6–3.

BOX 6–3
Piaget's views

Jean Piaget (1896–1980) was a Swiss researcher who became the guiding force in developmental psychology from birth through adolescence. While he also wrote about how children develop language and moral thinking, he concentrated on cognitive development. He published the basics of his theories between 1923 and 1932.

In 1921, Piaget began to study intellectual development in children; his work in this field would eventually span six decades. When he began, children were seen as little more than miniature adults, at least as far as intelligence was concerned. They were thought to differ from adults in the quantity of knowledge they possessed, but not in the quality. It was believed that people of all ages solved problems, remembered things, and thought about the world in much the same way. Piaget's conclusions changed this thinking; he was one of the first psychologists to recognize that humans are born as active, exploratory, information-processing organisms.

Piaget held that cognitive development occurred as a result of physiological growth and a child's interaction with the environment. A number of processes were involved in these qualitative changes. To Piaget, cognitive development meant adaptation and organization. Adaptation occurs as children change or adapt their *schemata* (i.e., their cognitive structures) to new information about the world. Adaptation has two processes: assimilation and accommodation. *Assimilation* is the process of incorporating new experiences; *accommodation* refers to changes in existing schemata to fit new information. It is through accommodation that people change their behaviours and knowledge to match their perceptions of the world. Imitation is an example of accommodation. Organization is the alignment of information.

Piaget held that children pass through four stages of cognitive development, which he labelled sensorimotor, preoperations, concrete operations, and formal operations. For each of these four stages, Piaget pinpointed a central cognitive leap, which he referred to as an *operation*. In Piaget's terminology, operations are systems or co-ordinated sets of actions for dealing with objects or events.

Piaget characterized the early years of life, from birth to about age two, as the sensorimotor period. Sensorimotor behaviours are acquired during infancy and are thought to be precursors to basic thinking and conceptual development. Children at the sensorimotor stage understand the world in terms of actions that can be performed on objects.

Newborns are equipped with reflex structures—for sucking, looking, grasping, and so on—that permit them to act upon the world. Through adaptation, these reflex structures develop into cognitive structures, which form the basis for acquiring knowledge of the physical world, and for understanding general principles.

During the sensorimotor stage, children gradually progress from reflexive to goal-directed and intentional behaviour. By means of a few reflex behaviour patterns, an unfocused curiosity, and the vaguest perceptions of the world, infants develop schemata of themselves and other people, and begin to recognize relatively permanent objects outside themselves. They gain considerable skill in handling objects and in responding appropriately to events around them. They begin to understand spoken language and to experiment with using it themselves. Their major cognitive milestone relates to object permanence: the realization that objects, people, and events exist even when they are outside their immediate experience. In normally developing children, the development of object permanence begins at about 8 months and is complete by about 18 months.

Piaget's preoperational stage spans from about two to six years (or later). For educational purposes, we can say that for most children the preoperational period extends until about third grade. Preschool children think quite differently from children of school age; the functioning of preschool children is not as reflective in nature. The older child does not simply know more than the younger; the cognitive structures that facilitate their problem solving are *qualitatively* different.

Children at the beginning of the preoperational period are starting to construct their knowledge on a conceptual plane, but they cannot yet think logically or abstractly, and they still tend to rely on perceptual analyses of situations rather than on conceptual references. At about age four children begin to be able to construct more complex images and more elaborate concepts. In the next three years or so, they add more and more information and learn more and more symbols. At this stage of development, children are ready to assimilate much new information.

The key development in the preoperational period relates to representational thought, which builds on object permanence. Representational thought actually begins at about 18 or 19 months, but becomes increasingly sophisticated during the preoperational period. Representational thought enables children to construct thoughts and images and use symbols; they can think about the past and also plan future actions. Representational thought is obvious in young children's dramatic and fantasy play.

The elementary school years, from about 6 to 12 years of age, are termed the period of concrete operational thought. As children become operational, their cognitive schemata, especially their thinking and problem-solving skills, become organized into concrete operations—that is, mental representations of potential actions. Concrete operations are the major development of this period.

As concrete operations develop, more refined methods of analysis are applied to new experiences; in fact, it is the new experiences that stimulate the development of concrete operations. In the period of concrete operational thought, children develop concepts based on many dimensions, not just one. They begin to understand conservation—for example, that the number of beans in a container is the same even if the teacher changes the shape of the container, and that no matter how often a ball of clay is reshaped, it is still the same amount of clay.

Students reach the formal operational period around the age of 12. Formal operational thought allows students to enter a new world of ideas and concepts; at this time they begin to hypothesize about relationships.

Piaget called himself a "genetic epistemologist" (*genetic* from innate structures, and *epistemology* from the study of how humans acquire knowledge). He was more interested in how children construct knowledge than in how they are taught or how they learn in the classroom. However, his ideas have been interpreted by educators and translated widely into instructional principles; and in that context they are often referred to as constructivist. The resulting principles have most often been applied in preschool and kindergarten programs which emphasize that children learn through discovery with a variety of materials, and that the teacher's role is not to instruct but to establish and direct an environment in which children can have a wide variety of experiences.

Because Piaget held that development depends on constructive activity, those following a Piagetian formula structure programs to encourage children to discover the world around them and to learn from their own experiences. The process of acquiring information, rather than the information itself, is central to this. The programs have these main components: active learning, language, experiencing and representing, classification, seriation, number, spatial relations, and time (Lay-Dopyera & Dopyera, 1990). Tasks are provided that call on children to identify real problems and to experiment with solutions involving processes such as measurement; and that require both divergent and convergent thinking. Teachers use questioning strategies that encourage children to reflect on their experiences and to predict future ones.

The essence of a Piagetian classroom is self-initiated activities; the children's own planning efforts are central. Each child is encouraged to interact with the materials in the environment as well as with the other children with the goal of acquiring new developmental skills by trial and error and by imitation. Spontaneous play is allowed and encouraged, for Piaget believed that such play is intimately associated with children's cognitive, physical, and socio-emotional development. Children play in centres where they interact directly with a set of learning materials. The Piagetian classroom stresses building things, making things, trying them out, making them work, and trying to answer questions about how and why they work.

LEARNING ACTIVITY 2

A great deal of rather unique terminology is associated with Piagetian ideas of how children learn. Some of the terminology is found in the text and in Box 6–3. Find out and explain to the class the meanings and applications of the following terms used by Piaget: reflex, schema, egocentricity, transductive thinking, seriation, operations.

Regarding structure, the teacher selects appropriate materials and options for activities, and arranges and equips the classroom to invite and encourage activity. Teachers provide materials that are challenging but not frustrating, and organize space to allow movement and play. They provide inviting and interesting activities in language, in representing experiences and ideas, in logical reasoning, and in understanding time and space.

The stress is not on discrete subject matter but rather on interdisciplinary topics and themes. When a thematic approach is taken, a variety of activities can be planned for children of widely diverging developmental levels.

Children with disabilities   Piaget's theory implies a developmental concept of children's learning. Programs for children with disabilities and for those at risk have increasingly reflected Piaget's influence. For children with disabilities, instructional programming decisions are made on the basis of each child's intellectual functioning rather than on the basis of a categorical orientation, such as "mentally retarded." Teachers provide activities that promote, for example, social interaction. For Juan, teachers would provide materials suitable for children in the late sensorimotor stage and that challenge him.

A central consideration in constructivism is the importance of prior learning; new knowledge is acquired by consolidating old knowledge through practice, and then extending that knowledge to new situations. Repeated trials of important concepts in various situations promote understanding. To teach Juan new skills, teachers would provide opportunities for many repetitions with the same and then different materials; this would promote both learning and generalization.

BOX 6–4

Helpful hints

- Provide experiences with other children through play and sharing.
- Provide frequent reinforcement for appropriate social behaviour.
- Provide children with experiences in which they can succeed. Use much positive reinforcement, such as praise.
- Provide large utensils for writing, painting, and cutting.
- Provide many opportunities for exploration and play.

- Emphasize activity and manipulation.
- Provide many opportunities for physical activity, but alternate periods of activity with quiet periods.
- Provide for much repetition of activities, at first with the same materials and then with different materials.
- Use much incidental teaching (see Chapter 12).
- Provide opportunities for imitating and modelling the behaviour of normally developing children, especially in language and social functioning;
- When necessary, break down tasks into small steps.

DEVELOPMENTALLY APPROPRIATE PRACTICE

The current emphasis in early childhood curriculum for infants or young children who are not disabled is on what is referred to as developmentally appropriate practice (DAP). DAP is not a specific or structured curriculum, nor is it a prescribed sequence; rather, it is a broad way of conceptualizing early childhood intervention—one that addresses all areas of a child's development through appropriate intervention. DAP also describes teacher intervention within the framework of the best traditions and practices of early childhood education. The DAP guidelines are organized around four components: curriculum, adult/child interaction, the relationship between home and program, and the developmental evaluation of children.

DAP comes from the cognitive school of thought. It is constructivist and is based strongly on the ideas of Piaget. Interventions such as those described above related to cognitive orientations and Piagetian classrooms fit within the concepts of DAP.

DAP is defined by the National Association for the Education of Young Children (NAEYC) as "the extent to which knowledge of children's development is applied to program activities" (Bredekamp, 1986, 1987). The guidelines for DAP generated by the NAEYC are a blend of empirical and conceptual literatures that provide information on pedagogical practices related to infants, toddlers, and preschool age children without disabilities (Salisbury, 1991)

The concept of DAP can be seen as linked to the problem of how to match the learning experience and environment to the child's developmental level. Essentially, DAP means instructing children at their own level of intellectual, social, and physical maturity. DAP is based on the assumption that if children are allowed to explore what interests them, those interests will guide them to choose and learn content that they are developmentally "ready" to learn (Noonan & McCormick, 1993).

The NAEYC's Developmentally Appropriate Practice Guidelines (Bredekamp, 1986) stress the following:

- DAP offers a wide variety of means for children to manipulate a wide variety of materials.
- It offers children opportunities to play alone and with others in sensory, constructive, and symbolic activities.
- It allows children to ask questions, and to develop concepts about themselves and the world.
- It provides children with opportunities to be physically active.
- It allows children to express themselves through words, art, and music.

Among the traditional curriculum models, only the behavioural model emphasizes the age-appropriateness of content. The developmental and cognitive-developmental models stress the developmental levels of individual children. What is provided in programs that stress developmentally appropriate activities differs from the developmental and behavioural curriculum of other preschool delivery models (Noonan & McCormick, 1993).

Children with disabilities DAP starts with a continuum of developmentally sequenced objectives, and then identifies activities within that continuum that the child is ready to learn (Lifter et al., 1993). It stresses what a child brings to the task; it responds to children's needs, abilities, interests, and cognitive goals. The dominant theme of DAP is to promote a whole curriculum—that is, a curriculum designed for the whole child. Thus, DAP is *not* a separate-subject approach with a skill-development focus; rather, it integrates all domains of learning. This integrative approach assumes that the context and means of development should be as normal as possible for each child. DAP programs stress child-driven and child-guided learning and exploratory play; children are expected to select and join in activities independently or in small groups under adult supervision.

Early childhood programs that ascribe to DAP emphasize a child-centred curriculum characterized by exploratory play and the making of individual choices, rather than a structured, teacher-directed curriculum with a specific set of objectives for all children. Teachers guide, support, and encourage; and they structure the environment so that children can interact, explore, and learn on their own (Wolery, 1991).

As we pointed out in Chapter 3, the appropriateness of the DAP guidelines for children with disabilities is not yet clear. Some authors (e.g., Wolery, Strain, & Bailey, 1992) note that for many children with special needs, DAP guidelines alone are not likely to be sufficient. Consideration must also be given to the unique learning needs presented by the disabled child, within the context of an environment and learning experiences that are chronologically age-appropriate. Thus, a four-year-old with severe impairments should be in a learning environment appropriate for typical four-year-olds, but at the same time should be provided with learning activities to match his or her unique needs. Others contend that DAP is appropriate for young children with disabilities and provides an adequate framework for early intervention efforts (Burton et al., 1992).

There is some agreement, however, that for children with disabilities, the term "developmentally appropriate" must be broadly defined, and be seen in two dimensions: age appropriateness and individual appropriateness.

Age appropriateness relates to the principle that the most important characteristic of a four-year-old with a disability is not that the child is disabled but that he or she is four years old. Content that is age appropriate features skills and activities typically engaged in by infants and young children who are not disabled. The skills stressed are those that develop confidence, intervenor responsiveness, and productivity. Children learn by interacting with adults and peers and with materials in the environment. While age appropriateness is important for young children, it gains even greater importance as students grow older. Age appropriateness can encompass more than activities. For example, a child of four should not carry a diaper bag or wear a bib. As we discussed earlier in this chapter, the skills that are individually appropriate are the functional skills children require in natural settings.

For children with disabilities, DAP involves conducting regular assessments through teacher observation and various other methods (see Chapter 8). Assessments highlight the activities to be targeted; these are often written down as goals and objectives on an individual program plan (IPP; see Chapter 9). The targeted skills are functional skills and also those skills which the child needs to follow the routines and activities of his or her various environments. Teachers work on these skills in the context of natural routines, such as dressing to go outside, preparing snacks, and clean-up activities.

A number of curricula that stress DAP have evolved. For example, the High Scope Curriculum (Hohmann, Banet, & Weikart, 1979) is based on Piaget's ideas and is an example of DAP. This curriculum has a cognitive-developmental theoretical orientation and strongly emphasizes problem solving, social development, independent thinking, and relationships. Questioning techniques are particularly important: "What has happened?" "How can this be made?" "Can you show me?" and so on.

The fundamental premise of High Scope is that children are active learners who construct their own knowledge from activities they plan and carry out themselves. An important aspect of High Scope is the teacher's role in guiding learning. Broad developmental milestones are used to monitor children's progress. However, teachers do not have defined subject matter to teach. Instead, they listen closely to what children plan and then actively work with them to extend the planned activities to challenging levels (Weikart, 1988).

MONTESSORI APPROACH

In the opening decades of this century, Maria Montessori, an Italian physician, developed early childhood programs to serve the needs of both normally developing and disabled children. Montessori's work is discussed in Box 6–5.

Montessori's approach is embedded in a philosophical system based on faith in the child's innate will to learn, on a belief in the unity of knowledge, and on recognition of the integrative nature of learning (Montessori, 1912). Montessori saw education as a means of assisting the psychological development of chil-

BOX 6–5

Maria Montessori

Maria Montessori (1870–1952), the first woman in Italy to earn a doctor of medicine degree, was greatly influenced by Joseph Sergi, the Italian anthropologist who attempted to revolutionize educational practices by studying children. Montessori began to study children's development seriously in 1906; in 1907 she established a Casa dei Bambini (Children's house) in the slums of Rome. She directed her efforts toward children of the poor. Fifty to sixty children from the ages of two-and-a-half to seven attended the school for eight to ten hours a day in what Montessori called a prepared environment.

Montessori was instrumental in establishing educational and rehabilitation programs for retarded children. She also demonstrated how these children could be helped to live fuller, more meaningful lives. Throughout this work, she insisted that mental retardation was an educational, not a medical problem (Montessori, 1912; 1917).

Montessori drew heavily on the sense-training methods developed by two pioneer special educators, Jean Marc Itard and Edouard Seguin. Like them, she believed that all learning takes place through the senses and can therefore be improved by training the senses.

Montessori developed a "prepared environment" in which children were free to use materials of their own choice and at their own pace. She wanted each of the materials to be used in a specific manner to provide a segment of the self-education she envisioned. Her materials provided experiences with length, breadth, height, colour, texture, weight, size, and form. For example, she designed a series of puzzles and peg boards, as well as small-motor tasks that encouraged eye/hand co-ordination.

Montessori wrote many books about her philosophy and practices. The Montessori method soon spread. Alexander Graham Bell brought Montessori to the United States in 1910, and he and his wife did much to promote the Montessori model of early childhood education.

Despite early enthusiasm, pure Montessori methods did not persist in North America. Interest petered out mainly because of a lack of trained teachers. However, many of her special materials were later adapted and used extensively, and some aspects of the Montessori methods were incorporated into other early childhood programs. There are few modern preschool programs that do not reflect some aspect of Montessori's philosophy, whether it be respect for the child, child-size furniture, or freedom to select activities.

In the 1960s there was a rebirth of interest in Montessori programs. Today, Montessori programs, or adaptations of them, have again become a viable and important alternative in early childhood education. Montessori schools continue to emphasize the development of small-motor skills and respect for the child's accomplishments.

dren, rather than as teaching per se. She believed that children develop through an unfolding of inborn characteristics, but she also insisted that certain environmental conditions must be in place if these inborn traits and abilities are to develop normally. She did not believe that normative behaviour at any given age should be accepted as necessary behaviour for that age level, although she *did* hold that children pass through "a series of sensitive periods" during which they are especially attuned to particular aspects of learning.

Montessori stressed not ages and stages but rather the provision of appropriate activities to foster concentration, self-confidence, and self-acceptance. She proposed that children choose their own activities, and believed that it is the educator's job to provide activities appropriate to the abilities of the individual child. The teacher serves as a model for children in extracting learning experiences from the environment, but without intruding too much of his or her personality into the situation.

Montessori felt that children need to organize their often chaotic perceptions of the outside world and build a sense of predictability and security (Kramer, 1988). Essential to the Montessori approach is the *prepared environment*; in fact, much of Montessori's effort focused on constructing environments in which children would have opportunities for appropriate "occupations." Each environment has definite space structuring. Materials are designed to represent reality. Children use real things instead of playthings, and real tasks are performed. Children are thereby encouraged to do tasks that adults do.

Montessori was skilled in designing special materials; she measured the educational appropriateness of these by how hard the children concentrated as they interacted with them. There are four basic types of materials: those for daily living, such as personal grooming, cooking, and clothing; sensory materials (visual, auditory, tactile, and olfactory); academic materials for language, reading, writing, and math; and cultural and artistic materials.

The child is first given a "fundamental lesson" in which he or she is shown how to take materials from a shelf, how to arrange them on a mat, and how to return them. After the child has explored the equipment, the teacher introduces the vocabulary that represents the concepts the child has been exploring.

Materials are introduced gradually. Only one type of each equipment is in the classroom. This helps children learn to respect the work of others and to cope with the realities they will meet in daily life. The appropriateness of the materials is measured by the degree of concentration, involvement, and satisfaction that the child experiences. When the child begins to experiment with possible new uses or begins to use an apparatus in fantasy play, it is time to introduce similar materials of greater difficulty.

Montessori's materials were all designed on the metric system. They are self-teaching in the sense that they vary in only one dimension at a time. They are self-correcting in that if children order the materials incorrectly, the errors will be obvious and can be corrected. This affords all children far greater autonomy and freedom to pace their own learning efforts.

Some of the Montessori equipment is designed to develop the skills necessary for future academic work. For example, in materials for handwriting preparation, children are shown how to lift and manipulate knobs on metal stencils; the point here is to develop finger and thumb co-ordination. They are then provided with paper and pencil and shown how to use the stencils to draw basic forms. Later, sandpaper letters are provided for developing "muscle memory" of the letter forms (Lay-Dopyera & Dopyera, 1990).

Children with disabilities The premise of the Montessori approach is that children will learn spontaneously if they are provided with a well-organized environment, tasks suited to their developmental level, and freedom to learn at their own pace. Programs are designed to enhance development in sensory skills, motor skills, and language. While it is true that children with disabilities will require more teacher direction than their peers, the environmental arrangements of Montessori schools are appropriate for young children with disabilities. The adapted materials are appealing; so are the approaches designed for children to work with these materials at their own pace.

Selecting an Approach for Children with Exceptionalities

The field of early childhood education includes several areas: infant, preschool, kindergarten, and the early elementary grades. Given this mix, early childhood education does not have a cohesive orientation or set of practices. Early childhood programs have evolved in various ways, and a number of models are available. Some programs are strongly committed to a particular model; others are more eclectic; most are continually being modified to be more immediately relevant to the needs of young children. Most models fall on a continuum, with the differences relating to content, structure, and methodology. We can see this in the outline of models in Table 6–1. However, all programs and almost all models have this as an underlying theme: the providing of a warm, supportive environment in which children can reach their full potential.

TABLE 6–1: Models in early childhood education

Model	Basic premise	Curricula; methods
Behaviourist	All learning results from environmental stimuli, particularly those which are rewarding or punishing. All behaviour must be overt and measurable.	Meticulously planned environment and program. Clear objectives, using task analyses; systems of reinforcement.
Cognitive-developmental	Stresses how children learn concepts, understand the world.	Active involvement with the environment; using skills and knowledge for problem solving. Focus on memory, language, thinking, problem solving.
Developmental	Normal physiological development produces steady, organizedpatterns of behaviour; learning results from the interaction of maturation and environment.	Stress on initiative, self-directed learning, manipulation of environment.
Functional	Extension of behavioural model; not a complete program.	Stresses acquisition of functional skills—life skills, skills for independent living, adaptive skills.

Head Start	Children need enrichment or programming to overcome deficits. Many programs include health, nutrition. Focus on parent involvement.	Teacher directed, small groups, behavioural orientation.
High Scope	Planned curriculum founded on Piagetian principles. Used with normally developing and disabled children.	Self-initiated learning. Stress on problem solving, language, developmentally appropriate practice.
Montessori	Provision of appropriate activities; teacher as facilitator.	Planned environment, special apparatus.
Piagetian	Theory-based developmental model; constructivist. Children construct their own knowledge in interaction with the environment.	Interaction with the environment stressed.
Portage	Home program for infants and toddlers. Parent training model.	Developmental curriculum using natural contexts and routines.

For children with special needs, there is no consensus about which model is the most useful. Indeed—as we pointed out at the beginning of this chapter—there is a lack of firm data to guide model selection. Moreover, the field is changing rapidly, and practices that are recommended today may be obsolete tomorrow.

Traditionally, the curriculum models that have been applied in early intervention for infants and young children with special needs are the developmental model, the developmental-cognitive model, and the behavioural model. Many early intervention programs merge two sets of principles: developmental and behavioural. Thus, developmental principles provide the content of teaching, and behavioural principles provide the methods.

Each model or combination of models has its advantages and its drawbacks. Educators have long debated whether directed learning (Head Start and behaviourism) is more or less effective than self-motivated learning (constructivist models). Some have seriously questioned whether the developmental model is useful for children with significant disabilities.

Many principles that arise from behavioural psychology remain important in the training and education of young children with disabilities, especially when those children have severe or multiple disabling conditions. Prompting, cuing, reinforcement, and other behavioural techniques have been found to be successful with this population.

Maturationalist (developmental) models use the concepts of maturation and readiness. They focus on helping children reach developmental norms, and hold that a child's behaviour reflects a certain stage of development. These models lack the specificity of behavioural programs, and emphasize those aspects of development that are least influenced by environmental factors. However, the normal sequence of development may not be an appropriate template for decisions about the educational and social needs of young children with severe disabilities. As teaching guides, theory-based models (such as those based on Piaget's work) are probably more useful than scales based on simple developmental milestones. In a theory-based model, items are organized around a specific skill and sequenced in an appropriate fashion (Bailey & Wolery, 1984).

In selecting a model for children with disabilities, educators must be pragmatic. Program models must be constantly modified to ensure their immediate relevance to young children and their families. Moreover, rigid adherence to one model will not allow personnel to meet the needs of all children. Programs must be adaptable, and pay attention to the particular strengths and weaknesses of each individual child. The chosen curriculum should be able to respond to each child's current level of skill and interest, and should be able to emphasize each child's unique pattern of development.

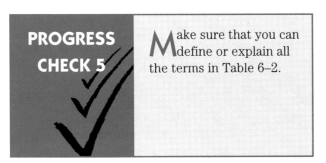

PROGRESS CHECK 5

Make sure that you can define or explain all the terms in Table 6–2.

TABLE 6–2: **New terms and ideas**

child development	maturational lags
curriculum	mental retardation
developmental milestones	model
developmental stage	reinforcer
functional skills	

SUMMARY

1. Within the field of early childhood education, teachers identify themselves with a variety of orientations, perspectives, and styles. Programs may be founded on a distinct philosophy or approach, or they may be eclectic and draw from many models.

2. Most models in early childhood education can be broadly categorized as behavioural or cognitive; in many ways, these schools of psychology constitute opposing philosophies. According to behaviourists, development occurs as a result of learning; this is in direct opposition to the views of Montessori and Piaget and their followers, who believe that new learning occurs as a result of development.

3. Behavioural psychology has contributed many techniques to the field of early intervention. Behavioural orientations are based on the learning principles of behavioural psychology. Behaviourists describe human development and learn-

ing as resulting from interactions with the environment that allow individuals to experience the relationships among stimuli, actions, and the consequences of actions. In this process, reward and punishment are central. For the behaviourist, only behaviour that can be observed and measured has psychological or educational value. Models based on behavioural principles emphasize the role of the environment in learning and employ basic behavioural principles to construct favourable environments. The chief goal of behavioural programs is repertoire expansion—that is, teaching, generalizing, and maintaining skills across domains.

4. Because it emphasizes task analysis and small accomplishments with much reinforcement, the behavioural model seems particularly well suited to children who are severely disabled.

5. For children with disabilities, functional approaches are an extension of the behavioural orientation. In functional approaches, skills to be taught are selected on the basis of their future usefulness. One basis for determining whether a skill is important is whether it represents a key behaviour at a particular stage of development (i.e., whether it is necessary for success in daily functioning, either now or in the future).

6. Biological-developmental theorists describe growth in holistic-interactionist terms. They hold that human development is genetically determined, and that because development is largely governed by maturation, the environment is a secondary concern. Thus, children's learning and thinking evolve systematically over time. Maturationalists generally stress that children develop as they grow older, whatever their earlier experience. They also suggest that experiences and tasks be provided that will allow children to build on the skills and knowledge they already possess.

7. Most curricula for children with severe disorders have adhered to a biological-developmental or a cognitive-developmental approach; however, there are some fundamental controversies regarding the utility of applying a developmental model for children with severe disabilities. It is argued that many young children with disabilities display developmental sequences that differ considerably from those observed in nonhandicapped children; it follows that it cannot be assumed that sequences of behaviour typically found in nondisabled children are relevant to severely handicapped children.

8. Cognitive theorists describe psychological growth in holistic, interactionist terms. They hold that from birth, organisms use, assimilate, and construct conceptions of their world. There is interaction between the environment and a child's innate abilities; it follows that children construct their own meanings of the world. Cognitive-developmental theory strongly emphasizes problem solving and individual thinking. Programs focus sharply on the whole child, and learning activities are highly experiential. These models encourage co-operation among peers, peer direction, spontaneous discovery, and problem solving.

9. Piaget's theories about children's cognitive development and thought processes have led to a clearer conception of how a child's own activities are central to

his or her understanding. Piaget postulated a sequence of universal stages of cognitive development, which he saw as occurring as a result of physiological growth and the child's interaction with the environment. Piaget's basic ideas have been highly influential in early childhood education.

10. Developmentally appropriate practice (DAP), recommended by the National Association for the Education of Young Children (NAEYC), is a broad term that has to do with identifying activities a child is ready to learn from within a continuum of developmentally sequenced objectives. DAP is based on the idea that children will learn when given support and guidance within a framework of child-initiated activities that promote active engagement of the child. The curriculum is fitted to meet the needs of the child, not vice versa. There are two components to developmentally appropriate programs: age appropriateness and individualization.

11. Maria Montessori moved theory into the practical and concrete world. She developed ways of working with children that contrasted sharply with the practices of her time. She began with mentally retarded children and then derived and proposed general principles of education that held wide appeal and were later adapted to normally developing children.

12. There are a number of different program models in ECSE. We still do not know which model is most effective for children with disabilities. If programs are integrated and developmentally appropriate, it is probably best if teachers are eclectic and draw what they need from various models.

CHAPTER 7
Creating the environment

CASE STUDY

Josie

Three-and-a-half-year-old Josie has been enrolled in the local daycare centre for almost a year. In this full-day program, Josie is beginning to enjoy the materials and activities. She especially likes story and circle times, and singing. Josie showed some initial shyness, but this faded quickly and now she interacts with her peers very well.

Josie is legally blind, the result of a congenital condition of unknown origin. She retains a small amount of residual vision in the left eye, and this seems to provide her with some light stimuli. Intervention for Josie began in the first months of her life. She now uses a white cane for mobility and is learning to be more skillful. Because she still has some vision, glasses have been prescribed for her, but she resists these vigorously.

Josie was the first child with a disability to enrol in this daycare centre. At first, the staff were hesitant about accepting a child with such an obvious disability and such special needs. They worried that they would not be able to program for, communicate with, or manage a child with a severe visual impairment. Also, they weren't sure how a visual impairment affected a child's development, or how to modify the class program, the environmental arrangements, and the play areas. They had some additional concerns about the other children, who began to "play blind." However, this phase did not last long. A psychologist explained that it was only a stage, and that it does help children to learn about the limitations imposed by blindness.

The teachers quickly realized that their expectations about Josie had been bounded by stereotypes about the disability, and that they had been wrong to consider the visual impairment first, rather than the child. They soon found Josie to be a bright, outgoing child who participated in almost all the centre's activities, including play, group times, and outdoor activities. Sometimes, in fact, Josie was *too* eager to try new experiences; as a result, certain environmental precautions, especially in outdoor play, were necessary. Josie has some difficulty judging heights, and changes in contour and surface texture. The teachers have had to learn ways to make Josie a little more careful in these situations without making her dependent on them.

Indoors, few adaptations have been necessary. The teachers are careful to keep walking spaces clear of obstacles, to always tell Josie if something has been moved, and to leave doors open or shut consistently. At first, a buddy helped Josie with transitions between activities, but she quickly learned her way around the centre alone.

Although Josie participates in all of the centre's activities, the teachers have drawn up some individualized goals and objectives for her. For visually impaired children, the broad goal of early intervention is to strengthen the unimpaired sensory channels. To this end, the teachers have provided additional activities for her in the auditory, kinesthetic, tactile, olfactory, and taste modalities.

Josie has also needed a little help with her language skills. Too often, she uses "verbalisms"—that is, words that have no experiential basis. To correct this, Josie needs more direct interaction with people and objects, as well as practice in language arts, descriptive and conversational skills, and role playing. The only specialized help Josie needs at the centre is a visiting teacher, who works with her on orientation and mobility skills. Josie's IPP is shown later in this chapter.

The first thing the specialist did was work with the teachers to acquaint Josie with the layout of the classroom. This process had four stages. After Josie and the teacher established a *key landmark*—the door to the classroom—Josie worked on *perimeter orientation*—that is, the configuration of the entire classroom. The teacher talked Josie through the peripheral boundaries and explained the key furnishings in each area. They then moved on to *cross-room exploration*, which involved Josie learning to move from one centre to another. The specialist showed the teachers how to give Josie clues by clapping hands or tapping a table. Finally, Josie learned about the furnishings and equipment in *specific centres*.

TEACHERS OF STUDENTS OF ALL AGES MUST KNOW how to organize environments in an effective way. Well-organized environments promote a warm and supportive space in which optimal learning and socialization can take place and problem behaviours are kept to a minimum.

In preschool settings, effective organization of the environment is especially critical. The overriding aim of early childhood programs should be to create an environment in which all children can maximize their development. Settings should encourage quality interactions between children and materials, activities, and people.

Studies to identify influences on child development have shown that children's use of materials and the ways they interact with peers and adults are particularly significant factors in learning. It follows that if children's potential is to be fully realized, both the learning environment and the children's own characteristics must be considered. Early childhood personnel must organize environments that provide three types of stimulation: sensory, affective, and social. Environments must be effective in shaping behaviour; in stimulating play, curiosity, and movement; in facilitating social interactions; and in promoting learning and development across all domains.

For the child, every aspect of the preschool experience is affected by the environment. For the teacher, environment and curriculum are inseparable. This means that an early childhood environment is not one single thing; rather, it includes many different components. In preparing and maintaining the environment, teachers must pay attention to access, traffic patterns, visual impact, the arrangement and use of space, light and sound sources, the selection and use of equipment and materials, and material storage. Still other components of the environment are the curriculum, the pattern and quality of interactions, the presence of other persons, the amount of structure, the organization of time, procedures for meeting with parents, rules for working with aides and volunteers, and the rules for children's behaviour.

When young children with disabilities are being integrated, environmental organization is particularly important. In this regard, the key is to ensure "that environments for handicapped infants and preschoolers facilitate children's development of social, motor, communication, self-help, cognitive, and behavioral skills, and enhance children's self-concept, sense of competence and control, and independence" (Bailey, Palsha, & Huntington, 1994, p. 198).

The process of organizing the environment includes making environmental interventions and adaptations. *Environmental interventions* are when teachers physically rearrange the setting to foster interactions; this can mean restructuring play areas, providing activities that promote social interaction, and providing a socially competent group. Interventions can also consist of exposing the children to alternative strategies for achieving competence; this can mean changes in the targeted skill or skill sequence; in the ways that small groups are formed and taught; in the level of participation expected; in the kinds of materials used; and in the nature of cues and support required. Environmental interventions are discussed in relation to skill development in Chapters 10 to 15.

Sometimes integration demands special modifications and adaptations. Whether these mean changes in space, in activities, in scheduling, or in structure will depend on the child's individual needs. For example, Nancy, the deaf child we met early in this book, can be assisted by some quite specific environmental alterations. Because Nancy learns entirely through visual modes, important strategies for her include provision of a stimulating visual environment and natural lighting to assist speech reading. A carpeted floor and sound-proofed ceilings would help her get the most from her hearing aid. Josie, although legally blind, has some residual vision in one eye. She too needs strong natural light in a stable space where she can learn to move with comfort and confidence. For Darrin on his scooter board, space between equipment and dividers is necessary so that he can move from activity to activity with ease.

This chapter presents some ideas on how the learning environment can be adapted—in the sense of space, activities, and materials—both generally and for specific groups of children with disabilities. We include outdoor space in this, and discuss how a well-designed, integrated playground can permit disabled and nondisabled children to play together. Materials and toys are also discussed in this chapter. (Toys for specific groups of children are examined in Chapter 11.) We also discuss some specific adaptations that children bring to the classroom, such as wheelchairs and hearing aids. Further aspects of environment creation and management are addressed in later chapters. Scheduling is discussed in Chapter 10, and classroom management in Chapter 12.

BOX 7–1
Visual impairments

In simplest terms, the human eye can be seen as having three parts: the eye itself, which picks up visual messages; the optic nerve, which transfers the messages; and the brain, which interprets the messages. Images are passed through the eye and along the optic nerve to the brain by light. When anything stops or hinders the passage of the light, visual problems occur.

Many of us are well aware of myopia, hyperopia, and astigmatism; all three problems occur when the light does not fall on the retina correctly because the eyeball is too long or too short. Such minor visual impairments are extremely common. Severe visual impairments and blindness, such as we see in Josie and Kasha, are low-incidence conditions.

A vision specialist, usually an ophthalmologist, assesses visual acuity and functioning. Eye examinations are given to identify any refractive errors (myopia, hyperopia, astigmatism), which can then be corrected; to obtain information about visual abilities; to measure visual fields (i.e., angle of view); and to make recommendations that will promote optimum visual functioning.

The most common procedure for measuring central vision acuity uses the Snellen Chart, which consists of a series of letters, numbers, or symbols, which must be read from a distance of about 6.5 metres. Each line is a different size and corresponds to a standard distance at which its items can be distinguished by a person with normal vision. This gives the measure 20/20 vision. The Symbol E Chart is especially suitable for young children and for those who cannot read. With this chart, only Es pointing in different directions are used.

The results provide important information for teachers. The amount of residual vision a child has depends greatly on the type of visual impairment. So does how children use their vision. The results also suggest whether the eye condition is stable or deteriorating, and whether it is operable.

Teachers may be the first to notice that a child has a visual impairment. These are some signs of mild visual impairment:

- One eye turns in or out.
- In near work, the child squints, or closes or covers one eye.
- While looking at near or far objects, the child rubs eyes often, or squints, or shakes his or her head.
- The child tilts head or crosses eyes.
- The child seems afraid of walking down stairs, climbing, or running freely.
- The child often falls or bumps into objects.
- The child holds objects very close to the eyes, or very far from them.
- The child's eye movements seem abnormal.
- The child complains of fuzzy or blurred vision.
- The child has reddened eyes or eyelids, encrusted eyelids, frequent sties, frequent eye infections, swollen eyelids, or watery eyes.

Sight is one of the most important of the human senses. A severe sight impairment affects many other areas of a child's functioning, most particularly motor and mobility skills. Blind infants acquire early motor skills such as sitting and standing at about the same time as other children, but they may be slower in crawling and walking. Delays in walking until 16 to 19 months are common in blind children; and even children with sufficient vision for orientation and mobility may show delays in ambulation, as well as a lack of confidence. Factors that contribute to delays in mobility include a lack of interest in the environment owing to the visual loss, a lack of models for ambulation, and a lack of visual righting reactions (which impedes the development of balance).

Visually impaired children may also be slower than their peers to acquire self-help skills such as dressing, feeding, and toileting. As well, blind children often have special needs relating to self-awareness, self-esteem, and social skills. Visual impairment causes unique differences in how a healthy self-image emerges; it also tends to interfere with spontaneous social activity and communication. Blind children face obstacles in obtaining the full benefits of peer interaction. They may have trouble acquiring interpersonal skills. They often behave in ways that decrease effective interaction with peers.

Children with severe visual impairments may fail to make expected eye contact with peers, and typically will not smile. When they do not look at people, this is often interpreted as disinterest rather than as a manifestation of the condition. These children possess no sense of appropriate head and facial movements during conversation. The visually impaired child is unable to utilize those visual clues which are necessary for the modelling and feedback that are the foundation of social skill acquisition. These children miss many of the important nonverbal cues that teachers and peers would otherwise provide through facial expressions, gestures, and body language (Scott, 1982).

The early development of visually handicapped children is often more a function of early experiences, family support, and stimulation than of the degree of visual impairment. For visually impaired preschoolers such as Josie, early experiences in integrated settings create a sense of belonging and self-reliance. Integration helps children born with visual deficits to learn what the culture expects in the way of behaviour and mannerisms. Sighted and visually impaired children learn from each other, make friends, and recognize their strengths and abilities relative to others.

In early childhood, children with severe visual impairments need training in all the other senses; this helps them compensate for the loss of vision. Attention must be paid to their gross motor skills (for mobility) and fine motor skills (for independent functioning). These children tend to use their hands in broad, sweeping motions, and fail to acquire precise search and grasp skills. As a result, they have weak hands and fingers and so need to take part in activities such as clay manipulation. They also benefit from squeeze toys, peg boards, and puzzles.

Some children require consistent vision stimulation. Visual skills include attention to lights and objects; tracing and scanning; and figure–ground discrimination. With body image, students need to learn to identify body parts. Visual perception encompasses object discrimination, the use of pictures, sorting and classification, and sequencing.

Environmental planning

Teachers enhance children's physical and mental development when they create play environments that are both complex and accessible. All environments, for both normally developing and disabled children, have some common characteristics and serve certain common functions. These features characterize all good environments for young children:

- They are aesthetically pleasing. Classrooms should be safe and tidy. A neat and clean activity centre is more likely to prompt use.
- They are orderly and consistent—neither confusing nor too subdued. In most early childhood settings, bright displays of children's creative expression dominate. These are appealing to the eye and reinforcing for children.
- They provide nurturance and reinforcement. A nurturing environment is pleasant and warm and promotes a sense of security and trust.
- They foster personal identity.
- They encourage the development of competence.
- They provide opportunities for growth.
- They allow both social interaction and privacy. There should be retreat areas (i.e., places for informal socialization and for privacy). Programs serving severely disabled children often contribute to maladaptive behaviour by ignoring individuals' needs for privacy (Baker, 1980).
- They have individual work areas.
- They are free of physical barriers.

- They provide repetition and multiple coding. Programs must be rich with information for the senses and have a range of environmental stimuli.

- They promote the children's engagement with the environment. Children's behaviour develops and changes through the relationship between the child's behaviour and environmental stimuli. Much evidence points out that a carefully managed classroom can significantly improve a child's behaviour. Often, caregivers do not have the time or expertise to implement detailed behaviour management procedures; for this reason, it is critical that the physical and programmatic features of early childhood programs work together to stimulate appropriate behaviour, prevent behaviour problems, and maintain an atmosphere that supports exploration and stimulates cognitive growth.

The process of adapting the environment for children with disabilities is only a variation on the process of adapting the environment for all children. All children need an appropriate, stimulating, and challenging environment. Simply placing a child with a disability in a supportive and stimulating environment is not enough: a number of modifications in environment, planning, curriculum (i.e., program), assessment, and attitudes may well be necessary in order to enhance the developmental outcomes for young children with disabilities.

The actual physical environment is the first consideration. Teachers should analyse the classroom's physical environment from the perspective of the exceptional child and make any necessary modifications to ensure that activities are accessible. They will probably find that when equipping a classroom to accommodate children with disabilities, they will have to consider safety, space, lighting, and abundant opportunities for movement.

If children with mobility problems are at the centre, teachers will also need to accommodate special mobility devices and positioning needs (see Chapter 13). Also, children with visual impairments such as Josie may have special equipment for mobility and for vision. Nancy, our deaf child, will use an individual hearing aid.

LIGHT

The design and placement of walls, windows, and doorways affects the behaviour of those using the area. Some aspects of a setting, such as the size and shape of rooms, the placement of windows, and the floor and ceiling materials, will be static and so difficult to change. Even so, some modifications can always be made for children with disabilities, especially for those with sensory impairments of vision or hearing.

Lighting should be considered. Speech reading (lip reading) by a deaf child is easier in a room with natural rather than fluorescent lighting. When speaking with the child, teachers should ensure that the light is on the teacher's face rather than the child's.

Lighting is equally important for a child with a visual impairment. Here, the type of impairment determines lighting needs. Many children with visual impairments require bright, natural light. Josie, for example, requires as much natural light as possible so that she can fully use her residual vision. However, some children with a visual impairment need muted lighting—especially when the visual disability is the result of albinism.

SPACE ARRANGEMENTS

Another consideration in environmental planning is the organization of available space. Spatial organization determines the degree of structure and responsiveness. That is, the way physical space is used signals to the children what they can do and how active they can be.

In an integrated program the major considerations in planning the indoor space are the same as for any regular preschool or child care program. Spaces should be attractive and usable by all. The playroom should be open, with a variety of play areas accessible to children. Open arrangements ensure that there is no visual obstruction. Barriers should be no more than 50 to 120 centimetres high.

Children show more goal-oriented behaviour and less passivity in open environments than they do in more closed arrangements (Dunst et al., 1986). Social interactions between disabled and non-disabled children are more frequent when play areas contain few barriers and when play materials can be used by more than one child at a time (Raab et al., 1986). As well, open arrangements have a positive effect on staff supervision practices, and this in turn can lead to high levels of child engagement.

Cubbies, bulletin boards, materials, and chalkboards should be within the reach of all children. Each child needs an individual storage space. To give children a sense of personal ownership, bins, cubbies, and boxes may be used. To encourage autonomy, children need to be able to change their space, and to be able to make decisions about where things belong and about how they are kept.

SAFETY

The environment must be safe for young children. That means it must be in good repair and free of hazards. In particular, spills must be wiped up right away, floors must be kept clean, and pushing or running in the classroom or the halls must not be allowed. For children with disabilities, the early environment should be childproof. This involves the following:

- Modifying or padding sharp edges of furniture or materials.
- Supervising play materials with small parts.
- Being certain that paint on walls, toys, and so on is lead free.
- Covering electrical outlets.
- Keeping medical and cleaning supplies locked away.
- Covering hot-water faucets with protectors.
- Supervising play at water tables and when using gross-motor play equipment.
- Using floor play for most activities.
- Ensuring that standing and climbing equipment is sturdy, and using it under close supervision.
- Having nonslip floor coverings.
- Keeping toys off the floor.
- Removing equipment that is easily overturned.
- Keeping disposable plastic gloves or plastic bags in the bathroom area for handling diapers and other toileting procedures.

It is important to teach all children safety precautions associated with the use of a walker, crutches, or a wheelchair. Note that wheelchairs need extra room. The child with a physical disability should be taught to place crutches and other aids in places where others will not trip over them.

STORAGE

Early childhood programs require a great deal of storage, both accessible storage within the classroom and closed storage. Generally, place in open storage only those things you wish children to use.

Children need to learn the appropriate use of materials by experimentation; for this reason, current materials should be displayed. When toys are stored on shelves and within children's lines of sight and within their reach, play is encouraged. Here are some ideas for displaying materials:

- Make sure that an array of standard items is always available in low storage.
- Use shelves rather than toy boxes for storing and displaying materials. Montes and Risley (1975) compared the use of shelves and boxes and found that storing manipulative toys in boxes increased the amount of time children spent selecting toys; this reduced active play time.
- Store large items such as blocks and trucks on open shelves; place small items such as beads, cubes, and crayons in containers.
- Have plenty of room on the shelves.
- Show children how and where things are to be stored, and insist that they follow these expectations.
- Set up a system for sharing toys.

For some children, too many materials on display is distracting. For others, the use of toys is closely tied to individual goals and objectives (e.g., promoting individual or co-operative play, or learning to share). In these situations, teachers may find it helpful to be more structured in the storage and use of toys.

When fewer toys are available, crowded shelves are eliminated and sharing, co-operative play, and peer modelling of imaginative and creative play all increase. It is useful to label and mark toys by different categories (e.g., sensorimotor) or by age levels and then to rotate groups of toys. Use all categories of toys: manipulatives, building toys, play materials, dramatic play objects, and visual-motor toys. McGee and colleagues (1991) suggest that teachers consider these approaches:

- Make an inventory of toys; code them according to dimensions of size, complexity, developmental level, category, and sensory quality.
- Divide the toys into 12 sets of 10 items each, with at least one toy in each set representing each dimension. For example, have one toy in each set at a low developmental level (6 to 24 months) and one at a high level (4 to 6 years).
- Keep two rotation sets in the classroom at any one time. Begin with sets 1 and 2. At the end of the week, remove set 1 and replace it with set 3. Keep up this ro-

LEARNING ACTIVITY 1

Spend some time in an early childhood setting. Using the steps outlined by McGee and colleagues, make an inventory of the toys. Code them for size, complexity, developmental level, category, and sensory quality.

tation so that each week there is a new set of toys. However, dolls, dress-up costumes, and books should remain in the environment at all times.

ACTIVITY AREAS

Many early childhood programs use activity areas (or centres). Activity areas are an appropriate use of space; there is evidence that children become more engaged in activities when the indoor space is arranged in well-defined activity areas (Moore, 1986).

Independent and semi-independent use of activity areas is a reasonable goal for most preschoolers with special needs. Children with severe or multiple disabilities may need activity areas that address more basic skills, or they may need additional support such as adult intervention or adaptive equipment.

Centres should invite children to come, see, do, and learn. Well-defined and effective activity areas have certain characteristics:

- They are carefully planned and organized to meet the needs of the children using the centre.
- They have a specific location with visible boundaries.
- The activity areas are linked, both physically and conceptually.
- The activity areas don't "distract" each other. Teachers must anticipate that different activities will occur at the same time and plan space so that they don't disrupt one another. Block building, for example, is a noisy activity, so the centre should be placed as far as possible from quiet areas such as the reading centre.
- The arrangements allow control by staff. For example, if the teacher wants to label children's paintings during an art activity, the art area should allow visual scanning of the rest of the room.
- There are surfaces for both work and sitting.
- There is adequate space for both storage and materials display.
- The colours are bright, and the materials are soft.
- For children in wheelchairs or using other ambulatory aids, the activity tables are set away from the walls so that children can reach them from all sides.
- The furniture is the correct size. Tables should meet children below the chest. Tables with semicircular "bites" allow children to get closer. A rim around the edge prevents small objects from being knocked off (Deiner, 1983; Lay-Dopyera & Dopyera, 1990; Olds, 1987).

Many types of activity areas are found in early childhood settings: a "discovery centre," dramatic play, block building, art, books, and so on. Below, we outline some of the major types.

Dramatic play   This activity area, found in almost every preschool, allows children to act out real-life roles. It often takes the form of a housekeeping centre.

Dodge and Frost (1986) suggest that changing the contents of the dramatic play area and supplementing children's knowledge with both direct and vicarious experiences, such as books, film strips, field trips, visitors, and discussions, can result in increased use of the area.

It is important to keep the dramatic play centre neat and orderly—especially the clothes and equipment. Eliminate or monitor closely the use of materials that a number of children may use, such as combs and brushes.

BOX 7–2
Josie's IPP

NAME: *Josie*
CENTRE: *Greenheath*
AGE: *3—6*
SUPERVISOR: *Ms. Jones*

Report number: 2
Josie has been in the centre for almost a year. During this time, she has been working on individual goals and objectives embedded within the daily routines and activities of the centre.

Progress
Two overriding goals were established for Josie when she first entered the setting. The first was to develop security in the environment and in moving about in it. The second was to help Josie develop her other senses, especially audition and touch.

Assessment
At the request of the parents, an assessment of Josie's progress was undertaken. The full assessment included a psychological report as well as observations and informal checklists provided by the teachers.

The results of a vision assessment were also available. It showed Josie's acuity to be in the range of legally blind. However, it also showed that she used her residual vision to the maximum extent (except for the glasses).

Present levels of functioning:
Cognitive: The report of the psychologist confirms the observations of the teachers: Josie is functioning somewhat above the norm. This can be seen in her test results, and in her language, problem-solving skills, and activities at the centre.
Language: Josie demonstrates strong language skills, although she requires more experience in some areas. She asks many questions and shows much natural curiosity.
Behaviour: Josie is an outgoing child and is well accepted by her peers. She enjoys group work and small-group play.
Motor: Josie's gross motor skills are developing; she receives ongoing assistance with orientation and mobility from a specialist teacher. Fine motor skills are lagging a little, probably because of the visual impairment. Josie needs many more concrete experiences, and to learn by doing.
Adaptive equipment: Josie is learning to use a white cane, although she rarely uses it in the school setting. She has had glasses prescribed, but is extremely adverse to wearing them and has become quite adept at forgetting the glasses or hiding then in her cubby.

Long-range goals
To strengthen the other senses.

Short-term objectives
To improve auditory skills through identification and localization of sound.

Blocks

Blocks provide children with opportunities to learn many concepts, such as problem solving and height and size. They also encourage dramatic play, social interaction, and co-operation. Block play facilitates muscle and eye/hand co-ordination and offers multisensory experiences.

At the centre there should be both wooden blocks and hollow blocks. There should be sufficient materials that a number of children can play; this will keep disputes to a minimum. Especially helpful are toys that have a built-in tolerance for error, such as blocks that fit together even if the child does not match them perfectly (Deiner, 1983). For children in wheelchairs, provide sided oven trays or cookie trays for blocks.

Procedures:

a. *Identify familiar sounds on a tape. Repeat patterns of drum beats, hand claps, feet stamps.*

b. *Find the direction of a sound. Attract auditory and then visual attention by ringing a bell near the object to be looked at.*

c. *Use noise-making toys.*

d. *Search for a loudly ticking clock.*

e. *In small groups, identify "Who said that?"*

Objective: To improve tactile discrimination.

Procedures:

a. *Identify pictures and objects through touch. Match objects to pictures done in sandpaper.*

b. *Match picture to object and describe orally.*

c. *Match and sort textured materials.*

d. *Match and sort block shapes by touch.*

e. *Surprise bag of familiar objects to identify.*

Objective: To improve taste and smell awareness.

Procedures:

a. *Smell box of safe but not really edible items such as toothpaste and orange peel. (Care in this area is crucial, as Josie may not be very discriminating regarding what is safely edible.)*

b. *Simple food preparation.*

Objective: To improve social interaction through teaching appropriate smiling behaviour.

Procedures:

a. *Reinforce Josie whenever she smiles appropriately.*

b. *Model appropriate smiling behaviour (use touch).*

c. *Tell Josie how important it is to smile at other individuals. Have her practice smiling at the teacher, and reinforce.*

d. *Prompt smiling in natural play situations through direct instruction, such as "Josie, smile when you look at Teresa."*

e. *Prompt smiling in natural play situations through indirect comments or noticing another child smiling, such as "Josie, look at Teresa's big smile" (after Bailey & Wolery, 1984).*

Objective: Visual stimulation, to encourage the use of residual vision.

Procedure: Provide slide projector, flashlight, mobiles, and bright objects during free play. Use incidentally.

Objective: To prompt Josie to wear her glasses.

Procedures:

a. *Tell Josie, "We'll put your glasses on for a little while," when she is involved in an activity. Begin with periods of two or three minutes.*

b. *Monitor wearing glasses, comment favourably, reinforce.*

c. *Gradually extend time for wearing during free play. At the same time, extend to other areas such as small-group time.*

Blocks are popular toys with young children.

Sand and water play

Sand and water play and play with clay, plasticine, and playdo provide similar positive experiences. This type of play provides excellent sensory experiences, helps develop physical knowledge, and allows many opportunities for role playing, social interaction, and the development of language skills.

Children with a visual impairment may not want to take part in this type of play; they use their hands for information gathering and may not want to get them dirty. However, they will be missing out on exploratory behaviour, and should be encouraged as much as possible.

Reading, language arts

Reading and language centres give children a chance to be quiet, to relax, and to be exposed to books and other language materials. It may be a good idea to provide two or more copies of popular books. The centre can also include a tape recorder, a flannel board with story pictures or magnetic letters, and writing materials.

For children who are visually impaired, such as Josie, use larger pictures or materials. Totally blind children require materials that provide information through the other senses; these children may enjoy textures and "scratch and sniff" books. Visual materials need to be relatively uncluttered, consisting of simple stimulus patterns. For example, photographs of single, real, everyday objects are probably of more interest than picture books with busy detailed drawings. Teachers can also introduce storybooks that have clear plastic overlap pages with braille. These books, called touch-and-see books, are available from many local libraries and local branches of the Canadian National Institute for the Blind (CNIB).

Children with physical disabilities may require specialized equipment. Page turners and book stands will assist them in reading, and magnetized pencils and equipment will be helpful for writing and drawing. Children who show little interest in books may use the centre more if materials are made more familiar and personal. For example, a child might read and reread a captioned book of his or her own photographs from home.

Art

Art activities provide opportunities for creative expression, for practising fine and perceptual motor skills, and for applying language concepts relating to form, shape, colour, texture, and spatial

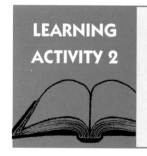

LEARNING ACTIVITY 2

Prepare a lesson plan showing how you would introduce Josie to playing with clay or plasticine. Include another peer and add social interaction as an objective.

A reading/writing centre is important in an early childhood setting

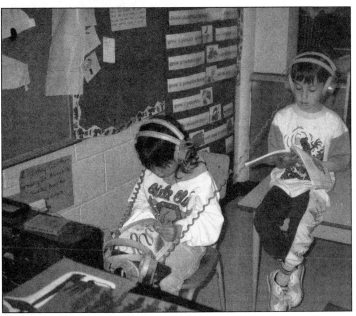
Many preschools are equipped with listening centres.

relationships. (Children's art and art activities are discussed in Chapter 13.) The degree of planning and structure in the art centre depends on the developmental level of the children. Painting on an easel, for example, is more restricting than finger painting on a tabletop.

Woodworking   This is the setting for practising many motor and grasping movements. Children here are provided with the opportunity to use wood and real tools in a constructive manner. The woodworking centre needs a tool storage pegboard, low shelves for tools that cannot be hung, small containers for nails and other small items, and a work space.

Some children with disabilities may need tools made of a material other than wood. Styrofoam pieces can be used for hammering, screwing, and sawing.

Computer centre   The microcomputer, with its adaptability and re-active characteristics, can be an integral part of the preschool environment. Young children are enthusiastic about computers and show curiosity, playfulness, and positive affect when working with them (e.g. Corning & Halapin, 1989).

Three-year-olds take longer to acclimatize to the keyboard than do five-year-olds; otherwise, there are no other major differences in how younger and older preschoolers use computers (Essa, 1987; Sivin, Lee, & Voltmar, 1985). Very young children can use the standard keyboard, change software, and work together at a computer station with minimal instruction. Among elementary children, interest persists even after months of using programs such as LOGO (Clements, 1985); in preschool children, attention spans are longer with computers than with other activities (Hutinger, 1987).

Among young children with disabilities, computers have been used to enhance functioning and assist in the learning of specific tasks. Whether they are

Computers hold many benefits for young children with disabilities.

used as educational tools or as prosthetic devices, computers provide sensory input, enhance mobility, develop cognitive and language skills, strengthen motor and perceptual functioning, and facilitate communication (Clements, 1985).

Computers can stimulate cognitive functioning. Garner and Campbell (1987), for example, used computers in integrated environments to develop specific cognitive skills in a wide variety of functional activities. Computer programs are simple, based on the way children learn. Children may first learn about cause and effect: by pressing a switch when prompted by an artificial voice, they can make a happy face appear. Then they can learn to choose between two possibilities—for example, to press switches to choose certain pictures of toys. They may then proceed to games in which they match a stimulus picture to one of two choices on the computer. A correct match operates a toy or appliance (Behrmann, 1984).

Computers have the potential to facilitate social interaction among both disabled and nondisabled preschoolers. The computer can act as an equalizer, allowing children who are physically disabled or speech/language impaired to engage in social interactions. Alternative input devices allow children with the most severe physical limitations to enjoy independent access to computer programs that can be played with a friend. For example, a computer program called Switch Handler allows severely disabled young children to engage in a variety of activities not previously available to them, including computer-generated turn-taking activities.

For other special needs children who are not often interested in other people or comfortable with them, a computer may serve as a catalyst for social interaction. In computer environments, children who work in pairs spontaneously teach, help, and praise each other, and ask more questions of each other than of their teachers (Borgh & Dickson, 1986).

For nonvocal children, computers with built-in speech promote autonomy. One child used a computer with voice output to give Simon Says commands to classmates (Mirenda & Schuyler, 1988). For disabled preschoolers, computer activity is more effective than toy play in stimulating vocalization (McCormick, 1987).

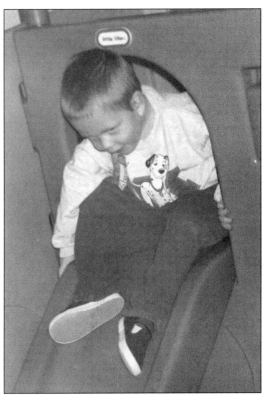

A centre should be set up with sturdy indoor equipment.

Selection of Equipment and Materials

In the preschool or kindergarten classroom, children need many opportunities for activity, exploration, and manipulation. Play equipment should stimulate interest, spark curiosity, and provide graduated challenges. It should increase spatial awareness; develop fine and gross motor skills; encourage creativity and imagination; and encourage self-sufficiency and self-esteem. Activities must be designed and materials used that provide an adequate blend of familiarity and novelty. Each planned activity should offer all children a chance of success at some level.

Equipment should cover a broad range of developmental levels. In general, normally developing children around age two respond well to blocks, dishes, pull and wind-up toys, and dolls. Three-year-olds prefer books, clothes, puppets, and such toys as a barn with animals or a street with houses and stores. Kindergarten and early-elementary children respond best to toys with many pieces and to puppets and action figures (Owens, 1991; See Box 7–3.

BOX 7–3
Play Equipment

Because more learning takes place between birth and six years than at any other time in a child's life, parents and early childhood educators tend to be especially concerned about the impact of toys during this period. Toys are sheer fun for children, but they are also important tools for understanding the world. Toys have amusement value, and assist in a child's physical and mental development, and facilitate interaction between parent and child—and all of these things simultaneously.

Toys and play materials best enhance an infant's exploratory play if they can be manipulated in a variety of ways that infants can perceive. For example, toys that make sounds when moved are better when the sound-making parts are visible, as with a bell whose clapper children can see and touch, or a rattle made of a clear material. Simple, attractive, homemade playthings can be as effective as commercially made products.

In our culture, toys are usually manufactured products purchased for the sole purpose of entertaining children. As such, they reflect the range of variety and sophistication of our complicated world. There are excellent toys as well as horrible rubbish. Millions are spent each year on toys, and certainly some of this money is spent badly (and even harmfully), either because the toys don't last, or because they are given at the wrong age, or because they are potentially dangerous.

Each year, the toy industry in the United States introduces more than 5,000 new products (Mergen, 1982) and racks up over

$12 billion in sales (Oppenheim, 1987). Barbie has generated over one billion dollars in sales over her career. In 1980 a doll named Strawberry Shortcake revolutionized marketing for toys by earning over one billion dollars in her three-year stint of popularity. In 1985 toy manufacturers spent a total of $160,866,500 on television advertising alone (Oppenheim, 1987).

Today's toys are no longer sold as single items; they are often accompanied by entire lines of merchandise. For example, Strawberry had her friends Lemon Meringue and Peaches 'n Cream; she also had movies and a television cartoon, and accessories and accommodations; she was on linens and lunch boxes, notebooks and greeting cards, pyjamas and a host of other consumer goods. Through advertising, children decide they want a certain toy and its accompanying lines. Soon, however, trends change. Thus begins the cycle of child wants toy, then child gets toy, then child ignores toy (Erickson, 1993).

Even in this world of technology and gadgetry, it still appears that children prefer simple toys. Gottfried and Brown (1986) conducted an experiment in which children were offered a choice of two rooms. One room contained a wizardry of mechanical toys, the other ordinary blocks. At first, most children chose the room with the mechanical toys. Eventually, however, they became bored with these, and soon all of the children were playing in the room with the blocks.

When choosing toys for home and school, consider these points:

- Choose toys that allow freedom of imagination—that allow children to experiment. It is important that children invent their own playthings, and that parents and teachers allow children to use toys in their own way. Rarely do children use toys in the way the manufacturer intended (Erickson, 1993).

- The more play possibilities a toy has, the more interest it has for children. Versatile toys are those which can be used in many ways by many children.

- Quality is important. One doll with many dresses that will last is preferable to a toy that breaks in a few hours.

- The size of the toy should be appropriate for the child. Huge stuffed toys may appeal to adults, but they are often too unwieldy for small children.

- The material should be appropriate. Wood and plastic are best for young children.

- The toy should be safe, with no pieces that can be chewed, swallowed, or poked.

If children are to enjoy the instruction, the task's difficulty must be appropriate to current levels of performance. That is, the task must be slightly beyond the child's present ability so that it is challenging. It must not be boring, or too easy, or so difficult as to seem insurmountable (Noonan & McCormick, 1993).

Toys and activities should promote social interaction among non-disabled and disabled children, as well as the specific goals and objectives for the child with special needs. Some equipment and materials have a greater potential than others for promoting social interaction. For non-disabled preschoolers, wagons, hollow blocks, dramatic play materials, and games that require two players are best (Quiltich & Risley, 1973). The same has been found for preschoolers with disabilities (Peterson & Haralick, 1977; Stoneman, Cantrell, & Hoover-Dempsey, 1983). Dolls and housekeeping materials also encourage socially interactive play.

BOX 7–4

Helpful hints

Working with children with visual disabilities

- Check the lighting needs of each child.
- Don't move furniture or equipment without first telling the child.
- Make the child aware of low-level landmarks such as variations in flooring (wood, tile, rugs of different textures, and so on). Also, use mid-level landmarks of varying configurations: large metal wastebaskets, fuzzy stickers, braille labels, and the like.
- Provide vivid, concrete, practical experiences.
- Encourage the use of other sensory modalities in exploring the environment, and the use of any remaining vision to interpret visual stimuli more efficiently. Multisensory approaches combine inputs from more than one sense at a time; in so doing they provide extra information to the child and, thus, more depth to the concepts being formed.
- For children with poor vision, provide higher-intensity visual stimulation to arouse interest. Objects should be shiny, brightly coloured (preferably in primary colours), and of reasonable size. They should be presented close to the eyes, and there should be strong contrast between the objects and the background.
- Provide relatively uncluttered visual materials; such materials should offer simple stimulus patterns.
- Allow children to hold objects as close to their eyes as they wish. Children will find their own optimal viewing distance.

- Avoid glare on furniture and paper.
- Use materials with good tactile characteristics.
- In art, define the boundaries of the paper by using picture frames taped to the paper. Or glue string around the edge of the paper.
- Children with severe visual impairments rely more on language; the teacher must "talk things through." Use language to help children focus their vision as well as to provide feedback. For example, "I hear some children going downstairs. Do you remember when we went down yesterday? I wonder where the children are going."
- Be specific in language. Do not use artificial, contrived, or unnatural verbal behaviour.
- Provide many clues to the environment. For example, alert the child to the bubbling of an aquarium for the science area, a rug for the reading area, and wind chimes for the outside door (Deiner, 1983).
- When speaking to the child, stand still. A moving voice is difficult for a blind child to follow.
- Teaching visually impaired children means dealing not only with those who have uncorrectable problems but also with those who refuse to wear their glasses or corrective patches. If children do not tolerate their glasses, begin with periods of five to ten minutes when the child is absorbed in some other activity.
- If the child wears glasses, make sure they are clean.
- Always verbally alert the child. That is, let the child know when you arrive and leave.
- Help the child identify individual voices, especially in unfamiliar settings.

ADAPTING TOYS

Many commercial toys are unsuitable for a significant proportion of children with special needs. Children with visual impairments need more colour and texture in their toys. Those with severe disabilities need very simple equipment. Children with physical and motor difficulties may find it difficult or physically impossible to play with ordinary toys (Jackson et al., 1991).

Toys can be adapted in many ways. For Josie, there can be adaptations in colour (use only primary colours) and texture (cover the bases of some toys with sandpaper). For children with physical disabilities, the size of toys can be increased, or pieces added to make grasping easier (see Chapter 13). Also, toys can be electronically adapted.

There are some commercial toys available that are voice activated or require merely a puff of breath or a tilt of the head. For children in wheelchairs, radio-operated trucks and cars are used to provide interactive play.

Some toys can be converted with special switches. Physically disabled children need simple on-and-off or directional electronic switches. These serve for play. Note also here that switches and battery-operated toys are very useful for teaching simple cause-and-effect relationships, and for improving motor control and co-ordination.

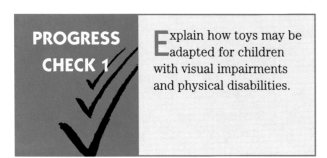

PROGRESS CHECK 1

Explain how toys may be adapted for children with visual impairments and physical disabilities.

Many types of switches are available. Switch designs are based on the child's physical limitations and on the nature of the motor or cognitive skill being taught. Examples: a shadow switch works when the child waves a hand over the photo cell and blocks the incoming light; a touch switch requires only one touch on a large surface; a motion switch works when it is tipped five degrees down from horizontal; with a puff switch, the child blows to operate a toy.

Specialized Equipment

Adaptive equipment equipment customized to meet the physical needs of individual children. It is any device designed or modified to lead individuals with disabilities to independence.

When children have sensory limitations or health or neurological disorders, their medical needs and technological demands must be met before they can benefit from classroom experiences. Besides adapted toys, some young children with disabilities require specialized equipment to optimize their functioning. Equipment is especially important for children with deficits in mobility or with sensory impairments. Usually, the equipment is selected or recommended by professionals such as audiologists or therapists, and brought to the classroom with the child. For children with special equipment needs, occupational and physical therapists provide the most effective management strategies. When these professionals are not available, at least some responsibility falls on the teachers, who should develop some familiarity with the equipment. It is helpful if teachers can change a battery in a hearing aid, arrange seating for a child with a physical disability, or move a wheelchair in a way that is safe for both the child and the teacher.

Children with physical disabilities need specially adapted furniture and toys.

Prosthetic devices used to replace lost functions and/or provide support; they duplicate normal body movements as nearly as possible while restraining normal functions as little as possible.

Orthotic devices assist a limb's action.

Adaptive devices devices that make living easier such as toileting aids, and Velcro fasteners on clothing.

Along with physical equipment, there is a range of equipment now available that can greatly improve quality of life for young children by allowing them more control over events in their environment. Simple examples are adapted spoons and switch-adapted, battery-operated toys; complex ones are computerized environmental control systems (Parette, Hofmann, & Van Biervliet, 1994).

Adaptive equipment and *assistive technology* are general terms for these devices. **Adaptive equipment** may be defined as any device designed or modified to lead individuals with disabilities to independence (Raschke, Dedrick, & Hanus, 1991, p. 25). An *assistive technology* device is an item, piece of equipment, or product system, whether modified, customized, or acquired commercially, that is used to increase, maintain, or improve functional capacities of disabled individuals (s. 602 (a) (25) IDEA, 199).

Adaptive equipment is a broad category that includes the prosthetic, orthotic, and adaptive devices that children use to increase their physical, motor, or sensory functioning. There is quite a lot of overlap in these categories.

Prosthetic devices replace lost functions, or provide support, or both. They duplicate normal body movements as closely as possible while restraining normal functions as little as possible. Often they are used for mobility. The most common mobility devices are braces, crutches and wheelchairs. The use of this equipment is discussed in Chapter 13. **Orthotic devices** assist a limb's action. For example, for a child with a movement dysfunction, special spoons, forks, and dishes make eating and drinking easier. Many children use a "spork"—a combination spoon and fork. Other eating implements have Velcro straps so that the child can handle and control them more easily. **Adaptive devices** make living easier. They include toileting aids (portable urinals), Velcro openers on clothing, and TTDs (telephone machines) for deaf people.

Much of the current technology requires pre-academic readiness skills, and most of it operates through one dominant modality (e.g., touch for keyboards, vision for monitors). However, there are newer devices that allow for alternative modalities—for example, there are now voice-activated computers and captioned TV programs (Sawyer & Zantal-Wiener, 1993). Instruments that permit cognitively disabled persons to control devices in their environment are becoming more available. As a result of miniaturization, use of lighter materials, and higher capacities for information processing, many technologies are becoming less noticeable and obtrusive.

VISUAL AIDS   Children with severe visual impairments use specialized equipment and materials. Prescription devices and low-vision aids can do much to maximize a child's vision potential, especially when combined with visual stimulation. Glasses are the device of choice; other visual aids—magnifiers, telescopes, and so on—are generally not used by young children, as they demand too much motor and intellectual competence.

HEARING AIDS   Children with hearing impairments will use some form of amplification. Hearing aids can be worn by infants as well as by children and adults. Most hearing-impaired children benefit from amplification, especially when auditory training begins early. Even a profoundly deaf child can benefit from a hearing aid. Even a few distorted fragments of sound can help immensely in the acquisition of speech and language.

Hearing aids are primarily sound amplifiers. They can help children to develop their residual hearing, to improve the audition of their own voices, to use speech in a purposeful way, and to expand their vocabulary and language ability. Note that hearing aids may alleviate the problems of hearing loss, but they cannot eliminate the problems altogether.

Outdoor Space

Every preschool should have an appropriately designed and furnished outdoor play area. Outdoor play does much to develop physical and social skills in young children; it also contributes to their intellectual understanding of the world and to their emotional growth. Going outdoors provides a break from indoor activities for both adults and children, and has obvious health benefits in that it gives children an opportunity for exercise and movement in the fresh air and sunlight (Bailey & Wolery, 1984).

A playground attached to an early childhood program should be considered an outdoor classroom. It should be a learning environment that meets curriculum objectives by encouraging child-initiated, teacher-supported activities that are both stimulating and safe. Playgrounds should be constructed to foster children's intellectual and social development and to strengthen their physical abilities. They should allow children to manipulate the environment; this will strengthen their sense of autonomy and achievement.

Tremendous strides have been made in understanding the play needs of children, and recent research has provided a much better understanding of what makes an effective outdoor learning environment. The keys things to provide seem to be these: a rich diversity of natural experiences, new and different challenges every day, and opportunities for dramatic play. For all children, outdoor play areas should be designed to do the following:

- Encourage children to use all their senses.
- Allow children to feel independent and to improve their self-image by independently manipulating the environment.
- Foster communication and social contact with other children.

- Enrich fine and gross motor skills by providing a variety of activities that require responses at varying degrees of difficulty.
- Provide a broad range of media to help develop cognitive skills.
- Promote an atmosphere that fosters recreational and creative play (Raschke, Dedrick, & Hanus, 1991).

Many young children with disabilities face special problems in outdoor play. Regarding children with disabilities, there are two major challenges in outdoor play—to allocate enough time for outdoor play and experiences, and to ensure that a high-quality outdoor play environment is available.

For children with disabilities, outdoor activities are important. (Note that some parents or doctors may restrict it for some children.) Preschool children should go outside at least once in the morning, and again in the afternoon if the program is full-day. However, many programs, particularly those for children who are severely disabled, have been reluctant to take children outdoors. Reasons include the need for close supervision, reluctance to take the time to help children get dressed and undressed, and a fear that the child with a disability may be more likely to get sick (Bailey & Wolery, 1984).

Too often, outdoor play environments have failed to accommodate children with disabilities. For example, when confronted with swings and slides of traditional design, children with physical disabilities are often left on the sidelines to watch other children. Older children with moderate levels of intellectual disability lack the repertoire of skills for using outdoor playground facilities fully (Watkinson & Muloin, 1988).

Adaptive playgrounds

Adaptive playgrounds play environments modified to enable children with physical disabilities to become more independent.

Adaptive playgrounds are play environments modified to enable children with physical disabilities to become more independent (Raschke, Dedrick, & Hanus, 1991). They should be designed for children who crawl, slide, and roll as well as for those who walk and run. When a playground that integrates children with special needs is being developed and designed, accessibility and safety are primary concerns. The following are basic considerations:

- Provide plenty of space. Children are more likely to trip, bump their heads, or become trapped if space is limited at corners, paths, gateways, and so on. Avoid sharp turns on pathways; children who use mobility hardware such as walkers and wheelchairs need more room to negotiate turns.
- Avoid overcrowding of equipment; allow for space and manoeuvrability here also.
- Develop alternatives to steps for entering the playground and buildings. Use ramps.
- For wheelchair participants, slopes must have reasonable grades. Slopes should not rise faster than 1:24–28 (paths) or 1:16–17 (ramps). Handrails should be provided where appropriate, particularly on slopes.
- Flat pathways should also have handrails so that some children can temporarily discard their wheelchair or crutches.
- Manoeuvring can be difficult on uneven surfaces. Pathways should be made of a hard, smooth substance. Do not use loose gravel, rough brick, or cobblestone. If loose surfaces such as gravel or bark are used for pathways, provide alternative access on a harder surface.

- Pathways should run to all structures and play areas. Paths should be at least one metre wide.

- On pathways, avoid using drain covers with slots; these can too easily trap wheelchairs or walkers.

- Cracks in hard-surface pathways sometimes create steplike physical barriers; these should be repaired.

- Private, intimate spaces are very important for some disabled children. Such spaces should allow them to see the main areas of the playground where other children are playing. Often they need to watch from a place where they feel secure before venturing into the main part of the playground.

- Seating, with backs and arm rests, should be available throughout the play area to accommodate children and their parents.

- Place picnic tables along side paths. The table side paralleling the pathway should not have a bench; this will allow easy access by wheelchair participants.

- Easy-access shelter areas should be provided for cover from sun and rain.

- Easy access to toilet facilities is necessary.

- The play area should be constructed of generally soft materials—sand, timbers, tires, grass, and so on. Land contours and natural environment components, like bushes and trees, which offer shade and wind protection as well as aesthetics and a sense of enclosure, should be considered.

- Sand and water play areas, as well as gardening areas, should be elevated to a height of one metre, with indentations to accommodate wheelchairs.

- Crawl tunnels are popular with all children, but should be large enough to accommodate wheelchairs. A diameter of at least two metres is needed, and the surface of the throughway should be of a hard substance. Avoid using piping or conduits, which can cause head injuries and skin abrasions.

- Slides can be modified and embedded in the side of a hill. Access to the top can be by ramp, or by spaced steps that allow a child to leave his or her wheelchair at the bottom and then "climb" by easing up backwards using arms, shoulders, and back.

- On climbers, the space between the rungs should be less than half the height of the child.

- While standard swings can be used by most children, children who are more severely disabled will need vestibular and box swings (Jambor & Gargiulo, 1987; Raschke, Dedrick, & Hanus, 1991).

- The playground should provide visually impaired children with opportunities to learn from physical cues. For example, it should provide them with practice in walking on uneven ground; with help in developing balance, direction, and independence; and with opportunities to improve touch and hearing. It is important to provide textures; visually impaired children should be exposed to dirt, gravel, sand, grass, wood, and rock formations, as well as to hard and soft, and rough and smooth materials (Jambor & Gargiulo, 1987).

PROGRESS CHECK 2

Make sure that you can describe or define the terms in Table 7–1.

TABLE 7–1: New terms and ideas

adaptive devices
adaptive equipment
adaptive playgrounds
assistive technology
orthotic devices
prosthetic devices

SUMMARY

1. Those working in preschool settings have the responsibility for organizing and managing a classroom.

2. The importance of a carefully arranged environment for facilitating the social, motor, language, and cognitive development of young children has been well documented by researchers.

3. A good environment should be socially as well as physically responsive. Careful planning of the environment is important for skill acquisition, skill facilitation, generalization, and nurturance. Settings are not noticeably different when children with disabilities are integrated.

4. In an early childhood setting, the provision of unstructured experiences is essential. Indoor and outdoor equipment should be attractive and appealing, and should be set out in such a way that groups of children enjoy the maximum opportunity to play without interference or obstruction. Activities may include a dress-up corner, a block corner, a sand pit, a puppet theatre, water play, shopping, and a train set.

5. An attractive, interesting, and well-managed classroom will capture the interest of young children with disabilities. A good environment has educational and therapeutic value to these children. It must be planned carefully to provide spaces that are, safe, healthy, nonrestrictive, and normalized for children with disabilities.

6. Materials should be appropriate, accessible, and sufficient in quantity. They should stored so as to be inviting to the children, and in such a way that children know to put them back after use.

7. When the quantity of materials is limited, sharing increases.

8. Computer applications have been used to improve functioning and to promote the learning of specific tasks. Computers also assist social interaction.

9. A child with a disability may be unable to manipulate educational materials. In such cases, some physical adaptations to the regular preschool environment will be necessary, and certain environmental precautions will have to be taken.

10. Assistive or adaptive devices, such as wheelchairs, hearing aids, braces, and special cutlery, are used by many children with disabilities. For people of all ages, such devices are constantly being developed and improved to enrich education and enhance quality of life.

11. The playground should be considered an extension of the classroom.

12. When play areas segregate children with disabilities from their nondisabled peers, they become obstacles rather than facilitators of opportunity. Playground designs should be carefully thought out to meet the needs of children with disabilities.

C H A P T E R   8

Assessment Practices in Early Childhood Special Education

CASE STUDY

Billy

Laura works in a large and busy daycare centre in Winnipeg. She has been there for more than four years and enjoys the work, the other staff, and, especially, the children. At the centre, the children generally choose and initiate their own activities, with the teachers offering support and direction as needed. A number of children with disabilities are at the centre, and the program has been modified to accommodate their special learning and social needs.

Four-and-a-half-year-old Billy has been attending the centre since he was two years old. Increasingly, Billy is a concern to the teachers and his parents and a source of irritation to the other children. He is so highly distractible and has such a short attention span that he does not make optimal use of the educational materials and activities, and his constant movement detracts from the learning experiences of his classmates.

At the centre, Billy has always been known as an active child, but now he wanders aimlessly, lacks an attention span, concentrates poorly no matter what the task, and is showing minor aggression toward peers. Compared to school-age children, preschoolers (especially infants) tend to exhibit higher activity levels and are more easily distracted by competing stimuli. But even at two-and-a-half, and in a group of very active two and three year olds, Billy's excessive activity did not pass unnoticed. It seemed that the bright, busy centre, full of children and games and toys, was often too much for Billy to deal with.

Billy is now four, and his activity still seems aimless. He finds it difficult to concentrate on any task. He seems impelled to run from activity to activity, picking up toys, dropping them, touching and knocking and stepping on them, never finishing anything, and rarely staying with an activity for more

than a few minutes. He asks many questions but rarely waits for an answer. He likes to tell stories to the teachers, but they are always jumbled, with the words "falling all over each other" with little sequence. During circle time, Billy squirms and fidgets, touches and pokes the child next to him, plays with the teacher's shoes or with the rug, rolls on his haunches to stare at the ceiling, and is generally distractible and inattentive.

For people like Laura who work in child care centres, life is busy and full. On any given day, hundreds of details demand attention. One of the many things that teachers do is observe children's social, play, and communicative behaviour. Most often this is done informally. In Billy's case, however, Laura and the other teachers have observed his progress carefully and recorded such things as how long he stays with a project and how he interacts with his peers.

An interview with Billy's mother revealed details about his behaviour in other settings, as well as the family's perceptions of the problem. The mother told the teachers that Billy had been an active, wakeful baby and a "veritable terror" as a toddler. He walked early, at about ten months, and from then on was into everything. By the time he was two, he never seemed to be still. He was up and running through the house first thing in the morning and was extremely difficult to settle at night.

After much careful observation and after taking many detailed notes, the teachers, with the mother's approval, decided to discuss Billy's behaviour with a psychologist. The psychologist tried some formal tests with Billy but had very little success. However, her observations and those of the teachers pointed to some type of attention problem. A pediatrician confirmed this with a medical diagnosis of Attention Deficit Hyperactivity Disorder (ADHD).

With the mother and the psychologist, the teachers met to decide how to help Billy play more co-operatively, attend better, and extend his concentration. They developed a program for him within the context of his normal daily activities. Its main emphasis was on helping him generalize newly learned skills to other environments. Billy's individual plan is found in Box 8–2.

THERE IS LITTLE DOUBT THAT EVERY TEACHER working with young children in early childhood or early elementary programs has met a child like Billy. Often, the behaviour of these children is simply more intense and more active than that of their same-age peers. Children like Billy move more, ask more questions, talk more, and are more distractible and impulsive and less task oriented.

Laura and the other teachers observed Billy carefully because both they and the parents noted a disturbing quality in his development—most particularly in his high rates of excessive movement. He seemed to do everything too much and too fast, except for concentrating and paying attention—and of those he did too little.

In taking the time to observe and analyse Billy's performance, Laura and the other teachers were entering the realm of assessment. Assessing learning, social behaviour, and emotional needs is a major part of what all early childhood teachers do (Bredekamp, 1987). Much of this assessment is done informally, through ongoing observation. Assessment is a collaborative process that involves the school, the child, the family, and the community.

In early childhood settings, observation is one of the most common assessment procedures. Perhaps without even being aware of it, teachers are constantly observing children's growth and development. They observe the steady progress in normally developing children, and may be the first to identify deviations in behaviour and learning that predict future problems. For children with disabilities, observations provide essential information about the child's progress and about the effectiveness of programs. As well, these observations can be highly useful to others who are involved with the child. An audiologist, for example, needs data on how a hearing-impaired child is responding to specific amplification.

Along with observations, early childhood personnel may use a variety of standardized measures. The National Association for the Education of Young Children (NAEYC) (1988) found four categories of these in use: achievement measures, readiness tools, developmental screening measures that test a child's ability to acquire skills, and IQ tests.

Assessment in early childhood education (or during any level of schooling) is not intended to label a child or to propel him or her toward special education. The basic purposes of assessment are to collect information, to clarify the "whys" of a child's performance and behaviour, and to make decisions. The notes and close observations provided by Laura and the other staff about Billy were part of an assessment process, the purpose of which was to make decisions that would enable Billy to improve his behaviour, learning, and socialization within the centre. The concrete result of the decisions was an individual program that included extra assistance for Billy in the areas where he was showing lags.

Assessments are done for *all* children: for those who are developing normally, and for those who seem to be adjusting poorly in some aspect of their development (behavioural, social, emotional, or communicative, or some combination of these). For children with disabilities, assessment is more complex and many special methods are used. Educational assessments consider those behaviours—such as social, communication, motor, and self-care—which relate to the child's ability to function adequately. They determine how the child learns best, the behavioural characteristics that affect learning, and whether there are any sensory or motor impairments relevant to achievement and performance. Other assessments for children with special needs relate to various medical and psychological considerations.

Assessment serves little purpose if the process is undertaken merely to collect data. For all children, but especially those with disabilities, assessment and intervention should be intertwined—that is, assessment activities should be embedded in the curriculum and allied with preventative programs or early intervention programming. The effectiveness of programs depends greatly on the continuity between early assessment and intervention: without a diagnosis, we cannot devise a program for a child, and without an assessment, we cannot arrive at a diagnosis.

For children with mild and moderate disabilities, assessment mainly involves providing information on functioning levels in the various developmental domains, and on the type and degree of deviant behaviour being manifested. For children with severe and multiple disabilities, assessment is more complex and far-reaching and includes medical variables.

In order to work with children with disabilities, early childhood educators must be familiar with three major areas of assessment. First, they should develop at least a nodding acquaintance with the formal and informal measures used by psychologists, speech clinicians, and other professionals. Teachers are rarely directly involved if assessment is for placement in special intervention programs, or for diagnosis, or for describing the child's cognitive abilities relative to others. However, personnel in early childhood programs should be able to interpret the information presented in psycho-educational reports. Second, early childhood personnel should be aware of the variety of assessment techniques that are employed for determining children's strengths and weaknesses. Third, those intervening with young disabled children should be comfortable using developmental scales and checklists that supplement and document their own observations.

In this chapter we present an overview of the assessment process in early intervention. We stress those aspects of the identification process in which early childhood personnel are most likely to be involved. In particular, we examine the area of observation, for there is no substitute for it: people who come into professional contact with preschoolers must be alert to the signs that a child may have a difficulty. Early childhood personnel can develop skills in identifying potential learning and behavioural difficulties so that appropriate referrals and interventions can be made.

The goals of this chapter are to enhance students' skills in informal measures such as interviews and observations, and to alert them to the many other types of measures that may be employed. Assessment is also addressed in the chapters that follow this one, specifically in reference to various developmental domains.

Hyperactivity a child's frequent failure to comply in an age-appropriate fashion with situational demands for restrained activity, sustained attention, resistance to distracting influences, and inhibition of impulsive response. That is, an excess of motor activity for a child's age and situation.

BOX 8–1
Attention Deficit Hyperactivity Disorder

The number of children diagnosed with Attention Deficit Hyperactivity Disorder (ADHD) has increased sharply in the past decade. This does not mean that ADHD is a new problem. Rather, the increase is a result of new terminology, new diagnostic techniques, and a greater understanding of what the problem actually is.

For a long time, all types of attention disorders and excessive motor activity were subsumed under the general term hyperactivity. Physicians have long been aware of hyperactivity in children. The condition was first described in 1845 by a German physician, Henrich Hoffman (Cantwell, 1975). A hundred years later, researchers in the new area of learning disabilities paid a great deal of attention to hyperactivity, which was then and is now one of the most common childhood behaviour disorders. As physicians, researchers, and educators studied it, they concluded that it was actually one of a group of related conditions. It is now estimated that between 3 and 20 percent of all elementary school children are hyperactive. Also, at least three boys have the disorder for every girl (Wicks-Nelson & Israel, 1991).

ADHD is characterized as comprising developmentally inappropriate levels of sustained attention (inattention), poor impulse control (impulsivity), and poor regulation of activity level to situational demands (hyperactivity). The disorder is often associated with other conditions such as learning disabilities, conduct disorders, academic underachievement, and social skills deficits (Barkley, 1989).

Attention is the "process of tuning in to sensory information" (Bailey & Wolery, 1984) and requires engagement or active participation. As children mature, they improve their ability to control their attention, to discriminate between what is and what is not important, and to adapt their attention to details of situations. They are able to maintain attention for longer periods because they are less easily distracted.

Children with ADHD are inattentive. Any strong stimulus can divert their attention. These children often fail to finish what they have begun; they don't seem to listen, are easily distracted, have difficulty concentrating and paying attention, and don't stay with a play activity (Alderson, 1993). Most authorities agree that the attention problems found with ADHD are more serious and more basic than those of hyperactivity alone (Henker & Whalen, 1989).

These children are also impulsive. They often act without thinking, shift too often from one activity to another, have difficulty organizing themselves, need much supervision, speak out of turn, and don't wait their turn in games or in groups. They show angry outbursts, may be social isolates, blame others for their problems, quickly get into fights, and are very sensitive to criticism (Alderson, 1993).

Hyperactivity is defined as "a child's frequent failure to comply in an age appropriate fashion with situational demands for restrained activity, sustained attention, resistance to distracting influences, and inhibition of impulsive response" (Routh, 1980, p. 57). Hyperactivity means an excess of motor activity for a child's age and situation. Hyperactive children display rates of motor behaviour that are too high for their age group; they indulge in excessive, nonpurposeful movement. Hyperactive children are more distractible; they show shorter attention spans and lower frustration tolerance, as well as impulsive behaviour patterns. They are poorer at tasks requiring sustained attention. They have difficulties in problem solving and planning (see Reardon & Naglieri, 1992). The hyperactive child runs and climbs on things excessively, can't sit still, is fidgety, has difficulty sitting still, bothers peers, and is always on the go. Even when asleep, the child shows excessive activity and other sleep problems (Alderson, 1993).

Longitudinal research shows that children with generalized hyperactivity have a very early onset of problems (Gillberg & Gillberg, 1988). Typically, signs of hyperactivity first appear in early childhood, often by the age of three and sometimes even in infancy. The mean age of onset is four years (Alderson, 1993; Barkley et al., 1988). The problems associated with hyperactivity persist and affect academic and social functioning. Among hyperactive children, conduct disturbances and academic deficits are common. Misconduct is noted in as many as 70 percent of cases (Barkley, 1990).

ADHD is a medical diagnosis. The prevalent opinion is that the cause of ADHD is found in the central nervous system—specifically, that it results from faulty regulation of norepinephrine, a neurotransmitter (Alderson, 1993). Given an early and accurate diagnosis, and provided that the child is regularly observed by both the parents and the physician, ADHD can be controlled with minimal disruption. It is most often controlled through medication; the hope is that drug therapy will permit better peer relationships and an improved self-image, and increase pleasure in attaining competencies.

The two most commonly used drugs for controlling ADHD are Ritalin and Dexedrine. Both are psychostimulants. Ritalin is the first choice, probably because it produces fewer side effects. Ritalin is used for hyperactive behaviour in as many as 90 percent of cases (Kavale, 1982).

At least in the short-term, these drugs are clearly effective. They decrease motor activity, diminish impulsive responding, and improve attention. In fact, while on stimulant medication ADHD children are sometimes indistinguishable from normal children (Fishburne, 1989). However, when they are taken off the medication, their academic performance decreases to pre-treatment levels (Famularo & Fenton, 1987).

Early Identification

The whole notion of early childhood special services for children with disabilities and their families rests on the two principles of early identification and early intervention. One is the corollary of the other. Early identification serves no purpose if it is not followed by early intervention; and appropriate early intervention rests on adequate and accurate early identification.

Early identification is the process of identifying an exceptionality or a high-risk condition as early as possible in a child's life. It is based on the idea that potentially disabling conditions can prevented, or at least ameliorated, if detection and intervention are early enough.

Several writers have proposed that there are three categories of children who can benefit from early identification and early intervention (Zeitlin & Williamson, 1986). We encountered these groups in Chapter 2:

Early identification the process of identifying an exceptionalness or a high-risk condition as early as possible in a child's life.

- Environmentally at-risk children, who are biologically sound, but for whom delayed development is probable because of physical or social circumstances such as poverty, neglect, or abuse.
- Medically or biologically at-risk children, who have a history of health conditions (such as prematurity) that are known to be potential threats to development.

- Disabled or developmentally delayed children, whose congenital disorders, sensory impairments, neurological dysfunctions, or significant delays in major areas of functioning have already been established.

Such children are identified early in a number of ways. Early identification can be performed through prenatal screening. Other conditions, such as Down syndrome, are apparent at birth. Parents may be the first to identify infants who are not reaching their developmental milestones at the right times. Deaf infants, for example, cry and coo and even babble just like children who hear normally. However, they stop this vocalization by about 10 months. When they do, and when they fail to develop their first words at about 12 months, parents may well become suspicious.

The early identification of children with mild disabilities is more difficult. For example, a child with a mild intellectual disability is often not identified in early childhood. Such a child usually shows no physical anomalies, and usually does not lag very far in reaching developmental milestones; it is not until the child faces the complexities of reading and writing in a formal school program that learning problems become obvious. Similarly, as we pointed out in Chapter 2, learning disabilities are by definition linked to formal school achievement. Children who demonstrate hyperactive behaviour and attention deficits may be identified in the early years; those with more subtle learning and behavioural problems may not be identified until much later.

PROGRESS CHECK 1

Define the three groups of children for whom early identification is most important. Why are mild disorders so hard to identify in early childhood? To what signs could a teacher be alert?

Assessment in Early Childhood Environments

DEFINING ASSESSMENT

Assessment is a very broad construct that includes measurement, evaluation, and testing. These three refer to processes for making informed decisions about a child's needs. Even so, they don't mean exactly the same thing.

Assessment is the most inclusive term. Assessment is something we all do almost every day. When we check and compare the prices on different cans of asparagus at the supermarket, we are making an assessment. When we read the TV guide synopses of different movies and then select one, we are making an assessment. Even when we select the clothes we will wear for the day, we are making an assessment based on the weather, where we are going, and other factors. In other words, **assessment** is simply the process of gathering data in order to make a decision. In the field of education, the assessment of a child who is at risk or disabled involves gathering information on the child in various contexts using various means so that we can decide on the most appropriate educational placement for the child and the most suitable individual program.

Assessment the process of gathering data in order to make a decision.

Measurement involves assigning numbers to something. It answers the question "How much?" The third term, evaluation, answers "What does it mean?" We often use tests—tools or measures designed for a specific purpose—to measure and evaluate. For example, a psychologist may try to find out what level of mental ability (IQ) Billy has. To do this, she may use a test such as the Wechsler Preschool and Primary Scale of Intelligence–Revised (WPPSI-R). She would write down Billy's scores and then be able to say that Billy has an IQ of a certain amount (measurement). She could then compare Billy's scores to those of other children of the same age to see how Billy is functioning (evaluation). When the results of this data gathering are used to plan an intervention for Billy, the entire process in known as assessment.

In recent years, practices in early childhood assessment for learning problems have improved considerably. The main changes have been in the types of tools and measures preferred, in the environments used for assessment, and in the flexibility of the procedures. Also, early childhood personnel are now more likely to be involved. Assessment is still a complex process that involves diverse procedures, rationales, tools, and personnel. The process is shown in Figure 8–1.

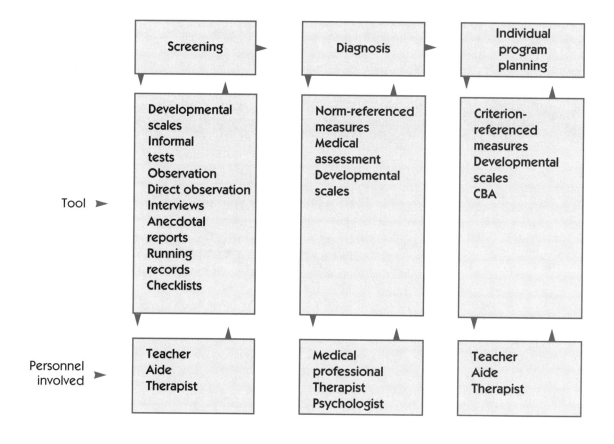

FIGURE 8–1

The assessment process in early childhood settings

As Figure 8–1 shows, assessment in early childhood settings generally serves three purposes: screening, diagnosis (direct testing), and IPP planning. We can mention here that children are also assessed for readiness for specific programs (particularly kindergarten). Also assessed are entire programs (program evaluation).

In the assessment process, a single test, person, or occasion is not sufficient. For a complete picture of a child, data must be gathered from various sources, using various instruments, in various settings, and on many occasions.

The term screening is used in both medicine and education for activities to identify children who face a high probability of delayed or abnormal development. For example, we noted earlier in this book that the Apgar test is given to all newborns to pinpoint problems in neonatal functioning.

When we talk about **_screening_** in education, we are referring to a classroom activity that generally occurs before direct testing. Screening for young children is defined as "a global process of surveying the behavior of children in an attempt to detect the existence of general developmental problems" (Neisworth et al., 1980). That is, screening looks at large groups of children and begins to identify those who may have difficulties in behaviour and learning.

> **Screening** a term used in medicine and education to refer to developmental and health activities that are intended to identify at an early age those children who have a high probability of exhibiting delayed or abnormal development.

Screening is a first step in determining whether children need early intervention or special services, such as a modified or individualized educational program. Note, however, that screening is not a valid diagnostic tool; it should only be used for making referrals to in-depth assessment (i.e., to direct testing).

The optimal time for screening is still a matter of debate, but there is increasing evidence that supports preschool screening as a way of preventing more complex learning difficulties later in life.

For diagnosis (also referred to as direct testing), standardized measures are used. Direct testing is used when the professional wants to know how the infant or preschooler responds to a standardized stimulus, request, or specific set of materials. Direct testing is essential for determining a specific score for a child, and for comparing a child's performance with that of other children (Bailey & Wolery, 1984).

Program planning is done after the child is identified for early intervention. The assessment provides information about the child's current levels of functioning. Teachers and others can then pinpoint strengths and weaknesses and prepare individual goals and objectives in the form of an IPP (see Chapter 9).

These three processes—screening, direct testing, and program planning—require a variety of materials and procedures. The tools for screening are not the same as those used for direct testing or for creating IPPs, although to some extent they overlap and complement each other. Screening and diagnosis are likely to involve both norm-referenced and criterion-referenced procedures. The ongoing instructional evaluations that are part of IPP monitoring rely on criterion-referenced measures which focus on the child's mastery of skills and tasks rather than on the child's relative standing in a group.

PROGRESS CHECK 2

Explain the term screening as it relates to young children with special needs. What is the difference between screening and direct testing? As an early childhood teacher, in which process are you more likely to be involved?

WHY ASSESS?

The general objective of assessment in educational circles is to make appropriate decisions about children that will facilitate their educational and psychological development. Within that general objective, the early assessment of young children allows educators to do the following:

- Diagnose disabling conditions.
- Identify children who are at risk for disabilities and who may require more in-depth evaluation, remediation, or medical treatment.
- Identify children who are experiencing developmental (maturational) lags.
- Identify children who are not developing language at a satisfactory rate and who may require additional instruction.
- Predict a child's future level of functioning.
- Prescribe appropriate treatment.
- Prevent secondary conditions.
- Suggest appropriate education placement.
- Understand the child's problems so that they can plan educational experiences to maximize the child's strengths. An assessment presents a detailed picture of performance across a variety of domains; thus, teachers can develop appropriate instructional goals.
- Provide services during the preschool years, which are critical. Early identification may prevent later underachievement. In one study, called Project Child, half the children who were later identified as having disabilities could have received more effective remediation if their difficulties had been diagnosed earlier (Vacc, Vacc, & Fogelman, 1987). Research indicates that regardless of the type and amount of subsequent intervention, earlier diagnosis is associated with better school performance after five years.
- Evaluate a child's success as a function of program variables and as a function of changes over time.
- Evaluate the success of the program.

Assessment is used to identify conditions and to pinpoint the nature and character of the child's problems (e.g., difficulties with attention or fine motor coordination, or sensory limitations). It details the needs, which can then be addressed. For example, "mental disability" is not a helpful assessment result, but "slow in reaching developmental milestones in motor and language skills" is. Assessment also proposes possible remediation strategies.

As based on assessment data, the decisions made about a child may be minor or far-reaching:

> The decisions made by assessment are actually a continuum ranging from informal transitory types of decisions to those having far reaching consequences for the child. At one end are day to day decisions to encourage more social interactions for a withdrawn child, provide an anxious child with a little more attention, spend time with another on counting skills, etc. At an intermediate point in the continuum are decisions that begin to involve others such as deciding to discuss aggressive behaviour with the parents of the child. At the far end are serious and far reaching decisions such as referring a child for psychological assessment or initiating a therapeutic program for a child. (Hoge & Wichmann, 1994, p. 1)

Collecting the Data

When we discussed family needs assessment in Chapter 5, we noted that there are three basic methods for collecting information: tests, observations, and interviews. The same three basic methods are used in child assessment. The measures are used alone or in combination and can serve a single purpose or many objectives and purposes. The methods used are differentiated by the type of data that is collected as well as how those data are collected.

TESTS

Tests controlled and structured procedures that attempt to elicit particular responses that the child might not demostrate spontaneously.

Every student is familiar with tests. Most have written hundreds of them in school and college or university. In formal terms, a test is an observation of behaviour. ***Tests*** are defined as controlled and structured procedures that attempt to elicit particular responses that the child may not demonstrate spontaneously (Bailey & Brochin, 1989).

In this section we are interested in three major categories of tests: norm-referenced, criterion-referenced, and curriculum-referenced. Some of these tests are employed in the screening process; others are used in direct testing; some can be employed in both screening and direct testing. Further, some tests focus on only one aspect of development. An IQ test, for example, is a norm-referenced measure used in direct testing that focuses on cognitive development. Other measures concentrate on language or motor skills or play behaviours. Many other tests are multidimensional; that is, they assess a number of domains of development.

> ## LEARNING ACTIVITY 1
>
> Most students are familiar with the multiple-choice format for tests. Consider your past experience with such tests and the information you have read so far in this chapter, and prepare three multiple-choice questions. Test other members of your class with your questions.

Norm-referenced tools

The main purpose of some measures is to indicate a child's developmental level relative to that of other children. When an individual child's performance is compared with that of a normative group (i.e., of other children of the same age), the instrument is referred to as ***norm-referenced***.

Norm-referenced instrument when an individual child's performance is compared to the normative group consisting of other children of the same age.

Norm-referenced tests are ***standardized***; that is, they have standard procedures for administration and scoring. The value of standardization is well illustrated by Donald Bailey and Mark Wolery (1984), who ask us to consider five teachers who are trying separately to determine whether a child can cut with scissors. The results are likely to vary considerably with the teacher's materials, procedures, and scoring criteria. One teacher may use blunt scissors, another pointed ones. One may use newsprint, another notebook paper, another cardboard. One teacher may have the child cut a shape, another may ask for a straight line. In the end, we have five different conclusions about the child's performance.

Standardized refers to instruments that have standard procedures for administration and scoring.

Standardized tests provide precise materials, strict administration procedures, predetermined criteria, and careful scoring. The accompanying test manuals explain exactly how to ensure consistent and unbiased administration. For each subtest, a precise set of directions tells the examiner the following: where to begin; how to present the items; what to say; what type of help, correction, and reinforcement to offer; when to stop; and how to score the responses. Spontaneous behaviour and the child's presenting behaviour are carefully noted.

The great advantage of standardized tests is that they allow a child's performance to be compared to that of other children (the normative group). However, such tests are better at pinpointing developmental delays than at facilitating program planning. Standardized measures tap into isolated intellectual and language abilities; they do *not* yield information on functional skills of the kind that is relevant to a child's IPP and useful in the context of daily activities (Notari & Bricker, 1990).

Criterion-referenced tools

Norm-referenced measures do not provide a lot of information that is directly relevant to a child's educational program; they are more concerned with comparing the child's performance to a norm. Assessment for the purposes of programming typically uses criterion-referenced measures, because these focus on a child's mastery of skills or specific tasks.

Criterion-referenced measures (also called content- or objective-referenced tests) measure success or failure in meeting some predetermined objective. Their main purpose is to indicate a child's specific skills. Teachers can compare the child's performance to a specific level or rating, and then track that child's progress over time. This flexibility of use makes criterion-referenced tests among the most valuable in the assessment field (Berdine & Myer, 1986).

The items in criterion-referenced tests are selected for their importance to school performance or daily living. They typically list items in a developmental sequence that indicates the average age at which the skills should be accomplished. When missed, these skills typically become teaching targets.

> Criterion-referenced measures (also called content—or objective—referenced tests) measure success or failure in meeting some previously determined objective. Their primary purpose is to indicate a child's specific skills so that teachers can compare a child's performance to a specific level or rating as well as to the child's progress over time.

Curriculum-referenced measures

Curriculum-referenced testing (or curriculum-based assessment) is a special form of criterion-referenced testing. Curriculum-referenced tools are similar to criterion-referenced ones, except that predetermined criteria are not necessarily set, and the test is always related to what was taught in the classroom. These measures provide information about a child's status in regard to a prespecified curriculum sequence; this is possible because assessment covers the same materials as those presented during instruction.

Curriculum-based assessments for infants and young children have been developed to strengthen the links between assessment and programming. Only skills that can be taught are selected. Children are first assessed on the objectives to be learned. Skills are then sequenced in a hierarchical, logical teaching order (Blankenship, 1985). The child is then evaluated as to how well the target objectives have been achieved.

The Assessment, Evaluation, and Programming System (AEPS) (Bricker, 1993) is an example of a curriculum-based assessment tool. The AEPS establishes individualized goals and objectives and offers a guide for selecting content and strategies.

INFORMAL MEASURES

Standardized psychometric and other measures are still widely used in early childhood assessment. But while groups such as the National Association for the Education of Young Children (NAEYC) recognize the value of such testing, they are cautious, stressing that standardized measures are only one source of information. NAEYC encourages educators to conduct assessments that are directly related to the curriculum and that involve the performance of natural rather than contrived skills. Suggested methods include anecdotal reports, running records, language samples, interviews, and observations, but are not restricted to these (NAEYC, 1988, 1991).

It is now common practice to employ a combination of developmental scales, observations, observational checklists, interviews, and formal intelligence tests. When several different measures are used, discrepancies and inconsistencies in each child's profile become more apparent. All of the data can then be used to present a full and detailed picture of the child's functioning; such information later helps shape the individual program.

INTERVIEWS

In **interviews**, information is gathered by conversation or direct questioning. Interviews are an important component of the screening process and serve a number of functions. For example, an interview with a kindergarten teacher may be appropriate when a child is being readied for transition to the public school system (see Chapter 16).

> Interview a method of gathering information by conversation or direct questioning.

Interviews as part of the assessment process are generally with a child's parents. In fact, an assessment is incomplete without the careful collection of data from parent interviews. Parents have this singular advantage: they are able to provide information about specific types of behaviour in a variety of settings over a much longer time than is available to the examiner during a typical assessment session (Bagnato, Neisworth, & Mussen, 1989). Because parents can provide information about the child's abilities that is not obvious in testing or teaching situations, parental insights about the child complement information from other sources regarding the child's abilities and educational needs.

Parent interviews may be structured and formal or unstructured and informal. In either case, they provide opportunities for both teachers and parents to take stock of the child's program in a leisurely fashion. Interviews with parents also foster collaboration, and this ultimately leads to a productive relationship between parents and professionals. They provide an opportunity for teachers and caregivers to get to know each other, and this sets the tone for a positive and sensitive working relationship.

Teachers should be well prepared for formal interviews. At the conference, they should have on hand all necessary documentation such as anecdotal reports, narrative descriptions of the child's behaviour, collections of work, photographs, and results of assessments. For more formal interviews, a number of questionnaire and interview forms have been constructed for use with parents, teachers, and other key informants. These can provide important information about various aspects of a child's progress.

Interviews are most effective if the interviewer is a good listener and asks questions that reveal information about the child from the parent's perspective. Parents may be asked in general terms if they have any particular concerns about their child's development; or they may be asked to observe and report on specific behaviours (Diamond & Squires, 1993). Alternatively, the parents may describe what a typical day is like with the child: what the child does well and likes to do, what the child needs help with and tends to avoid, recent progress or changes in the child's behaviour at home, and the child's interests (Noonan &

McCormick, 1993). Parent/teacher interviews generate information about the family's perceptions of their child, about significant events in the family's and the child's life such as transitions and medical procedures, and about priorities and preferences for services. The parents may also suggest specific techniques for maximizing performance.

OBSERVATIONS

All teachers observe children. It is something that teachers do rather well. It is estimated that an elementary teacher's observations can predict with 80 percent accuracy which children will experience academic failure.

Observations by parents and teachers serve a number of purposes and have a number of advantages:

- They sample a child's typical behaviour and provide information on how a child uses—or fails to use—relevant skills in natural contexts.
- They look at the whole child and at how well the child uses skills to meet the expectations of the environment.
- They provide essential information on how a child functions in a setting, for all those involved with the child.
- They allow informal assessment of many important skills—for example, peer interaction, communication, independent functioning.
- They can be used to examine various behaviours and the context in which they occur.
- They can be carried out by a range of personnel.
- They are particularly valuable when it is necessary to document spontaneous behaviour.
- They help teachers make a more rapid and accurate assessment of the assistance that will be required both inside and outside the preschool centre.
- They provide data that help shape the individual program.

Observations take many forms. They are often casual and informal, but they can also involve precise and specific notation. Some common ways to collect observational data include sampling, anecdotal records, diaries (running records), and checklists. Videotaped recordings of behaviour in familiar, unfamiliar, structured, and unstructured settings also provide valuable information. Videotapes made at intervals allow teachers and clinicians to establish a learning program for a child over time (Donlon & Curtis, 1972).

Direct observation

Direct observation involves teachers observing closely and then documenting their observations. Direct observation techniques permit children's behaviour and achievements to be assessed in the context of normal daily routines. Data recording may be as simple as a narrative system, or it may be more sophisticated, with codes to score language skills, motor behaviour, and so on. With direct observation, occurrences of a particular prespecified behaviour are recorded at the time the behaviour is occurring. Behaviour is best recorded in natural settings; this means professionals or parents observing the infant or preschool child in natural situations such as the centre, the home, the park, and the shopping mall.

Not all behaviour can be documented: we must sometimes be content with a sample. With sampling, systematic observations of a child are undertaken over

> Direct observation when teachers observe closely and document the observations.

at least a week. There are different sampling strategies; which one is used depends on the type of behaviour being observed. Generally, we want to assess how long and how often an unusual or disruptive behaviour occurs.

Event sampling is used to track specific behaviours, such as aggression or temper tantrums. There are two types of event sampling. A *frequency count* is used for behaviours of relatively short duration—for example, to count the number of times a child hits another child. *Duration sampling* indicates how long something goes on, and is used for behaviours such as crying or temper tantrums, which can vary considerably in length.

To illustrate event sampling, let us consider Robert, who demonstrates a variety of physically aggressive behaviours such as slapping, punching, and generally aggravating the other children in the room. In using direct observation techniques, the teacher would measure Robert's behaviour. Over a period of at least five days, she would record a checkmark on a tally sheet each time Robert exhibited physical aggression. The average number of aggressive behaviours in the five days would become the baseline, which is something like a profile of the behaviour. If a program to improve Robert's behaviour is undertaken, the teacher can quickly measure his progress by comparing his current behaviour to the baseline. For an illustration, see Figure 8–2.

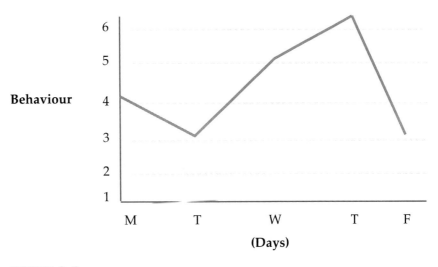

FIGURE 8–2

Event sampling

Anecdotal records   Another method for quickly recording a child's behaviour is with **anecdotal records**. Anecdotal records focus on specific behaviours in specific settings at particular times. The anecdotal notes should describe the context of the child's overall behaviour—that is, the setting, the participants, and the social context. Aggression in outside play may well be quite different from that which is seen in the art activity centre.

Although informal, anecdotal reports should include a precisely written narrative of the child's behaviour. For example, a teacher may observe Jimmy aggressively taking a truck from another. The report may also state that "in the

Anecdotal records
brief global
statements of events
important to a
child's performance.

outdoor area, Jimmy demanded that Jack give him the truck to ride. When Jack refused, Jimmy punched Jack and took the truck. A teacher intervened and Jimmy was placed in time out for two minutes."

When anecdotal reporting is careful, systematic, and periodic, it holds considerable value. These reports provide documentation of environmental antecedents (what happened before the behaviour), and of responses to the behaviour. When written regularly, the teacher can substantiate specific behaviour patterns. The records may provide warnings of future problems, and glimpses of undiscovered potential. Haphazard reports, on the other hand, can lead to incorrect assumptions. Incidents chosen for reporting should be selected because they are typical of a recurrent type of behaviour displayed by a particular child; or, conversely, because the behaviour is highly atypical for the child.

Anecdotal reports should be brief but as complete as possible. They should contain the following:

- The child's name.
- The time, activity, setting, day of week, and date.
- The name of the person making the observation.
- A precise description of the behaviour, in nonjudgmental terms.
- The events that preceded and followed the behaviour.
- Any information obtained from other sources, such as another teacher or a teacher's aide.
- Additional comments; for example, how did the behaviour make you feel? Although teachers may indicate their own feelings, this subjective reporting should be clearly distinguished from the behaviour itself.

Anecdotal reports should be written as soon as possible after the incident. After the anecdotal report is written, the child must be observed further in a variety of settings, to confirm or discount the presence of a chronic difficulty (Winzer, 1989).

Chronologues

Unlike anecdotal records, which focus on particular instances of behaviour, chronologues (also called running records or diaries) provide descriptive summaries of *all* of a child's actions in the environment. Chronologues are used when an observer wishes to record all relevant events over a period of time. They are narrative descriptions, and are useful when the teacher is interested in what generally occurs and the sequence in which things happen. However, they may be difficult to interpret because the information is not organized in any meaningful fashion. They are also very time-consuming and need constant attention.

Case studies

A case study (or case history) is a detailed description of many phases of a child's life; it includes health history, family history, school performance, formal assessment, and so on. A case study indicates milestones, such as the child's development of language or fine motor skills.

Checklists

Many teachers use checklists with precise and specific headings to formulate and organize their notes on individual children. Table 8–1 shows a checklist. It includes process (ability) and product (activity) headings suitable for preschool children.

TABLE 8–1: Example of a teacher checklist

		Yes	No	Comments
Speech	• speaks clearly	☐	☐	
	• points a lot; uses gestures instead of speech	☐	☐	
	• speaks quietly	☐	☐	
	• mispronunciations of common words	☐	☐	
	• dysfluency; stutters	☐	☐	
Language	• uses many words	☐	☐	
	• names objects, people, events	☐	☐	
	• enjoys discussion	☐	☐	
	• recalls experiences	☐	☐	
	• relates experiences in sequence	☐	☐	
	• listens to others	☐	☐	
	• follows simple directions	☐	☐	
	• enjoys stories	☐	☐	
	• reads to self or out loud	☐	☐	
Play	• engages in solitary play	☐	☐	
	• wanders	☐	☐	
	• destructive	☐	☐	
	• shares toys	☐	☐	
	• takes turn in games	☐	☐	
	• plays co-operatively	☐	☐	
	• engages in dramatic play	☐	☐	
Social	• likes parent to stay until familiar with a new situation	☐	☐	
	• secure in new situations	☐	☐	
	• relates to other children and to adults	☐	☐	
	• has concern for others	☐	☐	
	• makes friends easily	☐	☐	
Behaviour	• demands attention	☐	☐	
	• short attention span	☐	☐	
	• becomes angry or frustrated	☐	☐	
	• tantrums	☐	☐	
Self-help skills	• takes care of self	☐	☐	
	• puts on coat, mitts	☐	☐	
	• toilet trained	☐	☐	
	• uses toilet independently	☐	☐	
	• washes up	☐	☐	
	• feeds self	☐	☐	
	• drinks from cup or glass	☐	☐	
Motor	• hops on one foot	☐	☐	
	• balances on small plank	☐	☐	
	• catches ball	☐	☐	

	Yes	No	Comments
• enjoys being outside	☐	☐	_____
• uses puzzles	☐	☐	_____
• cuts with scissors	☐	☐	_____
• cuts out a prescribed shape	☐	☐	_____
• draws a person	☐	☐	_____
• co-ordinates hand movements	☐	☐	_____
• writes own name	☐	☐	_____

PROGRESS CHECK 3

Explain the various types of informal assessment that may be used in an early childhood setting. If you were working with Billy, the child introduced in the case study, which methods would you use? Explain your choice.

Parents may join with teachers in observing the child's learning and behaviour. Methods of accomplishing this use tools that are designed to make assessment a shared responsibility between parents and professionals. Both parents and teacher rate the child on observed performance; they then share their findings and select goals.

Assessment Approaches

Assessments are undertaken to gather data about a child's performance and behaviour so that decisions can be made about which intervention is best. A number of very different procedures make up the assessment process.

MEDICAL ASSESSMENT

A huge variety of medical procedures are used with children with disabilities. Some of these are carried out at birth or even before. ***Prenatal screening*** examines fetuses that may be at risk. Procedures for this include amniocentesis, chorionic villi sampling, and other measures that can identify fetuses with Down syndrome and other chromosomal and genetic abnormalities. Ultrasound can identify such problems as spina bifida and orofacial defects. In the delivery room, each infant is given an ***Apgar screening***, which looks at colour, respiration, muscle tone, heart rate, and reflexes. Most infants score close to the total full score of 10; infants who do not score well on the Apgar screen may be considered high risk.

Some conditions, such as Down syndrome and spina bifida, are obvious from birth; others may appear in infancy. For example, the cries of infants who are autistic or neurologically impaired tend to be different from those of normally developing infants, and while all infants are born with primitive reflexes, most of which disappear after about six months, in children with cerebral palsy, many of these primitive reflexes will persist.

A medical examination should be a routine part of the diagnostic process in education, and it should include vision and hearing tests. Ophthalmologists

Prenatal screening **examines fetuses who may be at risk.**

Apgar screening **neonatal tests that look at colour, respiration, muscle tone, heart rate, and reflexes.**

check both visual acuity and visual functioning; audiologists are chiefly concerned with assessing hearing and recommending and fitting amplification equipment; otolaryngologists concentrate on ear, nose, and throat problems that affect hearing and speech.

ASSESSMENT OF MENTAL ABILITY

IQ tests, which measure mental ability, are probably the best known and most controversial of the norm-referenced measures. IQ tests assess a child's performance and intelligence against the norms of other children of the same age. Examples of some commonly used measures of mental ability are shown in Table 8–2.

TABLE 8–2: Measures of mental ability

Instrument	Age range	Features
Bayley Scales of Infant Development (Bayley, 1969)	1 month to 42 months	Developmental. Assesses cognitive, fine and gross motor, socio-emotional.
Columbia Mental Maturity Scale (3rd. ed.) Burgemeister, Bluma, & Lorge, 1972)	3–6 to 9–11	Used for evaluating ability in normally developing and variously handicapped children. Requires neither verbal response nor motor skills.
Detroit Tests of Learning Aptitude (Baker & Leland, 1967; Hammill, 1984)	3 years to adult	Specific subareas may be selected.
Hiskey Nebraska Test of Learning Aptitude (Hiskey, 1966)	3 1/2 to 18 1/2	Normed for hearing impaired students; nonverbal instrument.
Kaufman Assessment Battery for Children (Kaufman & Kaufman, 1983)	2–6 to 12–6	16 subtests in a mental processing scale and achievement scale. Assesses nonverbal cognitive ability.
Leiter International Performance Scale (Leiter, 1948)	2 to 12 years and up	Samples variety of functions. Untimed.
McCarthy Scales of Children's Abilities (McCarthy, 1972)	2–6 to 8–6	Picks up just about where the Bayley leaves off; 15 subtests that provide a general estimate of intellectual functioning and a profile of abilities. Looks at short-term memory, co-ordination, hand dominance.
Merrill-Palmer Test of Mental Ability (Stutsman,1948)	18 months to six years	Highly attractive manipulatives; low language demands.
Wechsler Preschool and Primary Scale of Intelligence–Revised (Wechsler, 1989)	3–0 to 7–0	General cognitive ability.

For people of all ages, IQ testing is extremely controversial. Early childhood educators consider assessments of individual development and learning to be essential tools for program planning and implementation (Bredekamp, 1991). Even so, many query the need for psychological assessments in early childhood education. They point out that IQ testing is tenuous because cognition in children changes rapidly, and often in an uneven way; and that IQ tests give global scores that reflect only a limited sample of a young child's abilities.

Even with the many cautions, psychometric assessments are still widely used. Advocates stress that they are essential for a complete understanding of a child's development because cognitive skills are closely related to skills in other domains, especially language, social functioning, and behaviour.

Typically, early childhood personnel will not be involved in psychological testing. Because IQ tests are delicate instruments and need careful interpretation, they are only administered by psychologists and others with special training. However, early childhood teachers may receive a report documenting the psychologist's findings about a certain child. A clear report will provide the following:

• The child's maturation levels (what the child is developmentally capable of in various areas).

• A perspective of the child relative to children of similar age generally (as opposed to the child's classmates).

• An indication of overall intellectual functioning, reasoning, thinking, and problem-solving ability.

LEARNING ACTIVITY 2

Ever since they were devised in 1905, IQ tests have been controversial. Check some other references such as psychology and educational psychology texts. Write a brief paper on the criticisms that surround IQ tests for individuals of all ages.

• A profile of learning abilities, cognitive strengths and weaknesses, and modality strengths.

• A profile of underlying deficits in processing (perception, language).

• An indication of attention and memory skills.

• Test behaviour (effort, attitude, response to structure, and so on).

• Social, emotional, and personality considerations.

• Suggestions for appropriate teaching approaches (Brown, 1992).

INFANT ASSESSMENT

The main purpose of infant assessment is to provide information about an infant's strengths and weaknesses so that intervention strategies can be planned. Infant assessment has three components: the professional has the opportunity to interact with the child, to observe the reactions of the parents, and to develop an understanding of the infant's functioning in the environment.

There are no tests available that can adequately assess intelligence in newborns or reliably predict later intellectual development. However, a number of procedures have been designed that can measure the infant's developmental state. Most of these focus on sensorimotor tasks: gross motor behaviour, vocalization, and language behaviour. Generally, a six-month-old would be assessed on recognition of people and objects, motor co-ordination, alertness, awareness of the environment, and vocalization.

The most widely used standardized test of cognitive ability for infants and preschoolers is the Mental Scale of the Bayley Scales of Infant Development (Bayley, 1969, 1994). Although the Bayley Scales were standardized for normally developing children, much research has focused on their use with disabled children. Cook and colleagues demonstrated that the Mental Scale of the Bayley Scales was a stable instrument for predicting cognitive performance in developmentally at-risk infants between 6 and 12 months. In particular, the Bayley scales can indicate the nature and extent of a child's difficulties.

The full Bayley Scales consist of a mental ability test and a motor scale. The 163 mental test items and 81 motor scale items are based on skills typically found in children in the sensorimotor period or a few months beyond it. At 16 months, for example, a mental ability measure is being able to build a tower with three small cubes after demonstration by the examiner. A motor measure is the ability to stand on the left foot alone.

Another commonly used cognitive test for children functioning in the sensorimotor period is the Ugiris and Hunt Scale of Infant Psychological Development. This scale and its adaptations (Dunst, 1980; Fieber, 1977) are criterion-referenced measures based on Piaget's sensorimotor constructs. They measure sequential steps in sensorimotor development: means/end relationships, visual pursuit and object permanence, causality, gestural imitation, verbal imitation, construction of objects in space, and behaviour relating to objects.

Intervenors may use developmental screening, which provides an assessment of the child's developmental status in order to determine whether the child is likely to experience delays in development (Meisels, 1988, 1989). Comprehensive screening ensures that all aspects of a child's growth and development are checked so that comparisons can be made within and across domains. Parents can be included in the assessment process. Two widely used assessment procedures in which parents are active participants are the Minnesota Child Development Inventory and the Denver Prescreening Developmental Questionnaire.

PROGRESS CHECK 4

Explain when, how, and why a psychologist would use the Bayley Scales. Describe the scales themselves and the type of information they yield.

DEVELOPMENTAL ASSESSMENT

Developmental perspectives view behaviour in terms of a natural progression in areas such as cognitive development, fine and gross motor development, and language and social behaviour development. The developmental approach to assessment is founded on the assumption that children progress through stages, and that knowledge of these stages can be employed so as to highlight qualitative and quantitative differences between children.

Essentially, developmental approaches consider whether a child has attained basic developmental skills; they compare the exceptional child with normally developing peers in different domains of development. As we pointed out in Chapter 6, a developmental curriculum model, based on developmental assessment, does not have the confidence of all those in ECSE. Some professionals consider the developmental approach as the most appropriate for pinpointing lags or problems in one or more areas of growth; others stress the need to examine immediately functional skills, and worry that developmental scales may not focus on important social or cognitive strategies. They question whether it is useful or efficient to examine skills that *seem* age-specific and prerequisite but may not be important to certain relevant tasks.

The developmental approach to assessment is based on the use of developmental scales. These provide guidelines, which in turn provide a baseline. If the child fails an item, it is rewritten as an instructional objective, under the assumption that skills must be taught in the same order they are acquired by non-disabled children. For example, if four-year-old Johnnie does not reach the expressive language milestones normally seen in four-year-olds, we may say that he demonstrates expressive language at the level of a child of only 30 months and is therefore 18 months below the norm for expressive language development. Specific training would begin at Johnnie's developmental level (30 months) and attempt to provide experiences to address the deficits.

Developmental assessment often uses norm-referenced tests, which determine the extent of deviation from the norm. Developmental scale items are typically drawn from standardized tests designed to differentiate children who are not developing normally at an expected rate. Sometimes developmental scales are not standardized; instead, teachers use simple scales of developmental milestones that are compilations of information taken from various scales and charts.

A broad range of measures are available for developmental screening and assessment. Examples of developmental scales are shown in Table 8–3.

One of the most widely used scales is the Denver Developmental Screening Test, which was developed for children from one month to six years of age. The Denver is a screening instrument; its main purpose is to sort out from a large group of children those who may be at risk for developmental lags, and who should be referred for further evaluation.

The Denver surveys a child's functioning on landmark developmental tasks relating to gross motor skills, fine-motor adaptive skills, language behaviour, psychosocial ability, and so on. It consists of 105 items arranged in four sections: personal-social skills, fine motor and adaptive skills, language skills, and gross motor skills.

The Denver is easy to administer and score. A child's performance is measured against an age scale that represents the functioning of normal children. By comparing the child's performance to the norm for each activity, examiners can estimate developmental delays.

TABLE 8–3: Examples of scales and measures

Scale	Age	Features	Subtests
Battelle Developmental Inventory (Newborg, Stock, & Wnek, 1984)	Birth to 8 years	Comprehensive developmental tool based on developmental milestones. Estimates functioning across domains and generates a total developmental score. Not normed on children with handicaps, but test manual describes uses with children with disabilities and adaptations for sensory and motor impairments.	341 items in five assessment domains: personal-social, adaptive, motor, communication, and cognitive.
Behavior Rating Scale for Autism and Atypical Children (Ruttenberg et al., 1977)		Uses observation. Designed for autistic children.	Eight scales that measure relationship to an adult, communication, drive for mastery, vocalization, expressive speech, sound and speech reception, social responsiveness, body movement, and psycho-biological development.
Bracken Basic Concept Scale (Bracken, 1984)	2–6 to 8–8 years	Includes both a diagnostic and a screening test.	
Brigance Diagnostic Inventory of Early Skills (Brigance, 1978)	Birth to 7 years	Developmental and readiness.	Cognitive, speech and language, fine and gross motor, self-help, socio-emotional.
The Callier-Azusa Scale (Stillman, 1978)	Birth to 6 years	Deaf-blind, severely and profoundly handicapped. Used by someone familiar with the child so that typical behaviour can be observed in natural contexts.	18 subscales on five domains: motor and perceptual development, daily living skills, communication, and social development.
Carolina Developmental Profile (Lillie, 1975)	2 to 5 years	Developmental.	Cognitive, speech and language, fine and gross motor skills.
Denver Developmental Prescreening Questionnaire	3 months to 6 years	Parent report.	

Scale	Age	Features	Subtests
(Frankenburg, Fandal, & Thornton, 1987)			
Denver Developmental Screening Test (Frankenberg, Dodds, & Fandal, 1975; Frankenberg et al., 1990).	Birth to 6 years		Assesses development in speech, language, fine and gross motor skills, self-help skills.
Developmental Activities Screening Inventory 2 (Fewell & Langley, 1984)	Birth to 5 years	Screening test. Adaptations for blind and deaf children.	
Developmental Profile 11 (Alpern, Boll, & Shearer, 1980, 1986)	Birth to 9 1/2 years	Relies exclusively on parent input.	Cognitive, speech, language, fine and gross motor, self-help, socio-emotional.
First Step Screening Test for Evaluating Preschoolers	2–9 to 6–2	Individually administered screening test for identifying developmental delays.	Eight subtests on quantitative reasoning, picture completion, visual position in space, problem solving, auditory discrimination, word retrieval, association, and sentence and digit repetition.
Miller Assessment for Preschoolers (Miller, 1982)	2–9 to 5–8 years	Overview of developmental status.	
Minnesota Child Development Inventory (Ireton & Thwing, 1974)	1 to 6 years	Parent report measure that uses a yes/no format.	320 items about child development and behaviour—gross motor, fine motor, expressive language, comprehension, self help, personal-social.

ECOLOGICAL ASSESSMENT

Ecological assessment is based on the social systems perspective. Ecological approaches broaden the traditional view of assessment: they view an individual's behaviour as a function of the values of the social system within which he or she is being evaluated; also, they consider the child's total "ecological system" (i.e., the various environments in which he or she functions). This type of assessment provides information on the child's functioning in various settings with various people. It also pinpoints the needs of the current environment, the next environment, and the home.

When the ecological approach is taken, assessment and intervention focus on real-life situations. The skills assessed and taught have functional meaning and are part of practical activities that fit into daily routines; they are also generalizable across different environments. This approach compares the child's current adaptive skills at home and in school with those likely to be needed in the future (Snell, 1987). It looks at environmental demands to determine which skills to assess; it identifies those skills which are most likely to be required at home, in school, or in the community, and which will increase self-sufficiency in those environments (Brown et al., 1979).

There are a number of methods for identifying and analysing routines and activities. One is to interview the parents or caregivers (this is sometimes referred to as an ecological inventory). The parents are asked to describe their daily routines and activities and the child's present participation in them. A second is the survival skills approach. Survival skills assessments and curricula are based on skills that early childhood educators expect or require of young children in child care, preschool, or kindergarten settings (Noonan & McCormick, 1993).

The Early Screening Profile and System to Plan Early Childhood Services (AGS, 1990) is an ecological approach to screening. It measures the cognitive, language, motor, self-help, social, and health development of children between two and six. It combines information from parents, children, and teachers in a brief yet comprehensive screen.

FUNCTIONAL APPROACH

The functional approach and the ecological approach are first cousins, both view children in terms of how well their current performance enables them to succeed in their environment. However, they emphasize somewhat different things: the ecological approach stresses assessment in natural environments; the functional approach stresses the skills needed in those environments. Functional assessment is important if a child is having problems in a certain environment. A child's age and degree of disability are critical factors to consider.

Functionality refers to the characteristics of skills needed for effective and individual coping in the daily environment. There are two components of functionality. The first is whether the skill will increase the child's ability to interact with people and objects in the daily environment. The second is whether the skill will have to be performed by someone else if the child has not been taught to do it.

The functional approach stresses the assessment of specific observable behaviours. It is based on the direct collection of performance data; on the identification of factors that affect performance, such as those under teacher control; on the presentation and examination of repeated teaching trials; and on close assessment to assess the success of teaching (Sugai & Maheady, 1988). It looks at elements of the child's behavioural repertoire that interfere with instructional

Adaptive behaviour the ability to respond to and function in the environment according to age and social standards. Behaviour that allows the child to interact with the environment and those in it in ways that are appropriate to age, context, and culture.

objectives; at appropriate steps to deal with the skill-inhibiting components of behaviour; at conditions that motivate the child to attend, or that elicit a response; and at the level of assistance the child requires to complete a task not accomplished spontaneously (Strain, Sainato, & Maheady, 1984).

Functional assessment provides a direct link between what is assessed and what must be taught, and encompasses ***adaptive behaviour*** (as does the ecological approach). Essentially, adaptive behaviour refers to how well a person is able to adapt to environmental demands. Many adaptive behaviours are highly visible skills that provide evidence of accomplishment (e.g., feeding oneself). Usually, the scales used to measure adaptive behaviour consist of lists of behaviours and are completed by someone close to the child—a parent, teacher, or primary caregiver.

Scales in common use include the Balthazar Scales of Adaptive Behavior (Balthazar, 1973, 1976); the Adaptive Behavior Checklist (Allen, Cortazzo, & Adams, 1970), and the Cain-Levine Social Competence Scale (Cain, Levine, & Elzey, 1963). The Vineland Adaptive Behavior Scale (Sparrow, Balla, & Cicchetti, 1984) is used with individuals from birth to adulthood. It has 297 items and provides a general assessment of adaptive behaviour.

PROGRESS CHECK 5

Outline the main features of ecological assessment and functional assessment. What are the similarities between the two approaches? What are the differences?

ARENA ASSESSMENT

Assessment procedures used to involve taking a child out of the natural environment. In current ECSE, the trend is toward assessing children in more naturalistic contexts, as opposed to clinical ones.

Arena assessment is an observational assessment approach in which staff from several disciplines focus on their particular domains within the context of play. Transdisciplinary Play-Based Assessment (Linder, 1990) is one example of an arena assessment approach. It is designed for children between six months and six years and provides observations in four areas: social-adaptive behaviour, cognitive skills, communication and language, and sensorimotor functioning. The Hawaii Early Learning Profile (Furuno et al., 1979) is also designed for use by multidisciplinary teams.

READINESS

Readiness testing is used to determine the child's readiness to benefit from a specific academic program—for example, a given level of a reading program—or the type of instruction to be used with the child at his or her current level.

Teachers who wish to use readiness measures will find a wide variety of popular ones on which to draw—for example, the Kindergarten Screening Instrument (Rivers, Meininger, & Batten, 1991) and the measures designed by Alfred H. Brigance specifically for child care centres, preschools, kindergartens, and ECSE programs.

The three Brigance screens assess developmental readiness and early academic skills for children from two to six. The Early Preschool Screen is for children of age two to two-and-a-half. The Preschool Screen is for children of three or four. The K and 1 Screen–Revised is for children of five or six.

The Brigance screens are easy to administer, simple to score, and cost-effective. Screening sessions take no more than 12 to 15 minutes per child. The process includes parent questionnaires. The Brigance screening devices gather information that typically is useful for program planning and referral-making, and for assigning children to groups. Examples of items in the Brigance screens are shown in Table 8–4.

TABLE 8–4: The Brigance screens—sequence of skills assessed

\# skills assessed
* optional advanced assessment

	Early preschool screen	Preschool screen	K and 1 screen
General knowledge and comprehension			
Identification of body parts	#	#	#
Identification of people in pictures	#		
Identification of objects	#	#	
quantitative concepts		#	
matching colours	*	*	
colour recognition		#	#
following directions			
Speech and language			
personal data response		#	#
picture vocabulary	#	#*	#*
verbal fluency	#		
verbalizes personal needs	*	*	
repeats sentences		#	
plural s and ing		#	
prepositions and irregular plural nouns		#	
articulates initial sounds		*	*
syntax and fluency			#
Gross motor skills			
standing	#	#	#
walking	#	#	#
jumping	#		
hopping	*	*	#
Fine motor skills			
block tower building	#	#	
draws shapes (visual motor)	#*	#*	#
draws a person			#
Math			
number concepts	*	#	
counts by rote		*	#
numerals in sequence			#

basic number skills	*

Readiness	
visual discrimination	#
recites alphabet	#
recognition of lowercase	#
letters (uppercase alternate)	

Basic reading skills	
auditory discrimination	#
basic preprimer vocabulary	*
preprimer-primer	*
oral reading	

Manuscript writing	
prints personal data	#

ACCOUNTABILITY ASSESSMENT

Instructors want to know if the teaching they are providing is really making a difference. Accountability testing (program evaluation) is carried out in order to make decisions about individual children and to identify changes that need to be made in entire programs. Program evaluations are used to determine whether a child has benefited from a particular program, and/or whether a teacher has been effective in instructing children.

LEARNING ACTIVITY 3

In this chapter, we have referred to the National Association for the Education of Young Children (NAEYC) a number of times. We have mentioned their attitudes and suggestions about assessment in early childhood education. List the main points made by the NAEYC that we have included.

Selecting an Approach

In infants and preschoolers, assessment is used to look for maturational lags and for problems that can be addressed through early intervention. Before assessing a child, examiners must know what behaviours they expect to see. For example, when testing a three-year-old, they must focus on behaviours usually exhibited by two- to four-year-olds. Such behaviours may include speaking in sentences of four to six words, building three-block pyramids, matching similar pictures, and buttoning. Problem behaviours might include a poor attention span, or failure to respond to oral language and visual symbols. A child might also be out of touch with the environment; this would appear as poor motor control, low body image, and poor visual and auditory discrimination. Examiners must choose tests and tools appropriate to these behaviours.

Tests are developed for specific purposes, such as screening, diagnosis, or intervention planning. It follows that tests should always be used for the purposes for which they were designed. Before selecting a test, the educator should consider the following:

- Which skill areas are included in the measure?
- Are the broad domains, such as language, self-help skills, and motor skills, divided into meaningful strands of behaviour?
- What is the age range addressed?
- Does the instrument reflect a developmental milestones model, a theory-based developmental model, or a functional model?
- Are suggested activities for training skills included in the test?
- Do the activities in the instrument provide adaptations for children with sensory or motor impairments? (Bailey & Wolery, 1984)

ASSESSMENT PROCEDURES

Not everyone agrees with assessment for very young children. The validity of using tests with young children and the tests themselves are the two long-standing sources of controversy. Some critics highlight the inadequacy of current screening and readiness measures for young children; and point out that all testing is less than perfect, and that many problems are associated with the measures used. For example:

- When working with young children, teachers may find a shortage of tools and be forced to use measures designed for older children.
- Many of the instruments available for assessment are of questionable reliability and validity; that is, they may not be consistent over time (from test to test) and may not assess what they claim to assess. For example, the Gesell Developmental Scales (Gesell & Amatruda, 1947), also known as the Gesell Maturity Scale, the Gesell Norms of Development, and the Yale Test of Child Development, were first published in 1925 and have since been used heavily by medical and allied professionals working with young children. Despite some updating, the Gesell scales suffer from a number of weaknesses and have been criticized severely for their lack of psychometric integrity (Meisels, 1985, 1987). Other studies have reported that less than half of infant developmental scales have satisfactory validity and reliability (Cross & Johnston, 1977; Walls et al., 1977).
- Test developers often ignore cultural and language variations, and some children may be disadvantaged by the measures themselves.

Others educators have pressing concerns relating specifically to the assessment of young children:

- The younger the child, the less confidence can be placed in the reliability and validity of assessment measures. Essentially, testing for young children simply tells us whether a child is reaching the developmental milestones within normal limits in a particular domain.
- Young children are not good test takers. Most are distractible and show a short attention span and transient responsiveness. They tend to tire easily and are often inconsistent in their responses. All of these factors make young children difficult to assess at the best of times.
- Obtaining co-operation from young children can be difficult. In contrast to older children and adults, they perceive no need to give "correct" answers or to "please" the examiner.

When assessing young children, assessors must administer materials rapidly and keep interest high.

• Even for highly trained personnel, very young children are difficult to assess. This problem relates both to administering tests and to interpreting results. Because children develop in variable patterns, and because there are wide variations in "normal" behaviour, interpretation cannot help but be tenuous.

The consensus is that for infants and preschoolers with disabilities, assessment is useful in the early intervention process. Most educators agree that some type of evaluation is essential in order to identify and diagnose problems, determine placement, and plan educational interventions. However, there are major differences of opinion about assessment, most of which are the same as those articulated about assessment for normally developing young children. Those working with children with special needs find themselves caught in a dilemma: they know that early identification is crucial for detecting developmental problems, yet they also know that the assessment process is fraught with hazards.

ADAPTING PROCEDURES

The assessment of any young child is difficult. The assessment of at-risk children and of those with disabilities is especially difficult. The more severe the young child's disability (or disabilities), the more true this is.

There are many reasons why. Problems in assessment arise because all children develop in complex and irregular ways; because assessment instruments are limited; because reliable prevalence data are lacking; and because knowledge is lacking about the relationship between social and biological factors in disabling conditions. The greater the disability, the greater the difficulties.

Accurate information about the performance of young children with special needs is lacking, for various reasons. For example, measures have generally not been specifically developed for the disabled population. Many tests are

BOX 8–2

Billy's IPP

Background information

Billy shows attention deficits, which are characterized by distractibility, difficulty in concentrating, and failure to complete tasks. He flits from toy to toy and activity to activity, never stopping to play for longer than a few seconds. He seems to have little or no attention span. However, his activity level is not really the problem; rather, it is his impulsiveness and lack of concentration. Billy's high distractibility and short attention span make it less likely that he will make the best possible use of the educational materials and activities. As well, his behaviour detracts from the learning experiences of classmates.

Assessment results/present levels of functioning

It is very difficult to make an accurate assessment of Billy's progress in the cognitive, language, and motor domains because his impulsiveness masks other areas of development. In language, for example, Billy loves to talk to the teachers and tells many stories about things that happened outside the centre. But he is always in such a hurry to get the words out that he jumbles them out of sequence. He does not appear to have lags in motor development—quite the contrary. He shows many gross and fine motor skills, but since he rarely concentrates for more than a few seconds, his construction skills, puzzle play, and so on are difficult to assess. Socially, Billy is meeting difficulties. The other children are not particularly willing to play with Billy, and this only increases his already rather aggressive behaviour. He is quite willing to take a toy from another child when he can't play in the group. For the most part, Billy is ignored rather than actively rejected by the other children, although some of the boys are beginning to respond to his behaviour with some aggression of their own.

Formal assessment was attempted, but the examiners had little confidence in their results. They reported that Billy was too distractible and impulsive to sit and concentrate for the time required to complete the various subtests.

The physician has recommended drug therapy for Billy. However, the mother is very unwilling to resort to Ritalin and has rejected the idea at this time.

General recommendations

The overriding goal is to help Billy curb his hyperactive and impulsive behaviour and play more appropriately. If this can be accomplished, the other problems of social acceptance and language may also be alleviated. For Billy, the number of activities and toys available will be restricted; at the same time, certain toys and activities that result in more social and interactive behaviours will be promoted.

Long-range goals

- To expand concentration span though activities in which the child is interested.
- To plan an activity, and to play with one or two other children for periods of 10 to 15 minutes with teacher monitoring.
- To provide clear-cut, consistent, and immediate consequences for behaviour.

Short-term objectives

- To improve concentration and behaviour. To this end, use much positive reinforcement. For example, play with Billy with a toy of his own choosing and invite one other child to play. Reinforce children for appropriate play behaviour.
- Use very short periods of time out (see Chapter 12) when Billy is becoming too excited or aggressive. Explain carefully to Billy the reasons for time out.

Young children are very difficult to assess.

standardized on the normally developing population, and many of the developmental scales are not normed on children with special needs. A common theme underlying much of the professional literature is that most standardized tests do not consider disabilities; thus, they are likely to be inappropriate or unfair to many children. Problems most frequently arise when a child's performance on a particular item is inappropriately influenced by the handicapping condition (Bailey & Wolery, 1989). Many of the tasks used in such tests must be eliminated because of motor difficulties, sensory impairments, and special problems present in the children being assessed. As well, exceptional children may show more restricted behaviour than regular children, and this may further decrease a scale's sensitivity (Garwood, 1982). Finally it is not clear which types of skills should be assessed in children with disabilities.

For children with severe and multiple disabilities, the problems are compounded. The assessment of these youngsters is particularly difficult for the following reasons:

- These children often show deficits in ability to establish relationships.
- Regular systems of reinforcement may be inadequate for these children.
- They usually have impaired communication skills.
- Their sensory abnormalities may result in unusual responses to sensory stimuli.
- They have attention differences.
- They may show abnormal motor behaviour.
- Clinicians must take into account the frequent co-existence of developmental disabilities, mental retardation, and neurological deficits.
- Autistic children especially have a need for sameness, and often demonstrate an inability to switch tasks. As well, autistic children demonstrate marked variability on test performance: they may do poorly on tasks requiring abstract thought, symbolism, and sequential logic, but perform well on tasks that demand manual and visual spatial skills (Cummings & Finger, 1980).

For young children who are at risk or disabled, it is vital that the examiner be flexible (Ulrey, 1982a, b). Flexibility is especially important for younger or more disabled children.

When young children with disabilities are being tested, rigid application of standardized procedures may result in false conclusions; for this reason, it is appropriate for examiners to modify procedures. For example, verbal tests may be eliminated from a battery, or a physical or occupational therapist may be called in to assist in handling and positioning techniques so as to maximize the child's performance. Those conducting assessments with young children with disabilities must consider several other adaptations that relate specifically to settings, standard routines, and the personnel involved. Areas for consideration include these:

- For an accurate and appropriate assessment, the examiner must establish rapport with the child and the family. When the parents are present, the child may feel more secure. Also, parents should be involved during the assessment process as a source of information.

- Assessment should be nonthreatening and should be performed in a naturalistic setting rather than a clinical environment. The best assessments are done in the classroom by the child's teacher. When minority and disabled children are tested in a familiar setting, they do better than when tested in unfamiliar settings (Fuchs & Fuchs, 1986).

- Multiple assessments should be conducted. The need is for ongoing assessment of the child in a natural setting in a child-centred situation.

- Assessments should be interdisciplinary. A team approach enables all members to see the child as a total being. This is better than each member concentrating on one part of the child's development. The size of the team will vary with the disability.

- Findings must be monitored frequently to reflect and encourage changes in the child's competency.

In assessment, there will be special procedural considerations. Many children have sensory or motor impairments that are likely to affect their ability to respond to standardized items. During the actual assessment, keep the following in mind:

- Keep the child motivated. Keep assessments short, intersperse quiet and movement activities, and use interesting materials.

- Be systematic. Some children may tolerate lulls in item administration; many will not. Testers need to plan carefully.

Support adaptation when the child must be placed in a certain position or provided some general form of support before being able to pass an item during an assessment.

- Adapt the response requirements as necessary. For this, there are three general techniques. With a ***support adaptation***, the child is placed in a certain position or provided with some general form of support so that the child can show whether he or she can pass an item. With a ***prosthetic adaptation*** the child is provided with a specific piece of equipment, such as braces or a hearing aid, so as to be able to demonstrate a skill. A ***general adaptation*** does not require support or a piece of equipment; instead, changes are made in the basic requirements of the task. Examples: a hearing-impaired child may need to perform communication tasks with sign language, and a child with a physical disability may be allowed to look toward the response instead of pointing manually.

Prosthetic adaptation the child needs a specific piece of equipment such as braces or a hearing aid to demonstrate a skill.

- Adapt the way the test is presented. For example, if the child has a visual impairment, hold a picture closer.

- Modify procedures. Often, this means allowing more time for timed tasks.

- Alter the test stimuli; for example, provide larger pictures or speak more slowly.

- Incorporate additional aids, equipment, and management procedures.

General adaptation one that does not require support or a piece of equipment but still represents a change in the basic requirements of the task.

- Limit the use of language to tasks that measure language skills; present other tasks using nonverbal techniques.

- When they are available, employ specially designed measures. For example, a number of scales are used to accommodate the scatter that is typical of children with infantile autism.

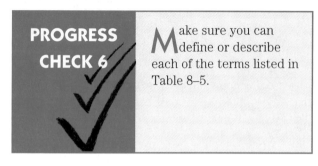

PROGRESS CHECK 6

Make sure you can define or describe each of the terms listed in Table 8–5.

- Consider other approaches to assessment besides developmental approaches using norm-referenced tools (see Bailey & Wolery, 1989; Langley, 1991).

TABLE 8–5: New terms and ideas

adaptive behaviour	interviews
anecdotal records	norm-referenced
Apgar screening	prenatal screening
assessment	prosthetic adaptation
criterion-referenced	screening
direct observation	standardized
early identification	support adaptation
general adaptation	tests
hyperactivity	

BOX 8–3

Helpful hints: ADHD

- Reflect and develop goals. Reflect on the data collected, the perspectives of other teachers, and the discussions you have had with the parents.

- Try various interventions. Each child with ADHD is different, and the same intervention will not suit all children.

- Stress positive reinforcement. For ADHD children, positive reinforcement (most often using secondary reinforcers) can be effective in reducing activity levels, increasing time on tasks, and improving academic performance (Fiore, Becker, & Nero, 1993).

- Channel excessive energy into more controlled activities, such as marching to a favourite tune.

- Do not allow too many choices. In painting, for example, three or four colours to choose from are better than ten.

- Hyperactive and impulsive children may especially benefit from direct suggestions for engaging in dramatic actions. Lay-Dopyera and Dopyera (1990) suggest that activities that involve conscious tensing followed by relaxation can be particularly effective for these children. They suggest that children become "racers." Here, they begin with actions such as shaking hands and giving autographs to the fans. They then become tight-set, with muscles hard and waiting for the starting signal. They then run a hard, quick race and follow this with total relaxation—collapsed, stretched out, and exhausted (p. 320).

- The impulsive child may benefit from dramatic activities that require conscious control of movement, such as moving slowly and then quickly. The child can follow a series of suggested actions, such as these: a cat stealthily approaching and then pouncing on a mouse; a little dog trying to steal a big dog's bone; or someone fishing, slowly reeling in a line to change the bait, and then rapidly reeling when there is a catch (Lay-Dopyera & Dopyera, 1990, p. 320).

SUMMARY

1. Assessment refers to the process of gathering information for the purpose of making a decision. The major benefit of early identification is that it allows early intervention to begin.

2. Children with special needs can be identified at any time. Children with severe disabilities and sensory handicaps such as deafness and severe visual impairment very rarely escape notice, and are usually identified quite early in life. For those with milder disabilities, the early childhood teacher is in a unique position: he or she is well placed to identify a child with a possible learning disability within the context of the peer group.

3. The trend is toward assessment in naturalistic settings. This means that teachers will play a greater role in the assessment process, particularly in the area of observation. Staff in early childhood programs should observe children on an ongoing basis and in a variety of situations.

4. Assessment serves one fundamental purpose: to find ways of promoting learning. Assessment procedures are employed to determine a child's developmental status, to arrange educational assistance, and to plan appropriate programs. Assigning labels is *not* the purpose of assessment; nor is comparing children to their peers.

5. Ongoing assessment employs a variety of tools and processes, which are used to monitor children's learning in all domains. These tools and processes include psychometric tests, achievement tests, criterion-referenced tests, developmental scales, adaptive behaviour scales, direct observation, and informant interviews.

6. Testing is but one of several strategies for gathering information about children; that being said, tests perform important functions when properly used.

7. When direct testing is used to assess children's cognitive skills, the procedures are referred to as psychometric testing, aptitude testing, or IQ testing. While normative measures may be useful in identifying disabilities and in arriving at a specific diagnosis, there are many difficulties associated with the use of standardized measures.

8. Psychometric tests are not suitable for a large proportion of children with disabilities; for this reason, other types of tools have been developed to measure a child's abilities in motor skills, language and communication, social behaviour, and self-help skills. Probably the most common measures are developmental scales founded on the developmental milestones attained by normally developing children at certain ages.

9. Although norm-referenced tests are sometimes employed, criterion-referenced tests are far more common. Criterion-referenced tests, unlike standardized tests,

do not compare the child's results to an age, grade, or performance norm. Rather, they attempt to measure the child's knowledge or skill in a particular area of learning. In curriculum-referenced testing, the child's abilities are assessed in the context of a predetermined sequence of curriculum objectives; each assessment item is linked to an educational objective.

10. Event sampling, which involves the measurement of specific behaviours as they occur, is one way to document direct observations.

11. One mode of gathering information is by asking parents. Caregivers are central to the assessment and intervention process, and teachers should actively solicit the views of parents as to which child behaviours are necessary and functional in the home and the community.

12. The most common infant assessment measures analyse a child's ability to solve tasks using combinations of motor, language, social, and cognitive skills.

13. Developmental checklists help to identify potential problems. An alternative to developmental scales is the adoption of a functional approach to testing that examines the child's performance within the context of naturalistic environments.

14. Preschool children present special assessment problems, both in the measures used and in the actual assessment. In the latter, the more disabled the child, the greater the difficulties in obtaining an accurate assessment.

CHAPTER 9

Individualizing Programs for Children with Special Needs

CASE STUDY

Cinta

When intervening with children with disabilities, early childhood personnel may find themselves participating on teams, collaborating with other professionals, paraprofessionals, aides, and volunteers; and working more directly with families. This is often a new experience for teachers. When told by her supervisor that she would be attending a formal team meeting, Lee felt a little worried. Certainly, in the daycare centre where she worked, Lee participated in almost daily meetings with her colleagues about the day's program, the children's progress, and general management and administrative issues. Now, however, the centre had integrated a child with a disability, and Lee was having to adjust, and team meetings were to be part of that adjustment.

Cinta, the child in question, was proving quite a challenge to the centre. When she first came, the staff were aware that the parents were newly arrived and that Spanish was the first language in the home. Because Lee speaks fluent Spanish, she worked with Cinta to maintain the first language and introduce the child to English.

As time passed, Lee began to have concerns about Cinta's progress in both languages. In many ways, Cinta appeared to be progressing through the normal stages of second-language development: she understood and used a few English words and seemed to respond to much that was said to her in Spanish. It was not the language that concerned Lee and the other teachers so much as the way Cinta tried to express the language. In both English and Spanish she seemed to have major deviations in her speech. Even taking into account how speech sounds are acquired in both languages, Cinta's gaps were very obvious. She consistently omitted many consonants, especially the high-frequency sounds such as *s*, *sh*, *t*, and *th*. For example, she called Lee "Mi Ee," and the supervisor, Mrs. Abrahamson, "Mi A–on." Her current best friend, Melissa, was "Mi–l–u."

When the speech therapist visited the centre, the supervisor asked him to observe Cinta's speech and language in child/child and adult/child interactions. After close observation, the therapist used a number of measures, moving from informal to more formal measures.

To begin, the therapist made a variety of objects and activities available to the children playing in a group that included Cinta. Then he recorded and observed Cinta's behaviour in this setting. This interaction was then evaluated in terms of the developmental level of linguistic performance, the social and regulatory use of language, the development of both Spanish and English, and phonology (the sound system of language). On a second visit, he used a language-sampling tool, the Teacher Analysis of Grammatical Structures (TAGS), and some formal measures of articulation and speech performance. Again, the assessment stressed both the first language and Cinta's emerging English.

It is extremely difficult to separate speech development from language development in the early years; in most children, the two are closely intertwined. In Cinta's case, however, language development was not the major concern. In Spanish, she seemed to be acquiring language in a normal sequence; in English, she was passing though the normal stages of second-language learning. However, there were many deviations in Cinta's speech that could not be attributed to learning two languages, and these were affecting her social interactions and communication in the classroom.

The therapist first recommended that Cinta have an audiological assessment. This assessment indicated that Cinta, while she wasn't deaf, had a hearing loss in both ears. She could hear speech but not the higher consonant sounds, and this was reflected in her own speech. Cinta's audiogram (see Figure 9–1) indicated that she had a bilateral (both ears) loss in the moderate to severe range.

Lee attended a team meeting, together with the audiologist, the speech therapist, Cinta's mother, and an interpreter. The goal of the meeting was to pool information about Cinta

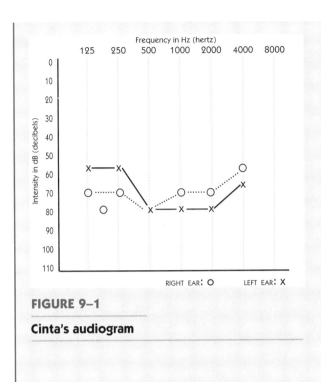

Frequency in Hz (hertz)

RIGHT EAR: O   LEFT EAR: X

FIGURE 9–1

Cinta's audiogram

and develop an appropriate program for her. The therapist explained the articulation errors and where they occurred in both languages. His findings were confirmed by the audiologist, who recommended hearing aids for Cinta and suggested some minor modifications to the preschool environment.

For Cinta, language experience will probably be the most critical type of intervention. Talking to Cinta, and reading to her and telling her stories, will increase her attention and communication skills. So will word games, and games involving rhyming and imitation, and access to records and videos. With Lee's input, the team discussed how oral language could be emphasized in the context of everyday routines using both Spanish and English. The mother agreed with the recommendations, and she and Lee decided on a plan to help Cinta accept her hearing aids. Cinta's individual plan is shown in Box 9–2.

GOOD EARLY CHILDHOOD EDUCATION SHOULD HELP young children accelerate their development, learn new behaviours, function more independently, and maintain positive advances. That being said, children with disabilities will probably have more difficulty learning from naturally occurring experiences. No matter how much fun the program is, no matter how attractive the toys, and no matter how stimulating the environment, without extra help young children with disabilities will probably not learn as easily as those who are developing normally.

In designing and delivering early childhood programs for children with disabilities, there are four main principles: the use of developmentally appropriate programs and practices; a focus on the family; the integration of services; and individualization (Canning & Lyon, 1990). In earlier chapters we addressed the first three of these issues: we stressed the need for developmentally and age-appropriate practices (Chapter 6), the integration of services based on consultation and collaboration (Chapter 4), and the importance of the family (Chapters 4 and 5). Implicitly or explicitly, we also emphasized that the essence of special education is individualization. Each child is viewed as having unique strengths and weaknesses, and programs are designed specifically to meet the special needs of individual children. This is true whether the child is in the infant or preschool years or in the formal educational system.

Early childhood educators have long recognized the presence of individual differences; many programs rely on written observations of children, which are then used to plan child-centred programs. For children with disabilities, we carry this one step farther.

BOX 9–1

Mild and moderate hearing impairments

A *hard of hearing* person has enough residual hearing to successfully process linguistic information through audition. In other words, such people can hear voices, however faint, or muffled. These people often but not always wear hearing aids. In contrast, a deaf person cannot hear voiced sounds, with or without a hearing aid.

Children with mild losses (25 to 40 dB) may have difficulty with faint or distant sounds. They may have problems in conversations, in groups, or in settings with much ambient noise. Those with moderate hearing losses (40 to 60 dB) often have difficulty with normal speech, especially in conversations, in groups, and in class discussions. Those with severe hearing losses (60 to 90 dB) have great difficulty even with loud or amplified speech, which seems faint and distorted. Those with severe losses require amplification and intense speech and language training.

Hard of hearing children can use spoken language adequately to transmit and receive information. They can use their residual hearing to develop speech and language skills, although they may use speech reading to supplement auditory skills. However, even with adequate speech and language skills, hard of hearing children may be at risk educationally.

Because childhood hearing impairment has ambiguous symptoms, it may be misdiagnosed, most especially in the case of hard of hearing children. The child may suffer from recurrent "on again, off again" otitis media, and present inconsistent responses. Moreover, many environmental variables, such as extraneous noises and distance from the speaker, can adversely affect the auditory comprehension of hard-of-hearing children.

If a child does not hear language, then the child's development of language will reflect these problems. Children who are deaf or hard-of-hearing require considerable intervention in the areas of health care, rehabilitation, therapy, and education. Generally, intervention involves two major components: medical and educational. Medical intervention tries to correct the physical causes of hearing loss and includes the amplification of sound through hearing aids. Educational intervention focuses on minimizing the educational and psychological consequences of hearing impairment, and takes the form of special education and related services.

Hard of hearing person one who, generally with the use of a hearing aid, has residual hearing sufficient to enable successful processing of linguistic information through audition.

For children with special needs, individualization often involves writing an individual program plan (IPP). These plans may be casual or structured, and appear in very different formats. Throughout this text, we have shown plans for different children; readers can see that plans follow different formats, contain different amounts and types of information, and involve different personnel. Also, the amount of direction for the teacher varies.

When a program is individualized, it does not mean the child will receive one-to-one instruction. Rather, it means there will be adaptations and modifications in one or more variables, including the environment, the schedule, the curriculum, the amount of teacher direction, and the way the groups are formed and taught. For some children adaptations will be minor; other children will place heavier demands on early childhood settings. For children who are mildly disabled, the main adjustments in a typical preschool program include a reduction in the physical and intellectual difficulty of the material provided, and extra aid and encouragement. The more severe the disability, the greater the adaptations will need to be, and the greater the amount of individualization.

We can see this in the case of Nancy, the deaf child in Chapter 2, and with Cinta, diagnosed as hard of hearing. In broad terms, both children are hearing impaired; however, each has completely different needs in the area of speech and language. Nancy's hearing loss is so great that she cannot hear voices even with the most sophisticated hearing aids. Nancy's information gathering will be largely visual, through speech reading and sign language. She will need consistent sign input; and when she reaches the formal school system, she will probably need a sign interpreter in order to function in a regular classroom.

Cinta obtains her information through audition, although the sound may be faint and a little distorted. She needs consistent auditory input, auditory training to stimulate her residual hearing, speech assistance in the sounds she is missing, and help getting used to listening to sound with a hearing aid. As she is also learning English as a second language, she needs many opportunities to use the new language, as well as encouragement to retain her native Spanish.

When teachers in the school system and early childhood personnel are confronted with having to prepare an individual program plan (IPP), they too often react negatively. Plans, they say, are too complex, take too long to prepare, and structure classroom interactions too much. None of this is really true. In an IPP we write down the goals we wish to help a child achieve, as well as the steps for achieving them. An IPP is an organizational document and a way for those involved with the child to communicate with each other. It is not written in stone; it can and should be changed as often as the needs of the child dictate.

There is no doubt that documenting what a child should accomplish in a set period can be time consuming. Note here that IPPs follow an assessment, and that all of those involved in the assessment process should contribute to formulating the IPP. Parent input is especially valuable; the goals set for the child should reflect the priorities that the parents hold for that child's learning.

We saw this part of the process in Cinta's case. All those involved—the audiologist, the speech therapist, Lee as the teacher, and the mother—provided input about the appropriate learning goals for Cinta. Wearing the hearing aids was an important goal for the mother and for the audiologist, while listening to and using certain speech sounds was important to Lee.

This chapter discusses the process of writing IPPs. Goals and objectives are the core of any IPP, and we will outline ways to prepare these.

Individualizing the Curriculum

As we discussed in Chapter 6, early childhood education models vary according to their philosophy, the children they serve, the site of service delivery, staffing patterns, the use of materials and activities, and evaluation techniques. This means that the goals and objectives of programs also differ.

Whatever the philosophy and model of a particular program, quality in early childhood programs depends greatly on the clear articulation of goals and objectives. Goals define the broad intent of the overall program model; they function as statements of expectations about the outcomes of programs and serve as

Most early childhood teachers expect children to develop at different rates and are prepared for uneven behaviour and rapid growth.

standards against which to measure a program's effectiveness.

Curriculum is the design and delivery of educational intervention and is always based on goals. Curriculum is defined as "systematic procedures for organizing educational activities; the procedures include both content (what to teach) and method (how to teach)" (Lillie, 1975, p. 2). Traditional curriculum may be seen as having four components: aims and objectives; the selection and organization of teaching experiences; teaching and learning strategies; and evaluation (Doxey, 1990).

For normally developing preschool and kindergarten children, both program goals and curriculum often focus on children's capabilities. The major goal of early childhood programs is to provide enrichment—that is, to expose children to social, cognitive, and other experiences that will enlarge and enhance their development. Programs are generally a mix of independent activities, teacher/child activities, and small- and large-group activities. Curriculum tends to centre on language arts, basic numeracy, creativity, and so on. Instruction is relatively unstructured. Children learn mainly through play; activities and materials are matched with their developmental levels.

For children with disabilities, the purpose of early childhood programs is intervention. Children's growth is stimulated and sustained in those areas of development where they are demonstrating lags; the children are taught skills that will allow them to develop as normally as possible. The three general areas of intervention are these: developmental, specific skills, and enrichment. Developmental areas include fine and gross motor skills, expressive and receptive language, and socio-emotional behaviour. Specific skill areas include self-help skills, pre-reading and pre-math skills, and communication skills. Enrichment areas include art and music. Not all of these areas will be included in an IPP. The IPP's goals and objectives only focus on areas of need.

One prominent characteristic of a curriculum for children with disabilities is its individual nature. Individualization is based on two principles: all children can learn, and all learning is legitimate. Most early childhood teachers expect children to develop at different rates and are prepared for uneven behaviour and rapid growth; thus, individualization "comes naturally" to them. With special children, individualization is carried a step further. An individualized curriculum is developed by a team, written in terms of long-range goals and short-term objectives, and founded on careful and ongoing measurement of a child's performance.

Individualization does not mean one-to-one instruction (although that may be a strategy). Rather, it means adapting and modifying the program and curriculum in ways that are compatible with the values of integration. Children with special needs should be placed in a centre where they can progress at their own level, where they are challenged to develop their potential without being swamped by a program beyond their grasp, where they can receive instruction in areas of need, and where they have opportunities to interact with normally developing children. At the same time, the program for a child with disabilities must fit with the centre's overall program: the needs of all children must be met, and the staff must be able to accommodate all needs.

Many of the modifications made for children with disabilities are beneficial to all children in the setting. The teaching methods are often almost the same, and many learning activities are appropriate for all young children.

The IPP

An IPP is a document that outlines the educational services and learning objectives for addressing a child's specific needs. It co-ordinates plans and services, personalizes and individualizes the child's program, and integrates the individual plan with the overall plans for the classroom group.

IPPs are influenced by a number of factors, especially the program model. The philosophy and curriculum influence assessment practices, learning objectives, teaching methods and strategies, the materials available, and child/teacher and child/child interaction. Even so, certain things appear on most IPPs:

- Child data.
- Conference data.
- Present levels of performance.
- Long-range goals.
- Short-term objectives.
- Instructional context.
- Broad suggestions for techniques or methods.
- Persons responsible.
- Assessment of the child's progress.
- An evaluation of the educational program.

Child data

Child data includes the child's full name, birthdate, chronological age, caregiver contact and telephone, centre, supervisor, and so on. Special needs such as medication, adaptive equipment, and feeding may also be included here. For example, on Cinta's IPP her amplification needs are included.

IPP data

Many plans contain various information about the IPP itself—for example, the names and positions of those attending the team meeting, when the IPP was drawn up, and whether the IPP is an initial document, a second IPP, or an evaluation document.

Present levels of performance

Assessment in early childhood education is predicated on one fundamental assumption: that when a child's disability or difficulty is iden-

BOX 9–2

Cinta's IPP

CHILD: *Cinta*
CENTRE: *Smithson*
DOB: *1 July 1990*
TEACHER: *Lee*

Medical information
Audiological assessment showed Cinta to have a hearing loss in the moderate to severe range.

Adaptive equipment
Behind-the-ear hearing aids.

Areas of need
Speech training, auditory training, developing proficiency in English, retention of first language.

Areas of strength
Normal cognitive functioning, appropriate social skills.

Assessment/performance information

Date	Test	Result
14-10-94	*Informal observations*	*Speech deviations.*
16-10-94	*TAGS*	*At almost normal levels in language; number of serious speech problems.*
	Articulation test	*Speech errors; use of consonants in initial, medial, and final position.*
24-10-94	*Wechsler Preschool and Primary Scale of Intelligence (WPPSI) Performance scale only*	*Normal cognitive functioning*

Persons responsible

Position	Name	Description
Teacher	*Lee*	*Stress oral skills; work proactively with therapist; model speech taught in individual lessons.*
Speech therapist	*Mr. Jones*	*Correct articulation errors, one hour weekly.*

Long-range goals
1. *Will participate in oral language activities on an individual basis and in small-group instruction.*
2. *Will imitate sounds correctly.*
3. *Will use residual hearing through auditory training activities.*
4. *Will wear hearing aid for prespecified times daily.*

Short-term objectives

1. *Small-group activities will focus on oral skills. For example, child will follow directions and find a treasure, or respond to simple discrimination of objects by giving a correct motor or verbal response. She can name and describe class members, as in "I see a person wearing a _____" "I see _____."*
2. *In incidental teaching episodes, the teacher will model correct sounds for Cinta to imitate.*
3. *In a small group, Cinta will participate in auditory training games [see Chapter 15].*
4. *To encourage Cinta to wear her hearing aids, the teacher should have her wear them for a pre-specified period (10 minutes) during free play or group time, and reinforce. Gradually extend the time for wearing the aids.*

tified early, problems can be ameliorated through early intervention, and the development of secondary conditions can be prevented. In effect, early identification is the natural corollary of early intervention.

Each individual plan is founded on an assessment that has been designed to discover the child's strengths and weaknesses in these areas: cognitive development, physical and motor development, socio-emotional development, and adaptive behaviour. Those preparing an IPP start with a record of the child's performance based on information derived from one or more assessments; they then pinpoint the child's present levels of performance and determine the skills the child needs to acquire. The assessment data should make it clear where a child is functioning and how that compares to normal developmental levels. For example, Cinta is four years old but has only acquired the speech sounds of a much younger child, and those not in the normal order of acquisition. With that information, teachers and a therapist can focus on helping her develop her speech skills. Or a fine motor assessment may show that five-year-old Jamie is functioning at a 30-month level in the motor domains. For him, objectives will stress motor skills beginning at Jamie's level of 30 months.

The process of taking assessment results, translating them into present levels of performance, and then using them to draw up an IPP is not as straightforward as it may at first seem. In fact, it takes much careful thought. Theories and assessment results cannot on their own determine goals and objectives. In determining instructional targets, we must start with the following: a basic understanding of child development, a knowledge of child assessment techniques, knowledge of the individual child (and of the implications for that child), good judgment, and, finally, the ability to relate developmental skills to the everyday demands of the classroom and to the demands placed on children.

Applying assessment information to IPP design involves three basic steps. First, the present levels of functioning are determined; this should result in a list of the child's

LEARNING ACTIVITY 1

Take any two of the case studies you have already read in this text. Read them carefully again, and divide the skill levels reported into skills that are developing normally, those that are delayed, and those that need remediation. Now prioritize the skills that need remediation in order of importance. Explain your reasons for the order of the objectives.

strengths and weaknesses. Next, these strengths and weaknesses are categorized as follows: skills that need remediation, skills that are delayed, and skills
within the normal range. Once this is done, skills are targetted for intervention
(long-term goals) and then written as short-term objectives.

Long-range goals

Goals and objectives are the core of the IPP. For children with disabilities,
goals and objectives are needed to help focus intervention services and to communicate the general and specific aims of an intervention among all those involved.

It is their specificity that differentiates goals from objectives. Long-range
goals are general long-term outcomes. A ***goal*** may be defined as a stated outcome
desired as a result of some action. Objectives are the increments in the progress
of learning. They are the steps for achieving the goals; they direct instruction and
learning on a day-to-day basis.

> **Goal**   a stated
> outcome desired as
> a result of some
> action.

Goals are broad general statements that help educators focus on the general
areas for which individualized programming will be provided. They indicate the
major learning experiences the child will have and the broad range of skills he or
she can be expected to attain. Long-range goals are usually written for one year,
except in the case of children with significant disabilities, whose long-range
goals may cover up to five years. When goals are written for one year, they are
annual goals. These annual goals are what the child can reasonably be expected
to achieve in that one year. Related annual goals can be grouped under broad categories called teaching goals; typically, these will be prioritized so that the most
important goals are addressed first. Billy, for example, does not play well with his
peers and has also failed to develop basic numeracy skills. At the centre, social
behaviours and peer interaction are more important at this time than numeracy. Goals on an IPP may also contain some of the major group-learning experiences, such as participating appropriately during circle time.

The process of defining goals requires much careful thought about desired
outcomes. Goals are generated by information about the child's present level of
performance and the skills needed for the environment. Typically, five to ten
goals are identified in those domains of functioning where the child is showing
the greatest lags.

When written down, goals should be phrased as specific expectations or
skills (as opposed to vague generic statements). For example, "learn to grasp" is
not specific enough; "places and releases object balanced on top of another object" is.

When selecting goals, team members should incorporate the parents' main
priorities. Planning should also consider the child's prior experiences and most
likely future. An IPP must take into account the physical and medical needs of
the child, and select skills that contribute to functional independence. It should
also consider goals that can be broken down into objectives that can be accomplished in small groups.

Goals should be developmentally and age appropriate and focus on the whole
child. One of the aims of early integrated intervention is to establish and maintain a synthesis in which all developmental areas are addressed in synchrony, so
that progress in one area supports progress in other areas. For example, a child
with a profound hearing loss needs to learn to utilize visual clues but also needs
to learn how it feels to play in the sand and build with blocks.

Short-term objectives

Once general goals have been defined, the objectives of a particular course of intervention can be established, along with appropriate teaching/learning strategies. An **objective** is a clear statement of exactly what a teacher wants a child to be able to do as a result of instruction. Short-term objectives state desired outcomes; they provide a flexible and personalized program for each child; and they set out a clear direction. They show the behaviour that a child will acquire in a specific period and indicate the degree to which the disability will interfere less with the child's functioning.

> Objective   a clear statement of exactly what a teacher wants a child to be able to do as a result of instruction.

Short-term objectives are provided for each annual goal and usually describe behaviour that can be acquired within three or four months. There is no exact rule, but generally three or four objectives are provided for each long-range goal.

Well-written objectives have some or all of the following characteristics:

- They have good form. Many objectives are written as behavioural statements. This means they include the behaviour or skill the child will perform, the conditions it will be performed under, and the criteria for acceptable performance. For example, "When given a bucket of blocks, Bill will construct a tower copying the teacher's model until he is successful on each attempt." This objective provides the skill (constructing a tower), the conditions (when given blocks and following a teacher's model), and the criterion for performance (on each attempt). Or compare these objectives: "The child will participate at circle time," and "The child will participate in group activities by requesting a turn." The latter objective requires a specific level of participation (requesting a turn); also, performance criteria can be established for it (two out of three approximations during each daily group over three consecutive days) (Notari-Syverson & Shuster, 1995).

- They are clearly stated. Good behavioural objectives are written as brief action statements; they use verbs and lend themselves to observation and measurement. In the example above, the verbs are *participate* and *construct*. Other appropriate verbs include apply, describe, recognize, repeat, copy, reproduce, choose, draw, classify, match, identify, and select.

- They describe behaviour. When appropriate verbs are used, teachers can more easily determine whether the child is performing the desired skill. Remember also that different observers must be able to identify the same behaviour.

- They are measurable and observable. A skill is measurable if it can be seen or heard and can be counted in some way—for example, by duration or frequency. For example, "Gains attention and refers to object, person, or event," is a measurable skill; "Gains a sense of self-importance" is not. "Understanding the story" is not measurable or observable; "Relates the story in sequence orally" is.

- They should be flexible. Objectives provide direction; they should encourage progress without pressuring the child to attain fixed standards.

> Tool skills   those that are instrumental in accomplishing the greatest number of other skills or functional skills.

- They allow the acquisition of a number of skills. Young children who are disabled should be instructed in such a way that they can learn many behaviours in a short time. Good objectives focus on tool (keystone) skills, or on general concepts as opposed to particular tasks. **Tool skills** are those which allow the greatest number of other skills or functional skills to be acquired. For example, an objective might state, "With paint in three colours, Juan will paint a mural with two other children." Such an objective opens the way to a number of strategies, such as peer mediation and incidental teaching, and to a number of skills, such as those relating to peer interaction, fine and gross motor development, the vocabulary of colours, and literacy (when a caption is added to the work).

- They should promote generality. Skills should be chosen that can be generalized across settings, materials, and people. For example, targeting the specific skill of placing blocks, balls, and triangles into a sort box excludes many opportunities for the child to practise other skills that represent the more general and useful concept of placing objects in a defined space (putting shoes in a shoebox, books in a particular space in a book rack, soap in a soap dish, and so on). Teachers should focus on the underlying concept of a skill, and modify and adapt materials as necessary (Notari-Syverson & Shuster, 1995).

- They should be functional. The functionality of objectives becomes more critical as the depth of the disability increases. Certainly, all children need functional skills, but those with significant disabilities have far greater needs. We discuss functional skills later in this chapter.

- They should be conceptually related to a hierarchical progression of long-range goals. That is, short-term objectives should be based on the established goals and on consistent instructional sequences that are designed to increase the complexity of a child's skills.

Task analysis breaking skills down into their component parts.

Long-range goals can be turned into short-term objectives through *task analysis*, a process in which skills are broken down into their component parts. All the small tasks that make up the larger skill are listed. The number of subskills depends on the task and on the individual needs of the child.

For example, a teacher may wish to teach a child to play with a ball. She will begin by performing a task analysis for the toy. The result will be a list similar to this one:

1. Pay attention to the ball.
2. Grasp the ball.
3. Pull the ball to the body.
4. Push the ball.
5. Open hands to retrieve the ball.

As another example, Donald Bailey and Mark Wolery present an analysis of requesting food and toys:

1. Child identifies (through pointing or some other response) various foods named by another person (milk, juice, cookie, apple, orange, grapes).
2. Child identifies (through pointing or some other response) various toys named by another person (wind-up chicken, blocks, busy box, clay, toy truck).
3. Child names (verbally, signs, or other conventional system) items of food shown by another person.
4. Child names (verbally, signs, or other conventional system) various toys as shown by another person.
5. Child imitates another person's model of "want" (verbal, signs, etc).

6. Child says (verbally, signs, etc.) "want" when shown one item (food, toys, etc).
7. Child says "Want (food or toy)" when shown same.
8. Child says "Want (food or toy)" when not shown same but when asked, "What do you want?"
9. Child says, "Want (food)" during snack and lunch times and when hungry.
10. Child says, "Want (toy)" during play times (Bailey & Wolery, 1984, p. 273).

After skills and concepts are broken down into steps, they are taught sequentially. A step that cannot be mastered is broken down into more basic steps.

TABLE 9–1: General guidelines for writing goals and objectives and selecting skills

Goals and objectives		Example
Stress skills that permit the child to participate in routine daily activities with non-disabled peers.	Can the skill be referenced to environmental demands or expectations?	Playing with a peer at the water table.
Ensure that the skill can be measured.	Does the skill contain or lend itself to determination of performance criteria?	Measurable: follows one-step. Nonmeasurable skill: will increase receptive language skills.
Select skills that represent a well-defined behaviour or activity.	Can the skill be seen or heard and can the skill be directly counted?	Observable skill: grasps block and builds tower. Unobservable: shows mobility in all fingers.
Choose skills that the child can perform with interesting materials and in meaningful situations.	Can the skill be be integrated into the normal routines of the centre? Can the skill be initiated easily by the child as part of daily routines?	Participating in a small group.
Select skills that stress a generic process, not a particular instance.	Does the skill represent a general concept or class of responses?	Fits objects into defined spaces. Puts mail in mailbox, places crayons in box, puts flatware into sorter.
Ensure the generalization of selected skills.	Can the skill be generalized across a variety of settings, materials, and/or other people?	Using switch on toy, computer, light.

Stress skills that are functional in the centre, at home, and in the community. Consider present and future needs.	Will the skill increase the child's ability to interact with people and objects within the daily environment?	Place objects in a container. Place cookie in paper bag, lunchbox in cubby, trash in bin, milk carton in grocery cart.
Stress skills that are appropriate.	Is the skill realistic and socially and educationally valid?	Pull off socks, take off boots.
Choose skills that can occur in a naturalistic manner.	Can the skill be taught in a way that reflects the manner in which the skill will be used in daily environments?	Uses objects to obtain another object. Uses fork to obtain food, broom to rake toy; steps on stool to reach toy on shelf.
Target skills that give the child more independence from caretakers.	Will the skill have to be performed by someone else if the child cannot do it?	Dressing, undressing. Cinta wearing her hearing aids.
Stress skills that are a priority for parents.	What are the parents' concerns?	

Source: Adapted from Notari and Schuyster (1993).

BOX 9–3

Helpful hints

With children who are hard of hearing:

- Be alert for the child's communication, and structure situations to encourage it.
- To increase the likelihood of communication, create situations in which children need assistance.
- Find and use many different ways of labelling the environment, encouraging communication, reading to the child, and increasing parent/child interactions.
- Use song cards as part of the routine. These inform the hearing-impaired child of the song to be sung; they also give all children the opportunity to choose the next song. The pictures serve as a reminder of the available choices.
- Structure science or art activities so that they require few verbal skills.
- Check every day that the hearing aid is working.
- Keep a spare supply of batteries.
- Watch the aids carefully, especially during outdoor play.

LEARNING ACTIVITY 2

Cinta is at your centre, and you wish to help her to respond to music on the piano and to play a simple musical instrument such as a tambourine. Break these two tasks into subskills using task analysis. Then write a behavioural objective for each subskill.

Educational goals and objectives should be embedded in routine activities and in naturalistic, everyday settings.

Instructional context The instructional context refers to the environmental variables that aid in the development of a behaviour. Educational goals and objectives should be embedded in routine activities and in naturalistic, everyday settings. Most of what infants and young children do should be fun; instructional strategies should be activity-based, and the instructional style should be enthusiastic and appropriate to the activities.

If teaching is to be meaningful, the skills taught must be easy to integrate with daily routines. Skills should be taught in ways that reflect how they are used in daily environments, and should be easy to transfer to home and classroom activities. For example, the skill "Walks between parallel lines 20 centimetres apart" requires that an artificial clinical or educational situation be arranged. On the other hand, "Walks avoiding obstacles" can be taught using naturalistic intervention strategies. The teacher will have many opportunities to integrate this skill with daily routines, taking advantage of naturally occurring antecedents and logical consequences (Notari-Syverson & Shuster, 1995).

Strategies Once goals and objectives have been identified, the next step is to select and sequence the most appropriate learning experiences for achieving them. Teaching activities and procedures are developed for each objective in the IPP. The selection of appropriate activities is an ongoing challenge. For example, activities for teaching colours to a child who is visually impaired (Josie) will be different from those used for teaching colours to a child with a cognitive delay (Rollo). We discuss strategies in Chapters 10 to 15.

In a sense, the IPP represents a philosophy of what should be taught rather than illustrations of how learning should happen. Examples of how to accomplish an objective may be written into it, but every approach, activity, or group interaction will not be. Some IPPs will include the specific equipment or materials to be used—for example, teachers may provide quite different puzzles for a child who is gifted and for one who is mentally retarded.

Persons responsible   The program also outlines the responsibilities of various people, such as the teachers or therapists who will assist the child. It shows the kinds of services to be provided (such as speech therapy), the type of instruction (individual or group), and the time to be spent on each activity (e.g., half an hour a day).

Assessment of child progress and program effectiveness   Each child's IPP should include a range of assessments of the child's progress and a detailed evaluation of the educational program. Teachers will structure activities to provide opportunities for the child to demonstrate whether the targeted milestones have been achieved.

Format of the plan   There is no such thing as a perfect IPP or a set IPP format. These plans may be formal and structured, or fairly casual and informal. Generally, the more handicapped the child, the more detailed and precise the IPP must be.

Determining instructional targets

For most children, IPPs are prepared annually, usually early in the year. Because the IPP is written before programming begins, the first individual education plan for a child with a disability is largely guesswork. The goals and objectives are hypotheses about what the child can and cannot do and about the child's critical needs.

An IPP is not a static document, nor is it a performance contract or written in stone. An IPP is a communication document that is constantly modified and changed to match a child's progress and needs. For example, a child who is visually impaired may well be visually impaired for life; but that child's needs will change, and not merely each year but perhaps each week or day (Deiner, 1983). One of Cinta's goals is to use her hearing aid at all times; once she accomplishes this, her next goal will be to listen actively with the aid.

IPPs are important in planning, but they are only a first step in the process of meeting the needs of the individual child. For a plan to be effective, the goals and strategies it proposes must be appropriate for the child's development, and it must be possible to meet the instructional targets within the context of the natural setting.

The major problem confronting teachers is this: how to determine and prioritize the skills that are important to teach. Skill determination is easier for children with mild disabilities, who generally follow the curriculum designed for their normally developing peers. The most complex IPPs are the ones for children with communication disorders, because language involves so many interdependent functions. Even so, the progression of skills and the strategies employed are similar to those for non-disabled youngsters (see Chapter 15).

When children have severe or multiple disabilities, it is difficult to determine what to teach—that is, what to teach first. Here, prioritizing skills and selecting the ones that represent important outcomes is a complex process. The type of handicap will partly determine where greatest emphasis should be placed.

In general terms, the child will need more structured programming to increase self-awareness and awareness of the environment. Educational needs will include language development, visual and auditory training, mobility training, and self-care skills. Psychosocial needs will include adaptive behaviour, group activities, life skills, and a range of socialization experiences.

The overriding criterion is functionality. The skills chosen for teaching should be ones that promote the child's meaningful participation in activities and increase his or her control over the environment; they should also be useful in the future. When working with these children, early childhood personnel must not only emphasize the development of basic skills but also anticipate future settings, and teach skills relating to these.

Functionality has to do with the usefulness of a skill. A ***functional skill*** is a behaviour or event that is critical to completing daily routines. The skill improves the child's functioning in present environments and facilitates transition to and participation in age-appropriate future environments. For example, sorting shapes to corresponding pictures of shapes is not a skill that a child is likely to use during daily activities; however, the child is likely to use the skill of matching lids to different containers. While both skills involve matching, recognizing, and sorting shapes, the use of functional objects such as containers and lids enables the child to learn a necessary skill that will foster independence in real-life situations (Notari-Syverson & Shuster, 1995).

For targeting skills, the following guidelines are often useful:

- Stress skills that are immediately functional or will yield results over time—that will enhance participation now or in future environments.

- Choose activities that minimize the need for adult assistance or direction.

- Choose activities that can be initiated by the child.

- Stress skills that promote interactions with others. Teachers should target behaviours (social, communication, motor, or self-care) that will result in a child being viewed more positively by peers.

- Be sure the child can master the skill. If the child's disability prevents mastery, target adaptations or alternative skills for full or partial participation.

- Select skills that a child is highly motivated to learn. Look for evidence of interest. The motivation for learning is there if the child is interested in particular topics or activities. For example, if the child always watches peers on the jungle gym or using the computer, or if the child always heads straight to the crafts table, consider ways to provide instruction in these activity contexts.

- Consider "moving" the child's behaviour, both vertically and horizontally. In other words, know when to expand the child's skill base and move to the next skill. Teachers can both strengthen already acquired skills and help children generalize them. They can also identify skills that are partially acquired or skills that are demonstrated in some contexts but not others, and then target mastery of these skills by providing practice in all natural environments (Bricker, 1986b; Noonan & McCormick, 1993; Notari-Syverson & Shuster, 1995).

Functional skills skills that help children to get along in their environments; behaviours that are critical for the completion of daily routines. These include dressing, eating, toileting, and participating in routine home and community activities.

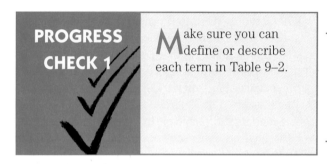

PROGRESS CHECK 1

Make sure you can define or describe each term in Table 9–2.

TABLE 9–2: New terms and ideas

hard-of-hearing
goal
objective
tool skills
task analysis
functional skill

SUMMARY

1. The major objective of programs for very young children is to provide quality care and to present opportunities and encouragement for every child to develop to full potential. In this light, early childhood education accommodates children who are disabled. Programs that include children with exceptional conditions are particularly useful when they are individualized so as to focus on the unique strengths and weaknesses of each individual child.

2. For each child with special needs, there will be an individualized program based on the child's unique strengths and weaknesses. Individualization means that special education and therapeutic activities are provided for each child.

3. Successful programming for children with special needs requires accurate assessment. Assessment results are translated into a plan of action, which is most often referred to as an individual program plan (IPP). As the name implies, plans are individualized for each particular child's unique needs.

4. An IPP contains placement and personnel information, specific objectives, time frames, and evaluation strategies. Other important factors contributing to a successful IPP are these: careful prior assessment, a team approach, a carefully drawn format, and thorough evaluation of the child's progress and of the approaches taken to intervention.

5. Goals are developed on an individual basis, and in a way that reflects the demands of the child's various environments. Individual behavioural goals must be developmentally appropriate as well as age appropriate.

6. An objective is an intended outcome stated in an observable and measurable way. Objectives are based on what the child needs to learn over a period—usually a year. Extra materials and activities may have to be provided to help the disabled child meet the objectives listed in the IPP.

7. Objectives often specify the conditions under which the behaviour will occur, and the acceptable levels of performance. To devise objectives, teachers use task analysis, a procedure in which large skills, such as dressing or putting on a sweater, are broken down into sequential components.

8. In setting goals and objectives, educators should consider five general issues: functionality, generalizability, measurability, suitability to the environment, and hierarchical relationships between long-range goals and short-term objectives.

9. IPPs must be responsive to changes in the child. The objectives need to be constantly reassessed in light of the child's behaviour, performance, and needs.

SECTION 4

Presenting the program

CREATING A WARM AND SUPPORTIVE environment and targeting skills by drawing up individual programs is only part of early childhood special education. Although effective teaching requires comprehensive assessment and effective planning, the real crux of ECSE is what happens in the day-to-day activities of the centre or classroom.

Sometimes people perceive special education as different or unique and unlike education for normally developing children. They equate special education with "curing" or at least alleviating disabilities so as to make children with special needs indistinguishable from their counterparts who are developing normally. But there is no magic in special education; the best teaching cannot restore sight, hearing, or sensation, or cure disorders. What special education does try to do is bring children to their optimal functioning across all domains.

A normal preschool or centre is the ideal setting for very young children with disabilities. In a natural setting, young children have many opportunities to build their cognitive, motor, language, and social skills by observing and copying their peers' behaviour, playing group games, playing with toys, and taking part in teacher-directed lessons.

When a child with any type of disability (or one who is gifted or talented) enters an early childhood program, the personnel adapt the environment and the program to suit the child's unique needs. Typically, the adaptations made will be multifaceted. Intervention for a young child with disabilities may be seen as involving *plan* plus *curriculum* plus *resources* plus *peers* plus *materials* plus *teacher methods* plus *teacher instructional skills and strategies*. Every intervention is unique; there is no such thing as one giant intervention.

In earlier chapters we explained how children with special needs have special requirements relating to the number of professionals involved, early identification and intervention, IPP planning, and environmental adaptations. The size and nature of groups, the degree to which children can choose activities, and the amount of teacher supervision may have to be adjusted for children with special needs. Children may need more structure and more small-group activities, and teachers may place greater focus on a child's individual goals and objectives. Generally, all of this is accomplished within the normal routines and activities of the centre.

How much teacher direction is necessary for special needs children is a point of contention. If teachers do not intervene enough, these children may flounder because the disabilities themselves interfere with the development of independence. But if teachers intervene too much, children may not develop age-appropriate independent behaviour. Adults—including teachers—whose expectations are too low may actually end up teaching reliance. Moreover, more teacher involvement has been associated with less peer involvement; it is *teacher-structured* activities that bring more peer involvement.

In this section we examine various aspects of program presentation, taking special needs and individualization into account. Two caveats are in order. First, the section is divided into specific developmental domains. However, this does not mean that the skills developed in a given domain (or curriculum area) are isolated from those developed in other domains. Nor do we recommend that separate interventions be designed for different domains. Rather, a holistic approach must be taken. Still, when children are in the early months or years it is appropriate to view language and speech, motor skills, cognition, and so on as separate skills.

Second, we present broad, generic approaches and some examples of activities and techniques. The activities should be seen as guides; by no means are they full listings of all the activities that could be presented, say, to improve listening skills or develop concepts. Also keep in mind that many of the ideas presented in this section are appropriate not only for children at risk and for those with special needs but for all young children. Furthermore, they can be adapted and structured for children at widely different stages of development.

Chapter 10 examines a number of strategies relating to peer-mediated models, environmental arrangements, incidental teaching, and so on. These strategies are also discussed in later chapters. For example, readers will find incidental teaching models for instruction in language, cognition, gross and fine motor skills, self-help skills, and socialization.

All learning activities for young children should be fun. Psychologists and educators have long recognized that for young children, play is the primary mode of learning, and research in child development has provided compelling evidence in support of this approach. Through play, children learn to explore. They learn flexibility, creativity, and self-directedness. They also develop their various sensorimotor skills, as well as their symbolic processes (Rogers, 1988).

It is hardly surprising that for all children, the importance of play as an element of or a model for early curricula has been widely recognized. Those intervening with young children must understand the stages of play, for most early intervention programs are founded on play. Chapter 11 discusses the theory and practice of children's play, both generally and for children with disabilities. For the most part, but not exclusively, when it comes to play children with disabilities follow the same developmental routes as their peers—that is, they develop the same skills in the same domains. Sometimes, however, children with special needs may require extra assistance to initiate interactions with peers and materials and to play appropriately.

Social skills develop in children in much the same way as other skills. Too often, however, social development is neglected for children with disabilities, because of the assumption that the child will automatically acquire social skills when exposed to normally developing peers. In Chapter 12 we look at the social interactions of children with disabilities and at strategies for improving their social skills. We also examine various ways of handling deviant and disruptive behaviour in early childhood settings.

Aspects of fine and gross motor development, self-help skills, and skills for independent living are explored in Chapter 13. This chapter also discusses adaptive equipment. Teachers can profit by learning how to transfer a child from a wheelchair to a toilet, how to position a child, and how to teach a child orientation and mobility skills.

Language and cognitive skill development are complex, multifaceted, and interdependent. From

the body of research that describes and explains the sequence of language development in children, we know that communication development is intimately related to other domains, most particularly social and cognitive development. At the same time, cognition depends on development in other domains. Chapters 14 and 15 discuss how teachers can foster development in the cognitive and language domains; they also present a number of strategies for children who are functioning at presymbolic levels in language and at the sensorimotor stage in cognitive development.

Eventually, children leave the early childhood setting and move to the formal school system. For children with disabilities and their families, the transition process is often stressful. In Chapter 16, we point out ways that personnel can prepare children for the transition, and some basic approaches that can be used to smooth the way for families.

CHAPTER 10
Generic teaching strategies

Kalim has been diagnosed by psychologists as severely mentally retarded. In children with severe intellectual disability, there are very often additional conditions, and this is the case with Kalim. She uses a wheelchair, has only minimal use of her left arm, and needs support to sit upright in a chair. Her vision is poor, and she needs glasses at all times. In communication, Kalim is functioning at presymbolic levels; she has only the most basic skills. She responds to her own name and to a few simple commands, but has not developed any expressive language. Kalim also suffers from a number of medical conditions and is categorized as medically fragile. Such children need ongoing medical management.

At one time, the severity of Kalim's disabilities and her concomitant functional problems (i.e., nonresponsiveness, nonvocal behaviour, serious health difficulties, and atypical motor responses) would almost surely have excluded her from a regular setting. Integrating severely disabled children is quite difficult. Generally, the more severe the disability, the greater the environmental and curricular modifications need to be. Kalim has physical disabilities that require special equipment, special positioning and handling techniques, special feeding techniques, and alterations in work, play, and rest schedules. Despite all this, the staff at the local centre are willing to accept Kalim, and to work with the family and with others involved with the child.

Everyone realizes that integrating Kalim will only be possible if everyone involved makes a substantial and co-ordinated effort. Kalim's disabilities will offer special challenges to those trying to provide normalized experiences for her. Educators may be called on to teach skills that most children are expected to learn at home (such as feeding, dressing, and toileting), and to provide care and perform procedures that are usually carried out by health care personnel. Also, they will have to work closely with other professionals, because children with severe and multiple disabilities require the services of a range of therapists, most specifically physical, occupational, and speech and language therapists.

At the centre, Kalim's inability to engage meaningfully with materials, activities, and people represents a real threat to her progress. Instruction is hindered by the presence of interfering maladaptive behaviours, and by difficulties adapting materials and techniques and identifying reinforcers to use in skill instruction.

Even small concessions allow a child to feel more powerful. To promote these, the teachers have joined a team to develop an appropriate individual program plan for Kalim. First, there are the skills needed for everyday functioning; second, there are basic survival and self-help skills, including movement; third, there are basic social and communication skills, such as those embedded in the daily activities of the centre. The teachers are working with various therapists and have learned how to handle and position Kalim using adaptive equipment (see Chapter 13). Ways are still being found to increase interaction between Kalim and the people, objects, and events in the immediate setting, and to eliminate deviant behaviours such as self-stimulation.

Kalim experienced her first interactions with other children in the preschool program. At first, she took little notice of the other children and their activities. As time went on, however, she began to take more interest. The teachers built on this by showing some of her peers strategies to prompt Kalim to wave or to play with a simple toy.

IN EARLY CHILDHOOD PROGRAMS, children learn to get along with peers and with adults in authority, and to interact with a variety of play materials. As we have pointed out more than once, some adaptations will be necessary to ensure that children with disabilities gain the full advantages of the placement. Adaptations and modifications help the child with a disability to function optimally, and to use all of his or her modalities; they also instil a sense of confidence, which helps to avoid secondary problems. Environmental adaptations should be only as special as necessary to ensure educational benefits (Biklen, 1985).

Children with mild disabilities may learn some things simply by being placed in a stimulating setting. For these youngsters, the major adjustments to the usual preschool program involve reducing the physical and intellectual difficulty of the activities and materials and providing more aid and encouragement. As well, teachers will place more stress on the cognitive, language, and social domains. When children like Kalim are placed in a setting, the adaptations made will be far greater, and a range of personnel will probably be involved (see Box 10–1).

BOX 10–1
Helpful hints

- Allow children to communicate to the limit of their abilities. It is all too easy to stifle a child's initiative by doing the talking, and to provide for the child's unrequested needs. Children whose development is delayed often need to be given more time to respond to and initiate communication. It is critical that caregivers continue to interact with the child who is disabled despite a seeming lack of response.

- Provide much support to the family. This is believed to be one way that early intervention may have a positive effect on outcomes, for both the child and the family (Dunst, Trivette, & Deal, 1988).

- Use multisensory approaches that combine inputs from more than one sense at a time; this will give extra information to the child, thereby providing more depth to the concepts being formed. Some form of movement is especially helpful.

- Use teaching aids that are tangible. Tactile and auditory input are the most effective.

- Use adapted toys (see Chapter 7).

- If children have characteristic behaviours such as hand waving, incorporate them into finger plays or sets of motions set to music (Deiner, 1983).

- Work proactively with therapists and other professionals.

- It may be helpful to use lights and music to cue activities. Signals can include flicking a light on and off, sounding a gong, or playing some familiar chord on the piano. Children must be taught to respond to such signals over a period of time and with repeated trials. For children with more severe disabilities, pictures arranged in a left-to-right sequence may help them understand a schedule. The teacher shows the individual pictures as the time for an activity arrives.

For a few children with significant disabilities, the modifications will be more major. A child with severe cerebral palsy will require assistance in mobility, positioning, speech, and motor areas. Physical, occupational, and speech and language therapists will also intervene with the child. For a child with spina bifida who is in a wheelchair or walker, teachers must ensure that the furniture is spaced far enough apart that the chair or walker can pass through easily. They must also see that the motor requirements of large-group activities do not present problems and that enough time has been allotted to change to new activities. Once a child with a visual impairment has learned the layout of the classroom, teachers must be careful not to move furniture or close doors that are usually open without first making the child very aware of the changes.

Educators of children with disabilities believe that children should learn motor, communication, social, and other skills within the context of preschool activities, in the natural setting where they will use the skills. They also hold that children with special needs require more "intentional" instruction, to optimize their growth and development.

The idea of providing children with disabilities with more adult direction to help them acquire skills does not go against the main concepts driving current practice in early childhood education for normally developing children. Developmentally appropriate practice (DAP) does not reject approaches that stress individualization or the use of direct instruction.

The fields of early childhood education and ECSE both promote the incorporation of instructional goals and curriculum content into normally occurring routines in the home, preschool, daycare centre, and kindergarten. The DAP frameworks do not articulate curriculum content, nor do they specify strategies that must be used. Rather, DAP embraces the notion of heterogeneous groups and promotes content that is directed toward a wide range of abilities and interests. The teacher is a matchmaker between child and materials; he or she understands when children are ready to learn and provides situations that support their learning (Bredekamp, 1986). Thus, DAP does not preclude the use of approaches such as systematic instruction or incidental learning, both of which are particularly relevant for children with disabilities.

In and of itself, regular early childhood education is not designed to intervene with young children with special needs. Most teachers in general, and preschool and daycare teachers in particular, are not trained to serve children with disabilities (Rule et al., 1985). Certainly, many preschool teachers have good instructional skills; but because they are trained to be facilitators of learning, they may not distinguish the need for certain children to be taught certain kinds of skills in settings that are adapted. However, the regular early childhood model and the teacher's instructional style can both be modified; as well, teachers are already familiar with many of the strategies and approaches used with special children, such as positive reinforcement and incidental teaching. Other approaches, such as Mand models and time delay, are more specialized but can easily become part of every teacher's repertoire.

This chapter outlines some of the generic teaching approaches and strategies that have been found effective in intervention with young children with disabilities. More specific applications are found in later chapters.

BOX 10–2

Developmental delay

Developmental delay is a broad category:

> [It is] a condition which represents a significant delay in the process of development. It does not refer to a condition in which a child is slightly or momentarily lagging in development or is at-risk of a delay. The presence of a developmental delay is an indication that the process of development is significantly affected and that without special intervention, it is likely that educational performance at school age will be affected. ("Developmental delay," 1991, p. 1)

Children who are developmentally delayed include those with significant delays or atypical patterns in their development, with or without specific diagnosis or identified etiology. The crucial word here is *significant*; these children have disabilities that are both severe and pervasive.

"Developmental delay" is often used synonymously with "pervasive developmental disorder." Depending on the types of disabilities seen and the presence of additional conditions, these children may also be classified as "multiply disabled" or "medically fragile."

Children with developmental disorders very often exhibit additional problems: mental retardation, perceptual motor dysfunctions, communication disorders, neurological impairments such as epilepsy, and so on. Many children with developmental delays have special health needs; when they do they are often referred to as medically fragile children. This latter category also includes children with chronic or progressive illnesses or with severe disabilities—for example, cystic fibrosis, congenital malformations, or neuromuscular diseases.

Children with developmental delays often find their world to be unpredictable, irregular, and full of confusion. Children have difficulty making sense of the confusing sounds, textures, and other stimuli that surround them. Often they have an additional condition, such as a visual or hearing impairment, that may distort, delay, or interfere with the accuracy of perception, making it hard for them to establish the identities and relationships of people and objects. For example, a deaf-blind child, or a visually impaired and mentally retarded child, may perceive only fragments of information. In the world of such a child, objects appear or disappear without any indication of where they have come from or where they have gone. These children do not see their mother place an object in their hand or watch the ball roll away. They do not know how others use the object or for what purpose it has been designed (see Winzer, 1996).

These children may demonstrate maladaptive behaviours, which fall largely within two classes. The first is aggressive behaviour, which may be self-directed (self-injurious behaviour) or directed toward others (Lovaas & Favell, 1987). Many children inflict serious injury upon themselves: they bang their heads against sharp corners, bite themselves, and gouge their own eyes. Aggressive behaviour can sometimes result in serious physical harm to peers, parents, and teachers. Often it results in the child being medicated, placed in restraints, and/or moved to a more restrictive environment (Lovaas & Favell, 1987).

The second class of maladaptive behaviours includes those which are stereotypic, ritualistic, and repetitive. The behaviours in this category include prolonged and repetitive body rocking, spinning, jumping, pacing, gazing at lights, twirling of objects, and excessive and repetitive vocalization. In physical terms, these behaviours are not as risky as aggression, but they are socially stigmatizing and may decrease the child's responsiveness to educational instruction (Lovaas, Newsom, & Hickman, 1987).

There are two main goals of any intervention: to decrease the behavioural symptoms that interfere with the individual's functioning;

and to promote the development of functions such as language, adaptive behaviour, and social and self-care skills. To these ends, a key objective is to help children get in touch and keep in touch with their environments. They need to learn **independent behaviour**, which is behaviour performed without the assistance of others (Bailey, Harms, & Clifford, 1983). Independent behaviour consists of **self-help skills**, which are those skills needed for independent functioning in relation to such basic needs as food and warmth.

For children with severe disabilities such as Kalim, curriculum must reflect all areas of development. However, training often emphasizes early developmental skills usually thought of as too routine or too basic to be part of a regular instructional program. Many children need to be taught a wide range of basic daily living skills such as independent eating, dressing, and toileting. They also require training in social interaction and communication, so as to learn how to relate effectively to others. Some children will need help to reduce or eliminate severe aggression, or strong and persistent ritualistic and stereotyped behaviours (Lovaas & Favell, 1987).

Teacher methods

Independent
behaviour
behaviour performed without the
assistance of others.

Self-help skills
those abilities
needed for
independent
functioning in
relation to such
basic needs as food
and warmth.

Pedagogy can be defined as the link between what a teacher wants children to learn and the children's actual learning. Two important components of pedagogy are the teacher's methods and the teacher's strategies.

Teacher **methods** refer to how a teacher interacts with children and what he or she does to teach. Teacher methods can be placed on a continuum between teacher directed to learner directed. High levels of adult structuring or teacher direction exist in situations where the teacher tells children what activity or task to perform, gives them directions for performing it, and offers specific praise or criticism for their performance. Low levels of structure exist where children choose their own activities and tasks and decide, without adult direction, how to carry them out.

Within general teacher methods, there are specific techniques and strategies; each of these offers a plan of action for approaching a task. **Teaching strategies** can be classified as natural or intrusive. The more a teaching strategy differs from typical learning experiences, the more intrusive it is. Thus, incidental teaching is a fairly natural strategy, while a teacher physically moving a child's feet on the pedals of a tricycle is intrusive.

Teachers employ a huge variety of strategies in their day-to-day interactions with children. A teacher is more likely to use a specialized strategy for a special needs child if he or she sees it as fair and reasonable; as attaining objectives; as successful in the past; as efficient in terms of time; as not difficult to implement; and as matching the theoretical orientation of the program at hand (see Odom, McConnell, & Chandler, 1993).

PROGRESS CHECK 1

Define and explain teacher methods and teacher strategies. Provide examples.

Approaches, techniques, and strategies

Methods   how a teacher interacts with children and what he or she does to teach.

The database on teaching young children with disabilities is relatively new, and interventions are drawn from two sources: regular early childhood education, and instruction with older children with moderate to severe disabilities. Because the field is so new and the research is only beginning, developing and individualizing curricula for young children with disabilities is an ongoing challenge. No cookbook formula is available. Adults must constantly revise, adapt, and modify approaches to meet the needs of individual children.

Certain general steps can be followed when adapting instruction:

1. Develop an appropriate IPP. We discussed the procedures for IPP development in Chapter 9.
2. Prioritize goals and objectives. Before anything else, children need the skills that will help them function effectively in their environment.
3. Identify activities that occur within the daily schedule and routines.
4. Identify IPP objectives that can be addressed within each activity.
5. Identify the nature of any adaptation needed to support individual needs.
6. Decide who will provide the adaptation.

Pedagogy   the link between what a teacher wants children to learn and the children's actual learning.

A variety of procedures exist to increase the motor, cognitive, social, and communication skills of young children with disabilities. Teachers will select and mix the strategies with which they feel most comfortable. There is no one strategy or bundle of strategies that works with every child; every intervention must be unique.

ENVIRONMENTAL STRUCTURING

When children with disabilities are successfully integrated, they interact socially and instructionally with non-disabled children. Children with disabilities require structured and systematic intervention directed toward their unique strengths and weaknesses. Their activities must be individualized, and their environment structured so that they can explore, interact, and learn. For this, teachers must provide guidance, support, and encouragement. This may involve modifying routines, groups of children, and play areas.

We discussed in Chapter 7 how the environment can be adapted to accommodate children with disabilities. To reiterate:

Teaching strategy   when a teacher teaches a learner to make a sequence of responses in order to reach the solution to a problem.

Skills   relatively small units of action or behaviour that are easily observed and occur in brief periods.

- The environment must promote skill acquisition. **Skills** are relatively small units of action or behaviour that are easily observed and occur in brief periods (Katz, 1988, p. 35). They are learned through observation, imitation, trial and error, directions, instruction, and drill and practice. The acquisition of new skills is easier when the proper equipment and materials are available. Children with disabilities often require individual or small-group instruction that is teacher directed and focuses on specific tasks.

- The environment should promote the teaching of new strategies. A strategy is a child's approach to a task; it includes how the child thinks and acts when planning, executing, and evaluating performance on a task and its outcomes (Deshler & Lenz, 1989). For children with special needs, teachers should provide many opportunities for performing a task over and over again.

Skill maintenance refers to children remembering learned skills and to the arrangement of the environment to increase the probability that a previously acquired skill will be demonstrated.

- The environment should stimulate **skill maintenance**, which refers to a child's ability to remember learned skills. Thus, the environment should be arranged to increase the likelihood that acquired skills will be demonstrated.

- The environment should emphasize **generalization**, which is also referred to as *transfer* and is defined as the process that enables individuals to respond to new situations in ways that were learned in earlier ones. Learning in one situation influences learning in another context; the end result is that children can use the skills outside the classroom in a variety of ways. Generalization is promoted when objectives are not disjointed and isolated but integrated. Rather than teaching a few discrete skills that are useful, teachers should emphasize instruction that promotes skill generalization.

- The environment should be designed so that children can learn many behaviours in a short time. During water play, for example, a child can be prompted to interact with peers, take turns pouring water into containers, and practise grasping water toys.

Schedules

Generalization the processes that enable individuals to make previously learned responses to new situations. Also called transfer. Learning in one situation influences learning in another context; the end result is that children can use the skills outside the classroom in a variety of ways.

Scheduling refers to who will do what and when they will do it. Establishing a schedule for classroom activities is an important component of successful programs because different arrangements produce different educational effects. For teachers, the schedule is a concrete manifestation of the program's concepts and goals. The daily schedule is determined in large measure by the orientation of the program planner, which may be behaviourist, or developmental, or Montessori, or some combination of these. For children, a schedule provides a comfortable routine in a predictable setting. The parts of the program that vary little from day to day become a framework for the program as a whole. Typically, routine times include arrival, snack time, toileting, transitions, and dismissal.

For all young children, the environment should be predictable. There are major benefits in providing a carefully planned daily routine:

- Proper sequencing of activities can positively affect children's behaviour (Krantz & Risley, 1977). There is a more positive atmosphere; there are also fewer clashes resulting from discrepancies between the teacher's expectations and the children's. Children know what to expect and become more secure and autonomous in their actions.

- A schedule may help children develop a sense of time.

- Schedules can facilitate learning by sequencing high- and low-activity periods, grouping skill components, and building reliance on established routines (Bailey & Wolery, 1984). Teachers should change activities often, interspersing serene activities with more active ones. In an all-day program, children need quiet periods and rest periods.

- A schedule provides an ideal context for teaching independent behaviours. Routine situations become a sort of scaffold in which responses become automatic and, eventually, more elaborate. For example, greeting time is especially important to young children. Routinely, teachers greet parents and exchange information if necessary. They then get down to the child's level and say "hi" or "good morning," and help the child perform standard behaviour such as taking off coat and boots. Other functional skills can be taught effectively through classroom routines, and through the use of a curriculum built on a framework of play.

- Through class routines, children learn to anticipate schedule transitions and to move from one activity to another with minimal staff supervision. When transitions are smoothly structured, children move as their individual needs dictate. Transitions that minimize or eliminate waiting for materials or activities promote engagement (on-task behaviour). Disabled children who learn to make transitions smoothly and quickly will find it easier later on to adjust to less restrictive environments, such as kindergarten (see Chapter 16).

  Schedule changes are particularly difficult for children with disabilities, who need the security and confidence that a predictable environment brings. Thus, when specialized staff are needed, scheduling and instructional arrangements should not interfere with the typical activities and schedule of the setting.

MEDIATED MODELS

Nearly all young children play, and young children in general learn through play and exploration with peers and adults. Children who are developing normally learn many things simply by being placed in a stimulating setting. They are encouraged to initiate their own activities and to develop at their own pace, without individualized instructional objectives. In contrast, children who are disabled often lack the ability to initiate their own activities in a large group setting. As a result, they may become isolated in a regular preschool classroom, and fail to develop as fully as they could. These children require more direct instruction and the use of mediated models.

Socially competent peers interact with one another in appropriate ways, which children with disabilities can learn through observation.

"Mediators" are people who help a child learn. There are two major types of mediators in early childhood settings: adults and peers. Adults include teachers, aides, and other grown-ups. A teacher who shows children how to do something is mediating the children's learning by modelling. Adults mediate by drawing the child's attention to specific aspects of an object or situation; by rearranging materials to facilitate completion of a task; and by presenting the child with selected materials.

Although the teacher may qualify as a mediator and model, a more potent model is often a respected or liked child. Peers are often excellent mediators, especially if they are willing to be trained and eager to assist a child with a disability.

Peer mediation

The potential benefits of peer modelling are cited as a justification for integrating disabled with non-disabled children in preschool settings. The use of peers as models in early childhood settings is based on several assumptions: Example is often a better route to mastery than explicit instruction. Socially competent peers interact with one another in appropriate ways, which children with disabilities can learn through observation. Also, children with disabilities like and admire their peers and for that reason have a natural tendency to imitate or model their behaviour. See Table 10–1.

TABLE 10–1: Peer mediation

Why use peers?	Example is a good route to mastery. Young children imitate more competent peers. Imitation is something that most young children often do spontaneously.
When to use peers.	In free play or small-group times for communication and social development.
Which peers to use.	Those with good behaviour, a willingness to participate, and an eagerness to assist the special child.
How to use peers.	Teach specific strategies. Monitor child/child interaction. Reinforce both children for appropriate behaviour.

Modelling refers to imitating behaviour in different situations. Modelling (also called imitation) is a natural way for children to develop new skills and to learn when and where certain behaviours should be displayed. From observing others, children form a conception of how new behavioural patterns are performed; later the memory serves as a guide for action.

Modelling   imitating behaviour in different situations.

During the early stages of development, parents are the most effective models. Later, as the child's world broadens, peers, teachers, and significant others also become models. In preschoolers, imitation of peers and adults is a frequent and ongoing process. Younger children seem to imitate more often than older children.

Peer interventions have the advantage of closely involving disabled children with their classroom peers; this may promote a more natural development of skills (Read, 1989). Particularly in the areas of language and social skills, the use of peers as models is an efficient and viable intervention strategy.

The usefulness of peer-mediated models (also called confederate interventions) is well supported by empirical and anecdotal research. The literature indicates that peer-assisted interventions offer a variety of benefits; in fact, these procedures may be as effective as teacher-implemented methods (e.g., Fowler et al.,1986).

In one study (Strain, Shores, & Timms, 1977), professionals trained preschool children to prompt their peers to interact and respond in a socially appropriate manner. The result was a "substantial increase in all subjects' social responding," and increased appropriate initiative behaviour by five of the six children (Strain, 1982, p. 99). Peer models can also benefit the educational and social progress of children with autism. Harris and colleagues (1990) explored the extent to which the language development of young children with autism might be influenced by being in a segregated versus an integrated classroom. They also examined the benefits to language development for a group of normal peers in an integrated class. The researchers documented substantial changes in language abilities of preschool children with autism who were exposed to an intensive language stimulation program; the language skills of the normally developing children in this class continued to grow.

Mere exposure to appropriate behaviour by peers does not automatically improve the skills of children with disabilities. Nor does peer mediation mean a bystander role for the teacher. In the most effective peer-mediated strategies, play activities are appropriately structured, peers receive training, and adults actively prompt and reinforce interactions. The teacher sets the stage, monitors the environment, and provides ongoing guidance as needed.

For peer-mediated interventions to be effective, specific peer initiations must be carefully selected and taught; the environment must be arranged in such a way as to promote interactions; peers must be trained to implement interventions; and daily intervention routines must be implemented (Strain & Odom, 1986).

The basic strategy of peer-mediated models is this: socially competent young children are taught to initiate interactions with less competent peers. Small children can be taught strategies such as establishing eye contact; describing their own or the other child's play; initiating joint play; and repeating, expanding, or requesting clarification of utterances made by the child with a disability (Goldstein, 1993). Peers can be taught to be play organizers, as in, "Let's play in the sandbox." They can share by offering to give or exchange an object. They can provide physical assistance, as in helping build block towers. And they can provide affection, as in patting and holding hands (Strain & Odom, 1986).

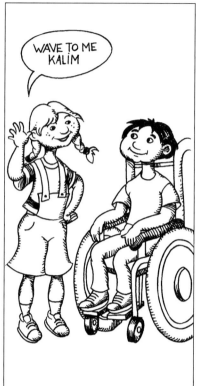

FIGURE 10–1

Posters for skill training

To prepare and implement peer-mediated models, these steps should be followed:

1. Appropriate peers are selected. The peers selected as models should have certain characteristics: they should comply with teacher requests; have regular attendance; play in age-appropriate ways; have no history with the target children, or a positive history; be enrolled in the same class; and express a willingness to participate (Strain & Odom, 1986).

2. Nondisabled peers are provided with ongoing training sessions. Normally developing children are taught how to direct, start, and organize play, and to offer assistance. Peer helpers receive role-playing training in which the teacher pretends to be another child. Various strategies are introduced—for example, the children can be taught to remind the special child how to do a puzzle.

   In the training session, the teacher first selects a skill such as waving back or using a toy in constructive play. One at a time, each component of the skill (i.e., each subskill) is introduced by the teacher, who uses a direct instruction approach. After a brief introduction and verbal rehearsal according to a prepared script, each child practises teaching the skill to an adult "actor." Each of the peers being trained has an opportunity to teach the skill while the other children watch.

As each subskill is introduced, adults model it; the peers then follow the model. Each child practises teaching the skill to an adult actor, who pretends to be the child with a disability. As the training sessions continue, the adult (as the disabled child) makes it progressively more difficult for the peer to encourage responses. The actor does this by initially ignoring the peers and by delaying responses for longer periods of time.

To help the children in the training session, a set of posters illustrating the strategy can be used as a prompt. The posters will have two or three panels and show one or two children teaching a skill to a disabled child. To elicit waving, for example, the first poster may show the child waving and waiting for the disabled child to imitate. The next poster shows the peer waving and saying, "Wave to me, Kalim." The third may show a physical prompt—that is, the peer moving Kalim's hand in a wave (see Figure 10–1).

3. Daily strategy training continues until each involved peer can independently perform a number of strategies with the actor on four consecutive trials.

4. The peer is assigned to a child with a disability for a 3 to 10 minute session of free-play activity. During this time, the teacher prompts and reinforces the use of strategies. The posters can be used to prompt use of the strategy.

5. The teacher monitors ongoing interactions—for example, by reminding children to play and by prompting play behaviour.

6. The peer gets a reward. Delivering reinforcement to peers enhances attention to those peers and facilitates observational learning (Brown & Holveot, 1982; Goldstein, 1993).

Adult mediation In teacher mediation, the teacher becomes the mediator of the child's learning experiences by working directly with the child. Teacher mediation activities include eliciting understanding from the children by asking guiding questions, supplying needed information, directing activity, challenging answers, requiring logical evidence for conclusions, and emphasizing the process of thinking, learning, and problem solving rather than the products. Among the many strategies that are subsumed under adult mediation, incidental teaching and direct instruction are important for children with disabilities.

LEARNING ACTIVITY 1

Use a role play of an instructor and groups of normally developing children. Go through the steps outlined above so that the "children" in the role play can learn to mediate with Kalim—that is, to wave to Kalim and have her respond. Make posters and use them as suggested in the outline.

Incidental teaching Mediated instructional approaches open the door for play interactions that provide a natural context in which to develop skills in many areas. One widely used teacher-mediated approach is incidental teaching, a specific form of naturalistic teaching that is applied to all domains but especially to those of socialization and communication. We can see this in Table 10–2, which presents examples of incidental teaching for promoting prosocial behaviour.

TABLE 10–2:   Incidental teaching of social behaviour: examples

Activity	Incidental teaching direction by teacher	Child interactive response	Anticipated response from peer(s)
Play Billy is playing with blocks and Susie (target child) is standing and watching.	"Susie, why don't you play with with Billy?" "Billy, share the blocks with Susie."	Susie sits down next to Billy and says "Me play too."	Susie begins to build a fort of blocks with Billy.
Lunch David (target child) needs help opening his milk carton.	"David, ask Dana to help you open your milk carton."	"Dana, please help me."	Dana helps David open his milk. David says, "Thanks."
Arrival Todd (target child) has trouble with the buttons on his coat.	"David, remember that Todd has trouble unbuttoning his coat. Why don't you show him how you unbutton your coat?"	David approaches Todd and says, "Todd, you want to unbutton your coat? Watch me."	Todd nods yes and approaches David. Todd watches David undo his coat and then tries himself.
Classtime Howard is walking from large group to the snack table and falls down.	"Mary (target child) look, Howard fell down. Let's give him a big hug and make sure he's OK."	Mary and the teacher walk over to Howard. Mary hugs Howard.	Howard hugs Mary and says, "Let's go eat."
Fine motor activity Paul (target child), who is mute but can work complex puzzles, is working a 20-piece puzzle.	"Look, Paul, Al needs help with his puzzle. Show him how to work it."	Paul shows Al where a piece of the puzzle goes and smiles.	Paul and Al take turns putting pieces of the puzzle in.

Incidental teaching
taking advantage of naturally occurring child-adult interactions in order to teach specific functional skills.

In its broadest definition, ***incidental teaching*** means taking advantage of naturally occurring child/adult interactions in order to teach specific functional skills. Incidental learning differs from intentional learning. Intentional learning is consciously goal directed; that is, a person intends to learn certain things and deliberately sets out to do so. In contrast, incidental learning takes place when a child is in a passive state but actively pursuing specific goals.

In essence, incidental teaching is a group of instructional techniques that are interactions between an adult and a single child where the child's behaviour serves to identify occasions for instruction. Incidental teaching is used typically when children show an interest in or involvement with materials, activities, and other children (Brown, McEvoy, & Bishop, 1991). When the child demonstrates an interest in some object or event, either by looking at it, asking for it, or examining it, the expression of interest is viewed as a request for instruction and the occasion is used as a teaching opportunity. For example, Cinta, the child we met in the last chapter, is painting at an easel when she points to a red area and indicates that the teacher should write a caption. As the painting is almost entirely red, the teacher prints, "See the red sun." She then uses Cinta's request for the word "red" to stress the language and the speech of the word; she may reinforce the concept further by going later to the doll centre with Cinta and playing with red doll's clothes.

Typically, incidental teaching episodes are brief. Because they are brief and occur when children are interested in materials, activities, or other children, problems with lack of attention and motivation are often minimal. As well, incidental teaching is designed to occur in everyday contexts, so training resembles that given to normally developing children. Further, incidental teaching focuses on episodes that are likely to evoke a positive response from peers.

The times for incidental teaching arise naturally in situations such as free play, and the occasions are used by the adult to transmit information or to give the child practice in developing a skill (Hart & Risley, 1975). For example, Janie is a socially withdrawn child. In a small-group format she has learned to ask a peer to share her toy. One day the teacher notices that Janie is not using this skill during free play but is standing off to one side and watching the other children play. She is observing another child playing with blocks, so the teacher prompts Janie to remember how to ask other children to share. Janie goes to the other child and asks her to share her blocks.

Incidental teaching is by definition not accidental, and must take place within a framework of careful planning by the teacher. There are five steps in incidental teaching:

- Ensure the child's responsiveness to the environment by providing opportunities that secure the child's attention.
- Maintain the child's attention based on the arrangement of environmental features as reinforcers.
- Elicit and sustain the child's interactions with the environment.
- Create elaborations of the child's behaviour.
- Work toward "conventionalizing" the child's responses. For example, use many other opportunities to teach Cinta the speech and language for "red."

DIRECT INSTRUCTION

Direct instruction refers to activity-focused, teacher-directed classroom procedures. Direct instruction is systematic and usually conducted according to an IPP. Lessons are appropriate for learning objectives aimed at a particular goal.

In formal activities, children remain in a group within a specified area and watch another person (usually a teacher) co-ordinate an activity. In informal activities, children can obtain a variety of materials at any time and use them in a variety of ways. Since non-disabled children do not exhibit skill deficits, too much reliance on formal activities or direct instruction is restrictive for them. For children with disabilities, however, direct teaching may be necessary. This may involve, for example, teaching how to use materials independently.

Direct instruction procedures include prompting, shaping, and reinforcing; these are implemented in a precise and consistent fashion. Specific objectives to be attained are identified; appropriate stimuli to elicit the responses are arranged; learning sequences are programmed in small steps; and desired behaviours are reinforced. There is much documentation of the success of accomplishing specific academic objectives through **direct instruction**.

> Direct instruction activity-focused, teacher-directed classroom procedures.

Reinforcement

In Chapter 6, we discussed behavioural models and approaches in early childhood education and pointed out that many of the principles of behaviourism are used

---

BOX 10–3

In the classroom

Child Place is a fairly typical centre. One supervisor, two teachers, and two aides are on staff; together they care for and teach 35 children between two and almost six. Students from the local community college are often at the centre on practica training, and sometimes a parent volunteer is present. A number of children with identified special needs are enrolled, and there are two other children about whom the staff are developing some concerns. Various therapists come to the centre regularly to work with and offer assistance to these children.

On a very typical day in October, the following incidents occurred during free play in the various centres. Each involved children with identified special needs.

In the block centre the student teacher, Jane Lin, was working with three children on a small-group activity. Each child had individual objectives that related to improved peer interactions, listening in a group, improved language, and the development of fine motor skills through functional activities. Jane played with the children, focusing on their specific objectives within the context of the group interaction. She demonstrated and prompted tasks, provided many opportunities for listening and conversation, and used much reinforcement for correct behaviour. To a child who needed a block, for example, she said, "Ask Jamie for the block that you need," rather than simply giving the child a block. She then reinforced the child's request with "Good. Now you have the yellow block."

Ms. Johns, one of the teachers, was printing captions on children's paintings in the art centre. Cinta, whom we met in Chapter 9, was very proud of her work. She tugged at Ms. Johns and told her, "Red." Following the child's initiation (and her interpretation of the painting), Ms. Johns printed "See the big red sun." She read the caption to Cinta and

by teachers at all levels every day. We pointed out that early intervention practices tend to be rooted in behavioural psychology, and are especially pertinent to children with disabilities. Box 10–3 shows some activities at a typical centre. As you can see, Ms. Johns, Ms. Locke, Ms. Hall, and the student teacher are using a variety of strategies to assist learning and prompt appropriate behaviour. Consciously or unconsciously, they are employing some principles from the behavioural school of thought.

Positive reinforcement Of all the principles that arise from behavioural theories, that of positive reinforcement is the most important for teachers. In behaviourist terms, ***positive reinforcement*** is a consequence that increases the likelihood of a response being repeated. Behaviour that is reinforced tends to increase in frequency, magnitude, or probability of occurrence. Thus, reinforcement is defined by its effect; children quickly learn that certain behaviours function to obtain desired objects, activities, and services.

In a classroom setting—indeed, in any situation—reinforcement is used to shape or produce new behaviours as well as to maintain or modify existing ones. Children respond well to reinforcement and rapidly learn that certain behaviours bring a positive response, whether it be a smile, a pat on the back, or some more tangible reward such as a gold star.

> **Positive reinforcement** a consequence that increases the likelihood of a response being repeated.

---

prompted the speech of the word "red." To follow up on this incidental teaching episode, Ms. Johns and Cinta went to the doll corner to find red clothes for a doll.

In another centre in the playroom was Juan, the child we met earlier. When Juan first entered the centre, he tended to wander rather aimlessly, observing other children but not joining in. With some encouragement from the staff, he began to interact with materials, and to a lesser extent with peers. The staff also tried to teach Juan the rules and routines of the centre. On this day Juan had just finished with a nesting toy and seemed ready to move toward the art centre. Ms. Hall, involved with another child, said quietly: "Juan, pick up the toy and put it on the shelf and then you can go and paint."

Ms. Hall was playing with Janet on an inset puzzle. Janet was having problems choosing the correct pieces and inserting them properly in the puzzle frame. Ms. Hall began to help by first placing a piece in the puzzle herself. Then she pointed to the next piece and physically helped

Janet manipulate it into the frame. After Janet placed the first few pieces in this manner, Ms. Hall offered her praise: "Good girl, you've put the pieces in." For the next pieces of the puzzle, the teacher pushed two choices toward Janet, who selected the correct piece. Instead of physically helping Janet turn the piece, Ms. Hall gave verbal directions: "Turn it around. Will it fit? Yes, now turn it a little more."

In another part of the classroom, events were not moving along quite as happily. Lee wanted a toy truck that Marcus had and asserted his wants with cries and shouts and finally with kicks until the teacher, Ms. Locke, intervened. She told Lee he had to go and sit on a small chair away from the group for three minutes. Ms. Locke then sat with Marcus and played with the truck, giving Marcus much praise as they proceeded. At the end of the three minutes, Lee was allowed to rejoin the group. When he sat and began to play amicably with Marcus, Ms. Locke provided positive feedback: "I like the way you and Marcus are playing together."

At the preschool level, teachers should use much positive reinforcement, especially if the child has a disability. Reinforcement with preschoolers with disabilities shows many positive results. For example, Guralnick (1976) observed a child with special needs and found that the child engaged mainly in solitary play. Having the child observe two peers playing associatively or co-operatively had no effect on social play. When peer modelling was combined with reinforcement, significant increases in associative and co-operative play were noted.

Research demonstrates two problems in using reinforcement. First, teachers do not employ positive reinforcement well enough or often enough. This is true at all levels, from preschool to the secondary grades; also, the use of positive reinforcement tends to go down as grade level increases. For example, Strain and colleagues (1983) looked at kindergarten to grade two classrooms and found that the teachers used more negative than positive feedback. Children received relatively little positive attention when they performed appropriately; when they obeyed a teacher request, there was only a 10 percent chance that they would be recognized or rewarded.

The second problem revolves around the amount of reinforcement provided. Infants and young children should live and play in reinforcement-rich environments in which they learn that their behaviour has a predictable effect on their social and physical interactions. However, for infants and young children with disabilities, the encouragement that occurs naturally is often not adequate. They may not notice the encouragement, or the encouragement may not be powerful enough relative to the skill difficulty. For these children, reinforcement must be structured and systematic.

Types of reinforcers Reinforcers are classified as primary or secondary. *Primary reinforcers* satisfy inborn biological needs, such as food, drink, warmth, and sleep, and strengthen the behaviour they follow. As they are necessary to perpetuate life, it is assumed that primary reinforcers are innately or naturally reinforcing (Winzer, 1995).

Secondary reinforcers are initially neutral or meaningless; they acquire their reinforcing value by being associated with primary reinforcers or already established secondary reinforcers. There are three main types of secondary reinforcers: token reinforcers, activity reinforcers, and social reinforcers. All may be used in classrooms. Token or activity reinforcers should always be accompanied by a social reinforcer.

Token reinforcers include buttons, poker chips, bottle caps, and so on. These reinforce behaviour in the same way that money does, through being associated with or exchangeable for other primary or secondary reinforcers.

Activities that are allowed if certain conditions are met are included as *activity reinforcers*. Younger students will often work very hard to earn the right to clean the blackboard, hand out snacks, and so on. Activity reinforcers include task-embedded reinforcement—for example, reinforcement gained when puzzle pieces fit together.

Activities are connected to what is referred to as the *Premack principle*. This simple principle is sometimes referred to as Grandma's Law, as in "Eat your vegetables and then you can have dessert" (Winzer, 1995). We can see an example of the Premack principle in Box 10–3. With Juan, Ms. Hall is making the pre-

---

Primary reinforcers those things that satisfy inborn biological needs, such as food, drink, warmth, sleep, or sex, and which act to strengthen the behaviour that they follow.

Secondary reinforcers those which are initially neutral or meaningless but acquire their reinforcing value by being associated with primary reinforcers or an already established secondary reinforcer.

Token reinforcers initially meaningless items that attain reinforcing value when they are associated with, or exchangeable for, other primary or secondary reinforcers.

Activity reinforcers activities that are handled in a specific way.

Premack principle a more preferred consequence should be made contingent (dependent) on a less-preferred task.

Social reinforcers verbal or nonverbal actions that provide attention or communicate approval.

Instructional reinforcers motivators that are introduced strictly for the purpose of teaching or of increasing the strength of a particular skill.

Negative reinforcement occurs when an unpleasant stimulus is immediately taken away or removed from the situation as a consequence for a behaviour, with the effect of increasing the probability that the behaviour will

ferred activity (painting) contingent on completion of the less-preferred task (picking up and returning the nesting toy to its storage place).

Social reinforcers include verbal or nonverbal actions that provide attention or communicate approval. Social reinforcers are the easiest to use in classrooms, for they can be given quickly and efficiently. In classroom situations, teachers indicate approval in many ways: they smile, wink, pat a shoulder, or say, "Well done!" All of these forms of teacher approval have a powerful effect on children's behaviour (see Winzer, 1995).

In Box 10–3, Ms. Hall uses social reinforcers with Janet: she praises her success in the hope that the reinforcement (praise) will make the behaviour more likely to appear again. Ms. Locke uses positive reinforcement with Lee, but her reinforcement is even more potent and therefore even more likely to ensure that a positive behaviour will appear again. Ms. Hall praises Janet for successfully completing a puzzle; Ms. Locke uses feedback to tell Lee exactly what aspects of his behaviour she likes.

Instructional reinforcers are used strictly for teaching or improving a particular skill. Care must be taken in the use of instructional reinforcers, as there is always the possibility that the skill acquired will not be maintained after the reinforcers are withdrawn.

Sometimes children do not have to be reinforced directly. Seeing a model receiving positive reinforcement increases the likelihood of the same appropriate behaviour being strengthened. We see this with Lee (see Box 10–3). This is referred to as "vicarious reinforcement."

Negative reinforcement　With ***negative reinforcement***, an unpleasant stimulus is immediately removed from a situation as a consequence for a behaviour; the effect is to increase the probability that the behaviour will occur again (Skinner, 1953). There are many examples of negative reinforcement in daily life: a driver will fasten his seatbelt to stop the unpleasant buzzer; a mother will pick up her infant to stop the fussing and crying; students study to avoid parental nagging; or a window is closed on a cold day. In each case, the aversive situation is terminated by the response, and the likelihood increases that the behaviour will occur again (Winzer, 1995).

Negative reinforcement and punishment are often confused, although they are not the same thing at all. Negative reinforcement *results in* behaviour—children perform behaviours that allow them to escape or avoid aversive stimuli. In negative reinforcement, the aversive stimuli *precede* the response; in punishment, the aversive stimuli *follow* the response. In the case of Lee, time out should have been aversive, as he was removed from the group. Negative reinforcement occurs when the time out is complete and he rejoins the group. The cessation of re-

PROGRESS CHECK 2

Explain positive reinforcement and the various types of reinforcers that can be used. Also explain negative reinforcement and provide some examples from your own experience.

In the following two situations, make up a scenario in which positive reinforcement may be used:

1. John Brown is desperately trying to quit smoking. His wife is helping him.

2. Josie, our child with severe visual impairments, needs to wear her glasses at the centre but refuses to do so and has become very good at "losing" her glasses.

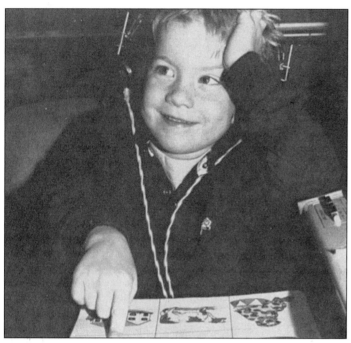

All forms of teacher approval have a powerful effect on children's behaviour.

moval from the group should increase the likelihood that he will not wish to be placed in time out again.

Using reinforcement   The art of providing reinforcement lies in finding responses to reinforce, identifying appropriate responses, and noting the effect on the learner (Schermann, 1990). Reinforcers can be anything a child finds pleasurable. Children differ in what is and is not reinforcing to them and in the amount of reinforcement they need. Something that is reinforcing for one child or in one situation may not be reinforcing for another child or in another situation.

Generally, it is not necessary to use edible reinforcers at a centre, except perhaps with younger children or children with disabilities, who may not readily respond to teacher attention or praise. Primary reinforcers can be very useful when teaching a new behaviour, because when chosen properly they work rapidly (Winzer, 1995). For most children, however, verbal and symbolic reinforcers produce better results that tangible reinforcers. Young children work hard to obtain praise, and the effects of verbal reinforcement and praise are about as strong as monetary rewards or candy.

Shaping **the teaching of new skills or behaviours by reinforcing learners for approaching the desired terminal behaviour.**

Shaping   When using reinforcement to teach a new behaviour, we don't always wait for a perfect response to occur. In behavioural learning, ***shaping*** means teaching new skills or behaviours by reinforcing learners for approaching more and more closely the desired end-behaviour.

In shaping, children are reinforced for performing behaviours that are in their current repertoire but also for stretching themselves toward new skills. Educators use shaping when children cannot learn all the steps in a task or behaviour at once. They teach the behaviour in small steps and reinforce successive approximations until the desired response is given.

The process of shaping is shown in Figure 10–2. As you can see, it is essentially a series of steps; each step or accomplishment is rewarded until the child can perform an entire sequence.

Shaping is successful when children can move rapidly from success to success. This requires careful task analysis on the part of the teacher, as well as frequent reinforcement as children accomplish each step. The steps to follow in shaping a behaviour are as follows:

1. Define the target behaviour. The goal should be a challenge; also, it must be possible for the child to receive frequent reinforcement on the way to reaching it.

2. Decide what behaviour to build from.

1. Define target behaviour.	Colour-match three cards with colours.
2. Decide what behaviour to build from.	Will match one colour in one minute with help.
3. Establish a reinforcer.	Will earn special play with the teacher.
4. Outline a series of steps to get to the target behaviour.	Match two colours without assistance. Match four colours in different objects without assistance.
5. Start training at first step of 4 above.	
6. Shift to new criterion.	
7. Repeat until target is reached.	
8. Set new target if necessary.	

(After Becker, 1986)

FIGURE 10–2

Shaping

3. Establish a reinforcer.
4. Start training with the first criterion. Only reinforce behaviour that meets a given criterion.
5. Shift the criterion. Gradually change the response criterion for reinforcement in the direction of the target behaviour.
6. Reinforce any behaviour that is vaguely similar to the target behaviour. For example, any vocalization beginning with "b" is reinforced as an approximation to "bottle" (Noonan & McCormick, 1993).
7. If the child is not successful, return to the earlier criterion.

Prompt anything that assists the child in making a desired response, such as a teacher pointing to something or modelling how something is done.

Prompts To help a child perform a behaviour correctly, the teacher may use various prompts. A ***prompt*** is anything that helps the child make a desired response—for example, a teacher pointing to something or modelling how something is done. Prompts precede the performance of a behaviour and lead to the correct response in a given situation; they are a way of helping the child know what responses will be right.

Prompts are fairly natural, and we all use them every day. The mother of a ten-month-old infant says "shoe" and points to the object; the grade five teacher uses a pointer to stress words on the chalkboard; in a television studio, someone holds up the laughter and applause cards (Winzer, 1995).

There are many types of prompts. After natural prompts, the least intrusive are verbal; the most intrusive involve full physical assistance. The types of prompts include these:

- *Natural prompts* are objects or people in the environment that bring a response. Juan, for example, is standing in front of an easel but not doing anything. He sees Ms. Hall coming and is prompted to dip his brush in the paint.

- *Indirect prompts* are when someone asks a question or makes a statement about something that needs to be done. For example, "Would you like to close the door?"

- *Direct verbal prompts* are more specific: "Close the door, please."

- *Gestural prompts* are those natural movements we use, such as beckoning a child to come.

- *Model prompts*. If we return to Ms. Hall and Janet for a moment, you will remember that Ms. Hall is helping Janet complete a puzzle and using demonstration, prompting, and praise. She prompts behaviour through modelling in order to increase Janet's interest and motivation.

- *Instructional prompts* can be as subtle as a glance or as intrusive as physical guidance. By simply looking at a toy that needs to be picked up, the teacher may prompt the child to comply.

- *Visual/pictorial (environmental) prompts* provide assistance such as colour coding, or pictures telling the child what to do, or an identification picture on a child's cubby.

- *Tactile prompts* involve touching the child. We can give partial or full physical assistance.

Prompts should be faded or withdrawn as soon as possible so that the child learns to perform the behaviour without constant help or reminders. In the case study, Ms. Hall is using a number of prompts with Janet: she places the correct puzzle piece herself (model prompt); she points to the correct piece (physical prompt); she moves Janet's hand (physical prompt); and she verbally instructs Janet in how to complete the task (verbal prompt). She is shaping Janet's responses to the puzzle by first giving many prompts and then gradually fading them so that Janet is taking more of the steps on her own.

Tactile prompts involve touching the child and giving partial or full physical assistance.

Cues   A cue means giving children a warning before they are expected to do something. Flicking the lights for clean-up time is a cue. In the context of instruction, a cue is a prompt that directs attention to a particular dimension of a stimulus or task. Pointing and saying "Pick up your spoon" is a cue because it directs the child to a specific object. Cues are more effective when they direct attention to the most important features of the stimulus; thus, pointing to the handle rather than to the bowl of the spoon is more precise, since it directs attention to where the child must place his or her hand (Noonan & McCormick, 1993).

Time-delay procedures   The time-delay prompting strategy is a systematic "wait procedure" that relies on fading prompts. The time delay procedure was first described by Touchette in 1971 when he was teaching students with severe disabilities. Since then, much research has been undertaken on time delay strategies. Time delay has been described as a nearly errorless learning method that transfers control from a teacher's prompt to the naturally occurring stimulus (Schuster & Griffen, 1990); and as probably the least intrusive way to teach a child to initiate an interaction, and to assist responding.

Time delay is simple to apply. It is most often used with children with significant disabilities, especially for prompting communication and language. In time delay, the teacher begins by helping the child complete the task with some type of prompting. Then the prompt is systematically delayed; that is, the teacher waits a predictable number of seconds before helping. For example, when the child shows interest in an object or activity or needs a particular object (food, materials, toys) or an action (assistance), the adult waits for the child to emit some behaviour related to that object or activity, such as looking at the adult and saying, "More."

The steps of a time delay procedure are as follows:

1. The adult is close to and looking at the child. The adult faces the child with an expectant look and displays the desired object.

2. The adult delays any action following child attention to material. That is, the teacher waits a specified time for the child to request or label the desired object. The adult is silent but maintains eye contact.

3. If the child responds, the adult provides the desired object. The adult praises the child, and immediately offers the material or assistance when the child verbalizes appropriately.

4. A verbal prompt follows incorrect child responses (Halle, 1984).

5. Further prompts, such as physical prompts, are then used as necessary. (See Chapter 15 for further applications of the time delay procedure.

PROGRESS CHECK 3

At the centre, Kalim shows interest in a soft blue-wool ball. The teacher wants Kalim to vocalize in order to obtain the ball. Describe how she would stimulate vocalization using a time delay procedure.

BOX 10-4

Kalim's IPP

NAME: *Kalim*

CONTACT: *Mrs. S.*

DATE OF BIRTH: *12 January 1991*

HOME: *555-1111*

CHRONOLOGICAL AGE: *4–1*

BUSINESS: *555-2222*

SUPERVISOR: *Ms. Jones*

EMERGENCY CONTACT: *555-3333*

MEDICAL NEEDS: *Kalim is a medically fragile child. Protocol is attached.*

ADAPTIVE EQUIPMENT: *Wheel chair, glasses, adapted toys using a rocking lever switch.*

Personnel

- *regular teachers and supervisor*
- *physical therapist for individual therapy with Kalim, and for demonstrating seating, postural control, positioning with staff*
- *language therapist to teach basic communication using alternative method, working proactively with teachers*
- *psychologist for ongoing assessment of Kalim—a resource for teachers as necessary*

Long-range goals

- *To develop attention to the environment: attending to stimuli, tracking stimuli, engagement of objects and people; to sit and look upon request; to develop the ability to consciously observe what others are doing.*
- *To react to sensory stimuli by using tactile, motor, visual, auditory, taste, and smell modalities.*
- *To respond to caregiver communication: sig-*

Chaining   Chained tasks demand skills that require two or more separate yet sequential responses to be completed before the technique is accomplished. Examples include hand washing, tooth brushing, and cooking.

Chaining is a technique for connecting a sequence of simple responses to form a complex response that would be difficult to learn all at once. Chaining requires task analysis—breaking the task down into small steps. The number of steps that come from the task analysis and the number performed by the teacher depend on the needs of the individual child (see Chapter 9).

There are two types of chaining: backward and forward. In backward chaining, the teacher does every step in the sequence except the last one. In forward chaining, the child does the first step and the teacher completes the task.

Below is an example of a chained procedure. Teachers may record progress by using the code PP for physical prompt, VP for verbal prompt, and NP for no prompt needed.

nalling and communicating intention.

- *Functional use of selected motor skills and adaptive skills. Grasping and reaching, object permanence, means-end behaviour, space (such as putting things in or on top of), and construction (as in building).*

Strategies

- *Properly position using a bolster chair.*

- *Use facilitation techniques (physical guidance and encouragement) to help Kalim achieve normalized postures and movements. Physically help her carry through actions she has difficulty understanding with words or other actions.*

Short-term objectives

1. *Wave to peers when prompted.*
2. *Use adapted toys on request. Reach for, grasp toy.*
3. *Imitation, such as dropping objects in a pot.*
4. *At snack times, respond to "More." Use time-delay procedure. Generalize to toy play.*
5. *Grasping. To stimulate arm movements, select toys that produce a result when moved, such as a mobile.*

Correctly activates simple toy. Activates light, easy-to-move toys such as balls, toys on wheels, roly-poly toys, and large, bright, noise-making toys such as bells and drums. Take Kalim's hand to the toy rather than taking the toy to the child. This helps in ear–hand coordination, establishing object permanence, sound localization, and identification.

Object permanence. The beginning steps of object permanence may be demonstrated by the ability to locate an auditory signal and then follow it as it moves.

In a forward chaining procedure, the teacher would initiate the process by prompting the child to take the coat from the hook and then assisting with all of the other steps. As they proceeded, he would expect the child to perform more of the steps alone.

	M	T	W	T	F
Take coat off hook.					
Place on floor upside down.					
Stand at neck of coat.					
Bend over.					
Put hands in armholes.					
Flip coat over head, push arms into armholes.					
Start zip fastener.					
Zip up coat					

(After Deiner, 1983)

SMALL-GROUP INSTRUCTION   Instruction with two or more children simultaneously is referred to as small-group instruction. Group instruction is widely used in early childhood settings. The format of small groups is familiar to all early childhood teachers: Children are gathered into groups for a specific activity with one teacher. The teacher presents the activity, and children participate for a set period. Groups often have a theme or a purpose. Themes are organized around a unit curriculum approach; for example, Valentine's Day can be a theme in February.

Group activities are used to expand children's knowledge, inquisitiveness, and problem-solving abilities. To this end, group activities encourage behaviour such as listening, sharing, taking turns, and attending, in a variety of ways.

Child groups vary in composition, in type of interaction (with both the teacher and the other members), and in content of instruction. Heterogeneous groups include children with different functioning levels; homogeneous groups include children functioning within about twelve months of each other.

In homogeneous groups, children are likely to have similar goals and activities. Because a homogeneous group may not include models for the children with disabilities to imitate, some children with severe disabilities may not participate. For children with disabilities, heterogeneous groups are more effective.

For all children, teachers should try to have one group period a day. For each 15 minutes of instruction, the focus of attention should be changed three times; that is, there should be different activities at least every five minutes (Lay-Dopyera & Dopyera, 1990). In group instruction, teachers should use stories, singing, movement, discussions, language activities, and cooking.

When children with disabilities are present in an early childhood setting, the resulting discrepancy in skill levels of the children with disabilities and their normally developing peers often makes it difficult for teachers to plan meaningful activities for all children. When teachers use additional small-group instruction in the context of an activity, this problem is overcome; teachers can focus on individual learning objectives, but still use heterogeneous groups for modelling.

For the following reasons, small-group instruction is an appropriate and effective means of teaching children with disabilities:

- There are many major learning experiences in groups.
- Small groups provide opportunities for children with special needs to participate in mainstream educational and social situations. And as there are fewer children, everyone has more opportunity to participate.
- Smaller groups are easier for the teacher to control.
- Groups advance social interaction among the members. (This is the major rationale for group instruction.) Teachers can identify one social behaviour, such as sharing, and embed it in group teaching.
- In groups, peers naturally reinforce each other, and this enhances a child's motivation.
- Small groups make the most efficient use of instructional time.
- Small groups provide opportunities for observational learning.

- There is independent work, such as attending to task, and there is instructional work, such as following group directions.
- Teachers can choose activities that incorporate a number of different learning objectives and that are adaptable to various ages and skill levels. In a small group, the learning objectives of individual children can be targeted. When more than one child has the same objective, instruction is enhanced through reinforcement, peer modelling, and the repetition of the same procedures.
- Small-group work facilitates generalization of skills. For children with the same objectives, teachers can use different materials and instructional stimuli. When children observe different stimuli associated with the target response, generalization is facilitated.
- For children from non-English speaking backgrounds, groups encourage the development of language.
- Groups increase the probability of later placement in less restrictive environments. The ability to work in groups is important in formal school settings (see Chapter 16).

To ensure that children with disabilities are fully participating in the group and that their specific objectives are being addressed, teachers make certain decisions prior to teaching. They make decisions about when and how a specific child's objectives will be included, and choose instructional techniques that facilitate participation in the group. As well, teachers decide which age group is best for the child's specific objectives, and which size of group is most manageable. Teachers are well advised to use groups of only two children at first and then systematically increase the size of the group.

There should be frequent and appropriate participation by all the children in the group. Normally developing children as young as two can be taught group participation skills such as sitting in a group for 5 to 15 minutes, taking turns, and paying attention and following instruction while surrounded by many distractions. Children with disabilities may need to be taught group behaviour. During instruction, teachers should consistently reinforce group behaviour.

There are many techniques to enhance participation:

- Attention signalling—for example, the teacher raises a hand and says "Look."
- Response signals, such as when children answer when pointed to.
- Varied pacing. Pacing refers to the speed at which the teacher moves from one child to the next in the group, and may be rapid or slow. Generally, teachers should use quick pacing and move from one child to another rapidly.
- Pauses for emphasis and attention, and rhythm and volume variations. Teachers leading a group can create a rhythm of loud, soft, fast, slow. This will sustain child attention.
- Selective attention. Praise children who are attending and participating.
- Intentional mistakes. These violations of expectations mean that a predictable response is changed (see Lay-Dopyera & Dopyera, 1990).
- Partial participation. Here, teachers modify the requirements for group activities. They may ask a child for only a portion of a response. For example, a child may

try to grasp a toy and reach out his or her hand for it, but then the teacher helps the child grasp the toy and puts it in his or her lap.

- Adaptive participation, as when an alternative means of response is allowed. For example, the child may wear a Velcro strap in order to grasp toys (Noonan & McCormick, 1993).

- Group responding, as when children respond together. This response may be verbal (singing songs, rote responses such as counting, and so on) or motor (for example, finger plays). Group responding increases the opportunities for every child to participate in the group.

- Group contingencies. These involve an instructional arrangement whereby reinforcement is provided when all the group members demonstrate a required response (Noonan & McCormick, 1993).

Arranging small groups   Earlier in this chapter we pointed out the importance of predictable schedules. Most preschools, whatever their philosophy, follow roughly the same routines, and their schedules are usually designed around certain activities. Thus, there is typically a short period for storytelling and other group activities, when children learn to pay attention to the teacher; and a show-and-tell, during which they pay attention to each other. Free play, various other activities, snack time, and outdoor play are also included in most programs. The following schedule is fairly typical:

8:45–9:00	Greet children and parents.
9:00–9:20	Large-group circle time (days of the week, show-and-tell, and so on).
9:20–9:50	Free play (with table play activities, art, sand/water play). Teachers direct the child to a particular activity, or present new options and let the child choose.
9:50–10:00	Transition time/bathroom.
10:00–10:20	Snack time.
10:00–10:45	Outdoor/motor play.
10:45–11:05	Free play.
11:05–11:25	Large-group circle time (language activities).
11:25–11:30	Prepare to go home. (O'Connell, 1986)

From an ECSE perspective, the only activity that is missing from this schedule is individualized instruction time. The question arising is how to use some of the time in the traditional schedule for more direct instruction for children with disabilities while still providing all the activities of the natural setting.

In a regular preschool schedule, a typical free-play period is characterized by child-initiated activities with materials designed to promote fine motor, perceptual, language, cognitive, and creative skills. The functional skills developed through these activities—which include puzzles, beading, colouring, painting, and water and sand play—are often the same ones that children with disabilities need most to develop. Part of the free-play period can be modified to provide children with disabilities with scheduled, direct instructional time, during which they can learn specific skills for utilizing the classroom materials (O'Connell, 1986; Radonovich & Houck, 1990).

If this period is designated a small-group instruction session instead of free play, the teacher will have to change roles so as to provide structured direction. This will involve identifying the skills to be taught and the activities in which the child will participate, the goal being to ameliorate skill deficits. Centres are the appropriate setting for these small groups. Since group assignments are not fixed, groupings will change daily or weekly with the nature of the planned activities, the skills of the children, and the availability of volunteers. Nonhandicapped children are excellent models and can help the children who are disabled.

Figure 10–3 shows one week's planned activities for a small-group instruction period. Each group's composition will vary with the nature of the activities and the degree of teacher instruction and feedback the children with special needs require. During the 15-minute period, each child with a disability should receive at least five opportunities to perform the response, with the teacher providing prompts and corrective feedback or reinforcement.

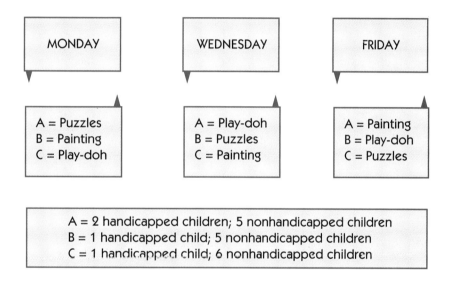

From Managing Small Group Instruction in an Integrated Preschool Setting by J.S. O'Connell, Teaching Exceptional Children, Vol. 18, 1986, 166-171.
Copyright 1986 by the Council for Exceptional Children.
Reprinted with permission.

FIGURE 10–3

Schedule

In puzzle play, as an example, a group of children have been assigned to do puzzles (Group A). The puzzles may range in difficulty from a simple, three-piece, noninterlocking puzzle to a twelve-piece interlocking puzzle. Careful planning has ensured that a puzzle is available for the appropriate functioning level of the child with a disability. At the acquisition stage of learning, children with disabilities should not be allowed to select their own materials.

PROGRESS CHECK 4

A number of rather difficult terms and concepts appeared in this chapter. Make sure you can define each of the terms in Table 10–3. Also, explain a situation where each term would apply. For example, what is a secondary reinforcer, and when, how, and where would it be used?

The non-disabled children quickly learn the designated routines for handling the materials. While modelling appropriate puzzle behaviour for the group as a whole, the teacher can physically prompt the two children with disabilities in Group A to complete the response. As the other children begin to put their puzzles back together, and perhaps start on new ones, the teacher provides instruction to the children who are disabled through commands and prompts, using corrective feedback and reinforcement (O'Connell, 1986; Radonovich & Houck, 1990).

TABLE 10–3: New terms and ideas

activity reinforcers	Premack principle
direct instruction	primary reinforcers
generalization	prompt
incidental teaching	secondary reinforcers
independent behaviour	self-help skills
instructional reinforcers	shaping
methods	skills
modelling	skill maintenance
negative reinforcement	social reinforcers
pedagogy	teacher strategy
positive reinforcement	token reinforcers

SUMMARY

1. Teachers intervening with children with special needs may have to adapt their methods to some extent. Their methods will tend to be more teacher directed.

2. Teachers must arrange the learning environment and design instructional activities so that children can perform the desired behaviours over time (i.e., maintain or retain the behaviour) and in a variety of settings and situations (i.e., generalize the behaviour). Intervention may also consist of exposure to alternative strategies for achieving competence.

3. Scheduling is a critical component in any program. Precise scheduling is even more essential when teachers must co-ordinate one-to-one, small group, and large-group activities to meet the needs of all children.

4. A daily routine provides predictable sequences.

5. It is widely recognized that an important aspect of successful integration has to do with structuring activities so as to involve non-disabled children with their peers who are disabled. The use of peers as models has long been recognized as an efficient and viable strategy, particularly in the areas of language and social skills.

6. Incidental teaching is a well-validated procedure for promoting language development and social skills acquisition. The strategy is used to support independent and child-initiated behaviours where the child's behaviour serves to identify occasions for instruction. Incidental teaching is a child-initiated process and is conducted most effectively in natural settings. Typically, teaching episodes are brief and are conducted during unstructured activities.

7. In direct instruction, prompting, shaping, and reinforcing procedures are implemented in a precise and consistent fashion.

8. One of the most powerful tools in the repertoire of any teacher is positive reinforcement. Positive reinforcement involves using various kinds of reinforcers to increase the likelihood that a behaviour will be strengthened. Positive reinforcers are generally categorized as primary or secondary.

9. Reinforcers are used to increase the likelihood that a behaviour will be repeated. In general, the younger or more disabled the child, the more effective tangible reinforcers are.

10. Shaping is used when the desired response is not one the child can perform already, and when there is no way to prompt the response. In shaping procedures, approximations of a behaviour are reinforced until the correct behaviour is performed.

11. Group instruction is widely used in early childhood settings.

12. Children with disabilities can be provided with scheduled, direct instructional time in supervised small-group sessions, during which they learn the specific skills they need to interact with classroom materials.

CHAPTER 11
Children's play

CASE STUDY

Joe and Katie

Joe and Katie are the same age and in the same preschool group. However, they are very different in their abilities, especially in language and gross and fine motor skill development and in their social interactions with peers and adults in the environment. These differences can be seen in the way they play, the skills they are acquiring, the tasks they undertake, and the ways they interact with their peers and respond to adults.

Joe is a normally developing four-year-old who is into the stages of dramatic and sociodramatic play. Of course, he still enjoys many of the activities termed sensorimotor and constructive play and engages in much rough-and-tumble play outside with his friends. Katie encounters many more difficulties in play in any mode or setting. In fact, her play is quite unlike that of other children at the centre, and often her repetitious and mechanical movements do not seem like play at all.

Quite early in life, Katie was diagnosed as having infantile autism. Her parents first noticed differences in Katie's behaviour when she was only a few months old. The child did not look at people, did not seem to track objects, and did not enjoy being picked up and cuddled. Katie cried excessively, and her mother could rarely comfort her.

Now that Katie is four, the differences between her behaviour and that of her normally developing peers is very noticeable. Katie rarely looks at anyone and does not engage in any social interactions with her peers. She does not seem to understand any language and therefore does not use any speech and only a little of what could be called expressive language. The latter consists of a few gestures used consistently to indicate that she wants food or drink. Katie is very graceful and seems more adept in gross motor skills than in other areas, but she is not yet toilet trained.

Katie's play is quite different from that of her peers. She does not choose among all the toys but always selects a small shiny car, which she will play with for hours, sitting on the mat and spinning the wheels. Nor can Katie be persuaded to work and play in any of the activity centres. Only occasionally do the teachers succeed in involving Katie in playing with other children.

It was hoped that Katie's entry into a regular preschool program would stimulate her language and enhance her social skills. There has been some improvement, albeit a small one, and this is encouraging. Many of the other children have sat with Katie and tried to interest her in other toys and games. While her interest so far has been marginal, she does seem to be responding to the other children in the environment more often and in more positive ways.

The single goal for Katie is more sustained social interaction with her peers and teachers. Simultaneously, behaviour, language skills, and cognitive skills should also improve. For half an hour once a week, a speech therapist works with Katie on a one-to-one basis on language development. Katie's IPP is shown later in this chapter.

CHILDREN SPEND MOST OF THEIR WAKING HOURS at play, acquiring the skills, values, and ideas that are crucial for growing up. They run and jump and chase each other and so develop their bodies; they play with words and ideas and develop their minds; they play games and dramatize fantasies, thus learning social skills and moral rules.

Because of its importance to development across many domains, the play of normally developing children has become an area of intense research. The central issue has been, and still is, whether play significantly influences cognitive growth. Various theoretical models have been developed based on different perspectives. Jean Piaget, for example, discussed play from a cognitive-developmental perspective; Mildred Parten documented play as social development.

Despite the accumulation of knowledge about play, we do not yet know if ideas about normally developing children can be generalized to children with disabilities. This is because the play of young children with disabilities has not received the attention it deserves (Guddemi, 1990), perhaps because traditional programs for these youngsters have stressed skills, not play.

Some researchers favour the proposition that the play of children with special needs requires more structure, and is less sophisticated and more functional than the play of typical children. But there is also support for the hypothesis that the play of children with disabilities is not so different from that of typical children. At the very least, it may be developmentally appropriate (see Malone & Stoneman, 1990). Others have looked at specific deficits in the play of children with disabilities, and point out that many special children may be deficient in play skills; they must be taught how to play, how to choose an activity, how to get started, and how to use materials independently.

Of all disabling conditions, infantile autism and blindness seem to have the greatest impact on the development of sensorimotor and symbolic play. Children with infantile autism such as Katie are so special in their play and other behav-

BOX 11-1

Infantile autism

Infantile autism is a condition that is identified in children before 30 months. Autism is often classified as a developmental delay because of the pervasive nature of the condition. With autism, every aspect of a child's functioning is affected. Autism reveals itself in fleeting eye contact, the failure to form attachments, and disrupted relationships. Children have difficulty in developing language skills, in learning to communicate, and in relating. They display bizarre behaviours and body movements and sometimes suffer inordinate fears.

One of the most noticeable results of autism is that children have severely impaired relationships with all the people in the environment. Autistic children show severe self-isolation. They never begin to establish normal human attachments; they are extremely alone from earliest infancy and are unresponsive to other people. They seldom initiate contact and appear distant, aloof, or in a shell (Winzer, 1996).

Autistic children tend to have severely impaired communication skills and are unable to use language appropriately. Researchers are now fairly certain that autistic children have incurred some damage to the brain. This damage may affect the language centres in particular. Almost 50 percent of autistic children fail to develop any speech (Cummings & Finger, 1980); among those who are also mentally retarded, this figure is even higher. In the other 50 percent, the acquisition of language and speech is severely delayed. Facial and gestural expression of emotions can also be abnormal. Affected children fail to use gestures appropriately, and do not interpret accurately such

iours that they are exceptions to all the rules. Children with autism demonstrate significant delays in the development of symbolic play. For autistic children, play—especially make-believe play—as a vehicle for learning about objects and events does not appear to be intrinsically motivating (Lifter et al., 1993). These children are more likely to ignore toys and engage in self-stimulating behaviour. Even when these children do play, they use toys in an unusual manner. It follows that helping Katie to play more naturally and with a greater variety of materials and increasing amounts of peer interaction is of major importance. Even though objectives in the context of play may seem unnecessary, they are needed to ensure the right play activities for Katie (see Box 11–5 for the objectives for Katie).

Other children with disabilities will not require the intense and consistent interventions that Katie needs. However, they may need some extra assistance, especially in dramatic play. Teachers may need to structure play situations and social interactions more. When they do this in free-time play periods, equality of performance between disabled and non-disabled peers is achieved. The activity—whether it be blocks, puzzles, or dramatic play—assumes major importance, and the child with a disability can interact with peers on a more equal level. The child's disability is no longer the focus of attention. Each child is using the activities and materials at his or her own level, and the achievements of every child are praised and accepted.

In this chapter we outline the theoretical models of play as developed by Piaget, Parten, Smilansky, and others, and show how they relate to the day-to-

clues as eye contact, body posture, tone of voice, and facial expression (Hobson, 1988).

Some children with infantile autism move gracefully and show strong motor skills development. But even these children may not be toilet trained or capable of dressing themselves. It is not unusual to find ten-year-olds with autism who are not yet toilet trained.

Autistic children often exhibit strange and inappropriate behaviours: self-stimulation (e.g., string twirling, constant humming), self-mutilation (e.g., arm pinching, face slapping), and strange ambulatory patterns (e.g., toe walking, bunny hopping). They are obsessively insistent on "sameness." They use objects stereotypically and inappropriately and are preoccupied with music (Winzer, 1996).

Their play behaviours are unusual. Their only strong attachments are toward inanimate objects. Children who are autistic are fascinated by things that spin. They can sit for hours holding a toy car upside down, endlessly spinning the wheels. Unlike other children, they are virtually impossible to distract from this behaviour.

Children who are autistic need structured intervention in life skills and communication. Training begins with establishing their self-concept. Children must learn who, what, and where they are in order to realize that they are separate from others. Once they are aware of themselves as separate beings, they are ready to establish basic relationships. They then learn basic social behaviours, such as communication, and are trained to refrain from socially unacceptable actions. Unfortunately, owing to their unresponsiveness and lack of communication skills, they are very hard to train. Few receive academic training beyond basic levels (see Winzer, 1996).

day activities of a preschool setting. We discuss the characteristics of play observed in children with disabilities and point out ways that teachers can help these children develop more stimulating play behaviour and improve interactions with peers. Since toys are an integral part of the process of learning about the world for children, we will also discuss these, and indicate specific toys that are most suitable for particular groups of children. Note here that all the chapters in this section stress the principle that play is the major mode of learning and skill acquisition for children. This means that the discussions in this chapter can be applied to all other domains of development.

The development of children's play

Although research has isolated different aspects of play behaviour, play has never been precisely defined. However, play has several essential characteristics: it is intrinsically motivated, freely chosen, pleasurable, and actively engaged in by the participants (Hughes, 1991). Play is what we do when we do whatever we want to do—when we do not have to follow a routine or meet the expectations and directions of others.

Many people believe that it is through play that children develop physical skills, expand their cognitive grasp of the world, and develop social skills and roles. The confidence that children gain by learning to direct and control play increases their ability to enjoy themselves and to acquire life skills that are essential to well-being.

Not everyone agrees with this perspective. Some educators disdain play as frivolous and unworthy of serious consideration or, even worse, as a negative influence. For example, Maria Montessori viewed play as developmentally irrelevant.

Even among educators who value play, there are a number of different views about how it benefits children's development and functioning. Some see play mainly as a means for creating pleasure and improving quality of life. In a similar vein, others see it as a way to cast off tensions and concerns and to work out feelings about relationships. Still others believe that a child uses toys, daily routines, imagination, and friendships to learn about life.

A widely held perspective is that play is the foundation on which human culture rests (Huizinga, 1970). Play exists because all humans instinctively yearn for arousal and stimulation, and play is one means to finding both.

Others see play as an important means through which physical, cognitive, and social skills are strengthened and honed. Those who adopt a cognitive stance view play as having primarily a cognitive function—as the child's major way of learning from earliest infancy (Weininger, 1979). Otto Weininger observes: "Play has to do with exploration, curiosity, sensory-motor activity, social activity, verbal imitation, and divergent thinking" (1990, p. 15).

STAGES OF PLAY   As we find in other domains of development, such a cognition, there is a progression in the way children play—in what things they play with, how they play with them, and with whom they play. Various researchers have attempted to define these stages along cognitive or social lines. Table 11–1 shows the stages of play as outlined by Jean Piaget, Mildred Parten, and S. Smilansky.

TABLE 11–1: Stages of play

Age	Piaget	Parten (1932)	Smilansky (1968)
0–2	Practice	Solitary	Functional
3	Perceptive	Onlooker	Constructive
4		Parallel	Dramatic
5		Associative	
6		Co-operative	
7	Team play		Games with rules
14	Adult play		

Each of these researchers uses a somewhat different terminology to define the various stages (and other researchers use still other terminologies). These terminologies differ with the orientation of the researcher and with the theoretical perspectives from which children's play is viewed. The different terminological systems are explained in Box 11–2.

Jean Piaget

Piaget's theories about play have been widely accepted as the most definitive and comprehensive in developmental psychology (Fink, 1976). Piaget collected much of his early research with his own children; he also spent a great deal of time watching other children play and asking them about the rules of their games.

Piaget saw play as a characteristic feature of early childhood that disappeared with the onset of rational thought (Eckler & Weininger, 1988). Piaget viewed play as an activity in which children, instead of being pressured to adapt to reality, manipulate reality to serve their own purposes. Play consists of activities done "for the mere pleasure of mastering them and acquiring thereby a feeling of virtuosity or power" (Piaget, 1945/1962, p. 89).

Piaget viewed play activity as essential to cognitive growth—as the vehicle for infants to advance through a series of increasingly sophisticated ways of understanding the world. He considered play to be assimilation, which is one of two processes that all individuals use to achieve equilibrium in their lives. Through assimilation we change the world to match our present cognitive abilities. In playing, the child takes the world and makes it into whatever he or she wants it to be: a box becomes a race car, a blanket becomes a house, the child becomes a fantasy figure or a superhero.

Starting in early infancy (Piaget's sensorimotor period), infants build up an understanding of their world through self-initiated exploratory play, using all the cognitive skills available to them. They manipulate objects, usually small ones, for reasons that have nothing to do with biological needs such as hunger, thirst, or warmth. They mouth, shake, stack, and toss familiar and novel objects. Thus, a rubber ball is something to squeeze, and a cup is something to hold, put in the mouth, or drop from the side of the high chair. Much learning occurs this way.

BOX 11–2
Terminology

Term	Description
Piaget	
Practice	Equivalent to sensorimotor practice play; characterizes the sensorimotor period. For example, shaking a rattle.
Mastery	Play that helps children to master new skills, especially physical skills; includes almost any skill that the child feels motivated to learn. As children grow, it increasingly includes activities that are clearly intellectual, such as play with words or ideas.
Symbolic (perceptive) play	Emerges in the second year at the end of the sensorimotor period, reaches a peak at age four, and declines after age six. Children appear to mould reality to their own caprices without rules or limitations.
Team play	Beginning with the onset of concrete operations, games with rules predominate.
Parten (1932)	
Solitary	Children sit and look at others or perform simple non-goal oriented activities alone, with materials different from children within solitary speaking distance; no interest in activities of others. Solitary play is indicative of immaturity and decreases with age.
Onlooker	Watching others, perhaps talking to others but no entry into the play situation.
Parallel	Playing independently with toys similar to those being used by others in close proximity; no attempt to play with others.
Associative	Playing with other children; no role assignment or organization of activity. Interactions not sustained. Children interact, sharing materials, but they don't seem to be playing the same game.
Co-operative	Playing in an organized group.

Smilansky (1968)	
Sensorimotor	Play that captures the pleasure of using the senses and motor abilities such as playing in food and finger painting. Often involves the actions of one's own body such as in skipping or dancing.
Constructive play	The manipulation of objects to construct or to create something such as building with blocks.
Symbolic (dramatic) play	A playful representation of an actual object or experience.
Sociodramatic	Dramatic play in cooperation with play other persons.
Games with rules	The acceptance of prearranged adjustment to the rules.

Young children enjoy dressing up as part of fantasy play.

Take, for example, the tiny child trying to place differently shaped objects in an unusually shaped container. The infant will find that some objects fit and some do not, some can be squeezed and forced in and some cannot, some objects fit only when turned in a certain way, and so on. Through this activity, the infant is building a meaningful and useful understanding of spatial relations, texture, size, shape, and directionality (Caruso, 1988).

In their second year of life, as they become more mobile, children further exercise their senses through practice play. In this later stage of the sensorimotor period, children often reproduce acts they have seen adults perform, such as talking on the telephone and drinking from a cup. Late in the second year, children begin to use objects and toys in a variety of ways. They begin to replace themselves with a toy as the active agent of play; for example, the child will now place the cup in a doll's mouth rather than his own.

During their first two years, children have been developing the two cognitive skills that form the basis for the further development of play and other skills. At about eight months, infants begin to develop object permanence. **Object permanence** is defined as knowing

Object permanence knowing that things exist even when their presence cannot be perceived.

Represententational thought the ability to imagine things or events not present and represent them in some way.

Dramatic play the substitution of an imaginary situation to satisfy personal wishes and needs.

that things exist even when their presence cannot be perceived. The child now realizes that objects exist even when they cannot be heard, touched, or seen. "Object" here refers to both physical and social objects (i.e., both things and people). In normally developing children, object permanence is in place by the age of two.

A second crucial cognitive step that begins late in the sensorimotor period is the development of ***representational thought***, which is the ability to imagine things or events not present and represent them in some way. Representational thought, which continues to develop through the period of preoperational thought, depends on the development of language as a symbol system. Once children are capable of symbolism, they can both create and accept an arbitrary relationship between an object and an idea. Once children have developed the capacity for object permanence and its next step, representational thought, they can indulge in ***dramatic play***, which involves the substitution of imaginary situations to satisfy personal wishes and needs.

During the preschool years, pretending is a favourite activity. Children are old enough to think symbolically but too young to really distinguish reality from fantasy. Things that have been encountered but not fully incorporated are re-created in fantasy, reworked, and gradually assimilated. While engaged in sociodramatic play, children act out complex social situations that involve the reconciling of players with differing needs and background experiences and with contradictory views.

A number of investigators have followed up on Piaget's descriptions of the changes that occur in young children's play and exploration. In general, this research not only confirms Piaget's basic observations about children's play, but also extends and refines them (Caruso, 1988). Later investigations clearly support Piaget's contention that the development of exploratory play in infancy has a predictable sequence; action serves as the basis of knowledge, as shown in the gradual progress from self-centred play to play involving the outside world. Representation and pretend play begin late and develop slowly. Pretend play becomes more sophisticated, shifting from play involving self, to self/object play, to object play exclusively (Lamb & Bornstein, 1987).

PROGRESS CHECK 1

Outline the stages of play presented by Piaget. Now return to the discussion of Piaget's theory in Chapter 6 and review the stages of play in terms of his general stages of cognitive development.

Mildred Parten

In contrast to Piaget, who looked at play in terms of cognition, Mildred Parten investigated the social aspects of play. In her classic research on children's play, she observed five types of play among two- to five-year-old children in nursery school (see Table 11–1).

S. Smilansky

A frequently examined model of play is the one devised by Smilansky (1968), who suggested three categories: functional, constructive, and pretend (dramatic) play. These categories form a developmental hierarchy corresponding to stages of cognitive development. *Functional play* emerges first and is the major type of play during the sensorimotor stage. *Constructive play* and *dramatic play* emerge during the preoperational stage, in that order. *Games with rules* come into prominence in the concrete operations period.

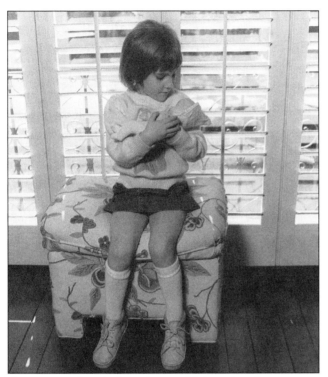

Some researchers believe that as children play, they practise adult roles.

Functional play involves simple muscular activities (such as an infant playing with a rattle) and repetitive manipulation of materials (such as stacking and knocking over blocks). In functional play, children practise and repeat skills.

The period from two or three to seven years represents the constructive stage of play. Children now use play materials to build something. When constructive play appears, children begin to create representations of aspects of the physical world. In doing so, they learn about various materials. Functional play seems to be the most common form of play during the first two or three years of life. Starting around age two, both constructive and dramatic play begin to increase, with constructive play accounting for 40 percent of all play by age three-and-a-half (Christie & Johnsen, 1987).

Pretend play becomes more frequent and more complex with each passing year. Between two and seven years of age, children involve themselves so intensely in role playing that they use and develop their minds in ways that cannot be duplicated in formal training. Horgan (1990) holds that a child's sense of humour starts to form at around the same time symbolic play begins. As children pretend to eat or sleep or put on make-up, they almost always laugh.

While children are engaged in dramatic (pretend) play, they often try to integrate new and puzzling encounters and situations into their understanding. As they structure their activities, they invent ways to make the actions of adults and peers fit their own conceptions of the world. They do the same for things they have seen in the media, especially television.

By the time they are four or five, children are engaging in sociodramatic play, which is a later version of dramatic play. Sociodramatic play is make-believe play about social situations. It usually occurs in the context of a story or a specific plan of action focusing on a role identity. This is where children play mother or father or doctor or fire fighter. Lay-Dopyera and Dopyera (1990) point out that in sociodramatic play, children take on an identity not their own ("Let's pretend I'm _____"), convert common objects to imaginary uses ("Let's say this is a _____"), and set up imaginary conditions ("Let's pretend we're downtown and _____").

Social play in early childhood seems to afford crucial experiences that would be hard for adults to provide and that would be difficult to acquire at a later stage of life (Hartup, 1983). While a child can engage in dramatic play alone, sociodramatic play is play involving others. Because true social play involves interaction with other children and co-operation, it requires several cognitive abilities that aren't necessarily required for the lower levels of social play.

According to Smilansky (1968), sociodramatic play provides children with practice at adapting scattered experiences to the demands of a particular role, and thereby contributes to their development. Children must discern the central features of the role behaviour and simultaneously take into account the physical context and the ideas and actions of others. Through play, children improve their understanding of various situations and learn about role relationships and the associated behaviours of mothers, fathers, doctors, nurses, and so on. Such complex involvement is also believed to develop powers of observation and abstract thought (Lay-Dopyera & Dopyera, 1990).

Typically, sociodramatic play represents the first effective social education in a child's life (Lay-Dopyera & Dopyera, 1990). In social play, children learn to initiate and maintain friendly relations with peers. Social play also provides children with more opportunities to work co-operatively with a greater variety of children than would be offered in the home or in the neighbourhood. By learning to play with friends, children learn reciprocity, nurturance, and co-operation more readily than they would by interacting with adults (Eisenberg et al., 1985). Social play helps children learn, practise, and explore appropriate social roles; it also encourages co-operative behaviour, allows practice in language skills, and improves children's abilities to pursue independent tasks (see Weininger, 1990).

Dramatic play declines but does not disappear as children enter middle childhood. Between four and seven, children begin to play games with rules. Many of these games, such as musical chairs, involve sensorimotor activities.

The ability to distinguish play from reality develops in the third stage, from eight to thirteen years. Children now find other ways to satisfy their desires, and rely less on make-believe. Their social horizons begin to expand, and team play becomes more important than individual role-playing. They become more interested in the environment and seek out play situations and toys that will help them explore that environment. The final stage of play begins when the child is about fourteen. At that point, natural creativity, love of play, and the desire to learn have to be kept alive through proper stimulus and encouragement (Wittenberg, 1979).

Gender differences   There are gender differences in play; however, researchers are unsure whether these differences stem from genetics or socialization or a combination of the two. This is discussed in Box 11–3.

Children who are exceptional

Play is a universal form of expressive behaviour; nearly all young children play. Young children in general learn through play and exploration with peers, materials, and adults. This is equally true for children with disabilities. For them, play is enjoyable and fulfils the same functions as it does for normally developing young children. As well, play may facilitate the development of other behaviour, and may normalize their interactions with others.

Play problems are quite common and can be seen in both disabled and nondisabled children. Normally developing children who lack experience may demonstrate problems in play. Not interacting with peers or materials is a play problem.

BOX 11–3

What the research says about gender differences

Several sex differences have been identified with regard to the cognitive play categories. Boys engage in more functional play; girls are more likely to engage in constructive play (Johnson & Roopnarine, 1983). Gender differences also appear to be connected to the social quality of constructive play: girls engage in more solitary constructive and parallel constructive play than boys (Hetherington, Cox, & Cox, 1979; Pellegrini, 1982). Very early on, gender differences are also seen in pretend play. Boys are more likely to refer to buildings and repairing vehicles, and to prefer action toys and toy vehicles. Girls refer to preparing meals or caring for babies, and prefer art activities, dolls, and dancing (Carter, 1987; Wall, Pickert, & Bigson, 1989).

The toys that children select echo these differences. Even very young children tend to play with sex-typed toys. In a daycare setting with a range of toys, boys played with trucks, trains, and tools; girls played with dolls and tea sets, or with neutral toys such as blocks (Atkinson et al., 1990). Other research confirms this; boys play with toy vehicles and construction toys, and they play action games. Girls prefer art activities, doll play, and dancing (Carter, 1987). Boys seem to develop sex-typed preferences for toys earlier and more consistently than do girls (Gibson & Chandler, 1988).

In the preschool years—and indeed throughout childhood—boys typically spend more playtime outside, engaged in gross motor activities such as running, climbing, and playing ball. Generally, boys play in larger groups, and their play is rougher and takes up more space. Also, they are more likely to play on the streets and in other public places. Many if not most boys' activities involve playful aggression and competition, as in *rough and tumble play*, which accounts for between 11 and 15 percent of playground behaviour among both preschoolers and school-age children (Pellegrini, 1988).

In rough and tumble play we see mimicry of aggression, although this play is really quite different from real aggression. (We can tell this from the children's laughing faces, which look so different from the frowns and scowls of aggression.) Rough and tumble play is both fun and constructive, and develops interactive and gross motor skills. Rough and tumble play occurs among children who have considerable social experience, often with each other. It is three times more likely to occur among boys (DiPietro, 1981). Rough and tumble play is related to boys' social problem solving and popularity. It requires negotiation skills and constant redefinition of situations (Humphreys & Smith, 1987). Boys learn to handle social problems, such as dominance and leadership. They also learn to share materials, space, ideas, and power.

Girls spend more time indoors, typically at activities that demand fine motor control and relatively lower activity levels, such as arts and crafts, sewing, and dressing and undressing dolls. When they do play outside, girls are more likely to engage in co-operative, turn-taking games.

Boys tend to play with boys and girls with girls. This preference for same-sex play partners is evident even in infancy; so is the tendency for masculine play to be more aggressive (Maccoby, 1980).

Children who lack experience may wander, and be anxious and aloof, and may be rejected or ignored by their peers. Children may be dabblers (i.e., start something but don't continue). Wanderers don't make play choices or engage in active play. Sometimes, lack of play skills may first appear to be a discipline problem.

The play problems observed in children with disabilities may be more complex and pervasive. The type of disability affects play behaviour; the greater the disability, the greater the play deficits that are likely to be seen. As we already pointed out, severe visual impairment and infantile autism seem to have the greatest negative impact on the development of play skills.

Even a mild learning problem or disability can hinder a child's early social development and early and subsequent play behaviour. Children with mild disabilities seem to develop play skills in the same sequence as their peers, and can do most of the things other children can do. But they may lag in developing the skills needed for higher levels of play, and in the social skills needed for effective interaction. Mildly disabled children in play groups are less successful in peer social interactions than their younger and same-age normally developing peers.

Children with language disorders may lag in development of play. Verbal exchange seems to be necessary to sustain symbolic play; for this reason, delays in verbal language ability may restrict the emergence of co-operative make-believe play involving the symbolic use of objects and sophisticated peer interaction (Higginbotham & Baker, 1981).

In young hearing-impaired children, communication deficits interfere with normal play development (Higginbotham, Baker, & Neill, 1980). Hearing-impaired children tend to engage in less complex and less social play than children who hear normally (Esposito & Koorland, 1989). Higginbotham and Baker (1981) found that hearing-impaired preschoolers between 47 and 66 months of age preferred solitary constructive play, while hearing children of the same age preferred co-operative dramatic play.

Children with mental disabilities seem to make more limited toy selections and to use less social and pretend play (Fewell & Vadasy, 1983). These children may choose only one toy and show little interest in interacting with other children. Mentally retarded children have been found to engage in more sophisticated play when playing alone as opposed to with peers. It may be that peers are a distraction that results in less sophisticated play (Malone & Stoneman, 1990).

Some children with intellectual disabilities and more significant problems will not know how to use any of the materials—paint brushes, crayons, scissors, and so on—and may not learn through observing others. Children who are severely retarded seldom act on play materials in a constructive manner; they tend to engage in repetitive, nonfunctional actions with toys, such as banging and throwing (Wehman, 1977).

Play requires experience and opportunity; this alone places restraints on children with severe physical disabilities. A physical impairment can affect a child's range of motion, physical strength, co-ordination, communication, and interaction with instructional toys and materials. These children may have different first-hand knowledge and experience than their peers because they cannot explore the environment the way other children can. For example, sensorimotor children with cerebral palsy rely more on visual exploration and less on tactile exploration of toys than do children developing normally (see Rogers, 1988).

Social variables may interfere with the play behaviour of children who are physically disabled. Their different appearance (i.e., physical impairments, adaptive equipment) can serve as a barrier to social interaction. Many children with disabilities are seen by both nonhandicapped adults and by other children as unattractive. Normally developing children may be fearful or uncertain of the child's appearance, or may feel it would lower their status with their peers to be seen interacting with the disabled child (Bailey & Wolery, 1984; and see Chapter 12).

Visually impaired children may be substantially delayed in sensorimotor play, and may exhibit delays or deficiencies in symbolic and social play. Abnormalities in symbolic play seem to be related to the limitations imposed by the impairment.

In discussions of the behavioural deviations of children who are autistic, play disorders are consistently cited. Evidence indicates that the play of children with autism is quite different from that of mentally retarded and other exceptional children. For autistic children, the salient issue is not delayed play, but play that differs in topography, pleasure, and complexity. Their play is often obsessional, mechanical, and repetitive, and there is a marked absence of both co-operative play and of innovative pretend play. Perhaps because of the language deficits that invariably characterize infantile autism, their play is striking in its lack of fantasy and its sterile, repetitive, ritualistic, and solitary nature (Winzer, 1996).

These children do not seem to know how to use play forms. In a room full of toys, an autistic child is more likely to ignore the toys and engage in stereotypic self-stimulating body movements. If the child does play, toys are used in a deviant fashion. Typically, unusual preoccupations, such as memorizing timetables, are pursued single-mindedly to the detriment of other activities (Rutter, 1985).

Assessing play skills

While the higher forms of social play are more connected with more mature children, in fact all forms of play can be seen in early childhood. This means that play provides a rough estimate of developmental levels. For time to time, teachers need to stand back and observe children's use of materials, the age appropriateness of their play, and the way they play with peers.

Play for young children who are disabled serves the same function as play for other young children: it is a mechanism for learning (Rogers, 1988). Observing the play of children with disabilities is crucial to the evaluation of learning, since it provides the teacher with information about readiness, preferred strategies, levels of performance, and skill generalization. As teachers observe children's play they can note, for example, the child who has problems with puzzles; the one who is unable to correct a poor choice of piece placement; and the one who has difficulty paying attention to details in puzzle pictures or piece shapes. During construction activities they can observe the child who has difficulty putting pieces together; who shows poor concentration in simple tasks; who relies on very basic constructions; and who engages in stereotypic play.

More formal assessments of children's play can be made. Play assessment is user friendly—natural, nontraumatic, and enjoyable for both the child and the teacher. It shows what children can do rather than what they cannot do (Weber, Behl, & Dummers, 1994). Play assessment should take place in a natural setting, in a child-centred situation rather than a clinical environment.

The usefulness of play as an assessment tool was first reported by Parten (1932), whose description of the developmental changes associated with a typical child at play is still appropriate. Many professionals still use the Parten scale as one component of a comprehensive assessment strategy when assessing the social and emotional functioning of children with special needs. Teachers may note, for example, a lack of progression from solitary into parallel and associative play.

The best possible instruments for assessing play have yet to be developed. The first formal measure to assess play was a series of eclectic scales based on Piaget's stages of development. Today's tools are more refined, and have practical applications for both assessment and intervention, but they still aren't as advanced as those now available for assessing children's cognitive, linguistic, and motor skills.

Play assessment tools assess and define a child's strengths and weaknesses in the areas of sensorimotor and symbolic play abilities, and assist in planning appropriate strategies for intervention. A sampling of tools is shown in Table 11–2.

Targeting play skills

There are two ways to target play skills. The teacher could target the skills shown by normally developing children. Alternatively, the teacher could identify the child's current level of functioning within identified developmental sequences and build on that repertoire.

Generally, children with mild disabilities will follow the sequence of skills development seen in normally developing children. To pinpoint the skills to target, teachers can conduct a toy inventory; this will identify the toys that non-disabled children play with during free play. This is accomplished by observing children at 30-second intervals for 20 minutes and recording the frequency with which each toy is used.

Children with significant retardation and multiple disabilities may not be able to benefit in all ways from play activities. For these children, a play assessment should first determine present levels of functioning. When a child has more deficient skills, a more structured program will be required. Some special children require focused and purposeful instruction that uses techniques such as modelling and demonstration, prompts, verbal guidance, and systematic reinforcement (Safford, 1983). Activities and toys should focus on eight aspects of child development, in this order: awareness of sensations; balance and big movements; dexterity and eye/hand co-ordination; vision; space/time awareness; personality/socialization; language; and imagination and creativity.

LEARNING ACTIVITY 1

In Chapter 8 we discussed a procedure called arena assessment. Explain how this is used, the instruments that may be used, and the personnel who may be involved. Stress how the child's play is central to arena assessment.

TABLE 11–2: Assessing play skills

Tool	Ages	Special features	Strategies
Assessment of Play Behaviour (Largo & Howard, 1979)		Allows assessment of the frequency of play schemas observed and elicited from young children.	A standard set of toys is chosen to elicit symbolic play. Toys are presented to the child in a particular order. The child first plays freely with the toys, then the evaluator attempts to prompt various kinds of play.
Hypothesized Sequence of Development of Exploration/ Play (Belsky & Most, 1981)	Early in the sensorimotor period.	Covers most of the play milestones. Useful for screening.	12 play behaviours, beginning with mouthing and continuing through symbolic substitutions. Uses two standard sets of toys presented to a child as free play.
Play Assessment Scale (Fewell, 1984, 1988)	Two-month level extending to 36-month level.	Developmental measure.	Contains 45 sensorimotor and symbolic play behaviours arranged in developmental order. Specific toys are grouped to stimulate particular kinds of play. Most items can be passed without the use of language.
Symbolic Play Checklist (Westby, 1980)	Begins at nine months.	Integrates language development, cognitive aspects of play, and social aspects of play.	Series of 10 steps based on normal development according to chronological age.
Trans-disciplinary Play-based Assessment (Linder, 1989, 1990)	6 months to 6 years.	Functional approach.	Assesses cognitive communication, sensorimotor and socioemotional development.

BOX 11–4

Helpful hints

- Observe, to gain insight for selecting individual activities and materials.
- Take advantage of opportunities to expand play.
- Encourage exploration and experimentation with materials.
- Avoid interrupting play.
- Let children know you are interested by encouraging them to talk about their play.
- Be available when needed for assistance.
- Label toys to increase communication skills. (Eheart & Levitt, 1985)
- Special efforts in promoting play should be concentrated on children who are passive and who do not demand much attention or stimulation.

Adapting activities

Play is important because children spend a great deal of time occupied with it. So all children should be prompted to participate where possible. Children with disabilities may not be able to fully benefit from play activities because of the limitations resulting from their disabilities, but every child can benefit in many ways, and each deserves the opportunity to participate. The challenge for early childhood educators is to take advantage of the inherent appeal of play to create meaningful learning experiences.

In the classroom, play is approached in much the same way as other areas. The role of the teacher in play mainly involves creating an environment for play and providing opportunities for play to occur.

Small children need different types of play: exploratory play, toy play, social play, and structured game play (Beers & Wehman, 1985). All these types of play require different skills, as well as different prompting strategies on the teacher's part.

TOY PLAY

Toys are not the goal of play. Rather, they help children acquire many new skills and encourage them to explore their world and discover themselves. Toys can help a child become aware of the environment; they promote self-initiated play and independent activities. Toy play provides opportunities for children to learn shape, size, and colour discrimination. Sensory awareness (visual, auditory, tactile) can be heightened by play with a variety of toys. Toys can help children develop motor skills, both gross motor (balance, mobility) and fine motor (grasping, dexterity, eye/hand co-ordination).

Toys also help children to develop basic educational skills and—perhaps most importantly—to enjoy personal relationships. Infants as young as six months are more likely to be social with one another when toys are present (Hay, Nash, & Pedersen, 1983). As children develop, they use toys in play more and more. By eighteen months, toddlers play appropriately with toy telephones, dishes, and tools. They like to play dress-up, and dolls and stuffed animals become more important. Four-year-olds use a far wider variety of toys and use them in more complex ways.

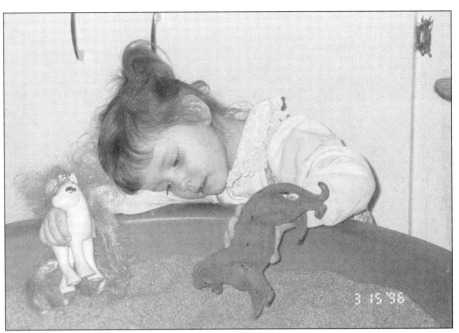

Toy play provides opportunities for children to learn shape, size, and colour discrimination.

Many toys are generic, and most children will use and enjoy them. However, some children lack natural curiosity and will require adult help and direction for play, as well as toys carefully selected to meet their needs. When selecting toys, we must consider the abilities and disabilities as well as the special preferences of each child. We should choose toys that encourage and reward a child's strengths and that foster the development of new skills and a greater sense of confidence and self-esteem.

For the child with an intellectual disability, play should be directed toward activities that bring the child into contact with objects and thereby stimulate his or her perception of the world. For children with intellectual disabilities, the toys used by other children are suitable. Improvised toys include plastic containers that encourage initiative as the child discovers a small toy inside each. Or teachers can help make a "My own …" book with photographs or pictures.

Play is one of the best ways for children with visual disabilities to gain the concrete experiences they require. Large and sturdy toys instruct them in manipulative skills and provide a sense of achievement. Play also teaches children how to seek out interactions with adults. Following are some special considerations for choosing toys for children with severe visual disabilities:

- Toys should develop the curiosity that may be lacking in the child.
- Toys should stimulate the senses of hearing and touch (size, shape, texture, weight, and so on).
- Tactile and auditory dimensions are particularly important. Materials can be adapted to emphasize tactile and auditory learning modes. Adding some sand to the fingerpaint, for example, gives the child greater tactile experiences. Sewing cards made with cardboard and a large punch allow tactile feeling.

- There should be good contrast between objects and background.
- More intense visual stimulation may be needed to arouse interest. Shiny objects in primary colours are best. For example, nesting boxes and stacking rings tend to hold attention because of their colours.
- If necessary, toys should be presented close to the eyes.
- The child will need encouragement to develop efficient and effective hand use; it is important to provide the child with toys that are interesting to feel and that have movable parts.
- Toys that encourage mobility and that exercise large muscles are especially desirable.
- Co-ordination toys will help the child develop fine muscle movement; they will also improve discrimination skills.
- Objects and toys should be of reasonable size.
- Toys should be sturdy. Children whose sight is impaired use their hands more and tend to be harder on toys than sighted children.

Toys to encourage good play skills in a child with a hearing impairment need not be special; the toys that interest the deaf child will be the same as those that hearing children enjoy. However, some toys should be chosen with a view to encouraging play at close range between parents and child, or between the child and other children. The best toys are those that present everyday situations such as family figures and transportation, and those that encourage dialogue. Toys that make noise (preferably with different levels of pitch and loudness) can provide a form of auditory training. Other toys include nesting boxes, blocks, puzzles, and games that link sounds, pictures, and words.

Toys for children with physical disabilities such as cerebral palsy must match for both age and degree of disability. Some children will have poor hand function, spastic movements, or difficulties with finger control. Others will require practice at pounding, banging with their fists, or using both hands. A wide range of construction toys is available, and teachers can select and adapt them to suit the child's abilities. Following are some considerations for selecting toys for children with physical disabilities:

- To develop both the weak and the strong muscles, select toys that encourage the use of two hands.
- For very young children, the soft and textured latex squeak toys found in pet stores are generally preferable to children's toys, as it takes much less pressure to generate a rewarding squeak.
- Toys should be especially durable; choose very sturdy toys.
- Toys should not contain too many small parts that are difficult to grasp. To adapt toys, add extra width to the handles so that they are easier to grasp. Attaching knobs to wooden puzzles makes handling easier. Materials can also be enlarged; for example, the child may be able to play dominoes if the pieces are 15 rather than 5 centimetres long (Peterson, 1987).
- Toys should be constructed so that they do not roll out of reach too easily. Toys can be mounted to a sturdy base to stop them from sliding out of reach. To secure fine motor toys, use baking pans with raised sides.

- Adapt toys electronically, as was discussed in Chapter 7.
- Large toys can be adapted. For example, add Velcro straps to the pedals of riding toys to prevent feet from slipping. A tricycle can be adapted by moving the handlebars to an upright position so that the child does not have to lean forward.

Children with significant disabilities may not select toys, play appropriately, or interact with peers. Some children with severe developmental delays will engage in repetitive, nonfunctional behaviours and show little or no interest in toys. In order to develop the skills necessary to explore the environment, these children need opportunities for exploratory and manipulative play and experience in handling, manipulating, and exploring objects. Toys for developmentally delayed children should encourage and extend communication skills, present everyday life skills, encourage expressiveness, and interest the children in imaginative play.

Toys should be extremely simple and provide repetitive action and sound. For a child who is disinterested in play, an action toy with a simple single function is more likely to stimulate play than a stuffed toy. Individual toys are a powerful motivator. Provide each child with a hobby box that focuses on the child's strongest preferences, interests, and abilities. To select appropriate toys, conduct an inventory of the toys the child seems to prefer; choose simple toys that require similar skills—for example, a truck, a set of blocks, and a ball. Battery-operated toys can be wired to a switch so that the child can control them and choose among them.

For children with severe disabilities, the opportunity to make choices should be built into play activities. For example, the teacher can place pictures of various activities a few inches apart on a piece of heavy cardboard; the child can select an activity by placing a fist on the appropriate picture (Hirst & Shelley, 1989).

The autistic child needs to be provided with toys that do not require imagination or complicated language. Also, the toys must be deliberately provided, as children will not explore and discover them for themselves. Children who are autistic enjoy water, mud, and sand play. Constructional toys such as puzzles and Lego are of interest to them; however, the interest is not in the product or the picture puzzle but rather in the process of fitting the pieces together. Autistic children may bring their own toys to the centre. Toys are important to the autistic child in that they can provide familiarity and reassurance. Note that autistic children often break the toys of other children.

When considering toys for a gifted child, remember that a toy may be boring to play with but interesting to take apart. Creative children often impose their own ideas on a mundane object to make it suitable for them. We discuss this later in the chapter.

SOCIAL PLAY

In early childhood, social development and friendship formation are intimately associated with play activities. In children with disabilities, social play of all kinds and at all levels is often lagging. Direct teacher intervention may be necessary to get these children to play with others. Teachers may encourage the child to participate, suggest ways to get involved, and physically help the child.

BOX 11–5
Katie's IPP

NAME: *Katie*
DATE OF BIRTH: *12 September 1990*
CENTRE: *Maple Arms*
DIRECTOR: *Ms. M.*

Previous assessment results

A number of formal and informal assessments have been attempted with Katie. However, the results are extremely tenuous. She would not co-operate on any formal measures so any results arise from observation only.

Present levels of functioning

Communication

Katie does not use any expressive language except consistent vocalizations to indicate hunger or thirst. Her receptive language is unknown but she gives few indications that she is developing in this area appropriately.

Motor

Katie has good fine and gross motor skills. However, she shows no indication of toilet training yet.

Social

Only rarely will Katie interact with staff or peers. She prefers to play alone with a single toy. She rarely has gaze-to-gaze behaviour and does not respond to the initiations of other children. Katie's inappropriate play behaviour with toys suggests that she can benefit from an intervention to develop play skills. Teaching her to play with popular toys may also increase interactions with peers.

Behaviour

Most of the time, Katie follows the rules of the centre. She goes to a location during free-play time but can rarely be persuaded to join in group sessions.

Recommendations

Children with autism have difficulty in responding to multiple cues. Regarding group activities, keep the group as small as possible to minimize outside distractions, and present only one task in a session.

Long-range goals

- *to explore various activities*
- *to engage in activities that require rhythmic movement*
- *to ride and guide large wheeled toys*
- *to improve play skills. Katie will engage in independent and co-operative play for up to ten minutes.*

They may encourage co-operative activities that are centred on joint tasks and provide common goals—for example, "Build a tower."

Dramatic play provides a safe outlet for energy and an opportunity for children to try out roles without fear of judgment. It also allows children to be part of a group. Some children can take full advantage of dramatic play. In fact, to engage in it, most children need only the time, the opportunity, and the props. Others, especially those with disabilities, need teacher assistance. Children with disabilities may not have developed the representational thought, the communication, or the perspective taking that are necessary for full participation in dramatic play. Training in sociodramatic play may increase children's play skills and their performance on cognitive skills (Johnson, Christie, & Yewkey, 1987).

A number of strategies can be used to stimulate play behaviour in children whose abilities to initiate activities and to be independently involved are not

- *to make a choice within an activity*

Objective

When given two toys during playtime, Katie will select the desired toy by gazing and reaching toward it.

Procedure

1. *Require Katie to sit with the teacher on a rug.*
2. *Present the target toys.*
3. *Guide Katie physically through the subskills. For example, place her hand on the ball and say "Roll the ball." Physically help her carry through an action she has difficulty understanding in words or other actions. The teacher may say "Roll the ball" while the aide places Katie's hands on the ball and then positions and releases it with a rolling motion. Pair physical and verbal prompts.*
4. *Give encouragement and praise for even small progress. Fade the physical prompt.*
5. *Teacher models the subskill.*
6. *Use verbal prompts only.*
7. *Cue prompt such as "let's play."*
8. *Self-initiation has occurred when Katie will play merely on presentation of the toy. (see Capone, Smith, & Schloss, 1988)*

Objective

When presented with a ball, truck, or set of blocks, Katie will engage appropriately in reciprocal, self-directed play 80 percent of the time on three consecutive trials.

Procedure

1. *Place the toys in front of Katie.*
2. *Verbally prompt her to choose a toy. If she does not respond, guide her hand to the toy.*
3. *Model play behaviour with the toy.*
4. *Reinforce Katie for any interaction or imitation. Use edible reinforcers if necessary.*
5. *Shape play behaviour with further reinforcement.*

Objective

Katie will observe and show an obvious interest in what other children are doing. She will imitate other children as they engage in water play, sand play, puzzles, playdo.

Procedures

Seat Katie opposite another child and occasionally point out what the other child is doing. Reinforce both children.

well developed. This includes normally developing children with deficient play skills as well as those with mild disabilities. In Chapter 12, we go into further detail on developing social behaviours.

The following techniques may be appropriate for many children:

- If a child needs direction toward an activity, keep in mind the type of activity and that child's individual objectives. For example, large toys encourage the formation of large, action-oriented groups; small, intricate toys encourage the formation of smaller groups that tend to stay in one location and play quietly. Gross motor skills may be encouraged in the first, language in the latter.
- Pairing a disabled with a non-disabled child yields far higher levels of social play than when a disabled child is paired with another disabled classmate (Guralnick & Groom, 1987). This may be because of the more proactive social initiations

of non-disabled children and the positive regard in which disabled children hold their normally developing classmates.

- Introduce co-operative play activities and a variety of toys that can be used by more than one child at a time. For example, crayons encourage solitary independent activity, while a shovel and pail requires two players.
- Place a child in charge of a play centre so that others will come to the child for materials.
- After children (especially those who lack confidence) have created a block structure or other similar product, ask if they would like to see themselves with the work. Hold up a mirror (preferably the large, stand-up metal variety) so that they can see themselves standing beside it. Or take a Polaroid picture (Lay-Dopyera & Dopyera, 1990).
- Provide informal teacher intervention in the form of participation in or direction of the activity. For example, when children seem unable to successfully engage in sociodramatic activities, the teacher may wish to structure the experience and invite the children to play specific roles. In initiating sociodramatic play, the teacher sets the stage by providing specific materials. The teacher then provides children with roles. He or she can initiate the interaction by saying, "Pretend that you are coming into the bakery and that you are very hungry." "Why don't you pretend that you are the customer at the bakery and I'll be the clerk?" The teacher can demonstrate how specific objects can be used to represent other objects, as in "We can pretend these long blocks are bread and the round ones are cakes." As the interaction continues, the teacher prompts children to stay in their roles (Kohler & Strain, 1993; Lay-Dopyera & Dopyera, 1990, p. 322).

Game play

Games are an integral part of children's play. Organized games for young children should be simple and noncompetitive. Many children with disabilities can join in games, learning the movements and rules by imitating their peers.

Deaf children can easily join in the games of their hearing counterparts, although they will probably need to be instructed carefully in the rules because they cannot pick them up by listening to peers. Visual impairments make children's participation in games more difficult. Another child can act as buddy to help them learn what to do. As a general rule, autistic children do not like to play with other children. Simple games of catch and hide-and-seek with objects can be carefully introduced, but there is no understanding of competitive games because for the autistic child, there is no concept of winning (Wing, 1980).

Children who are retarded, and those with severe disabilities who are confined to a wheelchair, find it very difficult to join group games. When children cannot walk or crawl or raise their arms to catch and throw, special accommodation must be made. Cynthia Hirst and Eva Shelley (1989) describe a number of games that children in wheelchairs can play.

In Pin the Kite in the Sky, a simple relay game, the teacher tapes blue paper to the wall and then provides one paper kite for each child. The child holds the kite and is pushed to the wall. He or she is helped to tape the kite to the wall and is then pushed back to the starting line to touch off the next child. When pushed to the wall next time, the child must retrieve the kite.

Red Light, Green Light requires a red sock (a stop sign) and a green sock (a go sign). The socks are placed on either arm of one child or held in either hand. One child acts as a signal raiser. When the green sock is held up, the chairs of the other contestants are pushed forward. When the red sock is held up, their chairs must stop. The object is to be first over the end line. The game continues until each child has had a turn to be the signal raiser.

Children who are gifted

Gifted children are more perceptive and develop an understanding of their environment more quickly; for this reason they enjoy richly expressive play experiences much sooner than other children. Fiscella and Barnett (1985) investigated the play styles of a group of gifted and nongifted preschool children and found that the gifted children were more advanced in physical, social, and cognitive play. However, they were not different from their peers in degree of humour or in the general affect they demonstrated.

All children must be allowed to play freely, and play should be an integral part of the preschool curriculum for gifted children. Too often, we look on the play of gifted children as merely one more avenue for an educational experience, or we try to encourage advanced developmental outcomes. This is a mistake; with gifted children, we must not always try to make the play educational or beneficial. These children need a chance to be carefree and frivolous and to play just for the sake of playing, the way all children do. Much learning occurs when there is play, but there is no lasting end product, and children should not be forced into producing something that is acceptable by adult standards.

Gifted children learn as they imitate others or themselves, and as they use objects to manipulate or represent other things. These children often look beyond the basic functions of objects, and use toys in creative and unique ways. Creative children will probably impose their own perceptions on mundane objects; some will even make an uninteresting toy interesting by dismantling it. (However, not all children who dismantle toys are creative: some are angry or destructive.)

Teachers and parents should choose toys that do not "do" too much. Gifted children delight in making their own things, so the toys that are of greatest value to them, and that encourage the most creative activity, tend to be basic in design and to lend themselves to all sorts of possibilities.

Gifted children are often interested in materials considered appropriate for much older children. It is important that the parent disregard the manufacturer's suggested age ranges and select toys that match the child's advanced functioning.

Make sure that you can define all the terms in Table 11–3.

TABLE 11–3: New terms and ideas

constructive play
dramatic play
object permanence
representational thought
rough and tumble play

SUMMARY

1. Good teachers have always known that children's play is a powerful learning process, especially in the early years. The importance of play as an element or model for early curricula is widely recognized. Play is generally considered vital to cognitive learning in young children, and important in social, motor, and language learning.

2. In the past few decades, the role of play in children's development has been a subject of major interest and controversy among educators and psychologists. The manner and sequence in which play skills develop has been conceptualized in many ways by different authors. The concept of play may be approached from various angles, including physical play, play as preparation for formal learning, play as cognitive development, and play as social development.

3. For a comprehensive understanding of the complexities of play behaviour, Piaget's work is well worth noting, but other variables should also be considered.

4. As children develop, the nature of their play changes; it advances from the repetitive and constructive modes of the sensorimotor period to become more dramatic. At the same time, playing alone gives way to playing with another child or in a group. The beginnings of dramatic play coincide with the achievement of symbolic thinking. The growing ability to engage in make-believe play during the preschool years reflects and perhaps promotes advances in cognitive development.

5. As they develop, boys and girls engage in fairly different kinds of activities and games.

6. Many researchers have noted the importance of play for normally developing children; the play of children with disabilities has not been as fully researched, so our understanding of it is not as fully developed. However, the growing consensus is that children with disabilities develop play-related behaviours in the normal sequence. That being said, children with special needs require more structure, and their play is both less sophisticated and more functional than the play of children who are developing normally. A key factor affecting the development of play is the type and severity of the disability.

7. The types of play most important for children with disabilities are exploratory play, social play, toy play, and structured game play.

8. Toys promote children's play. While most children will use the same toys, special toys and adaptations are helpful to particular groups of children with disabilities.

CHAPTER 12
Promoting social skills

During his first day in the preschool program, Brian hit another child and took that child's toy. None of the staff were unduly concerned at this time. Learning to share and to inhibit aggression is an important part of training at the preschool. Besides, they reasoned, it was the first day, and Brian needed time to adjust to the new situation and new rules and to the many children in the environment. A staff member spoke to Brian about his behaviour and soothed the other child by returning the toy. The incident should then have been forgotten.

But as the year went on, the staff and the other children could not forget or ignore Brian's behaviour. On the contrary—his verbal and physical aggression, his screaming, his outbursts of frustration when corrected, and his increasing number of temper tantrums made him a focus of attention. Most of the other children began to ignore him; a few retaliated with slaps and kicks of their own.

With some reluctance, the staff began to discuss whether Brian could remain in the setting. His chronic disruptive behaviour went far beyond what is seen in a typical preschooler, and the usual sanctions, such as a sharp reprimand or removal from the group, did not seem to have much effect.

An interview with the mother was both enlightening and frustrating. She denied that Brian could possibly have a behaviour disorder. "His father is very strict with him," she argued, "and he never misbehaves at home." She, too, had rather rigid rules, and these Brian followed for fear of quick punishment. She described how Brian conformed to her expectations or he would receive "a sharp slap." Sometimes, however, she gave different responses to the same behaviour, such as a hug or a kiss.

For early childhood teachers, a child like Brian presents a difficult dilemma. They know that nearly all young children display aggressive or excitable or even bizarre behaviours at one time or other; they also know that young children's affective and social behaviour is in large measure not the product of inborn characteristics but rather is constantly being modified by experience. They also realize that parents bring highly subjective expectations, values, and reactions to the raising of their children: behaviour that one parent views as too aggressive or active, another may dismiss as normal. The result is that without meaning to, some parents neglect or exacerbate their children's developmental difficulties. The harsh and somewhat erratic discipline that Brian's mother provides in the home may be contributing to his aggressive behaviours rather than easing them. Even at age two, children from aggressive homes are more aggressive than other children in contexts where other children would not be (Patterson, 1982).

Teachers are responsible for the well-being and learning of all children in the learning environment and cannot allow one child to disrupt the preschool experience for everyone. Ambron (1980) reported that some child care staff are more permissive, more tolerant of disobedience and aggression, and less inclined to set standards and directions for behaviour than parents are. This is clearly not the case in Brian's setting: the staff set high standards for behaviour and self-control for all the children in their care.

Rather than simply eliminating Brian from the centre, the staff have decided to initiate a special program to help him develop social skills and interactions with his peers, while at the same time working to eliminate the disruptive and deviant behaviour. Also, they will work with him to eliminate his disruptive and deviant behaviours. They will provide opportunities for him to engage in activities appropriate to his stage of development, and avoid involving him in activities that are likely to be uninteresting or stressful. They will also teach him social skills through peer modelling, and provide much reinforcement for appropriate behaviour. When misbehaviour does occur, time out procedures will be used.

A special program for Brian could produce a number of positive effects for him, for the other children, and for the staff. For the staff, the assessment of Brian's behaviours may be telling. Before a program is designed and implemented, the deviant behaviours must be carefully assessed (for type and frequency) so that the most crucial behaviours to eliminate can be targeted. When this is done, any sort of "halo effect" is eliminated (that is, the duration and frequency of Brian's outbursts and aggression are not exaggerated). Note here that a focus on poor behaviours may be masking any appropriate behaviours that Brian sometimes demonstrates.

Brian's behaviour will not improve overnight. Even so, increasing the attention paid to his positive behaviours may on its own improve his affective functioning. Also, the other children at the centre will serve as appropriate role models, and this may have positive effects on their functioning and behaviour.

The teachers must also consider the parents. They must try to help Brian's mother understand how to control his behaviour at home and in other settings.

An extract from Brian's IPP is shown later in this chapter.

AN IMPLICIT GOAL OF SCHOOLS FOR CHILDREN of all ages is to foster growth and development in many non-academic dimensions such as personality, morals, and social skills. Many parents and practitioners believe that the main value of early childhood education lies in socialization. And, in fact, research shows that the greatest benefit that good daycare provides is improved social skills.

Socialization is a broad concept that essentially means learning to interact appropriately with adults, peers, and the environment. It includes personal and social growth, mastery of the environment, emotional growth and stability, feelings of self-worth, self-expression, and self-image. An important facet is that children develop self- control and learn how to behave appropriately in specific environments.

Establishing good relationships with peers has been described as one of the most important accomplishments of early childhood (Guralnick, 1986). Teachers will encounter many children who have problems in socialization. Some will be excessively shy or withdrawn; others will fail to interact with peers or materials; still others will engage themselves little (or not at all) with either people or objects. Some children prefer to wander, or to observe others, rather than play with other children; they passively watch an adult or child, but without smiling, laughing, or reacting in any way.

As more and more children with disabilities are integrated into regular programs, teachers will

Some children fail to join their peers in play activities but wander or only observe other children.

also meet children who, because of the nature of their disability, are lacking in social skills. Because many children with disabilities encounter problems in social functioning, increased opportunities for social interaction are a vital part of successful integration into environments with normally developing peers. For these children, the acquisition of academic skills is generally not viewed as being as important as the acquisition of social skills.

Children who lack socialization skills are often categorized as having a behaviour disorder. Children like Brian are often disruptive, aggressive, and destructive. They are not developing internal controls, and this results in behaviour problems that are chronic, pervasive, and demanding. The behaviour of these children can consume inordinate amounts of teacher time, disrupt the environment, and harm the learning and the peer interactions of other children.

Procedures to improve social skills for children who are withdrawn, who are disabled, or who are behaviourally disordered, are an important part of early childhood curricula. For some children, environmental adaptation, peer and teacher mediation, modelling, and training in specific social skills are effective approaches. For children like Brian, teachers will also require techniques for handling the overt and disruptive behaviours.

In this chapter we discuss ways to improve social functioning in the preschool environment. We look at ways to develop specific social skills in children with disabilities; here, the focus will be on teacher- and peer-mediated interventions. We also offer some suggestions to help teachers more effectively manage preschool environments and chronic and disruptive behaviour.

Some children with behaviour disorders may withdraw from people in the environment.

BOX 12-1
Behaviour disorders

When children deviate significantly from what is considered normal behaviour for their age and the behaviours persist over time, they are categorized generally as children with behaviour disorders. Many of these youngsters actually show the same behaviours as other children; but they show them far more often, or far more intensely, or not often enough, or not intensely enough. Non-disabled children may hit, spit, swear, and throw tantrums occasionally. Behaviourally disordered children do so far more often, for more prolonged periods, and with far greater intensity (Winzer, 1996).

In special education, behaviour disorders form an elastic category that includes children who display different types of conduct disorders; anxiety and withdrawal; immaturity; hyperactivity and attention deficits; psychoses; and social maladjustment. All of these result in difficulties in adjustment. The severity of disturbance may range from mild to serious and debilitating. These children pose a particular challenge to early childhood personnel in the areas of management, attention, co-operation, and peer relations.

Generalized fear or anxiety is a strong feeling of uneasiness or apprehension that occurs in anticipation of something unpleasant. Anxiety is quite common in children. Many are apprehensive of new situations but are able to deal with them after their initial anxiety. Anxiety is considered abnormal when it arises in situations that most people can handle with little difficulty. Anxious children show a tendency to develop physical symptoms, pains, or fears associated with personal or school problems (Winzer, 1996).

We addressed the topic of ADHD and hyperactivity in Chapter 8. Recall that behaviours frequently associated with ADHD include high activity levels, low task persistence, short attention span, distractibility, and impulsive responding.

By far the greatest number of children categorized as behaviourally disordered have conduct disorders. These children exhibit **antisocial behaviour**, which refers to either overt, aggressive, disruptive behaviour or covert antisocial behaviour. Both types involve repeated infractions of socially prescribed behaviour patterns that violate social norms and the rights of others (Kauffman, 1989; Loeber, 1985).

Children with conduct disorders refuse to comply with requests, rules, and the conventional limits of behaviour. Their behaviour is not age appropriate. Children with conduct disorders are often overactive and difficult to control as preschoolers (Martin & Hoffman, 1990). They may be somewhat more fussy and irritable than normal, or they may exhibit aggressive behaviour and irregular patterns of eating and sleeping.

Out-of-control children behave aversively at least three times as often as normal children. Two commonly observed behaviours are various forms of aggression (such as hitting, biting, and kicking) and temper tantrums. Temper tantrums are common among two- and three-year-olds as they strive toward independence. Two-year-olds have many more moments of clinging, of tantrums, and of stubbornness as they vacillate between independence and self-determination. Among normal children, unfocused temper tantrums diminish during the preschool period and are uncommon after age four (Hartup, 1974). In behaviourally disordered children, tantrums are more likely to continue; a 12-year-old throwing a temper tantrum is demonstrating clearly inappropriate behaviour.

Most children become more aggressive as they develop. They use aggressive behaviour to overcome resistance. But with some children, aggression becomes a dominant theme in social interactions. Children learn that they can get others to do what they want by causing them

Temper tantrums are not uncommon in young children.

distress. At an early age, these children learn patterns of attack and counterattack, and learn them so well that they become blind to alternative ways of solving conflicts.

As a form of behaviour, aggression is difficult to define. *Aggression* may be seen as any form of behaviour that is intended to hurt another, either physically or verbally, or intended to injure property. Psychologists have distinguished two main types of aggression: hostile and instrumental (Feshbach, 1970). *Hostile aggression* seems to occur for its own sake and is its own goal. The bully who steals from a smaller child or calls the child names is exhibiting hostile aggression. *Instrumental aggression* is directed toward achievement of a nonaggressive goal and involves quarrelling over an object, territory, or privilege. A child may want something another child has and first try a series of nonaggressive tactics—such as asking or offering to trade—to attain the object. Finally, he or she resorts to aggression—grabbing, punching, and using verbal abuse or other antisocial behaviours (Winzer, 1996).

Aggression is a developmental process. When children first start playing with other children as toddlers, they are rarely deliberately aggressive. They might pull a toy from another child, but the object is to obtain the toy, not to hurt. As children grow older, the frequency of deliberate physical aggression increases, normally reaching a peak sometime during the preschool years, and then declining. This decline is especially apparent for instrumental aggression. Hostile aggression also becomes less frequent, but it does not decline as rapidly.

Before age three, children usually express their anger through undirected temper tantrums, hitting, and angry cries. Between three and six, the expression of aggression undergoes several related changes. After age three, disputes with playmates rather than parents are the main cause of angry outbursts (Harris, 1986). Children become more retaliatory and begin to express their anger verbally by scolding, insulting, or threatening others (Harris, 1986). Physical tussles over possessions decrease, while the amount of verbal aggression (such as threats and insults) increases. Hostile aggression, in which one child attempts to hurt another even though there are no possessions at stake, makes its appearance at this time (Hartup, 1974).

Parental attitudes and child-rearing techniques are often critical in the development of aggressive behaviour. Family conditions may predispose a child to develop behaviour problems, or precipitate maladaptive behaviours. It was long ago proven that family variables are good predictors of early forms of antisocial behaviour and later forms of delinquency. Families of antisocial children are characterized by harsh discipline, little parental involvement with the child, and poor monitoring and supervision of the child's activities (Patterson, De Baryshe, & Ramsey, 1989). With one antisocial parent, the child is at significant risk of forming an antisocial personality into adulthood; with two antisocial parents, the child is at even greater risk (Robins & Earls, 1985). In other words, aggression is multigenerational: children in aggressive families are more likely to be aggressive, and in turn,

Television is a major socializing agent for young children.

their children are likely to be more aggressive (Huessman et al., 1984).

However, many other forces may also be at work. Children learn aggression in many ways: by observing parents, siblings, friends, and characters from television and films. As well, children are more likely to be aggressive if they have opportunities to practise aggression, especially if no unpleasant consequences follow. When aggression is rewarded, it is reinforced. A young child who slaps another to obtain a special toy will consider the toy a reward for poor behaviour if no one intervenes (Winzer, 1996).

The problems created by the behaviour of aggressive children should not be underestimated. Children with conduct disorders often lack social skills and possess unfortunate personality traits that elicit dislike and rejection from others. Additionally, children do not grow out of conduct disorders. Children who are excessively aggressive and defiant develop intense and far-reaching interpersonal problems. Childhood aggression is recognized as a strong predictor of later behaviour difficulty in adolescence and early adulthood (Griffin, 1987; Lefkowity et al., 1979; Olweus, 1979).

PROGRESS CHECK 1

From the information presented in Box 12–1, outline the major characteristics of children who are withdrawn, and of those with behaviour disorders. As well, return to Chapter 8 to find the characteristics of children with ADHD.

Antisocial behaviour
overt, aggressive, disruptive behaviour, or covert antisocial acts; repeated infractions of socially prescribed behaviour patterns that violate social norms and the rights of others.

Social development

Socialization is the means by which individuals become reasonably acceptable and competent members of their society. Through socialization, we acquire discipline, skills, knowledge, ambitions, and empathy for those around us; these things allow us to participate in the life of the family, and later of the school and the community (Winzer, 1995).

During early childhood, children develop rapidly in self-confidence and social skills. They move toward *social competence*, which is defined as "the ability of young children to successfully and appropriately select and carry out their interpersonal goals" (Guralnick, 1990, p. 4). Social competence requires social and communication development; the growth of independence, and of meaningful and productive relationships with peers; and other factors that contribute toward becoming socially acceptable. Social competence is also situation-specific—for example, many children who are mildly disabled are perfectly competent interacting in their own homes. With less forgiving peers, they may not be.

Aggression any form of behaviour that is intended to hurt another, either physically or verbally, or intended to injure property.

Adaptive behaviour, which is essentially behaviour that allows the child to interact with the environment and those in it in ways that are appropriate to age, context, and culture, is an important component of social competence. *Social skills*, another component of adaptive behaviour, are defined as "those responses, which within a given situation, prove effective; or in other words, maximize the probability of producing maintaining, or enhancing the positive aspects for the interactor" (Foster & Ritchey, 1979, p. 626).

Social competence is developmental. Its acquisition involves many complex processes that begin in infancy and are mediated by caretakers. In the home, for example, parents often remind preschoolers to ask nicely and not to order others around, to eat properly, to share, and to monitor their volume and tone in speaking. Once in a preschool, normally developing children are likely to learn many things from teachers, peers, materials, and toys, such as aspects of verbal interaction, turn-taking, sharing, and social interaction.

Hostile aggression aggression that seems to occur for its own sake and is its own goal.

Egocentrism refers to the self-centred quality of the preschool child's thoughts and behaviour. Young children are centred on themselves and experience everything in terms of themselves; they act as if everyone else thinks exactly the same way they do, knows exactly what they mean, and so on. As children develop, cognitive growth permits them to gradually learn the social rules and customs of the society and to develop a greater appreciation of the roles, motives, and feelings of others and themselves. As children become less egocentric and develop more social competence, they begin to see things from the point of view of others.

Instrumental aggression aggression directed toward achievement of a non-aggressive goal; involves quarrelling over an object, territory, or privilege.

PROGRESS CHECK 2

Discuss the concept of egocentricity. Provide examples from the behaviour of young children you have observed.

Children with disabilities

Many children with disabilities lag in social competence; this in turn affects their degree of social interaction. Research shows that about 75 percent of children enrolled in preschool special education programs experience difficulties or delays acquiring peer-related social competence (Odom, McConnell, & Chandler, 1993). In an integrated setting, deficits in the social domain are considered to be more of a deterrent to success than problems with academic readiness.

Socialization the means by which individuals become reasonably acceptable and competent members of their society.

Children with disabilities may demonstrate the behaviour of much younger children, or they may display somewhat different behaviour. Often they will ignore, disrupt, or direct social aggression toward other children. Also, children with disabilities initiate far fewer social exchanges than their normally developing counterparts and tend to engage in shorter sequences of reciprocal interaction (Beckman & Lieber, 1994).

Children with disabilities may fail to respond readily to initial overtures from others. This lack of response may further isolate the child, by serving to discourage interaction. Problems such as echolalia or a failure to respond when greeted by a peer may extinguish any naturally occurring social interactions initiated by normally developing peers.

Social competence the ability of young children to successfully and appropriately select and carry out their interpersonal goals.

Children with disabilities placed in regular preschools are more likely to be socially rejected by peers and to display social isolation. They tend to place extra

Adaptive behaviour the ability to respond to and function in the environment according to age and social standards. Behaviour that allows the child to interact with the environment and those in it in ways that are appropriate to age, context, and culture.

Social skills those responses which, within a given situation, prove effective; in other words, that maximize the probability of producing, maintaining, or enhancing the positive aspects for the interactor.

Egocentrism the self-centred quality of the preschool child's thoughts and behaviour, and the child's inability to see something from another person's perspective.

demands on the teacher's time. They are less attentive and are more often the recipients of negative behaviour from normally developing children (see Hundert & Houghton, 1992). Normally developing children may ignore children with disabilities because they fail to notice—or misinterpret—those children's attempts to communicate or play. When children are excluded by their peers, their opportunities to try out and practise critical social and communication skills are severely restricted.

Some children are socially rejected. Children with disabilities may be rejected because they are part of a rejected group, and sometimes because of their own actions. For example, a seven-year-old normally developing child told interviewers that a child with a severe disability was messy at snack and lunch times. The other children viewed the child as "gross," and no one wanted to look at her (Demchak & Drinkwater, 1991).

Children with learning disabilities, behaviour disorders, and mild mental retardation are more likely to be rejected; those with physical, health, and sensory deficits are often isolated (Gaylord-Ross & Haring, 1987; Horne & Ricciardo, 1988). Even if they are not ignored or actively rejected, children with disabilities may not be warmly accepted. Preschoolers are aware of differences and disabilities, and react by favouring their normally developing peers (Brown, Ragland, & Fox, 1988). Non-disabled preschool children tend to prefer non-disabled playmates during free play activities; non-disabled children demonstrate more than twice as much positive peer interaction with non-disabled classmates (Cavallaro & Porter, 1980; Peck et al., 1988). When only children who are disabled are available, non-disabled children tend to engage in more isolated play and to interact less socially. At the same time, children with disabilities either show preferences for playmates who are also disabled, or show no preferences (Cavallaro & Porter, 1980).

Some research suggests that as the developmental levels of children with disabilities decrease, so does social interaction. Non-disabled children tend to interact less often with peers who have more severe conditions. Observations by teaching staff indicate that children with more visible handicaps are often the last to be included in play or to be chosen in some games.

Many studies on social interaction have focused on specific groups of children. For example, in a set of detailed observations of the free play behaviours of Down syndrome toddlers (Ray, 1975), it was found that delayed toddlers exhibited low rates of many specific social behaviours. Nondelayed toddlers had twice as many peer contacts and were more likely to point to other persons or objects, to wave at other persons, and to smile or laugh. Children with Down syndrome talked significantly less than their nondelayed peers, and their social interactions were more likely to be with adults.

Peer interaction for hearing-impaired children may be different in both quality and quantity from that of hearing children. Hearing-impaired children interact far less. They show low levels of interaction because of delayed linguistic skills. Deaf children lacking speech cannot use greetings or open a conversation; they are unable to sustain a dialogue and have difficulty responding to peer initiations.

The more speech a child has, the more communication with peers there is. When hearing-impaired children integrated into a regular nursery school were studied (Brackett & Henniges, 1976), the investigators found that children with the least speech tended to segregate themselves, interacting only minimally with hearing classmates.

Children with severe visual impairments face obstacles in social interactions. They do not indulge in as much spontaneous social activity as other children, and they often behave in ways that decrease their effective interaction with peers. Blind children, for example, often do not smile or wave unless specifically instructed.

From the very beginning, children who are severely disabled are at a grave disadvantage in social interactions. At the age where normal children are developing most rapidly, the multiple deficits of children with physical handicaps prevent them from interacting with the environment in ways that are critical to the development of social, motor, cognitive, and communication skills. Thus, they are doubly limited—by their delayed physical development, and by their limited ability to engage with the environment in ways that stimulate development (Warren, Alpert, & Kaiser, 1988).

Children with severe physical or multiple handicaps may not be able to reach beyond their own bodies, may not recognize others in the environment, and may be obsessively engaged in such self-stimulating behaviours as light gazing or hand flapping. Such children find it difficult to establish any spontaneous social interactions. Other physically handicapped children may lack the motor movements relating to social interaction, such as waving or smiling.

Children with autism and other severe developmental disabilities exhibit substantial deficits in social interaction (Rutter & Schopler, 1978). Autistic children have severely impaired relationships with parents, peers, and others in the environment. They demonstrate aggressive and stereotypic behaviours that can seriously jeopardize their ability to function in a normal environment.

PROGRESS CHECK 3

Outline some of the particular social problems that teachers may observe in children with disabilities. Discuss why such children may be ignored or actively rejected.

BEHAVIOUR DISORDERS

Many children with disabilities demonstrate deficits in social interactions. They show ***problem behaviour***—that is, behaviours that make it difficult for them to interact with peers, parents, teachers, and others. A smaller group of children with disabilities may show specific behaviour disorders. At the same time, we very often see behaviour disorders in children who have no other disabling conditions (Brian being an example).

In special education, behaviour disorders constitute a distinct category, but one that is broad and fluid. This is because of the wide range of behaviours exhibited by young children, the types of inappropriate or deviant behaviour that may by manifested, and the subjective nature of processes for identifying behaviour disorders.

The classification of behaviour disorders is generally seen to encompass a variety of behaviours. These are children with conduct disorders; children with problems related to attention deficits and motor excess (ADHD); children who are anxious and withdrawn; and children with severe psychoses such as childhood schizophrenia. The final classifications, social maladjustment and juvenile delinquency, typically concern adolescents and are not discussed here.

Problem behaviour behaviours that make it difficult for children to interact with peers, parents, teachers, and others.

All young children display rapid and uneven development and wide variations in behaviour. It is difficult to determine when a behaviour has become serious enough to demand attention. Also, behaviour is very much "in the eye of the beholder." What one teacher describes as deviant, another may see as excessive but within normal limits.

All of this wide variability means that there is no such thing as a typical behaviourally disordered child. However, there are some common characteristics seen in many children with behaviour disorders:

- They show behaviours that do not compare favourably with those of other children at the same developmental level. They deviate significantly from their peers in quantity, quality, and modes of expression.
- There is a failure to develop inner controls over behaviour. The child may be impulsive, distractible, hyperactive, and disruptive.
- The child exhibits inappropriate behaviours or feelings under normal conditions.
- The child exhibits a relatively high number of problem behaviours.
- The manifested behaviours are generally unacceptable to adults and peers.
- The child is unable to build or maintain satisfactory interpersonal relationships with peers and teachers.
- The behaviours interfere with expected performance relative to chronological age. Children show an inability to learn that cannot be explained by intellectual, sensory, or health problems.
- The child continues and even increases the behaviours unless structured and systematic intervention occurs (see Kauffman, 1991; Winzer, 1996).

Assessment

For children with disabilities, careful assessment is a necessary prerequisite for planning, implementing, and evaluating programs. However, when they attempt to assess children's social skills, teachers and others are entering an area fraught with contradictions and difficulties. Some of the problems stem from the fluid and changing nature of the behaviour of all young children, others from the tools available for assessment.

In young children who have special needs or are at risk, social and emotional development is the most heterogeneous category that can be assessed. A broad range of skills may be assessed:

- *Peer relations and awareness of others*. Does the child share, take turns, comfort others, show leadership? Or is the child aggressive and often engaged in conflict?
- *Play skills*. Does the child engage in solitary, parallel, associative, co-operative, small-group, and large-group play? Or does the child show a lack of progression from solitary toward parallel and associative play?
- *Relations with adults*. Is the child independent, or does the child exhibit clinging behaviour, excessive dependence on adults, and/or many requests for unnecessary assistance?

- *Personal development*. Does the child show self-confidence, curiosity, concentration, and the ability to shift attention? And does the child avoid danger?
- *Adaptation to change*. Is the child stable and controlled, or frustrated, withdrawn, tearful, fearful, and/or excitable?

No instruments are available that can accurately predict social and emotional problems in young children, and there are no standardized tests that look specifically at the social interaction skills of very young children. Various methods for collecting information about child behaviour include direct observation, analysis of anecdotal records, interviews with parents, and psychological and educational assessment.

The most direct way of collecting information on social interactions is to record observations made in a social context. The main reason for observation is to gather information on how a problem manifests itself in an actual setting. Observation focuses the type, quality, and frequency of behaviour; it also compares a child's interactions with those of other children of the same age.

Checklists, often teacher constructed, are widely used. An example of a teacher checklist for social skills is shown in Table 12–1.

TABLE 12–1: Social skills checklist

2 years and up	Yes	No	Comment
Takes directions from adults not within the family.	☐	☐	
Initiates own play.	☐	☐	
Claims and defends a possession from other children.	☐	☐	
Separates from major caretaker without crying.	☐	☐	
Makes constructive use of toys, blocks, paints, and so on.	☐	☐	
Pretends to engage in role play such as putting a doll to bed.	☐	☐	
Shares objects and gives up objects belonging to others if helped to do so.	☐	☐	
Attends to music or a story for about ten minutes.	☐	☐	
Takes turns under adult direction.	☐	☐	
Makes a choice when prompted.	☐	☐	
Shows increasing preference for co-operative play.	☐	☐	
Knows own name and refers to self using name.	☐	☐	
Spontaneously greets people; demonstrates courteous behaviour.	☐	☐	
Wants to use identical equipment to the child next to him or her.	☐	☐	
3 years and up			
Follows rules in a group game led by an adult.	☐	☐	
Takes turns with other children.	☐	☐	
Plays near and talks to other children.	☐	☐	
Shares possessions.	☐	☐	
Respects the property rights of others.	☐	☐	

	Yes	No	Comment
Plays interactively with other children, borrowing and lending materials.	☐	☐	
Tells own sex.	☐	☐	
Performs simple chores in preschool setting.	☐	☐	
Continues activities without constant reassurance.	☐	☐	
Shows sustained interest in interactions with others, without continued adult support or direction.	☐	☐	
Attends to music or a story for about 20 minutes.	☐	☐	
Participates in large-group teacher-directed activities.	☐	☐	
Able to share the teacher's attention with others.	☐	☐	
Attends in a one-to-one learning situation for five to ten minutes.	☐	☐	
States own name.	☐	☐	
Co-operates with adults most of the time.	☐	☐	

4 years and up

	Yes	No	Comment
Enjoys short periods of solitary independent activities.	☐	☐	
Plays with two or three other children co-operatively for 20 minutes.	☐	☐	
Dresses up for imaginative play.	☐	☐	
Expresses emotions verbally.	☐	☐	
Plays imaginatively with cars, blocks, and so on.	☐	☐	
Remains quiet when adults are speaking.	☐	☐	
Cleans up after play when directed.	☐	☐	
Will participate in constructive outdoor play without direction.	☐	☐	
Co-operates with other children in some project.	☐	☐	
Initiates conversation with an adult.	☐	☐	
Participates in organized games with adult direction.	☐	☐	
Has a favourite friend.	☐	☐	
Contributes ideas to peer play.	☐	☐	
Persists with tasks.	☐	☐	
Attends to the person speaking.	☐	☐	
Asks for assistance when appropriate.	☐	☐	
Follows routine requests or limitations.	☐	☐	
Attends to music or a story for up to 30 minutes.	☐	☐	
Shows an interest in creative activities.	☐	☐	

Another checklist that may prove helpful to professionals is the Social Observation of Mainstreamed Environments (SOME) checklist (Johnson & Mandell, 1988), shown in Figure 12–1. The SOME is designed to relate a child's proficiency in social skills to the behavioural expectations of an early childhood environment. The SOME is intended to examine a specific child's performance; it is not meant for group use.

Child's name: _____   Date: _____

Individuals observing the child: _____

Settings in which the child was observed: _____

Behaviour	Child's performance	Classroom expectations	Comments	Resolution
1. Asks for help when needed				
2. Plays well with others.				
3. Obeys class rules.				
4. Attends to task for short periods of time.				
5. Completes task with minimum of adult assistance.				
6. Initiates interactions with peers.				
7. Initiates interactions with adults.				
8. Observes other children.				
9. Imitates other children.				
10. Makes simple designs.				
11. Practises turn taking.				
12. Respects others' belongings.				
13. Respects others' feelings.				
14. Follows simple directions.				
15. Uses verbal vs. nonverbal means to express feelings.				

Other recommendations _____

Signatures _____

From A Social Observation Checklist for Preschoolers by R. Johnson & C. Mandell, *Teaching Exceptional Children*, Vol. 20, 1988, 18-21. Copyright 1988 by the Council for Exceptional Children. Reprinted with permission.

FIGURE 12–1

SOME checklist

There are 15 items on the SOME checklist, with space for additional items that may be considered important. The items represent the behaviours generally seen as important to successful integration at the preschool level. A range of personnel can complete the SOME checklist, which requires observations of the child in a variety of settings (classroom, bus, home, playground) and during different types of activities (free play, snack time, teacher-directed activities). A minimum of 10 to 15 minutes should be allocated to each observation. The SOME can also be used to make placement decisions, to establish social development goals, and to pinpoint objectives for a child's individual program (Johnson & Mandell, 1988).

There are four columns on the SOME checklist. The first column is used for recording whether the child demonstrates the desired behaviours. A plus (+) is used if the child shows the desired behaviour, a minus (-) if the child does not.

The second column is used for indicating which social behaviours the classroom teacher considers important. The third column provides space for recording concerns or observations relating to any of the child's behaviours. For example, "Child plays well with one other" might be written here to indicate that the child plays well in a one-to-one situation but withdraws in larger groups.

A sample of additional tools is shown in Table 12–2. A full listing of socio-emotional scales for preschoolers is found in Hoge and Wichmann (1994).

TABLE 12–2: Assessment measures

Burks Behavior Rating Scale—Preschool and Kindergarten (Burks, 1981)	3 to 6 years	Completed by teachers with 18 scales that include excessive anxiety, withdrawal, dependency, excessive aggression, and resistance.
Child Behavior Checklist (Achenbach, 1991)	Various checklists for different age levels.	Completed by parents.
Early School Behavior Scale (Pianta, 1987)	4 to 7 years	Parents respond on competence, anxiety, and conduct problems.
Behavior Screening Questionnaire (Richman & Graham, 1971)	3 to 6 years	Interview designed to be administered to mothers on problems relating to concentration, control, dependency, and so on.

Targeting skills

Social skills assessments have two main purposes. They establish which behaviours (social, communicative, motor, or self-help) will result in a child being viewed more positively by peers. They also identify skills that will increase participation in present and future environments.

For all young children with disabilities, needs in social skills must be considered when goals are being established. Teachers must consider whether the child has a behaviour problem or a behaviour disorder.

When children show social skill deficits (behaviour problems), the skills targeted should be those that will increase social interaction with peers. Skills

LEARNING ACTIVITY 1

Use either the teacher checklist or SOME with a very young child. Administer and score carefully. Keep in mind confidentiality, and make sure you have the necessary permission before doing this.

necessary for social interactions include smiling, positive physical contact, sharing, and verbal complimenting. The emphasis should be on teaching appropriate social skills, rather than on waiting for inappropriate skills to develop and then remediating them.

When a child is identified as having a behaviour disorder, the first step is to establish how serious it is. Teachers should begin by considering what will happen if a formal intervention is not implemented, and the effect of the behaviour on the child's overall well-being. They should also consider the frequency, intensity, and durability of the behaviour, and whether the behaviour is age appropriate. Some "inappropriate" behaviours are actually immature behaviours that are typical of young children at certain ages.

If the behaviour rarely occurs, is not too serious, or is not likely to persist, or if it is developmentally age appropriate, a special intervention program may not be necessary or a decision to implement such a program may be delayed for a while. On the other hand, if the behaviour significantly interferes with the child's learning, if it may lead to the child being excluded, or if it is physically harmful, it must be seen as a serious problem that calls for a special intervention program (a behaviour reduction plan) (see Bailey & Wolery, 1984).

Promoting social interactions

A main objective of integrated programming is to increase the frequency with which children with disabilities engage in social interactions with less disabled or normally developing peers. Through peer contact, children with disabilities observe more appropriate models for social behaviour, have access to responsive social partners, and engage in normalized social experiences.

The integration of mildly disabled with non-disabled children can result in frequent social interactions between the two groups, with little teacher intervention. In classroom settings, the children with disabilities may acquire social and certain communication skills from their non-disabled peers through both structured and naturally occurring interactions.

Often, however, children's social behaviour does not improve spontaneously in an integrated setting. For children who are moderately or severely impaired, additional structure and training by the teacher will almost certainly be required. If social and intellectual integration is the goal in integrated classes, then teachers should introduce programming to ensure that integration does indeed occur.

Successful social integration depends on the attitudes, strategies, and techniques of the adults in the setting. In fact, adult behaviour may be the most important factor in determining the nature of children's interactions and the degree of social integration experienced by children with disabilities.

Unless they implement planned interventions in integrated programs, teachers cannot be sure that social interactions between disabled and non-disabled preschoolers will occur (Raab et al., 1986). A number of procedures can be used to promote social interactions between children in early education settings. The three main categories of social intervention are these:

- *Environmental interventions.* Teachers rearrange features of the classroom to foster interaction. This can include restructuring play areas, providing activities that promote social interaction, and providing a socially competent peer group.
- *Peer-mediated interventions.*
- *Child-specific interventions.* Teachers provide direct instruction—for example, they prompt children to engage in interactions or role playing (see Odom, McConnell, & Chandler, 1993).

The type of intervention depends on the child and his or her needs. For example, Antia, Kreimeyer, and Eldredge (1993) found that for hearing-impaired children, environmental supports did more than social skills training to foster social interactions.

At times, interventions to promote socialization and teach social skills will not be enough. When a child has a behaviour disorder, teachers will have to direct energy toward discipline, classroom management, and the controlling or eliminating of inappropriate behaviour.

ENVIRONMENTAL STRUCTURING

Social interaction is a critical part of development for preschool children. Children should be provided with all possible opportunities to interact with others in activities that interest them. Children are more likely to interact if they share a setting with other children (especially if those other children know how to interact), and if there are materials available with which they can play together.

Social interactions increase when teachers structure play situations. Teachers can promote play between children by organizing the environment to increase and maintain peer interactions. To this end, a number of general strategies can be employed:

- Reduce the environmental barriers between play and activity areas. Social interactions between all children are more frequent when play areas contain few barriers and when play materials can be used by more than one child at a time.
- Provide a variety of toys or play units that can be used by more than one child at one time. A social toy requires or encourages interaction among children. For instance, crayons encourage solitary independent activity; a game, on the other hand, usually requires at least two participants.
- Provide many manipulative materials. Sand, clay, and blocks promote social interactions between children that range from early parallel and associative play to the most advanced co-operative play.
- Place a child with a disability with a normally developing peer in a play situation. As they work side by side, one child will often imitate or comment on the actions of the other; this will lead to increased interaction and joint activity.
- Reinforce disabled and non-disabled children for interacting with one another.

Activities can be structured to increase children's interactive play behaviour. For example, the following sequence can be followed:

1. *Parallel play.* The child is aware of and will tolerate one other child playing next to or at the same activity. Strategies include telephone conversations, where two children face each other with their own telephones and the teacher prompts children in a typical conversation. Children can play "colour concentration," in which two children face each other and the teacher lays colour cards face down. Children take turns choosing two cards to match. The teacher can also use two sets of objects, such as two blocks or two toy animals, and have children seated on opposite sides of a divider. One child arranges his or her materials and then gives directions for the other child to do the same.

2. *Awareness, appreciation of others, physical contact.* Children will tolerate and willingly take part in activities involving physical contact with other children. Strategies include story time, where the adult encourages children to sit in compact groups; or movement, where the teacher and children hold hands and dance to music. Children imitate the teacher's steps, such as hopping or jumping.

3. *Showing an interest in others.* Children will observe and show an obvious interest in what other children are doing. Children can use toy telephones for greetings or for opening and closing conversations. One child can give directions while another builds Lego toys or playdo models.

4. *Sharing.* The child allows others to play with a preferred activity or toy for a short time. This includes a show-and-tell table or book sharing.

5. *Co-operative play.* The child willingly participates in co-operative play with others. Activities to promote co-operative play include construction, decorating a table, making a group mural, packing toys away, using large puzzles that require more than one child, establishing a shopping corner, and cooking.

6. *Joining in activities.* The child willingly joins in unstructured games with others.

7. *Accepting rejection.* The child accepts it when others do not allow him or her to join in their group activities, or when they indicate that they do not want to play.

8. *Imaginative play.* This includes music and movement, listening to animal noises, animal songs, role playing, and dress-up and tell.

9. *Class group skills.* The child will sit, follow instructions, and participate in group class activities (see Chapter 10) (Anon).

PEER-MEDIATED STRATEGIES

Another approach to teaching social skills to young children in integrated settings is peer modelling. As we explained in Chapter 12, in a peer-mediated approach, normally developing peers are trained to help children with disabilities improve their social interaction.

For the development of social skills, peer-mediated strategies have certain distinct advantages. When teachers use peer-mediated strategies, they modify the learning environment so that it supports children's social interactions with peers. Specifically, they systematically encourage students to practise prosocial behaviour with their peers during typical preschool activities (Brown, Ragland, & Bishop, 1989).

Peer mediation procedures have certain standard components, which preschool teachers utilize during songs, games, and other activities. These components include the following:

- Instructions to encourage children to interact with one another.
- Frequent modelling of prosocial behaviour, with opportunities for children to observe peer interactions.
- Frequent behavioural rehearsal of functional social responses.
- Acknowledgement and praise for children's social interactions with peers (Brown, Ragland, & Bishop, 1989, p. 9).

BOX 12–2

Friendships in early childhood

Peer interaction varies with age, and children's understanding of friendship changes as they develop. Friendships develop from the parallel play and momentary interactions of two-year-olds to the close intimacy of female adolescents.

Friendships are relatively rare in the first two years of life. Very young children tend to have fleeting friendships that are defined by moment-to-moment actions and show little stability. Before the first birthday, a meaningful interaction between two children is rare; in the first year, contacts between infants tend to be brief and loose. Ten-month-olds treat other children as if they were inanimate objects—they pull their hair, poke at their eyes, and babble to them.

At about 12 months, true social exchanges begin and patterns of play become more peer oriented. These follow a developmental pattern. By 18 to 20 months, children can co-operate and take turns with a playmate. They initiate play with each other, and arguments become more frequent and more intense. By 20 months, toddlers become involved in complementary exchanges—for example, offering and receiving toys. Two-year-olds will work together to build a block tower, talk to each other on the telephone, and imitate each other jumping from a couch. At the same time, ownership becomes important. Taking toys and winning out become serious affairs.

After age two, peers become increasingly important in children's social lives. In young children, friendships are relatively superficial: they are quickly formed and quickly broken. Rapidly changing allegiances are a normal part of development. For young children, friends are people to play with. Friendships begin and end quickly, and moment-to-moment actions define friendships. What matters are shared activities and who has the blocks or the tricycle.

Children begin to hold their own in social interactions at about age three. Preschoolers often begin their social interactions by establishing their individuality. That is, they tell each other their names and ages and show off any interesting toys, garments, or skills they may have. Imaginary friends—an example of pretend or dramatic play—come along at about age three. These are most common among first-born children and only children.

TEACHER MEDIATED STRATEGIES

In a teacher-mediated approach for promoting social interaction, the teacher interacts with the children with disabilities in various ways designed to increase positive behaviour with peers. Teacher-mediated approaches concentrate on teaching children specific prosocial behaviours through modelling, shaping, coaching, and development of cognitive skills (Gresham, 1986; Hollinger, 1987); they also prompt children to engage in interactions and role playing. Also, through role playing, peer tutoring, and reinforcement, teachers try to change the attitudes of normally developing children toward their disabled peers.

BOX 12–3
Helpful hints

- Try to create a warm atmosphere characterized by acceptance without permissiveness.

- Establish routines; set clear limits to behaviour.

- Be consistent in demands and expectations.

- Be alert to what everyone is doing. Constantly scan the room visually.

- Visually display behaviour—for example, make a poster showing a child playing with blocks.

- Remember that in large measure, young children's affective and social behaviour is not the product of inborn characteristics and is constantly modified by experience.

- Convey the idea that you like the child even if you do not find the behaviour acceptable.

- Provide models of nonaggressive responses to aggression-provoking behaviour.

- Provide reinforcement for nonaggressive behaviour; do not allow positive reinforcement for aggressive behaviour.

- Provide opportunities for all children to engage in activities appropriate to their stages of development. Avoid involving them in activities that are likely to prove uninteresting or stressful.

- Provide opportunities for children to help each other.

- Make directions short, simple, clear, and redundant.

- Stress conversational skills, such as asking about other people's interests, responding to others' questions, and maintaining an extended conversation by taking turns to comment on a topic.

- Give anxious and withdrawn children a role in dramatic play.

- Sit the anxious child close during group time.

- For the rejected child, clarify communication and prompt interaction.

- Where possible, allow large blocks of time for play (60 to 90 minutes). Long play periods encourage greater social and cognitive activity, enable reluctant children to become involved, and allow play to evolve in different directions (Christie & Wardle, 1992).

SOCIAL SKILLS TRAINING

Many early childhood education and special education teachers have argued that social skills instruction should be an integral part of every preschool curriculum. But even with these arguments, and with the emphasis on socialization that characterizes early childhood education and ECSE, specific and structured training in social development has too often been neglected. The assumption seems to be that the child will automatically acquire social skills when exposed to normally developing peers. This is not usually the case.

Positive social skills in preschool form the foundation for positive peer relations and friendships in later life. They enable children to acquire and practise pivotal language skills, and help them learn other important skills such as conflict resolution. Children with positive social skills can also learn how to respond to and display social affection (Hartup, 1983).

Social skills encompass a myriad of verbal and nonverbal skills. Important social skills for young children include the following:

- Making appropriate facial expressions.
- Establishing eye contact.
- Greeting people appropriately.
- Entry skills (e.g., gaining entry to a peer group).
- Sharing and having a conversation; maintaining an extended conversation by taking turns commenting on a topic.
- Modulating tone of voice.
- Listening in a constructive way (e.g., pausing for a response).
- Requesting more information when appropriate; asking questions of peers and responding to questions.
- Saying "please," "thank you," and "excuse me."
- Extending and receiving invitations in appropriate ways.
- Giving verbal and nonverbal compliments and positive feedback.
- Acquiring a desired toy.
- Negotiating a new playground.
- Gaining teacher attention in a positive way.
- Maintaining acceptable habits of cleanliness, grooming, and health.
- Inhibiting reactions to stimuli to stem inappropriate outbursts.
- Selecting appropriate choices based on probable consequences (i.e., self-management skills).
- Handling teasing.
- Resolving conflicts with parents and friends.

These skills are fundamental to the social development of children. One way to judge their importance is simply to think about how the absence of such skills would affect the child's ability to function within the group and the family.

Because children with disabilities often face delays in acquiring social skills, these skills may have to be taught to them deliberately. A social interaction program could be introduced for the class as a whole, or training could be directed solely at children who show deficits. In the latter case, training would take place in those settings where the social behaviour would most naturally occur.

Among children who are mentally retarded, learning disabled, or behaviourally disordered, social skills interventions have been fairly successful. Hundert and Houghton (1992) found that during training, children with disabilities increased their rate of positive social interaction to levels comparable with those of normally developing children in their class. However, in this study the increased rate was not maintained, nor was it transferred to other settings.

Direct teaching can be used for social skills training. For example, to teach sharing, the teacher can use the following steps:

1. Reinforce the child for any observed instances of sharing.

2. Reinforce peers for sharing. Be sure the target child observes the peer reinforcement.

3. Serve as a model for sharing, verbally describing what you are doing and why.

4. Practise individually with the child through role play. Teach the child how to share; also teach appropriate responses when the child is not ready to share ("I am not quite finished, but I will let you use it in a minute").

5. Prompt appropriate responses or initiations during free play. For example, if Jane is apparently finished with a toy, the teacher could say, "Jane, since you are done with the tricycle, why don't you ask Leonard if he wants to use it?" (Bailey & Wolery, 1984, p. 232).

FIGURE 12–2

Feelings

Source: Beaven-Browne (1993).

Role playing is a valuable strategy for training preschoolers to solve problems in social situations. In role playing, teachers provide a theme and the children act it out. As well, puppets can be used to act out different scenarios. Children are asked to play act with the puppets and then to generalize in play situations with other children. The teacher provides positive feedback for prosocial behaviour.

INCIDENTAL TEACHING   These procedures help children to get in touch with their feelings and to work out conflicts. Children can also be prompted to talk about and express their feelings. Teachers can use a "clock" to initiate the discussion (see Figure 12–2).

We have mentioned incidental teaching a number of times in this text as an appropriate strategy for developing communication and social skills. In incidental teaching, the teacher provides an adult or a peer to model appropriate social behaviour, as well as to prompt and shape appropriate social responding. Individual teaching interactions are typically very brief and distributed or spaced over a period of hours and days. Teaching occurs in the natural environment. In incidental teaching of social behaviours, teachers should do the following:

1. Identify which children could benefit from additional social interactions throughout the day.

2. Identify classroom situations and circumstances that would allow incidental teaching of social behaviour with the children.

3. Plan various methods of encouraging social interactions. For example, some children may need physical prompts; others may need verbal prompts.

4. Wait until the children have ample time to observe and respond to a child and his or her peers.

5. Be observant and sensitive, and follow the lead of the child by allowing him or her to identify potentially reinforcing situations.

6. Systematically encourage the children who are selected for incidental teaching of social behaviours to interact with classmates who are socially sophisticated.

7. Try to make social interactions as pleasant as possible, and be prepared to interrupt and redirect children if the interaction becomes disruptive in the classroom (Brown, McEvoy, & Bishop, 1991).

Classroom management

Classroom management the way in which teachers manipulate the classroom environment to minimize disruptions and give all children the optimum opportunity to engage in appropriate behaviour and reach learning and social goals.

Ideally, all children should develop internal controls and exhibit self-control. But very young children do not have the cognitive skills necessary for complete self-control; thus, one of the greatest challenges in working with young children is helping them learn to get along with other children.

There are minor conflicts and misdemeanours that teachers encounter and handle every day; then there are children like Brian. Both in preschool or in the formal school system, teachers will encounter children who are disruptive and who fail to comply with requests and basic rules.

Controlling behaviour and teaching discipline and self-control is one aspect of the broader construct referred to as classroom management. In general terms, **classroom management** refers to "the way in which teachers manipulate the classroom environment to minimize disruptions and give all children the optimum opportunity to engage in appropriate behaviour and reach learning and social goals" (Winzer, 1995, p. 627). In early childhood, classroom management has been described as "what a teacher does to keep children constructively engaged

Behaviour management all the ways in which teachers control inappropriate and disruptive behaviour, as well as ways in which children are taught discipline and to control their own behaviour.

Discipline helping children to learn to guide their own behaviour in a way that shows respect and caring for themselves, other people, and the physical environment.

Preventative discipline strategies and procedures that militate against any discipline problems arising.

in activities that are developmentally and educationally appropriate" (Lay-Dopyera & Dopyera, 1990, p. 209).

Classroom management includes planning curriculum, organizing procedures and resources, arranging the environment, maintaining children's progress, and anticipating potential problems. Within the construct of classroom management, ***behaviour management*** refers to all the ways that teachers control inappropriate and disruptive behaviour, as well as the ways that children are taught discipline and to control their own behaviour. ***Discipline*** is defined as helping children learn to guide their own behaviour in ways that show respect and caring for themselves, other people, and the physical environment (Derman-Sparks, 1988).

There are three major facets of classroom management: the physical environment, daily routines, and guidance strategies (behaviour management). In earlier chapters we discussed the environment and scheduling. Here we touch on these again and also take a closer look at rules and routines. This section also examines how teachers can help children develop internal controls, and discusses how best to handle infractions and misdemeanours.

PREVENTING POOR BEHAVIOUR

Managing children can be a challenging and frustrating task, whatever their age, grade, or functional level. No matter how well teachers manage their classroom or centre, and no matter how conscientious, consistent, and fair they are, there will inevitably be some children who fail to respond as positively as others and who consistently test the teacher's authority (Winzer, 1995).

The best way to handle inappropriate behaviours is to prevent them from happening in the first place. ***Preventative discipline*** refers to strategies and procedures for preventing discipline problems. Good preventative discipline means a warm and interesting environment, logical routines, clear rules, much positive reinforcement, and children who are aware of the consequences of misdemeanours.

The physical environment

Teachers help children learn self-control by providing an environment that facilitates the transition from external controls to internal controls. Within that environment, teachers must encourage positive interactions with adults and peers, call attention to others' points of view, encourage communication, ensure that children develop constructive ways to solve differences, and promote co-operation rather than competition. Teachers try to keep conflicts between children to a minimum, and to eliminate aggressive behaviour by ensuring that children develop constructive ways to settle differences.

Much misbehaviour can be prevented if the work space is well organized, utilizes space efficiently, permits orderly movement, and minimizes distractions (see Chapter 7). Probably the single most effective management technique for behaviour control is visual scanning of the room; this is necessary for safety, for keeping all children on task, and for discipline. The environ-

PROGRESS CHECK 4

Explain these concepts: social competence, classroom management, discipline, and preventative discipline. Now relate all of these terms to Brian and his experiences at a preschool centre. If you were working with Brian, which methods of classroom management and behaviour control would you favour? Explain.

ment should be structured so that the teacher can scan the class with maximum efficiency.

Rules and routines

Classroom management is quite different for preschool children than for those of school age. For many youngsters, preschool is the first encounter with the routines of a structured day and the first time they are challenged to get along with their peers in a restricted area for an extended period of time. Children must learn to work and play independently in close proximity to others, and to play co-operatively with peers.

To ensure smooth functioning of the setting, adults set up timetables and schedules as well as systems of rules and routines. As we discussed earlier, schedules bring predictability to the children's environment and are the basis of smoothly operating transitions. Rules and routines serve the same purpose. Routines make the environment predictable; rules tell children the limits of their behaviour.

Routines are the general organizational strategies that everyone soon learns. For example, children learn the routines of picking up and returning toys, putting their belongings in their cubbies, and sitting down to eat a snack. Small children need to be consistently reminded of routines, helped to comply with them, and reinforced for appropriate behaviour.

Rules define the limits on behaviour: "Walk, don't run," "We don't hit other people," and so on. In older classes, teacher and students often devise rules together. Rules for very young children are usually devised by the teachers alone. Preschool rules usually focus on the safety and well-being of everyone in the room rather than on punctuality and completing homework. Young children may not fully understand rules; their suggestions, especially in regard to penalties for rule breakers, tend to be extremely draconian.

For young children, physical and psychological limits (rules) make the world more manageable, more secure, and more understandable. Children need a predictable environment where they can face new challenges with confidence, and they need limits on their behaviour to help them develop self-control.

The limits teachers impose must be both necessary and developmentally appropriate. Teachers must be sensitive to the interpersonal needs of small children and set limits that will help them to develop initiative and to expand their autonomy. While a permissive, unstructured setting is not beneficial, neither should rules be rigid and inflexible. The more rigorous the performance demands placed on children, the more difficulties they will encounter.

The list of rules should be short, directly relevant to the children's experiences and to the needs of the setting, and phrased in positive terms. "Don't fight about the tricycle" is not a good rule; the more general "Share with other people" is.

All children should be expected to follow the rules as far as possible. However, young children may not understand the rules or know how to obey them, even when they are clearly stated. Mrs. Jones and Billy, for example, may have quite different definitions of sharing.

Behaviours that conform and do not conform to the rules need to be directly discussed and/or taught. For example, the rule "Walk quietly in the classroom" can be stressed in the following manner:

1. State the rule and clarify the terms. For example, "What is walking quietly?" "When would you walk in the room?"

Routines the general organizational strategies that everyone soon learns.

rules define the limits on behaviour, such as "Walk, don't run," or "We don't hit other people."

2. Discuss the reason for the rule. For example, "What would happen if everyone made a lot of noise?"

3. Give examples and test the rule. Use role playing, modelling, or pictures to accompany the written rule.

4. Establish the consequences for breaking the rule. The consequences for poor behaviour must be explicit, predictable, and logical. If Brian is hoarding all the blocks, for example, an appropriate response is to specify the behaviour (keeping all the blocks), remove materials or the child, and praise the behaviour (of another child acting appropriately or when Brian acts appropriately).

5. Review the rule often.

Reinforcement

In Chapter 10 we discussed the value of consistently reinforcing appropriate behaviour to increase the likelihood that it will occur again. As a technique to prevent minor behaviour problems, reinforcement is valuable. Especially among older children at a centre, praise and blame can become powerful tools; children are now aware of themselves and how others perceive them.

The basics of reinforcement are these:

*   Reinforce often and consistently for positive behaviours.
*   Ensure that the correct child is reinforced.
*   Ignore minor deviations when possible, but reinforce good behaviour.
*   Make other children aware of the reinforcement. When they see another child being rewarded, they may improve their behaviour.
*   Use secondary reinforcers such as verbal praise rather than primary reinforcers.
*   Use praise judiciously; provide feedback often. "I like the way you're building that tower" is more reinforcing than "Good building." "Thank you for pouring the juice" will provide more information than "Good boy."
*   Match reinforcers to the individual child, as necessary. Kalim may respond to having her hand patted, Juan to a diary that goes home to his mother every day, Nancy to seeing the teacher clap her hands in approval, and Martin to a smile and a wink.
*   Use additional amounts of reinforcement for children with disabilities. Reinforce target behaviours based on individual objectives.

HANDLING INAPPROPRIATE BEHAVIOUR

Despite our best efforts to teach appropriate skills, inappropriate behaviours and minor conflicts will erupt in any setting where there are groups of children. On an almost daily basis, teachers will encounter misbehaviours such as defiance, temper tantrums, and bad language. Sharing, co-operation, and peer relations are often brand-new skills; children need time to develop them, and this will test the teacher's patience. Teachers will intervene in many conflict situations among children and handle many instances of child aggression.

Conflict   a dispute of incompatible behaviours or goals.

In many studies, ***conflict*** is defined as a dispute of incompatible behaviours or goals (Shantz, 1987). Conflict is always dyadic (social) and varies from minor verbal bickering to unrestrained physical combat. Quarrels between children, although frequent, are likely to be short and quickly forgotten. They usually last between 12 and 31 seconds (Eisenberg & Garvey, 1981; Houseman, 1972). Hay

(1984) reported a median occurrence of five conflicts per hour among preschool children across 20 varying settings.

Conflicts between children are developmental in nature and can be slotted into three categories. The most common involve *possessions*. Younger children have more disputes over objects than older children (see Peterson, 1992). Older children have more conflicts over *behaviour and territory*—that is, over actions or lack of actions—and over who is factually right or wrong (Shantz, 1987). The third type of conflict children resort to is *verbal and/or physical aggression*. This is seen in both older and younger children and in about one-quarter of all conflicts (Hay & Ross, 1982).

Because conflicts are so subtle in nature, careful observations and consistent strategies must be used to help children resolve them effectively. When quarrels seem to be getting out of control, teachers must intervene by directing children to alternative activities or requiring that they conform to the rules for sharing and co-operation.

Conflict and aggression are not the same thing. Aggression is more serious, as well as more physical (as in hitting or biting), than conflict (see Box 12–1). During early childhood, children need to learn when and how to modify their

BOX 12–4
Brian's IPP

NAME: *Brian*
SUPERVISOR: *Mary Jones*
DATE OF BIRTH: *March 12, 1991*
CONTACT: *Mrs. S.*
CHRONOLOGICAL AGE: *4–1*
PHONE: *555-7777*
CENTRE: *Sunny View*

Background Information
Brian is a child who is developing normally in the cognitive, physical, and language domains. It is his overt, acting out behaviour that is causing problems. This has been discussed with the mother at some length.

For Brian, the ultimate goal is an improvement in social skills and peer relations and a concomitant reduction of disruptive behaviour. Brian's behaviour reduction program will include: a focus on activities of his own choosing at which he can be successful;

prompting to take more initiative at the centre; positive reinforcement for appropriate behaviour; and strictly monitored time out procedures for misdemeanours and aggressive behaviour.

Long-Range Goals
*Improvement in independent performance.
Improvement in group instruction and peer-related activities.
Promotion of peer social and communication skills.
Encouragement of expression of feelings.*

Short-Term Objectives
1. *Attempt to have Brian take more initiative in a positive way. For example, allow him to deliver small messages to adults, assist in snack time, or take leadership in a group game.*

2. *Help Brian to play with one other child in a construction activity of Brian's choosing.*

3. *Explain the time out procedures to Brian. Use non-exclusionary time out for three minutes as a consequence of misbehaviour.*

aggressive impulses, partly because by school age, aggressive children are decidedly unpopular with peers as well as with teachers.

Very aggressive children are often noncompliant and will not attend to any activities or instructions. When a serious behaviour problem is present, and teaching a new skill or modifying the environment is not an adequate or complete solution, a ***behaviour reduction plan*** may be needed. This refers to a set of actions that a teacher takes when a child, despite management efforts, continues to engage in behaviour that is not acceptable.

Time out procedures

Behaviour reduction plan a set of actions that a teacher takes when a child, despite management efforts, continues to engage in behaviour that is not considered acceptable.

Time out from positive reinforcement the withdrawal of access to reinforcers for a specified period of time.

Time out (i.e., from positive reinforcement) is the withdrawal of all reinforcers for a specified period of time. Time out procedures assume that the setting, which includes the teacher, the peers, and the materials, has value as a positive reinforcement, and that removing children from ongoing activities will halt their behaviour. If the time in the environment is interesting and reinforcing, only very brief periods of time out will be necessary. If the classroom environment is not rich in reinforcement, or if time out gives the child an opportunity to get out of activities he or she does not find reinforcing in the first place, time out will not be effective.

In early intervention programs, time out is one of the most commonly used procedures for reducing inappropriate behaviours. It has been used with a variety of behaviours in preschool children. Studies show that it reduces aggressive and disruptive behaviours (Clark et al., 1973), inappropriate language responses (Wulbert et al., 1973), tantrums (Solnick, Rincover, & Peterson, 1977), and oppositional behaviour (Wahler & Fox, 1980).

Fee, Matson, and Manikam (1990) examined the use of a nonexclusionary time-out procedure. Children wore a "time-out" ribbon around the neck or wrist. Happy Face emblems were attached to these, and children chose their favourite colour. The ribbon, when worn, signalled that children were entitled to participate in activities and to receive positive reinforcement from the teacher for such things as taking turns in talking and remaining seated during group activities. A child who demonstrated a disruptive behaviour first received a warning. If he or she did not comply within five seconds, the wristband was removed for three minutes and the child could not participate in ongoing activities or receive reinforcement. Peers were also instructed not to look at or talk to the child. This procedure was successful in reducing disruptive behaviours.

Another research team (Porterfield, Herbert-Jackson, & Risley, 1976) used a technique referred to as contingent observation with children aged one to three. When a child exhibited disruptive behaviour, the infraction was explained and a more appropriate alternative suggested: "No, don't take toys from other children. Ask me for the toy you want." Then the child was required to sit and watch class activities from the side of the room. After one minute, the child was asked if she or he had learned the more appropriate behaviour: "Do you know how to ask for a toy you want?" If the child said "Yes," he or she was allowed to return to the class activity. If the child did not respond, said "No," or was engaged in some inappropriate behaviour such as crying or yelling, time out was extended.

After another minute or so, the adult would return and ask the child again. Once the child rejoined the group, praise was given for appropriate behaviour. This combination of time out and modelling was shown to be an effective approach to changing disruptive behaviour.

Time out regimes vary in the manner and degree to which access to reinforcement is denied (see Skiba & Raison, 1990). Variations include these:

- *Planned ignoring.* This simply removes social attention from the child for a given length of time.
- *Non-exclusionary time out.* The child is not removed from the classroom environment, but access to reinforcement is restricted by some means; for example, the child might be required to sit on the periphery of the room.
- *Exclusionary time out.* This requires the individual to be removed from the area of reinforcement, although not from the classroom. For example, a child may be required to sit behind a screen or bookcase located in a remote area of the room.
- *Seclusionary time out.* Here, the child is entirely removed from the classroom situation, often to a special time-out room. (Note: In these last two variations, the child is unable to view class activities or to model the appropriate behaviours demonstrated by other students.)

Before using time out, teachers should explain the procedure to the children, including when and why it will be used. Once the process is in place, an adult should warn a child once for an infraction and then use time out. As a rule of thumb, Christophersen (1988) advises that time out should never exceed five seconds for infants (7 to 15 months old), three minutes for toddlers (15 to 36 months old), or five minutes for three-year-olds. Five minutes is seen as the maximum length of time out for a child of any age.

Punishment

Punishment does little to deter unwanted behaviour and with young children should be used sparingly if at all. In children, punishment generates anger and brings greater conflict. Punishment does not answer the "why" of poor behaviour, nor does it teach appropriate behaviour, nor does it suppress behaviour; in fact, it may lead to other unacceptable behaviours emerging, and it may be used by children as a negative means of gaining attention from adults (see Winzer, 1995).

In and of itself, punishment does not lead to acceptable behaviour. Punishment, if used at all, should be used as part of a two-pronged attack. The first prong is to carry out the punishment in order to suppress the undesirable behaviour. The second is to make it clear to the child what he or she should be doing and then reinforce the positive behaviour. For example, Ms. Locke wants to eliminate Lee's aggressive behaviour and at the same time strengthen his co-operative play behaviour. Thus, she positively reinforces all instances of the appropriate behaviour, as in playing amicably. Lee is unlikely to engage in aggressive behaviour when he is playing happily.

Maladaptive behaviours

Because of their many areas of need, it is very difficult to integrate children with severe disabilities. These children often have severe developmental delays as well as other disabilities and various unconventional behaviours.

Children with severe disabilities may demonstrate a range of maladaptive behaviours. The most frequently observed inappropriate behaviours in these children are noncompliance, physical aggression, self-stimulation (often called stereotypic behaviour), and self-injurious behaviour (Wehman & McLaughlin, 1979). Other commonly found inappropriate behaviours include destruction of materials, temper tantrums, and a host of annoying actions ranging from teeth grinding to throwing toys.

Children with significant disabilities require structured approaches that focus on positive interaction with children, adults, objects, and events in the immediate setting. We want these children to interact conventionally with others, first on a one-to-one basis, then with peers, and then in small groups. Maladaptive and stereotypical behaviours must be targeted early because they interfere strongly with socialization. They are offensive to many non-disabled children and may repel social contacts.

Highly structured behaviour programs are often successful in softening or eliminating self-stimulating and self-destructive behaviours. With self-stimulation, the Premack principle often works well (see Chapter 10).

Involving parents

In Chapter 8 we pointed out the value—indeed, the necessity—of parent interviews during the assessment process. At all other times, the staff are well advised to confer with parents on particular items relevant to child's progress, especially when any sort of behavioural intervention is taking place.

Educators must be able to communicate effectively with parents. A first rule to remember is to communicate a lot. Talk, write, smile, telephone, confer, and visit. Preschool personnel should speak to parents often and through many different channels. For example, in the mornings and evenings, when the parents pick up their children, teachers can position themselves at the door so as to be able to discuss smaller questions with parents.

A daily report card of the child's activities will reassure the parents and keep them informed. Another excellent communication method involves sending a notebook back and forth each day between centre and home.

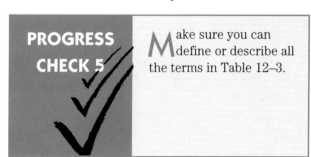

PROGRESS CHECK 5

Make sure you can define or describe all the terms in Table 12–3.

TABLE 12–3: New terms and ideas

adaptive behaviour	instrumental aggression
aggression	preventative discipline
antisocial behaviour	problem behaviour
behaviour management	routines
behaviour reduction plan	rules
classroom management	social competence
conflict	social skills
discipline	socialization
egocentrism	time out
hostile aggression	

SUMMARY

1. Social skill development is one of the primary tasks of early childhood education. Early intervention programs place strong emphasis on peer-related social competence. For children with disabilities, social acceptance by peers must become a major focus of early intervention.

2. Social skills and adaptive behaviour are two parts of a broader construct, social competence. Problems in socialization cover a broad spectrum of deficits. Substantial evidence indicates that young children with disabilities often demonstrate poorly developed social competence and pervasive and long-term difficulties in their social interactions with peers and adults. Social skills and adaptive behaviour are crucial areas of development for children with disabilities.

3. The more severe the disability, the lower the percentage of social interactions with non-disabled peers.

4. One of the most serious problems for early childhood personnel is how to deal with disruptive, antisocial children. Extremely aggressive and highly disruptive children are not rare, and form the major portion of those identified as behaviourally disordered.

5. Having a friend and being someone's friend are very important to preschool children.

6. Social assessment uses observations in natural settings, interviews with parents or caregivers, and rating scales.

7. Because children with disabilities may encounter difficulties developing social skills and using them appropriately, their successful integration into regular preschool programs requires carefully planned and systematic procedures that result in positive social interactions with children who are not disabled.

8. One strategy for promoting social interaction is a teacher-mediated approach; here, the teacher interacts with children with disabilities in ways that increase positive behaviour with peers.

9. Teachers must initiate structured social-skills training. The importance of social skills intervention is supported by the literature on peer acceptance, which indicates that children with early peer difficulties are at risk for a number of negative outcomes.

10. Another approach to promoting social contact between children with disabilities and their non-disabled peers is to train the latter to initiate social interactions and teach the former to interact appropriately.

11. All children need to learn self-control, sharing, and positive peer interactions.

12. Time out involves cutting off all reinforcement for a period of time. Time out procedures vary in the extent to which the child is removed from positive reinforcement following an inappropriate behaviour. Time out may be exclusionary (the child is removed from the environment for a given period of time) or non-exclusionary (the child remains in the environment but is denied access to reinforcement for a given period of time). Time out is only effective if the environment from which the child is removed is more interesting and reinforcing than the time out area.

CHAPTER 13

Motor skill development

CASE STUDY

Kenny

Five-year-old Kenny is a clumsy child. Depending on whether you talk to his teacher, his mother, or his brother, he is described as unco-ordinated, clumsy, or a klutz. Kenny's gross motor skills lag behind those of other five-year-olds, and many fine motor tasks are beyond him.

Kenny's language, cognitive functions, and social skills all seem to be developing normally. But as he grows older, his lack of motor agility is casting a pall on other activities. The other children in Kenny's group are learning skills such as tying laces, spreading with a knife, and using scissors. Outside, the boys are climbing and running, riding and jumping. Organized games such as baseball are just beginning to be incorporated into the play of the older children. Although he tries very hard to imitate and join in with his peers, Kenny does not yet seem to have the readiness for a range of motor skills, especially in the fine motor domain.

The deficits are not quite as obvious in the playroom because Kenny tends to choose activities where he can use simple equipment. He likes cars and trucks and simple wind-up toys but avoids more complex toys, such as Lego or puzzles with many pieces.

Because of his poor co-ordination, Kenny's functional skills are also lagging. He seems to become confused with dressing and undressing and will end up with both arms in one sleeve of a sweater. Even the Velcro tabs on his sneakers give him trouble; he cannot do them up tightly or evenly.

By six or seven, nearly all children hold their pencils as adults do. Kenny has not developed here and often holds his pencil in a vise-like grip. As well, when using a pencil or a paintbrush, Kenny has not yet decided on a dominant hand. He uses both hands and will often change the brush at the midline.

In the early childhood years, teachers can easily observe vast physical changes in children and accompanying advances in motor skill acquisition. Compared to other children of the same age, Kenny shows lags that are outside the normal range. Because his lacks are fairly obvious, the teachers have not conducted any assessment except observation and a casual checklist of motor skills. With this data, they have decided on three major strategies for Kenny. The first is to provide him with as many opportunities as possible to develop motor skills and to engage in skills and activities over and over again. This is easy in a centre filled with toys and equipment. The teachers make sure that Kenny engages in activities at which he can succeed but still be challenged. For example, he avoids the climbing equipment, but the teachers have been working on having him step through an obstacle course that requires some jumping and climbing onto low equipment.

The second strategy is to make sure that Kenny has some success daily. For example, the teachers have adapted an art project so that Kenny can use tearing instead of scissors. The third strategy focuses on functional activities such as putting on and taking off boots. The teachers have task analysed each of the important dressing activities and are helping Kenny acquire the steps.

A possible IPP for Kenny is shown later in this chapter.

THE PERIOD FROM AGE TWO OR THREE TO AGE SIX is usually called the early childhood or preschool period. Sometimes this period is referred to as the play years, because while children are playful and active at every age, the years of early childhood are the most playful and active of all.

Being active is the nature of children; they seem to have about a thousand muscles that want to move and only a very few that want to sit still. Young children are active, picking up and discarding toys and running from one side of the playroom to the other. The younger the child, the more active he or she is likely to be. Two-year-olds are the most active of all; after that age, motor activity decreases year by year. There is also a hereditary component in activity: boys tend to be more active than girls. The difference, which shows up in infancy, increases steadily so that by age eight only about one girl in five is as active as the average boy (Eaton & Yu, 1989).

The development of efficient motor skills is critical for social and physical independence in the home, community, child care, and preschool environments. Gross motor skills allow children to run and jump and play and be active. Fine motor development contributes to independence in most daily living, advanced play, and school skills. As well, motor skills and movement are an integral part of tasks in other domains: cognitive, communication, social play, and self-help.

As in all other domains, we see much variability in children's motor development; the normal range is very wide. Teachers of preschool and young elementary school children need to be aware of the variations in physical and fine and gross motor development. Cutting, pasting, drawing, colouring, printing, tying, and so on will be much easier for some children than for others. Some will be able to run, hop, jump, skip, and catch with ease; those who are slower to develop will have trouble with many or all of these skills. A few children will mirror Kenny; they will be developing within normal frames in other areas, but in motor skills they will show lags beyond what could be considered normal.

For children with disabilities, motor development may be lagging or quite deficient. Motor disabilities and deviations have been associated with a variety of physical handicaps, including cerebral palsy, spina bifida, and muscular dystrophy. As well, we can identify motor delays in children with the more severe forms of retardation, with multiple disabilities, and with visual impairments, and even in some children who are deaf.

Motor skills are integral to almost everything a child does or wants to do in the environment. Deficient motor skills can affect cognitive development because they hinder the young child's ability to manipulate and explore. Similarly, development of social skills may be hindered because efficient motor skills are necessary for many forms of play with peers. Motorically disordered children cannot manipulate toys and other objects, or join in dramatic and pretend play or rough and tumble play. Nor can they engage in jumping and skipping games.

TABLE 13–1: General checklist for motor difficulties

	Yes	No	Comments
Body image	☐	☐	_____
Can identify major and minor body parts	☐	☐	_____
Can draw a person	☐	☐	_____
Balance, static and dynamic	☐	☐	_____
Can stand on one foot	☐	☐	_____
Can squat	☐		_____

	Yes	No	Comments
Can tiptoe	☐	☐	_____
Can walk on walking board and balance beam	☐	☐	_____
Balances in movement to music	☐	☐	_____
Uses outdoor boards for climbing	☐	☐	_____
Activities are appropriate to age	☐	☐	_____
Judges heights accurately	☐	☐	_____
Rides 2/3 wheeler bike	☐	☐	_____

Co-ordination

Runs	☐	☐	_____
Climbs	☐	☐	_____
Jumps	☐	☐	_____
Trots	☐	☐	_____
Marches	☐	☐	_____
Gallops	☐	☐	_____
Hops	☐	☐	_____
Hops on one foot	☐	☐	_____
Skips	☐	☐	_____

Visual motor

Throws	☐	☐	_____
Kicks	☐	☐	_____
Catches a ball	☐	☐	_____
Throws a ball at a target	☐	☐	_____

Visual perception, awareness

Able to match and correct a poor choice of piece placement in puzzle play	☐	☐	_____
Pays attention to details in puzzle pictures or piece shapes	☐	☐	_____

Manual dexterity

Has the ability to put puzzle pieces together	☐	☐	_____
Good concentration	☐	☐	_____
Builds	☐	☐	_____
Threads	☐	☐	_____
Models clay	☐	☐	_____
Pours	☐	☐	_____
Inserts toys	☐	☐	_____
Hammers	☐	☐	_____
Does up and undoes buttons	☐	☐	_____
Picks up small items	☐	☐	_____
Cuts or snips with scissors	☐	☐	_____
Holds a crayon or brush with the correct grasp	☐	☐	_____
Puts large blocks or bricks on one another so that they balance	☐	☐	_____

Fine motor

Shows variety in marks and colours on paper	☐	☐	_____
Shows spontaneous progression through normal stages	☐	☐	_____

	Yes	No	Comments
Cuts with scissors	☐	☐	
Writes own name	☐	☐	
Cuts out a prescribed object	☐	☐	
Handedness and dominance	☐	☐	
Right-handed	☐	☐	
Left-handed	☐	☐	
Mixed	☐	☐	
Co-ordinates hand movements	☐	☐	
Has left-to-right awareness	☐	☐	
Other	☐	☐	
Stereotyped play	☐	☐	
Unusual fear of equipment	☐	☐	
Child avoids activities requiring skills he or she feels are lacking. Concentrates on free movement, for example, but resists guidance to attempt controlled movement activities.	☐	☐	
Excessive fatigue and lack of stamina	☐	☐	
Persistent noisy breathing on exertion	☐	☐	
Repetitious episodes of blank staring and briefly unco-ordinated movement, particularly if accompanied by unusual eye or hand movement	☐	☐	
Lack of strength or avoidance of use of one limb or side of the body	☐	☐	
Noticeable lack of bladder or bowel control	☐	☐	
Unusual, excessive, or extraneous movement of body parts (e.g., facial grimaces or hand tremors)	☐	☐	

Physical disabilities affect learning in other ways. Learning will be hindered when the child has experienced a great many medical procedures that lead to long periods of recuperation as well as missed time in the classroom. At a centre, these children get tired easily and have limited vitality, short attention spans, and limited mobility. As well, independence and daily living skills are adversely affected by physical disabilities. Children may experience problems in daily living activities such as getting in and out of a wheelchair, and in and out of a car or bus, and transferring from a wheelchair to a toilet.

In this chapter we examine motor skills and ways in which programs may be adapted to assist children's functioning. While we acknowledge that art and music do much more than develop motor skills, we discuss both of these curriculum areas in this chapter. Arts and crafts is an important form of play and crucial in the development of fine and gross motor skills. As well, every child can enjoy and learn some aspect of music, regardless of the type and severity of the disabling condition.

In this chapter we also examine adaptive equipment, ways to handle and position children, and orientation and mobility training for children with severe visual impairments.

BOX 13–1
Motor delays

When physical development is mildly delayed, it usually follows the sequences of normal development, except that it proceeds more slowly. Children who show mild delays in the motor domain may demonstrate a variety of behaviours that have to do with co-ordination, body image, and laterality.

General inco-ordination refers to a lack of muscular control. Motorically disordered children may walk with an awkward gait, be unco-ordinated in physical activities, and have more than average difficulty in running, jumping, skipping, and throwing and catching a ball. These children may demonstrate balance problems or spatial disorganization, evidenced by poorly developed concepts of space and a distorted body image.

Body image is a mental image of one's own body. The concept includes awareness of the body and its capabilities; of the interrelationship of body parts; and of the relationship of bodies to the environment. Knowledge about body image provides a stable base for making other judgments, especially about visual relationships.

It is also important to the acquisition of mobility skills. When children have body image problems, they may not be able to organize themselves within their environment. They may be clumsy, and slow in dressing and undressing; they have difficulty putting on sweaters and socks and show problems walking across the room without touching or knocking into furniture.

Kinesthetic refers to knowledge of the movement of our own bodies and muscles. It is part of haptic development, which includes the development of touch, a knowledge of body movement, and concepts of position in space. Children with kinesthetic and haptic problems meet difficulties in touch and body movement.

Laterality refers to an internal knowledge of the differences between left and right; *directionality* is an awareness of left and right outside the body. When children have developed a sense of laterality they can project it onto concepts in external space, such as *up* and *down* and *in front* of and *behind*.

Children may also have problems with spatial relationships. Spatial relationships involve the child's recognition of an object's position in space and of one object's location relative to another. Children with spatial problems often bump into things or knock things over (see Winzer, 1996).

Physical and motor development

General inco-ordination **a lack of muscular control.**

Body image **a mental image of one's own body.**

Laterality **an internal knowledge of the differences between left and right.**

Physical development refers to the acquisition of postural control and the movement patterns necessary to produce functional motor acts. "Motor" is a term used in discussing muscular movement. Thus, *motor development* is the process through which a child acquires movement patterns and skills. *Motor learning* involves using the body in such ways as to make the best use of what is perceived (Gibson, 1978). *Motor skills* are skills related to the development and use of the muscles and limbs. *Motor control* is the process by which the brain and the muscles work together to produce co-ordinated skilled movement. Finally, *motor imitation* involves the child's ability to match or copy the verbal and nonverbal behaviour of a model (Bailey & Wolery, 1984).

Motor development, like physical development, follows a predictable sequence. Infants indulge in a range of motor activities of increasing complexity that spill over to other developmental domains. By six months, most babies can reach,

PROGRESS CHECK 1

Box 13–1 describes problems with co-ordination, body image, laterality and directionality, and spatial relations. Explain these terms and then relate them to the behaviours that Kenny shows. Have you met children exhibiting any of these problems? Describe the child and the behaviour.

Directionality an awareness of left and right outside the body.

Physical development the acquisition of postural control, and the necessary movement patterns to produce functional motor acts.

Motor development the process through which a child acquires movement patterns and skills.

Motor learning involves using the body in such ways as to make the best use of what is perceived.

Motor skills those related to the development and use of the muscles and limbs.

Motor control the process by which the brain and the muscles work together to produce co-ordinated skilled movement.

grab, and hold on to dangling objects. Most children can sit alone at seven months, pull themselves up on furniture by nine months, and take their first steps at twelve months.

From about 12 to 24 months, children are called toddlers because of the characteristic way they use their legs, toddling from side to side. By 15 months, the toddler is experimenting with different forms of walking, such as running and dawdling. Even at age two, the child is still quite clumsy, falling down often and sometimes bumping into stationary objects. Even so, two-year-olds can walk on tiptoe, stand on one foot with assistance, jump with both feet, and bend at the waist to pick up an object.

Between the ages of two and six, children are able to move with greater speed and grace. Their bodies grow slimmer, stronger, and less top-heavy, and the brain matures to permit more body co-ordination. They also become more adept at focusing and refining their activity. The result is a steady improvement in various motor skills.

As their muscular ability increases, children discover that they can lift and manipulate objects that defeated them earlier, and this contributes to their growing self-confidence. In fact, many preschoolers think of themselves as able in *all* areas, from physical to intellectual skills. Many studies have demonstrated that preschool children regularly overestimate their own abilities—partly because they do not spontaneously compare their abilities with those of others (Ruble, 1983).

There are steady increases in height and weight as children's body proportions change. Between two and six, children add almost seven centimetres and gain about two kilograms a year. Until about puberty, both sexes follow very similar paths of physical development: at the same age, they are about the same size and can do about the same things. Between boys and girls, there seems to be little difference in strength until around six years, and the lead that boys take from then on does not become pronounced until adolescence (Salkind, 1990).

The three most important principles in physical development are these: the cephalo-caudal, the proximo-distal, and the principle of readiness. *Cephalo-caudal* refers to the fact that growth extends from the head downwards. *Proximo-distal* refers to the fact the growth extends from the torso outwards. Infants are able to grasp voluntarily at two months but cannot accurately control their reach. Increasing arm control enables infants to hit, then reach for, and finally grasp for objects. *Readiness* means that a child must have the physical maturation and the opportunities to learn before he or she can perform a physical skill. For example, it would not be reasonable to expect a 12-month-old baby to ride a bicycle, because the child's muscles and balance are not sufficiently matured. No amount of training or social encouragement will prompt the child to acquire this skill—he or she is simply not biologically mature. On the other hand, four-year-olds who are physically ready to ride a bicycle need to be given opportunities that take advantage of their level of physical maturity (Winzer, 1995).

Physical development is also closely tied to maturation of the central nervous system (cns). During early childhood, the brain develops faster than any other part of the body; there is a clear link between what children can do and the myelinization of the brain. (In simple terms, myelinization occurs as the structures of the brain are coated with myelin, a substance that allows the synapses of the brain to meet and function effectively.) In children, differences in cns maturation rates result in differences in the ability to control and especially to co-ordinate different parts of the body. Neural maturation is clearly seen in motor activities. Most three-year-olds find it difficult to march or to ride a tricycle, because these activities require the use of alternating sides of the body. Most five-year-olds can hop on one foot, a skill that requires fluid co-ordination between the two halves of the brain. No matter how hard they try, most three-year-olds cannot master this skill (Sutherland et al., 1988), as the brain has not matured sufficiently.

The principles of physical development—especially the principle of readiness and the proximo-distal principle—are important in early childhood education. Readiness means that children must have the maturation to perform motor tasks and must be provided with the opportunities to do so. For most young children, opportunity is not a problem: children who are developing normally learn many motor skills in their day-to-day experiences, wherever they are. They may practise their motor skills in a well-equipped nursery school with climbing ladders, balance boards, and sandboxes, or at home using their own furniture for climbing, or outside using boxes for crawling and fences for balancing. However, even given plenty of instruction and opportunities to participate, children who lack the physical maturation needed to succeed at fine and gross motor tasks and manipulations are unlikely to improve their skills until this maturation takes place. We can see this in the case of Kenny.

Gross motor skills
large body movements such as running, climbing, and throwing.

The proximo-distal principle is also important in early childhood because it relates to gross motor and fine motor skills and their timelines for development. **Gross motor skills** involve large body movements such as running, climbing, and throwing. **Fine motor skills** involve small body movements—usually use of the hands. Jumping is a gross motor skill; picking up a penny is a fine motor skill. Because growth occurs from the torso outwards, gross motor skills develop earlier than fine motor skills.

Fine motor skills
those that involve small body movements and refer to the muscles of the hand.

Gross motor skills develop early. As every teacher of young children has observed, two- and three-year-olds rarely sit still at a table or a desk. Instead, they prefer to run across the room, climb on a chair, or push large objects. All of these activities require gross motor skills and the use of large muscles. Fine motor skills are much harder for the preschooler to master; for most children, gross motor skills will outpace fine motor skills.

Fine motor skills develop in a reasonably predictable fashion as the areas of the brain associated with eye/hand co-ordination become more fully myelinated by about age four. As children develop fine motor skills, they gain control over their wrists and fingers; this enables them to hold

PROGRESS CHECK 2

Many terms are used to describe development in the motor domain. Explain the terms *motor, motor development, motor learning, motor control, motor skills,* and *motor imitation.*

a pencil properly, play musical instruments, sew and cut, and create works of art. Nevertheless, fine motor development is not really complete until adolescence, and many skills are not possible for young children. Preschoolers labour endlessly to tie their shoelaces, put toothpaste on a brush, and get their jackets zipped.

CHILDREN WITH DISABILITIES

When we consider motor problems, we look at two broad groups of children. The first group includes those like Kenny. The motor development of these children may not be proceeding normally. Whether the problem is seen as a lag or as a mild disability depends on how far their development deviates from generally accepted norms. In these children, delays in gross motor skills are almost always accompanied by fine motor delays.

These children may show general unco-ordination, poor knowledge of body image, and poor spatial relationships. They may have problems with laterality and directionality, and may be confused about directions, handedness, and temporal concepts. They may also show visual motor problems and will not succeed in working puzzles, stacking blocks, drawing people, or copying designs (see Box 13–1).

BOX 13–2

What the research says about handedness

There is really no way to determine a baby's handedness in the first year or two. Most babies start out ambidextrous, although some signs of hand preference are evident in early infancy, suggesting that hand preference is genetic (Corballis, 1983).

Hand preference becomes increasingly distinct during early childhood. By the age of three or so, most children have adopted a dominant hand. Many three-year-olds hold a crayon, pencil, or brush much as adults do, but may continue to have difficulty guiding these tools within precise markings (Lay-Dopyera & Dopyera, 1990). As well, sometimes preschoolers use their nondominant hand to paint or to write simply because their other hand is busy doing something else.

By five or six, most children consistently prefer to use one side of the body in dealing with the world. By age five, more than 90 percent of all children are clearly right- or left-handed. Yet hand preference remains somewhat flexible, since a child can be forced to use his or her less preferred hand.

Although estimates vary, about 17 percent of the entire population is in the sinistral (left) camp. Of this approximate number, only about 4 percent are true left-handers, meaning that they process linguistic information in the right hemisphere of the brain. The rest seem to have their speech centre in the left brain, or possibly language skills are shared between the hemispheres. Left-handedness is found almost twice as often in males (McKean, 1987), and more often among twins.

It has been believed that children who prefer their left hand are generally less well co-ordinated and more disposed toward reading disabilities and other problems than right-handed children. Recent research suggests that this stereotype may be exaggerated. Tan (1985) examined the correlations between handedness and motor competence among four-year-old preschoolers. Of her sample of 512 children, 448 (90 percent) were right-handed, 41 were left-handed, and 23 had no hand preference. Tan found no difference in motor skills between right- and left-handed children, but noted that children lacking a hand preference performed less well than the other groups. Tan concluded that left-handed children may be assumed to be less well co-ordinated than right-handed children because their motor skills look so different. She also concluded that a lack of hand preference may be a sign of a developmental lag in motor skills and suggested that such children receive direct training to enhance their motor co-ordination.

The second group includes children with significant physical and motor disabilities. In this book we have already met a number of children with serious motor problems. Darrin, if you remember, has cerebral palsy, and Kalim is severely mentally retarded and has associated motor delays. For these children we have discussed the developmental consequences, and toys and their adaptations; we have also touched on adaptive equipment.

Musculoskeletal impairments those that affect body movement and functioning but are not caused by neurological damage.

Physical problems with associated motor disabilities and deviations may be a result of cns damage or a neuromuscular disease. Cns damage includes cerebral palsy and spina bifida. Cerebral palsy, a motor disorder often accompanied by other disabilities, is one of the most common crippling conditions in children. Neuromuscular diseases cause ***musculoskeletal impairments***, which affect body movement and functioning but are not caused by neurological damage. Some of these conditions are characterized by a weakening and wasting away of muscular tissue. In muscular dystrophy, for example, there is progressive muscle weakness.

The body's bony and physical structure must be intact and must function adequately for a child to attain normal development in physical skills. Children with spina bifida, muscular dystrophy, cerebral palsy, or another orthopedic condition that causes deviations of the bones, muscles, or joints, exhibit abnormal functioning and are unable to some degree to handle their bodies.

In normally developing children, physiological development produces steady, organized patterns of behaviour. In contrast, children with serious physical delays or impairments, or with neuromotor disabilities, may not progress through the normal sequence of physical development. Motor skill development may be splintered. Skills may be missed in the normal sequence, or may be acquired partially, or may develop in an atypical fashion (Illingworth, 1980). For example, a child may not crawl but may learn to use a scooter board.

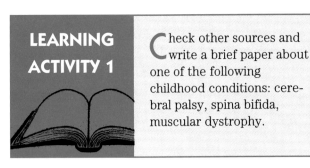

LEARNING ACTIVITY 1

Check other sources and write a brief paper about one of the following childhood conditions: cerebral palsy, spina bifida, muscular dystrophy.

Assessment of motor skills

When young children are assessed, all the main areas of development are considered. When a child has a disability, physical development is always a prominent part of the assessment. Often, physical and motor assessments are the first ones undertaken, usually by medical professionals and paraprofessionals. When motor skills specifically are examined, most assessments focus on the number of motor milestone skills performed by the child. Assessments for children with mild motor delays are quite different from those for children with serious physical disabilities. This is also true of interventions.

For children with mild motor delays, a comprehensive motor assessment considers whether both fine and gross motor skills have been attained within normal developmental milestones. Children with mild motor delays may be identified within the everyday context of classroom activities. Often, teachers' observations will pinpoint minor motor delays or difficulties. Some areas to watch for are shown in Table 13–1.

TABLE 13–2: Motor scales

The Hawaii Early Learning Profile (Furumo et al., 1979)	0–36 months	Designed for multi-disciplinary team use.	Gross- and fine-motor sections include 146 and 93 items, respectively.
The Peabody Developmental Motor Scales and Activity Cards (Folio & Fewell, 1983)	Birth to 7 years	Standardized scales.	Gross and fine motor skills.
Test of Gross Motor Development (Ulrich, 1985)	3 to 10 years		Gross motor skills.

A child's art will provide information about motor skills and many other domains of development. The teacher can learn much about the child's developmental level, and discover his or her abilities, interests, thoughts, and priorities. Children's figure drawings are an especially good reflection of cognitive awareness, visual motor development, and social maturity.

Motor skills can also be assessed by traditional developmental tests that include hopping, jumping, and other functional skills. A small number of standardized scales are available (see Table 13–2).

For children with more severe disabilities, a motor assessment is usually conducted before skills in other domains are assessed. For children with severe disabilities and motor impairments, regular assessments of development and motor movement are important for a number of reasons. For one thing, all physical anomalies are not discovered in the neonatal period. As well, we need to know how functional motor skills are developing, since these relate to the child's ability to perform necessary daily activities. We also need to know what types of skills a child has developed and how they are used.

For motor assessments, early childhood personnel should rely on the expertise of physical or occupational therapists. Because these people have an in-depth knowledge of the neurobiological system, they are able to recognize the impact of specific impairments on movement and stability. The therapist will conduct an assessment of the physical domains that considers physical status, mobility, and functional aspects (how the child uses motor skills). The assessor will probably observe and test the following:

- Head control in various body positions, such as supine, prone, and sitting.
- Posture and righting reactions. Children may not have righting reactions (i.e., the motor control needed to be upright and aligned).
- The effect of different body positions on functional motor control.
- The status of primitive reflexes and higher-level automatic reactions.
- Muscle tone, which refers to the resting state or tenseness in a muscle. This may be too high (hypertonia or spasticity), or too low (hypotonia or flaccidity), or fluctuating (athetosis).
- Movement.
- Specific motor milestones such as rolling, sitting, and walking.
- Fine motor skills.
- The technical complexity of necessary specialized equipment and devices.
- The functional aspects of mobility and self-care, such as how much assistance the child needs, generalizing of the performance, the amount of time needed to accomplish functional tasks, and the techniques and approaches for functional tasks (Copeland & Kimmel, 1989; Haley, Hallenborg, & Gans, 1989).

TARGETING SKILLS

Intervention for motor skills development typically relates to one or more of these areas: strength, physical and motor fitness, postural control, eye/hand co-ordination, object manipulation, positioning, mobility, adaptation, generalization, sensorimotor integration, and spatial awareness (Fewell, 1993).

Intervention for children with mild physical delays or disabilities will usually target the normal sequences of gross and fine motor skill development. For many physically and severely disabled children, the treatment of motor deficits is a large part of early intervention and requires teachers, therapists, and parents to work as a team. Especially in the case of children with cerebral palsy and other motor disabilities, teachers should consult with a physical or occupational therapist about positioning and handling before teaching motor skills. The child will only be able to perform certain activities, no matter how much reinforcement is provided.

When children have severe physical delays or disabilities, the skills targeted should be functional and should include choices. Functional objectives emphasize the physical components of daily activities, as well as skills for independence. A child with a

A child with a disability should be encouraged to move as independently as possible.

disability should be encouraged to move as independently as possible. Thus, when going from circle time to a learning centre, the child should walk, crawl, or manipulate a wheelchair, but should *not* be carried. Also, placing pegs in a board aids in fine motor development but is not really related to future needs. Pulling on socks develops similar motor areas and also provides a living skill.

A number of commercial motor curricula are available for use with young children. These include Fit for Me (Karnes, 1992), Body Skills (Wender & Bruininks, 1991), and the Peabody Developmental Motor Activity Cards (Folio & Fewell, 1983).

Promoting skill development

Young children have tremendous potential for physical growth. They need many opportunities for activity, exploration, and manipulation, as well as opportunities for the development of motor skills. Physical education at the preschool level provides a means for children to develop physical and motor fitness, fundamental motor skills and patterns such as throwing and jumping, and skills in games and dance. The average child needs about 270 minutes to achieve an independent goal in motor skills (Wessel & Kelly, 1986). Structured activity should be part of the daily program.

When teachers are promoting motor skill development, they often use physical guidance as an intervention procedure or they provide activities that encourage the child to practise motor skills. As far as possible, motor skills should be developed within the context of purposeful activities and daily routines. Fifteen-minute practice segments, well spaced, will be more efficient than a massive dose of four straight hours.

GROSS MOTOR SKILLS The opportunities for gross motor activities are numerous, and involve both indoor and outdoor play. Here are some examples of gross motor activities:

- Throwing a ball at a large target.
- Catching a rolled heavy ball. Provide a large ball that requires some strength to throw about.
- Using carpet tiles as stepping stones.
- Climbing in, carrying around, and crawling through large cardboard cartons.
- Throwing beanbags. Children in wheelchairs can attach these and other objects to the chair with string, for easy retrieval.
- Catching a balloon. Use balloons for throwing, batting, and chasing.
- Tossing rolled-up socks into a laundry basket.
- Walking along a wide, curving ribbon.
- Following footprints on paper.
- Tumbling on a mat.
- Playing games. Game formats are important for motor skill training. They increase maintenance and generalization and promote social interaction (Bailey &

BOX 13–3
Kenny's IPP

NAME: *Kenny*
DATE OF BIRTH: *22 March 1991*
CENTRE: *Sunny Dale*

Present levels of functioning

Cognitive: Psychological assessment shows normal cognitive development. The psychologist did note that Kenny showed some difficulty in manipulating the small blocks and puzzle pieces in the performance scale of the test.

Communication: Language is developing at a normal rate, and there is no evidence of speech deviations.

Motor: Kenny shows substantial lags in both fine and gross motor skill development. He is functioning about 18 months below his expected level.

Social: Kenny's lack of motor skills sees him excluded more and more often from the outside play of his peers. At the centre, he prefers to play with younger children.

Long-range goals

1. To improve motor skill co-ordination.
2. To develop manipulative skills, fine motor skills, manual dexterity, and eye/hand co-ordination.
3. To develop a range of skills and techniques such as drawing, painting, and cutting.
4. To improve body image.

Short-term objectives

1. Engage in a variety of activities that require balance and bodily control. Suggested activities—
   - *Pick up and match a pair of balloons.*
2. Explore the use of various implements such as brush and pencil. Suggested activities—
   - *Finger painting in paint, shaving cream.*
   - *Use large brush with water on chalkboard or brick surface.*
   - *Use oversized crayons for drawing.*
   - *Use commercially bought special grip for pencil.*
   - *Provide tools that give free-flowing movement of the fingers, hand and arms, such as large crayons and large paintbrushes.*
3. Will point to body parts. Suggested activity— Play Simon Says.

Wolery, 1984). For example, children can take part in relay races where they walk, run, jump, hop, or skip while holding hands with a partner.

- Rolling down a slope.
- Bouncing on a giant tire.
- Jumping on a low board.
- Pushing a doll in a pram or a wheelbarrow full of sand.
- Running obstacle courses. Construct an obstacle course in which running spaces are interspersed with blocks or old tires that can be climbed or jumped from. Shape the course so that children can begin again once they have completed one cycle.
- Walking up and down ramps.
- Bouncing on trampolines.
- Walking between the rungs of a ladder placed on the ground.

- Crawling through barrels.
- Stepping through tires on the ground.

Children who are severely disabled have fewer skills and need an array of activities that are appropriate to their developmental level. For the severely disabled child, activities should be designed by a physiotherapist. Motor and muscular activities are most appropriate. The children develop self-confidence as they move through their environment; they learn that moving can be effortless and fun, and their body image comes into sharper focus. Gross motor activities are also worthwhile for children who are developmentally delayed. They develop concentration and perseverance, and this increases their attention span and improves their play patterns.

Gross motor activities may include crawling, rolling, walking up and down stairs, running, grasping objects with the hands, throwing, catching, balancing, jumping on and off objects, stepping over and into objects, bouncing, climbing, kicking, rolling an object, reaching and batting at a bobbing toy, and practising sitting balanced while watching a puppet show.

FINE MOTOR SKILLS

Many educators consider the development of fine motor skills an important part of the preschool curriculum. In her day, Montessori agreed with them. Common materials for fine motor development are puzzles, blocks, and sorting toys. Visual motor activities include colouring, cutting, tearing, and clay modelling. Some fine motor activities are listed next:

- Picking up objects with tongs.
- Drawing with crayon or finger along a wide path.
- Threading jumbo beads on a stiff lacing.
- Stacking foam bricks.
- Finger plays. Use those that allow a child to use the whole hand, not just the fingers.
- "Fishing"—that is, attaching magnets to sticks and going fishing for paper fish that have paper clip mouths.
- Playing with water and sand. Provide utensils for measuring and pouring. Children with poor motor co-ordination can learn to dig, lift, and pour, and to make comparisons about height and weight.
- Modelling with clay. This helps children develop the muscles of their hands as they roll, squeeze, and manipulate the material. Use plastic rolling pins and cookie cutters.

To enhance body and space awareness:

- Filling in body details and clothes on a silhouette provided by the teacher.
- Dressing a doll.
- Making puzzles of body parts.
- Playing simplified Simon Says naming body parts.
- Moving like a rag doll.
- Using action songs.
- Copying the teacher's movements, such as "point to the nose."

For children with severe disabilities, fine motor activities are selected by the occupational therapist. These activities will include tactile play (painting with shaving cream, finger painting, play in sand, wheat, or water, nature collage, hand and foot prints, soap bubbles, cooking, playdo); fine manipulative play (stacking, threading, posting, sorting, matching, fishing, Lego); and body image and imitative play (bathing and dressing dolly, dressing up).

Many fine motor tasks are performed while seated. Postural stability in a sitting position is critical to fine motor skills. We explain methods for positioning and posture later in this chapter.

BOX 13-4
Helpful hints

- Very young children seem to have an endless supply of energy and limited attention spans, so expecting them to engage in long periods of quiet work is futile. Provide many opportunities for physical activity, and alternate active periods with quiet ones.

- Be aware that most adaptive equipment is large and heavy, and that children need to learn its use.

- Lack of progress in, or deterioration of, motor skills is a cause for concern. Observe children carefully.

- Make adaptations in the environment and in play materials so as to enhance opportunities for interactions among all children.

- Provide large toys to develop gross motor skills, but also puzzles, blocks, painting tools, and clay to promote small muscle development.

- Provide large utensils for writing, painting, and cutting.

- Provide many opportunities for exploration and play.

- Emphasize activity and manipulation.

- Incorporate motor objectives in all activities. For example, it is just as important to focus on walking when going to the table for a snack as it is when practising walking in a straight line.

- Stress functional skills such as typing, zipping, dressing, and undressing.

- Remember that any adaptive device has a limited lifespan because of the growth and development of the child.

Art activities

Art activities are important in the early childhood curriculum. In the motor domain, art develops basic skills such as fine motor dexterity, eye/hand co-ordination, and manual dexterity. Art activities are just as important for reinforcing experiences in other areas of the curriculum. During art activities, children think about what to draw or paint, manipulate a tool, view their work, and perhaps explain the end product. In doing all this, they are experiencing a sequence of events far broader than just motor skills.

Art activities enhance cognitive development by enriching children's knowledge of themselves and their environment; they also encourage decision-making and, it follows, independence. Finally, art helps develop problem-solving skills and encourages sensitivity to a range of materials.

The major objectives of an art program will include all or some of the skills outlined in Table 13–3.

TABLE 13–3: Major objectives of art programs

- Teachers develop children's manipulative skills, fine motor skills, manual dexterity, and eye/hand co-ordination by providing tools that promote free-flowing movement of the fingers, hands, and arms, such as large crayons and large paintbrushes.
- They develop the children's large muscles such as in the hands, arms, shoulders, and back.
- They develop children's tearing and cutting skills.
- They develop a range of skills and techniques in children such as drawing, painting, and cutting.
- They develop children's ability to consciously observe what they are doing.
- They develop children's reactions to sensory stimuli by using tactile, motor, visual, auditory, taste, and smell modalities.
- They encourage the children's exploration of various tools such as pencil and paintbrush.
- They expand children's concentration spans through activities in which the children are interested.
- They develop children's problem-solving skills.
- They develop children's colour recognition.
- They develop children's autonomy, so that they select a place to work, make a choice within an activity, clean up after an activity, and explore various activities.
- They increase children's self-esteem through success, and encourage expression of feelings.

Art has much therapeutic and diagnostic value for the child with special needs. Art activities help children develop in social, emotional, motor, sensory, and cognitive areas. By producing art, children with disabilities begin to understand, organize, and utilize concepts.

BOX 13-5
Cerebral Palsy

Art is a developmental process. Kellogg and O'Dell (1969) are well known for their analysis of the spontaneous art work of preschool children. When they examined about one million drawings by children aged 4 to 14 attending art classes, they concluded that certain scribbles and forms developed innately. Usually children were able to draw simple shapes spontaneously before they were able to copy them.

The human face is by far the favourite subject of preschool drawings. Younger children carefully draw the eyes, nose, mouth, and ears and then indicate the rest of the body almost as an afterthought, rapidly sketching the arms and legs as stiff lines and the hands and feet as circles. Only later do details of clothing and background begin to appear. By the age of five, most children have progressed beyond rudimentary stick figures, but their drawing still reflects their distinctive view of the world. Heads tend to be disproportionately large, and people tend to be larger than the background objects (Salkind, 1990).

Children acquire drawing as a form of writing very early and continue to use it well into the sixth and seventh years. After learning how to hold a pencil, preschool children show a consistent age-related progression from scribbles to recognizable forms (such as circles and lines) to representational figures.

Scribbling is a very important activity for the young child. Kellogg describes scribbling as the "placement" stage. Scribbling seems to be a universal natural step in development; it serves as a foundation for more differentiated behaviour in a number of areas. Young children scribbling should be seen as attempting to master raw materials that at some later date they will use to communicate. They scribble everywhere, and wise adults will provide ample opportunity for children to scribble. If paper and pencil or crayon are not available, children will find other means for engaging in these same processes. The media may include sticks in dirt; mud on walls; fingers in food, feces, sand, snow, or steam on a window; and so on (see Lay-Dopyera & Dopyera, 1990).

The scribbling of a young child passes through three stages—disordered scribbling, controlled scribbling, and named scribbling. During disordered scribbling, the child seems to be satisfied with the kinesthetic sensations as he or she makes random markings on whatever is handy, using whatever tools are available. During controlled scribbling, the child gains some visual control of lines. This happens as the child discovers a relationship between the kinds of motions made, the appearance of marks on the paper, and the relationship of these lines with the outside world. However, much remains random. Three-year-olds tend to plunk their brushes in the paint, pull them out dripping wet, and then push them across the paper.

Drawings become more symbolic during the second and third year and show a steady increase in complexity and sophistication. Kellogg characterizes the time between about three and three-and-a-half as the "shape" stage, because children begin to create geometric shapes such as circles.

During the "design" stage (three-and-a-half to four-and-a-half), children continue with shapes. By three-and-a-half or so, children typically begin to give their drawings names. A scribble that looks no different from previous ones may be described as "This is my daddy," or "I'm eating." This is seen by some art educators as an important landmark in a child's self-expression (Lay-Dopyera & Dopyera, 1990). Once children begin to name and intentionally embellish their representations, they may increasingly use drawing and painting and other art activities as a means for recording images of things experienced (Lay-Dopyera & Dopyera, 1990).

The "pictorial" stage (four to five) is when drawings represent something. Markings are no longer random. Five-year-olds take care to get just enough paint on the brush; they plan where to put each stroke and stand back to examine the final result (Allison, 1985). By five, children have developed their own unique style of drawing (Gardner, 1980). All finger paintings may look the same to the viewer, but by now each is as individual as the child.

Most children enjoy art activities, and all should have the opportunity to learn the feel of paint and the effect of using different body parts to make a mark. Keep in mind, however, that some children may be more hesitant than others. Children with severe disabilities may not know how to use a paintbrush or manipulate clay. Children with severe visual impairments are often hesitant to get their hands dirty and may not like to fingerpaint. Many autistic children seem to enjoy drawing, yet they tend to copy things they have seen rather than make up their own pictures.

ADAPTING THE ART PROGRAM

Few adaptations are necessary to make an art program enjoyable for most children. However, to stimulate learning, a few changes ought to be tried for specific groups of children. For children who are hearing impaired, print making and pattern recognition activities (e.g., vegetable prints) may enhance visual attention and discrimination. For children who have speech delays, blow painting and straw painting develop the muscles of the mouth and teach breath control. If a child has an attention deficit, limiting the choice of colours or materials and using masking tape around the table or easel will help that child focus by creating an area for standing and working.

In many ways, art is a visual activity. For children who are visually impaired, art activities can be adapted to stress other sense modalities:

- Use scented markers with a specific fragrance for each paint colour, or use clay mixed with different scents.
- Add sand to acrylic paint.
- Use crayons on sandpaper surfaces.
- Make line drawings with glue.
- On an easel, make a black mat and use beige or buff paper. Or use textured sandpaper for the boundary.
- Tape the edges of the paper to the drawing surface.
- Glue sandpaper to the sides of paint jars for grip and ease of identification.
- Use Velcro to attach jars and containers to easels and tables, or use rubber suction cups to secure the jars.
- Let the child use highlight pens on buff paper.

For children with physical disabilities, try the following:

- Use holders. To help children with motor problems, make paintbrush grips out of foam material or a piece of clay.
- Lengthen the handles of paintbrushes.
- Provide clay to encourage hand and finger use. As necessary, moisten the clay (just add water) to make it easier to manipulate.
- Use extra-large drawing crayons. Take broken pieces of crayon and bake them in an oven at 200 to 225°F for about 10 minutes to make crayon muffins.
- Use fingerpaint in a tray.
- Make a paintbrush out of a deodorant bottle by removing the top, filling the bottle with tempera paint, and snapping the top back in place.
- Use large chunks of sponge for painting.
- Use marking pens for free flow.
- Anchor the paper. Tape it to the table or easel.
- Use activities that require two hands, such as fingerpaint, clay, and playdo.

PROGRESS CHECK 3

Do you remember Josie, who has a severe visual impairment, and Darrin, who has cerebral palsy? You want to weave this week's art activities around the theme of autumn. Prepare a lesson plan and show the adaptations you would make in painting for Josie and Darrin.

- Paint large objects, such as boxes.
- To emphasize sequencing and patterning, use repetitious activities such as print-making.

Music and movement

Music and movement are interrelated areas that hold an important place in the early childhood curriculum. Music should be part of every child's environment; many skills may be developed through a music and movement program. In the preschool child, music activities take two main forms: manipulation/movement and singing. These lead to competencies in singing, playing musical instruments, listening to music, creating music, and moving expressively to music.

With music, children use their bodies, minds, and creative energy. The sound, whether soothing or stimulating, can promote social activity and teach and re-inforce skills from other curriculum areas. Movement helps children become aware of their bodies, teaches them how to relax, and develops rhythm and balance. Children can roll, crawl, jump on the spot, sway, bend and stretch, show variations in walking, stamp, and stand on tiptoe.

ADAPTATION

Children with disabilities may have less physical strength than children who are developing normally. Their movements may be limited, or they may have unwanted or uncontrolled movements. For these reasons, they will have some difficulty synchronizing their bodies to music. The spontaneous songs and movements of these children may be rhythmically irregular, with little regard for a consistent beat.

Early childhood personnel can help children with disabilities improve their co-ordination by providing many opportunities for them to practise their motor skills in a relaxed musical context. Music and movement can be used for relaxation, to increase body awareness and space awareness, and to enhance motor planning and rhythmic skills. Remember that movement is also an integral part of tasks in other domains: cognitive, communication, social play, and self-help.

Physical movement is a natural response to rhythm. The body should be the child's first musical instrument. By following a rhythm and imitating a movement, children develop the ability to integrate movement and audio-visual perception. By reacting quickly to changes in music, they develop control, balance, attention, concentration, and memory. By repeating rhythms, they develop memory and sequencing skills.

Music and movement skills develop in a definite order, from the simple to the more complex. The ability to maintain a consistent beat to music develops gradually over several years. Children can be encouraged to keep time to the beat through a number of teaching techniques, which can be applied individually or in small or large groups.

At first, children with disabilities can respond by clapping short rhythmic patterns or loud and soft patterns. They can move in time to the music, beginning with the arms, legs, fingers, feet, and so on. They can learn how sound and movement can be synchronized by wearing small bells on their ankles, wrists, or necks

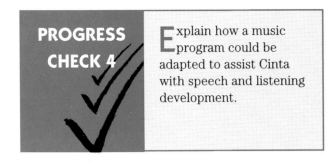

Explain how a music program could be adapted to assist Cinta with speech and listening development.

while dancing. Action songs that involve simple movements allow children to experience rhythmic movement without requiring them to synchronize the beat.

As their muscular co-ordination improves, children will begin to experiment with space and movement through rhythmic activities. While children will often imitate others during an open-ended movement activity, teachers can generally lead them to individualize their responses by asking them to focus on certain things, such as a different area of the body, a different position or area in space, a different style of movement (jerky, smooth, big, small) a new approach to imagery (a giant, in the snow, under water), or a different concept (louder, faster, higher). They can use their arms and legs to show how other things move, such as a turtle, an airplane, a kite, or a bird. Or they can be a rag doll or a tin soldier.

Props can help children develop body image, co-ordination, and knowledge of weight and texture. Dancing props can include paper streamers, silky scarves, long narrow strips of cloth, lightweight plastic tubes, flowing skirts and capes, paper flowers, and hoops.

Even children who can't join in fully enjoy creating sounds to accompany movement. Children who cannot move their legs can use their hands for clapping, waving, and so on. Or they can shake maracas or clackers in their hands to provide an accompaniment to those who are dancing.

Music offers many opportunities for speech and language training, social skills enhancement, and cognitive development. Action songs can be used for body awareness. Children can be told, for example, to "Keep the beat with your left shoulder," or "Only move your fingers in time to the music." Songs with a predictable sequence help children in memory development.

Music-making is beneficial for children with communication problems. Singing strengthens the muscles of the mouth and increases breath control. Blowing into instruments does the same thing. Children can toss balloons in the air and sing a note until they come to the ground.

Adaptations for mobility

As we pointed out in Chapter 8, children may use adaptive equipment, including orthotic and prosthetic devices, to improve their functioning. Adaptive equipment is often used for support, mobility, and positioning.

Equipment designed for mobility and to help children stand includes leg casts and braces, ankle/foot equipment, crutches, walkers, and wheelchairs. Positioning devices and strategies allow children with motor problems to achieve postures and movements that might otherwise by impossible or nonfunctional for them. Therapists may also design play equipment to increase spontaneous interactions with the environment and to practise movement skills.

Children with physical disabilities need many types of adaptive equipment for positioning and mobility.

ADAPTIVE EQUIPMENT

Orthopedic braces are for the lower extremities. There are three main types: short leg braces, long leg braces, and hip braces. A short brace would be used on the ankle joint, a long brace on the knee to the ankle.

Braces do not prevent contractures or develop walking skills; rather, they improve control and support. For children with cerebral palsy, braces are used mainly for control. They improve ambulation, control involuntary movements, and help to prevent or correct deformities. With spina bifida and muscular dystrophy, the braces are used mainly for support. Support braces weigh less than control braces (Venn, Morgenstern, & Dykes, 1978). When children are wearing braces, teachers should be alert to circulation problems, which may show up as swelling, coldness, change of colour, evidence of infection, or other skin problems (see Winzer, 1989).

Crutches are used during periods of temporary disability to help with balance and locomotion and to reduce weight on the lower extremities. When the disability is permanent or of long duration, crutches must be designed to reduce the weight the legs must bear and to provide stability and support. The surface on which the crutch may operate is important. If it is slippery, rubber-tipped ends, spiked ends, or tripod legs should be provided.

Walkers are upright devices used to provide support and movement. Supported standing forces weight-bearing that is necessary for the normal formation of the hip joints. There are different types of walkers, which can be modified in various ways. All provide standing support with forward-inclined standing. A scooter board is a wheeled board that a child propels with the arms.

Wheelchairs are designed for people who are unable to ambulate, or whose ambulation is unsafe and unsteady, or for whom ambulation is too strenuous. Wheelchairs come in a variety of shapes and sizes. They are manual or powered and can include many attachments. Most have arms that are lower in front and are designed to fit under a desk or table. Others have trays that serve as desks or provide a stable horizontal surface for presenting toys. Some are specially

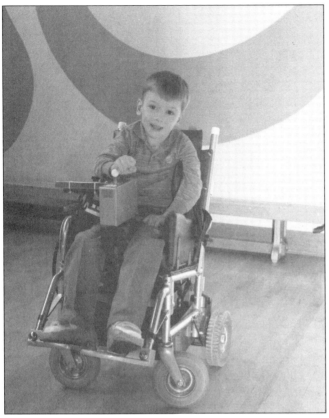

Children with physical disabilities need many types of mobility equipment, such as this electric wheelchair.

Carrying the way that a child with a physical or motor disability is moved.

Positioning how the child is seated or otherwise positioned.

adapted. A child with cerebral palsy may not be able to hold his or her head upright or play with toys at the midline of the body. He or she can use an adapted wheelchair with a head support and shoulder wedges to position the arms and hands forward in a position to play with toys.

POSITIONING   Promoting optimal postures and movement patterns for functional activities is an important objective for children with physical and motor disabilities. A carefully designed therapeutic intervention can increase skill acquisition. Areas of special concern are positioning and carrying. **Carrying** refers to the way a child with a physical or motor disability is moved; **positioning** is how the child is seated or otherwise positioned.

The way a child is handled and positioned affects movement abilities. There seems to be a significant relationship between sensory processing, postural control, and children's abilities to interact appropriately with the environment. As well, a child who is positioned properly finds it easier to maintain his or her body against gravity, and therefore easier to attend to a toy, the teacher, and other children.

Children with cerebral palsy have abnormal movement patterns: their coordination movements are inefficient and they retain primitive reflexes. Also, they may have inefficient righting reactions (which are those movements that bring or restore the body to an upright position).

Children with cerebral palsy and other physical disabilities must be handled in ways that normalize muscle tone and prevent the development of secondary muscular and structural disorders. Proper positioning can promote normal muscle tone and symmetry, provide stable and aligned posture, inhibit primitive reflexes, facilitate normal movement patterns, stabilize head and trunk control, and compensate for a lack of sitting balance (Bailey & Wolery, 1984; Clark & Allen, 1985; Copeland & Kimmel, 1989). Individual positioning is prescribed for each child.

Prosthetic equipment may assist in the therapeutic techniques of positioning and carrying. Equipment is selected based on its ability to increase the child's potential for movement and opportunities for learning. Equipment should provide support but still allow for active exploration. Prosthetic or adaptive equipment especially helps with positioning. Some children need support in a lying position and use adaptive boards, wedges, and bolsters. When furniture, pillows, or specialized equipment is used for positioning or carrying, the process is called *static positioning*.

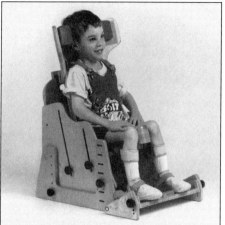

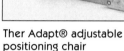

Ther Adapt® adjustable
positioning chair

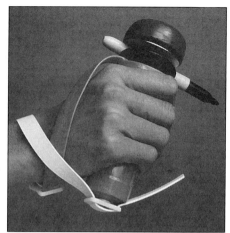

Knob holder

In static positioning the devices are fixed in place and cannot be easily adjusted in response to changes in muscle tone or movement or situational demands. An alternative to static positioning and carrying is *dynamic positioning*,
in which the adult's body (instead of equipment) is used to support the child
in the desired position. The advantage of dynamic positioning and carrying is
that the adult can respond immediately to child and situational needs. If the
child's tone increases significantly, for example, the resistance from static positioning equipment may further increase tone because of discomfort. With dynamic positioning, the adult can relax positioning constraints and then reinstate
support when the child's tone relaxes again (see Bailey & Wolery, 1984; 1992).
In dynamic positioning and carrying, the adult should provide support at key
points to help the child relax. Key points are the shoulders, neck, hips, and
knees (Bailey & Wolery, 1984; Parette & Hourcade, 1986).

In static positioning, positioning equipment is typically designed to place
the child in one or more basic postures in as normal a body alignment as possible. Equipment is used to maintain therapeutically beneficial positions or to facilitate normalized movements for children who have motor delays or disabilities
(Copeland & Kimmel, 1989). A number of types of equipment are used to provide
stable and aligned posture, normalize muscle tone, inhibit abnormal reflexes,
allow greater movement, and increase muscle strength. The main types are pillows, positioning inserts, and special seating.

Modular positioning systems, which use wedges or bolster seating, allow the
positioning of children of all ages, abilities, and sizes and help break up abnormal
patterns of muscle tone and reflexes. The wedge is a shaped piece of equipment
made of foam rubber or wood covered with padding; children lie on the wedge
with arms and shoulders over the edge. Bolsters are rolls or pillows that provide support. They support infants and small children in prone, seated, and side-
lying positions. Side-lying helps with body symmetry. Stomach-lying (prone) is
often used to encourage the child to raise his or her head against gravity; this increases extension of the body and weight-bearing on the arms. Supine (back-
lying) is often avoided, as it can result in abnormal posturing in some children.

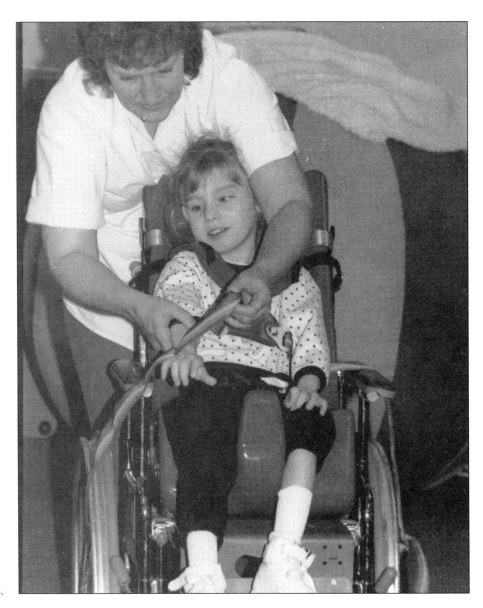

Teachers must know how to position children in wheelchairs.

For children with motor disorders, sitting may be difficult. Because children spend a lot of time sitting, it is important that they sit in the most beneficial position. They need to find positions that allow the best hand use, that are easiest for eye/hand co-ordination, and that present the least difficulties for balance. Several positions, such as cross-legged sitting, side sitting, and regular chair sitting, may be secure and comfortable.

The main objective in developing an adaptive seating system is to maximize the child's motor development and independence in functional activities. Proper adaptive seating equipment should inhibit abnormal reflexes and muscle tone, while also facilitating more normal body movement. A physical or occupational therapist should be consulted to determine the child's positioning needs—that is, the amount of support needed for an optimal seating position—and to guarantee accurate chair measurement.

Modified chairs are for children who have difficulty sitting well or who have abnormal hip and leg patterns. A special chair aligns the body, limbs, and head; flexes the hips, knees, and ankles; and brings the head and shoulders slightly forward. Adapted chairs include corner chairs, bolster chairs, and wheelchairs.

Postural stability is enhanced when the child is seated in a chair of the proper size. Chair inserts can be made using double-walled cardboard. Usually there will be an abduction block—a chunk of something the child's legs can straddle—to prevent the child from sliding to the floor. Dangling feet are harmful to children with motor problems; add a footstool so that the child's feet reach a flat, solid surface. Straps and other props are sometimes used to improve posture.

For floor sitting, it is best to have the child with cerebral palsy sit with his or her legs in front and together, bent at the knee if the child is athetoid, and straight if the child has spastic cerebral palsy (Deiner, 1983). If you have a child with cerebral palsy in your lap, have his or her legs straddle one of yours and hold the child around the middle.

A child who spends a large part of the day in a wheelchair must be carefully positioned—and regularly repositioned—so as to maintain a sitting posture that promotes good body alignment. This also helps prevent the muscle contractions that can result when nonmotoric children spend long periods of time in one position. Too long in an improper position in a wheelchair is uncomfortable. Inappropriate positions can result in problems with respiration, digestion, circulation, and normal physical development, and/or promote other physical deformities (Parette & Hourcade, 1986). The child should be repositioned every half hour or so.

Besides positioning children, teachers may have to transfer them, especially from a wheelchair to the toilet and back. The wheelchair is positioned alongside the toilet at about a 35-degree angle. The brakes are locked and the footrests swung away if possible. If the armrest can be removed, this should be hooked on the handgrip opposite the toilet. To leave the wheelchair, the child leans forward and places his or her hands around the lifter's waist or neck. The lifter then securely grasps the child by the belt, pants, or dress at the hips, locks the child's knees together with the lifter's own knees, and rocks back on the heels, simultaneously lifting and pivoting the child toward the toilet (King, 1987; Parette & Hourcade, 1986; Winzer, 1989).

Moving the wheelchair from place to place will also be necessary. When pushing a wheelchair down a curb, place one foot on the long pole at the back of the chair. Then grasp the handgrips firmly, tip the chair backwards, and gently lower the back wheels down the curb. To go up a curb, follow the same procedure, except lift the chair's front wheels onto the curb.

Teachers must ensure their own safety and the child's confidence when moving and positioning children. They should remember the following:

- Wear comfortable, sturdy shoes with low rubber heels to prevent the possibility of slipping.
- Always lift with the legs, not the back. When lifting, keep the back as straight as possible. Maintain a wide base of support by placing one foot in front of the other. Move the feet in short steps.
- Always tell the child what you are going to do.

People in wheelchairs report many negative experiences that range from being ignored or stared at, to having people use the chair as a piece of furniture, to encountering store fixtures that are too high and aisles that are impossible to negotiate. Borrow a wheelchair and spend a morning or an afternoon in it. Use it for all activities. Report on your experiences and feelings.

- Encourage the child to assist in positioning or transfer as much as possible.
- In a confined space, use the wall or furniture as a brace.
- Move the child slowly.
- Wait for the child to react.
- Be aware of the "feel" of the child.
- Children's feet should be supported and hips flexed.
- Feet should be stable on the floor, or on the footrest of the wheelchair (see Winzer, 1989).

Orientation an individual's knowledge of his or her position in space.

Mobility negotiating space.

ORIENTATION AND MOBILITY

Children with severe visual impairments will use specialized equipment and materials. They especially need equipment and assistance to develop orientation and mobility. **Orientation** refers to an individual's knowledge of his or her position in space; **mobility** refers to negotiating that space.

The developmental lags of blind children are precisely those that make successful mobility difficult. Mobility and orientation are extremely important for the young child with a severe visual disability. Training in orientation and mobility enables blind children to move with confidence and independence in their environment. To move freely and confidently, visually impaired children must know where they want to go, how, and in which direction. Because they have no sight to guide them, they must maximize the use of their other senses. They must also learn to use a travel aid correctly (Winzer, 1996). The prescription cane, sometimes called the white cane or the Hoover cane, is the most common travel aid used by children and adults.

All mobility techniques are meant to provide protection and information in various environments. The age of onset of the visual impairment does not predict an individual's success with mobility techniques (McLinden, 1988). Special teachers may introduce the white cane to children as young as three years of age. Also, young blind children can be taught to use specially adapted sensing devices. These can improve the locomotion and mobility of children as young as one year (Harris et al., 1985). Many work something like radar, sending out beams of ultrasound that cannot be heard by the human ear. When the beam hits an object, some of the ultrasound is reflected back to the device and converted into audible tones. For example, the Sonicguide supplies three kinds of information about an object: direction, distance, and general characteristics. The infant's Sonicguide uses a headband mounting and permits obstacle detection as close as 50 centimetres. The Canterbury Child's Aid is a binaural spatial sensor that reflects objects sensed from two receiving transductors mounted a small distance apart on an adjustable headband. Echoes are transduced into audible sounds, which are presented to the ears through small speakers or earphones. An object's distance is established mainly by the frequency: high frequencies signify faraway objects; the lower the frequency, the nearer the object (Harris et al., 1985).

TABLE 13–4: New terms and ideas

body image	motor development
carrying	motor imitation
directionality	motor learning
fine motor skills	motor skills
general inco-ordination	musculoskeletal impairments
gross motor skills	orientation
laterality	physical development
mobility	positioning
motor control	

SUMMARY

1. Children pass through vast physical changes in the preschool years. In normally developing children, motor development follows fairly regular sequences, with early skills prerequisite to later responses. Fine motor skills are refined later than gross motor skills.

2. Children master motor skills as their central nervous systems mature. Children are not born with fully developed nervous systems.

3. Across the board, boys are more active than girls.

4. To assist children in physical readiness, teachers should provide many opportunities for exploration and manipulation, for improving fine and gross motor skills, and for physical activities. Large outdoor toys, such as tricycles, wagons, and toy cars, allow much movement. Indoors, children need blocks, chalk, crayons, paints, clay, plasticine, puzzles, and other toys and games that involve creative play and manipulation. Children need plenty of activity but also a lot of rest, so quiet periods should be alternated with more active ones.

5. As a result of delayed development or neurological damage, many infants and young children with disabilities have physical development needs. These needs can spill over to affect other domains of functioning. When a child lags in movement and motor skill performance, all other activities are hindered. Restricted movement can interfere with a child's learning of cognitive and social skills.

6. Assessment of motor functioning is usually carried out by a therapist, who looks at muscle tone, primitive reflexes, posture, righting reactions, movement, fine motor skills, and so on.

7. In early childhood, opportunities to develop motor skills should be a part of the daily program.

8. Children with disabilities require activities to develop fine and gross motor skills. This will often mean that the environment must be adapted, and alternative strategies employed. For those with significant disabilities, the functional use of selected motor skills and adaptive skills will usually be targeted.

9. Art is a developmental process. For a child, art is nonverbal communication, Children begin to represent the world, and as they develop, the representation changes. After learning how to hold a pencil, preschool children show a consistent age-related progression: from scribbles, to recognizable forms such as circles and lines, to representational figures.

10. For many children with physical handicaps, physical, occupational, and speech therapy may be indicated.

11. Children with physical and motor problems often need unique and adapted furniture. Mobility, seating, and positioning are crucial considerations. Children may use bolsters, wedges, adapted chairs, braces, and so on. Consultation with a physical or occupational therapist is especially important in the case of children with cerebral palsy and other motor disabilities.

12. For children with severe visual impairments, gaining independence of movement is of the utmost importance.

CHAPTER 14
Developing cognitive skills

CASE STUDY

John and Carl

John and Carl are identical twins, now just four years old. The father teaches at the local university and the mother is an accountant. There are two older siblings, both boys.

The twins entered a nursery school at the beginning of this year. Last year they attended a two-morning-a-week program, but the parents felt that they needed more stimulation and challenge and more control in their environment. Left to their own devices, John and Carl turn their innate curiosity to all sorts of activities that often bring trouble from their parents and siblings.

When talking about their twins, the parents shy away from terms like *gifted* and *creative*. Nor do the teachers at the centre wish to label the children. However, relative to their peers, John and Carl seem to be functioning well above the norm.

Both boys are using language and vocabulary far above the level expected of children of this age. Moreover, both have made a strong beginning in reading and enjoy books. They sit in the reading corner and read books together, can identify many of the words, and are constantly asking the teachers to decipher new words for them. They recognize letters and know their sounds and can often work out the meanings of sentences from the context and by using the words they recognize as stepping stones.

The teachers do not hold any concerns about the progress of the boys. Their worry is how to provide activities that will continually challenge and stimulate John and Carl within the context of the daily routines and activities of the centre. Moreover, they need to provide support and advice to the parents. Parents of gifted children tend to be quite involved in their children's schooling, and John and Carl's parents often ask teachers how they can further help the children before they enter formal schooling.

When the teachers consulted a visiting psychologist about John and Carl, she began with a statement that at first surprised them. She said that nothing John and Carl were doing was extraordinary in its own right—even children of average ability are capable of reading, doing mathematics, and mastering spatial relationships. John and Carl were remarkable only because they had developed these skills so early—by four instead of seven or eight.

The psychologist also suggested that early programming for potentially gifted children was not a matter of difference but of degree. She compared the special methods to those used with children with mild disabilities: "With a child with a mild learning or behaviour problem, you slow things down. Activities are presented more slowly, concepts are presented in a logical, building order, and children are given many, many opportunities to do the same activity over and over again." She then suggested that the teachers simply turn the coin over: "We do not dramatically change a program or the curricula or the materials and activities for children with mild disabilities. Nor do we change it for children like John and Carl. What we do is quicken the pace—gifted children can learn about fifteen times faster than average children. We present many concepts and help children to integrate them by presenting small problem situations throughout all activities. And we don't need to do nearly as much in the way of practice. These children learn quickly and consolidate new skills in all sorts of ways."

The teachers appreciated the advice, but Ms. Jones, the aide, still had some concerns. She worried whether early reading was good for the boys and whether the kindergarten teacher the next year would appreciate two children who did not need to be taught beginning reading skills. The psychologist would not make any predictions about the kindergarten teacher, but she did stress that "the assumption that all children must begin reading at age six and progress at the same annual rate is, of course, nonsense that thoroughly contradicts the theory, research, and experience regarding individual differences" (Haberman, 1989, p. 285).

The psychologist's final suggestion concerned the structuring of individual programming for Carl and John. She noted that writing goals and objectives, even casual ones, on an IPP would help the teachers and the parents follow and monitor the twins' progress. This would also provide a clearer focus on strengths and pinpoint any weaknesses. Specific goals and objectives that may be prepared for John and Carl in the form of IPPs are shown in Box 14–4.

THE ABILITY TO ENTERTAIN COMPLEX THOUGHTS, communicate them to others, and reformulate them in light of new information is one of the most profound accomplishments of humans (Winzer, 1995). This process, called cognition, essentially involves learning and knowing. Cognition includes imagery, perception, thought, reasoning, reflection, problem solving, memory, creativity, all verbal behaviour, and the capacity for both logical and abstract thought. Cognitive skills do not develop separately and are not learned in isolation. They are integrally related to a myriad of communicative, academic, and adaptive skills and develop in the context of other activities. Language is always a crucial component.

The acquisition and development of cognitive skills depends on interactions with the social, motor, and language domains. For example, language plays a central role in concept development: the child must actively experience an item, have it named, and then interact further with it before he or she can express the name and any ideas about it. Teachers cannot ignore these interactions when intervening with and teaching young children—especially those with disabilities.

In this chapter we look at a number of areas related to cognitive development and examine intervention with two groups of children: those who show cognitive delays and those who are gifted. Because language and cognition are so intimately related, this chapter should be read in conjunction with Chapter 15. Many of the ideas on programming dovetail and are relevant to both cognitive and language development.

Creativity bringing new and usual responses to situations and problems.

Talent advanced skills in a very specific area such as in the visual or performing arts.

BOX 14–1

Giftedness

Because of its multifaceted nature and the many ways in which it can be manifested, giftedness is extremely difficult to define. A simple but workable definition would be that a gifted child is one who, by virtue of superior abilities, demonstrates consistently superior performance in one or more domains of human endeavour. ***Creativity***, which is often linked to giftedness, means bringing new and usual responses to situations and problems. ***Talent*** refers to advanced skills in a very specific area, such as one of the visual or performing arts.

The gifted population is heterogeneous, and not every gifted child will show all the same characteristics. With that in mind, here are some commonly seen traits:

- Unusual alertness.
- Long attention span. Louis and Louis (1992) found that a potentially academically gifted child will quickly become bored with old stimuli, even at three months.
- High activity level and less need for sleep.
- Smiling or recognizing caretakers early.
- Advanced progression through developmental milestones.
- Keen sense of observation.
- Extreme curiosity and excellent memory.
- Likes to learn and shows rapid learning ability.
- Abstract reasoning ability.
- A high degree of sensitivity.
- Perfectionism.
- Excellent sense of humour.
- Preference for older companions.
- Advanced ability with puzzles, mazes, or numbers. High-IQ children show early and rapid development of conceptual skills such as discriminating and labelling colours, identifying shapes, drawing, and working puzzles (see Silverman, 1986, p. 75).
- A craving for knowledge, and a desire to learn and to feel a sense of progress in learning.
- A desire to devour a subject and to spend long hours working on something of interest.

Gifted children learn more, faster and more easily than their age mates. When other children are learning to say their first words, these children are speaking in sentences; when others are rolling balls with playdo, these are trying sculpture. In preschool programs, gifted learners will surpass their age mates in several of the following characteristics: curiosity, persistence, autonomy, self-sufficiency, verbal facility, interest in reading,

interpersonal co-operation, and factual recall (Malone, 1979).

Preschool gifted children tend to demonstrate high levels of acquired knowledge, skill in specific academic areas such as arithmetic, and unusual levels of general information (Kitano, 1985). They learn to read sooner and continue to read at a consistently more advanced level. In specific skill areas, they may already perform as well as much older children.

Gifted children at the preschool level, or at any other level, are not gifted in everything. Especially in preschool children who are potentially gifted, we see dyssynchrony—that is, uneven development. This is especially true in motor skills. For example, writing with letters usually begins in late year two but more typically in year three. By the age of three and surely by age four, children can produce composites that mix scribble, drawings, and strings of letters. However, even when children know the letters, they probably do not possess the fine motor skills to form them well.

It is in the development of motor skills that potentially gifted young children are most like other children. On tests of fine and gross motor skills, they may score a little above the average, but not nearly as high as they do on cognitive tests. These children may be reading, but they are not able to hand-write, because their fine motor skills have not developed (Piirto, 1994).

This disparity between intellectual and physical development can cause problems for young gifted children, who may become frustrated because their hands will not do what their brains want. Disparities may also cause difficulties with teachers. There are some teachers who cannot accept that a child can read at advanced levels but can't write.

With their advanced functioning, gifted children enjoy learning and participation in centre activities. Generally, young gifted children interact well with their peers. They may assume leadership roles; for example, high-ability children are more likely to take a dominant role in group work at the computer (Bellows, 1987).

At the same time, young children may have little understanding or tolerance for peers who cannot learn as quickly. Sometimes the child may be bossy and unable to understand why others don't keep up. As preschoolers and in the primary grades, gifted children (especially those who are highly gifted) try to organize people and things. They invent complex games and try to organize their playmates. This often leads to resentment.

Many of us think of giftedness as a very special trait and would be pleased if our children were slotted into this category. We would predict, quite rightly, that if educated in a properly stimulating environment, our child would proceed through school with ease and then enter any of a range of jobs or professions.

But as we pointed out in Chapter 5, having a gifted child is not always a happy experience for parents. Sometimes the child's gifts cause tension in the family and create outside problems, such as teasing and rejection by neighbourhood children. In the family, the siblings may resent the special considerations, such as computers and camps, provided to the gifted child. Or they may resent it when the gifted child is treated differently or is reluctant to give up the spotlight. Parents may tire of the constant questions and become intimidated when the young child speaks and argues in almost adult terms. The gifted child may alienate his playmates by being domineering and bossy. Finally, many gifted children experience difficulties because of advanced social development. They often cannot find playmates whose interests match theirs; as a result, they often select older children for friends.

Cognitive development

Cognition the interaction of all the perceptual, intellectual, and linguistic abilities that are involved in thinking and learning.

The terms cognition and intellectual ability are often used interchangeably, although the meanings are a little different. Intellectual ability is the aptitude to perform tasks and to achieve in the environment. The concept of cognition is multifaceted and complex. In general, *cognition* refers to the interaction of all the perceptual, intellectual, and linguistic abilities that are involved in thinking and learning. *Cognitive development* refers to the thinking processes and how children understand and learn about their world. As children develop cognitively, orderly changes occur in how they understand and cope with their world. Thus, cognitive development relates to the methods a child uses to organize, store, and retrieve information for problem solving and generalization.

Cognitive development the thinking processes and how children understand and learn about the world in which they live.

Different theorists in the area of child development have different ways of conceptualizing children's cognitive development. One of the most accepted theories is the "age and stage" theory of Jean Piaget. If you remember our discussion in Chapter 6, Piaget divided cognitive development into four periods: sensorimotor, preoperations, concrete operations, and formal operations. Children at any given stage think differently from children at other stages, in both qualitative and quantitative terms. While children may progress at different rates, the stages themselves do not vary; thus, a child must pass through the sensorimotor period first, for the sensorimotor skills are necessary for basic thinking and conceptual development.

CHILDREN WITH INTELLECTUAL DISABILITIES

Children who have difficulties in cognitive development are generally referred to as mentally retarded, intellectually disabled, or intellectually challenged. To be judged as retarded, a child must have a tested IQ of 70 or below on a standardized test of mental ability, and also show deficits in adaptive behaviour.

Mental retardation is divided into the categories of mild, moderate, severe, profound. All children can learn, but the amount, pace, and complexity of learning is determined by the degree of intellectual disability. In this text we have met Juan, a child with mild mental retardation. Juan is lagging behind his peers in a number of domains, but he learns very well at the centre. In elementary school he will probably achieve one-half to one-third of what his normally developing peers will. Juan's disability is in the cognitive area but spills over to affect his language and social functioning to some extent. However, he shows no physical anomalies, or great gaps in motor development, or additional handicapping conditions.

This is in contrast to Kalim, our child with severe mental retardation. Kalim is lagging seriously in the cognitive, communication, and social domains, and her additional conditions place her in the category of multiply disabled and make her medically fragile. Kalim can certainly learn, but her disabilities restrict the amount and type of learning, as well as her attainment of independence.

GIFTEDNESS

Precocious children who demonstrate remarkable early development.

In almost every classroom and centre, teachers will encounter young children who seem to be more advanced than their peers across one or many developmental domains. These children may be ***precocious***—that is, demonstrate remarkable early development. Some of these children will be physically superior to their age mates; others will demonstrate high levels of creativity; often they will use language at advanced levels, and want to learn to read or be already reading. Some of these children will be categorized by educators as gifted, creative, or talented.

One of the most difficult tasks in special education is defining exactly what giftedness is and determining exactly who is gifted. For very young children, the difficulty is compounded because definitions of giftedness are often tied to academic prowess or a creative product such as a book, an essay, or a performance. When the term *gifted* is applied to young children, it essentially applies to potential rather than accomplishment; it requires guesses to be made about the future with limited information (Colangelo & Fleuridas, 1986). Thus, it is probably more appropriate to speak of children who are *potentially* gifted.

Various specific characteristics have been identified in children thought to be gifted quite early in life. The most potent is high verbal ability, which is a good indicator of IQ. In the United States, Gogel and colleagues (1985) surveyed 1,039 parents of gifted children. Seventy percent of the children were identified accurately by age three, most of them between one and three. Of all the characteristics that caused parents to suspect giftedness, "early verbal expression" was mentioned most frequently.

Many children who show early and extensive vocabulary development ask many questions, have good memories, and show an intense interest in books. They learn to read early and easily. One-half to three-quarters of academically talented children are reading by the age of five—and reading well (Piirto, 1994).

As we saw in the opening case study, programming for children such as John and Carl is special in degree, not kind: the regular early childhood curriculum simply needs extending and accelerating. However, the precise program dimensions and whether to program at all are matters of some debate (see Box 14–2).

BOX 14–2

Programming for gifted children in early childhood

Curriculum in early childhood education has often been designed to embrace conflicting goals. On one side is the academic-readiness perspective, which sees early childhood education as preparing children for academic success in later schooling. Proponents of this position advocate systematic instruction in a variety of prewriting and prereading skills in the years just prior to first grade (Stricklana & Ogle, 1990). On the other side are those whose stance reflects a traditional concern for putting the young child's social, emotional, and physical development first. Nowhere are these positions brought into sharper relief than in the care and education of potentially gifted children.

Over the past two decades, interest in the early stimulation of cognitive abilities and prevention of underachievement has led to the establishment of preschools for gifted children. However, most children who seem to be far advanced of their peers in some or all developmental domains are placed in regular early childhood programs. These young children require and deserve special programming, just as children functioning below the norm in some areas do. Attempts to provide special adaptations usually focus on three areas: parent assistance, skills training, and enriched curricula in the early childhood setting.

Some educators and parents adamantly favour early stimulation; they are tremendously eager to have young children develop as rapidly as possible, from the prenatal stage onward. They want the preschool years, once a time of play, fun, and finger paint, to become a fast-tracked academic experience. Because of this pressure to start children on the road to academics earlier and earlier, the early childhood curriculum—especially in kindergarten—has become a curriculum of literacy. More than any other area, literacy (reading) is stressed as the key component of early academics.

Other people oppose early identification and programs for gifted and talented children. They are aghast at the special arrangements (lessons, learning devices, computers, trips, vacations) many parents think they must provide (Lay-Dopyera & Dopyera, 1990). They see special programming as potentially harmful because of the way it hurries young children. They also point to the lower reliability of standardized measures for these children, and argue that children who are "early bloomers" may be misidentified as truly gifted (Kitano & Kirby, 1986).

The moderates in this debate argue for the many benefits they see arising from early identification and programming. Below are some of the more important reasons cited for providing gifted programs at the early level:

- Early programs may prevent later underachievement by challenging gifted children and supporting a positive attitude toward schooling.

- Enriched preschool programs nurture high potential and encourage gifted children to demonstrate their strengths.

- Early recognition and nurturance of talents will improve children's mental health.

- Early programs provide opportunities for parents and professionals to interact on issues of developmental needs and advocacy.

- Early programming is the best policy initiative for economically deprived children (see Stile et al., 1993).

- Creativity may very well be an innate trait that can be stimulated or crushed. Creativity seems generally to decrease as children get older—a tendency that may be accounted for by both age and culture.

Assessment

Cognitive development is assessed using standardized IQ tests. In Chapter 8 we discussed the pros and cons of using measures of mental ability with very young children. When standardized tests are used, they are used as part of a battery of observations and tests and are only used by trained personnel.

ASSESSMENT OF GIFTS AND TALENTS

In preschool, programming for gifted children must start with the accurate identification of gifts and talents. Early attempts should be made to identify and serve young gifted children. But while the importance of early screening for growth and developmental patterns is fairly well accepted for gifted children, the process is fraught with difficulties. In fact, despite the increased interest in early childhood education of the gifted over the past several years, many schools delay identification and services until the third or fourth grade (Stile et al., 1993). When early intervention is undertaken, the basic issues are who should assess, how to assess, and what to assess.

Young children who are potentially gifted can often be identified simply by observation. An 18-month-old child may use language in the manner of a much older child, or a three-year-old may tackle math problems that are taught in grade four.

Parents and other adults seem to be good at identification at this age, although parents usually underestimate rather than overestimate their children's giftedness (Chitwood, 1986). Parents' implicit beliefs about their children's ability levels closely relate to children's actual tested IQs (Louis & Louis, 1992). Parents are especially good at assessing creative thinking, abstract thinking, and memory abilities.

Potentially gifted children can be spotted by alert teachers. Teachers' ratings of young children's behaviour and characteristics have been shown to be fairly reliable and valid.

PROGRESS CHECK 1

Make a chart with two columns. In the first column place the traits of children with mild intellectual disabilities, in the second, the characteristics of young children who are gifted. How can you individualize programs for both groups of children in an early childhood setting? Explain in relation to centres and to small-group and large-group activities.

Teachers are good sources of information because they are required to observe children in relatively consistent circumstances (Martin, Hooper, & Snow, 1986).

Because giftedness is multifaceted and may manifest itself in many ways, it is difficult to select identification procedures and tools. As well as observation, more formal measures may be employed. As the search is for superior potential, not necessarily superior achievement, it has been traditional to include a measure of mental ability in identification procedures. Developmental scales are also used, as we need to examine progress in relation to developmental norms. Is a child, for example, ahead of his or her peers in the use of language, and if so, how far ahead?

Parents of a two- or three-year-old can answer certain questions. For example, can the child draw a person with at least some representation of legs, head, and eyes? Can the child recognize and correctly identify the numbers one to nine? Does the child read (i.e., instead of listening to) familiar stories and books?

Promoting Cognitive Development

For young children, training in cognitive skills focuses on attention, memory, concepts, language and gestures, mediation, problem solving, and logical thought. Any activity in any setting is a cognitive learning experience. Whenever children are interacting with the environment—building with blocks, riding a tricycle, playing with a doll, or even arguing with a pal about a wanted toy—they are developing their cognitive skills.

STRATEGIES FOR DEVELOPING COGNITIVE SKILLS

Cognitive development begins in infancy with the development of basic sensorimotor concepts and skills such as object permanence, causality, means-end behaviour, spatial relationships, schemas for relating to objects, and imitation. We discuss these later, in the section on programming for children with severe disabilities.

Many other cognitive skills develop in the years after infancy and before formal schooling begins at five or six. Preoperational children develop skills in classification and in representational play with objects. Such skills are generally seen as preparatory for later learning; however, many of them are functional in their own right. For example, problem solving includes the strategies children use to solve problems; logical thought refers to the child's understanding of reality.

Concept development

Cognitive development includes learning how to internalize the world so that objects and events can be grouped, classified, and organized in a manner conducive to efficient memory storage. The terms for these skills are *concept development* and *concept classification*. Both are basic to human cognition.

Although most of us could provide many examples of concepts, the term is not easy to define. One definition states that a concept is "a person's organized information about an item or class of items that enables the person to discriminate the item or class of items from other items and also to relate it to other items and classes of items" (Klausmieir, 1990, p. 94). Concepts have also been described as the fundamental structures for thoughts throughout a person's lifetime

(Prater, 1993, p. 51), as the fundamental building blocks of intelligence, and as structures that reduce the complexity of life by helping us organize a vast amount of information into meaningful units.

Roughly, a **concept** is an idea that includes all that is characteristically associated with it. That is, concepts are classifications of ideas, symbols, objects, and events; they are mental structures or representations that define how a set or class of entities, events, or abstractions are related. Every object, person, or event is made up of special characteristics or attributes; concepts are formed on the basis of relevant attributes shared by two or more objects, persons, events, or ideas. *Ball* may have the attributes of round, rolling, coloured, and toy; *apple* may be given the attributes of round, edible, fruit, and red, green, or yellow. A *dog* has legs, a tail, fur, and so on. Once children have learned the concept of *dog*, they can guess when they see a strange breed or size of dog that it is a dog because it has characteristics similar to their concept of *dog*.

The basic task associated with concept development is classification into categories. A category is a class or partition of objects; or a set of objects, or events, or people, or the like. **Categorization**, then, includes those processes which are involved in defining membership in categories. When children categorize, they treat two or more distinct entities as if, in some way, they were equivalent. For example, categorization occurs when a child sees a Great Dane and a Corgi and groups them both as dogs, or can place dogs and cats and lions in the larger category of animals.

> **Concept** an idea that includes all that is characteristically associated with it.

> **Categorization** the processes that are involved in defining categorical membership.

dogs

cats

yellow colour

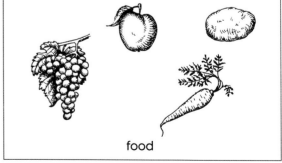

food

FIGURE 14–1

Concepts

Having developed some concepts, children can establish relationships between them; this provides propositions such as "cats are mammals." Children can then establish principles. For example, a child may first learn the attributes that go to make up the category of "birds." Having established that category, the child can move to a principle: "Winged animals fly."

The ability to develop concepts and to classify objects and events is an important preschool cognitive skill. Children show that they are able to learn concepts when they can identify a class of objects or relations by pointing out one or more instances of the class.

Matching and sorting tasks are either perceptual or conceptual in nature, or combine elements of both. Perceptual matching includes such activities as matching capital A to capital A, or small b to small b. In conceptual matching, a child is required to abstract an idea and then generalize to another instance. An example: matching capital D to small d, and capital G to small g. In the preoperational period, children's categories are largely perceptually bound (i.e., bound to what they can see). As they develop cognitively, their categories become more conceptually bound (i.e., bound to what they can reason).

Generally, children learn concepts in two ways: by observing the environment, or by definition. Certain types of concepts are more easily taught using certain procedures. For example, clearer concepts are more easily taught by highlighting their features and presenting the connecting rules; vaguer concepts are more easily taught by showing examples (positive and negative instances of the concept) (Hulse, Egeth, & Deese, 1980).

There are many techniques for strengthening children's concept development:

- Identify and teach the defining attributes of a concept.
- Use functional definitions of objects as well as descriptive ones: "We play with a ball, a ball is round."
- Stress basic concepts in conjunction with other skills such as language and maths.
- Keep in mind that the order in which concepts are introduced must correspond to the developmental sequence of learning. The concepts of *big* and *little* and *in* and *out* are learned early; temporal concepts come later. Five-year-olds will still talk about their birthday party happening after "three sleeps" rather than in three days.
- Start with concrete objects so that children can form a mental picture. Then move from the actual object to a colour photo, to a black-and-white photo, to a clear picture, to another picture, to a symbol, and finally to a word.
- Integrate concept learning with other objectives. For example, children may learn classification skills and expression of emotions at the same time in a card game in which they distinguish, label, and discuss facial expressions.
- Help children plan. For example, a mural-painting project can develop children's co-operation and problem-solving skills, as well as concepts.
- Use all the senses. For example, tell the child to "see the red ball," then "sit on the red square," then "eat the red candy," then "draw a red truck."

- Use movement for concepts such as *top, bottom, up,* and *down.* Children can sit on the top of chairs or place their hands on the bottom of the table. Or they can place two balls: one on top of the table, one on the floor.

- Have children follow directions. For example, bake (make) while following a written or pictured recipe, or put together a model from pictured directions (Owens, 1991).

- Integrate concept development with problem solving. This helps children make connections between experiences and understand integrative concepts. Problems are situations where the attainment of a given goal is obstructed, or where something is needed. Problem solving is the process used to eliminate the obstruction and secure the goal (Kodera & Garwood, 1979).

Dozens of tasks go into concept development. As examples, children can do the following:

- Match picture items by their function.

- Sequence pictures.

- Identify things that are used in the same way—for example, paint and crayon, or clay and plasticine.

- Describe concepts in their own words to peers.

- Make common object-and-action associations, such as a cup and saucer, shoe and foot, broom and sweep.

- Teach directions with construction toys, Lego, playdo, and clay.

- Make bodies big, small, tall, and so on; or use pictures to find an animal with a big tail, or a little tail.

- Devise their own classification systems. Craig Loewen (1990) suggests allowing children to develop a classification system for 50 or so assorted picture cards. The teacher first lays out all the cards; then the teacher and the children describe the pictures. Children then find two cards that have similar pictures, and the teacher asks, "Are there other pictures that can be added to the pile?" "How do you know?" This process is repeated until all the cards are sorted into piles.

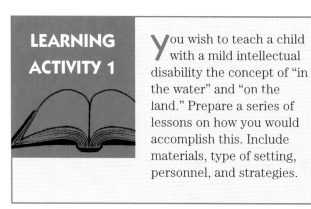

LEARNING ACTIVITY 1

You wish to teach a child with a mild intellectual disability the concept of "in the water" and "on the land." Prepare a series of lessons on how you would accomplish this. Include materials, type of setting, personnel, and strategies.

SERIATION

According to the work of Jean Piaget on children's cognitive development, the ability to seriate really begins during the period of concrete operations, which starts around grade one. However, children can be provided with many opportunities to develop this cognitive skill:

- They can sort objects that vary in weight, such as ping-pong balls, tennis balls, and golf balls.

- They can sort by height; for example, when everyone is standing in line, they would sort for tallest to shortest.
- They can sequence activities; this helps them focus on the order of tasks and ideas.
- They can "show and tell," to learn how to state information in logical sequence.
- They can sort picture cards into a sequence (see Figure 14–2).

apple

missing bite

core

teapot, cup

pour tea

drink tea

FIGURE 14–2

Picture cards

Questioning   One of the most potent methods available to teachers for fostering cognitive growth (and language) is to ask questions in a way that activates children's thinking. Problem solving should be an important aspect of questioning.

Questioning is not a test of what a child knows, and its purpose in not to find out something that you, as the teacher, already know. The point of questioning is to help the adult learn more about the child's understanding, and to pose additional challenges to the child. The questions adults ask should be meaningful to the children and designed to extend their thinking, to introduce and extend concept development, to stress new vocabulary, and to improve language abilities.

When teachers ask questions, certain kinds of questions are more educationally useful than others. Following are some important points to remember about questions:

- Children should be asked questions that extend their language. Avoid questions that result in yes-or-no answers. Instead, ask open-ended questions that begin with "How do you …" "Why …" "What happened …" and so on. For example, do not ask "Do you want to play with the doll?" Instead, "What do you want to do now?"

- During group time, use a game of questions. Tell children they cannot give a yes-or-no answer. For example, "Is your name Jim?" should get the response, "My name is Jim." In the same vein, "Do you like to play with blocks?" might lead to "I like the paints more" as a response.

- To teach new vocabulary, teachers can ask questions such as, "Is your clay too hard, too soft, or just right?" "How much water should we add to this clay—just a little, a cupful, or a half-cupful?" "What size trucks do you want for your highway?"

- Make questioning part of each activity. For example, children can plant a small garden. Follow-up questions and activities are shown in Figure 14–3.

- Facilitate thinking with "Why are you doing it this way?" "What is happening?" "Did it work?" and "Next time, how will you do it differently?"

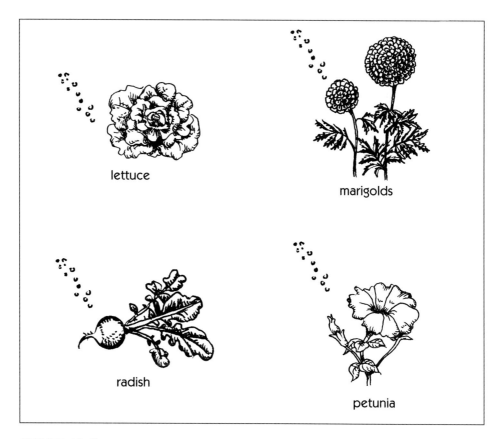

FIGURE 14–3

Questioning

PROGRESS CHECK 2

Explain how to help young children develop problem-solving skills. Relate your strategies to the theory of constructivism and developmentally appropriate practice as discussed in Chapter 6.

Intervention for children who are gifted

In many ways, children who are gifted need a faster track to stimulate their special gifts and enhance their interest in learning. However, we must not forget that they are children first. Programs should be developmentally appropriate, age appropriate, and individualized.

Gifted children require challenging and innovative programs that allow them to explore their abilities. Even in early childhood settings, they should be provided with opportunities for enhancing their creativity, for advanced learning and problem solving, and for developing literacy and numeracy skills. Teachers can expand and accelerate the regular curriculum so as to provide these opportunities. The main goals for gifted preschoolers are these:

- *Self-understanding.* Children must learn to accept and understand their own strengths and weaknesses and develop a healthy and realistic self-concept.
- *Independence.* Children must learn to make decisions and carry out plans.
- *Assertiveness.* Children must learn to stand up for themselves and to express their needs in mature and effective ways.
- *Social sensitivity.* Children must learn to understand the needs of others, to help others, and to co-operate with others. It is important for them to develop appropriate and effective interpersonal skills that focus on social perceptiveness, awareness of the needs of others, and social problem-solving strategies.

The following are also important:

- Friendship-making skills, so that children learn to interact appropriately with peers and adults.
- Social problem-solving skills, so that they learn to resolve conflicts without resorting to violence.
- Positive attitudes toward school and learning.
- The ability to commit to tasks.
- The ability to think creatively and productively. Partly, this means acquiring higher-level thinking skills, such as observing, predicting, classifying, analysing, synthesizing, and evaluating.
- The willingness to explore and take risks.
- Intellectual curiosity, and persistence in developing creative approaches to problem solving.
- Creative expression in a range of areas: art, dramatics, movement and dance, language, and so on.
- A strong foundation in traditional academic skills, with advanced work tailored to individual competencies. These children may be more ready to learn formal skills, such as reading, than are their age mates.

- Large and small muscle co-ordination and dexterity (see Roedell, 1985; Roedell & Robinson, 1977, p. 9).

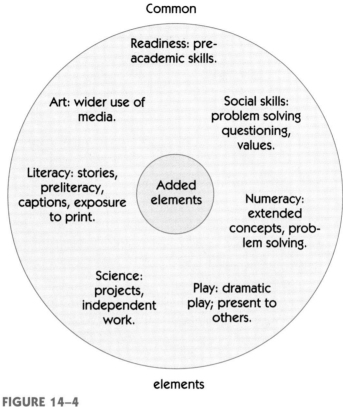

FIGURE 14–4

Programming for gifted children

ENVIRONMENTAL ADAPTATIONS The research clearly indicates that the early environment has a powerful impact on language and cognitive development (Davis & Rimm, 1994). To challenge and stimulate potentially gifted children, the environment should be rich in materials, manipulative experiences, exploratory activities, language stimulation, and social interaction. An atmosphere of inquiry and curiosity should prevail. Teachers should encourage the children to ask questions and seek solutions to problems that interest them.

Providing a variety of experiences will not automatically deepen children's understanding, or make them more aware of themselves and their environment, unless they assimilate the information into a usable framework. Adults working with gifted youngsters should do the following:

- Use curriculum that is concept focused, or theme and activity focused, and that is an extension of the units presented to the whole group. For example, in a unit on pets, explore unusual animals.

- Introduce many science projects such as growing plants.
- Provide opportunities for specific projects, such as building a dinosaur.
- Ask questions that require analysis and synthesis of information, and that consider many facets of a problem.
- Introduce new concepts by bringing in materials and ideas from outside the classroom.
- Encourage participation, without insisting on it at all times.
- Offer independent study, and allow for individual learning styles.
- Be positive, accepting, and open-minded.
- Make blank paper and writing materials available at all times.
- Make allowance for some noise during group activities.
- Provide activities in a variety of settings—tables, bookshelves, out of doors.
- Have child-centred bulletin boards displaying children's work.
- Encourage mentors and others to visit the school.
- Encourage peer praise and positive interaction.
- Encourage creative expression, fantasy, imagination, original art, and stories.
- Make use of computers.
- Provide girls with practice with building blocks, Lego, and mechanical toys to give them a firm start in the area of spatial visualization, which is one area where boys consistently score higher than girls (Gallagher & Gallagher, 1994; Karnes & Johnson, 1991; Smutny, Veenker, & Veenker, 1986, p. 99).

BOX 14–3
Helpful hints

- Use predictable books to help children learn about print. Because of the repetitious patterns and engaging story lines, these books are often eagerly reread by children.
- Use environmental print—signs, logos, food boxes—in dramatic play to help children learn about the forms and functions of print.
- Use many captions. When captions are used, the object is not to teach the child to read but to convey the message that words and pictures convey information in different ways.
- Employ a variety of materials and activities. Provide many new activities that challenge.
- Allow ample use of imagination.
- Use written language to record children's ideas and feelings and to indicate that words have a specific graphic representation.
- Ask many questions.
- Provide small-group projects in children's areas of interest.

EMERGENT LITERACY

In the past decade there has been a upsurge in attention to literacy development in young children. One reason for this is the concern about high illiteracy rates in the adult population; another is the wealth of information researchers have produced during the past 20 years relevant to how

Some children begin to read before they enter formal schooling.

young children learn language. The early years are no longer viewed as the approach to readiness for reading and writing. Literacy development is now seen as an ongoing process that begins in infancy with exposure to oral language, written language, books, and stories, at first in the home and later in other environments.

This new view is often referred to as "emergent literacy." However, the term seems to be used in two ways. First, it describes children's natural development of language and then literacy skills. Second, some authors also use the term to designate a type of teaching philosophy. In this usage, emergent literacy underlies the whole-language philosophy. Under this philosophy and teaching approach, literacy involves more than the ability to read and write. The contemporary concept of literacy sees the principal goal of language teaching as encouraging learners to use language to fulfil a greater number of language functions, such as thinking and problem solving (Dudley-Marling & Searle, 1991). It involves children being competent with written materials; and confident enough with those materials to take ideas and look at them critically, relate them to their own experience, and use them to enrich their lives. Whole-language approaches provide both functional and enriched language experiences for children and explore those experiences through a variety of meaningful materials.

Emergent literacy sees children's development of literacy skills as an outgrowth of natural modes of language development. It points out that young children, whose cognitive capacities seem limited, master a complex spoken language system in a very short time and with no formal instruction. It follows that "by understanding, respecting and building on the language competence of children, we can make literacy an extension of their natural language learning" (Ahuja, 1984, p. 38).

Emergent literacy means that the past emphasis in literacy teaching (i.e., teach them to read as early as possible and at exactly the same time) has been replaced by a determination to bring each individual child to reading in ways that will keep reading linked to feelings of competence and confidence. Children eventually arrive at an understanding of directionality, the alphabetic principle, and sound/symbol relationships. They read when they are ready.

The perspective of emergent literacy encompasses any experience a child has with the written word. It suggests that there are early steps in the process of learning to read that are not always recognized as part of a child's natural developmental preparation. Children learn many things *about* reading before they actually learn to read. They practise many other ways of using symbols before they come to understand the use of word symbols in reading. Emergent literacy is supported by providing simple books, pictures, and puzzles to infants and toddlers, and by expanding literary experiences to preschoolers by providing a rich print environment (Fox et al., 1994).

Studies of children who have not yet been taught to read and write demonstrate that natural encounters with print build a strong foundation for literacy. Literacy development begins with exposure to rich environments and interactions, long before children actually begin to read and write conventionally. Learning to read and write happens as children learn critical distinctions between art and written language, and between letters, stories, and other print forms (Franklin, 1992). Children may learn why dad writes a list before he goes shopping (the functions of print), where mom looks to read a story book (book conventions),

---

BOX 14–4

IPP for John and Carl

Present levels of functioning

Cognitive: Assessment indicates that both boys are functioning at least two standard deviations above the norm on a standardized IQ measure.

Language: John and Carl both demonstrate language abilities about three years above their chronological age.

Social: John and Carl need to interact and co-operate more with their peers. Perhaps because they are twins, they tend to spend all of their time together and often shut other children out of their play.

Motor: Both fine and gross motor skills are developing at a normal rate. Both boys are further ahead in gross motor skill development than in fine motor skills.

Academic readiness: John and Carl have both mastered reading with very little assistance.

Long-range goals

To challenge the boys in the areas of problem solving, numeracy skills, and independent work.

To promote greater interaction with peers.

Short-term objectives

1. Match John and Carl with two other children and have them build a special mural for the classroom. The myriad possibilities for working together are important for advanced social functioning.

2. Teach both children to be peer mediators with children not functioning to the norm.

and how to read Harvey's or K-Mart from commercial signs (environmental print).

Promoting literacy skills   Many early literary experiences that are worthwhile do not have an end product in the sense of something that can be seen on paper. Delight, joy, and interest encourage a child to want to speak and then, much later, to want to learn to read and write.

In preschool and kindergarten classrooms, dramatic experiences play an important and fundamental role in the facilitation of early literacy. When we provide sociodramatic play and other dramatic experiences along with reading and writing activities, we encourage children to develop their literacy skills. Dramatic experiences involve not only the encoding process (children bringing meaning to what they hear and read) but also the decoding process (children giving expression to that meaning). The dramatic process naturally incorporates a wide use of varied language functions, including the interactional, personal, instrumental, regulatory, and imaginative. These functions, because they are intimately connected with meaning for young children, further assist language development and early literacy (Mazurek, 1995).

Young children need a reason to use language, and through drama they may come to discover the purposes of reading and writing. We may use an entire story for dramatization, but we don't always have to. When we use a selected scene or incident from a particular story as the starting point for a drama, the focus shifts from the process of enactment to the exploration of the meanings of the story. The child's responses to the story are personally meaningful, and contribute to his or her understanding of the power of language, while extending language and literacy skills.

Young children may also be encouraged to create and dramatize their own stories. This provides them with a meaningful purpose for using language. At first, the teacher may simply act as a scribe and write out the children's stories for them. When the children directly observe their words being transformed into

Teachers should provide young children with many experiences involving printed materials.

writing. they may show an increased desire to read (i.e., so that they can write down their own stories).

For preschool children, reading books and having books read to them is a critical element in any natural literacy program. Children's language abilities improve when they are exposed to literature; this is ample justification for reading to them regularly. Wells (1986) carried out a longitudinal study of language and literacy and found that the quality and quantity of storytelling encounters between children and adults in the preschool years was an effective predictor of school achievement at age ten.

When teachers read often, young children learn to interpret literature by entering imaginative, fictional worlds, and by relating story content, themes, and motives to their own lives (see Franklin, 1992). New vocabulary and more complex sentence constructions become familiar through pleasant listening experiences. Children's language abilities expand when the literature to which they are exposed provides models that slightly stretch their existing abilities. As well, children develop a strong conviction that reading is its own reward—that it is not something done to please others or as a means to another end.

To convince children that books are worthwhile, adults should select materials about which they are personally enthusiastic. For those children who lack language facility because English is their second language or because they use a nonstandard dialect, stories with simple and clear wordings and phrasings are best (Lay-Dopyera & Dopyera, 1990).

PROGRESS CHECK 3

What is meant by emergent literacy? By whole language? How do these relate to drama, storytelling, and other experiences in early childhood settings?

Early reading

Reading is a sophisticated cognitive skill that requires perception, attention, memory, evaluation, thinking, decoding, sequencing, and finding implications. Reading involves manipulating symbols. Symbols stand for or represent something else; for example, a flag symbolizes a country. Spoken and written words are the most common symbols.

Children should never be forced into literacy. Young gifted children, however, not only talk and conceptualize at an advanced level, but can learn to read at age four or even three (e.g., Jackson, 1988). Some children teach themselves to read. They prod parents to read and ask, "What does that say?" or they pick up words from predictable books they have heard often. Children who begin reading on their own, without specific learning or drill, are often those who will be defined as academically gifted.

Preschoolers who invest the time and energy to learn to read share some common characteristics: an eagerness to learn, the ability to work independently, advanced knowledge, thinking ability, problem-solving ability, inquisitiveness, perfectionism, good memory, a long attention span, good judgment, the ability to produce original ideas and products, and a large vocabulary (Bryant, 1989; Smith, 1991). The deep comprehension needed for reading also takes verbal intelligence. Children who read exceptionally early have a certain aptitude for code breaking—especially the code of print (Jackson, 1988).

PROGRESS CHECK 4

Early childhood programs that ascribe to developmentally appropriate practice emphasize a child-centred curriculum characterized by individual choice-making and exploratory play. In such a setting, how would you stimulate emergent literacy and literacy skills in a young child who is beginning to read?

Children who learn to read early often teach themselves, using different procedures. Kamii (1985) observed that various young children demonstrated each of the following spontaneous strategies in teaching themselves to read:

- Focusing on the first letter of the word.
- Focusing on the word's configuration—its length and shape.
- Obtaining semantic clues from pictures and situations.
- Looking for familiar letters and letter combinations.
- Repetitive practice of spelling and copying words.
- Inventing and applying their own phonological system.

NUMERACY

All children must develop number concepts. Numeracy is closely tied to making sense of the world. Young children need "the freedom to explore, to conjecture, to seek, to validate, and to convince others" (Lappman & Schram, 1989).

As with reading, children develop numeracy concepts early and in a fairly predictable sequence. For example, at two-and-a-half a child can be quite definite about wanting two candies, not one. Preschool children use counting principles. They may not be able to count blocks accurately, but they will say 1 2 3 4 6 9 10, not 9 8 1 5 4. They later go on to learn concepts about numbers, measuring, money, spatial relations, time, and problem solving. Time is one of the most difficult of these concepts.

Children who are functioning above the norm often show advanced numeracy skills. By kindergarten, a gifted child may be counting by 5s and 10s and adding and subtracting. For these children, the regular curriculum should be extended. They should be provided with challenges in these areas:

- Sorting and matching.
- Saying numbers in order.
- Writing numbers.
- Arranging numbers in order.
- One-to-one correspondence.
- Recognizing shapes.
- Developing number concepts and manipulating numbers. For example, children can show all the ways that a given set of objects can be classified and sorted.

LEARNING ACTIVITY 2

Five-year-old Brett is in kindergarten. The teachers were surprised at his facility with numbers, especially when he showed them how to do multiplication. When Brett was assessed using the Test of Early Mathematical Ability, he scored above the 99th percentile. Prepare an IPP for Brett indicating the long-range goals and short-term objectives that would consolidate and extend his skills and interest in math within the context of the early childhood setting.

Craig Lowen (1990) uses matching and classification to develop number concepts. Children are provided with individual pails of buttons of various colours and asked to classify the buttons by colour. "Place all the black buttons together … Now put all the white buttons together." Then they are asked, "How many holes does each button have?" They can reclassify by colour and number of holes. As the game continues, the children are challenged to find other ways to classify and sort.

Children with severe disabilities

The characteristics of children with severe disabilities present many challenges to teachers. Many of these children do not have an efficient means of communication. In improving their quality of life, two areas must be emphasized: increasing their responsiveness to the environment and the people in it; and increasing the ability of caregivers to interpret their communications. In the early years, the main goals are to decrease their dependence on others; to increase their awareness of the environment; to teach them basic social, communication, and self-help skills; and to push their achievement levels as high as possible.

Typically, children with severe disabilities function at the sensorimotor stage of development. Sensorimotor development, which includes fine and gross motor development, refers to the continuously emerging interconnections between multiple sensory and perceptual systems (visual, auditory, tactile, kinesthetic, and olfactory) and motor systems (reflex, fine and gross motor control) (Neisworth & Bagnato, 1987, p. 91).

These children require training in a range of sensorimotor skills, beginning with basic attention and task engagement. The same skills underlie language development, as we will discuss in Chapter 15.

ATTENTION

Attention is a central cognitive process: if children are to learn successfully, they must attend to the environment. Attention is difficult to define. In general, it involves the process of tuning in to sensory information, using the senses to recognize, discriminate, and interpret stimuli, and focusing on the information for further processing. Attention also includes engagement or active participation, often referred to as on-task behaviour. Attention is developmental in nature and becomes more refined as a child matures.

When a child attends to something, he or she focuses on a stimulus and ignores distractions. Some observable behaviours typically associated with attention include eye contact, directed looking, visual tracking, directed body movements, and on-task behaviour. Nonattention and nonengagement are often evidenced by self-stimulating behaviour, wandering, aggressive behaviour, and inappropriate use of materials.

To begin to promote attention, the teacher may need to find a way to screen out extraneous noise. Then, to motivate looking, the teacher can introduce things that hold intrinsic interest for the child. A child will often look at a face before anything else, so once attention has been gained by face-to-face contact, an object can be introduced into the child's visual field. Since young children focus on details of shape and colour, brightly coloured woollen balls, for example, can be used to maintain eye contact. The teacher can gain the child's auditory attention by squeezing a toy that gives a noise cue. Once the child attends to a toy, the next steps are grasping the toy, picking it up, positioning it for appropriate play, and releasing it. Teachers can also provide battery-operated or simple wind-up toys; their repetitive action and sound help to develop attention spans.

TASK ENGAGEMENT

> Engagement (sometimes called task engagement or on-task behaviour) **the extent to which children are actively and appropriately involved with materials, people, or activities in the environment.**

Engagement, sometimes called task engagement or on-task behaviour, refers to the extent to which children are actively and appropriately involved with materials, people, or activities in the environment. It is the amount of time a child spends at developmentally and contextually appropriate behaviours in the social and nonsocial environment (McWilliam, 1991; McWilliam, Trivette, & Dunst, 1985). Engagement involves interaction with objects and people; thus, it includes manipulation, play, and use of objects, as well as verbal and nonverbal interactions with peers and adults (Rogers-Warren & Warren, 1984).

Engagement does not mean brief periods of paying attention or of productive activity; rather, it refers to sustained behaviour or the total duration of its occurrence. Moreover, a specific behaviour might be appropriate (engaged) in one setting but not in another. A four-year-old child with a speech delay who sits banging a toy on a table would not be considered engaged; a four-year-old with severe mental retardation and cerebral palsy who displays the same behaviour might be considered engaged (McWilliam, 1991).

When children interact independently with materials, activities, and people, they are demonstrating high rates of voluntary engagement. High rates of engagement are important for a number of reasons. First, when the rate and quality of engagement is high, other processes critical for development are at an optimal level. Second, engagement promotes learning. Children who persist in their work are likely to learn more and perform better in school than children who do not (Karnes et al., 1985). Thus, early engagement seems to predict success; the amount of time children spend at tabletop activities tends to be a predictor of future success in kindergarten (Hoy-Youngblood, 1986). Third and finally, studies have found that high engagement prevents or reduces behaviour problems.

The younger the child, the lower the rates of engagement. The parts of the brain that allow the child to sustain attention and screen out distractions become increasingly myelinated between the fourth and seventh years (Higgins & Turnure, 1984). This means that very young children are more likely to flit from activity to activity; they are also more easily distracted by visual and auditory stimuli.

At program entry, normally developing preschool children are engaged an average of 93 percent of the time, with a range of 76 to 100 percent (McGee et al., 1991). However, early childhood educators are unlikely to observe these high rates of voluntary engagement in young children with disabilities. Indeed, it is often very difficult to engage children who are disabled, and the more serious the disability, the more problems with engagement there are likely to be.

In increasing a child's engagement, the teacher has three tasks. The first is to identify the reasons for low engagement. There may be low levels of engagement because the child has neither the skills to perform the task nor an interest in doing so. However, the possible reasons for noncompliance and noninvolvement are many, and often they cannot be identified, especially when the child is severely disabled or autistic. The second task is to define the skills required to participate in a given activity and assess the child for those skills. The third is to intervene to teach the skills defined during the second task. This may mean providing the necessary structure to ensure that high rates of engagement occur in a variety of settings.

There are a number of variables that promote engagement. One of the main ones is the responsiveness of the environment. Engagement is related to environmental arrangements such as scheduling, types of toys, physical arrangements, the interaction between classroom materials, teacher contacts, and so on.

Frequent teacher attention will reinforce engagement, but on its own may not be sufficient. Because engagement depends on both the novelty and the appeal of materials, children need attractive and reinforcing materials. At the same time, they need responsive teaching—that is, teachers must elaborate on a child's behaviour and follow the child's lead. For example, a child may indicate a desire to participate in an activity by watching others and reaching toward a paint container. The teacher can position the child so that he or she can touch the paint container, and move the brush so that it makes contact with the child's hand (Fox et al., 1994).

Novelty is important in engagement. The best way to introduce a novel element is to embed it in a familiar routine or behaviour. For example, if the teacher always asks the child, "Give me a cup," and then changes it to "Give me a big cup," the child will focus on "big." As well, individualized materials are a powerful tool for increasing children's engagement levels. Activities such as music, dramatic play, art, carpentry, and water play are engaging activities.

Another variable related to engagement is the provision of opportunities for children to make choices. In general, children pay much more attention to objects they choose themselves. There is extensive research to support the view that increased opportunities for choice can increase participation and performance and decrease problem behaviour (e.g., Bannerman et al., 1990).

Imitation

Imitation the ability of the child to match or copy a model.

Imitation involves a child's ability to match or copy the verbal or nonverbal behaviour of a model (Bailey & Wolery, 1984). Starting from an early age, almost all children imitate. They imitate almost everyone—their parents, their older brothers and sisters, friends, playmates, television characters, and so on. They spend hours playing dress-up as daddy, the doctor, and the fireman. All of these are forms of imitation.

Imitation or modelling requires children to attend to specific demonstrated behaviour; to retain the information presented; to execute the modelled behaviour; and to be motivated to perform the behaviour. Imitation has two defining characteristics: it must duplicate the behaviour shown by the model, and it must be selective. The imitative response must occur after a particular behaviour by the model and not under a large number of other stimulus conditions.

Deferred imitation the repetition of an act seen at an earlier time.

Imitation may be immediate or deferred (i.e., delayed). ***Deferred imitation*** is the repetition of an act seen at an earlier time. Children mimic a behaviour pattern that they witnessed a day or two before but did not then perform themselves. Imitation is well in place by seven or eight months and becomes more frequent and more complex in the next several years. Delayed imitation is in place by the end of the first year—in Piaget's terms, at the end of the sensorimotor period, around the time symbolic play appears. Delayed imitation and symbolic play are related, as both require representational thought.

We must distinguish between learning to imitate and learning by imitation. *Learning by imitation* assumes that the child already knows how to imitate and uses imitation skills either to learn new behaviours or to learn how to adapt and apply previously learned behaviours. In *learning to imitate*, the child acquires the capacity to match his or her behaviour to that of a model (Parton, 1976).

Children with disabilities do not automatically imitate their non-disabled peers. For one thing, many children with severe handicaps must be taught how to imitate. Even then, there will be little imitation unless teachers structure the environment to encourage it. As well, when a child is disabled, any imitative behaviour may have to be systematically reinforced.

Specific strategies can be used to teach and facilitate imitation in early childhood settings. An important first strategy is to imitate the child. As training continues, teachers provide assistance as necessary to facilitate imitation, such as a mirror, and make imitation a rewarding experience. The adult can cradle the child, rock back and forth, and talk about the action. A large mirror provides feedback on the child's reactions. As well, children learn to imitate functional skills (such as the use of a comb).

Object permanence

Earlier in this text we discussed object permanence and its importance to the development of sophisticated play behaviours. We pointed out that the development of object permanence is essential to all cognitive, language, and social skills. It is a foundation for further cognitive milestones; the co-ordination of visual and motor functions forms the basis for later cognitive development in normally developing children.

Object permanence involves children's ability to realize that both physical objects and social ones (i.e., people) exist even when they cannot hear, touch, or see them. The following activities promote object permanence:

- Place a music box under a pillow.
- Play peek-a-boo behind a towel.
- Have the child find an object hidden behind a screen, then behind two screens.
- Have the child hide things in sand for others to find.
- Lose a toy in the sand and then ask, "Can you find it?"

Turn taking

Turn taking begins with teacher and child passing items back and forth as they are used. The following steps introduce this activity:

- Structure an activity for give and take.
- Follow the child's lead.
- Imitate the child.
- Wait for the child to take a turn.
- Signal the child to take a turn.
- Turn take on responses (MacDonald & Gillette, 1986).

Puzzles teach children many kinds of problem solving skills.

Means-end behaviour *learning to use objects and activities to accomplish a goal. Involves purposeful problem-solving using both objects and people. The ability to separate the procedures (means) for solving a problem from the goal (ends) of the solved problem.*

Means-end behaviour   ***Means-end behaviour*** refers to learning to use objects and activities to accomplish a goal. It involves purposeful problem-solving using both objects and people. It is the ability of the child to separate the procedures (means) for solving a problem from the goal (ends) of the solved problem (Bailey & Wolery, 1984).

When children use means-end behaviour, they repeat actions with a plausible outcome. Object manipulation, such as pulling a toy, is an example of means-end behaviour. So is when a teacher shows a child how to insert a puzzle piece: "If you turn the piece this way, it will go in."

Causality   ***Causality***, another foundation of cognitive skills, can be defined as children's recognition that events have causes—that behaviour can produce changes in objects (Bailey & Wolery, 1984, p. 165).

Causality children's recognition of causes for interesting events, particularly the child's realization that behaviour can produce changes in objects.

Switches and battery-operated toys are very useful for teaching simple cause-and-effect relationships, as well as for improving motor control and co-ordination. Cause-and-effect relationships provide answers to questions such as, "What will happen if ...?" and "Why does ... happen?"

PROGRESS CHECK 5

Explain how you would help a child with a severe disability to learn to imitate a wave.

PROGRESS CHECK 6

Make sure you can define or describe all the terms in Table 14–1.

TABLE 14–1: New terms and ideas

categorization
causality
cognition
cognitive development
concept
creativity
deferred imitation
engagement
imitation
means-end behaviour
precocious
talent

SUMMARY

1. Cognition refers to the many ways that humans gain knowledge through perception, memory, and thought processing. Cognition includes learning, remembering, categorizing, and organizing.

2. It is almost impossible to separate cognitive development from language and socio-emotional development in early childhood. Sensorimotor and other cognitive skills do not develop separately; their acquisition relates to the areas of social, motor, and language development.

3. As humans, we tend to think in concepts, not in scattered bits of information. A concept is a way of organizing information so that it is applicable to similar objects and events as well as to specific ones. Many concepts are learned through observation and experience.

4. Mediators facilitate a child's thought processes and problem-solving strategies.

5. Early programming for potentially gifted children serves as an opportunity to nurture high potential and encourage gifted children to develop their strengths.

6. Gifted children learn more, more rapidly, and more widely than their normally developing peers. One characteristic often seen in potentially gifted young children is advanced language skills. A group of children who are especially interesting are early readers—those who learn to read in preschool.

7. Children who are gifted require special projects, curriculum units, and questioning techniques. Their curricula need to include social and personal as well as academic goals.

8. Those taking an emergent literacy perspective do not separate literacy from other components of learning; rather, they view literacy as a natural part of the child's total development. Children learn many things about reading before they actually learn to read. They practise many other ways of using symbols before they come to understand the use of word symbols in reading.

9. To play and learn appropriately, a child must first be attentive. Engagement refers to active and prolonged participation in appropriate activities. Engagement depends on both the novelty and the appeal of materials in the environment.

10. Other important concepts in cognitive development are imitation, object permanence, turn taking, means-end behaviour, and causality.

CHAPTER 15
Promoting Skills in Speech and Language

CASE STUDY

Martin

Martin stamped his foot in frustration, picked up a small stuffed toy and hurled it against the wall, and then stalked off to a table and put his head down. For the next hour he sat there, cutting himself off from the teachers and the activities of the class despite repeated cajoling to join in.

No one was angry with Martin. But he was very angry with himself. Martin tries to talk and communicate, and the teachers try to understand him; when they can't, he lashes out in frustration. In recent months his outbursts have become more frequent and more intense. His peers have begun to avoid him, and his teachers and parents are becoming increasingly concerned.

Martin is almost four. He appears to be developing normally in the motor areas but his speech and language are lagging quite far behind other four-year-olds. He consistently adds syllables to words and mispronounces or substitutes the initial consonants. He is rather slow to speak, and when he does speak he often has difficulty recalling the words to use. He has problems with sequencing and cannot tell or repeat a small story in the correct order. He also shows gaps in his concept development. In a sorting game matching "hot" and "cold," for example, Martin could not sort the pictures correctly.

The teachers are well aware that Martin cannot yet be expected to have mastered all the sounds of English. But they also realize that his speech shows many deviations from that of a normally developing four-year-old. They are concerned about his language development and his delays in syntax, vocabulary, and sentence length and complexity. An additional problem is Martin's withdrawn behaviour and his growing tendency to sit alone and refuse to interact with the teachers, join in group activities, or play with peers.

The supervisor referred Martin to a speech/language therapist in order to obtain some details of his present levels of functioning in speech and language and to find out the best methods for assisting him. The therapist undertook an assessment that included speech and language development as well as cognitive functioning. She began by investigating the milestones in Martin's language development. To do this, she discussed Martin's progress with the staff and interviewed the mother. In her formal assessment of Martin's speech and language, the therapist assessed phonetic and articulatory language, morphology, and syntax. She also observed Martin interacting with the other children and recorded his linguistic behaviour, and later evaluated the information in terms of the speech and language that would be expected from a child of his age. Finally, she assessed his cognitive skills.

Broadly, the full assessment indicated that Martin is a child of normal intelligence who is demonstrating serious lags in speech and language. He may be said to have a *language delay* rather than a language disorder. This means that his language is developing in a normal sequence, but at a much slower rate than would be expected. Martin also shows a number of deviations in his speech. Some of these are attributable to his slow processing of language—he simply mixes up the message he wants to express. Others are due to his slower development in using the sounds of English.

Many of the minor speech deviations may be expected to correct naturally as Martin matures. It is his language delay that is of greatest concern at this time. Teachers must also worry about the development of an emotional overlay—an adverse reaction to learning difficulties. Martin's withdrawal and lack of interaction only compounds the language delay.

To help Martin develop stronger communication competence, the mother, the therapist, the psychologist, the centre supervisor, and the staff have devised an IPP for him that stresses development in both speech and language. (An extract from Martin's IPP is shown in Box 15–4). Training will take place in the natural environment, and the first priority will be to arrange that environment so that Martin will be in a position to use and respond to communication from adults and peers. Throughout the daily program, Martin will be exposed to as much natural conversation as possible.

THE ACQUISITION OF SPEECH AND LANGUAGE is a major learning experience for young children. While language development is a lifelong process, all the major developmental milestones are reached in infancy and the early childhood years.

Language acquisition is one of the most complex learning tasks children will ever undertake. Yet most children accomplish this task with ease. Normally developing children learn the essentials of their language at a very early age. By the time they are three, most children have developed an array of conversational skills that enable them to engage in extensive social and play interactions with their peers and others in the environment. The language explosion that occurs in the preschool years is most apparent in the growth of vocabulary—from about 50 words at 18 months to 200 words at age two, to between 8,000 and 14,000 words at age six (Carey, 1978). This means that between two and six, the average child learns between six and ten words a day.

Learning to communicate and understand the communication of others is one of the biggest challenges young children face. It is little surprise, then, that delays and disorders in speech and language are the most common and varied disabilities that teachers of young children will encounter. The percentage of preschoolers with speech and language problems ranges from 5 to 20 percent (Alberto, Davis, & Prentice, 1995).

Teachers will see children with phonological or articulation disorders, or with voice problems, or who stutter, or who have delayed or deviant language, or who have difficulties in expressive or receptive modes. Most often, these problems will be seen in combination. Speech and language difficulties may also spill over to affect other areas of functioning (Martin's reactions are fairly characteristic). Preschool children with limited communication skills are more likely to shorten their responses and to use nonverbal responses; they also tend to initiate communication with adults rather than other children (Rice, Sell, & Hadley, 1991). Because of the negative feedback they have received in the past, children with speech problems may talk only when absolutely necessary; they would rather respond with a shake of the head or a shrug. Also, children who are not successful in communication, such as Martin, often demonstrate negative, resistant, or attention-getting behaviour (Owens, 1991).

Speech and language problems often are associated with other conditions. For many young children with other disabilities, learning to communicate is not a simple or a naturally occurring task. Among these children, lacks in speech and language development are probably the most obvious deficits that early childhood teachers will see.

Nurturing competence and confidence in language is critically important in the early years, and it is imperative that serious speech and language difficulties be addressed as early as possible. The use of language is closely tied to cognitive

Language problems a range of difficulties with the linguistic code, or with the rules for linking the symbols and the symbol sequences.

Content the linguistic representation of what a person knows about the world of objects, events, and relations.

Form phonology, morphology, and syntax.

development and self-concept. Speech and language problems can impair a child's functioning in play and with peers and result in the development of secondary behavioural problems. As well, unresolved difficulties will hinder a child's future progress. Speech and language difficulties disrupt social relationships. They are strong predictors of school failure (Glascoe, 1995), and may indicate more pervasive disorders such as intellectual disability (Rescorla, 1989). Competence with language has a direct impact on a child's ability to learn to read and write later (Polloway & Smith, 1982).

Teachers look for strategies to teach communication to *all* young children, including those with disabilities, those from non–English speaking families, those who are lagging in development, and those who are preverbal. However, it is not yet clear which strategies for teaching communication are the most effective. Teachers use a wide array of procedures: singing, saying rhymes, holding the child while talking, imitating noises, and playing the many different games adults play with small children. Skilled teachers use descriptive feedback, directing, telling and explaining, question asking, modelling, and prompts and coaching statements. When necessary, they use teacher-mediated and peer-mediated strategies and direct teaching. They rearrange the environment and extend classroom routines. They use child-cued modelling, manding and modelling, time delay, and incidental teaching (Rogers-Warren & Warren, 1984).

BOX 15–1

Speech and language difficulties

Communication disorders are among the most common symptoms of developmental impairment in preschool children. An estimated 5 to 20 percent of children have communication disorders (Caplan, 1985).

Language problems encompass a range of difficulties with the linguistic code—that is, with the rules and concepts for linking symbols and symbol sequences. Language problems can affect a child's ability to recognize and understand spoken language, and to formulate correct sentences.

Content refers to the linguistic representation of what a person knows about the world of objects, events, and relations. Children with content deficiencies are well below age level in

expressive language and may demonstrate weak concept development. Children have a tendency to deal with objects or events in wholes rather than parts. They use overextensions—for example, they may call every animal they see a "doggie."

Form refers to phonology, morphology, and syntax, Children with difficulties relating to form may show restricted language and a reliance on gestures rather than speech. Children with syntax difficulties may use shorter and less complex sentences than their age mates. The vocabulary used by these children tends to be small, superficial, and reflective of weak development of underlying concepts.

Use refers to the functions of language (pragmatics). Children with problems here will talk about things out of order, produce rambling and repetitive utterances, and make unrelated statements. They tend to be more rigid and literal in their thinking: they lack the flexibility required for pretending, for playing word games, for laughing at riddles and jokes,

Use functions of language.

In this chapter we examine some aspects of speech and language development and discuss the consequences of deficits in these areas. We offer many strategies to improve the communicative competence of children with mild and moderate speech and language problems. For children with severe disabilities, who may be at prelinguistic or minimally linguistic levels, we also present various strategies that are effective in initiating or stimulating communication.

Language development

Speech disorders problems encountered in the oral production of language that interfere with communication.

Communication the transmission of information.

In all the enormous repertoire of human skills and abilities, communication is one of the most critical. In the broadest sense, *communication* is the transmission of information. Humans use communication to meet needs and desires, control environmental events, establish social relationships, and learn new skills and concepts.

At a simple level, human communication may be seen as consisting of three main parts, which are closely related. First, there is *language*, which may be defined as a rule-governed system that includes semantics, syntax, morphology, and pragmatics (the social use of language). We need a means to express language. For most people *speech* is the usual medium of expressive language—it and for effective social interaction.

Speech disorders are problems in the oral production of language that interfere with communication. Speech is impaired when it is ungrammatical, culturally or personally unsatisfying, or injurious to the speech-producing mechanisms (Perkins, 1977). There are many different types of speech problems; generally, they are classified as follows: phonological and articulatory problems; voice disorders; orofacial or structural problems; and problems of dysfluency.

It is difficult to separate phonological and articulation problems. Children with phonological impairments are often capable of producing the correct sounds but fail to do so consistently or when called for. They are aware of the effect of their errors on the listener's comprehension and will make adjustments to enhance verbal comprehension (Owens, 1991).

Articulatory disorders are characterized by omissions, substitutions, distortions, and additions of speech sounds. Omission errors refer to the leaving out of sounds in words, such as by substituting *pay* for *play*. Substitution errors occur when one consonant is replaced by another, such as *twick* for *trick*. Distortions involve deviations from normal speech sounds. For example, a lisp affects sibilant sounds such as the /s/ and /z/ sounds. Addition errors refer to the adding of a sound to a word. The extra sounds are usually added between blended sounds, such as *terain* for *train* (Winzer, 1996).

Voice disorders include voices that are too high, too low, too loud, too soft, or too nasal. Orofacial (structural) problems are often the result of different types of clefts. A child with a cleft of the lip and/or palate may encounter problems with swallowing, mastication, and correct respiration. Slow language development and delayed articulation are not uncommon in children with clefts.

Dysfluency refers to stuttering. Stuttering affects the rate and rhythm of speech and is characterized by blocking, repetition, or prolongation of sounds, words, phrases, or syllables.

is the sound system we use to express language. Speech is not the sole means for expressing language; many deaf people, for example, express language through a sign system. The third component of language is referred to as paralinguistics, which roughly means "beside language." Paralinguistics includes such things as stress, intonation, pauses, gestures, body language, our dress, and how physically close we are to others when we communicate (see Figure 15–1).

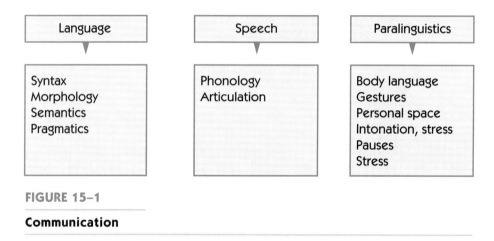

FIGURE 15–1

Communication

Language   a rule-governed system that includes semantics, syntax, morphology, and pragmatics (the social use of language).

Speech   the usual medium of expressive language.

Speech and language development begins at the moment of birth and evolves from nonverbal communication. Tiny infants quickly learn to produce sounds such as gurgling and cooing. They soon differentiate their cries so that they have an "I'm hungry" cry, a "Pick me up" cry, an "I'm bored" cry, an "I'm wet" cry, and so on. These early differentiated cries, together with smiling and eye-to-eye gazing, constitute the beginning of pragmatics, the social use of language. Infants attend to speech from a very early age and learn to respond to familiar voices.

Language is fundamentally a social behaviour, and communicative behaviour is always interactive. The quality of adult/child interactions is the single most important influence on a child's language development. Infants acquire early language through social interaction; the way parents speak to babies is believed to lay the foundation for language development.

By about six months, infants have begun to imitate the voiced sounds made by those around them. They engage in babbling—random sound play of almost infinite variety. At nine or ten months, they begin to imitate adults consistently. Children at this age produce intonation patterns similar to adult speech; they are able to reproduce the intonation patterns or melodies of the language they hear. In another six months they move to using single words (holophrasic speech).

The first meaningful speech of toddlers consists of single-word utterances about the world they know. They will not comment on taxes, wars, or the state of the economy, but they will mention familiar foods, people, clothing, and routines (Owens, 1988). Most children pass the major milestone in language development—the construction of simple sentences—at the end of their second year. At the same time, they begin to become increasingly aware of listeners' needs for information, and are soon able to communicate with people outside the immediate family.

Between the third and fourth years, language is established in all its main forms. By this time, children can speak about things and events that are distant in time and space; they are able to describe events of the past and expectations of the future as well as present experiences. By the age of four, most children have achieved a great deal of language maturity. By the time they arrive at school, they have a firm linguistic base—that is, a sophisticated grasp of semantic and syntactic rules, and an ever-expanding vocabulary. By age six, children are sophisticated language users. They can not only talk better, but they have become aware of how language is used. Six-year-old children can recognize the nuances of language, and begin to take delight in jokes and riddles that rely on ambiguity (Winzer, 1996).

In the early years, it is difficult to separate speech acquisition from language acquisition. Do keep in mind, however, that speech is a mechanical production of language: language can exist without speech, but speech cannot exist without language. In young children, speech acquisition is orderly and is closely associated with chronological age and with physical and intellectual maturation.

Speech development depends on having something to say (language) and the opportunity to say it (social interaction). It also depends on the development of the speech mechanisms and articulators: the pharynx and larynx, the tongue, the palate, the lips, and the teeth. The production and modulation of breath flow is also important to speech production.

There is a progression in development of language sounds, and many of the errors made by young children are part of the developmental process. Although four-year-olds are more than 90 percent intelligible in their speech, children do not develop all the sounds of English until later. Many preschool children have difficulty with /r/, /s/, /j/, and /z/, and with blends such as /ch/ and /sh/, which may not be perfected until about age eight. The last English sound that most children acquire is the /zh/, as in *leisure* and *measure*.

> **PROGRESS CHECK 1**
>
> Outline the major stages in children's language development. Stress form (syntax and morphology), content (semantics), and use (pragmatics).

Children with speech and language problems

Children show great variability in their speech and language acquisition and development. For children with communication exceptionalities, speech and language skill levels fall outside what could be considered normal parameters. These youngsters encounter difficulties in acquiring and using speech and language.

A child's language is delayed when there are problems in the formation, expression, or understanding of language. A child who has a ***language delay*** is lagging behind others of the same chronological age; a four-year-old may have the semantic (vocabulary) development of a three-year-old and the morphological and syntactical skills of an even younger child. The child may demonstrate poor concepts, an inability to follow directions, lack of speech, speech confusion, poor word comprehension, or restricted vocabulary. Martin, the child in the opening case study, shows a language delay.

Language delay the child is lagging behind others of the same chronological age.

Some children with language delays catch up to their peers as they mature; others respond well to early intervention. However, some children with language delays may not close the gap. These children show such difficulties in developing language in a normal progression that they may never attain adult levels.

Language disorders are far more complex than language delays; they are also much more difficult to remediate. Children with **_language disorders_** may have the rudiments of a language code and may comprehend language more easily than they produce it, but they show large gaps in linguistic development and display little consistency in their various deficits (Winzer, 1989). Language disorders may manifest themselves in speech, either at the phonological or grammatical level; in the comprehension of specific concepts or of language structures; or in some combination of these areas (Winzer, 1989).

Young children make speech errors when learning to talk: mispronunciations and dysfluencies are common. Mispronunciations become speech disorders when they persist as characteristics in the speech of older children. Other speech disorders are seen when children lag very far behind normal development, when there are other problems such as with the voice, or when the lags affect a child's functioning and self-concept. Speech and language disorders and their effects are summarized in Table 15–1.

> Language disorders children show large gaps in linguistic development and display little consistency in their various deficits.

TABLE 15–1: **Effects of communication disorders**

Problem	Signs	Effects
Language	More than six months behind norms in reaching language milestones.	Slower in all elements of language acquisition and use.
Language disorders	May show impaired comprehension and poor verbal expression.	May not develop language in the usual sequence; fails to understand instructions; withdraws from group situations.
Articulation disorders	Abnormal production of speech sounds; speech not typical of chronological age.	May be ridiculed by peers; may have decoding and comprehension problems with respect to specific words.
Expressive problems	Difficulty in expressing language.	Hesitations, long pauses, repetitions, forgets words.
Fluency	Impaired fluency and rhythm.	Peer ridicule, oral difficulties.
Receptive problems	Difficulty in comprehending language.	Can't follow directions; can't sequence a story.
Voice disorders	Abnormal vocal quality, pitch, loudness, or duration.	Self-confidence may suffer; withdrawal.
Orofacial defects	Variety of clefts, such as cleft lip or cleft palate.	May have problems in feeding, speech, or respiration.

Source: Margret Winzer (1996). Reprinted with permission of the publisher.

CHILDREN WITH DISABILITIES

Problems in speech and language are considered to be a specific category of exceptional conditions. As well, speech and language problems cut across other areas. Many if not most children with other disabling conditions also show speech and language problems that further hinder their development. Some children with disabilities have only minor delays in speech and language. Children with more serious disabilities may not possess a linguistic repertoire at all, or may only have limited communication skills.

Children with mental retardation acquire language more slowly than normally developing children, although they follow the same general path in acquiring it. For example, studies suggest that the language development of Down syndrome children is quite similar to that of normal children (Tager-Flusberg et al., 1990). However, their language levels typically remain below those of normally developing children and are often below their own general mental age.

Children with mental retardation demonstrate delays in sentence length, sentence complexity, and speech sound discrimination. Their expressive language tends to be less complex, and some children have difficulty generalizing the rules of grammar. They do not gain as much information from verbal or nonverbal receptive language, and they do not decipher affective facial expressions as well as their peers (Adams & Markham, 1991).

Blindness poses an interesting linguistic challenge. In blind children, the hearing and speaking apparatus is intact, but the visual medium through which children form many of their real-world experiences is missing. Some researchers feel that blind children show lower language function than normal children; others hold that young blind children acquire vocabulary in the same way as sighted children, though there may be some differences in the percentage of words in each classification. As part of their information gathering, visually impaired children tend to ask more questions than other children (Erin, 1986).

Deafness and severe hearing impairments pose linguistic challenges both to the child and to the teacher. Speech and language are the areas most severely affected by a hearing impairment. In the case of severe hearing disabilities, children are impaired because of a primary dysfunction in a single aspect of the communication system. The physiological problem—lack of hearing—then spills over to affect other aspects of the system, further impairing the child's ability to learn and use language and to acquire speech.

Children with congenital hearing loss do not have the opportunity to practise the listening skills essential for developing speech and language. Here, however, the speech and language problems of individual children vary considerably. The relevant factors include the degree of hearing loss, the training and use of residual hearing, family dynamics, and the age of onset of the impairment. Children who acquire a hearing impairment after they develop speech and language may find it easier to develop communication skills; the later in life an impairment occurs, the greater the child's linguistic capabilities are likely to be (Winzer, 1996).

Children with physical disabilities may have motor disabilities that make intelligible speech impossible. The receptive language of these children may be far ahead of their expressive language so that they understand far more than they can express.

Children who are severely and multiply disabled find it very difficult to acquire the complex symbol system of language without enough sensory data to make language meaningful. They tend to remain at early stages of communication development for long periods of time.

The central role of language deficits and cognitive factors in infantile autism is well documented. For children with autism, adjustment is greatly hindered by their lacks in language. These children show deviant patterns in the quality and pattern of their language, not just language delays. Many children with autism seem to lack any knowledge of language or its uses. They demonstrate atypical language; echolalia is the most frequently cited language characteristic of individuals with autism who are verbal. Echolaliac children may repeat whole sentences parrot fashion.

ASSESSING LANGUAGE AND SPEECH

The issue of assessment for language proficiency in preschool and kindergarten is controversial. The major debate is simply this: Do we or do we not assess?

Those who argue against early language assessment point out that many children show minor delays in language development owing to general immaturity, and that some of these children will catch up to their peers without special intervention. They believe that the emphasis should be on language enrichment rather than assessment and remediation.

Others contend that many children do not catch up unless specific strategies to improve language and speech are implemented. They say we must identify delays and disorders early, because these negatively affect social integration, educational and personal achievement, and other areas of development. Many language delays can be identified by age two, and many speech and language impairments may be correctable within two years (Glascoe, 1991).

Even those who agree with early assessment point out the difficulties. Robert Owens Jr. (1991) describes language evaluation as "part science and part art" (p. 290). This relates to the age of the subjects, the variability in their functioning, the vast range of areas to be assessed, a relative shortage of appropriate tools, and the many possible settings for assessment. Communication should be assessed in multiple contexts and should sample from or include all settings in which the child normally has opportunities to communicate. Further, the types of measures used, the domains sampled, and the targeted skills are quite different for children with mild delays than for those who are functioning at prelinguistic or minimally linguistic levels.

Speech and language problems are generally assessed by a team comprising a psychologist, a speech clinician or therapist, a physician, and possibly an educator or a neurologist. A comprehensive assessment will consider some or all of the following:

- The case history. This gathers all pertinent developmental or behavioural data and usually involves an interview with the family.

- Any physical and psychological disturbances to normal language development. Before an assessment can proceed, these must first be ruled out. Assessment often includes a hearing test and perhaps an examination of the oral mechanisms.

- Receptive language comprehension: Does the child respond appropriately to gestures, words, short and complex sentences? Does the child understand songs and stories?

- Expressive language and vocabulary: Does the child use gestures, noises, jargon, baby talk, vocabulary, concrete and abstract words?

- Parts of speech: sentences and the mean length of utterance (mlu), simple and complex meaning, logical sequence, and range of ideas.

- Semantics. Semantics assessment focuses on determining a child's receptive and expressive vocabularies.

- Pragmatics. The pragmatic (social) functions of language are assessed to establish how children use their communication in social interactions.

- Auditory processing. This is concerned with the nature of the incoming auditory signal. Discrimination is especially important here.

- Articulation. Articulation assessment is a rapid and effective way of obtaining a sample of a child's speech. In its crudest form, the articulation test is a test of the child's ability to pronounce a certain number of words correctly. Articulation tests use picture-naming responses and typically test each consonant in the initial, medial, and final positions. Clinicians also try to determine whether there is a consistency in the child's error patterns. Children under four are usually tested in their ability to echo or imitate the clinician's model; children over four are usually asked to name either objects or pictures, to read words or sentences, or to describe objects.

- Fluency (i.e., the presence of stuttering or cluttering).

- Voice quality (i.e., the presence of unusual pitch or nasality).

Children with severe disabilities have problems imitating, responding to interactions, and using basic communication; thus, assessment focuses largely on prelinguistic communication behaviour. For children with severe disabilities, the assessment process combines ecological and developmentally based approaches. A speech and language assessment will examine the following:

- The child's understanding of sounds and gestures. This means observing the child's responses to environmental sounds, speech sounds, gestures, names, and requests.

- How the child uses communication. The therapist looks at how the child manipulates and interacts with the environment using speech and nonspeech means. Communication use includes how the child gains the attention of others, initiates play with caregivers and peers, and interacts in routine communication events, and whether the child anticipates and takes turns.

- The child's purposes for communication. It is essential to start by identifying the child's specific communication needs. To this end, the settings, people, and purposes for communication must be considered. Needs and interests are assessed by looking at the reasons for the child to communicate, the objects and activities the child prefers, and when and with whom the most appropriate interactions occur.

- Alternative methods of communication. These are discussed later in this chapter.

Another group of children who need specific language assessment are those who have serious hearing impairments or who are deaf. Clinicians assessing children with hearing impairments examine the following:

- The form, content, and use of language.
- The progress of speech development.
- The most appropriate communication mode for the child and the family. We return to this later in the chapter.

Given the complex and multifaceted nature of speech and language assessment, it is little wonder that a range of tools, measures, and informal procedures are used. To assess a child's language and speech, teachers and clinicians may use one or more of the methods listed below, depending on the data needed. General measures include the following:

- Formal tests. These are used to evaluate the child's language abilities and disabilities. Standardized language tests are available for both screening and diagnosis. They usually include normative data that indicate how children of various ages might be expected to perform. Children who perform below a certain score on a screening test are given further testing. There are only a limited number of standardized tests available for preschoolers (see Table 15–2).

TABLE 15–2: Assessing language

Measure	Age	Type	Subtests
Clinical Evaluation of Language Fundamentals–Preschool (CELF-Preschool) (Wiig, Secord, & Semel, 1993)	Preschool	Broad range of expressive and receptive language skills.	Basic concepts formulating labels, linguistic concepts, sentence structure, recalling sentences in context, word structure.
Peabody Picture Test (Dunn & Dunn, 1981)	2–6 to adult.	Receptive test.	
Preschool Language Scale (Zimmerman, Sheener, & Pond, 1979, 1993)	Preschool (1 to 8 years)	Individual scores for receptive and expressive language.	Individual administration.
Sequenced Inventory of Communication Development (Hedrick, Pratter, & Tobin, 1975)		Individual scores for receptive and expressive language.	
Test of Early Language Development (Arsick, Reid, & Hammill, 1990)	3 to 7 years	Language use, content, and form.	Individual administration.

- Observations of children's performance in spontaneous discourse. Teachers have many opportunities to listen to a child's language. Listening to what children say helps parents and teachers understand how they are processing information and how they are thinking and problem solving. Teachers can pick up certain warning signs in children's development just by listening. Thus, a child who is still overgeneralizing by using "doggie" for all dogs may well have problems in language development. In the same way, teachers can pinpoint speech problems. One strategy here is to make a tape recording or daily written record of exactly what the child says and compare this with the words he or she is trying to say. With this information, the teacher can prepare a list of the substitutions, omissions, or other problems in the child's speech.

- Language sampling. This is a type of direct observation. The objective is to collect a representative sample of the child's language and communication skills in natural settings. A spontaneous or elicited language sample consists of at least 50 and preferably 100 utterances, which are transcribed and analysed against normal language-acquisition norms.

- Checklists. These provide broad estimates of the child's functioning in speech and language. A sample checklist is shown in Table 15–3.

TABLE 15–3: Language checklist

Item	Yes	No
• Vocabulary is restricted largely to simple nouns, with a few verbs and the little words such as "the" and "but." Lacks content as expressed in adjectives, adverbs, and prepositions.	☐	☐
• Words and phrases are used but few proper sentences.	☐	☐
• Few pronouns used.	☐	☐
• Does not have much content to express; the themes the child talks about are very simple and unchanging (e.g., home and present activities).	☐	☐
• Asks only simple questions.	☐	☐
• Questions are often inaccurate or vague.	☐	☐
• The order of words used in sentences is jumbled, or words are so out of normal sequence that their meaning is impaired.	☐	☐
• Difficulty relating sequential events.	☐	☐
• Comments are often off topic.	☐	☐
• Disjointed conversational style, to a degree unusual for age and developmental level.	☐	☐
• Fails to use greetings and farewells appropriately.	☐	☐
• Shows little grasp of spoken instructions.	☐	☐
• Inattentive when listening to instructions.	☐	☐
• Looks constantly to peers and staff for visual clues.	☐	☐
• Poor memory for names.	☐	☐
• Difficulty comprehending new words and concepts.	☐	☐
• Has difficulty concentrating on a brief story, even when it is read individually	☐	☐
• Shows little grasp of the ideas expressed in simple picture stories.	☐	☐
• Lack of communication with peers.	☐	☐

Item	Yes	No
• Withdrawal or exclusion from group activities that require discussion, co-operation, or planning.	☐	☐
• Mispronounces sounds and words.	☐	☐
• Production of speech sounds in words is so unclear that he or she has marked problems in communicating with staff and peers.	☐	☐
• Uses few words.	☐	☐
• Points a lot.	☐	☐
• Speaks quietly.	☐	☐
• Uses nonverbal signals instead of speech.	☐	☐
• Omits small unemphasized words.	☐	☐
• The child has social problems or is clearly frustrated.	☐	☐

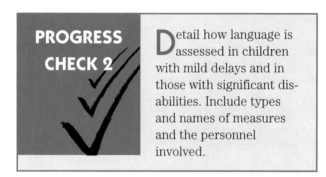

PROGRESS CHECK 2

Detail how language is assessed in children with mild delays and in those with significant disabilities. Include types and names of measures and the personnel involved.

TARGETING SKILLS

Language is made up of different elements, all of which must develop in tandem if a child is to achieve communicative competence. The main problem confronting teachers of young children with speech and language problems is determining which skills to assess and which to target for intervention. Children may require training in *all* aspects of understanding and expression. But the very complexity of language makes it almost impossible to target and teach everything that a language-impaired child needs to become a competent communicator. As well, the child may become confused if there are too many training targets.

For children with mild disabilities, the purposes of intervention are two: to teach a repertoire of linguistic skills that can be used for communicating in socially appropriate ways; and to stimulate overall language development (Warren & Kaiser, 1986a). The language development of normally developing children can guide the selection of training targets.

For children with severe or multiple disabilities, the communication skills to be targeted should be guided by a number of general principles:

- Teachers should find an appropriate balance between developmental and functional communication targets. In improving children's functional language, the first step is to identify their specific communication needs. Then teachers identify targets, and everyday situations relevant to those targets. Eating, dressing, and bathing are all daily living activities that provide relevant situations for preschoolers who are severely impaired to develop functional language.

- Language intervention should begin with the precursors to language. Children who are communicating at a level below age two have unique needs in language development. Often the goal of intervention is to initiate effective communication.

- For prelinguistic children, activities in the immediate environment form the basis for communication training (Owens, 1991). Since language is learned in a social environment, the centre should provide good linguistic models, and many opportunities for children to practise their skills. The best results are achieved when language training consists of continuous intervention in all naturally occurring activities and settings. Throughout the day, teachers should target present communication and presymbolic and symbolic behaviour within natural communication environments.

- Most training should be done in natural environments. For children with more severe deficits in speech and language, formal language training may involve brief lessons a few times a day. However, communication training with severely impaired children need not, and should not, be restricted to one-to-one therapy sessions.

- Generalization of training must be carefully planned.

- Activities should contain multiple components. For example, painting provides at least three opportunities for communication: obtaining access to the paint, the water, and the brush.

- Activities should lend themselves to repetitive action. When the child desires repeated actions by the caregiver, there are repeated opportunities for language use. Examples of repetitive activities include playing catch and being pushed on a swing.

LANGUAGE TRAINING

In a preschool setting, procedures for addressing speech and language difficulties are applied to two distinct groups of children: those with severe disabilities, and those with mild or moderate communication delays. These two groups receive different types of communication training (Bailey & Wolery, 1984). Children with mild disabilities may require only minor accommodations, such as more frequent repetition of the same activities with different materials. Children who are severely disabled need structured learning experiences and social intervention; these require staff time and resources.

For both groups of children, the key word in recent language intervention strategies is *natural*. Natural procedures take place in naturally occurring situations and pay attention to functional communication and conversational skills. There are a number of reasons for adopting the natural environment as the setting for language assessment and training:

- Language production is the result of interaction between the skills of the speaker and events in the environment; it follows that language is best taught through social interaction and naturally occurring events.

- A major problem in language training concerns the transfer of learned language from the training setting to the natural environment. Children with language disorders have more difficulty generalizing language skills; thus, it is by no means certain that language learned in clinical settings will generalize to other environments, including natural ones (Spradlin & Siegel, 1982).

- People in the child's natural environment can be the chief intervenors. Teachers and peers facilitate strategies.

- When training occurs in natural settings, it is bound to be functional, and this enhances the likelihood that new language will be maintained and generalized.

- Natural environments promote strategies such as incidental teaching.

- An exception should be noted here: It is possible that syntactic disorders respond best to direct teaching. Direct language instruction might be used at first, to introduce a new structure, which could then be generalized by means of interactive techniques.

Mild delays and disabilities

In our discussion of techniques for language intervention, we have arbitrarily divided children into two groups: those with mild delays, and those who are functioning at prelinguistic or minimally linguistic levels. Do keep in mind that many of the activities for the former group are beneficial for the latter.

The goal of training for children with mild or moderate delays is not absolutely correct grammar or pronunciation. Training should accelerate general communicative development and help young children communicate in a way that is understood by others and that seems comfortable for the child.

The techniques used to facilitate language development in children with mild or moderate disabilities are much the same as those used with normally developing children. Teachers provide the motivation to communicate, many opportunities for teacher/child and child/child interactions, and much peer and adult modelling. They focus on children's interests and create an atmosphere for realistic conversation. They help children use language to promote or regulate social interaction, and they develop the children's listening, attention, and memory skills. They also stress the language arts curriculum of listening, expressive language, and reading readiness.

Environmental arrangements

The first step in communication intervention is to adapt the child's environment. Environmental structuring is important for children who are shy or passive, for those with speech and language problems, and for children with disabilities that also hinder speech and language.

An environment that contains few reinforcers and few objects of interest, or one that meets children's needs without requiring language, is not a functional environment for teaching or learning language. The purpose of environmental intervention is to increase the number of opportunities for language use and to increase children's interest in the environment as an occasion for communication.

Both social and physical aspects of the environment should be considered. Adults mediate by providing a physical environment that allows many opportunities for language. They arrange classrooms so that there are materials and activities of interest to the children. A strong social environment provides many people to participate in formal and informal language interactions. The teachers set the scene, prompt dialogues that children can use with each other, and arrange the setting so that the children must communicate with caregivers to gain access to reinforcing materials or activities (Halle, 1984).

In arranging the environment to foster language development, consider the following:

- Focus on making language a part of children's routines.
- Provide access to interesting materials and activities.
- Create realistic conversational atmospheres where speech is valued.
- Focus on the children's interests.
- Provide many listening experiences.

A strong social environment provides children with many opportunities for language use.

- Provide adult and peer models who will encourage the children to use language, and who will respond to their attempts to do so.
- Establish a contingent relationship between access to materials or assistance and the use of language (Ostrosky & Kaiser, 1991).

Classroom situations, and equipment and materials, can be organized so that their use becomes an occasion for talking. For example:

- Some children may feel more comfortable beginning in a nonverbal mode. To encourage nonverbal co-operative activities, the teacher can suggest that two children work together to prepare for snack or to clean up. Or they can assign children to tasks that require joint effort—for example, moving an item that is too bulky for one person. To encourage fantasy or dramatic play on a nonverbal level, the teacher can begin by showing how to establish the fantasy: "The baby is hungry, Cinta. You can feed her?" (Hurvitz, Pickert, & Rilla, 1987).
- The teacher can provide only one plastic knife for children to share as they make fruit salad, only enough supplies for half the children, or inadequate portions of preferred materials such as blocks or crayons. This prompts language use, as children must request additional materials or share equipment to complete a task.
- The teacher can prompt children to make choices by presenting two or more options.
- The teacher can practise "sabotage"—that is, provide situations that children must problem solve. For example, the child may be given paint but not a paintbrush. A similar strategy is to place some materials out of reach. When materials are in view but out of reach, children will be prompted to make requests in order to receive the material. Or the teacher can create a situation in which children are likely to require assistance—for example, an unopened bottle of bubbles. The effectiveness of this strategy can be enhanced by showing the child the materials,

naming the materials, and then waiting for the child to make requests. Gaining the material is then reinforcing for the child.

- The teacher can provide an obstacle. This is similar to sabotage, but the child must do more planning to solve the problem. For example, ask the child to "Pour some juice," when there is no juice left in the jug. At snack time, give only two of the three needed items, such as a cup and a spoon but no milk. Can the child then remedy the situation or request the missing item?

- The teacher can use silly situations in order to get the child to comment. For example, the teacher tries to put the child's shoe on (Ostrosky & Kaiser, 1991).

- The teacher can provide unexpected situations or responses. For example, consider the following anecdote, provided by Halle (1984). Billy, a three-year-old severely disabled preschooler, is sitting at a table with two other children and a teacher. The teacher holds up a ball and goes around the table asking each child to label it. Billy does not attend or respond to the teacher's request. Next, the teacher introduces a cup and again goes around the table, with similar results. Three more objects are presented, and still Billy does not respond to the teacher's instructions. The next time Billy looks toward the teacher, he notices that the teacher's aide has quietly sneaked behind the teacher and is holding a ball just above the teacher's head without the teacher realizing it. Suddenly Billy smiles, excitedly begins pointing to the teacher, and vocalizes somewhat unintelligibly "ball" (Halle, 1984).

- Free play in the various centres provides many opportunities for commenting systematically, learning new vocabulary, developing concepts and conversational skills, and so on. Lay-Dopyera and Dopyera (1990) suggest that with water play, teachers look for opportunities to use words like *dry, wet, soaked*, and *damp*. With sand play, they can look for opportunities to use words like *damp, dry, sprinkle*, and *pack*. Block play encourages the use of words like *more, fewer, same, tall, taller*, and so on. As well, particular kinds of vocabulary can be encouraged by the kinds of props provided for sand and water play. Funnels, tubes, and containers encourage use of words like *into, out of, through*, and *half-full*. Containers of three different sizes promote discussion of *smallest, middle size, largest, more*, and *less* (Lay-Dopyera & Dopyera, 1990, pp. 289–290)

- Sociodramatic play puts intense demands on children's language abilities; at the same time, it encourages precision in language (Lay-Dopyera & Dopyera, 1990). Here, teachers can enhance language development by arranging play settings so as to encourage the use of newly acquired vocabulary. For example, if the children have just been on a field trip to the fire station, they will probably reenact the experience in play. In the play setting, objects should be available as well as photographs and illustrations of the places visited.

- In pretend play, both normally developing preschoolers and those with disabilities can be taught to enact sociodramatic scripts that provide a basis for interaction.

- Carol Westby (1992) discusses how to use a McDonald's menu to model various language functions using familiar themes. For example:

Requesting	I'd like a hamburger and a chocolate shake.
Directing	I'll get more bags. Please enter Michelle's order on the computer.
Reporting	I put pickles, onions, lettuce, and tomato on your hamburger. I burned myself with the grease from the french fries.
Predicting	There are lots of people here. I think we'll have to wait a long time.
Projecting into other's thoughts and feelings	She's in a hurry. She's mad because I didn't give her the change.
Reasoning	I don't have enough money, so I'll have to borrow some. I can't find a place to sit because there are so many people.

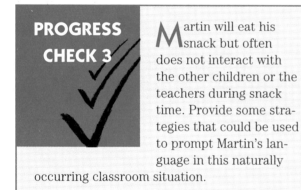

PROGRESS CHECK 3

Martin will eat his snack but often does not interact with the other children or the teachers during snack time. Provide some strategies that could be used to prompt Martin's language in this naturally occurring classroom situation.

Oral language skills Children learn what language *is* by learning what language can *do*. Often, an important first step is to help children control the environment nonverbally; in this way, they learn that language can be used to regulate others. When clear advantages to speaking are apparent, and positive rewards and supporting models are provided, these children will often adopt language for social regulatory purposes. Many activities can be modified so that children who are unwilling or unable to speak can still assume the regulatory role. The important element in regulatory activities is that the child is leading the activity and that the class is responding. Here are some examples of verbal and nonverbal regulatory activities:

- Imitative tasks are an excellent type of nonverbal activity. For example, the child assumes a particular body position that the others must imitate, or makes a block design that the class must copy.

BOX 15–2
Helpful hints

- Listen carefully to what children have to say.
- Remember that preschool children have short attention spans. Keep listening tasks short.
- Be careful with directions; carefully phrase, give directions one at a time, and repeat directions. Avoid using unnecessary words.
- After giving a direction, have the child repeat it to show comprehension.
- Repeat and reword if the child seems confused.
- Relate language to the children's environment. Match the language used to the children's experience. Use words and ideas that convey the children's own interests, needs, and experiences.
- Provide many opportunities for the children to give commands and ask for information.
- Give children opportunities to talk about their experiences.
- Respond to the child's intended message rather than correcting their pronunciation or grammar.
- Make a tape of you telling favourite stories and poems.
- Use rhymes to develop vocabulary.
- Use music, rhymes, and rhythms to encourage children's enjoyment of words.
- Use language in pretend play for different purposes: direction, explanation, prediction.
- Respond in a positive way to children's speech.
- Make children's language part of classroom reading materials. Use made books about shared experiences. Place labels around the classroom and on artwork (as captions).
- When children have severe disabilities, they learn best when the communication results in immediate and potentially reinforcing consequences (Caro & Snell, 1989).

BOX 15–3
Samples of children's regulatory language

	Attention bid	Command	Request for information	Statement of need or desire
leadership	Calling another child's name in order to indicate who should respond to a question, receive a token, or take a turn.	Get mat! You're next! March fast! Sit down! Quiet! Get that one!	Kimberley here today? Who want get juice? Who wants red one? What colour is this? What that?	Want Artis be snack server. Need every body help clean up. Want you go first.

- The child leads circle time by turning on the record player, shaking hands with classmates to greet them, pointing to the child with the next turn, giving out stars for attendance, and directing group songs.
- The child assigns jobs for the day, giving commands such as "Ron, get the mats."
- The child acts as messenger, especially when the recipient of the message is familiar with the meaning to be conveyed (e.g., "need book").
- The child chooses how class members will participate in a particular activity—for example, designating whether boys or girls will be first in line (e.g., "boys first").
- The child holds up pictures to be named and decides who will answer (e.g., making a request for information such as "Donna, what's this?").
- The child leads the group in a movement activity by calling out actions such as "March … Walk … Sit …" (Hurvitz, Pickert, & Rilla, 1987).
- The child leads an activity—for example, acts as a parking attendant in a garage and directs car parking.

Games in which the child directs other people are highly motivating (Owens, 1991).

Besides regulatory language, other aspects of oral (expressive) language should be fostered. Deficits in oral interaction skills prevent children with language problems from participating effectively in discussions, group time, and group projects.

In addition to exposing children to as much natural conversation as possible, teachers can stimulate and improve oral language skills in the following ways:

- By creating the need for speech. For example, if the child uses gestures instead of speech, the teacher can deliberately misinterpret the gesture and prompt speech.

	Attention bid	Command	Request for information	Statement of need or desire
social interaction	Calling another child's name (or saying Hey) in order to maintain social interaction.	Help me tie my shoe! Play here! Play with me!	Can you build it higher? Where ball? Why you cry? What's this?	Want to be your partner. Need paint. Need more.
dramatic play	Calling another child's name or 'pretend' name in order to create or preserve the atmosphere.	Setting: "Caring for baby" You be mommy! Sit down	Setting: "Caring for baby" Hungry? Want bottle? Why you cry?	Setting: "Caring for baby" Want milk. Need more

From Promoting Children's Language Interaction by J.A. Hurvitz, S.M. Pickert, & D.C. Rilla, Teaching Exceptional Children, Vol. 19, 1987, 12-15.
Copyright 1987 by the Council for Exceptional Children.
Reprinted with permission.

- By using daily events and happenings as the basis for comment and conversation. A resourceful teacher can make an exciting language-learning experience out of the most insignificant event—a lost mitten, a new toy, a dripping faucet.

- By modelling good language and pointing out child models. Children whose verbal language is developing slowly, but in normal sequence, will need practice in and models for many items. Modelling closely approximates the language-learning environment of nonimpaired children and is an effective strategy for children with language disabilities.

- By reading and telling stories. Teachers should consider reading the same stories over and over again, and using stories about events familiar to the children. The language should be predictable. For children with disabilities, stories might relate to their experiences with professionals.

- By creating a language book in the form of a diary. Interesting events in the child's life would be recorded. Simple drawings or photos could also be included, to act as prompts when other people read the diary with the child.

- By talking about things that interest the child and getting excited with the child.

- By following the child's lead and replying to the child's initiations or comments. Communication is maintained by conversational responses, not by saying, "Good talking." For example, "I saw monkeys" is related to "Monkeys are funny," not "Good talking" (Owens, 1991).

- By waiting patiently for answers to questions. For children with language problems, teachers should respond to the content rather than the correctness of the language—that is, stress the content of the answer rather than the grammar.

- By using puppets in dramatic play. Use a puppet as a listener; teacher is the prompter. Have the puppet request clarification, more information, or more complex sentences.

- By using expansions, paraphrases, extensions, and recast sentences. Here, the teacher responds to the child's statements and provides the child with additional information about communicating, especially about syntax. An *expansion* involves using the child's words in the child's order, but adding new words to make an expanded, grammatically complete sentence. So, when the child says, "Want apple," the teacher responds with, "You want an apple." With a *paraphrase*, the adult repeats a statement or question to elicit a reply—for example, "Want ball" to "Do you want the ball?" An *extension* follows the child's statement with different words. For example, if the child says, "I miss the bus," the teacher may respond with, "You missed the bus. Were you late for the dentist?" Using *recast sentences* involves repeating or restating the child's words in the correct form.

- By using indirect commands such as, "Tell Tommy what you want."

- By using finger plays. These are good for children with speech and language problems. They will not be self-conscious because they are within a group. When using finger plays, the teacher should pause often to let children fill in the missing word.

- By having children take part in stories that use different voices, such as "The Three Bears."

- By playing with vocabulary cards. The teacher turns over cards with two children. Say "What's this?" or "This is a ___." The teacher can also use sentence completion, or chaining—for example, "You're eating an ___."
- By using labelling, to stimulate vocabulary development and help fix ideas. Labelling, one of the most important communication skills, is the ability to associate a given symbol (i.e., word or sign) with a given object or event (Bailey & Wolery, 1984). Teachers should attach words to many things, either as single words or in short sentences.
- By giving the child a word or picture and asking him or her to make a little story. Or by giving the child a narrative beginning. This encourages sequencing.

Listening skills   To a great extent, receptive language depends on good listening skills. In an auditory training (listening) curriculum, children are taught to do the following:

- Attend to sounds.
- Attend to differences among sounds.
- Recognize objects and events from the sounds they make.
- Be alert to sounds.
- Use hearing for the perception of space.
- Use hearing for the perception of speech.
- Use hearing to control the production of speech (Michael & Paul, 1991).

A range of activities fit within a listening curriculum. Teachers can try these:

- Point out the names of sounds in the child's environment, and encourage parents to do the same when the child is riding in a car, out shopping, and so on.
- For sound identification and location, use record players, tape recorders, tape players, musical instruments, and shakers or rattles. Children can identify familiar sounds on a tape or find the direction of a sound.
- Have children make musical instruments—for example, tambourines out of paper plates, or maracas out of beans and paper cups.
- Use percussion instruments and the piano to show children vibrations.
- Have children copy rhythm patterns according to instructions.
- Help children match sounds to objects or activities. They can be shown pictures of vehicles and animals, and encouraged to imitate their sounds.
- Play games like "Who said that?" to help children learn to identify and distinguish between voices.
- Use finger plays with rhymes.
- Use many imitative activities such as Ring Around the Rosy, or familiar stories.
- Model good skills. Listen actively when children talk, and do not interrupt when the child is talking.
- Use puppets to prompt short conversations.
- Use small-group settings for auditory training (listening) games, and to improve concept development, expand vocabulary, and promote peer interaction. For example, use a loudly ticking clock and have the children close their eyes and tell the location of the tick. Ask simple questions, such as, "Where is Jim?" or "What

LEARNING ACTIVITY 1

Develop a listening component for Martin's IPP. Include long-range goals and short-term objectives, and examples of materials and strategies. Also, provide details on who will present the program, and the format such as circle time or a small group.

colour is your shirt?" Children should respond using phrases or complete sentences.

- Present sounds by voice or through tape. Children will imitate the sounds correctly.
- Expand vocabulary use through games, pictures, and movements using colours, adjectives, and so on.
- Use finger plays to teach concepts such as *big* and *little*.

BOX 15–4

Martin's IPP

Martin provides a clear example of a child with a language delay. Martin also demonstrates some of the deviations in speech development commonly seen in young children.

At this time, Martin's language use and social functioning are of greater concern than his speech difficulties—that is, his specific articulation errors. The main goal is to stimulate Martin's use of language at the centre through modelling and practice in listening skills.

Long-term goals
To improve expressive language used for reg-
ulatory and functional purposes.
To strengthen listening skills.
To expand vocabulary.

Short-term objectives
Improve oral (regulatory) language, listening skills, and social interactions.
Suggested strategies—
Place Martin with one other child and supply them with construction materials such as Lego or blocks. The teacher gives a short direction such as "Build a small red tower." Each child then takes turns giving directions.
Teachers can also prompt Martin to take leadership roles during various group activities.

Incidental teaching   The incidental teaching model developed by Hart and Risely (1975) can increase the appropriate use of language. Incidental procedures are especially good for young children with speech and language problems and for those with disabilities. Incidental procedures promote generalization of communication skills.

Incidental teaching is a practical response to the need for more child instruction and more child/caregiver interaction (Owens, 1991). It is useful in programs serving children who can initiate simple communications. With young children, the main benefits of incidental teaching are these: it teaches target skills effectively in the natural environment; it increases generalization of these skills; and it results in gains in the formal and functional aspects of language (Warren & Kaiser, 1986b).

In incidental procedures, teaching is conducted during instructional or unstructured activities for brief periods of time (see Chapter 10). For example, instead of teaching a preschooler to use two-word phrases by looking at picture cards and describing them, two-word phrases are taught throughout the day during free play, snack time, circle time, and story time when the child initiates speech (Noonan & McCormick, 1993). Or the teacher can use informal prompts to stimulate children's involvement: "Ask Jim if he needs help," "I think you will like this book," "Would you help me with ...?"

Systematic commenting   Systematic commenting is a close kin to incidental teaching. Teachers provide general conversational support for children's language.

Systematic commenting occurs when children are engaged in an activity and teachers talk to the children about the children's activity and their own, and describe the actions that the children are making (descriptive feedback). This parallel and self talk gives children a verbal description of actions in the immediate environment and may help children to note certain things that they might otherwise have only dimly perceived, and to express them in vocabulary and language.

With systematic commenting, comments should highlight the action or toy that is the focus of the child's attention. The teacher should emphasize verbal descriptions of the children's actions. The descriptive comments should stress the communication goals being targeted.

Activity-based teaching   Activity-based teaching is another variation of incidental teaching. In an activity-based approach, specific skills are taught in the context of ongoing classroom activities, especially play. With this approach, a high rate of teaching episodes is possible.

Activity-based teaching ensures a continuing degree of moderate novelty, provides many "natural" teaching incidents, and allows specific communication and language skills to be taught. The steps for activity-based teaching are as follows:

- Identify 12 to 20 age-appropriate activities that encourage interaction, particularly turn taking—for example, blocks, dress up, or colouring.
- Observe what engages the child's attention.
- Control the materials.
- Recycle activities about every two weeks.
- Play with the child. Correct and model targeted objectives such as language or social interactions.

Mand models   The natural environment is the best setting for language learning, However, children with more severe disabilities may require some one-to-one training. But as we pointed out earlier, skills learned in individual sessions often fail to generalize to the regular environment. The Mand Model Procedure was developed (Rogers-Warren & Warren, 1980) as a means of actively programming for the generalization of language skills.

Mand means verbally instruct ("command"). In the Mand model, the teacher follows the child's attentional lead but mands (instructs) the child to verbalize about the focus of his or her attention. The teacher provides a variety of play materials. As the child approaches the material, the teacher mands the child to describe the material: "Tell me what this is." Children who make appropriate responses are rewarded, and presented with the materials with a comment such as, "Good. You want the red truck." The teacher then prompts more complex utterances. If they are incorrect, a model is provided for imitation.

Mand models use teacher-initiated cues to elicit responses and provide correction procedures for errors. For example, assume the children are playing kitchen. One child, for whom expansion of basic vocabulary is a goal, reaches for detergent:

> Teacher: Tell me what you want. [mand]
> Child: That. [Points to soap]
> Teacher: Tell me what that is. [mand]
> Child: That.
> Teacher: Say soap. [model]
> Child: Soap.
> Teacher: That's right. Soap. Here it is.

The child is praised, the request is filled, and interaction continues (Jones & Warren, 1991).

The Mand Model has been used successfully with children with severe delays. Rogers-Warren and Warren (1980) placed three language-delayed preschoolers under the Mand model and found not only accelerated generalization of trained words and grammatical structures to the classroom but also improvements in aspects of the children's language beyond those taught in the therapy sessions. Rates of verbalization doubled to tripled from their baseline levels as the children's vocabulary and complexity of utterances increased.

Time delay

We discussed the general uses and applications of time delay procedures in Chapter 10. We pointed out that time delay is used to transfer control from a prompt to a more natural stimulus designed to evoke the target behaviour (Sulzer-Azoroff & Mayer, 1991).

Communication involves not only responding to another person's verbal mand, but also initiating conversation about various aspects of the environment. Time delay is used in language training to establish environmental stimuli other than verbally presented models and mands as cues for vocalization.

Time delay increases the number of occasions requiring communication, either by placing high-demand items within sight but out of reach or by withholding objects or assistance needed for a particular task. It involves inserting a period of time between the more natural stimulus and the prompt until the prompt can be discontinued altogether. These are the steps for a time delay procedure:

1. The child is trained to produce verbal requests for a desired reinforcer in response to a direct verbal cue, such as "What do you want?"

2. The facilitator withholds the cue while waiting for the child to vocalize spontaneously. When the child looks at an adult, the adult does not speak for a specified period of time unless the child does. If the child does not verbalize, the adult models or prompts the desired vocalization.

3. The child learns to respond to the naturally occurring stimulus rather than the adult vocalization (Owens, 1991).

4. As the child becomes better at communication, the teacher waits longer and longer before giving the prompt (Angelo & Goldstein, 1993).

Peer-mediated models   The ideal language-training setting is one in which the language-impaired child is engaged in some meaningful activity with a conversational partner who models appropriate language. One approach is to teach communication skills directly. Another is to teach peers to initiate and sustain communicative interaction with children who are disabled. This means that each conversational partner is a potential therapist.

The developmental literature provides many examples and ample evidence in support of the idea that normally developing children are able to initiate, maintain, and modify verbal interactions with peers. Recent studies of peer-training programs have found that normal preschoolers can be taught to use specific strategies to increase conversation during social interactions with exceptional children.

Goldstein and Ferrel (1987), for example, trained young peers as language mediators with language-disabled children. In another study, Goldstein and Wickstrom (1986) taught specific strategies to increase communicative interaction with behaviour-disordered, language-delayed children in an integrated preschool. Goldstein (1993) also used peer strategies for children with autism, and reported that when peers were prompted to use strategies with classmates with autism, they were able to increase communication.

In each of these studies, the normally developing peers succeeded in increasing the target children's initiation and response rates. In the study with the children with behaviour disorders (Goldstein & Wickstrom, 1986), impressive maintenance was demonstrated by two of the three language-delayed children, even when peers were no longer prompted to use the strategies.

When adults speak to children, their speech is generally shorter, syntactically less complex, and more redundant; it also relies more on attentional devices. Children use the same strategies when they speak to younger children. When interacting with children with disabilities, non-disabled preschoolers seem automatically to adjust their speech to the level of the special child (Guralnick & Paul-Brown, 1977, 1980). But while normally developing non-disabled children seem to modify their speech appropriately when interacting with children of similar age who exhibit general developmental delays, an exception may be for hearing-impaired children. Normally developing preschool children find it difficult to adjust their communication to hearing-impaired children (Vandell & George, 1981).

The studies by Goldstein and her colleagues indicate that peer mediations for language are successful after peers are trained in certain strategies. After training, peers may intervene in the following ways:

1. Establishing eye contact. In a play situation, the peer can say the target child's name and/or tap the target child's arm or shoulder.

2. Establishing joint focus of attention. For example, children can play in pairs—a blower and popper of bubbles, a hider and seeker of toys in the sand, a filler and dumper of pails, or a chooser and gluer of art materials.

3. Initiating joint play. The peer suggests joint play: "Let's make food for our picnic," or, "You drive the car and I'll work at the gas station."

4. Repeating or expanding what the target child said, or requesting clarification. For example, the peer may say, "The baby wants her bottle," after hearing "baby bottle." Or the child doing the prompting may say "What did you say?" if unable

to understand an utterance.

5. Describing their own or other children's play and commenting on ongoing activities. The peer clarifies his or her own play—for example, "My man is driving the car"—or describes the play of others, as in, "You gave the baby medicine."

6. Prompting requests.

TABLE 15–4: Overview of specific procedures to stimulate language

Incidental teaching	A well validated procedure to promote language development and social skills acquisition. The child's behaviour serves to identify occasions for instruction.
Systematic commenting	The child is engaged in an activity and the teacher makes descriptive comments that stress the targeted communication goals.
Activity-based teaching	Focuses specifically on the development and maintenance of language skills in play situations.
Mand models	Use teacher commands and fading of prompts so that children respond to natural stimuli, that is, to something this is reinforcing for them.
Time delay	Relies on fading prompts and the child being reinforced by the materials.
Peer modelling	Effective peer-mediated interventions take place where play activities are appropriately structured, peers receive training, and adults actively prompt and reinforce interactions.

Strategies for children with significant disabilities

The approaches and strategies we have just outlined are suitable for many children with speech and language problems. However, some disabilities affect language and speech development so adversely that even more specialized techniques must be used.

CHILDREN WITH HEARING IMPAIRMENTS   In this text, we have met two children with hearing impairments: Nancy, who is profoundly deaf, and Cinta, who is hard of hearing. While Cinta will probably learn quite well under the strategies outlined earlier, Nancy needs extensive curricular modifications to compensate for the learning handicaps that accompany severe and profound hearing impairments.

For deaf children, most loud speech is inaudible even with the most sophisticated hearing aids. Nancy misses the auditory aspects of communication. She receives all of her information through visual modes and thus has great difficulty developing speech and language. To compound this problem, few adults in her environment are proficient in sign language so there is no common mode of communication between her and her teachers.

In the preschool years a specialized teacher of the hearing impaired will assist Nancy in communication. The communication mode selected for Nancy will depend on her needs and on the wishes of her family. A number of communication methods are available, which can be broadly categorized as oral/aural or manual.

The oral/aural approach emphasizes speech and speech reading and uses amplification and auditory training as a vital part of education. It does not use sign language. Manual methods use sign language. Essentially, ***total communication*** uses speech, speech reading, and amplification, along with a school-based manual system. School-based manual systems such as Signing Essential English or Manual English are a marriage of necessity between American Sign Language (ASL) and English. Signs are presented in the order of English, with correct morphological structures.

Unlike school-based manual systems, American Sign Language (ASL or Ameslan) does not follow the semantic and syntactic structure of spoken language. ASL is recognized by linguists as a true language in itself, quite different from spoken language. Although most children are now taught through total communication methods, there is a mounting movement to teach very young children ASL and then teach them English when they enter formal schooling. This is, in effect, a type of bilingual education for deaf students.

In the early childhood setting, a number of environmental factors can help hearing-impaired children acquire language:

> **Total communication** uses speech, speech reading, and amplification, along with a school-based manual system.

- There should be good lighting. In particular, the teacher's face should be facing the light source. When it is, there are no shadows to distract and confuse the child.
- Adults should get down to eye level when speaking to deaf children.
- The child should be close to the speaker. Hearing aids function best within a metre or two of the speaker; speech reading is easiest at about two metres.
- The environment should be quiet so that the hearing-impaired child can receive the cleanest possible auditory message. Hearing aids amplify everything.
- Adults should speak only when the child is looking at them.
- Many labels should be used in the classroom.
- It is useful to preread a difficult story to the hearing impaired children in the group so that they are already familiar with the story line and language before the whole group gathers to hear it. This helps them develop self-confidence; it also enables them to fill in information gaps during the group situation.

CHILDREN WITH VISUAL IMPAIRMENTS   The communication skills of severely visually impaired children can be developed through role playing and through training in language arts, oral conversation, and social skills.

Children who are severely disabled

Children with severe disabilities require training in all aspects of understanding and expression. Approaches include incidental teaching, stimulation, Mand models, time delay, and formal training.

Children lacking efficient communication are often divided into two groups. The first group includes presymbolic children, who do not use signs, words, or pictures for communication. They may not possess a recognizable communication system, or they may use gestures such as pointing, or touching or moving objects. The second group includes minimally symbolic children, who use some visual, verbal, or tactile symbols, alone or in combinations (Owens, 1991).

Two general intervention strategies are used in communication training for presymbolic and minimally symbolic children. Intervenors focus on presymbolic training and communication training.

PRESYMBOLIC TRAINING   Presymbolic training is based on the belief that there are cognitive prerequisites for language acquisition. It includes cognitive, perceptual, social, and/or communication targets identified as significant in the acquisition of symbol use in non-disabled children. The skills that make up presymbolic training are those that are identified as characteristic of the sensorimotor stage of development: object permanence, imitation, causality, attention, and so on. We discussed these in Chapter 14. Within the general sensorimotor skills, specific presymbolic skills include the following:

- Startle and notice. The child startles to sound, quiets to a familiar voice, looks at the speaker, and may respond with smiling.
- Search for stimuli. The child localizes the speaker visually, observes mouth movements of the speaker, and searches for a speaker.
- Localization to stimuli. The child localizes sound accurately, responds to and looks at a person, and can gain intervention by nonverbal means.
- Facial and vocal imitation.
- Communicative gestures.
- Receptive language and symbol recognition.
- Sound imitation, which includes vocal shaping and vocal sequencing (Owens, 1991, p. 292).
- Symbolic play with objects.

COMMUNICATION TRAINING   When children lack the ability to understand others and express themselves, a means of communication is imperative so that the child can interact with the environment. "Communication first" approaches begin by establishing a communication system, which can later be expanded to employ symbols.

Training focuses on providing a basic communication system in a mode that is appropriate for the child and acceptable to the family. ***Communication mode*** refers to "the form in which the content of a message is expressed" (Sailor et al., 1980, p. 72). The three main modes of communication are vocal/verbal/auditory, which includes intonation, speech sounds, phonetically consistent forms, and spoken words; tactile, which includes touch, and signing in the hand; and physical manipulation, such as moving a partner's hand to a desired object (Owens, 1991). The mode selected will depend on the child's disability, the severity of the disability, additional disabilities, and the wishes of the parents.

> **Communication mode** the form in which the content of a message is expressed; the three primary modes of communication are vocal/verbal/auditory, tactile, and physical manipulation.

A communication-first approach is a functional approach to language that stresses nurturant and naturalistic language. It has been recognized recently that fewer presymbolic behaviours are necessary for symbol use than was originally believed, and that some augmentative communication can be successfully implemented with little or no presymbolic training (Owens, 1991). With this approach, initial communication skills are taught first. Teachers may begin with pointing—the first and most common way of responding for these children. The children are then helped to develop their turn-taking and generalized imitation skills. The training stages after this relate to lexical growth and the establishing of a basic vocabulary; to early symbol communication rules (Owens, 1991); and to participation in conversations that occur outside the training context.

Alternative methods of communication

When speech is delayed, or when there is reason to think it may be delayed or not develop at all—for example, when the child has multiple disabilities, including a significant hearing loss—alternative means of communication are considered. These alternatives are called ***augmentative communication.***

Augmentative communication refers to a general group of procedures designed to support, enhance, or augment the communication of nonspeaking individuals. Augmentative communication is used mainly by those whose speech communication is impaired by hearing impairments; by those with severe language deficits; and by those with severe neuromuscular or physical disabilities.

> **Augmentative communication** alternative means of communication.

Ideally, the selection of a communication mode is made by family and therapists together. The decision to use an augmentative communication system should take into account the child's language, cognitive, social, and emotional functioning. Motivation and the voluntary movement available to the child should also be considered.

Early in this book, and again in this chapter, we met Nancy, a child with a profound hearing loss. Nancy's parents would very much like her to acquire speech and the ability to speech-read. However, to help her communicate as early as possible, the parents are happy to have her learn sign language while she receives assistance to develop speech, speech reading, and the use of any residual hearing. On the other hand, Darrin, the child with cerebral palsy, hears and comprehends language but has great difficulty producing intelligible speech. Clearly, sign language would be inappropriate for Darrin, although a nonoral system such as Bliss symbolics should allow him to communicate adequately.

Augmentative communication   The two main types of augmentation are unaided and aided. Unaided approaches rely on gestures, signs, body movements, visual contact, signals, and pointing. The more symbolic the system, the greater the cognitive skills required. It follows that gestures are acquired more easily than speaking or ASL.

Signal communication uses simple yes and no signals, which may be movements of the head, hands, face, or eyes. Natural gestures include simple movements of one or both hands. For example, the word "eat" is indicated by tapping the lips with the fingertips of one hand. Natural gestures may vary from child to child. If a child consistently points to the mouth to indicate hunger, then everyone working with that child should use the same gesture. More formalized gestural systems include cue systems such as Amerind, which is built on the hand signals used by Native Americans. Amerind consists of about 250 signs, which may be used in any combination (Winzer, 1996).

Although sign language is typically associated with deaf children, studies suggest that it may be beneficial to a much larger population. Signing uses pantomime, gesturing, and other nonverbal communication to convey ideas, language, and vocabulary to young children. It may offer opportunities for language development; in prelinguistic children, it may facilitate the onset and development of spoken language (Kouri, 1989).

Aided approaches depend on picture or symbol systems. For example, Bliss symbolics is a complete language system that has been used successfully with children with severe motor disabilities and is simple enough to be learned by children too young to read alphabetic writing. There are other systems besides Bliss, some of which use pictures.

Symbol systems, including Bliss, are displayed on communication boards. A child's first picture communication board will have clear pictures or photographs depicting basic needs and activities: a cup, a toilet or pot, a bed, a toy, an item of food, and so on. Later supplementary displays could offer a choice of foods, drinks, or play activities. The child communicates by pointing to the appropriate pictures.

Technology has been a boon for individuals unable to use speech. Some of the most exciting and successful uses of electronic technology have been with nonverbal children and those with severe language disorders. For example, a portable

> **PROGRESS CHECK 4**
>
> Differentiate between aided and unaided approaches to augmentative communication. Provide examples of each. Which approach do you think would be easiest for a child to use in an early childhood setting? Which would be the most difficult for a teacher to implement? Explain.

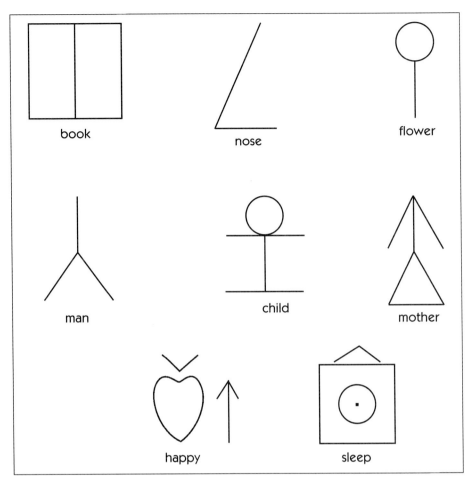

FIGURE 15–2

Examples of Bliss symbolics

audio-oscillator that emits a loud tone has been used to teach four simple signals (need, help, yes, no). Computers help many other children communicate more complex and subtle messages.

Nonspeech communication should not preclude speech therapy. Various studies have shown that speech attempts increase in frequency when nonvocal methods of communication are used (Mysak, 1982).

This child is learning to use a board system with Bliss symbolics.

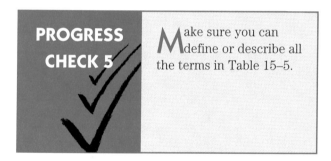

PROGRESS CHECK 5

Make sure you can define or describe all the terms in Table 15–5.

TABLE 15–5: New terms and ideas

augmentative communication	language disorders
communication	language problems
communication mode	speech
content	speech disorders
form	total communication
language	use
language delay	

SUMMARY

1. Human communication is incredibly complex. As a component of communication, language is a typically human activity. Language is a complex system of symbols, and of rules for using those symbols. Language is the product of all aspects of development: physical, sensory, social, and neurological. Speech is essentially a mechanical production of language.

2. The centre is a hub of linguistic activity. All day long, children listen to directions, peer exchanges, and teacher stories, and participate in group time. Children use their language to direct others, to ask questions, and to express their needs.

3. Early childhood teachers will encounter many children who are meeting minor delays in speech and language development. As well, most children with disabling conditions will manifest language and speech disorders. As children with disabilities have been mainstreamed into regular early childhood settings, their lack of social and communication skills has become increasingly apparent.

4. The variety of speech and language problems that may be found among preschool children is almost endless. Specific speech disorders relate to problems with articulation, voice, and fluency. Many young children show minor speech deviations that simply disappear with age.

5. Language assessment in the early years is especially difficult. In language assessment, it is important to compare cognitive and language scores. Formal language assessment is carried out by speech/language therapists. Areas for investigation include prelinguistic skills, receptive language, expressive skills, syntax, semantics, morphology, pragmatics, and phonology.

6. A language intervention should be a well-integrated whole; the various elements of language should be combined to enhance communication. Training should be in natural settings and use natural reinforcers. The linguistic environment should provide rich and varied language experiences. The form and nature of intervention for a child with a communication delay will depend greatly on how mild or severe the delay is.

7. Language use is promoted through environmental arrangements, materials and activities of interest, teacher mediation, and the availability of a partner with whom to communicate. Language strategies include incidental teaching, Mand models, and time delay. Other techniques to encourage language include reinforcing the child's attempts at communication, modelling language using short, simple sentences, and providing opportunities for children to interact with peers. Often the first step involves nonverbal communication contact.

8. To promote communication skills, teachers should arrange the environment to promote requests and comments by children and to support language-teaching efforts by adults.

9. The ability to direct or regulate others is an essential communication skill. Children require practice in regulatory language, oral language, and listening skills. Modelling and reinforcement are appropriate for children with mild and moderate delays.

10. When the teacher mediates the environment in response to children's use of language, social and physical aspects of the environment are linked to communication. Both peers and adults can be friends and partners in communication. Children with disabilities benefit when normally developing peers use specific communication strategies to communicate with them.

11. Children learn language through verbal and nonverbal prompts to produce language targets in combination with adult feedback. Prompts include models (re-

quests to imitate), mands (questions, instructions to verbalize), and cues (time delay).

12. Of all the needs of children with severe disabilities, the acquisition of communication skills is one of the greatest. Children who are communicating at a level below age two have unique needs in language development. Interventions are needed that focus on the early use of communication skills to engage others in conversational exchanges. To this end, methods used include child-directed modelling, Mand models, time delay, and incidental teaching. Often, the first step is to select the communication mode.

13. Prelinguistic training targets sensorimotor skills such as imitation, play, means-ends behaviour, and object permanence. Social skills such as attending and interacting with others are also prerequisites to communication. Prelinguistic teaching usually focuses on playing with objects.

14. Augmentative communication includes anything that augments speech or improves communication function. Augmentative communication is used with individuals who are hearing impaired; who have severe language deficits (including those associated with mental retardation); and who have severe neuromotor or other physical disabilities that affect the speech mechanisms. The choice of adjunct to communication is ideally made by family and therapists together.

C H A P T E R 1 6
Transition to the school system

In this text we have encountered a number of children with various types of disabilities and gifts and talents. These children are in different settings in different parts of the country and are taught and cared for by people with varied types of training. They come from homes that differ in multiple ways: family size and configuration, cultural background, socio-economic status, and the degree of acceptance and adaptation to the exceptional child.

Most of the children we have introduced have high-incidence conditions that affect behaviour and learning in some way. A few have serious developmental delays or multiple disabilities that seriously hinder their achievement and functioning. Generally, intervention with this latter group began in the first months and will continue throughout formal schooling, if not beyond.

One common experience for each child will be a transition from a setting serving very young children to the formal school system. All the children will move to kindergarten or grade one classes in their local school. The one exception is Nancy, the deaf child. After long pondering, her parents have decided to send Nancy to a school for the deaf. They reason that communication is Nancy's greatest need and that specially trained teachers can provide more speech and language input than is possible in a regular classroom.

Although kindergarten is not usually required, most of the children will enter available kindergarten programs. Kindergarten may be a half-day program or on alternate full days. Generally, the trend is toward full-day kindergarten. Research evidence (e.g., Gullo et al., 1985) suggests that this option need not place developmentally inappropriate demands on children.

As a link between preschool and grade one, kindergarten serves a transition function for children. The year in kindergarten is important, for it sets the stage for the child's school career and influences many other aspects of his or her life. For some children with disabilities, kindergarten may be a difficult experience: they may experience failure for the first time and begin to be labelled.

By the time they enter kindergarten, young children have mastered thousands of new skills. Nevertheless, it is estimated that 13 to 15 percent of all children—with or without disabilities—have adjustment difficulties (Barth & Parke, 1993). As well, the emphasis on academics in kindergarten programs places stress on children with disabilities and puts many normally developing children at risk. As we pointed out in Chapter 14, there is a growing trend toward instituting highly structured academic programs and readiness programs at the kindergarten level; many kindergartens are attempting to give young children an early start with the academic curriculum.

For children with disabilities, kindergarten is a critical and sometimes difficult transition period. Even children who seem ready for mainstream participation in kindergarten may encounter difficulties because they have not acquired the ability to interpret and act on subtle sound cues, such as facial expressions, tone of voice, and body language. For the first time, children may be labelled in some way. Depending on the organization and philosophy of the school, they may be taken out of class for resource room assistance or provided with an aide in the classroom. Even though kindergarten and grade one are considered part of the early childhood continuum, teacher expectations are different. The day is more structured and there is a greater emphasis on academic skills.

Most preschool teachers are aware of the stresses the parents will face during the transition, and of the new problems children with disabilities may face. In the final half-year of their time with the children, they will shift the focus of the preschool program to stress the skills the children will need in the next environment.

IN EDUCATIONAL CIRCLES, THE TERM "TRANSITION" was first used widely in relation to secondary school students, and most often referred to the movement from school to work. The term now has various applications, including the movement from a home-based program to preschool, from preschool to school, from elementary to junior high, and from hospital to home.

Transition is an increasingly important issue in regular early childhood education. One aspect of transition is the parents' involvement in their children's entry into other programs (Bredekamp, 1991).

In ECSE, the issue of transition has only very recently become a topic of formal investigation, and is only now being emphasized in the early intervention literature (Kilgo, 1990). When transition in early childhood has been considered, the main focus has been on transition from preschool to kindergarten or primary special-education programs; there has been less emphasis on procedures for transition from hospital to home, or from infant to preschool programs. The role of "sending programs" (i.e., of care providers working in the program the child is leaving) has been stressed over the role of "receiving programs" (i.e., of care providers working in the program the child is moving to).

Increasingly, however, transition programming is developing into an important area of responsibility at both ends of the process. In the United States, under Public Law 99-457, formal transition planning must be undertaken.

This increased interest in transition relates to both the family and the child. For the family, there has long been concern about alleviating the stress that comes with changing programs and systems and dealing with different personnel. For the child, the goals of transition planning are these: to select a placement that is appropriate for the needs of the child and supported by the child's parents; to ensure a smooth transfer of the child; to prepare the child to function in the next environment; and to ensure a smooth and rapid adjustment to that environment.

A number of tactics are now known to be useful in moving a young child with a disability from preschool to an integrated setting. These include a focus on family needs and expectations; assessment of the priorities and behavioural expectations of the new teachers; and direct observation of the behaviour of children judged to be successful.

In Chapter 5 we discussed the transition to an early childhood program. This chapter focuses on the transition to what will be, for the great majority of young children with disabilities, the public school system. We examine the skills children need to function successfully in more formal school environments, and strategies for involving parents in the transition process; also, we discuss how early childhood personnel can smooth the transition process.

Transitions

All definitions of *transition* have in common the idea that a transition is a passage or evolution, and not simply a matter of "here today, gone tomorrow." Transitions are not fleeting; rather, they are recurrent, life-long processes experienced by all individuals. They represent "critical episodes or phases in the life span of either families or individuals during which important developmental, social, and economic changes are likely to occur" (Mallory, 1995, p. 214).

In ECSE, *transition* can be defined as the process of moving from one program to another, or from one service delivery mode to another (Chandler, 1992). Transition is more than simply transferring records or relocating a child. The child's transition from a preschool to a public school program is a time of change for both the child and the family, and must be approached as such.

An Alberta study (Blakeley & La Grange, 1987) suggested that the transition from preschool to public school has always been a difficult one for children, parents, and teachers. Transitions should be carefully planned and undertaken. When they are, they help ensure continuity of services for young children with disabilities and their families.

TRANSITION AND THE FAMILY

There is a growing recognition that every family is a system and that any event involving a change in the life of a family can cause stress in that system.

Life cycle transitions are experienced by all families. In many families these transitions include the child's first step and first words, and various birthdays. When a child with a disability is a member of the family, these same transitions are important but there may be others: first encounter with the handicap, early childhood, school entry, adolescence, beginning adult life, and maintaining adult life (Fewell, 1986). Events of this latter type may magnify a child's special needs and create heightened stress in the family.

The transition from preschool to the formal system is one of a series of moves faced by the child and the family. Educators may see the transition to a regular program as a positive change, but this transition may be stressful for the parents (Hanline & Halvorsen, 1989). Placing a young child with special needs in a school program can be a difficult transition for the family because of the many difficulties associated with early transitions and because of the uncertainty that surrounds them.

The educational decisions that parents must make are a major cause of stress. Before a transition can even be planned, the parents must confront a variety of issues relating to the child's disability and continuing education.

The transition from the home or other services to a school program requires parents to spend a great deal of time and energy learning about the new educational system, the IEP process, their rights and responsibilities, special education and related services, and placement options. Placement decisions take much thought and are not made lightly or quickly. Nancy's parents, for example, spent many hours discussing the most appropriate placement for her.

During the period of transition, the child's eligibility for special education services is established and the child is often labelled officially for the first time as being different. Even when a mainstream placement in a regular school is clearly appropriate for a child, such a placement may cause problems for the parents, who are reminded daily of the lag between their child and other children at the school. Parents may feel socially stigmatized by the disability and isolated from other parents. They may worry about the social adjustment of their child and the availability of support services (Turnbull & Blacher-Dixon, 1980).

Stress also occurs because transitions result in changed roles and expectations. Preschool and public school programs differ on a number of dimensions, including location, personnel, transportation options, schedules, family support services, and methods of communication between home and teacher.

The transition to kindergarten may disrupt many of the patterns established in the preschool program. For families, the transition involves not only relinquishing ties with the familiar preschool setting, but also adjusting to a school that may provide fewer opportunities for family involvement and may place more complex academic and social demands on the child.

After the child begins to attend school, parents may be concerned about such matters as the implementation of the IEP, the delivery of related services, the competence of the teacher, the child's adjustment to the new environment, and even transportation. Parents must establish a trusting relationship with the child's new teacher and identify parent participation activities that best suit their particular family.

Parents may also be apprehensive about being separated from their child during school hours. They may feel a loss of control over daily activities and fear that the new teacher does not know the child well enough to provide appropriate care and instruction. Parents who have invested a great deal of time and energy providing daily care for their child may not know what to do with their free hours during school time (Hanline, Suchman, & Demmerle, 1989).

Families often encounter stress when their child makes the transition from early intervention services. Therefore, more emphasis must be placed on helping them deal with the transition process (Kilgo, 1990).

PROGRESS CHECK 1

State some reasons why parents feel stress when their disabled child moves from a preschool program to the formal school system. Are these reasons different from those that apply when the child is moving from the home to a centre? (Refer to Chapter 5.)

TRANSITION AND THE CHILD

The child's move from a child care or preschool program into the public school system may be the most abrupt and permanent break with the past that he or she experiences before leaving home as a young adult. For children, transition means severing bonds with preschool staff, making new friends, generalizing old skills to new situations, acquiring new routines, and exploring new environments. Children with disabilities will be facing a group of strange people, with all the inevitable separation fears this involves. They will have to learn the rules and consequences of an unfamiliar environment, as well as their place in the new hierarchy. In all this, they will be no different from any other children. The success of the transition will be influenced by the skills and behaviours the child exhibits during transition and by the match between those skills and the expectations of the receiving program.

Ensuring the transfer

Ideally, transition is designed to provide a seamless relationship between preschool and public school. The factors contributing to the success or failure of the process are multiple and complex. They relate not only to the child but also to the quality of the sending and receiving programs and the behaviour of the teachers, the family, and the community (Hains, Fowler, & Chandler, 1988). Especially important are the preparation, implementation, and follow-up that must be part of the process.

One key element in transition is planning. A successful transition is a series of well-planned steps. Good planning can help alleviate parental concerns. Also, the child's eagerness and excitement for school, and ability to transfer and maintain the skills and behaviours acquired in preschool, may depend on the care with which providers and families plan the transition.

In a well-planned transition, the parents are in control of their child's educational future, not just puppets in the hands of experts. While a transition is easier when a teacher gives parents information and a perspective on the process, it is critical that parents accept responsibility for decisions affecting their child and learn to advocate for their child. Parents need to feel central to the decision-making process; they must capitalize on their own resources and call on staff for resources, guidance, and back-up support.

The onus for initiating the transition is on parents or the preschool staff. It may be helpful if the parents and the personnel of the sending setting complete a written transition plan. An example is shown in Figure 16–1.

[Copy:] ____________________
Child: ____________________

The following plan states the steps that the parents of the above child and the staff will take to ensure the orderly transition to the school district for the child.

Recommended placement: ____________________
Neighbourhood school: ____________________
Step ____________________

	Person responsible	Target date	Date accomplished
1. The child is recommended for placement in ... The parents will contact the school principal.	Parents	______	______
2. Send records to receiving school; provide parents with copies	Preschool staff	______	______
3. Provide kindergarten teacher with preschool staff teacher's report	Preschool	______	______
4. Monitor progress	Parents	______	______

This plan is agreed to by the following parties: ____________________

FIGURE 16–1

Parent transition plan

From It's Time to Get Ready for School by B. Fiechtl, S. Rule & M. Innocente, Teaching Exceptional Children, Vol. 21, 1989, 63–65.

Co-operation is another key element. Preschool staff should try to work with the receiving program at some level. For example, it may be the preschool staff who have the richest information about the child's skills and how they will serve in a school setting; teacher observations and the results of any assessments completed in the preschool program can be of great value to the kindergarten or grade one teacher. Kindergarten teachers need observational data and assessment results if they are to individualize instruction to accommodate children who are disabled. Otherwise they may not teach the skills the children need (because they believe the children already have them), and overemphasize activities addressing skills children already have. Staff should organize for information and records to be given to the next placement.

Kindergarten teachers are often very interested in children's readiness for the new placement. In fact, the issue of children's readiness for school is presently receiving widespread attention from both professionals and parents. However, the idea of readiness is poorly defined and open to many interpretations, because teachers have different expectations for children and different definitions of success in the classroom.

An ideal approach would be for the preschool staff to identify the child's receiving teachers a year in advance, visit the classroom, and formulate a curriculum at the preschool based on the prerequisites of the programs to follow.

At the same time, the kindergarten staff could provide information about their program: the number of children and staff in the new setting; the amount of time allocated to various activities; the level of teacher involvement in those activities; the number of children participating in each activity; the type of seating provided; and the typical responses demanded in an activity (Sainato & Lyons, 1989).

IMPLEMENTING TRANSITION

Preparing for transition involves a number of components — preparing children and family members for the move to a new program, minimizing the disruption caused by necessary changes in services, supporting children and family members as they adjust to the new program, making subsequent adjustments to new experiences for the child and the child's family, and providing the child with the skills to succeed in the new placement.

An important role for any preschool teacher is to prepare children and families for the transition to the next environment, which is usually kindergarten (Donovan, 1987). In many respects, the most suitable instructional processes for children under five are no different from those for school-age children with disabilities (Sargent, 1988). In other ways, instruction at the preschool level is quite different from later instruction. Children in preschool programs do not sit at their desks for long periods of time. Nor do they have the attention spans (except perhaps in play) necessary for formal instruction, nor do they yet have the cognitive abilities required to learn effectively through teacher-dominated modes of instruction. Most preschool programs disavow structured educational experiences and drills and laborious instruction in basic concepts. Such activities may only inhibit a child's development, by reducing both creativity and initiative.

As the demands of the public school environment are different from those of the preschool, it follows that the skills the child needs for kindergarten are different from those needed for a preschool program. In kindergarten classrooms, there is a predictable and consistent schedule of activities. Kindergarten teachers require children to respond to directions given once to a large group; preschool teachers often give children repeated individual directions in small groups or on a one-to-one basis. There are provisions for free play in kindergarten, but these differ from those for younger children. As well, kindergartens place more emphasis on academic subjects or academic readiness. Literacy behaviour is stressed.

A kindergarten or grade one classroom does not allow for a one-to-one relationship between adult and child throughout the day; the child must spend much time in independent activities. Children must learn to follow group instructions; respond to group-directed teaching activities; follow rules and routines; work and play independently in close proximity to others; work and play co-operatively with peers; take turns; share; and wait. They are expected to develop the ability to attend to tasks; complete tasks successfully with a minimum of adult assistance; initiate interactions appropriately; and go along with simple classroom rules and routines. They must also understand how to ask for, offer, accept, and refuse appropriate help.

Preparing the child for the future environment is an essential component of transition. It is incumbent on early childhood personnel to identify the skills the child is expected to display in kindergarten, focus on the development of those skills, and demonstrate that the child does in fact possess the necessary skills.

It is logical to look at the next environment to determine the skills a child will need. If, for example, a kindergarten teacher considers a knowledge of colours to be a crucial skill for entry, then preschool staff are well advised to include in their programs work on recognizing, matching, and naming colours.

A number of studies have indicated which skills mainstream kindergarten teachers see as necessary for children with disabilities. There is evidence that teachers perceive as successful those children with disabilities who require less instructional interaction with adults during large-group and free-play activities (Walter & Vincent, 1982). Kindergarten teachers want skills that promote independence—for example, following directions, following classroom rules, attending to and following classroom routines, and participating in group activities (Hains, Fowler, & Chandler, 1988; Vincent, Brown, & Getz-Shaftel, 1981).

In a 1986 survey of 1,200 kindergarten principals, preparation for school and children's social and language development received more attention than academic achievement. Most of the principals who responded (62.6 percent) indicated that the main focus of their kindergarten program was preparation (academic and social readiness); 22 percent gave the main focus as academics (skills and achievement) (see Day, 1988).

Children who make the transition to kindergarten armed with the necessary survival skills and who use those skills in appropriate contexts are more likely to succeed in the educational mainstream than their peers without these skills (Fowler, Schwartz, & Atwater, 1991). To ensure that children adjust to their new programs, educators must begin to train them specifically for transitions—see Table 16–1. However, there can never be a universal list of transition skills, because classroom and teacher expectations differ too much. Note also that in the table, we have listed the skills that children should demonstrate in the new setting as optimal goals; these should not be seen as prerequisites for entry.

Teachers should always be aware that even though early childhood education can teach a range of new skills to young children with disabilities, and can change many behaviours that compete or interfere with learning, socialization, and communication, some skills and behaviours do not consistently transfer to or survive in the new school setting. Fowler and colleagues (1991) point out that there are no published data to answer the question of whether children who have received instruction in survival skills continue to use those new skills in appropriate contexts in new environments. Nor are there data to indicate whether children who have had instruction in survival skills are successful in mainstream kindergarten placements.

TABLE 16–1: Transition skills related to successful transition from preschool to kindergarten

Social behaviours and classroom conduct

Understands role as part of a group
Respects others and their property
Interacts and defends self without aggression
Plays co-operatively, shares toys and materials
Expresses emotions and affections appropriately
Takes turns; participates appropriately in games
Is willing to try something new
Follows class rules and routines
Lines up and waits appropriately
Imitates peer actions
Sits appropriately
Plays independently

Communication behaviours

Follows two- to three-part directions
Initiates and maintains peer interactions
Modifies behaviour when given verbal feedback
Asks peers or teachers for information or assistance
Recalls and follows directions for tasks previously described
Follows group instructions
Relates ideas and experiences
Answers questions
Communicates own needs and wants

Task-related behaviours

Finds materials needed for tasks
Does not disrupt peers during activities
Complies quickly with teacher instruction
Generalizes skills across tasks and situations
Follows task directions in small or large group
Replaces materials and cleans up work space

Monitors own behaviour, knows when a task is done
Begins and completes work at appropriate time without extra teacher attention
Makes choices
Stays in own space
Follows routine in transition
Uses a variety of materials
Seeks attention appropriately
Attends to teacher in larger group

Self-help behaviours

Recognizes when a problem exists
Avoids dangers and responds to warning words
Locates and cares for personal belongings
Takes outer clothing off and puts it on in a reasonable amount of time
Tries strategies to solve problems
Feeds independently
Cares for own toileting needs

The research does indicate that in kindergarten the skills most crucial for success are not naming colours or recognizing the letters of the alphabet, but social skills. These social skills are thought to include self-help skills, social interaction, play, and the ability to function independently. For example, the child may be required to sit quietly, work independently, and respond to group instruction.

Teachers can use various strategies to assist transition. First of all, the preschool environment can be altered to approximate the kindergarten environment. Social and academic skills acquired in the transition area will tend to generalize more easily to the kindergarten environment (Neisworth & Buggey, 1993).

If it seems important to the receiving kindergarten, preacademic and academic skills should be included in the transition plan. Preschoolers who have mastered academic skills such as understanding simple concepts, writing first name, and copying letters are more likely to succeed in regular classes (Chandler, 1993).

Teachers can alleviate many fears children have about a transition by including the following in the transition plan:

- Making field trips to the new school. The child will be less frightened of the unknown when given an opportunity to look in on the new class or program and meet the new teachers.
- Reading stories about the fun of new adventures and new friends.

- Helping children create a scrapbook about kindergarten.
- Role playing "going to the new school."
- Inviting the kindergarten teacher to the class (see Noonan & McCormick, 1993).

SUMMARY

1. The transition from preschool to public school programs is a transition not only for the child but also for the parents. When we discuss transitions, two main questions arise: the transfer of skills in children as they move to new programs and settings, and how parents cope with new routines.

2. For the child, the move to preschool is a move to a larger program with more children and new expectations. Children must learn interdependence, sharing, cooperation, teamwork, and group membership.

3. Little research has been done on transitions.

4. There is a growing recognition that each family is a system. Any event involving a change in family life causes stress in the system. This is especially true when the family has a child with a disability.

5. Because, transitions result in changing roles and expectations for families, they are difficult for parents. As turning points for families, transitions increase vulnerability to stress and the potential for problems. One factor in family stress is the nature of the child's educational program. Also, when making the transition into public school, a variety of issues related to the child's disability confront parents. Transition also means fewer opportunities for family involvement, more complex social and academic demands on the child, and a readjustment of family schedules and routines. Teachers can ease the transition to preschool by recognizing and respecting the concerns of parents. They can provide information about future placements and help parents make informed decisions.

6. Children's ability to maintain skills and their zest for learning may depend on the care with which the transition is made. Given the importance of the transition process to the child and the family, programs for successful mainstreaming should be one focus of the preschool curriculum.

7. Kindergarten teachers emphasize classroom skills that are conduct related and that promote independence—for example, following directions, following classroom rules, attending to and following classroom routines, and participating in group activities. Other skills for transition include social behaviour and self-help skills; motivation and problem-solving skills; preacademic and academic support skills; and task-related behaviour, conduct behaviour, and communication skills.

GLOSSARY

A

activity reinforcers activities that are handled in a specific way.

adaptive behaviour the ability to respond to and function in the environment according to age and social standards. Behaviour that allows the child to interact with the environment and those in it in ways that are appropriate to age, context, and culture.

adaptive devices devices that make living easier such as toileting aids and Velcro Fasteners on clothing.

adaptive equipment equipment customized to meet the physical needs of individual children. It is any device designed or modified to lead individuals with disabilities to independence.

adaptive playgrounds play environments modified to enable children with physical disabilities to become more independent.

aggression any form of behaviour that is intended to hurt another, either physically or verbally, or intended to injure property.

allergy (hypersensitivity) an abnormal and varied reaction that occurs following a contact with substances or agents which normally do not cause symptoms in other individuals.

ameliorative programs programs designed to assist children who are at risk for learning or behavioural difficulties, such as Head Start in the United States.

ancillary services areas and disciplines that support and complement special education.

anecdotal records brief global statements of events important to a child's performance.

antisocial behaviour overt, aggressive, disruptive behaviour, or covert antisocial acts; repeated infractions of socially prescribed behaviour patterns that violate social norms and the rights of others.

Apgar screening neonatal tests that look at colour, respiration, muscle tone, heart rate, and reflexes.

assessment the process of gathering data in order to make a decision.

asthma a variable, reversible obstruction of the airways characterized by the narrowing of bronchial tubes, swelling of tissues, and clogging of mucus.

at risk children who have increased vulnerability; they are more prone to developing some form of disabling condition.

augmentative communication alternative means of communication.

B

behaviour management all the ways in which teachers control inappropriate and disruptive behaviour, as well as ways in which children are taught discipline and to control their own behaviour.

behaviour reduction plan a set of actions that a teacher takes when a child, despite management efforts, continues to engage in behaviour that is not considered acceptable.

biological risk relates to infants and toddlers with a history of prenatal, perinatal, neonatal, or early developmental events that result in biological insults to the developing nervous system.

body image a mental image of one's own body.

C

carrying the way that a child with a physical or motor disability is moved.

categorization the processes that are involved in defining categorical membership.

causality children's recognition of causes for interesting events, particularly the child's realization that behaviour can produce changes in objects.

cerebral palsy a condition characterized by damage to the brain before, during, or after birth. A neurological impairment and one of the most common crippling conditions in children.

child a person undergoing the period of development from infancy to puberty.

child care   any arrangement for caregiving other than that provided by the parents.

child development   a series of patterned and predictable changes that foster a child's ability to cope with and master the external environment.

children with exceptionalities   those whose physical, cognitive, or emotional development falls above or below the norm. They require special education and related services in order to attain their full potential.

classroom management   the way in which teachers manipulate the classroom environment to minimize disruptions and give all children the optimum opportunity to engage in appropriate behaviour and reach learning and social goals.

cognition   the interaction of all the perceptual, intellectual, and linguistic abilities that are involved in thinking and learning.

cognitive development   the thinking processes and how children understand and learn about the world in which they live.

communication   the transmission of information.

communication mode   the form in which the content of a message is expressed; the three primary modes of communication are vocal/verbal/auditory, tactile, and physical manipulation.

concept   an idea that includes all that is characteristically associated with it.

conflict   a dispute of incompatible behaviours or goals.

congenital abnormalities   problems are generally present at birth.

content   the linguistic representation of what a person knows about the world of objects, events, and relations.

continuum of environmental (caretaking) casualty   environmental factors that range from healthy families to particularly adverse situations.

continuum of reproductive casualty   refers to reproductive factors; problems may range from relatively minor through to major difficulties.

contractures   the shortening of the tendons, to which children with cerebral palsy are prone.

creativity   bringing new and usual responses to situations and problems.

criterion-referenced measures (also called content—or objective-referenced tests)   measure success or failure in meeting some previously determined objective. Their primary purpose is to indicate a child's specific skills so that teachers can compare a child's performance to a specific level or rating as well as to the child's progress over time.

critical period   a part of the life cycle during which the organism is particularly sensitive or responsive to specific environmental forces. Outside this period, the same event or influences are thought to have little if any lasting effects.

curriculum   an organized and sequenced set of content to be taught.

cystic fibrosis   a genetically determined inborn error of metabolism that primarily affects the respiratory and digestive systems.

D

deferred imitation   the repetition of an act seen at an earlier time.

developmental milestones   various critical behaviours, such as sitting, walking, and using first words.

developmental stage   age-related behaviour changes that are predictable with increasing age.

diabetes milletus   a problem of sugar metabolism caused by a pancreatic disorder in the production of insulin, a hormone needed to metabolize glucose.

direct instruction   activity-focused, teacher-directed classroom procedures.

directionality   an awareness of left and right outside the body.

direct observation   when teachers observe closely and document the observations.

discipline   helping children to learn to guide their own behaviour in a way that shows respect and caring for themselves, other people, and the physical environment.

dramatic play   the substitution of an imaginary situation to satisfy personal wishes and needs.

E

early childhood education   a program that is concerned with the development and special needs of young children and their families, with particular emphasis on the preschool years.

early childhood special education   any program or service within the early childhood period. It can include home training, clinic-based programs, child care facilities, and nursery schools.

early identification   the process of identifying an exceptionality or a high-risk condition as early as possible in a child's life.

early intervention   the establishment of educational and support services for young children with or at risk for disabilities, and their families.

egocentrism   the self-centred quality of the preschool child's thoughts and behaviour, and the child's inability to see something from another person's perspective.

engagement (sometimes called task engagement or on-task behaviour)   the extent to which children are actively and appropriately involved with materials, people, or activities in the environment.

environmental risk   applies to infants and toddlers who are biologically sound but whose early life experiences are limited.

established risk   a diagnosed medical disorder with a known etiology (cause) that bears relatively well-known expectancies for developmental outcomes within varying ranges of developmental disabilities.

etiology   the causes of a disabling condition.

exceptionality   when the physical, cognitive, emotional, sensory, or behavioural development of an individual child is not within the norms that are established for all children of a particular age.

F

family needs   a family's expressed desire for services to be obtained or outcomes to be achieved.

fine motor skills   those that involve small body movements and refer to the muscles of the hand.

form   phonology, morphology, and syntax.

functional skills   skills that help children to get along in their environments; behaviours that are critical for the completion of daily routines. These include dressing, eating, toileting, and participating in routine home and community activities.

G

general adaptation   one that does not require support or a piece of equipment but still represents a change in the basic requirements of the task.

general inco-ordination   a lack of muscular control.

generalization   the processes that enable individuals to make previously learned responses to new situations. Also called transfer. Learning in one situation influences learning in another context; the end result is that children can use the skills outside the classroom in a variety of ways.

goal   a stated outcome desired as a result of some action.

gross motor skills   large body movements such as running, climbing, and throwing.

H

hard of hearing person   one who, generally with the use of a hearing aid, has residual hearing sufficient to enable successful processing of linguistic information through audition.

high risk   children have increased vulnerability; they are more prone to developing some form of disabling condition.

home visiting   a process whereby a professional or paraprofessional provides help over an extended period of time to a family in its home.

hostile aggression   aggression that seems to occur for its own sake and is its own goal.

hyperactivity   a child's frequent failure to comply in an age-appropriate fashion with situational demands for restrained activity, sustained attention, resistance to distracting influences, and inhibition of impulsive response. That is, an excess of motor activity for a child's age and situation.

I

imitation   the ability of the child to match or copy a model.

incidental teaching   taking advantage of naturally occurring child-adult interactions in order to teach specific functional skills.

inclusion   placing all children in the classrooms they would be attending if they did not have a disability.

independent behaviour   behaviour performed without the assistance of others.

infancy   the first two years of life or the period of life prior to the development of complex speech.

infant   derives from the Latin for "not speaking."

infants and toddlers who are disabled   individuals from birth to two years of age who are in need of early intervention services because they are experiencing developmental delays as measured by appropriate diagnostic instruments and procedures. Includes children who have a diagnosed physical or mental condition that has a high probability of resulting in a developmental delay. May also include infants and toddlers who are at risk for having substantial developmental delays if early intervention services are not provided.

instructional reinforcers   motivators that are introduced strictly for the purpose of teaching or of increasing the strength of a particular skill.

instrumental aggression   aggression directed toward achievement of a non-aggressive goal; involves quarreling over an object, territory, or privilege.

intervention   care and education aimed at influencing the direction and scope of children's developmental processes.

interview   a method of gathering information by conversation or direct questioning.

K

keystone skills   skills that allow children to learn a multitude of important behaviours.

L

language delay   the child is lagging behind others of the same chronological age.

language   a rule-governed system that includes semantics, syntax, morphology, and pragmatics (the social use of language).

language disorders   children show large gaps in linguistic development and display little consistency in their various deficits.

language problems   a range of difficulties with the linguistic code, or with the rules for linking the symbols and the symbol sequences.

laterality   an internal knowledge of the difference between left and right.

life cycle (life span) approach   this perspective sees the family as a unit that is moving through time and experiencing a series of events, tasks, and transitions. By looking at the family life cycle, it can be seen that the impact of the disabled child on the family changes over time.

M

mainstreaming   providing all exceptional students regardless of type and severity of disability, with an appropriate education alongside their normally developing peers as far as possible.

maturational lags   occur when children fail to develop within normal timelines.

means-end behaviour   learning to use objects and activities to accomplish a goal. Involves purposeful problem-solving using both objects and people. The ability to separate the procedures (means) for solving a problem from the goal (ends) of the solved problem.

mental retardation   substantial limitations in personal functioning, characterized by significant subaverage intellectual functioning, existing concurrently with related limitations in two or more of the following adaptive skills: communication, self-care, home living, social skills, community use, self-direction, health and safety, functional academics, leisure, and work. Mental retardation is manifested before age eighteen.

methods   how a teacher interacts with children and what he or she does to teach.

mobility   negotiating space.

model   a pattern or design that can be replicated or repeated.

modelling   imitating behaviour in different situations.

motor control   the process by which the brain and the muscles work together to produce co-ordinated skilled movement.

motor learning   involves using the body in such ways as to make the best use of what is perceived.

motor development   the process through which a child acquires movement patterns and skills.

ways as to make the best use of what is perceived.

motor skills   those related to the development and use of the muscles and limbs.

muscular dystrophy   a condition characterized by wasting away of muscular tissue and consequent progressive muscle weakness.

musculoskeletal impairments   those that affect body movement and functioning but are not caused by neurological damage.

N

nature   the range of traits, capacities, and limitations that each person inherits genetically from his or her parents at the moment of conception.

needs assessment   assesses current conditions and needs and provides information on what the parents' goals are for their child and for potential parent involvement in the program.

negative reinforcement   occurs when an unpleasant stimulus is immediately taken away or removed from the situation as a consequence for a behaviour, with the effect of increasing the probability that the behaviour will occur again.

norm-referenced instrument   when an individual child's performance is compared to the normative group consisting of other children of the same age.

nurture   all the environmental influences that come into play after conception, beginning with the mother's health during pregnancy and running through an individual's life span.

O

obesity   a body weight that is more than 20 percent greater than the average for one's age, sex, and body size.

objective   a clear statement of exactly what a teacher wants a child to be able to do as a result of instruction.

object permanence   knowing that things exist even when their presence cannot be perceived.

occupational therapists   support personnel with training in the biological and psychosocial sciences, the foundations of medicine, psychiatry, and prevocational skills development.

orientation   an individual's knowledge of his or her position in space.

orthotic devices   assist a limb's action.

otitis media   the most common form of ear infection in children. The lining of the middle ear becomes inflamed and the cavity filled with fluid; thus, the conduction of sound from the outer to the inner ear is hindered.

P

parent involvement   the process of actualizing the potential of parents; of helping parents discover their strengths, potentialities, and talents; and of using these for the benefit of themselves and the family.

pedagogy   the link between what a teacher wants children to learn and the children's actual learning.

physical development   the acquisition of postural control, and the necessary movement patterns to produce functional motor acts.

physical therapists   support personnel who are trained in medically based programs that usually include the study of the biological, physical, medical, and psychosocial sciences, as well as in-depth work in neurology, orthopedics, therapeutic exercises, and treatment techniques.

positioning   how the child is seated or otherwise positioned.

positive reinforcement   a consequence that increases the likelihood of a response being repeated.

precocious   children who demonstrate remarkable early development.

Premack principle   a more preferred consequence should be made contingent (dependent) on a less-preferred task.

prenatal screening   examines fetuses who may be at risk.

preventative discipline   strategies and procedures that militate against any discipline problems arising.

primary disability   the major condition affecting a child.

primary reinforcers   those things that satisfy inborn biological needs, such as food, drink, warmth, sleep, or sex, and which act to strengthen the behaviour that they follow.

problem behaviours   behaviours that make it difficult for children to interact with peers, parents, teachers, and others.

profound sensori-neural hearing loss   loss that affects the inner ear and the auditory nerve.

prompt   anything that assists the child in making a desired response, such as a teacher pointing to something or modelling how something is done.

prosthetic adaptation   the child needs a specific piece of equipment such as braces or a hearing aid to demonstrate a skill.

prosthetic devices   used to replace lost functions and/or provide support; they duplicate normal body movements as nearly as possible while restraining normal functions as little as possible.

R

reinforcer   an event or stimulus that increases the strength of a behaviour.

representational thought   the ability to imagine things or events not present and represent them in some way.

risk factors   the causes of potential disabilities. They are divided into three major categories— established risk, biological risk, and environmental risk.

routines   the general organizational strategies that everyone soon learns.

rules   define the limits on behaviour, such as "Walk, don't run," or "We don't hit other people."

S

screening   a term used in medicine and education to refer to developmental and health activities that

are intended to identify at an early age those children who have a high probability of exhibiting delayed or abnormal development.

secondary conditions   other conditions that are present or arise after the primary disability.

secondary reinforcers   those which are initially neutral or meaningless but acquire their reinforcing value by being associated with primary reinforcers or an already established secondary reinforcer.

self-concept   the perceptions of self that underlie, illuminate, and direct personality.

self-help skills   those abilities needed for independent functioning in relation to such basic needs as food and warmth.

service delivery   administrative arrangements for delivering assistance to exceptional children.

shaping   the teaching of new skills or behaviours by reinforcing learners for approaching the desired terminal behaviour.

skill acquisition   learning new skills.

skill maintenance   refers to children remembering learned skills and to the arrangement of the environment to increase the probability that a previously acquired skill will be demonstrated.

skills   relatively small units of action or behaviour that are easily observed and occur in brief periods.

social competence   the ability of young children to successfully and appropriately select and carry out their interpersonal goals.

socialization   the means by which individuals become reasonably acceptable and competent members of their society.

social reinforcers   verbal or nonverbal actions that provide attention or communicate approval.

social skills   those responses which, within a given situation, prove effective; in other words, that maximize the probability of producing, maintaining, or enhancing the positive aspects for the interactor.

social support approach   focuses on a family's functioning; stresses families helping themselves; sees informal support, such as the extended family and church, as more important than formal support.

special education   programming and instruction designed especially to suit the needs of an individual child who is exceptional.

speech   the usual medium of expressive language.

speech disorders   problems encountered in the oral production of language that interfere with communication.

speech pathologists (speech/language therapists) support personnel concerned with communication, its normal development, and its disorders.

stage theory approach   suggests that the parents of children with disabilities pass through orderly stages from grieving to acceptance.

standardized   refers to instruments that have standard procedures for administration and scoring.

stimulus   an aspect of the environment that can be specified in such a way that two or more observers can agree on when it is present and when it is not.

stress   the tension experienced when an event is perceived as harmful, threatening, or challenging to one's feelings of well-being.

stressors   the events or circumstances that give rise to stress; these internal or external events that threaten, harm, or challenge personal feelings of well-being.

support adaptation   when the child must be placed in a certain position or provided some general form of support before being able to pass an item during an assessment.

systems theory (perspective)   recognizes that actions in any part of the system affect the other parts, and that solutions to problems can only be found when the problem is properly defined in its larger environmental context. Influences are seen as multidirectional: each adult and child influences

every member of the household, and each family relationship affects all the other family members.

T

talent   advanced skills in a very specific area such as in the visual or performing arts.

task analysis   breaking skills down into their component parts.

teaching resourcefulness   the ability to provide children with experiences and instruction relevant to development that matches their needs, interests, and abilities.

teaching strategy   when a teacher teaches a learner to make a sequence of responses in order to reach the solution to a problem.

teratogens   environmental agents that may harm the developing fetus. Teratogens that can cause damage include prescription drugs, hard drugs such as cocaine and crack, nicotine, and alcohol.

tests   controlled and structured procedures that attempt to elicit particular responses that the child might not demonstrate spontaneously.

time out from positive reinforcement   the withdrawal of access to reinforcers for a specified period of time.

token reinforcers   initially meaningless items that attain reinforcing value when they are associated with, or exchangeable for, other primary or secondary reinforcers.

tool skills   those that are instrumental in accomplishing the greatest number of other skills or functional skills.

total communication   uses speech, speech reading, and amplification, along with a school-based manual system.

transition   the movement of children from one service program to another.

U

use   functions of language.

BIBLIOGRAPHY

A

Achenbach, T.M. (1991) *Child Behavior Checklist and Revised Child Behavior Profile*. Burlington, VT: University of Vermont.

Adams, K., and Markham, R. (1991) Recognition of affective facial expressions by children and adolescents with and without mental retardation. *American Journal on Mental Deficiency*, 96, 21-28.

AGS (1990) *Early Screening Profile*. Circle Pines, MI: American Guidance Services.

Ahuja, P. (1984) Helping children read through storytelling. *Reading*, 18, 37-43.

Arsick, Reid, and Hammill, D.D. (1990) *Test of Early Language Development*. Austin, TX: Pro-Ed.

Akerley, M.S. (1975) Parents speak. *Journal of Autism and Childhood Schizophrenia*, 5, 373-380.

Alberta Education (1982) *Early Childhood Services: Philosophy, Goals, and Dimensions*. Edmonton: Government of Alberta.

Aberto, F.M., Davis, B.L. and Prentice, L. (1995) Validity of an observation screening instrument in a multicultural population. *Journal of Early Intervention*, 19, 68-177.

Alderson, D. (1993, February) Attention Deficit Disorder. *Keeping in Touch*, 2.

Allen, D.A., and Affleck, G. (1985) Are we stereotyping parents? A postscript to Blacher. *Mental Retardation*, 23, 200-202.

Allen, D.A., and Hudd, S.S. (1987) Are we professionalizing parents? Weighing the benefits and pitfalls. *Mental Retardation*, 25, 133-139.

Allen, R.M., Cortazzo, A.D., and Adams, C. (1970) Factors in an adaptive behavior checklist for use with retardates. *Training School Bulletin*, 67, 144-157.

Allison, C. (1985) Developing direction of action programs: Repetitive action to correction loops. In J.E. Clark and J.H. Humphreys (Eds.) *Motor Development: Current Selected Research*. Princeton, NJ: Princeton Book Company.

American Association on Mental Retardation (1993) *Mental Retardation: Definition, Classification, and Systems of Support* (9th. ed.) Washington DC: AAMR.

Alpern, G., Boll, T., and Shearer, M. (1986) *The Developmental Profile*, 11. Los Angeles Western Psychological Services.

Ambron, S. (1980) Casual models in early education research. In S. Kilmer (Ed.) *Advances in Early Education and Child Care* (vol. 2) Greenwich, CT: JAI Press.

Angelo, D.H., and Goldstein, H. (1993) Effects of a pragmatic teaching strategy for requesting information by communication board users. *Journal of Speech and Hearing Disorders*, 55, 231-243.

Antia, S.D., Kreimeyer, K.H., and Eldredge, N. (1993) Promoting social interaction between young children with hearing impairments and their peers. *Exceptional Children*, 60, 262-275.

Apgar, V., and Beck, J. (1974) *Is My Baby All Right?* New York: Pocket Books.

Atkins, D.V. (1987) Siblings of the hearing impaired: Perspectives for parents. *Volta Review*, 89, 32-45.

Atkinson, R.L., Atkinson, R.C., Smith, E.E., and Bem, D.J. (1990) *Introduction to Psychology* (10th. ed.) New York: Harcourt Brace Jovonovich.

B

Bagnato, S.J., Kontos, S., and Neisworth, J.T. (1987) Integrated day care as special education: Profiles of programs and children. *Topics in Early Childhood Special Education*, 7, 28-47.

Bagnato, S.J., Neisworth, J.T., and Capone, A. (1986) Curriculum-based assessment for the young exceptional child: Rationale and review. *Topics in Early Childhood Special Education*, 6, 97-110.

Bagnato, S., Neisworth, J., and Mussen, S. (1989) *Linking Developmental Assessment and Early Intervention: Curricula-based Prescriptions*. Rockville, MD: Aspen.

Bailey, D.B. (1987) Preparing early interventionalists to work with families: Focus on collaborative goal-setting. *Topics in Early Childhood Special Education*, 7, 57-71.

———(1989) Issues and directions in preparing professionals to work with young handicapped children and their families. In J.J. Gallagher, R.M. Clifford, and P. Torhanis (Eds.) *Policy Implementations and PL 99-457: Planning for Young Children with Special Needs*, 97-132. Baltimore, MD: Paul Brooks.

Bailey, D.B. Jr., and Blanco, P.M. (1990) Parents' perspectives of a written survey of family needs. *Journal of Early Intervention*, 14, 196-203.

Bailey, D.B., and Brochin, H.A. (1989) Tests and test development. In D.B. Bailey and M. Wolery (Eds.) *Assessing Infants and Preschoolers with Handicaps*, 22-46. Columbus, OH: Merrill.

Bailey, D.B., and McWilliam, R.A. (1990) Normalizing early intervention. *Topics in Early Childhood Special Education*, 10, 33-47.

Bailey, D.B., and Wolery, M. (1984/1992) *Teaching Infants and Preschoolers with Handicaps*. Columbus, OH: Merrill.

——(1989) *Assessing Infants and Preschoolers with Handicaps*. Columbus, OH: Merrill.

Bailey, D.B., Jens, K., and Johnson, N. (1983) Curricula for handicapped infants. In S. Garwood and R. Fewell (Eds.) *Educating Handicapped Infants: Issues in Development and Intervention*, 387-415. Rockville, MD: Aspen.

Bailey, D.B., Harms, T., and Clifford, R.M. (1983) Matching changes in preschool environments to desired changes in child behavior. *Journal of the Division for Early Childhood*, 7, 61-68.

Bailey, D.B., Palsha, S.A., and Huntington, G.S. (1994)

Bailey, D.B. Jr., Simeonsson, R.J., Yoder, D.E., and Huntington, G.S. (1990) Preparing professionals to serve infants and toddlers with handicaps and their families: An integrative analysis across eight disciplines. *Exceptional Children*, 57, 26-35.

Bailey, D.B., Bysse, V., Edmondson, R., and Smith, T. (1992) Creating family-centred services in early intervention: Perceptions of professionals in four states. *Exceptional Children*, 58, 298-309.

Baillargeon, M., and Betsatel-Presser, R. (1988) Effets de gardinerie sur le comportement social et l'adaptation de l'enfant: Perception des enseignantes de la maternelle. *Canadian Journal of Research in Early Childhood Education*, 2, 91-98.

Baker, D.B. (1980) Applications of environmental psychology in programming for severely handicapped persons. *Journal of the Association for the Severely Handicapped*, 5, 234-249.

Baker, H., and Leland, B. (1967) *Detroit Tests of Learning Aptitude*. Indianapolis, IN: Bobbs Merrill.

Balthazar, E.E. (1973) *The Balthazar Scales of Adaptive Behavior: Scale 2, Scales of Social Adaptation*. Palo Alto, CA: Consulting Psychologists Press.

——(1976) *The Balthazar Scales of Adaptive Behavior: Scale 1, Scale of Functional Independence*. Palo Alto, CA: Consulting Psychologists Press.

Bannerman, D.J., Sheldon, J.B., Sherman, J.A., and Harchik, A.E. (1990) Balancing the right to habilitation with the right to personal liberties: The rights of people with developmental disabilties to eat too many doughnuts and take a nap. *Journal of Applied Behavior Analysis*, 23, 79-89.

Barkley, R.A. (1989) Attention deficit hyperactivity disorder. In E.J. Nash and R.A. Barkley (Eds.) *Treatment of Childhood Disorders*, 39-72. New York: Guilford.

——(1990) *Attention Deficit Hyperactivity Disorder: A Handbook for Diagnosis and Treatment*. New York: Guilford.

Barkley, R.A., Fisher, M., Newby, R., and Breen, M. (1988) Development of multi-method clinical protocol for assessing stimulant drug responses in ADHD children. *Journal of Clinical Child Psychology*, 17, 14-24.

Barth, J.M., and Parke, R.D. (1993) Parent-child relationship influences on children's transition to school. *Merrill-Palmer Quarterly*, 39, 173-195.

Baumeister, A.A., Kupstas, F., and Klindworth, L.M. (1990) New morbidity: Implications for prevention of children's disabilities. *Exceptionality*, 1, 1-16.

Baumgart, D., Brown, L., Pumpian, I., Nisbet, J., Sweet, M., Messina, R., and Schroeder, J. (1982) Principle of partial participation and individual adaptations in educational programs for severely handicapped students. *Journal of the Association for the Severely Handicapped*, 7, 17-27.

Baxter, C. (1980, July) Primary disability and secondary handicap: A rationale for the development of family oriented social intervention services. *Rehabilitation in Australia*, 27-34.

——(1987) Professional services as support: Perceptions of parents. *Australia and New Zealand Journal of Developmental Disabilities*, 13, 243-253.

Bayley, N. (1969/1994) *Bayley Scales of Infant Development*. New York: Psychological Corporation.

Beaven-Browne, P. (1993) Without a word: A classroom unit in non-verbal communication. *Teaching Today*, 12, 23-24.

Becker, W.C. (1986) *Applied Psychology for Teachers: A Behavior Cognitive Approach*. Chicago, IL: Science Research Associates.

Beckman, P.J. (1983). Influence of selected child characteristics on stress in families of handicapped infants. *American Journal of Mental Deficiency*, 88, 150-156.

Beckman, P.J., and Bailey, D.B. Jr. (1990) Preface, special issue on families. *Journal of Early Intervention*, 14, 195.

Beckman, P.J., and Lieber, J. (1994) The Social Strategy Rating Scale: An approach to evaluating social competence. *Journal of Early Intervention*, 18, 1-11.

Beckman, P.J., Newcomb, S., Frank, N., Brown, L., and Filer, J. (1993) Providing support to families of infants with disabilities. *Journal of Early Intervention*, 17, 445-454.

Beers, C.S., and Beers, J.W. (1980) Early identification of learning disabilities: Facts and fallacies. *Elementary School Journal*, 81, 67-76.

Beers, C., and Wehman, P. (1985) Play skill development. In M. Fallen and W. Umansky (Eds.) *Young Children with Special Needs*, 403-440. Columbus, OH: Merrill.

Behrmann, M.M. (1984) A brighter future for early learning through high tech. *The Pointer*, 28, 23-26.

Bellows, B.P. (April 1987) What does it mean? The composition of small groups for CAI. Paper presented at AERA, Washington.

Belsky, J. (1984) Infant day care and child development. Testimony before the US House of Representatives, September 5. In N. Salkind, (1990) *Child Development* (6th. ed.) Fort Worth, TX: Holt, Reinhart and Winston.

———(1986) A tale of two variances: Between and within. *Child Development*, 57, 1301-1305.

———(1987) Risks remain. *Zero to Three*, 7, 22-24.

Belsky, J., and Most, R. (1981) From exploration to play: A cross-sectional study of infant free play behavior. *Developmental Psychology*, 17, 630-639.

Belsky, J., and Steinberg, L.D. (1979, July and August) What does research teach us about day care: A follow-up report. *Children Today*, 21-26.

Bennett, A.T. (1988) Gateways to powerlessness: Incorporating Hispanic deaf children and families into formal schooling. *Disability, Handicap, and Society*, 3, 2.

Berdine, W.H., and Myer, S.A. (1987) *Assessment in Special Education*. Boston, MA: Little, Brown.

Berlin, C.M. Jr. (1983) Biological causes of exceptionality. In R.M. Smith, J.T. Neisworth, and F.M. Hunt (Eds.) *The Exceptional Child: A Functional Approach*. New York: McGraw-Hill

Bernheimer, L.P., Galtimore, R., and Kaufman, S.Z. (1993) Clinical child assessment in a family context: A four-group typology of family experiences with young children with developmental delays. *Journal of Early Intervention*, 17, 253-269.

Berreuta-Clement, J.R., Schweinhart, L.J., Barrett, W.S. Epstein, A.S., and Weikart, D.P. (1984) *Changed Lives: The Effects of the Perry Preschool Program on Youths Through Age 19*. Ypsilanti, MI: High/Scope Educational Research Foundation.

Biemiller, A., Regan, E., and Lero, D. (1987) Early childhood programs in Canada. In L. Katz (Ed.) *Current Topics in Early Childhood Education* (vol. 7) Norwood, NJ: Ablex.

Biklen, D. (1985) *Achieving the Complete School: Strategies to Effective Mainstreaming*. New York: Teachers College Press.

Black, M.M. (1991) Early intervention services for infants and toddlers: A focus on families. *Journal of Clinical Child Psychology,* 20, 51-57.

Blankenship, C.S. (1985) Using curriculum-based assessment data to make instructional decisions. *Exceptional Children, 52,* 233-238.

Blakeley, J.M., and La Grange, A.V. (1987, June) Continuity of educational experiences for children in grades K to 3: Educational perspectives. Paper at the Canadian Society for the Study of Education, Hamilton, ON.

Bloom, B.S. (1964) *Stability and Change in Human Characteristics.* New York: Wiley.

Bluma, S.M., Shearer, M.S., Frohman, D., and Hilliard, J.M. (1976) *Portage Guide to Early Education.* Portage, WI: The Portage Project.

Bochner, S., and Pieterse, M. (1989) Preschool directors' attitudes towards the integration of children with disabilities into regular preschools in New South Wales. *International Journal of Disability, Development and Education,* 36, 133-150.

Borgh, K., and Dickson, W.P. (1986) Two preschools sharing one microcomputer: Creating prosocial behavior with hardware and software. In P.F. Campbell and G.G. Fein (Eds.) *Young Children and Microcomputers*, 37-44. Reston, VA: Reston.

Bracken, B.A. (1984) *Bracken Basic Concept Scale.* Columbus, OH: Merrill.

Brackett, D., and Henniges, M. (1976) Communicative interactions of preschool hearing impaired children in the integrated setting. *Volta Review*, 78, 276-290.

Bradley, R.H. (1982) Socialization within day care: A brief review. *Infant Mental Health Journal*, 3, 156-161.

Bredekamp, S. (1986) *Developmentally Appropriate Practice.* Washington DC: National Association for the Education of Young Children.

———(1987) *Developmentally Appropriate Practice in Early Childhood Programs Serving Children from Birth Through Age Eight (Expanded Education).* Washington, DC: National Association for the Education of Young Children.

———(1991) Redeveloping early childhood education: A response to Kessler. *Early Childhood Research Quarterly,* 6, 199-209.

Bricker, D.D. (1978) A rationale for the integration of handicapped and non-handicapped preschool children. In M. Guralnick (Ed.) *Early Intervention and the Integration of Handicapped and Non-Handicapped Children,* 3-26. Baltimore, MD: University Park Press.

———(1982) *Intervention with At-Risk Handicapped Infants.* Baltimore, MD: University Park Press.

Bricker, D.D. (1986a) An analysis of early intervention programs: Attendant issues and future directions. In R.J. Morris and R.B. Blatt (Eds.) *Special Education: Research and Trends,* 28-65. New York: Pergamon.

———(1986b) *Early Education of At-risk and Handicapped Infants, Toddlers and Preschool Children.* Glenville, IL: Scott, Foresman.

———(1993) A rose by any other name, or is it? *Journal of Early Intervention*, 17, 89-96.

———(1995) The challenge of inclusion. *Journal of Early Intervention,* 19, 179-194.

Bricker, D.D., Bailey, E.J., and Slentz, K. (1990) Reliability, validity, and utility of the Evaluation and Programming System: For infants and young children (EPS-1). *Journal of Early Intervention*, 14, 147-158.

Brigance, A. H. (1977) *Brigance Diagnostic Inventory of Basic Skills.* Woburn, MA: Curriculum Associates.

———(1978) *Brigance Diagnostic Inventory of Early Development.* Woburn, MA: Curriculum Associates.

———(1980) *Brigance Diagnostic Inventory of Essential Skills .* Woburn, MA: Curriculum Associates.

Bristol, M., and Schopler, E. (1983) Stress and coping in families with autistic adolescents. In E. Schopler and G.B. Mesibov (Eds.) *Autism in Adolescents and Adults*, 251-278. New York: Plenum Press.

Brown, I.D. (1992, December) The teacher-psychologist relationship: A shared responsibility. *Keeping in Touch*, 2-3.

Brown, F., and Lehr, D.H. (1993) Making activities meaningful for students with severe multiple disabilities. *Teaching Exceptional Children*, 25, 12-16.

Brown, F., and Holveot, J. (1982) Effects of systematic peer interaction on the incidental learning of two severely handicapped students. *Journal of the Association for Persons with Severe Handicaps*, 7, 19-28.

Brown, L., Branston, M.B., Baumgart, B., Vincent, L., Falvey, M., and Schroeder, J. (1979) Utilizing the characteristics of a variety of current and subsequent least restrictive environments as factors in the development of curriculum content for severely handicapped students. *AAESPH Review*, 4, 407-424.

Brown, W.H., McEvoy, M.A., and Bishop, N. (1991) Incidental teaching of social behavior. *Teaching Exceptional Children*, 24, 35-38.

Brown, W.H., Ragland, E.U., and Bishop, N. (1989) A naturalistic teaching strategy to promote young children's peer interactions. *Teaching Exceptional Children*, 21, 8-10.

Brown, W.H., Ragland, E.U., and Fox, J.J. (1988) Effects of group socialization procedures on the social behavior of preschool children. *Research in Developmental Disabilities*, 9, 359-376.

Bruner, J., Roy, C., and Ratner, N. (1980) The beginnings of requests. In K.E. Nelson (Ed.) *Children's Language* (vol. 3). New York: Gardner.

Bryant, M.S. (1989) Challenging gifted learners through children's literature. *Gifted Child Today*, 12, 45-48.

Brynelson, D., and Cummings, H. (1987) Infant development programs: Early intervention in delayed development. In C. Denholm, R. Ferguson, and A. Pence (Eds.) *Professional Child Care and Youth Care: The Canadian Perspective*, 133-154. Vancouver: UBC Press.

Burgemeister, B.B., Bluma, L.H., and Lorge, I. (1972) *Columbia Mental Maturity Scale* (3rd. ed.) New York: Psychological Corporation.

Burks, H.F. (1981) *Burks Behavioral Rating Scales: Preschool and Kindergarten Manual.* Los Angeles: Western Psychological Corporation.

Burton, C.B., Hains, A.A., Hanline, M.F., McLean, M., and McCormick, K. (1992) Early childhood intervention and education: The urgency of professional unification. *Topics in Early Childhood Special Education*, 11, 53-69.

C

Cain, L.F., Levine, S., and Elzey, F.F. (1963) *Manual for the Cain-Levine Social Competency Scale.* Palo Alto, CA: Consulting Psychologists Press.

Calhoun, M.L., and Rose, T.L. (1989) Promoting positive parent-child interactions. *Teaching Exceptional Children,* 21, 44-45.

Cameron, R. (1989) Teaching parents to teach children: The Portage approach to special needs. In N. Jones (Ed.) *Special Education Needs Review*, 82-96. London: Falmer.

Canning, P.M., and Lyon, M.E. (1990) Young children with special needs. In I.M. Doxey (Ed.) *Child Care and Education: Canadian Dimensions*, 254-268. Toronto: Nelson.

Cantwell, D.P. (1975) *The Hyperactive Child.* New York: Spectrum.

Caplan, J. (1985) Evaluation of the child with delayed speech or language. *Pediatric Annals*, 14, 203-208.

Capone, A.M., Smith, M.A., and Schloss, P.J. (1988) Promoting play skills. *Teaching Exceptional Children*, 21, 54-56.

Carey, S.T. (1978) The child as word learner. In M. Halle, J. Bresnan, and G. Miller (Eds.) *Linguistic Theory and Psychological Reality.* Cambridge, MA: MIT Press.

Caro, P., and Snell, M.P. (1989) Characteristics of teaching communication to people with moderate and severe disabilities. *Education and Training in Mental Retardation,* 24, 63-75.

Carta, J.J., Schwartz, I.S., Atwater, J.B., and McConnell, S.R. (1991) Developmentally appropriate practice: Appraising the usefullness for young children with disabilities. *Topics in Early Childhood Special Education*, 11, 1-20.

Carter, D.B. (1987) The role of peers in sex role socialization. In D.B. Carter (Ed.) *Current Conceptions of Sex Roles and Sex Typing.* New York: Praeger.

Carter, E.A., and McGoldrick, M. (Eds.) (1980) *The Family Life Cycle: A Framework for Family Therapy.* New York: Gardner Press.

Caruso, D.A. (1988, September) Play and learning in infancy: Research and implications. *Young Children*, 63-70.

Casto, G., and Mastropieri, M.A. (1986) The efficacy of early intervention programs: A meta-analysis. *Exceptional Children*, 52, 417-424.

Cavallaro, S.A., and Porter, R.H. (1980) Peer preferences of at-risk and normally developing children in a mainstream setting. *American Journal of Mental Deficiency*, 84, 357-367.

Chandler, L.K. (1992) Promoting young children's social competence as a strategy for transition to mainstreamed kindergarten programs. In S.L. Odom, S.R. McConnell, and M.A. McEvoy (Eds.) *Social Competence of Young Children with Disabilities*, 245-276. Baltimore, MD: Brookes.

———(1993) Steps in preparing for transition. *Teaching Exceptional Children*, 25, 52-55.

Chess, S. (1987) Comments: Infant day care: A cause for concern. *Zero to Three*, 7, 24-25.

Children's Defence Fund (1987) *A Children's Defense Budget, FY1988: An Analysis of Our Nation's Investment in Children.* Washington DC: Author.

Chitwood, D.G. (1986) Guiding parents seeking testing. *Roeper Review,* 8, 177-179.

Christie, J., and Johnsen, E.P. (1987) Reconceptualizing constructive play: A review of the empirical literature. *Merrill Palmer Quarterly*, 33, 439-452.

Christie, J., and Wardle, F. (1992) How much time is needed for play? *Young Children*, 47, 28-33.

Christophensen, E.R. (1988) *Little People: Guidelines for Common Sense Child Rearing* (3rd. ed.) Kansas City, MO: Westport.

Clark, H.H., Rowbury, T., Baer, A.M., and Baer, D.M. (1973) Timeout as a punishing stimulus in continuous and intermittent schedules. *Journal of Applied Behavior Analysis*, 6, 443-455.

Clark, G.M. (1993) Is a functional curriculum approach compatible with an inclusive education model? *Teaching Exceptional Children*, 60, 36-39.

Clark, P.M. (1988) English as a secnd language in preschool aged children. In *Proceedings of the Australian Early Childhood Association 18th National Conference*. Canberra: Australian Early Childhood Association.

Clark, P.N., and Allen, A.S. (1985) *Occupational Therapy for Children.* St. Louis, MO: Mosby.

Clarke-Stewart, K.A. (1982a) Observation and experiment: Complementary strategies for studying day care and social development. *Early Education and Day Care*, 2, 227-250.

———(1982b) *Day Care*. Cambridge, MA: Harvard University Press.

———(1989) Infant day care: Maligned or malignant. *American Psychologist*, 44, 266-273.

Clarke-Stewart, K.A., and Fein, G.G. (1983) Early childhood programs. In P.H. Mussen (Ed.) *Handbook of Child Psychology (vol. 2) Infancy and Developmental Psychobiology*. New York: Wiley.

Clements, D.H. (1985) *Computers in Early Childhood and Primary Education*. Englewood Cliffs, NJ: Prentice-Hall.

Cohen, S.E., Parmalee, A.H., Sigman, M., and Blackwell, L. (1982) Neonatal risk factors in preterm infants. *Applied Research in Mental Retardation*, 3, 265-278.

Colangelo, N., and Fleuridas, C. (1986) The abduction of childhood. *Journal of Counseling and Development*, 64, 561-563.

Cole, K.N., Mills, P.E., Dale, P.S., and Jenkins, J.R. (1991) Effects of preschool integration for children with disabilities. *Exceptional Children*, 58, 36-45.

Cole, K.N., Dale, P.S., Mills, P.E., and Jenkins, J.R. (1993) Interactions between early intervention curriculum and student characteristics. *Exceptional Children*, 60, 17-28.

Cole, M., and Cole, S.R. (1989) *The Development of Children*. San Diego, CA: Scientific American Books.

Connell, D.R. (1987) The first 130 years were the fairest: Notes from the kindergarten and ungraded primary (K-1-2) *Young Children,* 42, 30-37.

Cook, R., Tessier, A., and Armbruster, V. (1987) *Adapting Early Childhod Curricula for Children with Special Needs*. Columbus, OH: Merrill.

Copeland, M.E., and Kimmel, J.R. (1989) *Evaluation and Management of Infants and Young Children with Developmental Disabilities*. Baltimore, MD: Brookes.

Corballis, M.C. (1983) *Human Laterality*. New York: Academic Press.

Cordesco, L.K., and Laus, M.K. (1993) Individualized training in behavioral strategies for parents of preschool children with disabilities. *Teaching Exceptional Children*, 25, 43-47.

Corning, N., and Halapin, J, (1989, March) *Computer Application in an Action-oriented Kindergarten.*

Wallingford, CT: Connecticut Institute for Teaching and Learning.

CEC, Council for Exceptional Children (1993) *Position Paper*. Division for Early Childhood: CEC.

Cratty, B. (1986) *Perceptual and Motor Development in Infants and Children* (3rd. ed.) Englewood Cliffs, NJ: Prentice-Hall.

Cross, L., and Johnston, S.A. (1977). A bibliography of instruments. In L. Cross and K. Goins (Eds.) *Identifying Handicapped Children: A Guide to Case-finding, Screening, Diagnosis, Assessment, and Evaluation*. New York: Walker.

Cummings, S.T., and Finger, D.C. (1980) Emotional disorders. In H.E. Rie and E.D. Rie (Eds.) *Handbook of Minimal Brain Dysfunction.* New York: Wiley.

Cummings, E.M., Ionatti, R.J., and Zahn-Waxler, C. (1989) Aggression between peers in early childhood: Individual continuity and developmental change. *Child Development*, 60, 887-895.

D

Darling, R.B. (1991) Parent-professional interaction: The roots of misunderstanding. In M. Seligman (Ed.) *The Family with a Handicapped Child* (2nd ed.), 119-151. Boston, MA: Allyn and Bacon.

Davis, G.A., and Rimm, S.B. (1994) *Education of the Gifted and Talented* (3rd. ed.) Boston, MA: Allyn and Bacon.

Day, B.D. (1988) What's happening in early childhood programs across the United States. In C. Warger (Ed.) *A Resource Guide to Public School Early Childhood Programs*, 3031. Alexandria, VA: Association for Supervision and Curriculum Development.

Deiner, P.L. (1983) *Resources for Teaching Young Children with Special Needs*. New York: Harcourt Brace Jovonovich.

Demchak, M.A., and Drinkwater, S. (1992) Preschoolers with severe disabilities: The case against segregation. *Topics in Early Childhood Special Education*, 11, 70-83.

Denholm, C.J. (1990) Attitudes of British Columbia directors of early childhood education centres towards the integration of handicapped children. *B.C. Journal of Special Education*, 14, 13-26.

Derman-Sparks, L. (1988) "It isn't fair:" An anti-bias curriculum for young children. In B. Neugebauer (Ed.) *Alike and Different: Exploring Our*

Humanity with Young Children, 8-15. Redmond, WA: Exchange Press.

Deshler, D.D., and Lenz, B.K. (1989) The strategies instructional approach. *International Journal of Learning Disability, Development and Education.*

Developmental delay: Questions and answers. (1991) *DEC Communicator, The Council for Exceptional Children,* 17, 1-4.

Devoney, C., Guralnick, M., and Rubin, H. (1974) Integrating handicapped and nonhandicapped preschool children: Effects on social play. *Childhood Education,* 50, 360-364.

De Vries, R., and Kohlberg, L. (1987) *Program for Early Education: The Constructivist View.* Chicago, IL: University of Chicago Press.

Diamond, K.E., and Squires, J. (1993) The role of parental report in the screening and assessment of young children. *Journal of Early Intervention,* 17, 107-115.

DiPietro, J.A. (1981) Rough and Tumble Play: A Function of Gender. *Developmental Psychology, 17, 50-58.*

Dodge, M.K., and Frost, J.L. (1986) Children's dramatic play: Influence of thematic and nonthematic settings. *Childhood Education,* 62, 166-170.

Donlon, E.T., and Curtis, W.S. (1972) *The Development and Evaluation of a Videotape Protocol for the Examination of Multihandicapped Deaf-blind Children.* Athens, GO: University of Georgia.

Donovan, E. (1987) *Preschool to Public School: A Teacher's Guide to Successful Transition for Children with Social Needs.* Syracuse, NY: Jowonio School.

Doxey, I.M. (1990) *Child Care and Education: Canadian Dimensions.* Toronto: Nelson.

Dudley-Marling, C., and Searle, D. (1991) *When Students Have Time to Talk: Creating Contexts for Language Learning.* Portsmouth, NH: Heinemann.

Dunlap, W.R. (1989) A functional classification for early childhood education. *Journal of Early Intervention,* 13, 73-99.

Dunn, L., and Dunn, L. (1981) *Peabody Picture Vocabulary Test—Revised.* Circle Pines, MN: American Guidance Service.

Dunst, C.J. (1980) *A Clinical and Educational Manual for use with the Uzgiris and Hunt Scales of Infant Psychological Development.* Baltimore, MD: University Park Press.

———(1985). Rethinking early intervention. *Analysis and Intervention in Developmental Disabilities,* 5, 165-201.

Dunst, C.J., and McWilliam, R.A. (1988) Cognitive assessment of multiple handicapped young children. In T. Wachs and R. Sheehan (Eds.) *Assessment of Developmentally Disabled Children,* 105-130. New York: Plenum.

Dunst, C.J., Johanson, C., Trivette, C.M., and Hamby, D. (1991) Family-oriented early intervention policies and practices: Family-centered or not? *Exceptional Children,* 58, 115-126.

Dunst, C.J., Trivette, C.M., and Deal, A. (1988) *Enabling and Empowering Families: Principles and Guidelines for Practice.* Cambridge, MA: Brookline Brooks.

Dunst, C.J., Trivette, C.M., and Cross, A.H. (1986) Mediating influences of social support: Personal, family, and child outcomes. *American Journal of Mental Deficiency,* 90, 403-417.

Dunst, C.J., Trivette, C.M., Hamby, D., and Pollock, B. (1990) Family systems correlates of the behavior of children with handicaps. *Journal of Early Intervention,* 14, 204-218.

Dyson, L., and Fewell, R.R. (1989) The self-concept of siblings of handicapped children: A comparison. *Journal of Early Intervention,* 13, 230-238.

Dyson, L., Edgar, E., and Crnik, K. (1989) Psychological predictors of adjustment in multihandicapped hearing impaired students. *American Annals of the Deaf,* 85, 9-14.

E

Eaton, W.O., and Yu, A.P. (1989) Are sex differences in child motor activity level a function of sex differences in maturational status? *Child Development,* 60, 1005-1011.

Eckler, J., and Weininger, O. (1988) Play and cognitive development—Development in preschoolers: A critical review. *Alberta Journal of Educational Research,* 34, 179-193.

Eden-Piercy, G.V., Blacher, J.B., and Eyman, R.K. (1986) Explaining parents' reactions to their young child with severe handicaps. *Mental Retardation, 24,* 285-291.

Edgar, E., Heggelund, M., and Fisher, M. (1989) A longitudinal study of graduates of special education preschools: Educational placement after preschool. *Topics in Early Childhood Special Education*, 8, 61-74.

Edmister, P., and Ekstrand, R.E. (1987) Preschool programming: Legal and educational issues. *Exceptional Children*, 54, 130-136.

Eheart, B.K., and Levitt, R.L. (1985) Supporting toddler play. *Young Children*, 40, 18-22.

Ehlers, V.L., and Ruffin, M. (1990) The Missouri Project-Parents as teachers. *Focus on Exceptional Children*. 23, 10-13.

Eisenberg, N., Wolchik, S.A., Hernandez, R., and Pasternak, J.F. (1985) Parental socialization of young children's play: A short-term longitudinal study. *Child Development*, 56, 1506-1514.

Eisenberg, A.R., and Garvey, C. (1981) Children's use of verbal strategies in resolving conflicts. *Discourse Processes*, 4, 149-170.

Eiserman, W.D., Shisler, L., and Hesley, S. (1995) A community assessment of preschool providers' attitudes toward inclusion. *Journal of Early Intervention*, 19, 146-167.

Elkind, D. (1986) Formal education and early childhood education: An essential difference. *Phi Delta Kappan*, 67, 631-636.

Elman, N.S. (1991) Family therapy. In M. Seligman (Ed.) *The Family with a Handicapped Child,* 369-406. Boston, MA: Allyn and Bacon.

Epstein, L.A. (1985) Family-based treatment for pre-adolescent obesity. In M. Wolraich and D.K. Routh (Eds.) *Advances in Developmental and Behavioral Pediatrics* (vol. 6) Greenwich, CT: JAI Press.

Erickson, S. (1993) Providing home made toys. Unpublished paper. University of Lethbridge.

Erin, J.E. (1986) Frequencies and types of questions in the language of visually impaired children. *Journal of Visual Impairment and Blindness*, 80, 670-674.

Esposito, B.G., and Koorland, M.A. (1989) Play behavior of hearing impaired children: Integrated and segregated settings. *Exceptional Children*, 55, 412-419.

Essa, E.L. (1987) The effects of a computer on preschool children's activities. *Early Childhood Research Quarterly,* 2, 377-382.

Esterly, D.L., and Griffin, H.C. (1987) Preschool programs for children with learning disabilities. *Journal of Learning Disabilities*, 20, 571-573.

F

Falvey, M.A. (1989) *Community-based Curricula: Instructional Strategies for Students with Severe Handicaps* (2nd. ed.) Baltimore, MD: Brookes.

Famularo, R., and Fenton, T. (1987) The effect of methylphenidate on school grades in children with attention deficit disorders without hyperactivity: A preliminary report. *Journal of Clinical Psychiatry*, 48, 112-114.

Fee, V.E., Matson, J.L., and Manikam, R. (1990) A control group outcome study of a nonexclusionary time-out package to improve social skills with preschoolers. *Exceptionality*, 1, 107-121.

Fenske, E.C., Zalenski, S., Krantz, P.J., and McClannahan, L.E. (1985) Age at intervention and treatment outcomes for autistic children in a comprehensive intervention program. *Analysis and Intervention in Developmental Disabilities*, 5, 49-58.

Feshbach, S. (1970) Aggression. In P. Mussen (Ed.) *Carmicheals Manual of Child Psychology* (3rd. ed) New York: Wiley.

Fewell, R.R. (1983) Assessing handicapped infants. In S. Garwood and R.R. Fewell (Eds.) *Educating Handicapped Infants: Issues in Development and Intervention*, 257-297. Rockville, MD: Aspen Systems.

———(1984) Play Assessment Scale (4th. ed.) Available from the author. Seattle, University of Washington.

———(1986) A handicapped child in the family. In R.R. Fewell and R.J. Vadazy (Eds.) *Families of Handicapped Children: Needs and Supports Across the Lifespan*, 3-34. Bellevue, WA: Edmark Corporation.

———(1988) Utilization of the Play Assessment Scale Workshop at Oregon. Cited in Weber, C. Behl, D., and Dummers, M. (1994) Watch them play, watch them learn. *Teaching Exceptional Children*, 27, 30-35.

———(1991) Parenting moderately handicapped persons. In M. Seligman (Ed.) *The Family and the Handicapped Child*. Boston, MA: Allyn and Bacon.

———(1993) Interventions to promote motor skills. In *DEC Recommended Practice: Indicators of Quality in Programs for Infants and Young Children with Special Needs and Their Families*, 91-94. Reston, VA: CEC.

Fewell, R.R., and Langley, B. (1984) *Developmental Activities Screening Inventory,* 11. Austin, TX: Pro-Ed.

Fewell, R.R. and Vadasy, R.J. (Eds.) (1983) *Families of Handicapped Children: Needs and Supports Across the Lifespan* Bellevue, WA: Edmark Corporation.

Fieber, N.M. (1977) Sensiromotor cognitive assessment and curriculum for the multihandicapped child. In B. Wilcox, F. Kohl, and T. Vogelsberg (Eds.) *The Severely and Profoundly Handicapped Child: Proceedings for the 1977 Statewide Institute for Educators of the Severely and Profoundly Handicapped.* Springfield, IL: Office of Education.

Fiechtl, B., Rule, S., and Innocente, M.S. (1989) It's time to get ready for school. *Teaching Exceptional Children*, 63-65.

Fink, R.S. (1976) Role of imaginative play in cognitive development. *Psychological Reports,* 39, 895-906.

Fiore, T.S., Becker, E.A., and Nero, R.C. (1993) Educational interventions for students with attention deficit disorder. *Exceptional Children*, 60, 163-173.

Fiscella, J., and Barnett, L.A. (1985) A child by any other name: A comparison of the play behaviors of gifted and non-gifted children. *Gifted Child Quarterly*, 29, 61-66.

Fishburne, G.J. (1989) Stimulant drug therapy and children with attention deficit disorder: An ethical issue. *McGill Journal of Education*, 24, 55-68.

Folio, M.R., and Fewell, R.R. (1983) *Peabody Developmental Motor Scale and Activity Cards.* Hingham, MA: Teaching Resources Corporation.

Foster, S.L., and Ritchey, W.L. (1979) Issues in the assessment of social competence in children. *Journal of Applied Behavior Analysis, 12,* 625-638.

Fowler, S.A., Schwartz, I., and Atwater, J. (1991) Perspectives on the transition from preschool to kindergarten for children with disabilities and their families. *Exceptional Children*, 58, 136-145.

Fowler, S.A., Dougherty, B.S., Kirby, K., and Kohler, F.W. (1986) Role reversals: An analysis of therapeutic effects achieved with disruptive boys during their appointments as peer monitors. *Journal of Applied Behavior Analysis*, 19, 437-444.

Fowler, W. (1975) A developmental learning approach to infant care in a group setting. In B.Z. Friedlander, G.M. Sterritt, and G.E. Kirk (Eds.) *Exceptional Infant Assessment an Intervention* (vol. 3), 341-373. New York: Brunner/Mazel.

Fox, L., Hanline, M.F., Vail, C.O., and Galant, K.R. (1994) Developmentally appropriate practice: Applications for young children with disabilities. *Journal of Early Intervention*, 18, 243-257.

Frankenburg, W.K., Dodds, J.B., and Fandal, A.W. (1975) *Denver Developmental Screening Test.* Denver, CO: Ladoca Project and Publishing Company.

Frankenberg, W.K., Dodds, J., Archer, P., Bresnick, B., Maschka, P., Edelman, N., and Shapiro, H., (1990) *Denver 11: Technical Manual.* Denver, CO: Denver Developmental Materials.

Frankenberg, W.F., Fandal, A.W., and Thornton, F.M. (1987) Revision of Denver Prescreening Developmental Questionnaire. *Journal of Pediatrics*, 110, 653-657.

Franklin, E.A. (1992) Learning to read and write the natural way. *Teaching Exceptional Children*, 24, 45-48.

Frey, K.S., Greenberg, M.T., and Fewell, R.R. (1989) Stress and coping among parents of handicapped children: A multidimensional approach. *American Journal on Mental Retardation*, 94, 240-249.

Friedman, C. T. (1989). Integrating infants. *Exceptional Parent*, 52-57.

Fritz, J., and Wetherbee, S. (1982) Preschoolers' beliefs regarding the obese individual. *Canadian Home Economics Journal*, 33, 193-196.

Fuchs, L.S., and Fuchs, D. (1986) Linking assessment to instructional intervention: An overview. *School Psychology Review*, 15, 318-323.

Furumo, S., O'Reilly, K.A., Hosaka, C.M., Inatsuka, T.T., Allman, T.L., and Zeisloft, B. (1979) *Hawaii Early Learning Profile.* Palo Alto, CA: VORT.

G

Gallagher, J.J. and Gallagher, S.A. (1994) *Teaching the Gifted Child* (4th. ed.) Boston, MA: Allyn and Bacon.

Galloway, C. and Chandler, P. (1978) The marriage of special and generic early education services. In M. Guralnick (Ed.) *Early Intervention and the Integration of Handicapped and Nonhandicapped Children*, 261-287. Baltimore, MD: University Park Press.

Gardner, H. (1980) *Artful Scribbles: The Signature of Children's Drawings.* New York: Basic Books.

Garner, J.B., and Campbell, P.H. (1987) Technology for persons with severe disabilities: Practical and ethical considerations. *The Journal of Special Education*, 21, 122-132.

Garwood, S.G. (1982) (Mis)use of developmental scales in program evaluation. *Topics in Early Childhood Special Education*, 1, 61-69.

Gaylord-Ross, R., and Haring, T. (1987) Social interaction research for adolescents with severe handicaps. *Behavioral Disorders*, 12, 264-275.

Gearheart, B., Mullen, R. C., and Gearheart, C.J. (1993) *Exceptional Individuals: An introduction*. Pacific Grove, CA: Brooks/Cole.

Gesell, A., and Amatruda, C.S. (1947) *Developmental Diagnosis* (2nd. ed.) New York: Paul B. Hoeber.

Gibson, J.T. (1978) *Growing Up: A Study of Children*. Reading, MA: Addison Wesley.

Gibson, J.T., and Chandler, L.A. (1988) *Educational Psychology: Mastering Principles and Applications*. Boston, MA: Allyn and Bacon.

Gillberg, J., and Gillberg, C. (1988) Generalized hyperkenesis: Follow-up study from age 7 to 13 years. *Journal of the American Academy of Child and Adolescent Psychiatry*, 27, 55-59.

Glascoe, F.P. (1991) Can clinical judgments detect children with speech-language problems? *Pediatrics*, 87, 317-322.

Goetz, L., Gee, K., and Sailor, W. (1985) Using a behavior chain interruption strategy to teach communication skills to students with severe disabilities. *Journal for the Association of Persons with Severe Handicaps*, 10, 21-30.

Gogel, E.M., McCumsey, J., and Hewitt, G. (1985, Nov/Dec.) What parents are saying. *Gifted/Talented/Creative*, pp. 7-9.

Goldberg, S., Marcovitch, S., Macgregor, D., and Lojkasek, M. (1986) Family responses to developmentally delayed preschoolers: Etiology and the father's role. *American Journal of Mental Deficiency*, 90, 610-617.

Goldstein, H. (1993) Use of peers as communication intervention agents. *Teaching Exceptional Children*, 25, 37-40

Goldstein, H., and Ferrell, D. (1987) Augmenting communicative interaction between handicapped and nonhandicapped preschool children. *Journal of Speech and Hearing Disorders*, 52, 200-211.

Goldstein, H., and Wickstrom, S. (1986) Peer intervention effects on communicative interaction among handicapped and nonhandicapped preschoolers. *Journal of Applied Behavior Analysis*, 19, 209-214.

Gottfried, A.W., and Brown, C.C. (1986) *Play Interactions*. Lexington Books.

Gough, P.B. (1991) Tapping parent power. *Phi Delta Kappan*, 75, 339.

Gowen, J., Johnson-Martin, N., Goldman, B., and Appelbaum, M. (1989) Feelings of depression and parenting competence in mothers of handicapped and nonhandicapped infants: A longitudinal study. *American Journal of Mental Retardation*, 94, 259-271.

Gowen, J.W., Christy, D.S., and Sparling, J. (1993) Informational needs of parents of young children with special needs. *Journal of Early Intervention*, 17, 194-210.

Grant, K.L. (1989, fall) Essential elements in the preparation of early childhood teachers. *NAECTE*, 23-24.

Green, A.L., and Stoneman, Z. (1989) Attitudes of mothers and fathers of nonhandicapped children. *Journal of Early Intervention*, 13, 292-304.

Greenman, J. (1988) *Caring Spaces, Learning Places: Childrens' Environments that Work*. Redmond, WA: Exchange Press.

Gresham, F.M. (1986) Conceptual and definitional issues in the assessment of children's social needs: Implications for classification and training. *Journal of Clinical Child Psychology*, 15, 3-15.

Griffin, G.W. (1987) Childhood predictive characteristics of aggressive adolescents. *Exceptional Children*, 54, 246-252.

Grossman, H. (Ed.) (1977) *Manual on Terminology and Classification in Mental Retardation*. Washington DC: American Association on Mental Deficiency.

Grunewald, K. (1974) International trends in the care of the severely and profoundly retarded and multiple handicapped. In F.J. Menaloscino and P.M. Pearson (Eds.) *Beyond the Limits: Innovations in Services for the Severely and Profoundly Retarded*. Seattle, WA: Special Child Publications.

Guddemi, M. (1990) Play and learning for the special child. *Day Care and Early Education*, 18, 39-40.

Guess, D., Sailor, W., and Baer, D.M. (1977) A behavioral-remedial approach to language training for the severely handicapped. In E. Sontag (Ed.) *Educational Programming for the Severely and Profoundly Handicapped*. Reston, VA: Council for Exceptional Children.

Guess, D., and Noonan, M.J. (1982) Curricula and instructional procedures for severely handicapped students. *Focus on Exceptional Children*, 4, 1-12.

Gullo, D., Bersami, C., Clements, D., and Bayless, K. (1985) A comparative study of 'all-day,' 'alternate-day,' and 'half-day' kindergarten schedules: Effects on achievement and classroom social behaviors. *Journal of Research in Childhood Education*, 1, 82-94.

Guralnick, M.J. (1976) The value of integrating handicapped and nonhandicapped preschool children. *American Journal of Orthopsychiatry*, 46, 236-245.

———(1981) Programmatic factors affecting child-child social interactions in mainstreamed preschool programs. *Exceptional Education Quarterly*, 1, 71-91.

———(1986) The peer relations of young handicapped and nonhandicapped children. In P.S. Stein, M.J. Guralnick, and H.M. Walter (Eds.) *Children's Social Behavior: Development, Assessment, and Modification*, 93-140. New York: Academic Press.

———(1988) Efficacy research in early childhood intervention programs. In S.L. Odom and M.B. Karnes (Eds.) *Early Intervention for Infants and Children with Handicaps: An Empirical Base*, 75-88. Baltimore, MD: Brookes.

———(1989) Recent developments in early intervention efficacy research: Implications for family involvement in PL99-457. *Topics in Early Childhood Special Education*, 9, 1-17.

———(1990) Social competence and early intervention. *Journal of Early Intervention*, 14, 3-14.

Guralnick, M.J., and Bricker, D. (1987) The effectiveness of early intervention for children wih cognitive and general developmental delays, In M. J. Guralnick and C. Bennett (Eds.) *The Effectiveness of Early Intervention for At-risk and Handicapped Children*, 115-173. New York: Academic Press.

Guralnick, M.J., and Groom, J.M. (1987) Dyadic peer interactions of mildly delayed and non-handicapped preschool children. *American Journal of Mental Deficiency*, 92, 178-193.

Guralnick, M.J., and Paul-Brown, D. (1977) The nature of verbal interactions among handicapped and non-handicapped preschool children. *Child Development*, 254-260.

———(1980) Communication adjustments during behavior request episodes among children at different developmental levels. *Child Development*, 55, 911-919.

H

Haberman, M. (1989) Thirty-nine reasons to stop the school reading machine. *Phi Delta Kappan*, 71, 284-288.

Hains, A.H., Fowler, S.A., and Chandler, L.K. (1988) Planning school transitions: Family and professional collaboration. *Journal of the Division for Early Childhood*, 12, 108-115.

Haley, S.M., Hallenborg, S.C., and Gans, B.M. (1989) Functional assessment in young children with neurological impairments. *Topics in Early Childhood Special Education*, 9, 106-126.

Hallahan, D.P., and Kauffman, J.M. (1991) *Exceptional Children: Introduction to Special Education* (5th. ed.) Englewood Cliffs, NJ: Prentice-Hall.

Halle, J.W. (1984) Natural environment language assessment and intervention with severely impaired preschoolers. *Topics in Early Childhood Special Education*, 4, 35-56.

Hamachek, B., and Kauffman, J. (1994) Special education in the United States. In K. Mazurek and M. Winzer (Eds.) *Comparative Studies in Special Education*. Washington, DC: Gallaudet University Press.

Hammill, D.D. (1984) *Detroit Tests of Learning Aptitude* (2nd. ed.) Austin, TX: Pro-Ed.

Hamre-Nietupski, S. (1993) How much time should be spent on skill instruction and friendship development? Preferences of parents of students with moderate and severe/profound disabilities. *Education and Training in Mental Retardation*, 28, 220-231.

Hanline, M.F. (1988). Making the transition to preschool: Identification of parent needs. *Journal of the Division for Early Childhood*, 19, 98-107.

Hanline, M.F., and Halvorsen, A. (1989) Parent perceptions of the integration transition process: Overcoming artificial barriers. *Exceptional Children*, 55, 487-492.

Hanline, M.F., and Knowlton, A.K. (1988) A collaborative model for providing support to parents during their child's transition from infant intervention to preschool special education and public school programs. *Journal of the Division for Early Childhood*, 12, 116-125.

Hanline, M.F., Suchman, S., and Demmerle, C. (1989) Beginning public preschool. *Teaching Exceptional Children*, 61-62.

Hanson, M., and Harris, S.R. (1986) *Teaching the Young Child with Motor Delays: A Guide for Parents and Professionals.* Austin, TX: Pro-Ed.

Hanson, M.J., Lynch, E.W., and Wayman, L.I. (1990) Honoring the cultural diversity of families when gathering data. *Topics in Early Childhood Special Education*, 10, 112-131.

Haring, N.G., and Bricker, D. (1976) Overview of comprehensive services for the severely and profoundly handicapped. In N. Haring and L. Brown, (Eds.) *Teaching the Severely Handicapped* (vol. 1) New York: Grune and Stratton.

Harris, A.C. (1986) *Child Development.* St. Paul, MI: West.

Harris, L., Humphrey, K., Muir, D.M., and Dodwell, P.C. (1985) Use of the Cantebury child's aid in infancy and early childhood: A case study. *Journal of Visual Impairment and Blindness*, 79, 4-11.

Harris, S.L., Handleman, J.S., Kristoff, B., Bass, L., and Gordon, R. (1990). Changes in language development among autistic and peer children in segregated and integrated preschool settings. *Journal of Autism and Developmental Disorders*, 20, 23-31.

Hart, B., and Risley, T. (1975) Incidental teaching of language in the pre-school. *Journal of Applied Behavior Analysis*, 8, 411-420.

Hartup, W.W. (1974) Aggression in childhood: Developmental perspectives. *American Psychologist*, 29, 336-341.

————(1983) Peer relations. In P.H. Mussen (Ed.) *Handbook of Child Psychology*, (vol. 4). 103-196. New York: Wiley.

Haskins, R. (1985) Public school aggression among children with varying day-care experience. *Child Development*, 56, 689-703.

————(1989) Beyond metaphor: The efficacy of early childhood education. *American Psychologist*, 44, 274-282.

Hawes, C. (1993) Early childhood care. In J.L. Roopnarine and J.E. Johnson (Eds.) *Approaches to Early Childhood Education*, 71-80. New York: Merrill.

Hay, D.F. (1984) Social conflict in early childhood. In G. Whitechurch (Ed.) *Annals of Child Development.* Greenwich, CT: JAL.

Hay, D.F., and Ross, H.S. (1982) The social nature of early conflict. *Child Development*, 53, 105-113.

Hay, D.F., Nash, A., and Pedersen, J. (1983) Interaction between six-month-old peers. *Child Development*, 54, 557-562.

Hayes, C.D., Palmer, J.G., and Zaslow, M. (1990) *Who Cares for America's Children?: Child Care Policy for the 1990s.* Washington DC: National Academy Press.

Hedrick, D.L., Pratter, E.M., and Tobin, A.R. (1975) *Sequenced Inventory of Communication Development.* Seattle, WA: University of Washington Press.

Henderson, A. (1989) Parents are a school's best friends. *Phi Delta Kappan*, 70, 149-153.

Henker, B., and Whalen, C.K. (1989) Hyperactivity and attention deficits. *American Psychologist*, 44, 216-223.

Hernicke, C.M., Beckwith, L. and Thompson, A. (1988) Early intervention in the family system: A framework and review. *Infant Mental Health Journal*, 9, 111-141.

Heshusius, L. (1986). Pedagogy, special education, and the lives of young children: A critical and futuristic perspective. *Journal of Education*, 168, 25-38.

Hetherington, E.M., Cox, M., and Cox, R. (1979) Play and social interaction in children following divorce. *Journal of Social Issues*, 35, 26-49.

Higginbotham, D.J., and Baker, B.M. (1981). Social participation and cognitive play differences in hearing-impaired and normally hearing pre-schoolers. *Volta Review*, 83, 135-149.

Higginbotham, D.J., Baker, B.M., and Neill, R.D. (1980). Assessing the social participation and cognitive play abilities of hearing-impaired preschoolers. *Volta Review*, 82, 261-270.

Higgins, A.T., and Turnure, J.E. (1984) Distractibility and concentration of attention in children's development. *Child Development*, 55, 1799-1810.

Hill, P.S. (1987) The function of kindergarten. *Young Children*, 42, 12-19.

Hirst, C.C., and Shelley, E. Y. (1989). They too should play. *Teaching Exceptional Children*, 21, 26-28.

Hiskey, M.S. (1966) *Hiskey-Nebraska Test of Learning Aptitude.* Lincoln, NA: Union College Press.

Hobson, R.P. (1988) Beyond cognition: A theory of autism. In G. Dawson (Ed.) *Autism: New Perspectives on Diagnoses, Nature and Treatment.* New York: Guilford.

Hofferth, S.L., and Phillips, D.A. (1987) Child care in the United States, 1970-1995. *Journal of Marriage and the Family*, 49, 559-571.

Hoge, R.D., and Wichmann, C. (1994) *An Evaluation Review of Interview and Rating/Checklist Instruments for Assessing Social-Emotional Competence in Preschool Children.* Ottawa: Psychology Department, Carleton University.

Hohmann, B., Banet, B., and Weikart, D. (1979) *Young Children in Action: A Manual for Preschool Educators*. Ypsilanti, MI: High/Scope.

Hollinger, J.D. (1987) Social skills for behaviorally disordered children as preparation for mainstreaming: Theory, practice, and new directions. *Remedial and Special Education*, 8, 17-27.

Holvoet, J., Guess, D., Mulligan, M., and Brown, F. (1980) The individualized curriculum sequencing model: 11: A teaching strategy for severely handicapped students. *Journal of the Association for the Severely Handicapped*, 5, 337-351.

Horgan, D. (1990) Learning to tell jokes: A case of metalinguistic abilities. In R.P. Honeck, T.J.S. Case, and M.J. Firment (Eds.) 208-213 *Introductory Readings for Cognitive Psychology*. Guilford, CT: Dushkin.

Horne, M.D., and Ricciardo, J.L. (1988) Hierarchy of reponse to handicap. *Psychological Reports*, 62, 83-86.

Houseman, J. (1972) An ecological study of interpersonal conflicts among preschool children. Doctoral dissertation, University Microfilms No. 75-12533.

Howlin, P. (1981) The results of a home-bound language training program with autistic children. *British Journal of Disorders of Communication*, 16, 73-87.

Hoy-Youngblood, M. (1986, February) Kindergarten readiness skills. In G.G. McGee, T. Daly, S.G. Izeman, L.H. Mann, and T.R. Risley (1991) Use of classroom materials to promote preschool engagement. *Teaching Exceptional Children*, 23, 44-47.

Huessman, L.R., Eron, L.D., Lefkowitz, M., and Walder, L. (1984) Stability of aggression over time and generations. *Developmental Psychology*, 20, 1120-1134.

Hughes, F.P. (1991) *Children, Play, and Development*. Boston, MA: Allyn and Bacon.

Huizinga, J. (1970) *Homo Ludens*. London: Maurice Temple Smith.

Hulse, S.H., Egeth, H., and Deese, J. (1980). *The psychology of learning* (5th. ed.). New York: McGraw-Hill.

Humphreys, A.P., and Smith, P.K. (1987) Rough and tumble friendship amd dominance in school children: Evidence for continuity and change with age in middle childhood. *Child Development*, 58, 201-212.

Hundert, J. and Houghton, A. (1992) Promoting social interaction of children with disabilities in integrated preschools: A failure to generalize. *Exceptional Children,* 58, 311-320.

Hurvitz, J.A., Pickert, S.M., and Rilla, D.C. (1987) Promoting children's language interaction. *Teaching Exceptional Children*, 19, 12-15.

Huston-Stein, A., Friedrich-Cofer, L., and Susman E.J. (Eds.) (1977) The relation of classroom structure to social behavior, imaginative play, and self-regulation of economically disadvantaged children. *Child Development*, 48, 908-916.

Hutinger, P.L. (1987) Computer-based learning applications for young children with special needs. In J.L. Roopnarine and J.E. Johnson (Eds.) *Approaches to Early Childhood Education*, 213-236. Columbus, OH: Merrill.

Hymes, J. (1991) *Early Childhood Education: Twenty Years in Review.* Washington DC: National Association for the Education of Young Children.

I

Illingworth, R.S. (1980) *The Development of the Infant and Young Child: Abnormal and Normal* (7th ed.) New York: Churchill Livingstone.

Ireton, H., and Thwing, E. (1974) *The Minnesota Child Development Inventory*. Minneapolis, MN: Behavioral Sciences, Systems, Inc.

J

Jackson, N.E. (1988) Precocious reading ability: What does it mean? *Gifted Child Quarterly*, 32, 196-199.

Jackson, S.C., Robey, L., Watjus, M., and Chadwick, E. (1991, fall) Play for all children: The toy library solution. *Childhood Education*, 27-31.

Jambor, T., and Gargiulo, R. (1987, October). The playground: A social entity for mainstreaming. *JOPERD*, 18-23.

Jenkins, J.R., Odom, S., and Speltz, M. (1989) Effects of social integration on preschool children with handicaps. *Exceptional Children*, 55, 420-428.

Jenkins, J.R., Speltz, M.L., and Odom, S.L. (1985) Integrating preschoolers: Effects on child development and social interaction. *Exceptional Children*, 52, 7-17.

Jensen, A.R. (1969) How much can we boost IQ and scholastic achievement? *Harvard Educational Review*, 39, 1-123.

Johnson, J.E., Christie, J.F., and Yawkey, T.D. (1987) *Play and Early Childhood Development.* Glenview, IL: Scott, Foresman and Co.

Johnson, R., and Mandell, C. (1988) A social observation checklist for preschoolers. *Teaching Exceptional Children,* 20, 18-21.

Johnson, T.E., Chandler, L.K., Kerns, G.M., and Fowler, S.A. (1986) What are parents saying about family involvement in school transitions; A retrospective transition interview. *Journal of the Division for Early Childhood*, 11, 10-17.

Johnson, J.E., and Roopnarine, J.L. (1983) The preschool classroom and sex differences in children's play. In M. Liss (Ed.) *Social and cognitive skills* 193-218 New York: Academic Press.

Johnson-Martin, N., Jens, J.K., and Altmeier, S.M. (1986) *The Carolina Curriculum for Handicapped Infants and Infants at Risk.* Baltimore, MD: Brookes.

Jones, H.A., and Warren, S.F. (1991) Enhancing engagement in early language teaching. *Teaching Exceptional Children*, 23, 48-50.

K

Kagan, J., Kearsley, R.G., and Zelazo, P.R. (1977) The effects of infant day care on psychological development. *Educational Quarterly*, 1, 109-142.

Kamii, C. (1985) Leading primary education toward excellence. *Young Children*, 40, 3-9.

Kaplan, P.S. (1996) *Pathways for Exceptional Children: School, Home, and Culture.* Minneapolis/St. Paul, MI: West Publishing.

Karnes, M.B., and Johnson, L. (1991) Differentiating instruction for preschool gifted children. In R. Milgram (Ed.) *Counseling Gifted and Talented Children: A Guide for Teachers, Counselors, and Parents*. Norwood, NJ: Ablex.

Karnes, M.B. (1992) *Fit for Me: Activities for Building Motor Skills in Young Children.* Allen, TX: Developmental Learning Materials.

Karnes, M.B., Johnson, L.J., Cohen, T., and Shwedel, A. (1985). Facilitating school success among mildly and moderately handicapped children by enhancing task persistence. *Journal of the Division for Early Childhood*, 9, 151-161.

Katz, L.G. (1988) Engaging children's minds: The implications of research for early childhood education. In C. Warger (Ed.) *A Resource Guide to Public School Early Education Programs.* Alexandria, VA: Association for Supervision and Curriculum Development.

Kaufman, A.S., and Kaufman, N.L. (1983) *Kaufman Assessment Battery for Children.* Circle Pines, MI: American Guidance Services.

Kauffman, J.M. (1977/1989/1991) *Characteristics of Children's Behavior Disorders*. Columbus, OH: Merrill.

Kavale, K. (1982) The efficacy of stimulant drug treatment for hyperactivity: A metaanalysis. *Journal of Learning Disabilities*, 15, 280-289.

Kazak, A.E., and Marvin, E.S. (1984) Differences, difficulties and adaptations: Stress and social networks in families with a handicapped child. *Family Relations*, 33, 66-67.

Kellogg, R., and O'Dell, S. (1969) *Analysing Children's Art.* Palo Alto, CA: National Press Books.

Kendall, D., Brynelson, D., and La Pierre, J.G. (1985) Infant development programmes in Canada. Unpublished paper, Infant Development Programme of British Columbia.

Kilgo, J.L. (1990) Early transitions. *DEC Communicator,* 17, 3.

Kilgo, J.L., Richard, N., and Noonan, M.J. (1989) Teaming for the future: Integrating transition planning with early intervention services for young children with special needs and their families. *Infants and Young Children*, 2, 37-48.

King, J. (1987) Handling physically handicapped students. Paper presented at MUN.

Kitano, M.K. (1985) Ethnography of a preschool for the gifted: What gifted young children actually do. *Gifted Child Quarterly*, 29, 67-73.

Kitano, M.K., and Kirby, D.F. (1986) *Gifted Education: A Comprehensive View.* Boston, MA: Little, Brown.

Klausmieir, H.J. (1990) Conceptualizing. In B.J. Jones and L. Idol (Eds.) *Dimensions of Thinking and Cognitive Instruction*, 93-138. Hillsdale, NJ: Erlbaum.

Klein, P.S., and Alony, S. (1993) Immediate and sustained effects of maternal mediating behaviors on young children. *Journal of Early Intervention*, 17, 177-193.

Knobloch, H., Stevens, F., and Malone, A.F. (1980) *Manual of Developmental Diagnosis.* New York: Harper and Row.

Kodera, T.L., and Garwood, S.G. (1979) Cognitive processes and intelligence. In S.G. Garwood (Ed.) *Educating Young Handicapped Children: A Developmental Approach.* Germantown, MD: Aspen Systems.

Kohler, F.W., and Strain, P.S. (1993) The early childhood social skills program: Making friends during the early childhood years. *Teaching Exceptional Children*, 25, 41-42.

Kouri, T. (1989) How manual sign acquisition relates to the development of spoken language: A case study. *Language, Speech and Hearing Services in the Schools*, 20, 50-62.

Kovach, J., and Kjerkland, L. (1989) *Final Report: Project Dakota 1983-1986.* Eagan, MN: Project Dakota Outreach.

Kramer, R. (1988) *Maria Montessori: A Biography.* Menlo Park, CA: Addison-Wesley.

Krantz, P., and Risley, T. (1977) Behavioral ecology in the classroom. In K. O'Leary and S. O'Leary (Eds.) *Classroom Management: The Successful Use of Behavior Modification* (2nd. ed.) New York: Pergamon Press.

Kuzemko, J.A. (1978) *Allergy in Children.* Kent, England: Pittman Medical.

L

Lahey, B.B., and Ciminero, A.R.(1980) *Maladaptive Behavior: An Introduction to Abnormal Psychology.* Glenview, IL: Scott Foresman.

Lamb, M., and Bornstein, M. (1987) *Development in Infancy: An Introduction.* New York: Random House.

Landerholm, E. (1990) The transdisciplinary team approach in infant intervention programs. *Teaching Exceptional Children*, 22, 66-70.

Langley, M.B. (1991) Assessment: A multidimensional process. In M.B. Langley and L. J. Lombardino (Eds.) *Neurodevelopmental Strategies for Managing Communication Disorders in Children with Severe Motor Dysfunction*, 199-250. Austin, TX: Pro-Ed.

Lappan, G., and Schram, P. (1989) Communication and reasoning: Critical dimensions of sense making in mathematics. In P. Trafton and A. Schulte (Eds.) *New Directions for Elementary School Mathematics.* Reston, VA: National Council for Teachers of Mathematics.

Largo, R., and Howard, J. (1979) *Assessment of Play Behaviors.* In S.J. Rogers (1988) Review of methods for assessing young children's play. *Journal of the Division for Early Childhood*, 12, 284-287.

Lavelle, A.M., and Keogh, B.K. (1980) Expectations and attributions of parents of handicapped children. In J.J. Gallagher (Ed.) *New Directions for Exceptional Children: Parents and Families of Handicapped Children* (vol 2.) San Francisco, CA: Jossey-Bass.

Lay-Dopyera, M., and Dopyera, J. (1990) *Becoming a Teacher of Young Children* (4th. ed.) New York: McGraw-Hill.

Lazar, I., and Darlington, R. (1982) Lasting effects of early education: A report from the consortium for longitudinal studies. *Monographs of the Society for Research in Child Development*, 47-195. University of Chicago: Press for the Society for Research in Child Development.

Lederberg, A.R., and Mobley, C.E. (1990) The effect of hearing impairment on the quality of attachment and mother-toddler interaction. *Child Development*, 61, 1596-1604.

Lefkowity, M.M., Eron, L.D., Walder, L.D., and Huessman, L.R. (1977) *Growing Up to Be Violent.* New York: Pergamon.

Leiter, R. (1948) *The Leiter International Performance Scale.* New York: Wiley.

Lewis, M. (1987) Social development in infancy and early childhood. In J.D. Osofsky (Ed.) *Handbook of Infant Development*, 419-494. New York: Wiley.

Lifter, K., Sulzer-Azaroff, B., Anderson, S.R., and Cowdery, G.E. (1993) Teaching play activities to preschool children with disabilities: The importance of developmental considerations. *Journal of Early Intervention*, 17, 139-159.

Lillie, D. L. (1975) *Carolina Developmental Profile.* Chicago: Science Research Associates.

Linder, T. (1990) *Transdiciplinary Play-Based Assessment. A Functional Approach to Working with Young Children.* Baltimore, MD: Brookes.

Loeber, R. (1985) Patterns and development of antisocial child behavior. *Annals of Child Development*, 2, 77-116.

Loewen, A.C. (1990) Primary mathematics instruction. Unpublished paper, University of Lethbridge.

Lojkasek, M., Goldberg, S., Marcovitch, S., and MacGregor, D. (1990) Influences on maternal responsiveness to developmentally delayed preschoolers. *Journal of Early Intervention*, 14, 236-273.

Lombardi, J. (1990) Head Start: The nation's pride, a nation's challenge. *Young Children*, 45, 22-29.

Louis, B., and Louis, M. (1992) Parental beliefs about giftedness in young children and their relationship to actual ability level. *Gifted Child Quarterly*, 36, 27-31.

Lovaas, O.I. (1982, September) An overview of the Young Autism Project. Paper presented at the Annual Convention of the American Psychological Association, Washington, DC.

Lovaas, O.I., and Favell, J.E. (1987) Protection for clients undergoing aversive/restrictive intervention. *Education and Treatment of Children*, 10, 311-325.

Lovaas, O.I., Newsom, C., and Hickman, C. (1987) Self-stimulating behavior and perceptual reinforcement. *Journal of Applied Behavior Analysis*, 20, 45-68.

Lussier, B.J., Cummins., D.B., and Alberti, D. (1994) Effect of three adult interaction styles on infant engagement. *Journal of Early Intervention*, 18, 2-24.

M

Maccoby, E.E. (1980) *Social Development: Psychological Growth and the Parent-Child Relationship*. New York: Harcourt Brace Jovavonich.

McBride, S.L., Brotherson, M.J., Joanning, H., Whiddon, D., and Demmitt, A. (1993) Implementation of family-centered services: Perceptions of families and professionals. *Journal of Early Intervention,* 17, 414-430.

McCarthy, D. (1972) *Manual for the McCarthy Scales of Children's Abilities*. New York: Psychological Corporation.

McCartney, K., Scarr, S., Phillips, D., and Grajik, S. (1985) Day care as intervention: Comparisons of varying quality programs. *Journal of Applied Developmental Psychology*, 6, 247-260.

McCollum, J.A., and Thorp, E.K. (1988) Training of infant specialists: A look to the future. *Infants and Young Children*, 1, 55-65.

McCormick, L. (1987) Comparison of the effects of a microcomputer activity and toy play on social and communication behaviors of young children. *Journal of the Division of Early Childhood*, 11, 195-205.

MacDonald, J., and Gillette, Y. (1982) *A Conversational Approach to Language Delay: Problems and Solutions.* Columbus, OH: Nisonger Center.

McDonald, L., Kysela, G.M., Siebert, P., McDonald, S., and Chambers, J. (1989) Transition to preschool. *Teaching Exceptional Children*, 22, 4-8.

McGee, G.G., Daly, T., Izeman, S.G., Mann, L.H., and Risley, T.R. (1991) Use of classroom materials to promote preschool engagement. *Teaching Exceptional Children*, 23, 44-47.

McKean, K. (1987) Introduction: New ways to measure the wisdom of man. In M.G. Walravens and H.E. Fitzgerald (Eds.) *Psychology 87/88*. Guilford, CT: Dushkin.

McLinden, D.J. (1988) Spatial task performance: A meta-analysis. *Journal of Visual Impairment and Blindness*, 82, 231-236.

McWilliam, P.J., and Winton, P. (1990) *Brass Tacks: A Self-Rating of Family-Focused Practices in Early Intervention.* Chapel Hill, NC: Frank Porter Graham Center, University of North Carolina.

McWilliam, R.A. (1991) Targetting teaching at children's use of time: Perspectives on preschooler's engagement. *Teaching Exceptional Children*, 23, 42-43.

McWilliam, R.A., Trivette, C.M., and Dunst, C.J. (1985) Behavior engagement as a measure of the efficacy of early intervention. *Analysis and Intervention in Developmental Disabilities*, 5, 33-45.

Mahoney, G., O'Sullivan, P., and Dennebaum, J. (1990) Maternal perceptions of early intervention services: A scale for assessing family-focused intervention. *Topics in Early Childhood Special Education*, 10, 1-15.

Mallory, B.L. (1995) The role of social policy in life-cycle transitions. *Exceptional Children*, 62, 213-223.

Malone, C. (1979) Gifted children in early childhood education. *Viewpoints in Teaching and Learning*, 55, 25-28.

Malone, D.M., and Stoneman, Z. (1990) Cognitive play of mentally retarded preschoolers: Observations in the home and school. *American Journal of Mental Retardation*, 94, 475-487.

Marcenko, M.O. and Meyers, J.C. (1991) Mothers of children with developmental disabilities. *Family Relations,* 40, 186-190.

Marchant, C. (1995) Teachers' views of integrated preschools. *Journal of Early Intervention,* 19, 61-73.

Marfo, K., and Kysela, G.M. (1985) Early intervention with mentally handicapped children: A critical appraisal of applied research. *Journal of Pediatric Psychology,* 10, 305-324.

Marfo, K., Browne, N., Gallant, D., Smyth, R., Corbett, A., and McLennon, D. (1988) *Early Intervention with Developmentally Delayed Infants and Preschool Children in Newfoundland and Labrador.* St. John's: MUN.

Martin, B., and Hoffman, J.A. (1990) Conduct disorders. In M.Lewis and S.M. Miller (Eds.) *Handbook of Developmental Psychopathology.* New York: Plenum.

Martin, R.P., Hooper, S., and Snow, J. (1986) Behavior rating scale approaches to personality assessment in children and adolescents. In H.M. Knoff (Ed.) *The Assessment of Child and Adolescent Personality*, 309-351. New York: Guilford.

Mayfield, M.I. (1988) Toy libraries in Canada: A research study. *Canadian Children,* 13, 1-18.

———(1990) Parent involvement in early childhood programs. In I.M. Doxey (Ed.) *Child Care and Education: Canadian Dimensions*, 240-253. Toronto: Nelson.

Mayfield, M.I., Dey, J.D., Gleadow, N.E., Liedke, W., and Probst, A. (1981) *Kindergarten Needs Assessment.* Victoria, BC: BC Ministry of Education.

Mazurek, C. (1995) Dramatic play. Unpublished paper, Lethbridge Community College.

Meisels, S.J. (1985) The efficacy of early intervention: Why are we still asking this question? *Topics in Early Childhood Special Education,* 5, 1-11.

———(1987) Uses and abuses of screening and school readiness testing. *Young Children,* 42, 68-73.

———(1988) Developmental screening in early childhood: The interaction of research and social policy. *Annual Review of Public Health,* 9, 527-550.

———(1989) Can developmental screening tests identify children who are developmentally at-risk: *Pediatrics,* 83, 578-585.

Meisels, S., Harbin, G., Modigliani, K., and Olson, K. (1988) Formulating optimal state intervention policies. *Exceptional Children,* 55, 159-165.

Mergen, B. (1982) *Play and Playthings.* Westport, CN: Greenwood Press.

Meyers, C.E., and Blacher, J. (1987) Parents' perceptions of schooling for severely handicapped children: Home and family variables. *Exceptional Children*, 53, 441-449.

Michael, M.G., and Paul, P.V. (1991) Early intervention for infants with deaf-blindness. *Exceptional Children*, 57, 200-210.

Miller, L.F. (1982) *Miller Assessment for Preschoolers.* Littleton, CO: Foundation for Knowledge and Development.

Mirenda, P., and Schuyler, A. (1988) Augmenting communication for persons with autism: Issues and strategies. *Topics in Language Disorders,* 9, 24-43.

Mitchell, A. (1989) Old baggage, new visions: Shaping policy for early childhood programs. *Phi Delta Kappan*, 70, 664-672.

Montes, F., and Risley, T.R. (1975) Evaluating traditional day care practice: An empirical approach. *Child Care Quarterly*, 4, 208-215.

Montessori, M. (1912) *The Montessori method.* A. George (trans.) New York: Stokes.

———(1917) *The Advanced Montessori Method: Scientific Pedagogy as Applied to the Education of Children from Seven to Eleven Years.* London: Heinmann.

Moore, G.T. (1986) Effects of the spatial definition of behavior settings on children's behavior: A quasi-experimental field study. *Journal of Environmental Psychology*, 6, 205-231.

Morrison, F. (1989) Child care for the 21st century: An overview and commentary. *Canadian Psychology/ Psychologique canadienne*, 30, 148-151.

Morrison, G.S. (1978) *Parent Involvement in the Home, School, and Community.* Columbus, OH: Merrill.

Moses, D., and Croll, P. (1987) Parents as partners or problems? *Disability, Handicap and Society*, 2, 1.

Mundy, P., Sigman, M., Kasari, C., and Yirmira, N. (1988) Nonverbal communication skills in Down syndrome children. *Child Development*, 59, 235-249.

Murphy, D.L., Lee, I.M., Turnbull, A.P., and Turbiville, V. (1995) The Family-Centered Program Rating Scale: An instrument for program evaluation and change. *Journal of Early Intervention*, 19, 24-42.

Murphy, M., and Vincent, L.J. (1989) Identification of critical skills for success in day care. *Journal of Early Intervention*, 13, 221-229.

Musselman, C.R., Wilson, A.K., and Lindsay, P.H. (1988) Effects of early intervention on hearing impaired children. *Exceptional Children*, 55, 222-228.

Myers, J. (1987) The training of dynamic assessors. In C. Lidz (Ed.) *Dynamic Assessment: An Interactional Approach to Evaluating Learning Potential*, 403-425. New York: Guilford.

Mysak, E. (1982) Cerebral palsy. In G. Shames and E. Wiig (Eds.) *Human Communication Disorders*. Columbus, OH: Merrill.

N

National Association for the Education of Young Children (1988) *Testing Children at a Young Age: Precautions, Position Statement*. Washington, DC: Author.

National Association for the Education of Young Children and National Association of Early Childhood Specialists in State Departments of Education (1991) Guidelines for appropriate curriculum content in programs serving children 3 through 8: A position statement. *Young Children*, 46, 21-28.

Neisworth J.T., and Bagnato, S.J. (1987) *The Young Exceptional Child: Early Development and Education*. New York: Macmillan.

Neisworth, J.T., and Buggey, T.J. (1993) Behavior analysis and principles in early childhood education. In J.L. Roopnarine and J.E. Johnson (Ed.) *Approaches to early childhood education*, 113-135. New York: Merrill.

Neisworth, J.T., Willoughby-Herb, S.J., Bagnato, S.J., Cartwright, C.A., and Laub, K.W. (1980) *Individualized Education for Preschool Exceptional Children*. Rockville, MD: Aspen Sytems.

Nelken, V. (1987) *Family-Centred Health Care for Medically Fragile Children: Principles and Practices*. Washington DC: Georgetown University Child Development Center. ERIC Ed. 303 000.

Nessner, K. (1990, winter) Children with disabilities. *Canadian Social Trends*, 18-20.

Newborg, J., Stock, J.R., and Wnek, L. (1984) *Battelle Developmental Inventory*. Allen, TX: DLM Teaching Resources.

Noonan, M.J., and McCormick, L. (1993) *Early Intervention in Natural Environments: Methods and Procedures*. Pacific Grove, CA: Brooks/Cole.

Notari, A.R., and Bricker, D.D. (1990) The utility of a curriculum-based assessment instrument in the development of individual education plans for infants and young children. *Journal of Early Intervention*, 14, 117-132.

Notari-Syverson, A.R., and Shuster, S.L. (1995) Putting real-life skills into IEP? IPSPs for infants and young children. *Teaching Exceptional Children*, 27, 29-32.

O

O'Connell, J.C. (1983) Children of working mothers: What the research tells us. *Young Children*, 38, 62-70.

———(1986). Managing small group instruction in integrated preschool setting. *Teaching Exceptional Children*, 18, 36-48.

Odom, S.L. (1988) Research in early childhood special education: Methodologies and paradigms. In S.L. Odom and M.L. Karnes (Eds.) *Early Intervention for Infants and Children with Handicaps*, 1-21. Baltimore, MD: Paul H. Brookes.

Odom, S.L., McConnell, S.R., and Chandler, L.K. (1993) Acceptability and feasibility of classroom-based social interaction interventions with young children with disabilities. *Exceptional Children*, 60, 226-236.

Olds, A.F. (1987) Designing setttings for infants and toddlers. In C.C. Weinstein and T.G. David (Eds.) *Spaces for Children: The Building Environment and Child Development*, 117-138. New York: Plenum.

Olweus, D. (1979) Stability of aggressive reaction patterns in males: A review. *Psychological Bulletin*, 86, 852-875.

Oppenheim, J. (1987) *Buy me! Buy me!* New York: Pantheon Books.

Ormerod, J.J., and Huebner, E.S. (1988) Crisis intervention: Facilitating the parental acceptance of a child's handicap. *Psychology in the Schools*, 25, 422-428.

Ostrosky, M.M., and Kaiser, A.P. (1991) Preschool classroom environments that promote communication. *Teaching Exceptional Children*. 23, 6-10.

Owens, R.E. Jr. (1988) *Language Development* (2nd ed.) Columbus, OH: Merrill.

Owens, R.J. Jr. (1991) *Language Disorders: A Functional Approach to Assessment and Intervention*. New York: Merrill.

P

Palmer, F.B., Shapiro, B.F., Wachtel, R.C., Allen, M.C., Hiller, J.E., Harryman, S.E., Master, B.S., Meinert,

C.L., and Capute, A.J. (1988) The effects of physical therapy on cerebral palsy. *New England Journal of Medicine*, 318, 803-808.

Parette, H.P., and Hourcade, J.J. (1986) Management strategies for orthopedically handicapped students. *Teaching Exceptional Children*, 18, 282-286.

Parette, H.P. Jr., Hofmann, A., and Van Biervliet, (1994) The professional's role in obtaining funding for assistive technology for infants and toddlers with disabilities. *Teaching Exceptional Children*, 26, 22-28.

Parten, M.B. (1932) Social participation among preschool children. *Journal of Abnormal and Social Psychology*, 27, 243-269; 28, 136-147.

Parton, D.A. (1976) Learning to imitate in infancy. *Child Development*, 47, 14-31.

Patterson, G.R. (1982) *Coercive Family Process*. Eugene, OR: Castalia Press.

Patterson, G.R., De Baryshe, B.D., and Ramsey, E. (1989) A developmental perspective on antisocial behavior. *American Psychologist*, 44, 322-335.

Peck, C.A., and Cooke, T.P. (1983) Benefits of mainstreaming at the early childhood level: How much can we expect? *Analysis and Intervention in Developmental Disabilities*, 3, 1-22.

Peck, C.A., Odom, S., and Bricker, D. (1993) *Integrating Young Children with Disabilities into Community Programs: Ecological Perspectives on Research and Implications*. Baltimore, MD: Brookes.

Peck, C.A., Palyo, W.J., Bettencourt, B., Cooke, T.P., and Apolloni, T. (1988). An observational study of "partial integration" of handicapped students in a regular preschool. *Journal of Research and Development in Education*, 21, 4-44

Peck, C.A., Wandschneider, M., Hayden, L., and Richarz, S. (1987, October) Development of integrated preschools: A qualitative inquiry into issues of concern to parents, teachers, and administrators. Paper at the Association of Persons with Severe Handicaps Annual Meeting, Chicago.

Pellegrini, A.D. (1982) Development of preschoolers' social-cognitive behavior. *Perceptual and Motor Skills*, 55, 1109-1110.

————(1988) Elementary-school children's rough-and-tumble play and social competence. *Developmental Psychology*, 24, 802-807.

Pence, A. (1989) In the shadow of mother-care: Contexts for an understanding of child day care in North America. *Canadian Psychology/Psychologique canadienne*, 30, 140-147.

Pence, A. (1990) The child-care profession in Canada. In I.M. Doxey (Ed.) *Child Care and Education: Canadian Dimensions*, 87-97. Toronto: Nelson.

Perkins, W.H. (1977) *Speech Pathology: An Applied Behavioral Science*. St. Louis, MO: C.F. Mosby.

Peterson, K.L. (1992) Helping student teachers understand conflict among preschool children. *Journal of Early Childhood Teacher Education*, 13, 15-18.

Peterson, N.L. (1987) *Early Intervention for Handicapped and At-Risk Children*. Denver, CO: Love.

Peterson, N.L., and Haralick, J.G. (1977) Integration of handicapped and non-handicapped preschoolers: An analysis of play and social interaction. *Education and Training of the Mentally Retarded*, 12, 235-245.

Phillips, D., McCartney, K., and Scarr, S. (1987) Child-care quality and children's social development. *Developmental Psychology*, 23, 537-543.

Phillips, D., McCartney, L., Scarr, S., and Howes, C. (1987) Selective review of infant day care research: A cause for concern. *Zero to Three*, 7, 18-24.

Piaget, J. (1945/1962) *Play, Dreams and Imitation in Childhood*. New York: Norton.

Pianta, R. (1987) Early Behavior Rating Scale. In R.D. Hoge and C. Wichmann, C. (1994) *An Evaluation Review of Interview and Rating/Checklist Instruments for Assessing Social-Emotional Competence in Preschool Children*. Ottawa: Psychology Department, Carleton University.

Piirto, J. (1994) *Talented Children and Adults: Their Development and Education*. New York: Merrill.

Plomin, R., DeFries, J.C., and McClearn, G.E. (1990) *Behavioral Genetics: A Primer* (2nd. ed.) New York: W.H. Freeman.

Polloway, E.A., and Smith, J.E. (1982) *Teaching Language Skills to Exceptional Children*. Denver, CO: Love Publishing.

Porterfield, J.K., Herbert-Jackson, E., and Risley, T.R. (1976) Contingent observation: An effective and acceptable procedure for reducing disruptive behavior of young children in a group setting. *Journal of Applied Behavior Analysis*, 9, 55-64.

Powell, D.R. (1990) Home visiting in the early years: Policy and program design decisions. *Young Children*, 45, 65-73.

Powell, T.H., and Ogle, P.A. (1985) *Brothers and Sisters: A Special Part of Exceptional Families.* Baltimore, MD: Brookes.

Prater, M.A. (1993) Teaching concepts: Procedures for the design and delivery of instruction. *Remedial and Special Education,* 14, 51-62.

Q

Quiltich, H.R., and Risley, T.R. (1973) The effects of play materials on social play. *Journal of Applied Behavior Analysis,* 6, 573-578.

R

Raab, M.M., Nordquist, V.M., Cunningham, J.L., and Bliem, C.D. (1986). Promoting peer regard of an autistic child in a mainstreamed preschool using pre-enrollment activities. *Child Study Journal,* 16, 265-284.

Radonovich, S., and Houck, C. (1990). An integrated preschool. *Teaching Exceptional Children,* 23, 22-26.

Ramey, C.T. (1981) Consequences of infant day care. In B. Weissbound and J. Musick (Eds.) *Infants: Their Social Environments.* Washington, D.C.: National Assocation for the Education of Young Children.

Raschke, D.B., Dedrick, C., and Hanus, K. (1991) Adaptive playgrounds for all children. *Teaching Exceptional Children,* 24, 25-28.

Ray, J.S. (1975, May) Free-play behavior of normal and Down's syndrome toddlers. In D.B. Bailey and M. Wolery (1984) *Teaching Infants and Preschoolers with Handicaps.* Columbus, OH: Merrill.

Read, L.F. (1989). An examination of the social skills of blind kindergarten children. *Education of the Visually Handicapped,* 20, 142-155.

Reardon, S.M., and Naglieri, J.A. (1992) PASS cognitive processing characteristics of normal and ADHD males. *Journal of School Psychology,* 30, 151-163.

Reschley, D.J. (1989) Incorporating adaptive behavior deficits into instructional programs. In G.A. Robinson, J.R. Palton, E.A. Polloway, and L.R., Sargent (Eds.) *Best Practices in Mental Retardation,* 39-63. Reston, VA: Council for Exceptional Children.

Rescorla, L. (1989) The Language Development Survey: A screening tool for delayed language in toddlers. *Journal of Speech and Hearing Disorders,* 54, 587-599.

Reynolds, A.J. (1995) Effects of a preschool plus follow-on intervention for children at risk. *Developmental Psychology,* 30, 787-804.

Rice, M.L. (1989) Children's language acquisition. *American Psychologist,* 44, 149-157.

Rice, M.L., Sell, M.A., and Hadley, P.A. (1991) Social interactions of speech-and language-impaired children. *Journal of Speech and Hearing Research,* 34, 1299-1307.

Richarz, S., and Peterson, K. (1990) Issues of integration based on a qualitative enquiry of parents, teachers, and administrators: Implications for teacher education. *Journal of Early Childhood Teacher Education,* 11, 14-15.

Richman, N., and Graham P.J. (1971) A behavior screening questionnaire for use with three-year-old children: Preliminary findings. *Journal of Child Psychology and Psychiatry,* 12, 5-33.

Richters, J.E., and Zahn-Waxler, C. (1988) The infant day care controversy: Current status and future directions. *Early Childhood Research Quarterly,* 3, 319-337.

Rimm, S., and Lowe, B. (1988) Family environments of underachieving gifted students. *Gifted Child Quarterly,* 32, 353-359.

Rincover, A. (1981) Some directions for analysis and intervention in developmental disabilities: An editorial. *Analysis and Intervention in Developmental Disabilities,* 1, 109-115.

Rivers, L.S., Meininger, L.K., and Batten, J. (1991, November) Kindergarten screening and program placement: Possible relationships. In J. Piirto (1994) *Talented Children and Adults: Their Development and Education.* New York: Merrill.

Roberts, J.E., Burchind, M.R., Koch, M.A., Fodto, M.M., and Henderson, F.W. (1988) Otitis media in early childhood and its relationship to later phonological development. *Journal of Speech and Hearing Disorders,* 53, 424-432.

Robins, L.N., and Earls, F. (1985) A program for preventing antisocial behavior for high-risk infants and preschoolers: A research prospectus. In R.L. Hugh, P.A. Gongla, V.B. Brown, and S.E. Goldston (Eds.) *Psychiatric Epidemiology and Prevention: The Possibilities,* 73-84. Los Angeles, CA: Neuropsychiatric Institute.

Robson, C., and Whitley, S. (1989) Sharing stories: Involvement in reading with inner-city nursery children. *Reading,* 23, 23-27.

Roedell, W. (1985) Developing social competence in gifted preschool children. *Remedial and Special Education*, 6, 6-11.

Roedell, W., and Robinson, H. (1977) Programming for intellectually advanced preschool children. ERIC No. Ed. 151-194.

Rogers, S.J. (1988) Review of methods for assessing young children's play. *Journal of the Division for Early Childhood*, 12, 284-287.

Rogers-Warren A., and Warren, S.F. (1980) Mands for verbalization: Facilitating the display of newly trained language in children. *Behavior Modification*, 4, 361-382.

Rogers-Warren, A.K., and Warren, S. (1984) The social basis of language and communication in severely handicapped preschoolers. *Topics in Early Childhood Special Education*, 4, 57-72.

Rose, D., and Smith, B.J. (1993) Preschool mainstreaming: Attitude barriers and strategies for addressing them. *Young Children*, 48, 59-62.

Rosenblith, J.F., and Sims-Knight, J.E. (1985) *In the Beginnning: Development in the First Two Years*. Monterey, CA: Brooks/Cole.

Routh, D.K. (1980) Developmental and social aspects of hyperactivity. In C.K. Whalen and B. Henker (Eds.) *Hyperactive Children: The Social Ecology of Identification and Treatment*. New York: Academic Press.

Ruble, D.N. (1983) The development of social comparison process and their role in achievement-related self-socialization. In E.T. Higgins, D.N. Ruble, Rule, S., Killoran, J., Stowitschek, J.J., Innocenti, M., Striefel, S., and Biswell, C. (1985) Training and support for mainstream day care staff. *Early Child Development and Care*, 20, 99-113.

Rule, S., Killoran, J., Stowitschek, J.J., Innocenti, M., Striefel, S., and Biswell, C. (1985) Training and support for mainstream day care staff. *Early Child Development and Care*, 20, 99-113.

Rule, S., Stowitschek, J.J., Innocenti, M., Striefel, S., Killoran, J., Swezey, K., and Boswell, C. (1987) The social integration program: An analysis of the effects of mainstreaming handicapped children into day care centers. *Education and Treatment of Children*, 10, 175-192.

Ruttenberg, B.A., Kalish, B.I., Wenar, C., and Wolf, E.G. (1977). *Behavior Rating Instrument for Autistic and other Atypical Children* (Rev. ed.) Philadelphia, PA: Developmental Center for Autistic Children.

Rutter, M. (1985) Infantile autism and other pervasive developmental disorders. In M. Rutter and L. Herson (Eds.) *Child and Adolescent Psychiatry: Modern Approaches*, 545-566. Oxford: Blackwell.

————(1987) Continuities and discontinuties from infancy. In M. Rutter and L. Herson (Eds.) *Child and Adolescent Psychology: Modern Approaches* (2nd ed.) Oxford: Oxford University Press.

Rutter, M., and Schopler, E. (Eds.) (1978) *Autism: A Reappraisal of Concepts and Treatment*. New York: Plenum.

S

Safford, P.L. (1983) Conceptions of special education: A quest for definition. In B.F. Nel, G.S. Jackson, and D.S. Rajah (Eds.) *The Changing World of Education*, 133-154. Durban, SA: Butterworth.

Safford, P.L. (1989) *Integrated Teaching in Early Childhood: Starting in the Mainstream*. New York: Pitman.

Sailor, W., Guess, D., Goetz, L., Schuler, A., Utley, B., and Baldwin, M. (1980) Language and severely handicapped persons: Deciding what to teach to whom. In W. Sailor, B. Wilcox, and L. Brown (Eds). *Methods of Instruction for Severely Handicapped Students*. Baltimore, MD: Brookes.

Sainato, D.M., and Lyons, S.R. (1983, December) A descriptive analysis of the requirement for independent performance in handicapped and nonhandicapped preschool classrooms. In P.L. Strain (chair) Assisting behaviorally handicapped preschoolers in mainstreamig settings: A report on research from the Early Childhood research Institute. Paper at the HCEEP/DEC Convention, Washington, DC.

Salisbury, C.L. (1991) Mainstreaming during the early childhood years. *Exceptional Children*, 58, 146-155.

Salkind, N. (1990) *Child Development* (6th. ed.) Fort Worth, TX: Holt Reinhart and Winston.

Salt, P., Galler, J.R., and Ramsey, F.C. (1988) The influence of early malnutrition on subsequent behavioral development. *Developmental and Behavioral Pediatrics*, 9, 1-5.

Sameroff, A.J., Seifer, R., Zax, M., et al. (1987) Early indicators of developmental risk: Longitudinal study. *Schizophrenia Bulletin*, 13, 383-394.

Sargent, L.R. (1988). Ensuring quality instruction. In K. Zantal-Wiener, Early intervention services for preschool children. *Teaching Exceptional Children*, 21, 61-64.

Satz, P., and Fletcher, J.M. (1979) Early screening tests: Some uses and abuses. *Journal of Learning Disabilities*, 12, 65-69.

Sawyer, R.J., and Zantal-Wiener, K. (1993) Emerging trends in technology for students with disabilities: Considerations for school personnel. *Teaching Exceptional Children*, 26, 70-72.

Scarr, S. (1984) *Mother Care/Other Care*. New York: Basic Books.

Scarr, S., and Kidd, K.K. (1983) Developmental behavior genetics. In M. Heath and J. Compos (Eds.) P.H. Mussen (series ed.) *Handbook of Child Psychology, vol. 2: Infancy and Developmental Psychobiology*, 345-435. New York: Wiley.

Schermann, A. (1990) The learning child. In I.M. Doxey (Ed.) *Childcare and Education: Canadian Dimensions*, 32-42. Toronto: Nelson.

Schindler, P., Moeley, B.E., and Frank, A.L. (1987) Time in day care and social participationn of young children. *Developmental Psychology*, 23, 255-261.

Schorr-Ribera, H.K. (1987) Ethnicity and culture as relevant rehabilitation factors in families with children with disabilities. In M. Seligman (Ed.) *The Family with a Handicapped Child* (2nd ed.) Boston, MA: Allyn and Bacon.

Schuster, J.W., and Griffen, A.K. (1990) Using time delay with task analysis. *Teaching Exceptional Children*, 22, 49-53.

Schwartz, R.H., and Yaffe, S.J. (1980) (Eds.) *Drugs and Chemical Risks to the Fetus and Newborn*. New York: Alan R. Liss.

Scott, E.P. (1982) *Your Visually Impaired Child: A Guide for Teachers*. Baltimore, MD: University Park Press.

Seefeldt, C. (1989) The knowledge base for early childhood teacher education. *Journal of Early Childhood Teacher Education*, 32, 407.

Seligman, M., and Darling, R.D. (1989) *Ordinary Families, Special Children*. New York: Guilford.

Shantz, C.U. (1987) Conflicts between children. *Child Development*, 58, 283-305.

Sharav, T., and Schlomo, L. (1986) Stimulation of infants with Down syndrome: Long-term effects. *Mental Retardation*, 24, 81-86.

Shearer, D.E. (1993) The Portage Project: An international home approach to early intervention of young children and their families. In J.L. Roopnarine and J.E. Johnson (Eds.) *Approaches to Early Childhood Education*, 97-111. New York: Merrill.

Shearer, M., and Shearer, D. (1972) The Portage Project: A model for early intervention. *Exceptional Children*, 39, 210-217.

Shonkoff, J.P., and Hauser-Cram, P. (1987) Early intervention for disabled infants and their families: A quantitative analysis. *Pediatrics*, 80, 650-658.

Shonkoff, J., and Meisels, S. (1990) Early childhood intervention. In S. Meisels and J. Shonkoff (Eds.) *Handbook of Early Intervention*, 3-32. New York: Cambridge University Press.

Shonkoff, J.P., and Meisels, S.J. (1991) Defining eligibility for services under PL99-457. *Journal of Early Intervention*, 15, 21-25.

Silverman, L.K. (1986) What happens to the gifted girl? In C.J. Maker (Ed.) *Critical Issues in Gifted Education*. Rockville, MD: Aspen.

Simeonsson, R.J., Cooper, D.H., and Scheiner, A.P. (1982) A review and analysis of the effectiveness of early intervention programs. *Pediatrics*, 69, 635-641.

Simon, E.P., and Gillman, A.E. (1979) Mainstreaming and handicapped preschoolers. *Exceptional Children*, 45, 463-464.

Sivin, J.P., Lee, P.C., and Voltmar, A.M. (April, 1985) Introductory computer experiences with commercially available software: Differences between three year olds and five year olds. Paper presented at AERA, Chicago.

Skiba, R.J. and Raison, J. (1990) The relationship between use of timeout and academic achievement. *Exceptional Children*, 57, 36-46.

Skinner, B.F. (1953) *Science and human behavior*. New York: Macmillan.

———(1971) *Beyond Freedom and Dignity*. New York: Knopf.

Slavin, R.E. (1988) *Educational Psychology: Theory into Practice*. Englewood Cliffs, NJ: Prentice-Hall.

Slentz, K.L., and Bricker, D. (1992) Family-guided assessment for IFSP development: Jumping off the family asessment bandwagon. *Journal of Early Intervention*, 16, 11-19.

Smilansky, S. (1968) *The Effects of Sociodramatic Play on Disadvantaged Preschool Children*. New York: Wiley.

Smith, C.B. (1991) Literature for gifted and talented. *The Reading Teacher*, 44, 608-609.

Smith, M.J., and Ryan, A.S. (1987) Chinese-American families of children with developmental disabilities: An exploratory study of reactions to service providers. *Mental Retardation*, 25, 345-350.

Smith, S.P. (1978) Some (not all) facts about asthma. *Journal of School Health*, 48, 311.

Smutny, J., Veenker, K., and Veenker, S. (1989) *Young Gifted Children: How to Recognize and Develop the Special Talents in Your Child from Birth to Age Seven*. New York: Ballantine.

Snell, M.E. (1987) *Systematic Instruction of Persons with Severe Handicaps* (3rd ed.) Columbus, OH: Merrill.

Snyder, L.S. (1981) Content and context in early lexical development. *Journal of Child Language*, 8, 565-582.

Solnick, J.V., Rincover, A., and Peterson, C.R. (1977) Some determinants of the reinforcing and punishing effects of timeout. *Journal of Applied Behavior Analysis*, 10, 415-424.

Sontag, J.C., and Schacht, R. (1993) Family diversity and patterns of service utilization in early intervention. *Journal of Early Intervention*, 17, 431-444.

Sparrow, S.S., Balla, D.A., and Cicchetti, D.V. (1984) *Vineland Adaptive Behavior Scale*. Circle Pines, MN: American Guidance Services.

Special Committee on Child Care (1987) *Sharing the Responsibility: Report of the Special Committee on Child Care*. Ottawa: Queen's Printer.

Spodek, B. (1973) Needed: A new kindergarten education. *Childhood Education*, 49, 191-197.

Spodek B., et al. (1982) *Early Childhood Teacher Education and Certification*. ERIC Doc. Ed. 227 946.

Spradlin, J.E., and Siegel, G.M. (1982) Language training in natural and clinical environments. *Journal of Speech and Hearing Disorders*, 47, 2-6.

Stainback, W., and Stainback, S. (1977) Teaching the profoundly handicapped in the public school setting. In M.A. Thomas (Ed.) *Developing Skills in Severely and Profoundly Handicapped Children*. Reston, VA: Council for Exceptional Children.

Stile, S.W., Kitano, M., Kelley, P., and Lecone, J. (1993) Early intervention with gifted children: A national survey. *Journal of Early Intervention*, 17, 30-35.

Stillman, R. (Ed.) (1978) *The Callier-Azusa Scale*. Dallas, TX: Callier Center for Communication Disorders, University of Texas at Dallas.

Stipek, D.J., and Sanborn, M.E. (1985, July) Teachers' task-related interactions with handicapped and nonhandicapped preschool children. *Merrill-Palmer Quarterly*, 31, 285-300.

Stoneman, Z. (1993) The effects of attitude on preschool integration. In C. Peck, S. Odom, and D. Bricker (Eds.) *Integrating Young Children with Disabilities into Community Programs: Ecological Perspectives on Research and Implementation*, 223-248. Baltimore, MD: Brookes.

Stoneman, Z., and Crapps, J.N. (1988) Correlates of stress, perceived competence, and depression among family care providers. *American Journal of Mental Retardation*, 93, 166-173.

Stoneman, Z., Cantrell, M.L., and Hoover-Dempsey, K. (1983) The association between play materials and social behavior. in a mainstreamed preschool: A naturalistic investigation. *Developmental Psychology*, 4, 163-174.

Strain, P. (1981) *The Utilization of Peers as Behavior Change Agents*. New York: Plenum.

———(1982). Peer-mediated treatment of exceptional children's social withdrawal. In P.S. Strain (Ed.) *Social Development of Exceptional Children*, 93-105. Rockville, MD: Aspen.

———(1990) LRE for preschool children with handicaps: What we know, what we should be doing. *Journal of Early Intervention*, 14, 291-296.

Strain, P.S., and Odom, S.L. (1986) Peer social interactions: Effective intervention for social skills development of exceptional children. *Exceptional Children*, 52, 543-551.

Strain, P.S., Lambert, D.L., Kerr, M.M., Stagg, V., and Lenkner, D.A. (1983) Naturalistic assessment of children's compliance to teachers requests and consequences for compliance. *Journal of Applied Behavior Analysis*, 16, 243-249.

Strain, P.S., Sainato, D.M., and Maheady, L. (1984) Toward a functional assessment of severely handicapped learners. *Educational Psychologist*, 19, 180-187.

Strain, P.S., Shores, R.E., and Timms, M.A. (1977) Effects of peer social initiations on the behavior of withdrawn preschool children. *Journal of Applied Behavior Analysis*, 10, 289-298

Strain, P.S., Steele, P., Ellis, T., and Timms, M.A. (1982) Long-term effects of oppositional child treatment with mothers as therapists and therapist trainers. *Journal of Applied Behavior Analysis*, *15*, 163-169.

Stricklana, D.D., and Ogle (1990) Teachers coping with change: Assessing the early literary curriculum. In L.M. Morrow and J.K. Smith (Eds.) *Assessment for Instruction in Early Literacy*, 205-218. Englewood Cliffs, NJ: Prentice Hall.

Stutsman, R. (1984) *Merrill-Palmer Scale of Mental Tests.* Los Angeles, CA: Western Psychological Services.

Sugai, G., and Maheady, L. (1988) Cultural diversity and individual assessment for behavior disorders. *Teaching Exceptional Children*, 21, 28-31.

Sulzer-Azoroff, B., and Mayer, G.R. (1991) *Behavior Analysis for Lasting Change.* Fort Worth, TX: Holt, Rinehart, and Winston.

Summers, J.A., Dell'Oliver, C., Turnbull, A., Beison, H.A., Santelli, E., Campblell, M., and Siegel-Causey, E. (1990) Examining the Individual Family Service Plan process: What are family and practitioner preferences? *Topics in Early Childhood Special Education*, 10, 78-99.

Sutherland, D.H., Ohlsen, R.A., Biden E.N., and Wyatt, M.P. (1988) *The Development of Mature Walking.* Philadelphia, PA: Lippincott.

T

Tager-Flusberg, H., Calkins, S., Nolin, T., Baumberger, T., Anderson, M., and Chadwick-Deas, A. (1990) A longitudinal study of language acquisition in autistic and Down syndrome children. *Journal of Autism and Developmental Disorders*, 20, 1-21.

Tan, L. (1985) Laterality and motor skills in four-year-olds. *Child Development*, 56, 119-124.

Task force on Child Care (1986) *Report of the Task Force on Child Care.* Ottawa: Status of Women, Canadian Government Publishing Centre.

Taylor, C., White, K.R., and Pezzino, J. (1984) Cost effectiveness analysis of full-day versus half-day intervention programs for handicapped preschoolers. *Journal of the Division for Early Childhood*, 9, 76-85.

Thorp, E.K., and McCollum, J. A. (1988) Defining the infancy specialization in early childhood special education. In J. B. Jordan, J. J. Gallagher, P. L. Huntinger, and M. B. Karnes (Eds.) *Early Childhood Special Education: Birth to Three*, 147-162. Reston, VA: Council for Exceptional Children.

Tingey-Michaelis, C. (1985) Early intervention: Is certification necessary? *Teacher Education and Special Education,* 8, 91-97.

Tjossem, T. (1976) *Intervention Strategies for High-Risk Infants and Young Children.* Baltimore, MD: University Park Press.

Tomlinson, R. (1982) Special needs in education. ERIC Doc. No. ED. 235 614.

Touchette, P.E. (1971) Transfer of stimulus control: Measuring the movement of transfer. *Journal of the Experimental Analysis of Behavior*, 15, 347-354.

Trivette, C.M., Dunst, C.J., Boyd, K., and Hamby, D.W. (1996) Family-oriented program models, help giving practices, and parental control appraisals. *Exceptional Children*, 62, 237-248.

Turnbull, A.P., and Blacher-Dixon, J. (1980) Pre-school mainstreaming: Impact on parents. In J.J. Gallagher (Ed.) *New Directions for Exceptional Children: Ecology of Exceptional Children* (vol. 1). San Francisco, CA: Jossey-Bass.

Turnbull, A.P. and Turnbull, H.R. (1986) *Families, Professionals and Exceptionality: A Special Partnership.* Columbus, OH: Merrill.

————(1990) *Families, Professionals, and Exceptionality: A Special Partnership* (2nd. ed.) Columbus, OH: Merrill.

Turnbull, A.P., Summers, J.A., and Brotherston, M.J. (1986) Family life cycle: Theoretical and empirical implications and future directions for families with mentally retarded members. In J.J. Gallagher and P.M. Vietze (Eds.) *Families of Handicapped Persons.* Baltimore, MD: Brookes.

U

Ulrey, G. (1982a) Influences of infant behavior on assessment. In G. Ulrey and S.J. Rogers (Eds.) *Psychological Assessment of Handicapped Infants and Young Children* 14-24. New York: Thieme-Shalton.

————(1982b) Influences of preschoolers' behavior on assessment. In G. Ulrey and S.J. Rogers (Eds.) *Psychological Assessment of Handicapped Infants and Young Children*, 25-34. New York: Thieme-Shalton.

Ulrich, D.A. (1985) *Test of Gross Motor Development.* Texas: Pro-Ed.

V

Vacc, N.A., Vacc, N.N., and Fogelman, M.S. (1987) Preschool screening: Using the DIAL as a predictor of first-grade performance. *Journal of School Psychology, 25*, 45-51.

Vandenberg, S.G., Singer, S.M., and Pauls, D.L. (1986) *The Heredity of Behavior Disorders in Adults and Children.* New York: Plenum.

Vandell, D.L., and George, B. (1981) Social interactions in hearing and deaf preschoolers. *Child Development, 52*, 627-635.

Venn, J., Morgenstern, L., and Dykes, M.K. (1978) Checklists for evaluating the fit and function of orthoses, prostheses, and wheelchairs in the classroom. *Teaching Exceptional Children, 11*, 51-56.

Vincent, L.B., Brown, L., and Getz-Shaftel, M. (1981) Integrating handicapped and typical children during the preschool years: The definition of best educational practice. *Topics in Early Childhood Special Education, 1*, 17-24.

Voeltz, L. (1980) Children's attitude toward handicapped peers. *American Journal of Mental Deficiency, 84*, 455-464.

——(1982) Effects of structured interactions with severely handicapped peers on children's attitudes. *American Journal of Mental Deficiency, 86*, 38-39.

Voysey, M. (1975) *A Constant Burden: The Reconstitution of Family Life.* London: Routledge and Kegan Paul.

W

Wachs, T.D., and Gruen, G.E. (1982) *Early Experience and Human Development.* New York: Plenum.

Wahler, R.G., and Fox, J.J. (1980) Solitary toy play and time out: A family treatment package for children with aggressive and oppositional behavior. *Journal of Applied Behavior Analysis, 13*, 23-39.

Wall, S.M., Pickert, S.M., and Bigson, W.B. (1989) Fantasy play in five and six-year-old children. *Journal of Psychology, 123*, 245-256.

Walls, R., Werner, T., Bacon, A., and Zane, T. (1977) Behavior checklist. In J. Cone and R. Hawkins (Eds.) *Behavioral Assessment: New Directions in Clinical Psychology.* New York: Brunner/Mazel.

Walter, G., and Vincent, L. (1982). The handicapped child in the regular classroom. *Journal of the Division for Early Childhood, 6*, 84-95.

Warren, S., and Kaiser, A. (1986a) Generalization of treatment effects by young language-delayed children: A longitudinal analysis. *Journal of Speech and Language Hearing Disorders, 51*, 239-251.

——— (1986b) Incidental language teaching: A critical review. *Journal of Speech and Hearing Disorders, 51*, 291-298.

Warren, S.F., Alpert, C.L., and Kaiser, A.P. (1988) An optimal learning environment for infants and toddlers with severe handicaps. In E.L. Meyen, G.A. Vergason, and R.D. Whelan (Eds.) *Effective Instructional Strategies for Exceptional Children*, 139-156. Denver, CO: Love.

Warren, W., and Hasenstab, S. (1986) Self concept of severely to profoundly hearing-impaired children. *Volta Review, 88*, 289-295.

Wasik, B.H., Bryant, D.M., and Lyons, C.M. (1990) *Home Visiting: Procedures for Helping Families.* Newbury Park, CA: Sage.

Watkinson, E.J., and Mulion, S. (1988) Playground skills of moderately mentally handicapped youngsters in integrated elementary schools. *Mental Retardation and Learning Disability Bulletin, 16*, 3-13.

Weaver, J.F. (1979) Collaboration: Why is sharing the turf so difficult? *Journal of Teacher Education, 30*, 24-25.

Weber, C., Behl, D., and Dummers, M. (1994) Watch them play, watch them learn. *Teaching Exceptional Children, 27*, 30-35.

Weber, C.U., Foster, P.W., and Weikert, D.P. (1978) An economic anaylsis of the Ypsilanti Perry preschool project. *Monographs of the High/Scope Educational Research Foundation*, N. 4.

Wechsler, D. (1989) *Wechsler Preschool and Primary Scale of Intelligence—Revised.* New York: Psychological Corporation.

Wehman, (1977) *Helping the Mentally Retarded to Acquire Play Skills.* Springfield, IL: Thomas

Wehman, P., and McLaughlin, P.J. (1979). Teachers' perceptions of behavioral problems with severely and profoundly handicapped students. *Mental Retardation, 17*, 20-21.

Weikert, D. (1986, winter) What do we know so far? *High Scope Resource: A Magazine for Educators*, 8.

————(1988) Quality in early childhood education. In C. Warger (Ed.) *A Resource Guide to Public School Early Childhood Programs*. Alexandria, VA: Association for Supervision and Curriculum Development.

Weininger, O. (1979) *Play and Education*. Springfield, IL: Thomas.

————(1990) Play: For survival. In I.M. Doxey (Ed.) *Child Care and Education: Canadian Dimensions*, 13-31. Toronto: Nelson.

Wells, G. (1986) *The Meaning Makers: Children Learning Language and Using Language to Learn*. Portsmouth, NJ: Heinemann.

Wender, J.K., and Bruininks, R.H. (1991) *Bodyskills*. Allen, TX: Developmental Learning Materials.

Werner, E.E. (1986) The concept of risk from a developmental perspective. In R.B. Keogh (Ed.) *Advances in Special Education, vol. 5: Developmental Problems in Infancy and the Preschool Years*. Greenwich, CT: JAI Press.

Wessel, J.A., and Kelly, L. (1986) *Achievement-Based Curriculum Development in Physical Education*. Philadelphia, PA: Lea and Felsiger.

West, J.F., and Cannon, G. (1987) Essential collaborative consultation competencies for regular and special educators. *Journal of Learning Disabilities*, 21, 56-63.

Westby, C. (1980) Assessment and cognitive and language abilities through play. *Language, Speech and Hearing Services in the Schools*, 9, 154-168.

————(1992) Whole language and learners with mild handicaps. *Focus on Exceptional Children*, 24, 3-16.

Whitebrook, M., et al. (1989) *Who Cares? Child Care Teachers and the Quality of Care in America. Executive Summary of the National Child Care Staffing Study*. Oakland, CA: Child Care Employee Project.

Wicks-Nelson, R., and Israel, A.C. (1991) *Behavior Disorders of Childhood* (2nd. ed.) Englewood Cliffs, New Jersey: Prentice-Hall.

Widerstrom, A.H., and Goodwon, L.D. (1987) Effects of an infant stimulation program on the child and the family. *Exceptional Children*, 11, 143-153.

Widerstrom, A. H., Mowder, B. A., and Willis, W. G. (1989). The school psychologist's role in the early childhood special education program. *Journal of Early Intervention*, 13, 239-248.

Wiig, E., Secord, W., and Semel, E. (1993) *Clinical Evaluation of Language Fundamentals-Preschool*. New York: Psychological Corporation.

Wilker, L. (1981) Chronic stresses on families of mentally retarded children. *Family Relations*, 30, 281-288

Wilker, L., Wasow, M.S.W., and Hatfield, E. (1981) Chronic sorrow revisited: Parent vs professional depiction of the adjustment of parents of mentally retarded children. *American Journal of Orthopsychiatry*, 51, 63-70.

Wing, L. (1980) *Autistic Children*. London: Constable and Co.

Winton, P.J., and Turnbull, A.P. (1981) Parent involvement as viewed by parents of preschool handicapped children. *Topics in Early Childhood Special Education*, 1, 11-19.

Winitz, H. (1975) *From Syllable to Conversation*. Baltimore, MD: University Park Press.

Winzer, M.A. (1989) *Closing the Gap: Special Learners in Regular Classrooms*. Toronto: Copp Clark Pitman.

————(1995). *Educational Psychology in the Canadian Classroom* (2nd ed.) Toronto: Allyn and Bacon.

————(1996) *Children with Exceptionalities in Canadian Classrooms (4th ed.)* Toronto: Allyn and Bacon.

Wittenberg, II. (1979, December) Toy choosing guidelines. *Child Focus*, 10-15.

Wolery, M. (1991) Instruction in early childhood special education: "Seeing through a glass darkly ... knowing in part." *Exceptional Children*, 58, 127-135.

Wolery, M., Strain, P.S., and Bailey, D.B. Jr. (1992) Reaching potential of children with special needs, In S. Bredekamp and T. Rosegrant (Eds.) *Reaching Potentials: Appropriate Curriculum and Assessment for Young Children*, 99-111. Washington DC: National Association for the Education of Young Children.

Wulbert, M., Nyam, B.A., Snow, D., and Owen, Y. (1973) The efficacy of stimulus fading and contingency management in the treatment of elective mutism: A case study. *Journal of Applied Behavior Analysis*, 6, 435-441.

Z

Zeitlin, S., and Williamson, G.G. (1986) Early intervention of infants and toddlers. *Teaching Exceptional Children,* 19, 57-59.

———(1988) Developing family resources for adaptive coping. *Journal for the Division of Early Childhoood,* 12, 137-146.

Zigler, E. (1987) Formal schooling for four-year-olds? No. *American Psychologist,* 42, 254-260.

Zigler, E., and Ennis, P. (1989) The child care crisis in America. *Canadian Psychology/Psycholgique canadienne,* 30, 116-125.

Zigler, E., and Valentine, J. (Eds.) (1979) *Project Head Start: A Legacy of the War on Poverty.* New York: Free Press.

Zimmerman, I., Sheener, V., and Pond, R. (1979/1993) *The Preschool Language Scale* (Revised ed.). Columbus, OH: Merrill.

Zinmeister, K. (1988, spring) Brave new world. *Policy Review,* 40-47.

AUTHOR INDEX

SUBJECT INDEX

Photo Credits

K. Bellesiles 309, 331
W. Chan 199
P. Chow 102, 141
courtesy Danmar Products Inc. 380 (right)
Y. de Rooy 126
M. Emme 125
T. Garke 205, 381
D. Hemingway 71
K. Mazurek 106, 165, 242

Prentice Hall Archives 28, 72
courtesy Fred Sammons Inc. 5
K. Smith (supplied by author) 12, 16, 33, 44, 53, 198, 201, 307, 403
L. Snider 379
D. Starrett 14, 168, 431
K. Stewart 277
courtesy TherAdapt® Products Inc. 380 (left)
M. Tomins 252, 261, 368
T. Wilson 288
M. Winzer 327, 328, 330